When Suicide Beckons

When Suicide Beckons

A
PSYCHOANALYST'S
MEMOIR

Bhaskar Sripada, M.D.

To my mom, my dad, and my wife,
without whom I would not be who I am.

Note on book cover

My dad, Captain Krishnayya Sripada, served in the Indian Medical Service during World War II, fighting on the Allies' side against the Japanese in Burma. The Gurkha knife that appears on the cover of this book belonged to him. He told me, "When you ask a Gurkha to show you his *kukri*-blade, he will politely show it to you, but will cut himself in the palm and draw a drop of blood before putting it back into its scabbard: once it is unsheathed, the *kukri* must taste blood."

Author's note

When Suicide Beckons is my memoir about suicide and the talking-cure of depression. I tell the story of a psychiatrist who became despondent after one of his patients killed himself. This book is a narrative account of the psychoanalytic treatment of a depressed person that will appeal to laypeople and clinicians interested in suicide. A person may commit suicide if they lose hope and believe their life is not worth living. However, the right treatment may be able to restore hope to a distressed individual who also doubts the value of their life. For psychoanalysts and those interested in depth psychology, I have included a preface and postscript explaining my views on the psychoanalytic process and describing my emotions, reasons, and experiences, which guided my actions. In the book, I describe our candid conversations and the thoughts, feelings, and memories evoked in me by my patient. I wrote about his analysis with my patient's consent. According to medical and psychotherapeutic reporting standards, all patients are de-identified. Therefore, I disguised and fictionalized all patient names, locations, dates, nationalities, addresses, etc., and all other personal information. In some parts of the narrative, one person represents the condensed Identities of several people; any resemblance to actual individuals is coincidental and unintentional. However, the details of my life are true. I portray historical figures accurately. Hence, the book is part memoir, part case study, and part fiction. Overall, this is a work of creative nonfiction.

CONTENTS

Preface	xiii
Acknowledgments	xxxv
Chapter 1	1
Chapter 2	10
Chapter 3	25
Chapter 4	34
Chapter 5	44
Chapter 6	55
Chapter 7	73
Chapter 8	84
Chapter 9	93
Chapter 10	107
Chapter 11	122
Chapter 12	135
Chapter 13	143
Chapter 14	154
Chapter 15	165
Chapter 16	173
Chapter 17	193
Chapter 18	205
Chapter 19	220
Chapter 20	231
Chapter 21	241
Chapter 22	250

Chapter 23 268
Chapter 24 276
Chapter 25 291
Chapter 26 305
Chapter 27 311
Chapter 28 317
Chapter 29 319
Chapter 30 332
Chapter 31 336
Chapter 32 339
Chapter 33 342
Chapter 34 344
Chapter 35 348
Chapter 36 355
Chapter 37 365
Chapter 38 375
Chapter 39 378
Chapter 40 388
Chapter 41 402
Chapter 42 408
Chapter 43 419
Chapter 44 433
Chapter 45 439
Chapter 46 451
Chapter 47 458
Chapter 48 469
Chapter 49 478
Chapter 50 482
Chapter 51 491
Chapter 52 500
Postscript 510
Index 527
About the Author 539

PREFACE

MY MEMOIR DESCRIBES AN ANALYSIS viewed through the eyes of a psychoanalyst. Jan (pronounced Yahn), a psychiatrist-in-training, became severely depressed after Amir, his own patient, committed suicide. When a young man kills himself, *his* world ends, but he leaves behind a dismembered family struggling with loss, grief, powerlessness, anger, and guilt. If the man were in treatment at the time, it would be a crushing blow also to his therapist. Indeed, the therapist may become so overwhelmed that he may be at risk of committing suicide.[1]

Memories are an essential part of a memoir and require no further justification. If the book is interesting, the reader bestows attention and further reading; fresh memories of his own may further reward the reader. But, do the analyst's thoughts, emotions, and memories of his life, evoked by treatment, contribute to the treatment of a given patient's analysis or the science of psychoanalysis? That is the question this book poses. I believe so. A psychoanalyst's personal training analysis. supervision, formal institute teaching, gut sense, and cumulative life lessons contribute to his attitude and interpretations. Thus, in this book, I describe my ideas, emotions, and memories in response to Jan in the analysis. Many of the analyst's childhood and life experiences are the roots of the analyst's interpretations and interventions. Some parts of the analyst's personality aid the analysis, while others inhibit it. Therefore, this memoir and accompanying case report also constitute a scientific communication. Although this book's

---

1 Regarding pronouns: Many of the vignettes in this book are dialogues between two men in a therapeutic environment, a situation where the generic "he" would generally be more natural than doubled pronouns ("he or she," "him or her"). I also use the generic "he" to avoid cumbersome locutions (e.g., "he or she," followed by "himself or herself"), I thank you, in advance, for your forbearance.

central concern is the analyst's experience evoked by the patient, his mentors and theories simultaneously influence him. So here, I outline critical analytic ideas and people that touched me; a literature review of approaches from the analyst's point of view is beyond the scope of this introduction. However, the opinions and reactions of analysts and others can further sharpen the appreciation of the analysis of ideas, emotions, and memories evoked by a patient's analysis for psychoanalysis. Psychoanalysis, since Freud, has evolved into a varied set of theories and practices, all using somewhat similar terms. I tried to integrate traditional and contemporary psychoanalytic wisdom using my professional judgment, freedom, and the notions of the unconscious, transference, resistance; in this introduction, I briefly clarify my position on some common analytic concepts.

I describe the first sixteen months of a three-year analysis of Jan, a doctor training to become a psychiatrist. After Jan's patient, Amir, killed himself, Jan became overwhelmed with grief, guilt, and self-doubt and sank into a deep depression. When he became distraught and did not leave the house for several months, his wife reached out to me. Jan and I met for two double sessions each week during this analysis. Although I offered Jan the couch, he never used it. Jan's danger of suicide receded after about three months of treatment. I thought of writing a memoir reflecting on my reactions to treating Jan. I shared the idea with Jan, and he consented to my writing about our treatment and allowed me to record the sessions for this purpose. Unfortunately, I could not record some sessions due to technical difficulties and oversights. To enable the reader to follow the flow of the analysis, I have omitted events and exchanges that seemed to be of marginal narrative value. For example, many sessions dealt with repetitive issues of guilt relating to Amir's suicide and anger directed at his father; anxieties about taking examinations; and administrative matters dealing with returning to work, applications for licenses, etc. So, rather than repeat similar sessions, I present selected sessions. They are sufficient to describe the analytic process and my reflections on it. I indicate the month of treatment at the start of many chapters to orient the reader. The reported sessions are sequential and chronological.

This book focuses on the psychoanalytic process and my responses to the ongoing analysis within each session during the initial, early, and middle phases of treatment. The first sixteen months of the treatment was the most productive period of the entire treatment. I do not describe the termination in this book, for a detailed report of every session of a whole analytic treatment would be of unmanageable length. Instead, I offer comments concerning the post-termination period in the postscript. Jan is a real person, disguised—at his request—to protect his identity.

In response to the patient's free associations, the analyst utters comments, clarifications, questions, and interpretations to help the patient. Taken together, the patient's free associations and the analyst's interpretations are public interpersonal, analytic events that a tape or video device may record. Thus, both patient and analyst have access to this interactive therapeutic information. Still, being active observers, the patient and analyst may attribute different meanings to the same manifest events, influenced by their respective histories and perspectives. However, this analytic public arena is restricted to the therapeutic setting and does not refer to the external world outside the analyst's office. In contrast to such public events are the contents of the analyst's thoughts, feelings, and memories.

Psychoanalysis and the analyst's inner world

Freud[2] recommended that analysts listen to the free associations of the patient with *gleichschwebende Aufmerksamkeit*—"evenly suspended attention": "The technique . . . is a very simple one. . . . It consists simply in not directing one's notice to anything in particular and in maintaining the same 'evenly suspended attention' in the face of all that one hears. . . . If the doctor behaves otherwise, he is throwing away most of the advantage which results from the patient's obeying the 'fundamental rule of psychoanalysis.'" (p. 211)

Thus, while listening to the patient, the analyst simultaneously scans his private inner world. Analysts have commented on the characteristics of the inner world, whether it be the patient or the analyst. For example, Kohut[3], stated that, "The inner world cannot be observed with the aid of our sensory organs. Our thoughts, wishes, feelings, and fantasies cannot be seen, smelled, heard, or touched. They have no existence in physical space, and yet they are real, and we can observe them as they occur in time: through introspection in ourselves, and through empathy (i.e., vicarious introspection) in others." (p. 459) Depending on the circumstances, this evenly suspended

---

2 Freud, S. (1913). "Recommendations to physicians practicing psycho-analysis." In J. Strachey (Ed. and Trans.), *The Standard Edition of the Complete Psychological Works of Sigmund Freud* (Vol. 12). London: Hogarth Press.

3 Kohut, H. (1959). "Introspection, empathy, and psychoanalysis—An examination of the relationship between mode of observation and theory." *Journal of the American Psychoanalytic Association, 7,* 459–483.

attention shifts between the patient's utterances and the analyst's experience in response to the patient. These include thoughts, imaginings, emotions, surprises, interests, conflicts, memories, wishes, fears, and doubts evoked in response to the patient. Unlike public and therapeutic analytic events, to which both the patient and analyst have access, the private experiences of the analyst are available only to the analyst. No tape recorder can access them. Because the analyst also attends to the patient's associations and takes analytic actions, evenly suspended attention's contents are elusive; they are a mixture of the unconscious, preconscious, and sometimes conscious responses. Moreover, the contents of the emerging evenly suspended attention are not isolated entities; their further connections lead to other areas of the analyst's past or present life outside the analysis.

Objectivity, transference, and the beginning of psychoanalysis

When Freud was formulating psychoanalysis, Cartesian dualism and Positivism dominated science. Based on the "method of doubt," seeking clarity and distinctness in his quest for truth and arguing that the subject could objectively measure an external object without influencing it, Descartes (1596-1650[4]) developed a dualism that became the basis of pre-twentieth-century Western science. Comte's Positivism[5] held that objective truths result from verified scientific propositions. The notions of positivism (inherent in classical science) and "objective truth" influenced early psychoanalytic practitioners. In response, they assumed analytic neutrality and adopted the ideal of the blank-screen analyst. They believed the analyst should be a blank screen on which the patient projects his transference, conflicts, and personality.

In addition, many analysts thought that an objective and neutral analyst was possible, necessary, and desirable. Many felt that the analyst's personality and private life were independent of their analytic interventions. According to this view, revealing the analyst's personal life was unwise. Therefore, in their clarifications, interpretations, interventions, and contract establishment (billing-payment, vacation, sickness, and gift policies), analysts technically shrouded themselves with a veil of neutrality to maintain a blank screen.

---

4 Descartes, R. (1968 [1628]). In *Meditation IV The Philosophical Works of Descartes Rendered into English*, by Elizabeth S. Haldane, C.H., L.L.D. and G.R.T. Ross, M.A., D.Phil., Volume I, 1968. Cambridge At The University Press.

5 Comte, Auguste (1855). *Positive Philosophy of Auguste Comte, Part I* translated by Harriet Martineau, Kessinger Publishing, Paperback, 2003

They hoped that such a precaution minimized suggestion and avoided influencing the patient. So, they believed an analyst's regular activity, covered by neutrality, did not require analytic scrutiny. Transference, according to the blank-screen model, is a patient-only phenomenon. Transference is based on the patient's childhood and current experiences and includes the patient's conscious or unconscious attitude or understanding of the analyst.

Although he did not write much about it, according to Freud (1910)[6], the analyst's "countertransference" results from the patient's influence on the analyst's unconscious, which interferes with successful treatment. Therefore, the analyst should recognize the countertransference and overcome it by further analysis. The chief significance of recognizing the analyst's countertransference is that it is no longer possible to claim neutrality and objectivity.

Analysts initially employed psychoanalytic metapsychology to describe the human personality. Thus, they used terms such as "forces," "energies," and "structures," derived from the natural sciences, for example, physics. This attitude, which assumed that analysts offered objective accounts of their patients and themselves, influenced their clinical discussions. For instance, in their case reports, analysts often referred to themselves objectively, in the third person, as "the analyst."

However, increasingly, analysts have developed terminology more appropriate for their discipline; interpretations uncover *meanings* within the psychoanalytic dialogue. The patient may agree or disagree with the analyst's meanings attributed to an event. Moreover, the patient can dispute the analyst's view, as the analyst is not a privileged observer. Recently, thanks to the influence of Kohut and others, many contemporary analysts have moved away from abstract metapsychological terms that foster an impersonal aura and describe the meanings contained in an analysis in "experience-near" personal terms.[7] I wrote the book from my first-person perspective in keeping with this trend.

The active participant-observer and a new definition of transference

In light of many modern twentieth-century discoveries, classical-science propositions gradually gave way to the contemporary appreciation of the

---

6 Freud, S. (1910) *The Future Prospects of Psycho-Analytic Therapy. The Standard Edition of the Complete Psychological Works of Sigmund Freud* 11:139-152

7 Kohut, H. (1982). "Introspection, Empathy, and the Semi-Circle of Mental Health." *Int. J. Psycho-Anal.*, 63:395-407.

active observer. Sullivan and others laid the groundwork for understanding the individual based on relationship networks. Harry Stack Sullivan drew attention to the analyst as a participant-observer who needed to pay attention to his own reactions to the patient.[8] Contemporary analysts questioned the blank-screen model of neutrality and transference as a patient-only phenomenon. While eschewing frank suggestion and manipulation, analysts recognized that their clarifications, interpretations, and actions always include a component of inevitable unconscious suggestion, based on their participant observership. This understanding resulted from the appreciation of the active observer within psychoanalysis, who inevitably contributes to his observations. According to this new view, the unavoidable analyst suggestion, where possible, must be made explicit from the analyst's or patient's perspective and may need to be subjected to further analysis. The following quote characterizes this abandonment of the possibility of objective neutrality and signals a new understanding of the patient and analyst relationship. "Transference is not only always contributed to by both participants, but each participant also has a valid, albeit different, perspective on it."[9] I adhere to Gill's new definition of transference and view the analyst's influence as inevitable.

Along with many other analysts, I have abandoned the impossible analytic goal of objective neutrality, previously considered possible and desirable. Instead, my view embodies the idea that both the analyst and patient are active perspectival observers who mutually influence each other.[10] Because of the analytic relationship, we assume that the patient's associations and the contents of the analyst's evenly suspended attention are also related. So, aside from treating the patient, the analyst's job changed from reporting neutral observations to explaining their contribution to the analysis. Therefore, this book describes Jan, my public interactions with Jan, and my private evoked reactions. However, in doing so, I emphasize both Jan and I were active contributors to the evolving treatment, and our respective manifest separate words, actions, and perspectives were mutually interacting.

8 Leston Havens. (1976). *Participant Observation*. New York: Jason Aronson

9 Gill, M.M. (1984). "Transference: A Change in Conception or Only in Emphasis?" *Psychoanal. Inq.*, 4(3):489-523.

10 Sripada, B. Kronmal, S.L. (1996). "Merton Gill and the Genesis of a New Psychoanalytic Paradigm." *Ann. Psychoanal.*, 24:67-81.

Transference and countertransference are indispensable psychoanalytic terms. Each analyst understands and uses "transference" and "counter-transference." Yet, because there are so many variants of psychoanalysis, there are many meanings and definitions associated with those terms. Still, because they are the backbone of much analytical work, each analyst should explicitly outline their understanding of these terms.

In this book, I offer a contemporary-psychoanalysis- and dynamic active-observer-based definition of transference. "Transference" is a term that explains the unconscious process of associated experiences. For example, conflicts, wishes-fears, emotions, and anticipations related to one person, time, place, thing, process, or function link up with another person, time, place, thing, process, or function. Such connections involve defenses and compromise formations, and are at the root of any experience. Furthermore, any experience combines predicted sensory qualities based on past learning and current sensory inputs.

There is a prominent unconscious entangling of different entities before the emergence of an event. Predictions and sensory inputs contribute to the emerging present and envelop prospective uncertainty. Our brain processes our expectations and sensory information relating to that event. If the two match, our expectations contribute heavily to the experience. If there is a significant discrepancy between predictions and sensory input, the ensuing surprise draws attention and incorporates more current sensory information. However, there is a relative retrospective clarity concerning its antecedents once an event has occurred. It is often easy to separate accurate from inaccurate predictions after an event. Thus, prospective entanglement often leads to retrospective disentanglement. For example, the players play the game on Sunday amidst much excitement and uncertainty. Knowing the game's outcome, the Monday morning quarterback criticizes decisions or actions undertaken by others after the event. Whereas the original acts of the players were undertaken prospectively with uncertainty and not knowing the outcome of an effort, a retrospective review has the clarity of hindsight and knowledge of the result of the action. Many emotional states, symptoms, defenses, compromises, or aspects of identity are not temporally discrete and spread across time, recur, or linger. So long as the patient does not understand the roots of his conflicts, he is often clueless, and uncertainty envelops his feelings and actions. Once the analyst and patient, working together, correctly interpret conflicts, the patient has a more precise understanding and is less constrained by unconscious factors. The patient and analyst have different perspectives and may agree or disagree on whether such entities belong to the past, present, or future and the degree of uncertainty or surprise that exists at a given time. Analytic scrutiny helps develop a coherent perspective that helps understand and explain the continuous transformation of present-future uncertainty into greater retrospective clarity. Despite this unavoidable dynamic of time passage, barring psychosis, denial, or other serious derailments, a person's experience can still be the basis of understanding, communications, dialogue, and actions. Analysis can help discern regularities and patterns to enable meaningful appreciation of the world. Despite the transference-based lack of absolute objectivity, the active participant, in concert with others, can develop a common language and guides for life engagement. Of course, understanding is provisional. Misunderstanding is remediable when correctable errors emerge; this involves continuous learning and self-correction.

The analyst's transferences constantly influence his observations because he can never objectively experience the world; this is true for any active observer. However, when the active-participant analyst and patient engage within the analytic situation, the patient's transferences influence the analyst's transference. Here, the analyst's and patient's transferences interact and mutually influence each other. Describing such complex dynamics requires terminology that is coherent and not too cumbersome. Using the same term, "transference," to describe the patient's and analyst's responses could lead to unintentional confusion or laborious communications. Analysts recognize that the patient and analyst mutually influence each other but distinguish between transference and countertransference. In the broad sense, transference in the clinical setting refers to all the patient's reactions to the analyst. In contrast, broad countertransference refers to all responses in the analyst evoked in the treatment. Thus, analysts understand that the patient's transference and the analyst's countertransference continuously influence each other.

In contrast to earlier analysts, who assumed their blank-screen procedure had assured neutrality, analysts began to be surprised by discovering clinical phenomena linked to the analyst's unconscious. Analysts began to describe their countertransference reactions to their patients, requiring acknowledgment and further inquiry. For instance, Lucia Tower[11] Forgot about the patient's session altogether—in the sense of a lapse of

---

11 Tower, L.E. (1956). "Countertransference." *J. Amer. Psychoanal. Assn.*, 4:224-255.

calendar-scheduling. and wrote a seminal paper on countertransference. Winnicott described hate in the countertransference.[12] Analysts realized that they could not count on the blank screen. The analyst's countertransference was no longer a private secret; it was a phenomenon that needed more understanding through study. At the manifest level, the patient's free associations are distinct from the analyst's interpretations, clarifications, and explanations.

The evolution of twentieth-century science and countertransference

In some ways, the evolution of the understanding of countertransference resembles the development of science in the twentieth century. The conventions of the classical science era shaped Freud's discoveries, often framed in absolute, objective terms with an omniscient perspective. The Occam's razor principle guided traditional or classical science in choosing the simplest or most parsimonious explanation.[13] The conventional analyst assumed an omniscient perspective, either consciously or unconsciously. The privilege and power inherent in that assumption enabled his interpretations a great deal of simplicity. In the classical view, reality exists independent of any observer's consciousness. Therefore, a neutral observer with the expertise and training, such as an analyst, could better grasp universal reality. As a result, he is qualified to analyze the patient's circumstances objectively. In contrast, in the contemporary view, an active observer, through the consciousness and perspective influenced by his location, time, and personality, infers reality. Here, although the analyst and patient participant-observers communicate, they maintain different perspectives. In particularizing the observer, the twentieth century's relativity, indeterminacy, and complementarity revolutionized science. Einstein (1956, pg. 1)[14] introduced the theory of relativity, which abandons the idea of an absolute or universal observer. Individual observers arrange events according to the criteria of "earlier" and "later;" based on their relative positions, observers experience time and sequence of events differently. Observers in different locations will perceive two

---

12 Winnicott, D.W. (1949). "Hate in the Counter-Transference." *Int. J. Psycho-Anal.*, 30:69-74.

13 Spade, Paul Vincent and Claude Panaccio, "William of Ockham", *The Stanford Encyclopedia of Philosophy* (Spring 2019 Edition), Edward N. Zalta (ed.), URL = <https://plato.stanford.edu/archives/spr2019/entries/ockham/>.

14 Einstein Albert. The Meaning of Relativity. Princeton University Press. New Jersey. 1956

events, A and B, differently. At one place, an observer may perceive A and B to have happened simultaneously, another observer may perceive A to have preceded B, and yet another observer may perceive B to have occurred earlier than A. Heisenberg (1958, pg. 50)[15] recognized that, in the subatomic sphere, there is no neutral observer; the scientist invariably influences what he observes, and that exact determination is impossible. According to Bohr (1962[16]), a scientific description of nature must include aspects of the observations themselves, the methods of observing, and the observer. Modern scientists struggled with baffling paradoxes in nature; in some experiments, light behaved like a particle, and in others, like a wave. In Bohr's view, conflicting accounts of events result from incompatible observation methods and do not imply any incompatibility in nature. Studying the same event using different approaches gives several partial insights into the event. Combining the results of such partial tests in a complementary manner, rather than choosing one and discarding the others, provided the best understanding of that event. While Occam's razor favors the simplest idea and suppresses all other hypotheses, contemporary science seeks to integrate several partial, specific particular perspectives of various active observers.

Edelman (1992, p. 66–8[17]) noted that the classical observer assumes an objective "God's-eye view," resulting in classical science disregarding the observer's mind, consciousness, and intentions. In contrast to the omniscience of classical God's eye views, modern science explicitly recognizes that every observer, based on his location (and personality), has a particular perspective. Thus, contemporary generalizations are not absolute or universal statements that apply to all observers; they are qualified and limited by specific observations, observational methods, and the observer. Arguing that the arrangement of a scientist's apparatus impacts their measurements and outcome, Edelman formulated modern scientific principles, which recognize the active observer's role in science. Edelman developed a framework for modern science that accounts for the active observer's (scientist's) mind, consciousness, and intention.

---

15 Heisenberg, W. (1958), Physics and Philosophy: The Revolution in Modern Science. New York: Harper & Row. p. 50.

16 Bohr, N. (1962), Light and life revisited. In: *The Philosophical Writings of Niels Bohr.* Woodbridge, CT: Ox Bow Press, 1962.

17 Edelman, G.M. (1992), Bright Air, Brilliant Fire: On the matter of the mind. N.Y:. Basic Books

There are two types of countertransference, narrow and broad. Narrow countertransference is often associated with traditional analysis and based on the assumption of the objective observer analyst. Although occurring in the analysis context, narrow countertransference overwhelmingly reflects analyst pathology. Broad countertransference is associated with the notion of the analyst and patient as participant-observers who have a mutually influencing relationship. The patient's dynamics evoke the broad counter-transference, which manifests in the analyst's experience. Therefore the broad countertransference is a gateway junction providing dynamic access to the personalities of both the analyst and patient.

By traditional analysis, I mean any theory that assumes the analyst's objectivity and neutrality; the analyst has privileges and grants himself powers not available to the patient. A traditional analysis views the patient's transference and the analyst's countertransference, when present, as related but distinct phenomena attributable to the patient or the analyst, respectively. When countertransference (narrow) is evident in traditional analysis, it is episodic and indicates some pathology in the analyst that impairs the analy-sis and necessitates some action (see below). However, if the analyst detects no countertransference, he assumes he is objective, neutral, and reasonably error-free and is providing the patient with accurate interpretations. Under such analytic conditions, where the analyst does not recognize his own coun-tertransference, the question of exploring an analyst's bias is practically moot.

However, an analyst's assumption of objectivity may be a dangerous illusion; if there is no overt evidence to the contrary, analysts can continue to believe that their observations are unbiased. Such an assumption is often associated with the analyst's power and privilege. An unconscious collaboration between the analyst and patient may make it difficult for any analyst's bias to be detected and rectified. An analyst may consciously or unconsciously desire the privilege and powers of being a person of author-ity; simultaneously, it may also be the patient's conscious or unconscious wish to place the analyst in such an exalted position. The patient is unlikely to challenge a traditional psychoanalyst when this dynamic is present. Thus, there is an increased risk of patient compliance or agreement with the analyst. Because its detection relies on the analyst's self-awareness, in such circumstances, the risk in a traditional analysis is for the narrow countertransference to go undetected.

As noted earlier, contemporary analysts assume that analyst and patient mutually influence participants-observers. Thus, the patient's transference and the analyst's countertransference are intertwined. The analyst's broad countertransference is, therefore, continuous and not episodic. This mutual influence can be summarized thus: *Analysts experience specific memories, emotions, and anticipations evoked by their patient relationships and interactions; these responses, in turn, shape their assessments, interpretations, and actions.* When an analyst employs the notion of broad countertransference, the analysts must continuously account for influences and uncertainties introduced by the active participant-observer analysts throughout the analysis. In contemporary treatments, the patient and analyst views help provide complementary perspectives. The patient's and analyst's perspectives may overlap, differ, or conflict in different areas.

When a traditional analyst detects narrow countertransference, the treatment is impaired, and the analyst's action is required to remedy it. However, in contemporary analysis, it is important to distinguish when the broad countertransference appropriately guides the treatment from when it is impairing it. In addition, contemporary analysts may also experience countertransference that is so intense or prolonged that it interferes with or disrupts the patient's analysis. When either a narrow or broad countertransference is interfering with the treatment, it becomes necessary for the analyst to seek consultation, enter a personal analysis, or transfer the case to another analyst.

In contemporary approaches, describing the separate patient and analyst perspectives, explaining the mutually influencing patient-analyst relationship and interactions, and integrating these views is a formidable and complex challenge. Moreover, because there is no single standard controlling authority, contemporary approaches can yield many ideas, that are difficult to conceptualize, integrate, teach, or learn. Though trained in classical psychoanalysis, I now take a contemporary approach to the analytic integration of my patient and my perspectives. This book provides clinical details of transference-countertransference experiences and my reactions through first-person accounts of the patient and myself.

A broad view of countertransference and the transference-countertransference matrix

Since the 1950s, psychoanalysts and psychodynamic therapists have held a broader view of countertransference. It is no longer seen only as an impediment to treatment. Instead, the analyst's countertransference is like a therapeutic laboratory because the patient's treatment evokes it. It may be the source of important information concerning the patient that the analyst can harness to understand and help the patient. In addition, countertransference can serve as a sensitive interpersonal barometer, a finely tuned instrument in social interaction. For example, a therapist who feels irritated by a patient for no apparent reason may eventually uncover subtle unconscious patient provocations that irritate and repel others, thereby keeping the patient unwittingly lonely and isolated. In this case, the root of the analyst's irritation lay in the patient's provocations that are the source of the patient's problems requiring treatment. In this broad view, the analyst must distinguish various ranges of countertransference. By understanding the analyst's benign broad countertransference identifications and resonances, the analyst can uncover the patient's identifications, preferences, and conflicts with other objects. However, at the other end of the spectrum of broad countertransference is severe or malignant countertransference, predominantly attributable to some unresolved pathology in the analysts. Thus, analysts realized that neutrality and objectivity, however desirable, are not possible. The analyst's private life mingles with the patient's analysis, and understanding this mixture is necessary to understand the treatment process.

An analyst can subscribe to a narrow or broad view of countertransference. Narrow countertransference is episodic. When present, it invariably interferes with the analysis and implies an analyst's psychopathology. Therefore, when present, the analyst must understand and correct it. In contrast, broad countertransference includes all analyst reactions evoked continuously in the relationship to his patient. Broad countertransference offers the analyst an ongoing stream of unconscious or conscious material and functions as an analytical laboratory. It may point to a prevailing analyst-patient identification (or objectification), help formulate patient dynamics, and aid treatment. Broad malignant countertransference includes processes seriously interfering with the therapy, predominantly attributable to some unresolved pathology in the analyst. When countertransference events emerge, they become occasions for a fresh look at the analyst's theory and practice, and can be occasions for the analyst's new self-learning.

Most psychoanalysts consider the analysis of the transference as a central aspect of analysis and acknowledge the importance of the analyst's inner world in aiding that effort. Since transference and countertransference are dynamically linked, relevant details of the analyst's countertransference must complement details of the transference analysis. Yet many analysts discuss their cases from the third-person point of view, offer theoretical discussions of their patients, and provide only a few details of their personal life evoked by the analysis. Moreover, there is no established psychoanalytic clinical tradition of accounting for the analyses from the analyst's first-person point of view. Therefore, while analytic peers do have a detailed appreciation of an analyst's theoretical applications in a case, they have little awareness of the personal ways in which the analyst's life influenced the interpretations offered to a patient.

The analysand's transference and the prevailing dynamics of the patient-analyst relationship at a given time shape the analyst's evenly suspended attention. Whereas the contents of the analyst's evenly suspended attention refer to the analyst's responses to that moment, the analyst's broad countertransference relates to all the experiences the entire treatment has evoked. This broad countertransference may include all the analyst's experiences of thoughts, imaginations, emotions, or memories from their own childhoods and lives, which resonate with the patient dynamics.

However, there is an increasing appreciation that both the patient and analyst are active participants in the analysis. Therefore, the patient's transference and the analyst's countertransference are conjoint products; they can be separated only at the manifest level. Thus, the principal goal of the analysis of interpreting the patient's transference needs a fundamental reformulation. The new understanding demands the analysis of the combined patient's transference *cum* analyst's countertransference.

Provided the mutuality and interactive aspects of the analyst and analysand are recognized, this central analytic task can be approached from any theoretical direction. These include the interpersonal (the mutual relationship of persons), intersubjective (the reciprocal relationship between subjects), self-other (the mutual relationship between a self and others), or the mutual relationship between participant-observers. Therefore, any analysis requires supporting clinical details about the patient and information about the analyst's particular response to the patient, regardless of the theoretical stance of the analyst. Often the analyst does not and does not have to divulge this information to the patient. Still, peer analysts need this comprehensive information to properly understand the combined roots of the patient's conflicts and sources for the analyst's interpretations and actions.

A theoretical construct is a generalization that applies to many or most patients. In contrast, evenly suspended attention and its resulting broad countertransference apply to a particular patient at a given moment. Therefore, the interpretation of an analyst is more likely to fit a patient when it is in line with the contents of the analyst's evenly suspended attention elicited by the patient. However, each analysand evokes the analyst's broad countertransference, specific to that case. Therefore, analytic interpretations precisely fit that patient when their sources contain evenly suspended attention (broad countertransference). The analyst's ideas about transference deal with inferences about the "other." In contrast, the contents of evenly suspended attention derive from the analyst's immediate self-history. Therefore, the contents of the analyst's countertransference, being the palpable experienced self-products, should be the analyst's foremost guiding lights. I attempt to reconstruct the transference-countertransference matrix and describe it in this book.

Prediction and learning from errors

Integrating psychoanalysis with biology and neuroscience yielded insights concerning predictions and surprises with clinical applications. For example, contemporary neuroscientists recognize that the brain functions as a constructive organ of prediction. The brain predicts sensory inputs and compares them with sensory information—the prevailing difference between the two measures the level of prediction error or surprise. When our internally generated brain predictions and sensory data relating to an event match, our expectations contribute primarily to that experience with only a necessary sampling of external inputs. However, whenever there is a significant difference between predictions and sensations, the subsequent surprise elicits attention and then incorporates more current information. Minimizing prediction error contributes to perception and self-organization.[18]

The neuroscience appreciation of prediction error and surprise lends itself to psychoanalytic applications. For example, the analyst unconsciously makes predictions about the patient, including the themes embedded in free associations. The analyst unconsciously, preconsciously, and consciously compares these anticipations with the patient's verbal and non-verbal

---

18 Friston K. (2012). Prediction, perception and agency. *International journal of psychophysiology: official journal of the International Organization of Psychophysiology, 83*(2), 248–252. https://doi.org/10.1016/j.ijpsycho.2011.11.014

expressions. This comparison yields an appreciation of matching areas (provisionally correct predictions) and mismatches that generate the analyst's surprises or prediction errors. Yet errors are inevitable. By taking note of these errors and acknowledging them where necessary, the analyst gradually adjusts his beliefs concerning the patient, improves the accuracy of empathic predictions, and develops a deeper understanding of the patient.

Play

Child analysts, including me, work with displacements of conflicts and emotions to toys and other objects, including transference to the analyst. Toys allow a child to play when words are insufficient to effectively bring a child's unconscious struggles into the therapeutic arena. The analyst enables the child to witness conflicts safely, as they are now externalized and rendered more tolerable through play. The analyst can interpret relevant dynamic, transference, or genetic (connected to significant others in the past) material once it has been consciously explored. Just as child analysts select toys for use in a child patient's play, I introduced movies, poems, and historical events into Jan's analysis. Although not common, many analysts use art, literature, and history, and it is not a technical novelty in adult analysis. For example, after a very draining session dealing with loss and guilt, Jan asked if I had any advice before stopping. He appeared to linger, and I thought a film would remind him of our sessions and help him through the challenging time. So, I intuitively suggested he see a particular movie also dealing with the theme of loss and guilt. Initially, I had some misgivings about making such a recommendation, but the results of subsequent conversations convinced me of the usefulness of such a maneuver. I freely used and described this technique. There are four aspects of such interventions. The analyst first explicitly introduces a movie, artwork, music, or historical event that may contain seeds to aid the patient's self-understanding while clarifying that the patient is under no obligation to pursue it. Second, the patient and analyst explore, at a distance, the dynamics displaced to such a situation removed from the patient. Third, the analyst interprets or the patient self-analyzes aspects of the art form that apply to the analytic-transference relationship, the patient's past life, or current relationships outside the treatment. Finally, the patient and the analyst can comment on the analyst's introduction of such an artifact. They can opine on whether it added to the richness of the analysis or was a waste of time.

Theories

The analyst's theories and life experiences guide his practice. Many unconscious factors attach to the analyst's transference to theory.[19] Due to this, any aspects of the analytic process can become idealized or devalued. Despite the prevalence of such unconscious and uncertain factors in the analyst's personality, the analyst uses his freedom and flexibility to decide the optimal path to treat the patient's problems, the analytic task at hand. Analysts develop theories or adhere to them in good faith, based on their life and professional experiences. The analyst's theories, the contents of his evenly suspended attention, and clinical results, taken together, are necessary to evaluate a psychoanalytic treatment. The primary professional obligation of the analyst is to his patient and the patient's treatment; he is not obliged to use a particular theory. It is not sufficient for the analyst to practice according to his preferred view, technique, or personality preference. The analyst must blend his approach or method to fit the patient's pathology and adapt to address illness, safety, and well-being. Therefore, whether an analyst subscribes to analytic neutrality or views patients and analysts as invariably influencing each other during psychoanalysis, judging any analysis must rest heavily on its effect on the patient. How did the treatment change the patient's manifest symptoms, suffering, complaints, and latent or deeper aspects of the personality? Did the analysis facilitate better insight, understanding, memories, and emotions associated with the self and others? Were unwanted surprises minimized by better anticipation, and was there better error detection and correction? If the patient suffered from self-destructive or suicidal tendencies, did the analysis better understand to manage such trends? Was the patient better able to manage conflicts, hostility, stresses, losses, and uncertainty? Was there increased capacity for work, love, and compassion? Progress along any of these lines counts for the analyst's good work.

Each analyst has a unique style. When an analyst is more talkative, the patient filters the excess and reacts to the heart of the analyst's communications; when an analyst speaks less frequently, the patient amplifies the analyst's words. Whether talking more or less, the analyst should be free and authentic; the patient will find a way to make the most of what the analyst offers. I experienced many feelings, thoughts, and memories

---

19 Rangell, L. (1982) "Transference to Theory: The Relationship of Psychoanalytic Education to the Analyst's Relationship to Psychoanalysis." *Annual of Psychoanalysis* 10:29-56

that did not end up as interpretations or interventions to patients. When a patient freely speaks and makes adequate progress through self-understanding, the analyst's observations, interpretations, and reconstructions complement the patient's effort. I believe this book is an example of the description of the flow of analysis, showing how patients' and analysts' words and actions are linked.

This book is simply a report of Jan's analysis from my perspective and includes my evoked responses. It does not claim to be a good or a good-enough analysis. I openly describe my thoughts, actions, doubts, and mistakes for the lay reader or analyst. I tried to correct my errors based on my judgment and Jan's feedback to the best of my ability. When suicide beckons to a patient, there is a high possibility that an analyst will experience stress and anxiety. An analyst may feel or behave differently where no one's life is at immediate risk. Nevertheless, when an analyst experiences anxiety, it is necessary to understand the private springs of such responses and how they influence the analyst's work.

Essential psychoanalysis and the unique analyst

Freud said, "It may thus be said that the theory of psychoanalysis is an attempt to account for two striking and unexpected facts of observation which emerge whenever an attempt is made to trace the symptoms of a neurotic back to their sources in his past life: the facts of transference and resistance. Any line of investigation which recognizes these two facts and takes them as the starting point of its work may call itself psychoanalysis though it arrives at results other than my own." (Freud 1914, p.16)[20]

Based on this statement of Freud's and his pursuit of studying the unconscious, I coined the term "Essential Psychoanalysis" to designate a form of psychoanalysis. Accordingly, Essential Psychoanalysis is any line of treatment, theory, or science that recognizes the facts of unconscious, transference, or resistance and takes them as the starting point of its work, regardless of its results.[21] My analysis of Jan and this book describing it are an example of Essential Psychoanalysis.

---

20 Freud, S. (1914). "On the history of the psycho-analytic movement." In J. Strachey (Ed. & Trans.), *The Standard Edition of the Complete Psychological Works of Sigmund Freud* (Vol. XIV). London: Hogarth Press.

21 Sripada, B. (2015). "Essential Psychoanalysis: Toward a re-appraisal of the relationship between psychoanalysis and dynamic psychotherapy." *Psychodynamic Psychiatry, 43,* 396–422. doi: 10/1521/pdps.2015.43.3.396.

In contrast, Extensive Psychoanalysis embodies the principles of unconscious, transference, and resistance. Additionally, it requires adherence to technical rules such as a minimum number of sessions a week and the use of the couch. Some of Freud's analyses did not adhere to his own rules. Freud also stated, "I must however make it clear that what I am asserting is that this technique is the only one suited to my individuality; I do not venture to deny that a physician quite differently constituted might find himself driven to adopt a different attitude to his patients and to the task before him." (1913, p. 111)[22]

Freud devised techniques to suit his personality. Since no other person has Freud's personality, each unique analyst must develop individually suitable strategies that fit his patient's needs. Each psychoanalyst must exercise individual judgment to ensure that the principles of psychoanalysis and the mission of helping lessen the patient's suffering persist through any clinical moment or clinical situation, theoretical idea, or piece of research. Following my freedom to integrate my thoughts, feelings, and memories as I treated Jan, I used conventional and innovative interventions to address his problems, the analytic task at hand. Of course, other analysts may not agree with the wisdom or usefulness of what I did. All criticisms, regardless of their direction, constructive or critical, are welcome; they further psychoanalysis.

Although the patient has no direct access to the analyst's reflections, the analyst can describe them to peers or the lay public to provide a more comprehensive context for their communications. To help the reader understand, the analyst needs to describe the experience of these fleeting, cryptic thoughts or symbolic happenings in ordinary language.

Psychoanalytic history has a rich tradition of case presentations. These describe the patient's initial complaints, defenses, dynamics, compromises, and transferences. In general, all analysts work with the most subtle details in the patient: verbal expression (including word choices, slips of the tongue, vocal range, timbre, omissions, and hesitations), non-verbal expression (body language, changes in appearance, and energy level), relationship to time (punctuality, eagerness, or reluctance to leave when the session ends), and more. In addition, psychoanalysts frequently communicate their theories and clinical findings using summarized case

---

22 Freud, S. (1913). "On beginning the treatment (Further recommendations on the technique of psycho-analysis I)." In J. Strachey (Ed. & Trans.), *The Standard Edition of the Complete Psychological Works of Sigmund Freud (Vol. XII)*. London: Hogarth Press.

reports. These often include dreams or illustrative vignettes dealing with unconscious, transference, self, other, intersubjective, or developmental patient dynamics. Such case reports detail the analyst's interventions, and countertransference, and assess the success or failure of the analysis. Often, they report on vignettes that focus on successful transference or dream interpretations, and sometimes the analyst's brilliance![23] Thus, summarized case reports have a recognized place in psychoanalytic tradition. In addition, however, there are examples of more exhaustive case studies. For example, in discovering the psychoanalytic method, Freud's Little Hans, Wolf Man, Rat Man, Anna O, Dora, and Schreiber provided examples of detailed case studies. In addition, Dewald[24] and Winnicott[25] discussed examples of analyses, and Gill and Hoffman[26] provided details of transcribed sessions. This book is an example of such an extensive case study. The patient and analyst are consciously, preconsciously, and unconsciously aware of their respective private realms, but both have access to the public analytic events. In this book, I describe analytic events of my treatment of Jan and offer my unique perspective of the analysis. However, neither I nor the book offers any information on Jan's private musings not expressed through his free associations. Had Jan authored a book about the analysis, his further personal musings could have become known, but he would not have had access to my inner world.

As you read this book, thoughts and images are bound to arise. They may be like mine or not. You may suddenly remember the horror of witnessing a man kill himself or the gentle passing away of a grandparent in sleep. It may be the taste of a favorite dish given to you by your smiling mom or the smell of her burnt toast. You may recall the childhood feeling of your mother leaving you at kindergarten, the excitement of your first kiss, or the thrill of your child's birth. The potential range is limitless. You may repeatedly return to the same scene, just as Jan often repeats his story, and the familiar words may evoke dullness and boredom. When reading a book, one usually wants to know what the author has to say; however,

23 Personal communication: Cliff Wilkerson.

24 Paul A., Dewald. (1972). *The Psychoanalytic Process: A Case Illustration*. 1972 Basic Books. New York.

25 Donald W. Winnicott. (1976). The *Piggle*: An Account of the Psychoanalytic Treatment of a Little Girl. Penguin. London.

26 Merton M. Gill and Irwin Z. Hoffman. (1982). *Analysis of Transference, Vol 2: Studies of Nine Audio-Recorded Psychoanalytic Sessions. Psychological Issues, Monograph 54.* International Universities Press Inc. New York.

you will get the most out of this book if you follow the road that leads to yourself. So put the book down sometimes, and reflect on your thoughts and feelings it evokes. The unique private revelations of your thoughts, emotions, and feelings spurred by reading this book are your reward and a measure of its value.

Life is hanging in the balance when death lurks everywhere; joy is a million miles away, and hope fades. This book describes how an analysis revived the spirit of someone who felt like a shadow of himself. Likewise, treatment alters both the sufferer and the healer. Treating Jan changed me, and I hope reading about it will move you, too.

~Bhaskar Sripada
Chicago, Illinois.
USA

ACKNOWLEDGMENTS

I AM GRATEFUL FOR THE HELP of many people who assisted in developing this narrative.

My most significant debt of gratitude is to Jan, who trusted me, first, to be his psychoanalyst and, second, to share his analysis for your benefit.

Cynthia Dunafon worked with me early on and helped me rein in a rambling story by offering editorial context and clarity. Her familiarity with the Bible was precious in clarifying references to it. Unfortunately, when she had to bow out due to health issues, I sought the editorial help of Dr. Chava Casper.

Through her probing questions, Dr. Casper helped me extend my thinking into many areas I had not considered, and her enthusiasm filled me with the hope that the book had value. She challenged my writing and thinking with her independent spirit and infused the final product with greater coherence and balance. The title of the book was her suggestion.

Although not directly involved in the writing of this book, Arnold Goldberg, Leo Rangell, and Merton Gill personally guided, mentored, and shaped my analytic identity. I either met or corresponded with each of them for between seven and ten years. Goldberg focused on the analyst anticipating the patient's self. Rangell showed the continuing relevance of the Oedipus Complex to the more profound understanding of man. Finally, Gill taught the centrality of transference in the analytic relationship. Gill, Rangell, and Goldberg subscribed to different but equally coherent psychoanalytic theories. After much effort to reconcile their mutual differences, they faced unavoidable conflicts and concluded that they could not resolve their theoretical disagreements. Despite my attachment to Gill, Rangell, and Goldberg, I used their ideas opportunistically. This book exemplifies my integration of their contributions to my style of analysis. My worldview differs from each of their views, but strives to allow greater freedom for both the patient and analyst.

I thank Peter Barglow, Maria Caserta, David Chandler, Ravi Dasika, Scott Davis, Steven Flagel, Prudy Guurguechon, Mazher Hussain, Hari Narayan Jandhayala, Gita Subba Rao and Subba Rao Jandhayala, Narayana Murty Jandhyala, Thomas Jobe, Karen Lupa, Ron Moline, Arthur Nielsen, Bhawani Prasad, Mark Smaller, Eva Sripada, Prabhakar and Padmashree Sripada, Padmini Sripada, Madhu Vallabhaneni, and Jesse Viner, for their thoughtful insights. In addition, I express my gratitude to Usha Mohan Reddy for ideas regarding the jacket cover and Kam Sripada for the cover photograph.

I also thank the team at 1106 Design for this book's final cover, interior page design, formatting, editorial, and other services. Finally, I thank Mark Smaller, Neal Spira, and Cliff Wilkerson for reviewing my book. With the support of all those who helped me, I tried to balance simplicity and elaboration. As a result, I hope the reader gets a good view of Jan's life through my eyes and a bonus glimpse of the responses of their own unique selves.

~Bhaskar Sripada
Chicago, Illinois
USA

CHAPTER 1

THERE WAS A FAINT KNOCK on my door. Before I could respond, Maria opened it and peeked in.

"I need your help," she said. She spoke with a faint Italian accent. Her tone was urgent.

"I'll try," I replied instinctively, pointing to a comfortable chair and motioning her to sit. But, instead, she perched tentatively on the chair's edge.

Over the past several decades, I taught many psychiatry residents, including Maria. She was a tall, attractive woman, about 30 years old. I didn't know her well, but I remembered her as quiet, composed, and shy. Now, however, she was flushed and animated, and she had entered my office before I answered her knock. I wondered what pressing issue had brought her.

"Do you remember Jan, my husband?"

Of course, I remembered Jan. He was another psychiatry resident. Several years before, he had worked with me for two months on the adolescent unit at Kennedy University Hospital. He came from Poland. He spoke English well, but with a strong Polish accent. So I had to concentrate on understanding him. When he worked with me, his mother was sick—some sort of cancer—and he was preoccupied with her illness. At one point, when his mother's medical condition had deteriorated, he came to me to request a week's vacation. It was a simple request, and I had no hesitation signing off on it. Jan was profusely thankful and almost held back tears of gratitude, a reaction that struck me as excessive. That memory arose in me now.

"Of course, I remember Jan," I replied.

"Jan is depressed. First, his patient, Amir, killed himself about six months ago. Although upset, Jan worked for a month after the suicide. Then

1

he failed the USMLE exam, and the department put him on administrative leave. He cannot return to work till he passes the exam. After that, Jan saw an analyst about three times and stopped. After that, he got worse and did not want to get out of bed. He has not left our house for about three months. So, now I am seeing you trying to get him help."

I usually experience anticipation associated with specific thoughts or feelings at the prospect of managing a new patient. So I look out for such intimations and try to make sense of them. Although Maria wasn't the patient, she had activated the process in this instance.

As I waited to hear about what else was going on, I noticed her eyes nervously but approvingly (or so it seemed to me) glancing at the bronze bust of Sigmund Freud on the mantle to the right of her chair, his visage exuding both kindness and intellect.

The Chicago Institute for Psychoanalysis presents each student this bust of Freud on graduation. To me, it was an announcement to the world that I had arrived. It was a cherished possession, a matter of immense pride, and represented years of training and sacrifice, also by my wife. The line from Virgil's *Aeneid* that Freud chose as the epigraph of *The Interpretation of Dreams* burst into my awareness: "*Flectere si nequeo superos, Acheronta movebo,*"[27] generally translated as "If I cannot bend the Higher Powers, I will stir up the underworld." It was a daring statement, even for someone whose dreams and actions *did* stir up the world.

I pondered Freud's eventful life and sought to remember something about him that might help me with Maria. A strange and banal memory came to me as I recalled Freud's observation, "*Pour faire une omelette il faut casser des œufs,*"[28] or, in simple English, "To make an omelet, you have to break some eggs." Freud was not talking food here, but sex: In dealing with patients, especially hysterical patients, it is impossible to treat a person with repressed sexual conflicts without breaking norms and mentioning sex. Freud saw no reason to feel any compunction about discussing normal or abnormal sexual facts. There is no danger of corrupting the human soul: Patients unconsciously have knowledge about such matters, and making them aware of the meaning of their latent thoughts benefits the treatment. In

---

27 Freud, S. "The interpretation of dreams." In J. Strachey (Ed. and Trans.), *The Standard Edition of the Complete Psychological Works of Sigmund Freud* (Vol. 4, p. ix). London: Hogarth Press.

28 Freud, S. "Fragment of an analysis of a case of hysteria." In J. Strachey (Ed. and Trans.), *The Standard Edition of the Complete Psychological Works of Sigmund Freud* (Vol. 7, p. 49). London: Hogarth Press.

short, Freud's advice to the analyst was not to pussyfoot around, be direct, and air out such thoughts—tactfully and at the right time.

Freud discovered that people unconsciously censor sexual ideas, often by innocently looking away. For example, after an embrace from Herr K, a young adolescent girl named Dora came to Freud for treatment, complaining of disgust and the sensation of pressure on her thorax[29]. Freud thought these two symptoms were displaced upward from her pelvis, where she had felt Herr K's erection. He courageously encouraged Dora to talk openly about her experiences. In contrast to traditional sexual mores, Freud thought that people could directly speak about sexual matters of every kind. He was cracking the eggs of an inhibited civilization to formulate ideas that would survive the ages.

Freud "discovered" what he admitted every nursemaid already knew: A boy loves his mother, a girl loves her father, and children have their own sometimes-fantastical ideas about sex. I don't know whether Freud moved heaven or hell, but he certainly shook up the Earth, although current science is less willing to accommodate many of Freud's beliefs and the psychoanalytic methods of his tribe.

Back to the office . . . but what did Freud and sex have to do with Amir's suicide? At that moment, I had no idea how any of these thoughts related to Jan or Maria. So I waited for more material but came up dry.

Maria continued, "After his patient killed himself, Jan worked for about two months and then failed the USMLE [the United States Medical Licensing Exam]. But, as you very well know, he has to pass it by the end of the third year, or he cannot be a doctor . . ." Maria's voice trailed away. Still sitting on the edge of the chair, she waited for me to speak.

I saw Maria's eyes anxiously glance around the room until her gaze fell on a painting on the wall of Kali, a Hindu goddess: Kali, the Dark Mother, the ruthless slayer of illusions, the goddess of death and time. After looking at the image for a moment, Maria abruptly recoiled and looked away. The myth of Kali and the demon Raktabhija burst into my consciousness. Raktabhija, a monster whose name means "blood-seed," acquired the magical power to clone himself. Whenever a drop of his blood spilled on the Earth, it became a clone. And every drop of blood from every clone became yet another clone. With his many clones and a vast army, he began to attack

29 Freud, S. (1905 [1901]). "Fragment of an analysis of a case of hysteria." In J. Strachey (Ed. and Trans.), *The Standard Edition of the Complete Psychological Works of Sigmund Freud* (Vol. 7). London: Hogarth Press.

all the gods. Knowing his powers, the terrified gods ran to Kali, imploring her to protect them and kill him.

Kali fell upon Raktabhija and his army with a frightful shriek, vanquishing his foot soldiers, elephants, and elephant riders. With her claw-like hands, she shoveled them into her mouth so that it dripped with their blood. Kali and Raktabhija were then left facing each other. Kali lifted Raktabhija off the ground, dismembered him, and ate him, extending her tongue to ensure that not a single drop of his blood would fall to Earth. Raktabhija was no more, and his dead and dismembered army lay strewn on the battleground.

Drunk with the blood of her victims and intoxicated by the taste of victory, Kali prepared to celebrate by adorning herself with tokens of a victorious battle, weaving a belt of dismembered hands, and draping herself with a garland of cut-off heads. She then began dancing furiously, trampling the corpses of her slain enemies. Fearing that Kali's fevered dance would threaten all the worlds, the gods tried to devise a way to break her trance and calm her down, but she would have none of it. Finally, in desperation, they dispatched Shiva, her husband, to bring her to her senses. Shiva called to her to stop, but she couldn't hear him. Desperate to get her attention, he threw himself amongst the corpses where she was dancing. Kali's foot was about to crush Shiva, her husband, when she abruptly recognized him and stopped herself.

The painting in my office (see the following page) captures this moment. Kali's blood-drenched tongue hangs out of her mouth in surprise as she suddenly recognizes her husband under her feet. Kali's jaw seems to have dropped in a gesture of shame. Her uncontrolled frenzy consumed her. She had lost track of herself and almost trampled her husband.

I bought the Kali painting at an unknown artist's street art fair in New Delhi. He spoke a Hindi dialect I could barely understand, yet I felt his deep devotion to the goddess. He called her "Mother" and portrayed her as fearsome and ugly, an old hag with pendulous breasts, a gaping mouth, bloodshot eyes, and claw-like fingers. Kali is riding a tiger, nude except for a belt of severed hands and a garland of skulls in other representations. In her arms, she carries a noose, a skull-topped staff, and the sword of Vengeance . . . and there is Shiva, fearful that she might inadvertently crush him underfoot. (In some versions of the myth, Shiva transforms himself into an infant. Kali, who has been deaf to all entreaties, hears the cry of her infant/husband and picks him up to nurse him, like any loving mother.

Picture of Kali, in my office.

(Who can ignore a screaming baby?) Whether as husband or baby, would it not be suicidal for a man to throw himself on the mercy of his wild, murderous, knife-wielding wife?

To those who cling to their unreal or illusory wishes and dreams, Kali appears as a demon and killer. However, to those who can distinguish between fulfillable wishes and dreams and those destined to remain unfulfilled, Kali is a benevolent and protective mother of truth. Kali's chief mission is the separation of illusion from reality. Kali teaches us that permanency is an illusion, change is inevitable, and death is inescapable.

Why does the terrifying Kali adorn the wall of my office? Suffering is often related to intolerable, strange, embarrassing, disheartening, tragic, or forbidden ideas and emotions hidden in plain sight or nestled in the recesses of our unconscious. A person may be disabled from conflict, anguish, the torment of nightmares, the daze of novelty, or blindness of hubris. He funnels these concerns into the analyst and asks, "Can you listen and accept and bear the weight of my true self? Can you understand my pain and help me?" The patient who feels that the analyst cannot, or does not want to, engage in his turmoil cannot fully participate in treatment. And the analyst who cannot bear witness to the patient's self-exploration is limited and cannot help that patient. Indeed, the *analyst's* avoidance may unintentionally foster the *patient's* avoidance. Kali shows how to attack illusions and evasions unsparingly and boldly seek understanding. Psychoanalysis is not the teaching of Emily Post's etiquette; it is a blood-and-guts deep dive. I want my patients to know I am there to serve them to the best of my ability. I will try to do this regardless of the nature of their suffering or their wishes. I hope the picture on my wall says to my patients, "Let your thoughts roam as far as they can into your fears and wishes. Self-knowledge will illuminate your path." Therefore, a picture of Kali, Shiva, and Raktabhija adorns my office.

I didn't feel pressured to respond. Instead, I wanted to listen to all the thoughts that came to me before I spoke. I wasn't sure how any of these thoughts could help Maria, who was concerned that her husband was falling apart and that her future was at stake. The death of a patient could make anyone sick, and losing the dream of becoming a physician at this stage could be devastating.

Then I remembered that, months ago, at a Residency Training Committee meaning I had attended, I had heard that Jan was in treatment at a Residency Training Committee meeting I had attended. "I thought Jan was seeing a psychiatrist," I said.

"He was," Maria replied. "He saw a shrink a few times, but he didn't click with him and gave up."

I noted that she used the word *shrink* somewhat derisively, but mostly, I saw the concern in her face that Jan had no clear avenue for help. I was saddened. Here, there was not a drop of treatment for Jan's depression in a sea of psychiatrists. I felt queasy, too, as an image of the Pied Piper of Hamelin hit me. I understood it immediately.

In the legend, the town of Hamelin is suffering from a rat infestation, and the people promise a big reward to whoever can get rid of them. A man with a pipe accepts the challenge and lures the rats to a river, where they drown. However, after he completes the job, the town refuses to pay him. Seeking revenge, the Pied Piper returns and plays his tune again and lures the boys and girls of Hamelin away—to drown or, in other versions, into a cave—never to be seen again. A lame child, unable to keep up with the others, remains alive and reports on what happened in one version.

I felt that Amir was like the Pied Piper, taking his life and his family's hopes forever. Amir's suicide was a powerful lure for Jan, like the Pied Piper's tune. Could Jan follow Amir into the cave of no return and commit suicide? Or could Jan become the lucky lame one who escaped the deadly cave with his life?

My wish to protect Jan's life was also to preserve my own hide: I didn't want a dead body on my hands. Yes, I feared that I did not want to be a failure. I needed Freud, my bronze hero, and Kali, my killer goddess, to keep my fears at bay. I felt a pang of guilt at the petty pride that made me hesitate. I would need courage to treat a potentially dangerous patient like Jan.

I also felt a little ashamed that I was hesitating. I rationalized that this was because—at the time—my practice was limited to outpatients. The depression that immobilizes a person to the point of not leaving the house for a few months could be severe depression, which sometimes requires inpatient treatment. I was not an inpatient psychiatrist. If Jan needed that, I could justify recusing myself. But what was it in me that made me feel that I might not be the right person to treat Jan? Jan must be drowning in self-blame. He needed someone who could empathize with him without blaming him. Could I be that person? I wasn't sure.

My father's name was Venkata Krishnayya Sripada, but I will refer to him throughout this book as *Nanna*, the word for "Dad" in Telugu, my native language. My mother's name was Kamala; I call her *Amma*, Telugu for "Mom."

During World War II, Nanna served as a member of the Indian Medical Service in India and Burma. There, he saw countless men die, had performed many amputations, and he'd had experience with treating many infected wounds. He spent the rest of his career as a general practitioner for the Indian Railways, but the war memories stayed with him the rest of his life.

Although Nanna witnessed the suffering and pain of soldiers during the War, he couldn't bear seeing his children in pain from even the mildest injuries. He was so concerned about the possibility of infection that he insisted on overzealously treating even minor cuts and abrasions. His healing was by the wet method: First, he washed the broken skin with water and covered it with gauze or cotton. Then he doused the bandage with a tincture of iodine or tincture of benzoin. This procedure produced a burning sensation as if a flame had been applied directly to the wound. To a child, it felt like pure torture. After a few days, the red-brown gauze, infused with tincture and clotted blood, was stuck to the healing wound. His peeling off the gauze set off another round of howling pain. No wonder we children avoided Nanna as much as possible if we got hurt; we submitted to Amma's ministrations instead. Amma used the dry method: She washed the wound with soap and water, and let it dry in the open air. She was the go-to doctor in the house.

Fortunately, my siblings and I escaped childhood without significant injuries. Nevertheless, both Nanna and Amma wanted to address the damage and manage the pain in dealing with our minor wounds. The main difference wasn't only the difference between the wet and dry methods of first aid: It was in their attitude toward our suffering. Nanna's love for us made it hard for him to tolerate our pain. He tended to blame us for our carelessness in becoming injured (and, unspoken, for causing *him* pain). Amma was more interested in doing what she could to heal the wound; blame never came into it.

When my children suffered slight injuries, I tried to behave like Amma and be as understanding and supportive as possible. I did feel Nanna's impulse to blame the victim for being careless, but I worked hard to suppress it. I knew that if this blaming attitude emerged in my interactions with Jan, who was already deeply depressed, it could be disastrous. So, I hesitated.

I am accustomed to having such fleeting thoughts and feelings. They reflect who I am and influence my style of treatment. But, like other analysts, I recognize that they may also echo the emotions of my patients. Thus, my hesitation and anxiety could very well be a manifestation of some element of Maria's or Jan's personality, but I had no way of knowing how so far. What was clear, however, was that Jan needed help.

As I sat there, remembering the tinctures of my childhood, I got a sense of how to characterize his problem, but as soon as I had it, that understanding slipped out of my consciousness, and I immediately forgot it. It upset me, but I decided to move on to Maria. Determined to do her best to get help for Jan, she had presented his predicament without self-pity, embarrassment, or denial. On the contrary, I could see that she was practical and realistic, and I appreciated her straightforwardness. It freed me to be direct, to be myself, so I got right to the point: "Do you think Jan is suicidal?"

"No, but he needs help *now*." She didn't hesitate to answer and seemed relieved that I'd been direct, too. Nevertheless, her speech conveyed her anxiety for her husband and herself.

"I hope you don't mind that I asked such a blunt question."

"No, I don't mind," she replied. "I appreciate your being direct. Unfortunately, I haven't been able to speak to anybody about this. I don't know what to do. I asked Jan to talk to somebody, but he won't."

I agreed that he needed to be in treatment. "I don't have an inpatient practice. I'm glad to try to help him, provided he's not so depressed that he needs to be in a hospital. It's unusual for a psychiatrist to call a patient to get treatment started. Treatment usually starts when the patient contacts the psychiatrist, but, if you wish, I'm glad to call him."

She gave me his number, and I dialed. When Jan answered the phone, he spoke slowly.

"H a l l o o."

I felt like I was speaking to a ghost. "Jan, this is Dr. Sripada."

Quickly coming to attention, Jan responded, "Yes, Dr. Sripada," and then, more hesitantly, "I . . . wasn't . . . expecting . . . a call."

"I'm with Maria. She told me that you haven't been feeling like talking to anybody in a while."

"Yes, that's true."

"I want to talk to you. I hope you'll agree to see me."

"Yes, I'd like to see you, too."

"How about tomorrow?"

"OK."

We made an appointment for the next day, and, because he lived far from my office, I recommended a double session. He agreed.

CHAPTER 2

On the way to the office the next day to meet Jan, I stopped at a farmers' market near my house and got in the long line of people sampling the strawberries.

As I waited, an image of Lydia, our babysitter for more than 10 years, came to me. It was worth the wait, for the strawberries were delightful. Lydia loved strawberries, and, like Jan, she was from Poland. My thoughts then moved to Jan. He had been avoiding contact with people for several months. The eerie tone of his voice had struck me on the phone. He'd cut himself off from the world and must have decided that isolation was his best strategy for life. Maria, his only link to the outside, was bravely standing by him, but she was terrified.

Jan had readily agreed to see me, but I wasn't sure what I could do to help him. There was nothing in my bag of tricks that seemed relevant. Jan wanted Amir to rise like Lazarus and remove his burden. I wanted Jan not to let his life slip away in pursuit of this miracle. I wondered if the sweetness of a moment—the sweetness of strawberries?—could touch him through his armor of pain and avoidance, whether it could make him think there might be other possibilities for him. So, I bought two boxes of strawberries—one for my family and one for him. The image of Citizen Kane popped into my consciousness as he revisited his burned-down house and, finding his half-charred cherished teddy bear, moved on. I hoped the taste of a sweet strawberry might revive some precious Polish memory and stir Jan to take a step on the path back to life.

Jan arrived at our appointed time. He was almost 40 years old, a good-looking fellow with black hair, rimless glasses, and a week-old stubbly beard. Jan looked a little heavier than I remembered him, less lithe and muscular. I extended my hand to greet him, and, without really looking at me, he raised his to meet it. His grip was inert and lifeless. I grasped his hand briefly with both of my hands to emphasize that I was fully there and wanted to do my best to help him. He looked up briefly but seemed to be in his own world. As he sat down, I reached for the box of strawberries and gave it to him.

"You didn't have to bring those," he said.

He seemed a little surprised and perhaps even annoyed. I wondered if he felt that I was treating him like a child, babying him with food, and resented me for the gesture. Nevertheless, I remembered the strawberries' sweetness and hoped it would lift his spirits, if only briefly. Just as a journey starts with a single step, his mood would have to improve one moment at a time.

"I brought them because I wanted to give them to you. I tasted the strawberries at the market and thought they were delicious. I thought you might enjoy them, too. I know you haven't talked to anybody in a while. You said you'd like to see me. . . . " I wanted to connect Jan's last words to me from the day before to where we were today, but before I could complete my sentence, he started to talk.

"Imagine the worst. That's what's happening to me. Like all physicians, I'm dealing with life-and-death situations, but I harmed my patient, unlike other physicians. As a psychiatrist, I drove a man to suicide. As a man, I love my wife, but I don't feel it. I'm alone, cut off from all other human beings. I have no future. I have no feelings. How can I mourn? Crazily enough, I feel jealous of my dead patient."

Jealous? Jan's unexpected declaration jolted me. *So he was jealous of a dead man?!*

That he had surprised me indicated the possibility and need for my future learning. Every surprise tells us that what we know is inadequate for the current situation. There must be new learning if we are to grasp the moment's lessons.

Before a concert, every orchestra tunes up according to the same preset routine: The oboe sounds the "A" note. The woodwinds follow, then the brass, and finally, the strings. The orchestra proceeds to the music, following the composer's sheet music and the conductor's guidance. All the musicians have a clear idea of the composition and their role in performing it.

There is no such prefixed composer-type design in analytic treatment. When an analyst meets a new patient, he can ponder only the *patterns* of possible futures: what he can contribute to this unknown patient, the panoply of emotions swirling within himself, and his state of readiness to interact with this patient. Before the first appointment with a new patient, I can consider memories of previous patients, but—unlike a musical instrument—I know I will have to tune myself differently to each patient. It is hard to describe the analyst's continuous self–other adjusting to match each patient. Until the analyst and patient settle into some preliminary pattern, the analyst must navigate their anticipation, memory, fantasies, hopes, and professional readiness to engage the patient. Ideally, the analyst is reasonably prepared for the patient.

When Jan said he was jealous of his dead patient, I was floored and baffled. Nothing in my experience had prepared me for that. But then, I remembered that I had considered the theme of courage when Maria first came to my office. Now, Jan had introduced a new idea—jealousy of a dead man—that was beyond my understanding. Only time would tell if I could tune in to Jan. His previous analysis had foundered because they could not share a workable wavelength.

Jan continued, "My patient killed himself, and I haven't been able to recover. Amir's suicide changed me completely. Its impact was more than I could ever have imagined. I always thought that I could manage life. I always found a way. I thought that life would always find a way, but I was wrong. It took some time, but now I realize there is no hope. There's something seriously wrong with me. I'll never make it. That's how I think."

I knew that Jan was depressed, but was he also suicidal?

Jan continued, "Also, soon after Amir killed himself, I had to take the USMLE. Until I pass it, I can't practice as a doctor. I've failed it several times. I've always passed exams with ease. Failing was new to me. It wasn't a question of what I knew or didn't know. It's as if I *decided* to fail. I did well on the practice exams at home, but in the exam hall, I froze. Whenever a question in psychiatry came up, I became anxious and overwhelmed, and I couldn't go on to the next question. I felt so compelled to answer those questions right that I just couldn't move on. I got stuck. I felt so guilty about Amir that it was like I had decided to fail. I've wanted to be a doctor all my life, but I don't deserve to be a doctor. I can't be a doctor. I can't be responsible. I don't want to be responsible for others.

"These were the thoughts that have been swirling around in me, and I can't stop them. I've had no one to talk to, and no one talked to me. Then, I didn't *want* to talk to anybody. I spoke to Maria, who is loving, kind, and generous. She wanted to help me, but I saw fear in her eyes when I spoke about my depression. I didn't want to overburden her with my guilt, let alone my thoughts about suicide, so I stopped sharing them."

Maybe wise, I thought. *Jan has enough human connection to care about her but, till now, not enough to get help for himself.*

Jan continued, "I withdrew. One day passed to another. Days and nights didn't matter. They all felt like nights. Days changed to a week. I didn't leave home. A month passed, and I didn't leave home. Three months passed, and I didn't leave home. I don't want to do this."

Jan seemed like a wooden statue; his face remained expressionless and flat as words poured out of his mouth like water through a breached dam. Often, depressed people so burdened by symptoms have slowed speech and difficulty communicating. Jan's coherent stream of thought amazed me. I was glad that he was talking, but I was still concerned that he might be suicidal. Most of what he had said until now made sense, but I didn't know what *this* was in "I do not want to do this." I wanted to communicate to Jan that I would do my best to try to understand him. And if I didn't understand something, we would stop and discuss it until I did.

I looked at him, made sure he was looking at me, and asked, "This?"

"Oh, *this* is being a doctor. When I got the call from you, you said you wanted to talk to me. You said you'd be *glad* to talk to me. No one had said that before. Maria told me later that she'd talked to you, and you called me with her in the room, and that you called as soon as she'd talked to you. I knew I'd never make it on my own."

Good, I thought. *Jan is aware of his wish to be a doctor and realizes he needs some assistance.*

"Maria knew it," Jan continued. "She knew I needed help. I don't know how I decided I would see you. I feel so guilty; I need to find out what makes me feel so guilty."

Was Jan guilty only about Amir, or was he also guilty about something else? And in the middle of all this heartfelt pain, he seemed detached from all feeling. As I was thinking, Jan's face suddenly turned red, and two streams of tears poured down his cheeks. I gestured toward the Kleenex on the end table near his chair. He ignored it; he was a proud Pole. He appeared to be saying, letting his tears flow, *I want to know myself, and I'm not ashamed of my pain.* Although he spoke profoundly about his feelings, he seemed lifeless; then, suddenly, his eyes seemed to flicker with . . .

. . . a spark of energy! "Here, I can talk easily. I can spill my guts."

Jan was aware that he was speaking freely, but what had gotten him stuck before? From Jan's perspective, I knew that it meant that he could talk freely *to me*. His chance use of the phrase "spill my guts" had me thinking freely, too, but I was thinking of *harakiri*! This came from an entirely personal stream of associations having to do with my own fear and fascination with suicide from years of listening to my father's war stories.

I was born several years after World War II ended. I came from a typical Indian family, with many uncles, aunts, and cousins. On most weekends and vacations, we visited family. There was always an exciting conversation about family matters, politics, and sports. Although all the family elders were adults during World War II and the declaration of Indian independence in 1947, my aunts and uncles rarely talked about either topic. Most of them worked for the railways, the judiciary, or other government jobs during the years preceding independence. Few family members joined Gandhi and gave up their jobs to protest the British; none were jailed for civil disobedience. Thus, my family had passively gone along with the British colonizers. Perhaps this left them with a sense of shame that they had not actively fought in the independence movement and cowed them into subsequent silence. On the other hand, I know of families with active discussions about the struggle for freedom, especially if their members had participated in it.

Since few of my uncles volunteered to serve in the War, the topic rarely arose in family conversations. However, on those rare occasions when it did come up, Nanna was open about his feelings about war. My uncles favored negotiations and compromise regarding political problems that faced the country, but my dad was open to confrontation. They saw him as crude, discordant, or beside the point. He was the bull in the Indian china shop.

At home, once every year, Nanna took out and cleaned his small stash of World War II memorabilia. First, he washed his black, rubberized, waterproof, mid-calf-high gumboots he wore walking through the wet mud during the monsoons while serving in Burma. He taught me first to turn them over and shake them, to roust any spiders or scorpions that may have nested inside. Next, he scrubbed and applied Brasso metal polish to his old buckles, buttons, and his Captain's epaulet stars and polished them. Next, he solemnly brought out his Gurkha knife, or *kukri*, cleaned it and applied Vaseline to the blade to prevent rusting. Then, he talked about the war, demonstrated marching and drills, and invited us to ask questions.

My older sister and I followed my dad to our terrace for our dad's drills most of the time. My other siblings did not attend these marches because

Nanna mostly talked about the dreadful responsibilities of doctors working under primitive battlefield conditions. He spoke of evacuating wounded soldiers taken by stretcher-bearers to the advanced dressing station, cared for in a Field Ambulance, moved to a Casualty Clearing Station, and then transferred to a Base Hospital. Death invaded life with little warning. Infected and gangrenous limbs were unceremoniously amputated with bone saws, as any delay could cost a life. As Nanna talked, you could feel the concern he had about his patients' pain, as he detailed the doses and methods of administering morphine to wounded and dying soldiers. Curiously, my older sister and I ended up being physicians.

Nanna described guns, bayonets, and hand-to-hand combat. The Japanese seemed to be winning early on, but the tide of battle turned. Defeated and disorganized, they retreated without burying their dead, so he also saw many putrid, bloated, rotting bodies. When he talked about the Japanese soldiers, he often used a British accent, speaking in a crescendo of rising emotion: "The Japanese are bloody blaggards, bloody bastards, and bloody buggers. Kill them! Bomb them!" At moments like this, he seemed transformed, so very not his usual friendly self.

During the knife-cleaning ritual, I once asked my dad why the Japanese deserved to be killed. He replied, "Because they used live Chinese, Burmese, English, and Indian soldiers and civilians for bayonet practice. They were the enemy, but I will also say the Japanese soldiers were brave and didn't fear death. If they could help it, they never surrendered, so they had to be killed. They committed *harakiri* if capture was inevitable."

Nanna then pretended to be a Japanese officer and reenacted *harakiri*. He sat down Japanese-style, kneeling on the floor with his legs folded underneath his thighs and resting on his heels. He took off his undershirt and unsheathed the *kukri*. He squinted his eyes to look Japanese, assumed a stolid demeanor, got a far-off look on his face, and pretended to draw the knife across his abdomen, starting from the lower left and moving to the upper right. While he did this, he pretended to be in great pain. However, he told us that what he was doing was only a show, but it was real for the Japanese officer who killed himself. He had witnessed *harakiri*. Despite some anxiety, I looked forward to these occasions, as there was always some exciting tidbit I learned about his fascinating past.

I learned from his stories that Allied soldiers tried stopping some of the Japanese from killing themselves, but they were just hell-bent on doing it and couldn't be stopped. As a physician, I now reflected on my luck that none of my patients had committed suicide. I cannot attribute such good fortune to any particular talent of mine: Any doctor can have a patient who commits suicide.

Thus, I identified two streams of thought: one, that Jan felt he could talk freely, and two, a series of childhood memories evoked by Jan's use of the phrase "spill my guts." I realized I was having difficulty listening with truly evenly suspended attention because the fear of Jan's suicidality was ricocheting through my thoughts.

Jan moved on to a new topic. "You're not the first psychoanalyst I've seen. The previous guy had an office downtown with a great view. Through his huge floor-to-ceiling glass window, I could see Lake Michigan. After days spent in the smallest room in my apartment, the open space outside his window made me feel unsafe. I thought of flying out, well, actually jumping out from the 23rd-floor window. He was polite and listened to me. His reactions were mild and mannerly, but I didn't feel any genuine personal reciprocity. I never felt comfortable talking to him. He would comment about what I said, and it felt pretty off the wall. I can't explain it better. We just didn't click. I couldn't tell him what I needed to."

What was it that Jan needed to say? Why didn't Jan click with him? What derailed the treatment? Although the previous analyst was likely part of the problem, I wanted to know what Jan had contributed to the stalemate. It might help me address issues early. I was anxious not only about Jan's suicidality but about my preoccupation with *harakiri*. Together, these might impair my ability to treat him. How long would it be before I, too, would have to deal with some issue that might abort the treatment? I know of analysts who have reputations as the best in their field, but people's judgments are susceptible to exaggeration. I've always felt uneasy when a patient said I was much better (or much worse) than other analysts, so Jan's initial ease with me offered no comfort. We analysts are all practicing an impossible profession. It has been my experience that when a patient singled me out as an excellent analyst, I needed to address the source of such excessive good faith. As they say in physics, the higher they rise . . . Jan's voice, which seemed to be louder than before, broke through my brief reverie.

Jan was animated now. "With you, we immediately went to Amir. I can't get him out of my mind. That's the problem. But I feel there may be a solution. Something has changed in me, just today. When I'm here, words come out easily. Now I feel I want to pass the exam and consider being a doctor, but I don't know how to do it."

I was relieved and felt my anxiety about Jan's suicidal potential drop, but I still had the memories of *harakiri* that he had evoked. While giving considerable weight to learning from my own life's experiences, I treat patients by the guiding lights of the founders and leaders who guided the evolution of psychoanalysis. Among the many illustrious analysts of the past, the contributions of two founders of psychoanalysis, Josef Breuer and Sigmund Freud, cannot be overstated. I thought about Breuer and Freud and Bertha Pappenheim (whom they called Fräulein Anna O), the first psychoanalytic patient. Here is a summary of Breuer's description of her case.[30]

Anna was a woman in her early twenties. Breuer saw her between 1880 and 1882.

Anna's father was sick with a sub-pleural abscess, and Anna and her mother took care of him. Anna herself had several symptoms during that time, such as hydrophobia, hallucinations, and cough. Breuer discovered that these symptoms were associated with Anna's thoughts and feelings. He found that the symptoms disappeared when she expressed the emotions related to the symptoms. For example, initially, Anna couldn't drink fluids. However, her hydrophobia disappeared after she expressed disgust at a governess who let a dog drink out of a glass.

Anna called the nexus of linked symptoms, associations, thoughts, memories, dreams, and feelings her "private theater." In her sessions with Breuer, she uttered whatever random thoughts and feelings occurred to her. She dubbed this novel treatment method a "talking cure" or "chimney-sweeping."[31] Those labels, coined by the first analytic patient, stuck.

Breuer became so engrossed in this young woman, sometimes devoting several hours a day to her treatment, that it took a while until he recognized that his wife had become jealous. He was guilt-ridden when he did and decided to terminate the therapy.

Breuer told Anna of his intention to stop her treatment, but that very evening, he was called back to her and found her in an agitated state, writhing with abdominal pain. When he asked what was wrong, she responded, "Now Dr. B's child is coming."[32] Breuer had viewed Anna as asexual until

---

30 Breuer, J. "Fräulein Anna O: Case Histories from Studies on Hysteria," in J. Strachey (Ed. and Trans.), *The Standard Edition of the Complete Psychological Works of Sigmund Freud* (Vol. 2, pp. 19–47). London: Hogarth Press.

31 Breuer, J. (1893). "Fräulein Anna O: Case Histories from Studies on Hysteria." In J. Strachey (Ed. and Trans.), *The Standard Edition of the Complete Psychological Works of Sigmund Freud* (Vol. 2, pp. 19–47). London: Hogarth Press.

32 Clark, R. (1980). *Freud, The Man and the Cause.* New York: Random House, p. 104.

that point, so he was utterly shocked. He concluded that she was in the throes of the hysterical birth of a phantom pregnancy. Alarmed, he fled from her and went on a second honeymoon with his wife. (So, Jan wasn't the first psychiatrist overwhelmed by a patient.)

A year after discontinuing Anna's treatment, Breuer confided to Freud that he was "quite unhinged and that [he] wished she would die so [he] could be released from her suffering."[33]

When Freud and Breuer first discussed Anna's case, they agreed that she was neurotic but differed fundamentally on what neurosis meant. Freud felt that sexual conflict was at the root of neurotic problems and saw hysteria as a sexual metaphor. Breuer, in contrast, did not consider sex to be a central theme in his understanding of Anna. He rejected the idea that a 23-year-old woman could have sexual feelings for a man about as old as her (by then) dead father. He never again wrote a single line relating to sexuality.

Ten years after this incident, Breuer asked Freud to consult on another case of hysteria. Freud labeled it a typical case of a fantasy of pregnancy and described how one of his own female patients leaped into his arms one day. He reiterated his conviction that hysterics suffer from sexual repression and that such an act illustrated the phenomenon of transference (redirecting emotions associated with someone in the patient's life toward the analyst). Breuer abruptly ended the discussion. According to Jones, Freud decided that "the recurrence of the old situation was too much for Breuer. Without saying a word, he [Breuer] took up his hat and stick and hurriedly left the house."[34]

Breuer and Freud were deeply affected by Anna O but in different ways. Whereas Breuer was frightened by his patient's sexual wishes, Freud bravely persisted in his quest to unlock the mysteries of sexuality. Freud complained that his isolation slowed his scientific progress because he had to rely on himself alone.

Psychoanalysis was always wet with the juices of life. It was never a matter of donning a surgical gown or operating in a sterile field where the doctor remained emotionally uncontaminated by the patient. My view is that it resembles the interaction of sun, seed, water, earth, and time needed to produce a harvest. It is not an intellectual exercise in human understanding alone; it needs to achieve results for real people in the real world.

---

33 Clark, R. (1980). *Freud, The Man and the Cause*. New York: Random House, p. 105.

34 Jones, E. (1953). *The Life and Works of Sigmund Freud* (Vol. 1, p. 226). London: Hogarth Press.

Anna O never married, but she continued to have thoughts about justice, law, and childbirth, writing, "If there is any justice in the next life, women will make the laws there and men will bear the children."[35] These are significant thoughts, even though they're not free associations according to the "fundamental rule."

All analysts learn about Freud's *fundamental rule*. Freud himself described it best: "So say whatever goes through your mind. Act as though, for instance, you were a traveler sitting next to the window of a railway carriage and describing to someone inside the carriage the changing views, which you see outside. Finally, never forget that you have promised to be absolutely honest, and never leave anything out because, for some reason or other, it is unpleasant to tell it."[36]

For me, having come from a railway family, there could not have been a more inspired metaphor.

When I was a child, my family lived in Kazipet, a small railway junction on the Grand Trunk Railway route that connected New Delhi to Madras. As I previously mentioned, the railways employed Nanna and most of my uncles on both sides of the family. The railways were a world unto itself. Nanna was the railway junction's only doctor. He treated all railway employees there and signed off on their sick leave, so his position was critical. He knew everyone in Kazipet who worked for the railways and loved to talk to them. He often took me to the station. The stationmaster showed me how they used Morse code to communicate and ensure trains did not run into each other. The first phone I ever saw was in the station. Nanna also arranged for me to go to the signal cabin, where the signalman described how he used a lever to switch the railway tracks.

Even the track ballast, the billions of stones that made up the rail bed, was a source of unique pleasure. As dusk settled, my friends and I would collect some promising-looking ballast stones and gather them in front of my house. We then took turns striking our choice stones. Although we celebrated every spark, we competed to see who could produce the brightest one. You might say that we generated a bit of social electricity.

Nanna took care of all the health needs of the closely knit railway community. My family belonged to the Railway Club. There I watched the

---

35 Jones, E. (1953). *The Life and Works of Sigmund Freud* (Vol. 1, p. 247). London: Hogarth Press.
36 Freud, S. "On beginning the treatment (Further recommendations on the technique of psycho-analysis I)." In J. Strachey (Ed. and Trans.), *The Standard Edition of the Complete Psychological Works of Sigmund Freud* (Vol. 7, p. 135). London: Hogarth Press.

stationmaster, conductors, guards, engine drivers, firemen, and others play billiards, badminton, cards, and other games, so they were no strangers to me. When I saw them, I greeted them by their names, and they were always happy to answer my questions.

Keith Coombs was a good Anglo-Indian friend while I lived in Kazipet. He was an engine driver's son. Once, when I was about 5 years old, Keith's father had shunting duty, rearranging cargo cars in the siding yard and on a spur away from the mainline. Keith suggested we visit his dad at work. So we walked to the siding, barely 50 yards from my house. His dad was expecting us and, when he saw us, he motioned us to join him and helped us up to the engine cabin. Keith's dad was a big, friendly man. He wore a red-and-white polka-dot bandana around his head, tied in a tail knot at the back. His hands were greasy, and he had a wad of cotton rags bulging in his pocket. He introduced us to his mate, a fireman, who showed us the coal bunker. The fireman opened the furnace door, shoveled in some coal, and let us look at the roaring fire as we felt a blast of hot air. The sweating fireman also had a bandana around his head.

When the flagman on the ground waved his green flag, Keith's dad engaged the throttle and eased the engine, which whooshed forward. It was deafening. He showed us other parts of the engine and named them, but I couldn't hear him because of the noise. Finally, he moved the behemoth forward and backward as it collected goods and arranged wagons in the yard. He lifted Keith to pull the whistle cord, and the engine went berserk with the noise. Then he lifted me up to have a turn. It was just a loose rope slung across the engine roof like a clothesline, and I had to tug it hard. The whole engine shook when the whistle blew. It was the most significant moment of my young life.

When I got down from the engine, I looked up and saw Mr. Coombs's smiling face. "Thank you, Mr. Coombs," I shouted. "I *really* enjoyed the engine ride."

"Y'rr w'lcome, m'boy," he shouted back in his thick Anglo-Indian brogue.

As I walked excitedly toward home, I heard the horn toot twice as the engine rumbled away. When I got home, Amma asked me how I had gotten soot and grime on the armpits of my shirt. "Keith's dad lifted me, and I pulled the engine whistle," I said. It was the proudest stain I ever got.

Those were the days of steam. For a young boy, a steam engine was a dream/nightmare come true. It was a living dragon. It ate coal fed by *coal-khalasis* (coal carriers), who walked up a ladder with a basketful of coal on their heads, crossed the gangplank, and poured it into the coal tender attached to the engine. One of my first ambitions was to be a *coal-khalasi*, climbing that ladder, balancing coal on my head. The engine drank water stored in water towers, fed to the tender through a water crane with a tube as wide as an elephant's trunk, and then discharged embers. The fireman removed the smoldering burnt coal and heaped it between the tracks before it turned to cold ash. The engine snorted steam like a dragon. And when it moved, the earth shook.

I thought the steam engine moved by squirting steam onto the wheels, which made them move, but I wasn't sure. When we had no school, I got up early and decided I would resolve the question. At the very least, I wanted to count the number of holes from which the steam poured out. It was my lucky day, because an engine was in the shunting yard, moving wagons around. I waved to the engine driver and sat down as close to the engine as I had the guts. I waited. My excitement mounted, and, finally, the moment arrived. As the engine started, it made a loud hissing, bellowing-clattering noise, and I was engulfed in steam before I could see from where the mist came. When the engine was still, at least I could see its parts, but smoke covered it with greater mystery when it started to move. I learned that steam felt hot at first and then got cold and wet. It was exhilarating, but it failed to satisfy my engine curiosity. I was no solver of problems; I was simply amazed by the world.

The railways had their dangers, too. There's a reason many train stations were home to three-legged dogs. I saw unlucky people, too, maimed by accidents. No one had to teach my siblings and me that life was dangerous. We knew! Indelible memories and anticipation of future scrapes kept the lessons of the tincture of iodine always alive.

The railways granted our family three railway passes every year to anywhere in India that had a railway station. We often used them to visit relatives, watching the world go by through the windows on the way. At that time, I was the third of four siblings. My parents subsequently had a fifth child.

When I was about seven years old, we went on vacation to visit the Taj Mahal in Agra. Amma had lived in Agra for several years when she was a girl, so she was especially excited. It was a bright day as the train approached Mathura, a town near Agra, and through the train window, we saw a peacock family. Then, to our delight, the peacocks suddenly took flight. For the rest of the ride, our conversation turned to the lively peacocks and the gifts of nature.

On our visit to the Taj Mahal, a street hawker persuaded Amma to buy a peacock-feathered fan. The fan echoed the excitement of our peacock sighting and came to symbolize it. Although I enjoyed the fan immensely, I remember hoping that the feathers came from naturally dead peacocks and not from peacocks killed for their feathers. I had no stomach for violence of any kind, let alone the needless taking of life, whether man or beast or fowl.

We then went into a store to purchase a miniature marble replica of the Taj Mahal.

Sensing he might induce us to buy more, the salesman displayed clay animals. He assured us that they would withstand rough play and offered proof. He held an elephant by its legs and threw it onto its back on the floor. It was unscathed! To me, the clay seemed to be magical. We bought a set of a dozen toy animals. That evening, I decided to retest and find out for myself how unbreakable the animals were. I picked the camel up by its back and flung it to the ground. To my surprise and dismay, one of the legs broke off. The joy of seeing the peacock family and the Taj Mahal evaporated. I showed the broken camel to Amma and Nanna. Amma said we could get some glue and put it back together. I was afraid that Nanna would get mad at me for being careless, but he laughed. And then he recalled that the salesman threw an elephant, which was sturdier than the camel. He also pointed out that the salesman threw the elephant onto its back, whereas I threw the camel with spindly legs. I was surprised and relieved that Nanna was far less critical than I had feared.

Those were the scenes I saw in the window from my past as I pondered Freud's fundamental rule.

Usually, it takes several months for a patient to get comfortable with the free-association method and feel safe enough to overcome the emotional censors that watch over our words and actions. Just because a patient is a psychiatrist (or a psychiatry resident) doesn't mean he will be able to let go and say everything that occurs to him.

Let me digress for a moment to explain the critical differences between the disciplines of psychiatry and psychoanalysis. Both psychoanalysis and psychiatry are methods of healing human suffering. Their pasts have intertwined, but they are evolving into more distinct realms. Psychoanalysis is based primarily on Freud's concepts, such as free association. It has traditionally been an outpatient treatment for neurotic individuals who can live independently and pay for such services. Some critics of psychoanalysis call such patients "the worried well" and consider free association a waste of time and money, an extravagant luxury. Psychiatrists lean more toward treating institutionalized patients with serious mental illness, although not exclusively.

Psychotropic-drug treatments for mentally ill patients started in the middle of the 20th century. Psychiatrists incorporated these neurochemicals into their practice as a complement to psychotherapy. They also investigated the brain and the genetic code and applied their knowledge from those efforts. As a result, most psychiatrists dispensed with free association, the definitive method of psychoanalysis. Instead, they merged biological and psychosocial approaches to mental illness in treating patients and their families.

In short, both psychoanalysts and psychiatrists seek to remedy emotional, social, and developmental impairment. Psychoanalysts focus on resolving emotional conflicts and repairing deficits using free association and interpretation, while psychiatrists use medication, individual, family, and group therapy, and other approaches.

There are disciplinary rivalries between psychoanalysis and psychiatry, even though many psychoanalysts are psychiatrists. Only physicians practiced psychoanalysis in the U.S. until almost the end of the 20th century. Today, the field of psychoanalysis is open to psychologists, social workers, and members of other clinical disciplines. However, one has to be a physician to be a psychiatrist. A psychiatry resident like Jan completes four years of advanced training in psychiatry after completing medical school. Most psychiatry residents glean preliminary notions of psychoanalysis and free association during their training, but they are generally not skilled in its practice. It was, therefore, a surprise to me that Jan was talking freely without any instructions from me.

Would it have made sense to tell Jan that he should say everything that occurred to him? Should I have imposed a rule when he seemed to be following it on his own? The key to psychoanalytic treatment is free associations themselves, not the fundamental rule concerning free associations. Still, no analyst can know for sure whether a patient is freely associating. A fluent and voluble patient can suppress thought and speak as though he withheld no idea. Often, it is only well into the treatment that a patient can free associate easily. And, in moments of excitement, when many associations occur at once, it is often impossible to report them all. The limited half-life of thoughts, the task of sequencing them, the limits imposed by speech, and the accommodations needed to answer questions from the analyst means that some thoughts will inevitably be lost. Given the caveats and qualifiers that accompany the concept of free association, analysts have no choice but to live with the uttered speech of the patient and whatever they can glean from their own responses.

Just as I had reluctantly said goodbye to Amma, Nanna, my family, and steam engines when I came to America, so, too, I reluctantly bade goodbye to the *rule* of free association, although not to free associations themselves. I felt a pang for the beloved and unexpressed train analogy. So, Jan did not hear the only rule of psychoanalysis. He didn't need to.

CHAPTER 3

JAN'S VOICE INTRUDED IN MY REVERIE. "At work, I just felt completely isolated and unsupported. I did get legal advice. The attorney said, 'Bad things happen.' He said that he would handle the case. He said I should move on and not contact Amir's family."

I felt I understood Jan's predicament: "You feel responsible for the suicide, though, and you can't move on."

"Correct," Jan answered angrily. "They wanted to put legal barriers between Amir's family and me."

I thought, *Yes, that's what lawyers do, and it's probably for your own good. You may not realize it, but there are situations where people may not talk to each other. They may dig a deeper hole for themselves.*

As if reading my thoughts, Jan added with disdain, "I don't care about that."

I realized that by deliberately sabotaging others' efforts to help him. Jan compounded his problem. I thought *You might not know what's in your best interest.*

Jan continued, "I want to know how I can help his family."

I thought *You wanted to help his family, but Amir's parents may want to cut your head off! What **you** want to do is not what's most important; what counts is what they will **allow** you to do. The key is not your intentions but their intentions. What possibilities does reality permit?* I shared none of these thoughts or questions with Jan, but I could see that his journey to getting well would be long and difficult.

Jan stubbornly persisted, "I want to know what I did wrong and acknowledge it. I caused a horrible and unnecessary waste of life. Amir was pure, and I cared for him."

I was amazed by what Jan was willing to do. He wanted to be bluntly honest and take the blame. He didn't seem to understand that the courtroom chamber is not a Catholic confessional stall. The judge is not a priest and could not grant absolution. Irrational guilt colored Jan's honesty. Of course, suicide is a waste of life. All life is pure, and its loss is a tragedy. But the question of negligence has to be proven in a court of law. Jan's attitude was like pleading guilty before a plaintiff even filed a petition. Most doctors in America would consider this professional suicide. It might seem courageous, but it would be stupid.

I wanted to be in tune with Jan's confessional spirit without egging it on, so I said, "It's tough. I know that you want to do your best."

As I had hoped, my words encouraged Jan to divulge more information. "I want to tell you about Amir," he began. "Amir was a handsome guy about 25 years old. He was a post-graduate Ph.D. student in physics. Anyone seeing him on the street would think that Amir was one of those geeky computer guys who could be a Trekkie or a fan of some sci-fi show on TV. For example, he often rode a bicycle to see me and carried a childish Pokémon helmet. He wore old jeans with the right pant leg rolled up and stretched, faded sweaters, perhaps from early adolescence. His face was clumsily shaven, with visible areas of unshaven hair on his chin or cheek. He often picked his nose and sometimes had an inflamed boil from his excavations. On the other hand, he was polite, likable, articulate, and soft-spoken.

"From the start, he wanted me to know he was no hillbilly. He said he was from a prominent family steeped in Arabic scholarship for generations. His family name was bestowed on his great-grandfather by the old Nizam, the ruler of Hyderabad more than 100 years ago, recognizing his erudition. Amir is the only son of a prominent professor; his mother is a respected doctor at the Zanana Women's Hospital in Hyderabad.

Is the only son? *Is?* So, for Jan, Amir was still a living presence.

Jan continued, "His father is an accomplished amateur Urdu poet. His mother lived several years in London during her training and was a fellow of the Royal College of Surgeons, specializing in Obstetrics and Gynecology. I heard that you were originally from Hyderabad. Is that true?"

"Yes," I replied.

"Have you heard of the Zanana Hospital in Hyderabad?"

"Yes," I said.

"Do you have any memories of it?"

Such questions from patients to analysts are common. In the early analytic phases, they signal the patient's curiosity about the doctor. They indicate the beginning of the unique patient–analyst relationship. This relationship will later become the focus of analytic scrutiny. Many analysts believe that they should not divulge any information about themselves but should redirect patients' questions, asking them what they think the analyst's answer would be to gain further details about the patient's imaginings. According to these analysts, answering such questions would contaminate the patient's evolving feelings for the analyst and interfere with the treatment. There is much to recommend this strategy.

Other analysts—including me—find that some patients may become frustrated that their analysts do not answer some questions; this itself may become an obstacle to further treatment. They believe that the analyst should weigh the pros and cons in each case in deciding how to respond to a patient's question. Furthermore, such analysts believe the patient's reaction to the analyst's answer may spark further inquiry. The crucial principle is that the analyst must strive to understand the patient's responses, answer the patient's questions, and respond authentically.

I took Jan's question as reflecting curiosity about me. Although I still saw him as potentially suicidal, I was glad that he was thinking about something other than Amir. He was no longer entirely consumed by feelings of worthlessness, guilt, and jealousy toward Amir. His question evoked several memories.

The first arose from that most primitive of the senses: smell. Zanana evoked a mix of sweat, blood, and amniotic fluid. To me, as a young man, it was the smell of sex, exhilarating and unsettling.

Zanana is an Urdu word referring to the part of a house reserved for women; the Zanana Hospital provided gynecologic and obstetric care to Muslim, Christian, and Hindu women. The first time I went to Zanana as a medical student, a few other male students on that rotation and I worked there surrounded by a sea of women. It was there that I learned to deliver a newborn and witnessed the miracle of life renewing itself.

On February 9, 1906, Mary, the Princess of Wales, laid the foundation stone for the Victoria Zanana Hospital. It was a place of excellence in both medical care and teaching when I studied there. The hospital had two gates. The outer one, an imposing iron grille, was about 10 feet high. The inner gate, fifty feet in, was maybe five or six feet tall and was made of sheet metal. It had a little door that only one person could pass through at a time. A hospital guard scrutinized every person who entered. Perimeter walls about six feet high surrounded the building, high enough to deter prying eyes. Cream-colored *chunam*, a quicklime plaster made from shell-lime and sand, widely used in India, coated the walls. Generations of men relieved themselves and spit betel juice on those walls, and, over time, they acquired a reddish-brown hue. In my memory, I could almost smell the urine and see the discolored *chunam*.

I recently visited the Zanana Hospital and found it shuttered. A new Zanana Hospital had replaced it. However, I could still see the inner gate through the rusted iron grille. There are no guards, no people, and no smells, but my memories are strong.

The Zanana Hospital sat on the south bank of the Musi River, which exuded a stinky smell—a result of the many open sewers of the old city of Hyderabad that drained into it. The Osmania General Hospital was on the north bank, where I spent many years as a medical student and intern. To get to the Zanana Hospital, I had to cross the dirty, smelly water of the Musi by going south over the Afzal Gung Bridge. A few palm trees stood out in the small, shallow islands in the river. On the banks of the Musi were *dhobis*, men and women who washed clothes. As I looked down from the bridge, I could see them rubbing soap into wet clothing laid on a stone slab. After rinsing each garment in the water a few times, the *dhobis* would lift it over their shoulders and, with a whooshing sound, swing it against the stone. They would then lay them all on the bank or hang them on ropes to dry.

The river itself was shallow and narrow. Not far from the *dhobis*, young boys often bathed water buffaloes. Untreated sewage and the effluence of local industries ran into the river, coloring it a dirty brown and adding yet another foul odor.

On the south bank of the Musi was the Salar Jung Museum, with its famous marble statue of Benzoni's veiled Rebecca. Rebecca's beautiful, shrouded face, which at once revealed and concealed, struck me with awe. I marveled at Benzoni's virtuosity, enabling him to make something so delicate and lifelike out of stone.

I knew that Jan was waiting for my answer.

"It smelled of women," I said.

I registered surprise in Jan's eyes in response that I had been so open in sharing my vivid associations. Then, to manage his surprise, I looked at Jan and said, "I remember the smell—the smell of sweat and sex. I remember the sounds—groaning and screaming of women in labor. And I remember the wonder in the mothers' eyes when they first held their babies—especially boy infants."

While I was on the obstetrical rotation, I delivered a girl infant. As soon as she came out, she vigorously pissed and screamed her lungs out. I counted that she had ten fingers and toes and examined her. I took the crying, kicking, and hearty infant to the mother's side and announced, "You have a healthy baby girl." The mother looked away and cursed "*lanje*" (bitch). It appeared that the mother wanted a boy. I felt sad that girls are sometimes not wanted. I imagined saying to the exhausted mother, "You have a beautiful, healthy baby girl. Are you not curious? She needs you to look at her and love her." I am glad to report that I was relieved, later that day, to see the mother lovingly hold the girl infant. I smiled at the mother, and she smiled back.

Over the years, I've learned that every second counts in analysis, especially those first ones right after the patient asks a question. A patient gauges the soul of a physician by how he responds to such queries. Jan nodded, and his surprise seemed to dissipate quickly. Then, before pursuing psychiatry, I remembered that Jan had been a radiologist specializing in gynecological radiology. I wondered if, with Jan's asking about my medical memories, his own medical identity was starting to reassert itself.

Jan continued with his story of Amir. "What a coincidence! Amir once told me, 'My mother often took me to the Zanana Hospital. It had a strong smell, a mixture of feminine odor and phenol used to clean and disinfect the floors. I would get headaches from it. It was so strong that it sometimes brought tears to my eyes."

I knew the smell of phenol, as well. It had a special meaning for me. About once a month, when Nanna was on a medical call, he stayed overnight at the Railway Hospital in Lallaguda. Amma would cook his dinner and put it into a *tiffin* carrier, and I would take it to him. *Tiffin* means "snack" or, more loosely, "food." A *tiffin* carrier is a stacked set of containers held together by a pin to transport or temporarily store cooked food. For example, one might put rice into one container, curry in another, soup in the next, and yogurt in still another. The *tiffin* carrier has a convenient handle that allows it to be carried by hand or slung on the handlebars of a bicycle.

When I first delivered Nanna's food, I had just learned to ride a bicycle and knew only how to balance and pedal. I used Nanna's bicycle, which, of course, was too high for me. I would walk the bike to the edge of the road and elevate myself by standing on the curb. I would get myself situated on the seat and then push off. Getting off was more straightforward: I just crash-landed. Amma and Nanna didn't know that I didn't know how to get on or off, so they sent me on errands. On the days I brought the *tiffin* carrier, I pedaled hard and was proud to bring Nanna his food, still warm. I waited while he ate and then took the *tiffin* carrier back. He patted me, thanked me, and proudly introduced me to his colleagues at the hospital. The hospital smelled of phenol. Every time I went there, I would encounter that phenol smell again.

Jan continued, "I remember my first session with Amir. He was talking about his background and culture. It was a world I knew nothing about. I wanted to understand, so I asked him lots of questions. He seemed to appreciate my curiosity and answered patiently. After he left that day, I wrote down what he'd said as much as I could. You never know when it might be helpful. Over time, I realized that hearing about his culture helped me understand my own culture and myself.

"They told us in our development classes that a person's first or most significant memory is important, but asking a patient about his first memory never worked for me. It seemed forced, and I often got information that I felt was meaningless or not believable. Still, because of what my teachers said, I tried to get into the habit of asking it. So, that first day, without much conviction, I asked Amir, 'What is your earliest memory?'

"He said he would tell me about a crucial memory, something that happened when he was nine, that he felt changed his life. There's an important day in the Muslim calendar called *Bakri Eid*, when they commemorate Allah asking the Prophet Ibrahim to sacrifice his son, Ismail. It's sort of like the story of Abraham and Isaac in the Old Testament. In the Muslim version, the Prophet Ibrahim blindfolds himself and goes to offer Ismail, but when he removes the blindfold, he finds a sacrificed goat lying on the altar and his son standing in front of him. Amir said Ibrahim's absolute devotion to Allah had greatly inspired his father.

"Muslims all over the world offer sacrifices on *Bakri Eid*. Ordinarily, they sacrifice goats or small animals, but occasionally they use a camel. The sacrificed camel provided meat for the festive foods for family and friends and the poor people in the neighborhood. He stressed that supporting the poor is an essential value in Muslim culture.

"So, when Amir was nine, there was a lot of excitement as *Bakri Eid* approached because his family was going to sacrifice a camel. Amir described everything in great detail. It was almost like I was watching a movie. The preparations started early in the morning. Amir saw the butcher unwrap a long knife from a leather bag and hand it to the knife sharpener. The knife sharpener used a pedal-driven machine that turned a circular stone. He put the knife against the stone for a few seconds, producing a screeching noise and a flurry of sparks. Then he brought the blade close to his eyes and inspected it. He repeated the process several times. Then he placed it at an angle so the sun's light would reflect off it. Then he handed it back to the butcher.

"Then, the camel came, led by seven or eight helpers. Amir was awe-struck, seeing such a big animal up close. The guests were relaxing, having tea, when his mother called him into the house to wash up and put on festive clothes. She brought him out to his father, who took his hand, and they walked together through the crowd. It was a big moment of pride for his father because he had organized the sacrifice for the community.

"The backyard was crowded with people from the neighborhood, including Amir's friends. The camel was standing, surrounded by the helpers. The ropes were slack, which gave it some freedom of movement, but it became restless and agitated after a while. At one point, Amir said he was near the camel, and it seemed to look him right in the eye. He wondered whether the camel knew it was there to be killed.

"Then the elders told everyone to move back to give the camel more room. Amir was standing next to his father. The butcher quietly approached the camel and then looked at Amir's father, who nodded silently. The man holding the rope around the camel's neck put his finger to his lips and scanned the crowd. The crowd went silent.

"The butcher approached the camel and gently touched its neck to feel for its blood vessels. He stood there and patted the camel, and the camel quieted down. Then, with one single, expert movement, he stabbed the camel at the bottom of its neck! The knife pierced the skin, and blood gushed down like a waterfall. The men tightened their grip on the ropes to limit the camel's movement. The camel weakened as the blood formed an expanding pool, and the men eased it onto the ground.

"Amir saw his father smiling, looking very proud, as the blood poured out of the camel's neck. He looked at Amir, but Amir turned his head away. His father put his hand on Amir's head, gently but firmly moving it so he would have to witness the whole sacrifice. Amir couldn't watch. When his father saw the fear in Amir's eyes, the pride disappeared, and he lost interest in Amir.

"The camel was dead, lying in a pool of blood. Everyone looked pleased because the sacrifice was perfect. Amir said one of the lessons of the sacrifice was that every Muslim man must be ready, if necessary, to kill not only what he hates but what he loves. Every Muslim boy must wholeheartedly celebrate the great sacrifice of Ibrahim. Everyone, adult or child, has to have the courage to witness and celebrate the sacrifice of the animal without doubt or fear. Amir felt he had failed.

"Amir had such clear memories of that day. Not surprisingly, it infected his dreams. The night after the sacrifice, he dreamt he was the butcher, even though he was only nine, and that, when the time came to kill the camel, he was paralyzed! Another time, he dreamt that his friends teased him because he was afraid to watch a camel sacrifice. And one of them mocked him for being what they call a *hijra*.

"A *hijra* is a transvestite eunuch. *Hijras* dress and exaggeratedly act like women. *Hijras* entertain or waylay people by clapping, cursing, singing, and obscene gestures. They suggest vulgar or prohibited sex through every action, like raping a woman or sodomy. Amir said people are embarrassed to be near them. They just give them money so they will go away. Many kids learn about sex and curses by listening to their songs. It's like it's their job to educate young children into the ways of the sexual and perverted world. Society puts up with them because no parent wants their child to be dangerously naive.

"*Hijra* also means 'eunuch.' Amir said that, in the olden days, some Muslim rulers had lots of wives and concubines. They castrated the men who had contact with the royal women—the guards, cleaners, medics, etc. The extent of castration depended on the nature of their job and proximity to the queen and royal female household. Amir described various types of castrations. Males who directly served the queen had their testicles and penises removed. Those in the harem but not in direct contact with the queen had their testicles removed but kept their penises. Amir used Urdu words to describe these various varieties and translated them for me. He said that using Urdu made him feel true to himself. I understand that feeling because I feel good when I use Polish words."

Jan looked at me for reassurance that I wanted to hear more about this obscure conversation. I nodded, and he continued, "Usually, Amir was a nervous fellow who fidgeted as he spoke, but he was unusually at ease describing the various forms of male genital mutilation. He was so calm and relaxed, and his clear and concise English struck me. It sent chills up my spine. Perhaps his ease with English and verbal precision came from his mother being a physician and living in London for many years. My psychoanalyst professors who taught us about Freud, the Oedipus Complex, and castration anxiety never mentioned the industrial applications of castration."

By now, I was not worried about Jan's suicidality. "We need to be stopping for today," I said. However, Jan seemed somewhat drained by the session's torrent of words.

"Thank you," he said. "It felt good to be able to talk."

CHAPTER 4

JAN STARTED THE NEXT SESSION where we had left off, discussing the fallout for Amir from the camel sacrifice.

"When Amir thought about the dream of being paralyzed trying to make a sacrifice, and when his friend teased him, he felt like a coward. He had run to his mother as a girl would. So he felt he was a wuss, too scared to participate in the sacrifice of the camel, while the other boys circled it, not fearful of the sight of blood and *enjoying* it!

"He also felt he was different from the other boys when it came to discovering what sex was. Kids in his town generally learned about sex from watching dogs. They would watch as dogs followed a bitch in heat. First, the male dogs competed to be close to her. Then, when she stopped, the dog nearest her would try to mount her. Some dogs just knew how to do it, but cowardly dogs would hesitate, even when they had a good chance, or they would let other dogs push them off. He worried that he would be like that, that he'd be scared and miss out.

"His father was a proud, macho type, and he wanted a fearless son. Amir wanted to be brave. The sacrifice tested his courage. He failed miserably, running to his mother rather than participating with enjoyment. Yet, even she wanted him to be brave.

"He wouldn't give himself a break. He said, 'Every day, cats eat mice. Death is everywhere. Why was I afraid to see the sacrifice, which is part of God's will?' From that day on, he couldn't get the image of the camel out of his head, and his fear made him ashamed. He said an ordinary, non-Muslim man could have a mixture of courage and cowardice, but a Muslim must have 100% courage. There's no place for even a drop of cowardice or doubt.

Amir let fear in, and it contaminated him. He felt it meant he wasn't a good Muslim. He decided he would never be afraid again.

"Over the years, he'd had recurring dreams of a camel head that transformed into his father's head or the other way around, and sometimes, *he* was a camel about to be sacrificed. He would see blood spurt in his dreams and wake up in a sweat. A few times, it took him a moment to realize that he hadn't been beheaded. It was sweat and not blood that covered him. Then, as an adult, he latched onto Francis Coppola's movie *Apocalypse Now.* In his mind, he would replay—again and again—the scene where Marlon Brando's head gets chopped off. He loved bloody, violent movies like that. *The Deer Hunter* was another one."

Jan paused, clearly overwhelmed, thinking about those gruesome scenes. "Amir was young. He was in his late twenties. He was a virgin and wanted to get laid. However, extreme anxiety got in the way of any sexual contact with women. His main problem was depression. I knew he was depressed. People who saw him before me said that he'd been depressed for a long time. A few times, I saw him less depressed but never happy.

"Amir was head over heels in love with a Chinese girl he called Ms . . . .—I'll call her Ms. Chen—but he had no clue how to approach her. I felt that it was my job to make him more marketable. So I tried CBT [Cognitive Behavioral Therapy], and it worked . . . until he sabotaged it.

"Ms. Chen often came to the gym at the same time Amir did, when it was not too crowded. They both usually used exercise machines at the far end of the gym. However, every time he wanted to make even casual conversation with her, he got tongue-tied and couldn't get even one word out. So I tried to find out why he was so shy. He said he was afraid that he would say something she would consider stupid.

"I told Amir that, in my experience, anything is good for a conversation. So I said, 'You could say to her, 'Hi. I'm going for coffee. Do you want to join me?' It would be a start, and he could go from there.

"Weeks and weeks went by. Nothing happened. Amir could never utter a word to her, but he continued to pine for her and moaned to me about his heartache. He would say, 'She's single. She's *so* sexy. She's just one step away.' He heard her when she spoke to others. Her voice was so sweet. She was so witty. He loved her voice. She even looked at him and smiled. But, in her presence, he couldn't open his mouth.

"'Why don't you write out a script,' I suggested. He could memorize a line! The first time he tried, it was an utter failure. Although he was almost 30, he was like an awkward teenager. Ms. Chen seemed unreachable.

"But I wasn't discouraged. It was a start. Although Amir forgot the script that time, he still had it. So I decided to encourage him and thought I gave him sound advice."

A question pressed for my attention: *Was Amir ready for Jan's direct help dealing with such social situations?* Instead, I asked, "What did you say to him?"

"I told Amir he could ask Ms. Chen even simple questions, like, 'What do you do?' or 'What are you studying?' Amir was well-read. He attended lectures at school and was familiar with pop culture. I said, 'Ask her what books she likes to read.' He wrote that down. He felt it was a reasonable question. He memorized it."

Jan continued, "One day, Amir finally spoke to Ms. Chen! As they were leaving the gym, he asked, 'Can I walk with you to the door?'"

"Ms. Chen smiled and responded, 'Of course,' and added, 'I work at a lab a few blocks away. Do you want to walk me there?'

"Amir was ecstatic. He was the happiest person in the world. That was the only time he wasn't depressed. Amir and Ms. Chen had coffee together. Then she invited him to her apartment. He was so happy to visit her there. Then he asked her to *his* apartment, and she came! She walked around the apartment, looked at his impressive books collection, and started a casual conversation. She stopped and looked at him and then moved closer and just stood there. And then she kissed him.

"Amir said that, by the kiss, he knew she wanted him to go further.

"But he left the room with some stupid excuse about getting her some water. Then, while he was gone, he phoned a friend in a panic and invited the friend over. When he told Ms. Chen, her mood changed. She excused herself and left the apartment abruptly.

"I felt sorry for him," Jan confessed. "He had what he wanted and got in his own way. He screwed up. Amir tortured himself for months after that for his 'stupidity.' It made him think of his dad: His dad often called him 'stupid.'

"Then Amir fell in love with Natasha, a Russian bombshell. He screwed up his courage to tell her he was attracted to her. She said to him, 'You're a nice guy, but I'm a lesbian. I've known I was lesbian since I was 7 years old. I'll always be a lesbian.'

"Amir was crushed but convinced that Natasha didn't know herself. He wrote her letters, imploring her to try being heterosexual and promising he would help. She wasn't interested. Amir followed her around and really annoyed her. One day, he followed her to the library and started pestering her. Natasha was at her wits' end. She told him, 'Go away. I don't want you. If you don't leave this minute, I will start to hate you!' Amir became dejected and blamed himself. After this, I felt maybe the treatment pushed him over the edge.

I wasn't sure what the word *this* meant, so I asked, "*This?*"

"After he killed himself," Jan said, "I felt that I maybe I'd pushed him to do things he had no business doing. Maybe he would have been better off jerking off alone and alive than tasting kissing and being dead. He never knew sex. He'll never know sex."

I appreciated Jan's plight but noted that he was speaking freely. That was important. I felt that the best thing I could do was help him unburden himself and wait until I had a clear invitation from him to speak—a question or a pause—or perhaps a clear thought within me demanding expression. I had nothin'.

Jan continued, "Amir talked about Muslim culture often. His father was strict and expected academic excellence. When Amir was a child, his father insisted that he read all the time, so he didn't play with other kids very much and never learned how to socialize. Maybe this is where he got his shyness, feelings of inadequacy, and fear of intimate contact. He tried to change, but . . ." Jan paused.

"Amir opened my eyes to many things. He lived in a completely different world than the one I live in. His ideas about women were so different from mine. Most women covered themselves from head to toe in a burka in his culture. His mother, who had spent many years in London and was an obstetrician, wore it only on ceremonial or family occasions. Amir thought that a woman was a lesser vessel than a man and must follow him. Then he moved to Chicago and met in-your-face women. They chose and were decisive.

"Before he met Ms. Chen, he was with Lisa. Lisa cared for him, but he despised women like her. Lisa was strong-willed and always decided where they should go. She forced him to do things he didn't want to do. Once, he grumbled because he had wanted to see an Arnold Schwarzenegger movie, and she wanted to watch *Friends*. He never told her that her decisiveness bothered him.

"He cried about her to me. She was the decision-maker. He thought that was *his* job; that was a man's role. He felt that they were like boyfriend and girlfriend because they were together. For her, it was more like a friendship, without any romantic or sexual undertones.

"I don't think I really understood what Amir tried to teach me about Muslim culture. He tried to explain, but I didn't get most of it. His mom wanted to hook him up with a girl in an arranged marriage. He didn't want it. He didn't like the idea of a woman in a *burka,* yet he couldn't be with a Western woman, either. He was caught in a no man's land or, more accurately, a no *woman's* land. He didn't know which land he belonged in. He had one foot in Islam and one foot in the West, and then he met a premature end. He didn't want to give up his traditions, and he couldn't adapt to a new world. He had no cultural balance. He was an alien in both worlds. He was like an uncut stone with so much potential. He was good and true. I knew him so well. I asked him all sorts of questions to try to understand him. I like to talk about him. I feel obligated to talk about him. He was a good man, and I thought highly of him. I cannot get him out of my mind.

"Amir knew I was going on a two-week vacation to Rome. Did he know I was going to get married? *I* didn't tell him, but it's possible he overheard it. I'll never know. He didn't leave a suicide note. The police found out that I was his doctor because my card was in his pocket. They called me a few hours before Maria and I boarded the plane and said he'd died of a gunshot wound. Later, I learned that the coroner determined it was suicide. I don't know if the gun was fully loaded or just one chamber. His favorite movie was *The Deer Hunter.* He often spoke about the horrible scene where the Vietnamese officer makes the prisoner blow his brains out playing Russian roulette.

"Before he left my office, Amir asked me to give him a sample of an antidepressant, and I did. Then, he left, saying that he hoped the medication would work and that he would see me in two weeks. I felt that he left my office with some hope.

"Sometimes, I was angry at Amir. He wasn't always straight with me. He never took medications as I prescribed them; he experimented with them. He would say, 'I wanted to know if I can be normal without them.' But, most important, his dishonesty took the form of delayed communications."

"For example?"

"He once said, 'I was suicidal three weeks ago. I went to the end of one of the Metra lines and climbed onto the bridge. Every time a train passed underneath, I leaned forward—thinking about jumping—barely keeping my balance.'

"After Amir killed himself, Dr. Amiss, my supervisor, told me, 'I was once in a similar situation. My patient wouldn't tell me that she was suicidal *at the time* she was suicidal; she waited for the feeling to go away before she told me! So finally, I told her I was unable to see her anymore. I couldn't work with someone who didn't give me a chance.'

"It wasn't only Amir's noncompliance. I feel I missed some important clues that he was suicidal. I feel responsible for causing a horrible, unnecessary waste of life. I knew he was depressed. I should have known that he was suicidal.

"The last time I saw Amir, he said, 'I stopped taking the medications two weeks ago.' I told him, 'The problem is not only that you don't take the medications as prescribed, but you don't tell me, so I don't know what's happening. I document what I think are your reactions to medications, and you're not even on them! I'm giving you suggestions based on what I see and what you tell me. Today, telling me that you had thoughts about killing yourself a month ago doesn't help you. When you're in real danger, we should focus on your safety, but we discuss much less important things. Besides, I don't know about the way you truly feel. You're working against yourself, and I feel like a fool. We need to communicate in real-time.'"

I appreciated Jan's frustration that Amir did not communicate in a timely fashion. Amir had been dishonest. Could something be gained now in trying to understand a dead person? The critical issue was the effect of Amir's suicide on Jan. Amir killed himself in a blaze of boldness, the boldness he wished he'd felt at the camel sacrifice. But with that pull of the trigger, he transformed *Jan* into a weak self, rather like himself. Amir's malignant depression infected Jan's desire to find hope for him, and the suicide infused Jan with depression and vacated Jan's hope. Amir's problem became transformed into Jan's problem. In the aftermath of Amir's death, Jan was now lost. Although these thoughts were my preliminary insight into the relationship between Amir and Jan, I couldn't translate them into sentences that I could convey to Jan.

Jan continued, "I spoke to another supervisor, Professor Williams. He felt that therapy was important but that Amir needed medication, too. He said that the human mind is like the painting of a landscape. In a depressed person, the sun is eclipsed; 'through medications, we paint a sun.'

"Although I liked the metaphor of the mind as a landscape, I didn't tell Amir about it. I told him, 'I need information from you. Don't cheat yourself out of the best treatment I can give.'

"Amir replied, 'Yeah, Yeah, I won't do it again. I'll be honest.' He said he wanted the medications. He smiled and reassured me, 'I'll take the medications every day.'

"After Amir killed himself, I couldn't bring myself to open my notes about him."

After a moment, Jan continued, "A deep sadness came over me while I was in Rome. I was *getting married*, but I couldn't get Amir out of my mind. He'll never know marriage. He'll never know intimacy. And maybe he could have. Even now, when I think of him, I feel sad. But, to me, in a way, he's still alive."

I noted Jan was not just sad but also confused. In his heart, Amir was still alive.

Impelled by the momentum of what he had just said, Jan continued, "I often compared my background with his background. I grew up Catholic. My father was Orthodox Catholic. My mom and my sister, Sofia, weren't Orthodox, but they had Catholic values. When I was young, I wanted to feel the transcendent power of the spirit that linked me with others and gave me a sense of true belonging. So after high school, I attended the Yag . . . ian University."

Here, Jan spoke fast and with a thick Polish accent that I couldn't follow him. However, I noticed that his demeanor and facial expression changed ever so slightly: pride, and then hurt pride? So, to expand on that momentary pride and repair it, I asked, "How do you spell it?"

Jan began to spell his *alma mater*'s name but suddenly found that he could not recall it: He tried "Jagellonian"; then he tried "Jagielonian," and then he became exasperated. He finally got it and added that it was an old Polish university.

Still agitated, he continued, "It's one of the oldest universities in Europe. After enrolling at the College of Medicine, I joined a monastery in a Dominican cathedral in Krakow. I woke up at 7 a.m. every day. I went to all the church meetings and kept a diary of my feelings. The group of students seeking new meaning in their lives was called The Movement for Liberation in the Holy Spirit. Priests from the cathedral were involved with the community. Some of the fathers or monks who led isolated, spiritual lives also lived there. I sought their guidance. I wanted spiritual support and a strong sense of belonging. One of the fathers . . . I forget his name . . . it was an Italian name . . . Augustine, was my guide. I went to confession with him regularly. We grew friendly, and he told me a little about his life.

When he was 20, he was engaged to be married, but he began to doubt the institution of marriage and called it off. Nevertheless, he found his calling in the church and became a Father in his thirties.

"I remember a girl I met there. Her name was Anna. She was immersed in The Movement and prayed as if her life depended on it. Many of the people there were into prayer and tried to get into trances to achieve a higher level of spiritual awareness. I worked hard to seek solutions through prayer. I pretended to be more engaged in worship than I really was, waiting for the Holy Spirit to enter me.

"I never went into a trance, though. Once, when the group was praying, Anna fell into a trance. She jumped onto a chair and got an ecstatic look in her eyes. Then she ripped off her clothes and stood there naked. Everyone was stunned. Nobody knew what to do. Finally, I decided to call an ambulance and get her to a psychiatric hospital. I went with her to the Kobierzyn Mental Hospital. That was when I understood that all things have limits, even prayer.

"I spoke to Father Augustine about her. He said, 'The spirit is always pure, but some bodies have a propensity toward insanity. For example, when a weak body traps the spirit, excessive prayer can bring out insanity. Although the spirit is pure, insanity manifests itself.'

"After that, I lost interest in spiritual matters. I believed in the Movement for two years, but then I lost my faith in prayer. Prayer was supposed to help good things happen, but Anna went insane. I feel that good things are supposed to happen in psychiatric treatment, but while in treatment, Amir killed himself. Can I have faith in medicine? Can I ever be a good doctor?"

"That's what we're here to try to find out," I said.

"Thanks for listening to me," Jan said.

"You had a lot to say," I replied. "To be continued."

As Jan left, he looked back at me. I saw a flicker of hope in his eyes and felt that he wanted to come back and talk.

I reflected on the contrast between Jan's previously expressionless face and today's hopeful eyes. Despite his grief, he could communicate clearly and share his feelings. Of course, he wanted me to know all the details of his interactions with Amir, but it was an odd experience to hear Jan discussing depression so clinically while he was so clearly depressed himself. That evening, I went on the Internet and searched for Jagiellonian University. I learned that Casimir III the Great founded the Krakow Academy in 1364. That was its name then. In 1491, Nicolaus Copernicus enrolled there. I then understood the pride that flitted over Jan's face when he mentioned studying there. Perhaps his difficulty in spelling *Jagiellonian* was related to whether he deserved to have been in such an esteemed institution. He certainly wasn't sure he deserved to belong to the medical profession, the do-no-harm vocation of Hippocrates.

I suddenly remembered a phrase that had occurred to me before I asked Maria if she thought Jan was suicidal: *Alterego Countertransference Identification*. In this context, *alter-ego* refers to another person very similar to the self. *Countertransference* refers to feelings or attitudes in a doctor toward his patient. *Identification* refers to how one person feels or behaves like another. In this instance, *Alterego Countertransference Identification* with a patient who committed suicide refers to a process by which a doctor identifies with the hopelessness of a patient who committed suicide and thus becomes suicidal himself. Unless corrected, it is a deadly problem for a healer to have.

I felt it was essential to acknowledge Jan's deeply felt relationship with Amir. Since Amir's suicide, though, Jan identified with Amir's hopelessness. For Jan to improve, I would need to help him de-identify with Amir, that is, to create an understanding of how he was *different* from Amir. This meant finding or creating areas unrelated to Amir that Jan found meaningful.

I surveyed the things in Jan's life that I knew held some interest for him. Even small details could be significant: His love for Maria (although he currently had difficulty expressing it), Maria's concern for him, and the hope for their future family all seemed promising. He was observant and had noted the "fear" in her eyes that kept him from talking to her more. I also remembered that Maria said Jan didn't speak to others, and Jan himself said he had no one with whom he could talk. Finally, I was glad to note Jan's pride-related affiliation to the Jagiellonian University. For someone so depressed, his memory and capacity for expression were remarkable.

Amir seemed to have been plagued by fearfulness. Unfortunately, when he finally found his courage, he used it to pull the trigger on himself. In reaction to Amir's death, Jan suffered a strange jealousy. I didn't yet understand Jan's jealousy and wasn't confident I could address it appropriately. That would have to wait.

I also noted that, although Amir was dead, Jan often referred to him in the present tense: For Jan, Amir was still alive. Thus, Jan's past intermingled with Amir's, casting a deep, dark shadow obscuring and confusing Jan's present experience.

Maria could give him all the love she had, and I could give him all the strawberries in Chicago, but Jan had to find his own will to live, thrive, and overcome his sadness. He had to rediscover that breathing was a vital pleasure and a responsibility that couldn't be transferred to anybody else. I understood Jan's depression, but his concern about going crazy was a mystery to me. This concern appeared in his story of Anna, who tore off her clothes in an ecstatic spiritual trance. Amir no doubt drove Jan crazy, but did Jan harbor a separate concern about insanity? Was there another shoe that Jan was going to drop?

CHAPTER 5

How does analysis work? How do analysts feel about treating patients? How does an analyst decide what to say and how to say it? These questions are hard to answer. Describing the process may be the best way to explain.

The starting point for treatment is usually the patient's *presenting complaint*. Determining how to treat that original problem—and, perhaps, the issues it obscures—involves understanding how the relationship between a patient and a doctor starts and grows. Just as a parent and a newborn child, or a dating couple, the analyst and patient are two people in a budding relationship. The analyst listens to the patient to detect, on a moment-to-moment basis, the small but meaningful patterns in the conversation. A newly recalled memory or an "Aha!" moment intensifies the process for the analyst or patient. At times, the conversation becomes shallow or gets stuck, indicating resistance. The patient may hesitate to describe associations; the doctor may make mistakes. Treatment, like love, can go awry. Because there are many conscious aspects of an analyst's actions, his errors should be easier to detect and correct. An analyst's focus on seemingly trivial trends in ordinary speech may seem picky to some. Yet, the treatment process sometimes illuminates significant aspects of apparently insignificant details. Now, back to Jan.

Jan walked in with a smile. He was carrying two cups of Starbucks coffee, graciously offering one to me, along with some packets of sugar—an unusual gesture from a client. I remembered that I had brought Jan strawberries with the hope of provoking sweet memories, and now he had brought actual sugar.

"Thank you," I said. "It was nice of you to bring me the coffee and, even more, the sugar. Last time, strawberries; this time, real sugar!"

We sipped our coffee.

"I called you the first time at the end of my conversation with Maria," I said. "It was soon after you had learned you hadn't passed the medical exam. When she asked if I could help you, I said I thought you were already seeing a psychiatrist. She clarified that you had seen someone briefly but that you weren't seeing him anymore."

Jan replied, "I saw that guy for two weeks in December, and then I stopped."

"When I spoke to Maria, I realized that, except for her, you were completely by yourself. That's when I called and said I wanted to see you. *I called you. You didn't call me.* When you answered the phone, your voice sounded like it was coming from the other side of life. I said, 'Jan,' and you replied in a ghostlike voice, 'H a l l o o?' You were isolated."

"I was," Jan said.

"You were somewhere else, but I felt you needed to come back into the sphere of life where you'd have a fighting chance. I felt that there was a need to reawaken some of your memories or interests. Even a modest movement in this direction would benefit you. So the first day, just before I saw you, I went to the grocery store to pick up a sandwich, and one of the ladies behind the counter told me to check out the strawberries at the farmers' market. It made me think of a Polish babysitter who worked with us for about 10 years. She loved strawberries and made some dish with cream or mayonnaise in it, so I thought maybe all Polish people like strawberries, so I bought some for you."

Jan laughed. "We love strawberries, but not strawberries with mayonnaise."

"Well, it takes all kinds to make the world. She was loving and generous to our children. I like strawberries, too. So when I tasted how sweet the strawberries were, I thought, *Let me take Jan some strawberries; maybe he'll come up with some sweet and healing memories.*"

"Strawberries are popular this season," Jan said.

The strawberries had bombed, but I didn't have the good sense to leave them alone. Sometimes, an idea lives beyond the time of its usefulness. "They're tasty. They make you feel good, at least for a few seconds, regardless of your previous mental state."

"Were they Polish strawberries or Yankee strawberries?"

I laughed heartily at Jan's phrase "Yankee strawberries."

Jan was serious and continued, "There's a difference. Some of the Yankee strawberries they sell in Dominick's or Jewel taste like cotton balls."

"I can't answer that question. I had just purchased the strawberries at the farmers' market in town. I assumed they were locally grown. I hoped they would remind you of something pleasant in your life."

This strawberry idea just wouldn't die. Sometimes, you want so badly for something to work, and when it doesn't, you just don't know how to kill it. It's a sign of overzealousness—and not a good sign.

Jan was pensive for a moment. "I see this story. I feel this story. It's a Polish way of evoking memories. I'll give you an example from a Polish movie called *Zmory*, based on a book by Emil Zegadlowicz with the same name. *Zmory* means "nightmare." It's the story of an orphaned boy who had a close relationship with his father but was more distant from his mother, who suffered from tuberculosis and focused more on her fragile condition than on her relationship with her son. Death, ignorant people, disappointment fill this coming-of-age story and shake the boy's faith in the sacred side of life. The boy started to talk to a kindly teacher and a good listener. The teacher peeled apples and threw the peels into a fireplace one day as they talked. The boy's father also peeled apples and threw the peels into the fireplace in his childhood. The smell of the burnt apples reminded the boy of his father and other warm childhood memories. I know what you were thinking of, but strawberries don't apply in my case. I can tell you what *would* have had the effect you were looking for. *Placek drozdzowy* is a Polish yeast cake, *sernik* is Polish cheesecake, and *makowiec* is Polish poppy-seed cake. My mother was a world-class expert at all of them. The smell of any one of them would have accomplished what you wanted."

I took account of my actions and tallied them. I checked one memory—*strawberries*—as rejected, but four associations—*Zmory, Placek drozdzowy, sernik,* and *makoweic*—as new significant material and recovered my inner composure. My thoughts now moved to jealousy. "When you first came to see me, you said—"

Jan jumped in to complete my sentence "—I'm dealing with life-and-death situations."

I replied, "That's true, in that Amir killed himself. However, you also said that you felt jealous of Amir. Do you remember saying that?"

Jan responded immediately, "Yes, I remember saying that. I knew I was on the edge of life and death, so I appreciated that you offered to help me.

When the thought of ending your life seems pleasant to you, . . . that's not a good thing. I've been thinking of many situations like that. When my mom died, I was depressed, but I felt more jealous than mournful with Amir. When you called me, I didn't feel the sad, empty feeling of the finality of someone dying. It was more of a pleasant feeling. I can't explain it. Jealous because someone treated death as a solution to life, and it worked. When death occurs, the problem of life is solved. I, however, am in the middle of life with no solution. Although she never said it, my mom suffered from pain at the end of her life. She appreciated whatever we did. I had a cousin in Poland who was a nurse and worked in a lab. My cousin drew her blood for tests. I went to the hospital and brought the results back home. My mom's liver functions were down, but some values showed temporary improvement on a day-to-day basis. Mom pretended that the news was good, even though she knew she was dying. I said my mom pretended, but maybe it was her guts. You have to know how to behave in such situations. She decided not to fear death, to recognize small improvements, and to enjoy every moment she had with her family."

"She was dying, and she knew it," I said, "and she was determined to die with dignity. She was also helping you and your family cope with the reality of her impending loss."

Jan was now crying as he spoke, "I think it takes a lot of courage. She invited people over whom she respected and cared about. She told them she would see her doctor, but she also wanted to speak to them and say 'hello' and find out what was going on in their lives. They knew her condition. She was saying final goodbyes. So many members of the family and neighbors came to say goodbye. Her ninety-six-year-old uncle came over, and they were joking around. He said her illness was violating the rules of the universe: He was older and waiting to be taken away, but she was the one being called. Mom died in 2004. Her uncle died in 2005. Amir died in 2005. My good friend Beata died a few weeks after my mom. I saw her for the very last time, right after my mom's funeral. When you know that you're facing death and can still make people around you feel better, that's extraordinary. This was one of Mom's last lessons. It was a good one.

"After Amir . . . ," Jan stopped, and then seemed to start over. "I never killed anybody in my life. But this is how it feels when you do it. In my mind, it is no different from taking a gun and shooting him. In this country, some people think that putting someone out of their misery is a humanitarian act, but I don't see it that way. He was overwhelmed by life and wasted it. Initially, I felt angry at Amir. Then I felt guilty. His death sapped the life force out of me. I didn't want to do anything. His death distracted me during my wedding and tainted it. I had the extremes of guilt and excitement at the same time. Everything I did, every step I took, I was thinking about him."

I wondered what Jan intended to say after he had said, "After Amir . . . ," but decided that he was speaking freely enough that it might be tactless and imprudent to go back to that truncated thought.

Jan continued, "I reached a crisis several months later. Despite the stress, I tried to take the USMLE. I studied or pretended to study—ha-ha—a lot, but nothing happened. You can take weeks and weeks to paint a picture, but if you don't put your heart into it, it will suck. I failed. I decided that I couldn't be a physician. I had no idea what I should do. However, I felt I shouldn't graduate from the residency program and become a psychiatrist. The crisis persisted, and I stopped going out of the apartment. Then Maria contacted you, and here I am.

"I used to imagine dream jobs. Before I came to the United States, I had many positions in Poland. The Polish medical system is different from the American one. Here, it's harder to cross over into an allied sub-specialty. I could work in several related fields, such as gynecology, oncology, and radiology. I worked for many years as an oncologist for women with cancer-related gynecological problems and on medical floors consulting for patients with addictions and pain. I used to dream of a perfect job that combined these fields into a new area of specialization. I had more experience than anybody in these overlapping areas, but when I began to doubt whether I should be a doctor, all those futures vanished."

"You're depressed and can't see the future."

"Yes, but coming to you and talking to you have helped more than anything. Before I saw the other psychoanalyst, I tried lots of antidepressant medications. They made me less depressed, but I didn't like them."

"Why?"

"It's hard to explain. Medicines do their job, but I found them unpleasant. It's hard to explain. I didn't experience true motivation. I wasn't myself. It reminds me of a depressed patient to whom I prescribed Prozac. He was impotent, and this contributed to his depression. After he took Prozac, he became *more* impotent. As you know, that's one of its side effects. I asked how he felt about it. He said he was less depressed and that one of the good things about taking Prozac was that he didn't care if he couldn't get a hard-on. That's the kind of relief you get when you take antidepressants. That's what antidepressants do." Jan laughed.

"I tried many psychotropic medications for adequate periods before I saw that analyst," he continued. "One of my supervisors said that trying medications even once can give a psychiatrist more empathy for patients. When I was on Zoloft, I didn't feel like myself. Being depressed felt more natural. I wasn't motivated to suppress my depression. Remeron was smoother and more pleasant, but it made me sleepy. I lost weight on Wellbutrin but didn't feel better. Effexor made me so anxious that I couldn't sleep. These were my experiences, though everyone reacts to them differently.

"I feel sorry for patients who have to take medications. When I saw patients, I explained their side effects. I even told some of them that I had tried them myself. Patients listened to me. They knew that I knew what I was talking about."

"Unlike most other psychiatrists," I added, chuckling. Jan laughed out loud at his unique therapeutic wisdom.

"Did you ever take any psychotropic medications?" Jan asked.

"No," I replied.

"At some point after you take Zoloft, you feel extremely sleepy. If you take it at 7:00 or 8:00 in the morning, or at 1:00 or 2:00 in the afternoon, you can't stop yawning. I mentioned this to a patient who had started Zoloft. He took it in the morning and was falling asleep during the day. So I told him to take the Zoloft at noon: 'You can yawn all you want to after dinner and go to bed early.' Patients said they liked that I knew the nuts and bolts of medications. In the past, I used to increase the dosage of medications rather casually. I would say to patients, 'Well, if 20 milligrams isn't working, let's go to 40.' I don't do that anymore. These medications are powerful!"

"I think you're indirectly saying that good treatment releases endogenous chemicals that can make you feel better," I said. "Medications ingested by a patient may deliver more than they need or more than they can tolerate. However, the doses of neurochemicals produced during successful psychotherapy are controlled—even if unconsciously—by the patient."

"There are published reports that compare CBT with antidepressant therapy," Jan responded. "They produce important and comparable changes in brain chemistry that functional brain imaging can reveal."

"Although yet unproven, I feel the same is true of non-Cognitive Behavioral Therapy," I added, "like psychoanalysis."

"I'm sure of this—words matter. If you say something a sensitive person doesn't want to hear, you can piss him off, even if you're trying to help him. That's what friends do. Words and actions change neurochemistry."

"There are no names for these sequences of chemicals," I said. "Rather than label them as 'chemicals,' laypeople usually call them 'compassion' or 'acts of kindness'; therapists know them as 'helpful words' or 'helpful actions.'"

Jan became pensive. "That's why psychiatry is an art. When I took the exam, words changed my outlook. Although I've been studying psychiatry for four years, I did the worst on questions relating to psychiatry. I did fine answering non-psychiatric questions, but I froze on questions that touched on the possibility of suicide. I could read and understand them, but I had an emotional block. I made stupid mistakes. I felt that most of the questions were trick questions. I read and reread the questions and couldn't leave them alone. I felt that they were trying to trick me. I became paranoid. I couldn't move."

Jan continued, "Maria told me most questions in psychiatry are testing your knowledge. For example, do you know the dosage range of medication? There's no hidden trick, but I was paranoid. If you're on the lookout for a trap, you can always find one. When I did the practice exams online, I answered thousands of questions in psychiatry. I did fine, but when I took the real exam, I flunked."

Jan's eyes narrowed, and he spoke intently, "This is how I began to feel jealous of Amir. After the suicide, Amir's problems were over. Whatever existential pain he had, it was over. But I was still dealing with it. *I* wasn't over it. I had passive suicidal thoughts at times like these, especially when driving. I tried to push such thoughts out of my mind as quickly as possible. Cars *do* crash. Accidents *do* happen—but I would never follow through. Before Amir killed himself, I never had thoughts of crashing or accidents."

"Occasionally, I drank, and the thoughts returned," he added. "For a Polish guy, that's normal."

"Did you ever drink and drive?"

"No," he replied. "It's bad enough to take your own life; it's unacceptable to take along some innocent bystander in an accident."

"Even when you were depressed, you always kept the welfare of others at heart: bystanders, Maria, your family. You're like your mother: You think of others."

He appeared pleased initially, and then a cloud settled on his face. "Yes, but *I* want to give up, and my mother never gave up. I'm not like her, but I would like to be like her."

"So, your mom didn't waste her sugar on you."

"What do you mean?"

"Sugar is like love and kisses. Your mom's love still affects you. She taught you how to care for others, and you learned that lesson well. But, on the other hand, maybe trying to care for impossible patients made you crazy."

Jan readily agreed. "Yes, I sure got crazy. I wish I had my mother's class. My mother achieved her goal. She was good, and she had two good children. Everybody liked her. Sofia and I were devoted to my mom. She suffered silently in pain because she didn't want to bother others. She was concerned about them. She never cried and complained or made others miserable with her pain. Sometimes, she suffered for no reason: In her last days, when she was in excruciating pain, she refused drugs that would have lessened her pain because she didn't want to wake up my sister or me to help her take them."

Jan continued, "Watching Amir deal with death was different. He was young and felt that he was at the end of his rope, that there was no other way—no way out. He lived with the feeling that nothing would change for the better. That's how depression talks. He had just enough energy actually to do it—to kill himself. For 10 years, he thought of killing himself constantly. Is it reasonable to put a man in the hospital for 10 years because he expresses suicidal thoughts? Some people like to collect stamps; he liked to collect thoughts of suicide. He said he didn't want to die like a coward. He hated the notion of taking poison to kill himself. He joked about some chemical called TIC 20—rat poison—saying that he didn't want to die like a rat. He was constantly pushing his limits with such thoughts. He was obsessed with the notion of chance and Russian roulette. You know, he was a mathematician. He had created many complex algorithms concerning chance in Russian roulette."

Then Jan pensively added, "I didn't know how to deal with a patient like that. I don't think anybody can really know. I spoke to a supervisor. He said Amir was involved in 'suicidal gambling,' but that's just a label. It doesn't tell you what to do with him. Amir was obsessed with the movie *The Deer Hunter* and the scene with the Russian roulette. Have you seen *The Deer Hunter*?"

"Yes," I replied.

"He talked about the number of bullets a gun can hold and the odds of the single bullet going off."

It is against my nature to ask questions of dead people, but I wondered if Amir had felt brave playing with such thoughts. Still, I asked, "Did you ever think of Amir's verbal gunplay as bold? That he was looking for a cure for his childhood cowardice when he couldn't bear to watch the camel sacrifice?"

"I think he felt brave talking about guns and his imagined, heroic death. I knew him well. I asked him specifically to describe how he felt when he had such thoughts: 'Amir, what goes through your mind when you think of playing Russian roulette?' He said that he couldn't describe it. He said perhaps I could imagine going near the railway station and thinking about touching the third, high-voltage rail.

"He asked me, 'Do you have the guts to imagine touching the third rail?' Then he laughed and said, 'The idea of death by electrocution doesn't attract me!' We did have a strange connection. He trusted me and told me things that nobody in his family knew, things none of his friends knew."

Jan sat back in his chair and sighed. "I've been through this kind of interior dialogue in my mind a hundred times. I almost feel bored."

I understood Jan's "boredom" to mean that he felt beaten and tapped out. He was experiencing resistance to continuing this chain of thought. "So bored that you don't feel like repeating it once more to me?" I asked.

I felt my eyes narrow in anticipation of his response. "No, not really," he said. "I see that *you're* not bored. I just realized that, although I thought about these things many times, I never actually said these words to anybody else. This is new. I was just telling you that Amir trusted me enough to tell me things that disgusted him about himself. He talked about his disgust at Internet porn and masturbation. He talked about his roommate, who was addicted to watching bestiality online. Amir hated bestiality and got angry at his friend, but his friend was always able to trick Amir into looking at it. Afterward, Amir had nightmares about it. Maybe it's most accurate to say that Amir was ambivalent toward bestiality. He hated it but was also attracted to it. It made him feel dirty inside, but he looked at it. We worked on it then, as I was practicing CBT with him. I felt that my job was to wean him away from his attraction to bestiality and toward romantic involvement with some attractive woman."

Jan continued, "When he had nothing social to do outside his apartment, he would revert to his hated Internet addiction and then become ashamed. Usually, the bestiality involved dogs and women. Amir would talk like this: 'When I masturbated, I thought of dogs copulating. That worked. When my mental image changed to Natasha or Ms. Chen and sex with them, something distracted me, like the thought that someone was watching me, and I just lost my erection. The same thing happened when I thought of Muslim women. Something got in the way, maybe the sound of a butcher sharpening knives. But when I thought of nothing and nobody, I could come. I could come easily with sensations only. No images."

I thought this was an example of a core masturbatory fantasy, er . . . fear.

I remarked, "The mystery of his life may lie in knowing the pictures and forbidden thoughts that the veil of his pure sensations hid."

"But none of it can be solved," Jan said. "He's gone."

From what Jan had told me, I came to feel that Amir was a bright young man who struggled, unsuccessfully, to integrate two identities: One was a strong, courageous Amir, personified by the butcher. His badge of honor is the blood on his shirt. The other Amir is weak, cowardly, loathsome, and worthless. But unfortunately, this persona was the one that Amir knew best and the one that overwhelmed his capacity for life.

Life and the camel always reminded him that he wasn't what he wished to be. I felt that Amir hated his weak self and struggled to be tough. He aspired to be socially successful, especially with women, about whom he fantasized and dreamt, but women and the good life always eluded him. Amir took to heart the American demand for success but had no place to hide his vulnerabilities. He struggled mightily but couldn't become the person he wanted to be. Finally, he decided to go out in glory by proving to himself that he could be bold. What more significant test of courage can there be than the courage to pull a trigger on oneself?

In the end, Amir unintentionally, but with Jan's collusion, managed to transfer his feelings of worthlessness to Jan. I knew that none of this would be relevant to Jan's analysis until he was less mired in his own depression and had become capable of addressing what went wrong between himself and Amir.

Jan continued, "I still feel that it's such a shame that he's not around. After I listened to him many times, he started to make sense to me."

"You made a connection with Amir, and he made a connection with you," I said, "but he had a tenuous connection to life. We can only speculate as to whether he devalued himself because of a heroic notion of courage, because he felt unworthy in his father's eyes, because of a mistake you made, or some combination. But I know you feel primarily responsible."

Jan responded, "Sometimes I want to talk to his father and mother, and sometimes that thought gives me nightmares. I want to help Amir's father deal with the loss of his son, but since I also feel that his expectations screwed Amir up, I don't feel that I could be of any use to him. So to some extent, I feel that what happened was Amir's father's fault."

"I think you're slowly coming to terms with the fact that you did the best you could, but your patient killed himself. It's unclear what you can do to help his family, but your thoughts about it are important for us here."

"There's nothing I can do now. My notes are an open book whether Amir's family wants to pursue legal action or not. What legal action will accomplish, I don't know. I, too, am suffering the loss of Amir, yet I want to do my best to help Amir's family. I'm willing to meet them if they come here, to listen to them and try to explain my point of view."

"Today, you talked about your mom and how, even in death, she had class. I think you want to demonstrate such class in helping Amir's family deal with the loss of their only son, but his family may or may not be able to benefit from your lofty motive. Your old uncle might say, 'When fate violates the rules of the universe, it's hard to know what to do.'"

"I understand what you're saying," Jan said, "but I also feel that Amir's father and mother have the right to talk face to face with the person they feel killed their son. After all, I may have been the last one who spoke to him."

CHAPTER 6

By this time, Jan had been in treatment for about a month. When starting an analysis, an analyst instructs patients to report their thoughts, feelings, sensations, wishes, memories, dreams—whatever occurred to them, regardless of whether it seemed relevant. I was aware that I had not yet instructed Jan about this "fundamental rule." For most patients, this is almost impossible to do at first.

It was an anomaly that I called Jan and asked him to see me; usually, the patient contacts the therapist. In introducing Jan to the role of psychoanalytic *patient*, I said, "I know you haven't talked to anybody in a while. You said you'd like to see me. . . ." I intended to follow up by telling him, as Freud recommended, to speak his thoughts as freely as he could. Perhaps I hesitated because I knew, from Maria, that he was having difficulty talking to anyone at that point, and I didn't want to make an impossible demand on him. Perhaps, because he had already seen another analyst, Jan knew the rules and started speaking freely. He was, indeed, associating. So I stopped trying to instruct Jan concerning the fundamental rule.

However, I felt that something other than free association was also at play: his moods. After only about a month into treatment, there was a vitality in Jan's demeanor and speech, and I felt that he was jumping too quickly from being depressed to being not depressed. I was concerned that the changes were occurring too fast. He hadn't learned any lessons from depression: What got him depressed? What situations made his depression worse? How could he guard against future depression? He had moved away from his depression so rapidly that I feared that his improvement was only skin-deep and that he had left himself open to another, future depression.

I might compare Jan's quick abandonment of depression to a young man who has just broken up with his girlfriend: At first, there are sleepless nights filled with loneliness, sadness, anger, and maybe remorse. Then, suddenly, he is captivated by some other woman's scent or a scarf, as he notices her glance or flowing hair, the fullness of her lips, or her graceful walk. He becomes preoccupied with thoughts of having sex with her. Romance (or lust) replaces sadness, and love becomes driven: It is desirable and a necessity for his everyday life. In an instant, his despair over the loss of the previous girlfriend evaporates. She's history. His sadness is gone. He's on to a new skirt chase.

Jan seemed in the middle of such a sudden transformation. His mood changed suddenly, but had he leapt too soon from depression to a kind of giddy enjoyment of our conversations? Of course, every analyst wants their patients to be curious about the treatment itself. When a patient overcomes the grief of the presenting complaint without much awareness of the root causes, the analysis can become no more than friendly banter. Psychoanalysts call this phenomenon *flight to health*. It often leads a patient to stop treatment before accomplishing significant analytic work. In such cases, despite the patient's apparent improvement, the analyst feels the anxiety that should belong to the patient. Thus, my concern about Jan's suicidality was not my only anxiety. Now, it included a mixture of his disavowed depression and my anxious response to that disavowal. If I were right, my next task would be to reintroduce the disavowed anxiety back to him.

Whatever the reason, I remained concerned about Jan's depression. As soon as Jan came into the session, he asked if I had anything on the agenda. "Yes," I said. "Do you remember anything we talked about last time?" I usually do not say anything to guide a session other than a greeting.

"Yes," Jan replied, "we talked about many things."

Jan didn't seem to experience my immediate question as curtailing his freedom to start the session or choose the topic of the conversation. Instead, he reacted to it as simply part of my friendly personality. Still, he paused for about half a minute and then continued, "I can tell you what I've been thinking in response to the session. There was mostly . . . what I was thinking was . . . I didn't have any certain point to which I could relate to my life . . . For example, you can say that you feel far from home or far from a person you love. After Amir's suicide, I distanced myself so that I couldn't connect to anybody or anything."

Good, I thought. *Jan is still in touch with his depression.*

Jan continued, "I had contact with Maria and my close friends, but I was emotionally cut off. I couldn't relate what I was feeling to anything that had happened to me in the past. Until then, my life had progressed in logical steps, one following another. But after Amir's suicide, I suddenly lost track of all the steps, and I couldn't go backward or forward. My memories were emotionally erased. I couldn't dream or imagine the future. I was stuck in an isolated present. I couldn't see how my life related to the rest of the world. All I could feel was that I shouldn't become a psychiatrist and quit even being a doctor.

"I couldn't try another specialization. So when I switched from gynecological oncology to psychiatry, I felt like this was what I wanted to do. Then, after I began the residency program, I realized that I was good at relating to patients' emotional lives. Even better, someone was paying me for doing what I like to do!"

Jan laughed heartily before continuing. "I was enjoying my psychiatry training. Then Amir's suicide came. First, I was shocked, and then I was angry at Amir."

I thought that Jan's anger would help get him back to himself. Anger clarifies the separation between one person and another. Jan's identification with Amir had blurred his identity and mixed it up with Amir's. He needed to de-identify from Amir.

"I'm not sure even now if I'm anywhere close to accepting what happened," Jan said.

I was glad that Jan was talking in the past tense, rather than when he said, "Amir *is* the son of . . ." Still, we needed a clear understanding of his acceptance of Amir's suicide.

Jan continued, "But today, I'm closer to accepting it than I was a few months ago. After the initial shock and grieving, I realized that actually—and I didn't realize this until after our last session—I had become isolated. I think this is what depression is. You don't think you're related to anything or anybody, even your spouse. I used to enjoy calling Sofia or my friends on weekends. Because of the seven-hour difference, weekends were a good time to call, so I'd call on Saturdays, Sundays, holidays. It was automatic. I just did it. After Amir killed himself, I called less. Sofia is the closest family member I have in Poland, and I also have close friends there. I just didn't feel like calling. I didn't check my e-mail for a few months. Letters, too. I was afraid Amir's mother or father might call or write to me, so I avoided everybody. It was my childish way of avoiding them."

Jan was aware of his avoidance, and I needed to acknowledge that. "In the past, you dealt with this tragedy through avoidance. Now you're trying to figure out who you've become and who you might be in the future."

Jan nodded. "True. Finally, Amir's mother wrote. She didn't say anything nasty; she just described how horrible she felt. She said that Amir was such a great guy: good and intelligent. She felt lost after he died. She wanted to understand. I knew where she was coming from. I felt pretty much the same."

Not exactly, I thought. I appreciated Jan's kindness, concern, and desire to help Amir's mom. But now, in addition to identifying with Amir, he was identifying with Amir's mother. I had nothing to add. I felt he was relieved that her letter was not hostile and that she didn't blame him, but I had a hunch her blame game was still to unfold, that she had merely put it off for now. She wouldn't be able to maintain this posture indefinitely, and, at some point, Jan would encounter an angry woman.

Jan continued, "I know that being connected to someone by blood ties . . . I can imagine if something happened to my sister. My feelings would be so much stronger. I can only guess how strongly she feels. What she described is the way I dealt with my feelings, too, until I saw you. This is in response to your question about what I remember from last time. You asked how it was from my point of view. This is it," he said, gesturing around the office. "This is my connection to the real world. This is how I realized what happened. This is how I reconnected. The connection began when I started to see you."

Jan saw the relationship between his treatment and his improvement. But that improvement seemed to me to be too quick, incomplete, fragile, and ununderstood. Still, my task was to amplify this connection and make the most of it. In addition to the memories of Amir and concerns for his family, Jan needed other experiences in his life. I thought that reliving or at least remembering some scenes from Polish life might jump-start a move in a positive direction.

Moreover, I had something specific up my sleeve. I'd recently seen a movie about a pianist when Germany occupied Poland during World War II. Despite his suffering and the horrors he'd witnessed, he found a moment of imaginative pleasure. Facing dread and the real possibility of death with every step or misstep, he found a way to keep his true self alive.

"Have you seen a movie called . . . *The Pianist?*" I asked, not quite sure of the title.

"With Harvey Keitel?"

"No, it's about a Jewish man struggling to survive in Warsaw during World War II. Roman Polanski was the director."

"Yes, Adrien Brody played the pianist, Władysław Szpilman. I was disturbed by it because it was about events in my country. Many American Jews consider Poland an anti-Semitic country. There is, in fact, a long history of marked ambivalence between Poles and Jews in Poland. There are many dark and horrible periods and some bright sides, too.

"Jews first started settling in Poland in 960. Then, like in many parts of Europe, many people turned against the Jews, and they were prosecuted."

"Prosecuted? Or persecuted?"

"Persecuted. There were riots against Jews and then pogroms, like in Russia. I can't begin to tell you the whole history. I've been fascinated by the history of Jews in Poland, and I have some personal experiences that make this a sensitive topic. My father's father was a typical Orthodox Catholic. My father's mother was an orphan. I found some evidence that indicated that her father was Jewish. However, my father never told me this."

As I listened to Jan, I remembered that he had referred to his "father" and his "mom." Also, from the tonal differences in how he said the two words, it was clear that *mom* was a term of endearment for him, while *father* indicated distance. Now I noticed that Jan used distancing terms when he talked about other "fathers'" family members.

For now, I decided to use his terminology, but to make doubly sure, I asked, "So, your father's mother's father was Jewish?"

"Most likely. My father never confirmed it. No one would talk about it. Many elders of my family simply said they didn't know. When my father was moving to a nursing home, I found some documents that made me think my father's grandfather was Jewish, and I remembered that my mom had mentioned it in passing when I was about eight. My mom wasn't prejudiced at all; she treated everyone the same. I got interested in Jews and read a lot about them when I started going to University."

"I read that the Jagiellonian University is about 600 years old," I said.

"Yes, Casimir III the Great started the university in 1364, but he died. King Wladislaus Jagiello re-established it in 1400. That is where it got its name. When I entered Jagiellonian University, I joined the Polish Jewish Society. I got mentored by some Jewish professors and read the Talmud."

He continued, "Once, my father became depressed and had to be locked up in a hospital at the Psychiatric Clinic on *ulica Kopernika*, Copernicus

Street. I visited him every day. He was there a long time, and he didn't shave the whole time. He had a long white beard when the hospital released him. I took him to the Jewish part of Krakow, called *Kazimierz*. In the middle of it is a street called *ulica Szeroka,* Wide Street, with two synagogues. One is an old synagogue that's now a museum; the other is a functioning place of worship. We arrived at the old synagogue at 3:45 p.m., just as they were getting ready to close.

"The lady was unhappy to see visitors since she was getting ready to close. I told her that I would appreciate it if she could show my father the old synagogue. I told her we wouldn't be long, and she let us in. My father wanted to say something to me, but her presence inhibited him.

"The minute we were alone together, he said, 'It's nice that you brought me here, but I'm not interested.' The synagogue was beautiful, completely restored after the war. As we were leaving, the lady said, 'Thank you for coming. If you want to pray, the synagogue is only a block away,' and she pointed the way to No. 40, where the active Remuh Synagogue was located."

Jan smiled. "My father became agitated. He became so angry that he couldn't speak. He was aghast that she mistook him for a Jew. Perhaps she thought he was a rabbi because of his beard. I had noticed it but hadn't said anything. I said goodbye to the lady, and we returned to the car. When we were in the car, I said, 'You became upset when the lady mistook you for a Jew.'

"My father became upset again and shouted, 'How could she . . . how could she even think it?!'

"'What's wrong?' I asked him. 'That you could be mistaken for a Jewish person? You have a beard and a big nose, just like mine. Why not?'

"Now, my father was *really* upset. 'These are the people who crucified Christ!' he yelled.

"'But Christ was Jewish!' I answered. 'They crucified one of their own! So, what's your problem?!"

"'You don't understand,' he said. 'You'll never understand. Jews gather all the power in the world by accumulating money. They're always in charge of the money. That's what you have to consider. That's what happened. That's what *is* happening.'

"'You feel very strongly,' I responded, 'but you don't make any sense.'

"'*You* don't understand,' he answered. 'You haven't lived long enough.'

"'I try to understand,' I said. 'I've read a lot about Judaism and the history of Jews in Poland, and I also joined a Jewish society.' Then, finally, my father turned his head away from me. That was one of the few times we had a conversation about Jews." 37

---

37 The tense exchange between Jan and his dad was a sample of their conflictual relationship. Jan's statement that Jews "crucified one of their own," struck me. Perhaps, Jan was using his father's idiom—Jews crucified Christ—to be provocative. I was sure Jan knew that Roman soldiers killed Jesus, but he was reflexively expressing a common Catholic belief that held Jews responsible for Jesus's death. It could be that Jan did not believe that Jews were accountable and misspoke, that this statement was a slip of the tongue. When Jan recounted how he threw his father's words back at him, I felt Jan was, unwittingly or otherwise, repeating an ugly trope that was inconsistent with his character.

What did Jan intend by the expression? At the time, I was not sure that I grasped the full weight of his words. Being neither Christian nor Jewish, my knowledge of both of these religions is limited. So, following this exchange, I looked into the life of Christ. I intend this footnote to fill in some information for others like me from non-Judeo-Christian cultures. The notion that "the Jews killed Jesus" is not only historically erroneous but was long an incitement to persecution and prejudice that the Catholic Church now decries.

Jesus was born in Bethlehem to a Jewish family; his mother, Mary, was married to Joseph, a carpenter. The four Gospels of Matthew, Mark, Luke, and John describe the life and teachings of Jesus but were written several decades after his death, based on popular oral traditions. To the extent that they supply a historical record, Jesus was crucified by the Romans under the instructions of Pontius Pilate, the Governor of the Roman province of Judea at the time.

According to these Gospels, Jesus came to Jerusalem during the feast of Passover. Jewish inhabitants welcomed Jesus when he entered the city, exclaiming, "Hosanna to the Son of David" (Matthew 21: 8–9). Jesus repeatedly railed against the avarice of the money changers, who facilitated the buying and selling of sacrificial animals, and the overseers of the Temple of Jerusalem, where the sacrifices were offered: "My house shall be called the house of prayer; but ye have made it a den of thieves" (Matthew 21, 12–13).

Pharisees, Sadducees, Essenes, Zealots, Nazirites, and others with differing beliefs and practices often congregated around the Temple in Jerusalem. The crowds who cheered Jesus supported his desire to "cleanse" the Temple. The Temple overseers who condemned Jesus may have felt that he was disrupting their mode of life and threatened their vested interests by stirring up the crowds.

In response to Jesus's actions, the overseers of the Temple and the judicial body, the Sanhedrin, arrested Jesus at night and tried him for violating the Sabbath, sorcery, and blasphemy, and for claiming to be the son of God. The Sanhedrin found him guilty and deserving of death. However, since Judea was a Roman province, only the Romans had the authority to conduct an execution.

Accordingly, the Sanhedrin turned Jesus over to Pontius Pilate, with the charge that Jesus claimed to be the King of the Jews and was, therefore, a threat to Roman rule. Initially, Pilate thought he was innocent and would have released him, but the Temple's overseers called for a demonstration favoring death for Jesus. "When Pilate saw that he could not prevail at all, but rather that a tumult was rising, he took water and washed his hands before the multitude, saying, 'I am innocent of the blood of this just Person'" (Matthew 27:24). Pilate then ordered Jesus's execution in the usual manner of the time: crucifixion. (Can one wash one's hands of actions performed by one's own hands?)

Thus, according to the Gospels, the ruling elite of the Jewish people—anxious to blunt Jesus's movement for religious and social reform—instigated his arrest and execution by the Romans. This chain of events was grotesquely simplified and distorted into the libel, "The Jews killed Jesus," and repeated over centuries by Church tradition, ignorant mobs, and fascist dictators looking for scapegoats. Blaming Jews for Christ's crucifixion has allowed anti-Semitism to flourish and caused immense suffering over the centuries to Jews who had nothing to do with his death.

"When I first came to the United States, I had a Jewish girlfriend for two years. She was from California. When we were dating, I spoke to my mom about her. 'I have this nice girlfriend, and she's Jewish. Her mother is a liberal Jew, but her father is Orthodox.'

"My mom said, 'OK. I'm glad for you.' I guess that during the following week, my mom mentioned this to my father. After that, my father became utterly paranoid. He thought this girl was a secret agent sent to seduce me and steal my money.

"I told my father, 'You have no evidence. I have no secrets that might interest a foreign government. I'm not participating in any secret research. I don't belong to any secret society. And I have no money that she can squeeze out of me.'

"On another occasion, I asked my father, 'Is your mother Jewish? Is there some Jewish blood in our family?' He became angry, and his face got red, but he shook his head 'no.' Then he asked, 'Who told you?'

"I didn't want to tell him that my mom told me. I told him I'd overheard it a few years before. In Polish, we have a proverb, 'Don't explain too much; only guilty people explain.' If you explain too much, you're probably guilty."

"I don't want to explain too much either, Jan," I responded, "but I want to clarify one thing. I want to explain why I thought about *The Pianist* and why I brought it up. In it, Brody is the accomplished pianist, Szpilman. In the scene I'm thinking of, he's in a concentration camp surrounded by German soldiers and doesn't want them to find him. Then, suddenly, he discovers a piano and is drawn to it. If he plays it, the German soldiers will hear. They'll discover him and kill him. But if he doesn't, he'll miss out on this almost impossible opportunity. So he sits on the piano stool, readies himself, and passes his hands over the piano keys while he imagines the music we hear in the background, but he dares not touch the keys. Do you remember that scene?"

"Yes, but it didn't take place in a concentration camp. It was in bombed-out Warsaw. I remember the scene: As he imagines himself playing the piano, his face is joyful."

I learned about anti-Semitism in Europe from reading about Freud's life and conversations with others at the Institute for Psychoanalysis. Unfortunately, my knowledge of what happened in Nazi-occupied Poland was thin. I was glad that Jan corrected me and clarified that the scene took place in bombed out Warsaw and not a concentration camp.

I said, "When he's pretending to play, he's presumably transported to the times when he *actually* played the piano, and he's reliving those precious moments. He never lost those connections. Those faraway notes were alive, a vital part of him. After Amir's suicide, I think that you lost connection with your past, with the life you had before. Earlier today, you said you felt isolated and cut off from yourself. Do you remember that? (Jan nodded) But perhaps, like Szpilman hearing the sounds of the piano, you can remember and reconnect to some vital experience from your past."

Jan was eager to reply. "I didn't understand when it was happening. I became disconnected without realizing it. I needed you to gain perspective and be able to look back. I was simply lost in my situation.

"I have to tell you about the previous analyst I saw. I didn't feel any connection to him. I felt probed and scrutinized, but I didn't feel helped."

"What did he say or do that made you feel that way?" I asked.

"I can't quite put my finger on it. He did all the things that you expect an analyst to do. He let me talk. He didn't interrupt too much. But when he asked questions, they seemed to be completely off. He wasn't in touch with what I was feeling. For example, suppose we were talking about isolation and how it connects with work. Then he asked, 'Do you like scrambled eggs?' You think, 'What is this f___ing Yankee question all about?' I didn't see why he would ask the questions he asked. They had nothing to do with anything we were talking about. That wasn't what I wanted. If he wanted to help me. . . ."

Jan laughed, recalling his exasperation and, in the process, lost his sentence. "Was something in me preventing me from participating in the treatment? After thinking about it for a long time, I concluded that that was not the case. My participation wasn't the main problem. He couldn't connect with me. I couldn't connect with him. We just didn't click.

"After listening to me for half an hour, why this crazy question? His body language and your body language are the same. Both of you are careful and are trying to understand what I'm saying and feeling. I realize that my accent isn't easy. It demands that you pay extra attention, and it's an effort. But when you ask a question, I feel all right. After I'm finished talking, the questions you ask seem relevant. I haven't felt you were off even once."

I laughed, relieved that I wasn't the one he was roasting but knowing full well that I was not forever safe from such a fate. But what relieved me most was that Jan was no longer as masochistic as he'd been when he talked about Amir. Now he could summon his bile. Hoping to extract some meaning from Jan's tirade, I said, "I'm laughing because you used a phrase that was catchy and also irreverent. How did you come up with 'f___ing Yankee'?"

"'Yankee' is how you refer to Americans in Poland, in Europe, in Latin America. Many people call America 'Yankeeland.' In casual conversation, they call it 'Yankeelandia.' I know it doesn't make any sense historically. Yankees are from the North and fought for the United States of America. Confederates are from the South and fought to form the separate Confederate States of America. Yet my friends call every person from the United States, North or South, a Yankee.

"The connection between people in Europe and South America, the places in the world I'm personally familiar with, is one of closeness. It's strong and deep compared to the superficial connections among people in the United States. So, for example, if one of my friends from Europe or South America asks, 'How are you?' they want to know. In Europe, even an acquaintance may tell you, 'My mom isn't well. She's in the hospital.'

"If a Yankee asks, 'How are you?' you have no idea what he means. You put on a smile and a Yankee grin and say, 'I'm fine, thanks. How are you?' When I first came to America, I made the mistake of giving someone an honest answer. I told them I was recovering from surgery. I saw terror in his face like I was a mental patient!

"When I first met Maria's grandma, she asked me about my family. She reminded me of my mother—the same body language and friendliness. The conversation lasted an hour and a half. More interestingly, she spoke only a few words in English, and I spoke very little Italian."

"When you went to see this analyst, what did you expect? What feelings did you have?"

"I think I saw him four times. When I entered the session, he was usually preoccupied with finishing his notes from the previous patient. He didn't seem quite there. His verbal communication was OK, but he didn't look at me, and I couldn't detect any warmth. He has an office on a high floor with a magnificent view of the city. From his office, you can see downtown Chicago and the Chicago River. It was impressive. I commented, 'beautiful skyline.'

"The guy responded, 'What makes you say that?'"

Jan laughed out loud, a hearty, mocking laugh. First, he felt that the analyst had misplaced priorities; then, mocking the analyst, Jan exaggeratedly repeated it twice, with increasing emphasis, 'What makes you say that? *What makes you say that?!*'

"In my head, I said, 'Look outside the window, you fool! It's beautiful!' I actually said, 'This is how it makes me feel. Just look!' He often asked questions like that. They seemed almost pre-programmed."

Jan continued, "Ten minutes before the session was up, I knew that I had 10 minutes, not because I looked at my watch, but because that's when he would become vigilant. He would say, 'We're almost at the end of the session.' I knew he was checking the time if he was reaching for his glass of water or a Kleenex. Maybe I was over-interpreting his body language or his quick look at the clock. Somehow, these small details put me off. Sometimes, when I get started, I can talk and talk and talk, especially when it's something important to me. For example, this topic is important to me. I also speak louder.

"It's possible that I'm not giving him enough credit. His office was in downtown Chicago, mostly steel and glass skyscrapers, so there was the Chicago skyline when I entered his office. However, what struck me was that his office had two massive windows that formed a wall of sheer glass. The glass started below knee level and rose to the ceiling.

"When I walked in, I was suddenly gripped by fear. For a moment, it felt like the glass didn't exist. And even if it did, I felt that if I flung myself against it, it would shatter, and I would go flying to the street below."

At this moment, I had a sense of hope that I could help Jan. I've already mentioned that I felt that Jan identified with Amir and that that was the source of his suicidal depression. However, in my judgment, he needed to appreciate their differences. Amir had concealed his suicidal ideation from Jan, but Jan was open about his with me. I don't know if Jan shared his suicidal thoughts with the previous analyst, but with me, he was able to express his fears and explain why he had to flee his last analyst. Thus, I felt hopeful that Jan and I could work together if Jan persevered in his treatment with me.

"I suddenly got scared," Jan continued. "Perhaps I didn't give him a chance. I may have attributed to him the danger I felt from his window. I just kept feeling that I might jump through it. I don't think he knew how I felt, but he was polite and listened to me. According to the book, his reactions were formal, and I didn't sense any reciprocity. I never felt comfortable talking to him. He would comment about what I said, and it felt pretty off-the-wall. The danger was from my depression, and I wasn't ready to go anywhere near it."

I felt that Jan basically understood the defensive avoidance of his sadness, which led him to thoughts about flying out the window, something he dodged by leaving his analyst.

"One day when I was driving to see him," Jan continued, "a Mexican guy cut me off on the highway and knocked off my side mirror. He was driving dangerously, like an asshole. My broken mirror was hanging off the side of the car, and I wanted him to stop. Instead, he tried to escape, so I drove in a way to cut him off. Finally, I succeeded, and he stopped."

I could see Jan getting more agitated. He reminded me of a child patient I had years ago, who was fixated on the Incredible Hulk and made raging noises like him.

"We got out of our cars, and he gave me his insurance card. I was angry, and I felt justified in my anger, so I stared him down and intimidated him. He was shaking. When I was a teenager, I got into many fights in Poland. For boys, it was how you established your position in the hierarchy. I was good at it. I had what it takes to be like that. When I looked at him, I suddenly felt 20 years younger. It was a setting to vent, but then I caught myself: 'What are you doing?' I asked myself. 'What am *I* doing?!'

"I've never done anything to anybody in this country. I've never even behaved aggressively, but I was so close at that moment. I could have beaten this guy up. If he had resisted me, I would have beaten him up, but then he couldn't stop apologizing. So that's what stopped me.

"I dropped my aggressive attitude when I went to University and turned completely to the other side. There was one exception: One day, my ex-wife and I were at the bar in a crowded restaurant, and she went to the washroom. A guy took her place and refused to give it back to her. I intimidated him and made him leave. Everybody supported me because he was a jerk. Anyway, it took some time for the Mexican guy and me to exchange insurance information and cool off, so, of course, I missed my session. When I saw the analyst the next time, I told him what had happened and that I was so glad I didn't hit the guy and end up in jail. And then the inane question came."

Jan laughed and then stopped—a dramatic prelude for his next piece of evidence against the analyst?—but he didn't speak.

"What did he ask?" I queried.

Jan looked embarrassed. "I don't remember . . . I just forgot."

Jan's moment of forgetfulness is called *repression*. I thought if I could get him talking again, he could deactivate the repression. "You must have felt relieved that you didn't hit the guy," I said.

"Yes."

"You could have been cooling your heels in jail."

"Precisely. Oh, yes—now I remember. The analyst said something that had nothing to do with what had happened! He said, 'You missed the last session. Do you think you were avoiding me?'"

I encouraged Jan to continue associating with his former analyst, and Jan had overcome his repression. He remembered that his analyst had asked whether he was avoiding him.

"The question was infuriating! I was in an accident! I had adrenaline pumping. I'm glad to be a free man. But all this guy could ask was whether I was avoiding him. He seemed narcissistic and so self-absorbed."

I asked, "What do you think of the situation with the Mexican guy now?"

"You see, my mom died a year ago. I used to call her frequently. When she died, I missed her so much. I couldn't accept that her death was final and permanent. I regret acting like the adolescent I used to be. I think it's an example of regression, which started when she died. But thank God, I still had some maturity and sense left in me. Sometimes, when people talk nonsense, you can make them realize that they're being foolish without hitting them. I managed to stop myself after the guy apologized. I hope I never again employ physical aggression. I enjoy talking to people, even in a fight. I may make them suffer, but I would never hurt anyone physically. In this country, there are legal ways to make someone feel pain. In some places, the only chance you have is when the person is in front of you. What's the best way to burn people when you're angry?"

"In this country, the way to burn people is to put a lawyer on their tail."

"So, in such situations, the Yankees are more civilized!"

So, Jan saw some benefits of the American Way. Despite what he said, Jan was a happy camper and glad to be an immigrant in America. His disparagement of Yankeelandia was just part of his attempt to manage his feelings about leaving home. The end of the session was near, but I wanted to acknowledge his experiences with his previous analyst before concluding the session. "Just as the psychiatrist is testing the patient, the patient is also testing the psychiatrist to see if he can be of help," I said.

"When patients come, I smile and appreciate that they're putting their trust in me," Jan responded. "You don't always have to be objective, cold, and distant. You should invite patients in and make them feel welcome. You make your presence felt. You try to be there."

"Well, the term on our combined presence for today is expiring. We have a few minutes before we stop for today."

Jan's face turned pensive. He appeared to have remembered something disturbing. "I understand we have to stop, but I just remembered something.

"My mother's parents' house was close to the Jewish quarter of our town. What now is a brick-and-mortar construction used to be a large wooden house with steep stairs at the front entrance and a huge terrace facing the garden in the back. I spent lots of time playing with my cousins, so I remember this house very well. I also lived there, as a toddler, when my mom was in a sanatorium with tuberculosis.

"When I was seven or eight, I heard that, when my Aunt Marta was a girl, she had a friend named Chaya who was shot and killed in front of my aunt's house. I was so shocked that I didn't ask any questions, but it changed how I felt about the place. After that, I didn't mind when my aunt and uncle tore it down when I was about ten years old and built a new house. At this age, I was not sure if death was permanent. After that, however, my aunt's place felt unsafe because I remembered that a girl was killed there.

"My Aunt Marta is a great storyteller, but she never really elaborated on Chaya's story. Not recounting an event was quite unusual for her. However, my aunt knows how to build suspense and includes impressive, funny, or dramatic punchlines. I loved to listen to her for hours. Whenever I had a question, she patiently and fully responded. In the back of my mind, I was curious about Chaya, but I didn't press my aunt for the whole story.

"In my adolescence, I visited the synagogue on *ulica Szeroka* and became interested in Jewish culture and traditions. Then, I started asking my aunt about Chaya. Each time, I felt that her answers were evasive and lacked her usual storytelling fireworks. Finally, after my mother died, we talked about their lives when they were young, and I asked her about Chaya again.

"Although she was not fully open, she was a little more forthcoming. She said she was 11 years old when the war began. Chaya was her friend. They played together a lot, often in my grandparents' garden. Chaya taught Marta some Yiddish and let her play with her toys. She was the daughter of a store owner who was one of the wealthier citizens in the town. Chaya was friendly and easygoing. They trusted each other with secrets and grew pretty close, even though their parents had no relationship.

"In September 1939, the Nazis occupied Mielec. First, they killed 200 Jews in the Jewish ritual slaughterhouse. Next, they burned the synagogue. Then, in October, the Germans went from house to house in the Jewish quarter, terrorizing them and forcing them into slave labor.

"On the outskirts of Mielec, there were many 'German villages,' where, before the war, Germans coexisted with Jews and Poles, but at this time, some of these young German villagers helped the Gestapo to intimidate, dehumanize, starve, and rob the Jews.

"Aunt Marta explained that, by 1942, Mielec was supposed to become *Judenrein,* free of Jews. My aunt remembered that Nazis surrounded the whole town on one cold night in March. They started to kill Jews who were unable to work and forced the rest to march toward the airport. On this march, if Jewish prisoners became weak, the Germans shot them and tossed them into a mass grave.

"My aunt wasn't sure what exactly happened at her friend Chaya's house. Her best guess was that Chaya was force-marched to the airport but managed to escape. She tried to return to her house, but the Germans swarmed all the surrounding streets. At some point, a German soldier spotted her. So she ran toward my Aunt Marta's house. Chaya banged on the door, but my grandma was too scared to open it. The soldier shot Chaya dead, and her body lay there for many hours. Eventually, someone, probably the sanitary services, took her body away.

"According to my aunt, Germans exploited tensions between Jews and Poles by setting them against each other. In other towns, the Germans forced everyone to watch hangings in town squares, including schoolchildren. The Germans left the dead bodies hanging by the noose for several days till the body broke off from the head and fell.

"Germans made Polish policemen hang Jews, and they made Jewish policemen execute Poles. Every time a German was killed by Polish partisans, the Germans randomly executed 10 locals.

"I've been thinking about what happened that day. For a long time, I wondered why my aunt was so cryptic in answering my questions for so long. Later, when I tried to clarify it with her, her eyes filled with tears. 'I don't really remember,' she said. 'It was such a long time ago.'

"Did my grandparents hear Chaya's frantic knock on their door? I'm sure someone did, but they were afraid to open it, terrified the Germans would kill them, too. My uncle Bozydar and some extended family members were part of the underground Polish resistance against the Germans. If you harbored Jews or anyone from the Polish underground resistance against the Nazis, you could be imprisoned, taken to a concentration camp, or shot. Every Polish person knew that and lived in constant fear. World War II was a tragedy for everyone in Poland. I know that my aunt still suffers from it. She lost a dear friend on her doorstep and can't remember. Maybe she remembers and feels too guilty to talk about what happened."

How should I have responded when Jan said he told his father, "But Christ was Jewish! They crucified one of their own. So what's your problem?" Should I have said, "It was only a small minority of Jews 2000 years ago who sought Jesus's death, and it was the Romans under Pontius Pilate who crucified him, not the Jews"?

Truth, understanding, and healing are all critical considerations for analysis at all stages of treatment. However, the realization of these goals depends on the patient, the analyst, and the treatment stage. There is an established and accepted technique in psychoanalysis for addressing conflicts between historical and personal realities.

Psychoanalysis heals suffering by understanding—preferably the unconscious's *self*-discovery—of the unconscious. The analyst aids the patient in many ways: by facilitating increased self-awareness, improving the management of anticipation and surprise, reducing internal conflicts, repairing developmental deficits, correcting errors, and fostering the acquisition of a broader range of adaptive choices. Listening to the patient's freely expressed thoughts, the analyst discerns the unconscious conflicts that underlie the symptoms, slips, and dreams that offer clues to his personality. Healing through psychoanalysis is primarily concerned with laying bare the stuff of the patient's unconscious.

Late in his life, Freud wrote "Analysis Terminable and Interminable," describing idealistic and realistic analytic attitudes toward analytic "truth." From the idealistic perspective that seeks complete analysis, Freud stressed "... that the analytic relationship is based on a love of truth—that is, on a recognition of reality—and that it precludes any kind of sham or deceit" (p. 248).[38]

In that same paper, Freud acknowledged that areas of the patient's life are "not currently active" in the analytic transference; this is from a realistic analytic perspective. Here, Freud suggested that sometimes it was better to leave some issues alone, even though there are areas of incomplete analysis. For example, he asked, "Could we, for purposes of prophylaxis, take the responsibility of destroying a satisfactory marriage, or causing a patient to give up a post upon which his livelihood depends?" (pp. 231–232)

An analyst does not have to choose *either* a realistic (acknowledging the unavoidable limitations of analysis) attitude *or* an idealistic (seeking a

---

38 Freud, S. (1937). "Analysis terminable and interminable." In J. Strachey (Ed. and Trans.), *The Standard Edition of the Complete Psychological Works of Sigmund Freud* (Vol. 23, pp. 209–254). London: Hogarth Press.

complete analysis) attitude for the entire analysis. The realistic approach is more suitable when the analyst and patient start treatment, and the goal of a fuller analysis is more suitable later on.

The analyst does not fully understand the patient's symptoms, defenses, and resistances at the beginning of treatment. The analyst doesn't know the patient well; they are strangers delving into potentially sensitive areas. The patient's previously untreated symptoms, inhibitions, anxieties, and narcissism (pride and self-esteem) demand caution and tact. At this time, it is easy to bruise the patient's vulnerabilities and self-confidence. Because the analyst's knowledge of the patient is limited, their interpretations will inevitably be tentative, incomplete, and sometimes unintentionally cause extra suffering. Initially, the patient is learning to be a patient. The analyst is learning how to engage the patient. At this stage, expectations should be modest.

The principle that I (and many other analysts) follow is to explore the emotionally charged and autobiographically lived events, like the patient's relationships to mother, father, and siblings. The analytic here-and-now events (including feelings toward the analyst) are more significant than are there-and-then events dealing with religious or political issues or even current events in the patient's life. The crux of a patient's childhood relationships is re-lived in the analysis, toward the analyst, through the mechanism of *transference.* Unconsciously, the analyst becomes a stand-in for the patient's mother, father, or other significant players. Feelings originate in childhood's emotional crucible, and the here-and-now transference re-engages them in. The treatment context is the best arena to explore and understand such feelings. However, sometimes such feelings are displaced onto religious figures.

In contrast to transference emotions, feelings displaced to religious or historical figures lack the transference element. So they are less amenable to analysis. Therefore, analysts usually focus on the patient's analyzable conflicts rather than dwell on religious or political interests, preoccupations, or clashes.

When a patient recognizes a slip or error and its antecedents, he discovers the unconscious *himself.* This awareness facilitates the patient's self-understanding and leads to the joy of discovery. When an analyst points out an error, he is, to some degree, instructing the patient about the unconscious. I could have corrected Jan's error and brought attention to his unconscious, but that would have risked embarrassing him and undermining his sense of control of his faculties, and deprived him of the thrill of discovering the unconscious.

Jan had just started the analysis, and I decided that it was better to address slips, prejudices, or errors after he showed more signs of awareness that they had occurred. And so, I let Jesus and the Jews pass without correction or comment.

CHAPTER 7

THE STORY ABOUT CHAYA SHOOK ME UP. I kept imagining the scene of a desperate child banging on the door, screaming for a chance to live, and being shot by a German soldier. I also thought of her friend Marta's sadness and guilt. I couldn't get the story out of my head.

Jan's account of his encounter at the synagogue with his father and our discussion of Szpilman in German-occupied Warsaw during World War II also reverberated in me. The Nazis exploited and murdered millions of Jews. Yet, until I left India, I didn't know a single Jewish person. Hearing about their tragic losses made me think of Hindu caste discrimination, suffering, tragedies, and killings suffered by Indians. With a sense of relief, I also remembered acts of kindness and benevolence that I had experienced.

According to social status, the hierarchical and hereditary ordering of society, from idealized to devalued, is the basis of the Hindu caste system. It is a social construct and the primary source of identity and discrimination in Hindu India. The main castes are *Brahmins* (priests), *Kshatriyas* (warriors), *Vaishyas* (traders and business people), and *Sudras* (artisans and farmers). Far removed from these four castes were the *Dalits* or *Untouchables* (scavengers, latrine cleaners, people who dealt with disposal of the dead). Brahmins were most idealized, and the Sudras and Dalits suffered most from discrimination.

Recent genomic studies of mitochondrial and nuclear DNA show that India is primarily a mixture of native Ancestral South Indians and Ancestral North Indians related to steppe people from Central and West Asia and

Europe.[39] Between 2200 BCE and 100 CE, there was a large-scale mixing of these groups. According to these studies, the Hindu caste system became rigid only after 100 CE, and the castes became isolated. Now, "no group is unaffected by mixing, neither the highest nor the lowest caste, including the non-Hindu tribal populations living outside the caste systems."[40] As a result, castes and subcastes have been largely endogamous for almost two thousand years.

India is striving to overcome the blight of this discrimination. India gained Independence from the British Empire in 1947. Despite the fundamental right to equality, India's Constitution allows for temporary special provisions (affirmative actions) to advance the interests of women, children, and the socially and educationally backward classes, Sudras and Dalits. These consist of a fifty percent reservation of seats in educational institutions and public-sector job opportunities for such groups. However, such special provisions' scope, duration, and desirability generate much political strife. Communities benefiting from the reservations want them expanded, and indefinitely extended. Those opposed hold that caste-based reservations violate the Indian Constitution's guarantees of equality for all and call for the end of caste-based quotas.

As I listened to Jan, memories from my childhood of friendly and intolerant relations among Indians of differing backgrounds bubbled into my consciousness. I believed that these memories were relevant to my treatment of Jan, as they alerted me to my internal maps of equality and discrimination. So I describe them.

I was born soon after India won its independence in 1947. During my childhood, a sense of freedom infused the country. Children of all castes and religions in the neighborhood played together without much adult supervision. We would just walk out of the house and play with whoever was there. There was occasional bickering, minor accidents, and scrapes, but nothing we couldn't handle ourselves.

Boys played cricket and chased wayward kites, and girls played hopscotch and jump rope. And boys and girls, together, played hide-and-seek, dodgeball, or badminton, or, when it was too hot outside, cards, Snakes and Ladders (like Chutes and Ladders), Monopoly, and caroms. We searched

---

39 Tony Joseph (2018). *Early Indians: The Story of Our Ancestors and Where We Came From.* Juggernaut Books. New Delhi.

40 David Reich (2018), *Who We Are and How We Got Here: Ancient DNA and the New Science of the Human Past.* Oxford Universities Press. The UK. pg. 136.

for birds, butterflies, and ladybugs. We imitated frogs and watched dogs copulate. Kids taught each other how to ride on rented bicycles. We saw movies together, and we sometimes did homework together. And in our house, I knew that when I returned home, my grandfather wanted us to wash our dirty feet, my dad wanted us not to make too much noise, and my mom wanted us to study.

My dad was an atheist and an equalitarian. According to Hindu tradition, each Hindu person can worship one, many, or no gods. Members of the same family often worshipped different gods. I grew up ignorant about the more profound implications of caste and religion. I knew that other kids belonged to different castes or beliefs, but it made no difference to our play. We were all friends.

I sometimes made incorrect assumptions about others' caste or religion. For example, among my friends, there were two boys with the same name: Narasimha. It is a typical Hindu name. We called Paala Narasimha "Milk Narasimha," because his family was in the dairy business. That made him a Golla or cow- or buffalo-herd Hindu caste member. He was about my age and his family lived in a corrugated-steel shed house that also sheltered three or four water buffaloes and several calves. They were massive beasts and, unlike cows, notorious for being stubborn and irritable. I always kept a safe distance from them, but he was unafraid of them. He lovingly talked to his water buffaloes as he milked them. He even knew how to coax milk from a grieving mother water buffalo. If a calf had died, their family would stuff the body with straw, and Narasimha would place it in front of the mother water buffalo to induce her to give milk. Whether it was the smell of the dead calf's skin or perhaps the wish for the calf's magical return, the buffalo, although grieving, still gave milk.

When I was about ten or eleven, I visited my friend Narasimha at his home. While distributing milk to nearby households that were their customers, he helped bathe and feed the animals. He invited me to watch him milk one of his water buffaloes that day. First, he gathered some hay, made affectionate sounds, showed the buffalo the grass, and then placed it within its reach. Then, taking a bucket of water and a clean pail from his house, he squatted on his haunches near the udder and held the pail between his knees. Speaking to the animal and cleaned its udder, stimulated its teats, and milked it. He set the vessel with milk on a nearby bench and covered it with a lid while still on his haunches. He looked at me and asked me to look at him. Bending a bit and opening his mouth, he squeezed the teat. Most of the milk squirted on his face, but a short stream fell into his mouth. "Warm and sweet," Narasimha exclaimed. "Warmth" made sense to me, but felt he did not mean sugar "sweet." Perhaps he meant the sweetness of natural fresh milk. Then he stood, pointed to the spot where he had sat, looked at me, and asked, "Do you want to milk it and get a squirt too."

I was surprised. Our family's milkman milked buffaloes in front of our house for a while. The milkmen carried water in one of their pails and, if given the opportunity, could deftly add water to the milk. Occasionally, I had to make sure their buckets were empty before milking began and that the milkman did not add water to it. (Later, we purchased milk in sealed plastic containers at grocery stores.) I observed that milking a buffalo could be challenging. When they are irritable and restless, they will not stand still for milking, and the milkman has to calm and soothe them before approaching their udders. As I surveyed the spot Narasimha cleared, the water buffalo suddenly loomed like a massive beast in front of me. I felt out of place and knew I was a stranger to the buffalo. Despite my curiosity, I said, "No," to Narasimha.

On one of my visits back to India a few years ago, Narasimha told me that his mother was ill, and we went to the old-age nursing home to visit her. Above her headboard was a framed picture of Christ, adorned with a prominent crown of thorns. A black-beaded rosary, a wooden crucifix, and a burning candle were on a nearby mantle. That was when Paala Narasimha told me he was not a Hindu *Golla*, but a Christian. In the more than 50 years I have known him, I had not known that! So, I give this example to show how far caste and religion were far from our minds during our childhood.

Another of my friends was Vinod, who belonged to the *Vaishyas* or business-persons caste. His dad owned several factories, and his family lived in a massive mansion. He often invited us kids to his house to play ping pong. For most middle-class children, ping-pong balls were expensive and always in short supply. Vinod thought that since all of us played, all the kids that played should chip in to purchase them. We had mixed feeling about this. After all, considering his family's wealth, he was in a better position to buy them. So we gently ribbed him for being *kanjuce*—stingy—when he asked for donations. However, we also knew that he was very generous, and *we* were using his house, play equipment, and hospitality. To celebrate our friendships, Vinod sometimes took us to fancy restaurants. It is clear to me now that our ribbing him for being stingy was a peculiar acknowledgment of his generosity, and *we* were the cheapskates. Fortunately, we were never too mean, and he took it in good spirit.

Brahmins, whether orthodox or secular, are vegetarians. Kids from other castes teased *Brahmin* boys like me by pretending to chop meat and yelling, "*Khiema!*" The word means "minced mutton," implying that we secretly loved (and ate) meat. I never craved meat. I have remained primarily a vegetarian.

In both instances I have mentioned, the teasing focused on something bogus: Vinod was generous, not stingy, and I didn't *want* to eat meat. Being teased as a *Bania* or a *Brahmin* was unpleasant, hurtful, and unnecessary, but I knew no example of caste bullying that needed parental intervention; the teasing was just a minor annoyance. I maintained relationships with my friends from other castes for more than 60 years.

Hindu Indians celebrate the harvest festival *Makar Sankranti* when the sun begins its northward journey, called the *Uttarayan,* and the northeast monsoon in South India comes to an end. This occurs in the month of *Poush,* in January, the month for flying kites. I grew up in Secunderabad, one of the many cities famous for kite flying and kite fights. The initial pleasure of kite flying is successfully launching the kite. Before long, though, it becomes competitive, in the form of kite fights, where the object is to cut the string of an opponent's kite.

Young kite flyers are pleased just to fly their kites and don't engage in kite fights. After about age ten, though, most kite flyers are looking for combat. They spread their strings with glue and powdered glass shards, thus converting each line into a cutting instrument (a *manja*). Thus weaponized the string, a combatant announces his desire to fight by bringing his kite near another. During a kite fight, the flyer seeks to maneuver his *manja* to quickly glide over the string of his opponent and saw it off. The loser feels it immediately when his string is cut, as the previously taut line goes limp in his hands. Humiliation! The winner yells "*Haffaa!*" with much jubilation. More humiliation. The loser must reel in his string in a hurry because it quickly falls to the ground. Other kids, on the ground, plunder it if they can, and you may not get back the remainder of your string. Even a bit of string has value. The lesson from kite flying is that there may be fierce competition in life, and there is no mercy sometimes. And if the loser does not even get back the remainder of the string? Ruination. Meanwhile, the cut-off kite wafts aimlessly in the wind, gently rocking toward Earth. As it nears the ground, kids who have been following its descent chase it with the hope of seizing this valuable trophy.

I lived near the Secunderabad Central Jail, with an extensive farm complex. The jail was adjacent to the Christian Home for the Aged. On the other side of the Home was the Bhoiguda Catholic cemetery. The prison housed the prisoners at the far end of its premises. Its backyard was a vast field that abutted our block. We could see the acres and acres of mint and spinach from where we lived. The cooling mint and fresh spinach perfumed the air when the breeze blew from the south on hot summer days.

A barbed-wire fence separated our block from the prison. Just outside the fence was a moat a few feet wide, full of wild plants, trees, and shrubs. I remember the poisonous Datura (*Datura stramonium*) plant, with its four- or five-inch white, trumpet-shaped flowers, and the wicked spines encasing its fruit. *Acacia arabica* (gum tree) hedges oozing drops of gum resin protected by sharp thorns lay in wait by the fence. And cacti with thorny leaves also stood guard. Together, the poison, thorns, and spines advised us kids to stay out and mind our own business, and warned the prisoners to remain in. (The jail is gone now, replaced by the new Gandhi Hospital.)

A low-slung wall about four feet high surrounded the Home for the Aged. This wall met the barbed-wire fence on the jail's perimeter and then turned 90 degrees to become part of the boundary wall that separated the jail from the Home for the Aged.

The prisoners worked in the luscious green fields under the watchful eyes of the jailers. (I never got close enough to see whether the prisoners wore leg irons.) There were stretches of hours or days when neither prisoners nor guards were in the fields. Many cut-off kites landed there, and we saw these intervals as golden opportunities to retrieve these treasures. Imitating older boys, a group of about six of my friends would break into the jail yard. A pair of tall boys would join and cup their hands to make a springboard so we could step up and leap onto the wall of the Home for the Aged. Then we'd cross over, jump into the restricted jail grounds, and run to grab the fallen kites before anyone else did. During such forays, I wondered what the punishment was for breaking *into* jail!

Growing up, I had a dear friend named Kanti; his father owned a wheat mill. I believe he belonged to the *Sudra* or labor caste. He was younger than me, perhaps by a year, but bolder. It was only with his guidance and encouragement that I overcame my hesitation and developed the courage to jump over that wall onto the jail grounds.

Behind my house was the backside of the Bhoiguda Catholic Cemetery. Although we never actually saw ghosts or demons, all the kids knew about them. They were the evil roaming spirits of recently dead people that might come to steal our souls, especially at night and in the vicinity of graves, especially newly dug ones. (We all knew about Hindu souls, but I was not sure if Christian souls were comparable to Hindu ones.) We avoided the ghosts by being outside only in daylight and staying away from most of the graves in the cemetery's front; for good measure, we tried to avoid doing bad deeds. However, at the back of the cemetery, though, there were giant banyan, neem, drumstick, guava, and tamarind trees with inviting branches that were irresistible for urchins like us. Occasionally, hordes of rhesus macaque monkeys roamed freely on these trees, gliding effortlessly from branch to branch. Even mothers with wide-eyed, wizened infants clutching them could jump and maneuver with ease. It was our dream to swing like monkeys.

I liked to climb guava trees and check out the guavas and would patiently wait for a nice big one to ripen. Sometimes, when the auspicious day came, I would climb up the tree to pluck the fruit and discover that a parrot had already taken the first bite, nibbling off the juiciest part! Climbing high up also enabled one to see further and find distant cut-off kites.

And this brings me to an incident of caste discrimination that stands out in my memory: One lazy Sunday in January, Kanti invited me to jump over the cemetery wall and climb a giant neem tree to search for cut-off kites. I'm guessing I was eight, and he was seven. He assured me that ghosts weren't real and that he had entered the cemetery several times. He noted how inviting the branches were and what a great view we would have from up high. Up we went. We watched the flying kites for a while. We marveled at the expertise, or its lack, in the respective flyers. We tried to predict the outcome of kite fights: which kite was king, which would survive and for how long, and which kite would soon perish.

Then I noticed that Kanti was distracted. Suddenly, he stopped talking and said, "Run." Being more agile than me, he started down the tree first. I looked down and, to my dismay, saw the cemetery *mali* (gardener) approaching. He broke off a branch from the tree, fashioned a switch, and waited for us. Kanti reached the ground first, and the *mali* gave him a few licks with the switch. Kanti was brave and took his licks without crying. Kanti waited for me as I nervously descended; neither of my parents ever spanked us. Despite my apprehension, I was relieved I didn't lose my grip and fall. The *mali* was waiting for me. With tears running down my cheeks, I grabbed my slippers, which I had left at the base of the tree, and struggled to get them on my wobbly feet. I waited for my punishment, telling the *mali*, "I'm sorry. I was wrong." "Get out!" the *mali* barked. "You should come here only after you die!" The *mali* chased us out of the cemetery without beating me, sparing me the pain and humiliation Kanti had suffered.

In that instant, I felt the *mali* didn't hit me because I was a *Brahmin*, but he hit Kanti because he was a *Sudra*. *Malis* usually belong to the *Sudra* caste. So how could the *mali* know that Kanti was not a *Brahmin* boy and I was?

All humans, regardless of their background, belong to the human species. Indians of all religions—Hindus of all castes, Muslims, Christians, Sikhs, Buddhists, and Jains—have the same claims to being Indian. In rural India, people live in small communities and know one another's backgrounds. Although people of different castes have somewhat different vocabularies and accents, there is no sure way to tell the differences among urban India. Could it be that the *mali* just took pity on me because I was crying?

Kanti and I should not have trespassed on private property. The *mali* could have given both of us a warning and spared us physical punishment, or he could have punished us both. Either action would have been fair. The *mali* chose discrimination, however. Since both the *mali* and Kanti were *Sudras*, the *mali* also could even have given Kanti the preferential treatment—sparing him and punishing me. He did the opposite. What sense does it make that the *mali* selected his own kind to disfavor and punish? These are paradoxes of human nature that defy easy understanding.

Kanti and I continued to be good friends for many more years. After I moved to America, I saw him several times when I came home to visit, and we had many good chats. So as far as I could tell, this episode didn't affect our friendship.

Kanti is dead now—felled by a heart attack—and I regret that I never talked to him about this incident. Perhaps someone with a bigger heart would have openly acknowledged the injustice right away. Although I felt guilty for having received preferential treatment, I was also glad not to have been whacked. Yet, I always admired Kanti's courage. He jumped into the jail yard before me.

If I had a chance to go back in time to when I was eight years old, I would tell Kanti, "I'm sorry about what happened to you. You didn't cry when the *mali* hit you, but I'm sure it hurt; everyone hurts when they get hit. I was scared and cried, but I was relieved not to get hit. What happened was unfair. The *mali* should have spanked both of us or shooed both of us away without lifting his hand." Neither the jail nor the cemetery ever tempted me again, but in one non-strike that favored me, the *mali* taught me that the Hindu caste system was rotten and unfair.

Another memory: In my early twenties, I visited my cousin, her husband, and their young guests in Warangal. Each of them had traveled widely, was knowledgeable about the arts and history, and had interesting stories. I was curious and young. I enjoyed listening to their beautiful conversations and their wit. I planned to visit for a few days and walk eighty-five miles from Warangal to Secunderabad as part of my discovery of India and the world. So, I was reluctant to leave such great company and trudge back home. I still remember the wonderful time I had in Warangal nearly half a century ago. I expected it would take me a few days, with breaks along the way. I carried a small backpack with some food and water. I walked a little more than twenty miles and was about ten miles from Jangaon. I drank the water faster than I had expected, my water bottle was empty, and I was thirsty. I stopped at a hut by the road and gently called, "O, Amma." A friendly-looking woman came out. She looked at me curiously, clearly surprised to see a tired city dweller. I showed her my empty water bottle and asked, "Can you give me some water, please?"

Before she answered, she asked, "*Meeru evaru?*" (Who are you?) At first, I was surprised by her question, but then I understood. From the context, I realized she wasn't asking about me as an individual, but rather, "What caste are you from?" For most of my life, I had lived in a big city or a bustling railway town, places where we took the cultural forces of modernization for granted. So when a person went to a public place, like a temple, a restaurant, or a train, no one would consider asking to know a person's caste. It was irrelevant. Besides, in those places, there was simply no way of knowing.

Here, about thirty miles from Kazipet, where I lived as a young child, I was dealing with an age-old Indian question. I wasn't sure how to respond, so I didn't reply immediately. Being my father's son, I didn't believe in caste, but I worried she wouldn't understand.

Although many Hindus, like Nanna and me, are trying to forge a new identity as a Hindu without a caste, it is difficult to achieve. Your caste is like your name: It becomes part of you but is given and maintained by culture. You may try to shed it, but others still apply it and don't acknowledge your renunciation. When Hindus become casteless, democracy will have truly arrived. But, until then, even in a simple conversation, one person will pigeonhole another into a particular caste.

The woman looked at me knowingly, for she guessed my caste from the way I enunciated the words "O, Amma." I didn't belong to her caste. I guessed she belonged to the laborer caste. She inquired, "*Bomanla [Brahmins]*?"

That isn't the word *Brahmins* use to refer to themselves, but a term used by non-*Brahmins*. I didn't view myself as a *Brahmin* but as an Indian. But that was not the time to explain my worldview. I needed water.

"I am a *Brahmin*," I answered, "but it doesn't matter."

"I have water if you wish," she said, "but the water is unfit for *Brahmins*!"

I was surprised and not surprised at the same time. This kindly woman was speaking from a tradition handed down through the ages. I was thirsty but also wanted to make my point. I replied in Telugu, "I'm thirsty. Water is the same for everybody. There's no one water for me and different water for you. *Manamuantha okate*" (We are all one.). She smiled in agreement and then brought out an earthen pot of cool water. After I drank, she asked if I wanted some for the road and filled my water bottle. I was happy for the water but even happier that two Indians from different castes and walks of life could touch each other. I turned and looked at her kind face before I departed. I could see that she understood my wish to erase caste distinctions and was willing to drop them herself. I thought of my own Amma (mom), who routinely offered water to visitors and workers in our house and to anyone thirsty. India is capable of change, and this woman near Jangaon was an example of someone ready to live in a genuinely democratic India. Both those with past privilege and those who have been the underprivileged need to warm up to equality. Equality is the magic of democracy.

I felt rejuvenated by the water, by her kindness, and by her acceptance of what I'd said. As I left, I bowed and brought my hands together in front of my chest, following an age-old Hindu tradition, and said, "*Namaste*." This gesture acknowledges the shared spark of divinity in oneself and the other. It says, "We are all the same in that we are all manifestations of the divine."

She, too, smiled and brought her hands together and said, "*Namaste*." Never did that simple Hindu greeting make more sense.

As I continued my journey (wisely taking a train the rest of the way), my joy in the woman's benevolence lingered. I felt many vocations admirably suited her. She could be a teacher and help kids realize their potential. She could be a politician and guide her community to a place of greater equality. She could be a judge and usher in an era of true democracy. But all this was not to be. She is trapped by caste, as is everyone else. When we limit ourselves because of caste, we all lose. If we try, perhaps the future can be different.

Although not related to caste, a couple of other incidents come to my awareness. When one of our neighbors constructed a four-story house with many apartments, I was pleasantly surprised that the family of

Younis Mohamed, the top student in my high school class, rented one of them. Younis approached his studies, especially mathematics, with discipline. He—and few others—took the time to work out all the corollaries to Euclid's theorems. Younis and I were friends, and I would often go to his house to do homework and learn from him. We would study in the small veranda separated from the rest of the house by a black curtain that covered the doorway.

About half an hour after we started working, we would hear a soft, loving, motherly voice calling from inside, "Younis *beta*, you've been studying for a long time. Please take some tea for Bhaskar *beta*." Younis would go into the house and return with two cups of tea. The word *beta* is a term of affection meaning "son" or "young boy." I rarely saw Younis's mother, but she called me "son" and was always a loving maternal presence over us. Then, after about a year, they moved away, and Younis left the school. I didn't say goodbye, and I never found out what happened to them.

One last story. Tahseen was a close friend of my family for more than thirty years. When I visited India recently, Tahseen was at our house, bemoaning his (Muslim) daughter's decision to marry a Hindu boy. His son had married a Hindu, but Tahseen didn't mind that. Hindu-Muslim marriages were OK if the *girl* was Hindu, but not the other way around. He said that many Muslim families share this view. I'm guessing Tahseen didn't seek out a Muslim shoulder to cry on, lest they blame him for rearing wayward children, but he had the good fortune to be able to talk to someone like Amma, then in her eighties. She listened to Tahseen and gave him coffee and said, in Urdu, "*Hum sub ek hein*" (We are all one.). In Amma's kind Urdu words, I heard an echo of my Telugu words to the woman near Jangaon so many years ago: We are all one.

These memories came to me as I tried to process Jan's story about Chaya. I grew up in an age of informality and simplicity. Riding a steam engine and breaking into a jail compound were everyday youthful exploits. Both would be highly irregular for my children, growing up in the U.S. Yet, my children and I had the good fortune of relatively benign childhoods. Unfortunately, Chaya and so many others were not so lucky.

CHAPTER 8

Some patients begin a session with "What were we talking about last time?" Others start with small talk, a few words about the weather, or the recent Bears or Bulls game, extraneous or tangential musings, expressed in the familiar surroundings of my office. With patient listening, such beginnings link to substantive emotions and ideas. What they begin with is of no consequence to any analyst. Whatever it is, I follow where it leads.

Jan arrived looking focused and resolute. There would be little chitchat today.

"I've been thinking about our last session. After I leave, I seem to continue our conversations, but with myself. I've learned to avoid the expressions 'I know for sure' or 'There's absolutely no doubt.' I never want to say those things again. I learned this when I worked as a gynecological oncologist in Poland."

Jan went silent like he was stuck.

"What made you change from using 'I know' to avoiding 'I know'?" I asked. "And why did you move from oncology to psychiatry?"

Jan regained his stride. "Oncology was a big influence in my life. Initially, I was excited about being an oncologist, but after a while, I became depressed. People close to me started dying of cancer. A former girlfriend died of cancer—on my ward and under my care."

God damn! I thought.

"It had been five years since we broke up. Then, early in the morning, I did rounds on the ward. A patient in the last stages of ovarian cancer, who looked like a bag of bones, had been admitted. As I did with all patients, I

84

talked to her and got her history when she whispered, 'You don't recognize me? I'm Nina.' I was stunned.

"I became disoriented. I didn't want to upset her by admitting that I hadn't recognized her. I said, 'Of course, I recognized you. I was looking at the chart. I'm sorry.' It bothered me that what I had just said wasn't true. I looked at the chart and then at her face. Then I reminded her, 'You know I'm so absent-minded.' I knew she knew this about me from the past."

"So, did you feel, 'I'm doing my best, but my patients are still dying! Now, my own past love is dying'?"

"Yes. Nina expressed hope because I was treating her, and she somehow expected that—by some miracle—I would cure her, but there are no miracles. Even when you put your heart into it, like in her case, she still died. There was another woman. She was a nice mom and had loving children. I tried everything I could, but I couldn't save her.

"To be fair, there were some survivors. A man who was suffering from advanced lung cancer was evaluated and assessed as not qualifying for surgery. We offered him chemotherapy, but he refused and went home to die. Six or seven years later, he returned. At first, we thought it was a case of mistaken identity—someone else's X-rays ended up in the file with his name—but we did a thorough investigation and confirmed his identity! You can never be sure. This was the only 'miracle' I witnessed in oncology."

To make sure Jan knew that I appreciated how hard the losses were for him, I added, "When patients died, it was heartbreaking for you."

Jan continued, "I faced death and dying every day. It built up. Ten or fifteen dying patients were admitted to my care every week. In most cases, my efforts were futile.

"I had a friend named Philip. I liked him very much. He enlivened any group he was a part of. We went on family vacations. We fished together and had good conversations. He was older than me and reminded me of my Uncle Adalbert. When Philip developed advanced colon cancer, he came to me for treatment. He went through chemotherapy and radiation, and went into remission. Then the cancer returned, and he ended up on my ward. Sometimes, you don't know what's better for patients—leave them alone or take heroic measures. Because of the inoperability of his cancer, I recommended palliative measures to lessen his pain and suffering. He died, and I went to his funeral."

Jan's account of his experiences of so many traumatic losses and with no way to deal with it moved me.

Jan went on. "Maybe that was a mistake. I went to the funerals of many of my patients. I wanted to be caring. I wanted to maintain a helping and trusting relationship with the surviving family members. Maybe I went too far because I ended up going to so many funerals."

"Did you get more depressed after so many funerals?"

"Yes," Jan replied immediately, "but at that time, I didn't know what depression was. I didn't know what was happening to me. I partied more and drank more, but I didn't see the connection. Now, of course, it's obvious. I wasn't detached. I was affected by what was happening around me.

"After Nina died and then Philip, I slowly came to realize that I wasn't equipped to do my job. I couldn't keep on living being an oncologist. I didn't feel like doing anything. I didn't feel like getting up in the morning. I didn't feel like taking a shower. I didn't feel like shaving. I didn't feel like brushing my teeth. I was simply lying in bed doing nothing. I didn't even watch TV. Time seemed to fly by, but I couldn't account for months. Suddenly, I had to tear off a few months from my calendar all at once. I remember feeling that there were only nights; I couldn't remember the days. I couldn't experience light or remember it. Those were literally dark times."

I thought that Jan fit a textbook description of major depression. "As a young and generous person, you put your heart into helping your patients until the sheer amount of suffering and death finally got to you and made you unable to function. How did the older doctors in your hospital who were treating similar patients deal with it all?"

"This is how I remember it: Their attitude was that treating patients was just routine work. They didn't put their emotions into it. In the ward where I worked, two doctors were alcoholics. Poland has a different culture than America when it comes to drinking. You have to drink *a lot* to be considered an alcoholic. Here in America, if you have more than twelve drinks a week if you're a man and more than seven if you're a woman, you're considered an alcoholic. In the '80s, when I started to experiment with alcohol, that was deemed normal in Poland. These guys were alcoholics, even by Polish standards. I'll call him Kris, one of them would get drunk three or four times a week. I didn't hang out with him, but he was my mentor. He taught me everything I knew about gynecological oncology and brachytherapy.

"He was a good person. He was kind and loving to his children. He liked people, and people liked him. He kept up with the field of oncology and was a good and thorough doctor. Patients especially liked him. But he was quite crude."

"How so?"

Jan paused a moment as he searched his memory. "Oh, he had a sexual joke for every occasion. I can't explain because I can't remember any of his jokes right now. I'm sure you've come across such a person. He was a doctor with the mind of a truck driver. The other guy became the director of the unit. I knew that, on some level, both guys were losers; they weren't going anywhere. I couldn't imagine spending the rest of my life with them. In Poland at that time, it was a sort of tradition that if you started working in a hospital, there was a good chance that you would die in that hospital. So when I talk about it or think about it, I get upset and have to stop. I don't want to continue."

Here, again, I saw evidence of Jan's resistance. He could no longer continue to communicate his thoughts. Everyone, patients and non-patients alike, sometimes reach such limits, even if they don't recognize why. Such stops may reflect the suppression of thoughts or feelings; in treatment, they are signals of resistance to the communication of free associations. Jan could no longer bear the weight of his memories and their emotions. He had reached the limit of his tolerance for his despair. His silence indicated his turning away from such or other unwelcome thoughts or feelings. When therapists feel that the resistance represents a dangerous situation, they must act decisively to protect the patient from harm. Barring such hazardous conditions where the doctor preempts the patient's freedom and works against the patient's will, the analysis relies on the patient's free associations. Most of the time, the analyst addresses the resistance, but I let it go that day: Jan had done enough heavy lifting for the day.

This event was important because I got to see variations in Jan's depression. In moving past the pain of Amir's suicide to another hurt, Jan demonstrated he could break free from the all-encompassing feelings about Amir's suicide. I felt hopeful that, from this non-Amir depression, he would become re-involved in the human landscape. By encouraging him to expand the range of his emotional experience, he could get a sense of having choices in his life. Especially when he remembered or felt some satisfaction or joy, he would feel a degree of relief from his tragic sense. Now we or, more specifically, he would have to probe other areas. Jan had signaled the end of his capacity to pursue this theme from his past, but some ancillary thoughts and feelings connected to it might still be available to him. I felt that tapping into his medical knowledge—something related but less emotion-laden—might be a good place to begin.

"What is brachytherapy?" I asked.

"The term *brachytherapy* encompasses several internal radiation techniques used in cancer treatment. Irradiation is one of the methods of treatment for certain cancers. Sometimes this is done by placing seeds or pellets with radioactive radium in the tumor to target the areas affected but spare surrounding tissue. Around the time I started practicing, a new afterloading treatment became available. We often used it for cervical-cancer cases. You positioned metal applicators to target the tumor. After taking X-rays, you calculated the irradiation dose, and you delivered radioactive pellets pneumatically through the applicators. Unfortunately, most applicators I worked with were unwieldy. To avoid using the applicator, you could deliver the radioisotope through the device with your bare hands; but this method is unsafe for the oncologist because it exposes him to a lot of radiation.

"I want to give you some idea of our radiation exposure. It's like getting a few chest X-rays every day. That's a lot of exposure. The greatest risk is to the hands, face, and eyes because you must look closely at the cervix while quickly positioning the applicator. After three or four procedures a day, I was tired. It did something to my body. We did have protective gloves, but, as I just explained, they reduced our coordination, so we didn't always wear them. Instead, we wore regular surgical gloves, even though they didn't protect us from radiation. We could have used metal forceps to keep the radium away from our hands. But again, it wasn't convenient because you had to spend more time with your nose close to both the vagina and the radiation."

Jan paused and seemed to be switching gears. "I've seen many men maltreat women. You could say that they're cruel. Women would certainly say so."

I thought that cruelty was a new topic, and it wasn't about depression, so perhaps it held some promise.

Jan was already talking. "I'm speaking of highly educated people, like physicians. You know the drama of the hospital is on the wards, where physicians see their patients. This was our stage. When we saw patients, the professor, the star among the physicians, was in front. Usually behind him—and it was usually a *him*—was a docent. This was an associate professor hoping to become a professor when the professor died or retired. Other junior faculty followed the docent. The medical students gathered in the back.

"On the gynecological wards, some women knew the hospital routine and came prepared to present themselves to the doctors, so to speak; other women weren't familiar with our practices or simply didn't care. So, some vaginas were clean and presentable; others were not.

"The professors often made jokes about the women, especially if they smelled bad. And sometimes, they were cruel. For example, they joked about the 'fish market,' an inside joke when the smell was strong. Kris, who I told you about before, would refuse to examine such a patient. Instead, he'd say, 'Tell her to freshen herself up.' He didn't even talk directly to the women. Medical students in the back who didn't hear what happened would often come across weeping women after his cruelty."

I felt that Amir was deceptive and wondered: *Does Jan think Amir was cruel to him by withholding critical information?*

Jan seemed adrift for a moment. Then he said, "I got lost in what I was saying. Oh, yes, I was talking about irradiation, metal forceps, and danger to the hands. If you used your hands, you could do it quickly. With forceps, you struggled for 10 minutes. It was simpler to use your hands, so that's what I did.

"The older physicians gradually did fewer and fewer procedures to lessen their radiation exposure. The younger physicians also had ways of limiting their exposure. For example, when I did brachytherapy, my working day was only six hours long, and I had eight weeks of vacation a year. In addition, they gave extra money to people based on their radiation exposure. That gave me the chance to travel and get additional training.

"To specialize in radiation therapy, I had to study the physics of radioactivity and know both the side effects on the human body and the risks involved in dealing with specific radioactive isotopes. So from the beginning, I knew the risks."

I asked, "So, the risk is not only to the patient. It's to you, too?"

"Yes."

Early in the session, Jan had been overwhelmed as he described his experiences as an oncologist. But now, he had overcome his resistance, whatever it was, and resumed talking. I felt there were similarities in his struggle to deal with death and dying as an oncologist that had made him leave oncology and his current struggle coping with the death of his psychiatric patient. Separate from that, as I indicated earlier, I thought Jan's main problem was that he had identified with his suicidal patient. This identification was unconscious, and I could not directly address it right now if it was unconscious. Jan would have to become aware of this identification first.

Amir had killed himself as a way to confront his fear. He wanted to be bold enough to pull the trigger—only that would satisfy his doubts about being a coward. Amir may have died playing Russian roulette. His "cowardliness" following the camel sacrifice may still have been haunting him. I had to test whether Jan saw any such similarities in his own life, such as not using the gloves that would have protected him from radiation. If Jan saw similarities, we could work together to enable Jan to make self-protective changes in himself now and in the future.

"You said it was simpler not to use gloves, but it was like playing Russian atomic roulette, no? Radiation roulette!"

Jan responded, "Of course. I knew I couldn't do this for the rest of my life. It was too risky. But separately, medical failures resulted in dying patients, including my ex-girlfriend and friend, making me feel I couldn't be so close to death. I didn't feel good waking up in the morning and going to work knowing I would see more death and dying."

"There was so much death around you. That's why you got depressed in the past. Then you got better and put distance between death and you, and now Amir's death has gotten you down again."

Jan agreed. "No doubt! The deaths accumulated, and I can bear only so much. A girl, Joanna, had a severe form of sarcoma. She was super-intelligent. She spoke five languages. You don't meet people like that very often. She was clearly gifted. I felt that her fate was stupid. Fate had no right to pick on her. Fate had no right to take her. She was in a lot of pain, and I would talk to her. She grew attached to me. When I was on call, the nurses would call me when she wanted to talk. All this stuff runs together . . . when I tell you one story, I have all of them in my mind. I believed in medicine, but medicine was failing me.

"At one point, I joined a reformed Catholic monastery because I wanted to believe; the name of the monastery could be translated roughly as The Movement of Salvation of the Holy Spirit. Religious men with many student followers run this place. A girl went into a trance, went crazy, and ripped off her clothes. Oh, yes—I've told you this story before. Sometimes I remember things with such power that I have to repeat them."

Conversations or monologues written by great authors are gripping and draw the reader into the story's heart. In real life, conversations are often dull, and monologues have no listeners. Psychoanalysis has its own unique conventions, where dullness may be a façade, and seemingly dull monologues have an attentive listener. Here, a patient has the opportunity to speak in whatever manner they feel inclined. Even if the patient's words are an uninterrupted soliloquy, ideally, the analyst is always listening. Themes evolve slowly, and moments of insight may be few and far between. Thoughts are often idle or repetitious. Patients suffering from severe trauma often repeat phrases, ideas, or stories. In regular conversations, repetition is often cut off by impatient listeners or those eager to speak themselves. Therapy welcomes repetition and looks for minor variations among versions. In this haystack of words, the analyst—and often the patient—look for important clues. Why are some ideas, emotions, or memories "sticky," and what do they mean? The search is a labor of professionalism and love that is slow, unpredictable, and dependent on chance discoveries.

Any psychoanalytic description must do justice to the minute variations of a patient's outpourings in treatment. A traumatized person says the same things over and over again. Consequently, throughout this book, I describe trauma with representational repetitiveness. Hence I impose a degree of monotony on you, the reader. That is the nature of trauma and the process of working through it. If you try to snuff out that burning candle, you may spread the fire into hidden, unknown areas. Patients often feel re-injured by a therapist's clumsy attempts to hasten treatment. A patient may take the analyst's attempt at hastening treatment, although well-intended, as evidence that the analyst does not understand or does not want to understand him. Treatment requires evocation and re-experiencing of powerful traumas several times before they are tamed. "I understand that you need to tell the story again," I said.

Jan continued. "She fell onto the floor, and everyone believed that the Holy Spirit was entering her. Then her eyes rolled back, and she extended her arms as though she was reaching for the Holy Spirit. Showing her naked body was inappropriate in a church, so people tried to cover her up and subdue her, but she fought to free herself. She must have felt that she was full of the Holy Spirit. Now I find the whole scene funny and ridiculous. She was overloaded with the Holy Spirit."

Jan laughed as he recalled the scene. "As that girl tore off her clothes, my beliefs came to an end. I knew she was psychotic. After that, I shifted to medicine."

Consent

Analysts recognize that an analyst's personal analysis, theories, conflicts, fears, and hopes influence the analyst's actions. In addition, significant people in an analyst's past and present, and his entire history, culture, idols, beliefs, predictions, prediction errors, and error corrections also influence analytic attitudes, interpretations, interventions, and actions. Psychoanalytic literature has a rich history of cases describing the patient's free associations and actions, the analyst's interpretations, and other interventions. All analysts use the analyst's inner world, but no established psychoanalytic clinical tradition exists to report on the contents of the analyst's evenly suspended attention and their associated linkages. I wanted to shine a light on this area.

At this point, I felt that Jan was no longer seriously depressed. I wanted to write a memoir detailing an analysis from my perspective and detailing my responses to his ongoing analysis. I discussed such a project with Jan and asked Jan if he would consent to record our sessions to assist in this purpose. Jan had been a researcher himself and knew the formal-consent process and its components, such as the study's purpose, explanation of procedures, description of risks and discomforts, benefits, confidentiality, noncoercive disclaimer, and my willingness to answer his questions. If he consented, although disguised and de-identified, sensitive material he shared with me would become public. The benefit of his consent would accrue to the science of therapy and not him. For example, analysts may get a deeper picture of the analyst's experience of the analytic process and the sources of his interventions. I told him that his participation was voluntary and that he could withdraw his consent at any time. I also clarified that I would continue to treat him even if he declined to consent. However, Jan consented.

CHAPTER 9

THIS SESSION MARKS THE START of the third month of Jan's treatment. Jan was preoccupied with preparing for the exam that would allow him to continue his training. During Jan's sick-leave absence, the program reassigned his cases to other residents. We now spent most of the time discussing his exam anxieties and his professional self-doubts and managing them. He questioned his ability to become a good psychiatrist and to be worthy of his patients' trust . . . ever. As he worked through his trauma, he went over and over his concerns. Gradually, the frequency of the repetitions decreased, and the pain lessened somewhat. Finally, after considerable preparation and much anticipation, Jan took the exam. One evening, he called me on the phone and announced that he had passed. I congratulated him and welcomed him into the community of certified physicians and psychiatrists. I recalled that a few months after Amir committed suicide, Jan failed his exam. He had been on administrative leave for about six months.

As both a patient and a physician treating patients, Jan occasionally felt his lack of experience acutely and questioned the quality of help he could provide. This concern cropped up often in our sessions, especially regarding patients who seemed vulnerable to suicide.

I had felt all along that Jan identified with Amir and had been anxious that he himself might become suicidal, so I was glad to hear about his attempts to understand the dynamics of the relationship between a doctor and his patient. These attempts to understand his patients helped Jan to start to come to terms with his own experience with Amir and the responsibility he had and would have toward future patients.

Jan was devastated by Amir's death and wanted to do his best for his future patients. But, of course, every therapist wants and intends to protect the lives of his patients and diminish their suffering and pain. Therefore, when there is a danger to the patient's or any other's life, the physician or therapist directly or through appropriate referral must act to safeguard life. However, the physician or therapist can't breathe for a patient; that responsibility belongs to the patient and is not transferable. And when a patient conveys the wish to harm himself, the healer should act to protect his patient's life, though a patient who is hell-bent on killing himself can always find a way.

It was a jubilant Jan who arrived at the next session. "I passed!" he exulted, even though he had already told me.

"Congratulations!" I said again. I felt his joy and relief. By the time he took the exam, he had regained his desire to be a doctor and a psychiatrist. Failing would have meant having to rearrange his entire future. Passing meant he could reconnect to his previous life as a physician and the one he imagined going forward.

Jan immediately started to describe his work as a psychiatric resident. "I had my first meeting with my superstar supervisor, Dr. Schwartz. It started awkwardly, though, and I managed to make him feel bad. I was seeing a patient just before the time for our appointment. Five minutes before the session was to end, the patient started talking about his suicidal thoughts. Since I'm very sensitive to suicidal communications, I was trying to figure out what to do and lost track of time. It took about 10 minutes to come up with a satisfactory plan."

Jan continued, "When I went out, I saw an anxious, agitated-looking guy sitting in the waiting area. I didn't think that *he* was Dr. Schwartz and went looking for the secretary at the front desk to find out if Dr. Schwartz had arrived. She wasn't there, so I asked the guy, 'Do you know where the front-desk person went?'

"He acted irritated and almost barked, 'No, but are you Dr. Jan _____?' It was Dr. Schwartz!

"I replied, 'I'm sorry. I got delayed by a suicidal patient. Please come into my office.'

"It took him a long time to reply, and then he said, 'OK. OK. Not a problem. Not a problem.'

"He's an interesting guy. He spoke to me about some of the papers he's written, and we lost track of time. He probably stayed longer than he had planned. He told me a story about a patient who had begun psychoanalysis as a young man and remained in analysis almost his entire adult life. He was now 95 years old but had remained in good mental and physical condition. Schwartz told him that he himself had developed a heart problem. His coronary arteries were blocked, and his doctor had recommended bypass surgery. The old man said to Schwartz, 'Don't do it. You know doctors. All they want to do is squeeze money from you. You may die from the surgery!' After the surgery, the old man went to the ICU and ran into Schwartz's son. 'Where's the body?' he asked, assuming that Schwartz had died in surgery. Schwartz told me he was irritated that the old man had shown up at the hospital.

"'So,' I said to him, 'it sounds like the old man was starting to treat you not as a psychoanalyst, but as a person.'

"Schwartz said, 'There's more to it than that.' He then told me about a paper he was writing. I'm happy that he's my supervisor. But, he also has this preoccupation with death and dying. He said that he's worked with children dying of cancer and their parents.

"I want to talk to Dr. Schwartz and get supervision from him about an old Polish woman patient I'll call Teresa. I saw her for two years before Amir committed suicide and resumed seeing her. For those two previous years, Dr. Alvear-Reverte supervised me on this case.

"The story with her is that she's divorced, and she lost her son. He was a perfect child. No drugs, no legal problems, and he had done well academically. Unfortunately, he took his first girlfriend on a car ride and died in a car accident. When I picked Teresa up from the medication-management clinic, she was in a state of shock. She briefly became psychotic. She was extremely anxious. Before coming to the psychiatric clinic, her internist had put her on high doses of Xanax, which—as you know—is often habit-forming and sometimes addictive. OK, what I'm now going to say isn't arrogant. I feel she needed a Polish psychiatrist. I doubt that a psychiatrist from anywhere else could succeed because certain Polish traditions intersect with modern life. Poles have this tremendous respect for doctors. You do whatever the doctor says, regardless of how you feel. I worked with her for two years and weaned her off the Xanax.

"Teresa created a shrine to her son in her house. His room was left intact as if he were still living there. She arranged his clothes and personal items as they were on the day he died. She said she would go into his room and look at pictures of him for hours. As she looked at the pictures, she would sometimes hallucinate and begin to imagine things: She imagined her son waving his hand at her, and she believed this meant that he was still alive somewhere. This would make her happy for a while, and then she would cry. She was hoping to revive him by looking for signs of his presence. Sometimes, when she saw her blanket bunched up in the morning, she felt that her son had come and visited her in the night while she was asleep.

"After two years, I asked her to start removing one shoebox-full of stuff every week and putting it in the garage. If she couldn't do it for one week, that was OK. Each week, she and I would discuss the items she took out. Once she started, she kept going. Along the way, she had a lot of resistance and reservations. She was honest. At one point, she told me that she didn't like my treatment and was causing her problems. I reminded her that she didn't have to do it every week. I even told her that she could always bring things back to his room if she changed her mind. Eventually, she emptied the room. Now, she has a tenant living there, and she's glad for the regular income. And she threw away all the stuff in the garage! I like to reason with patients. I don't like to push them to do anything. I just want to know what happened. Dr. Alvear-Reverte and I came up with this idea, and it worked.

"Another problem that we worked on was her belief that her son had been deliberately killed. She wrote some letters to urge the authorities to investigate the accident. She wanted to write the 'killer.' She started with something like, 'You are probably with your family and feeling good, but I want you to know how I feel as a mother. Every day, I get up, thinking that my son is alive. Then, every day, I have to rediscover that you killed him. Every time, I feel like you stabbed me in my heart.' I asked her, 'Why do you want that guy to know how you feel?' She kept revising the letter over several months. Then she went to Poland for a month. When she returned, she told me, 'I don't feel that sending the letter is a good idea anymore.' This is how she mourned the loss of her son."

"I have two questions, I said. "First, did Schwartz get back to explaining what he meant by, 'Well, there's more to it'? Second, what did Alvear-Reverte say about Teresa?"

"No, Schwartz didn't get back to 'it.' Probably he meant that my comment might be a small and insignificant part of understanding his 95-year-old patient. As for Alvear-Reverte, he never says anything. I spoke to him about our interactions and ideas and asked him some questions, but he never answered questions. I discussed Teresa's letters. He enjoyed the process of her revisions. I called him after Amir killed himself. He said, 'Jan, the machine has started.'"

"The machine?"

"The machine is the process by which the university deals with deaths and other critical incidents.

"Alvear-Reverte said, 'The patient's family may contact you, but the university review is moving; no one can stop it or change it. So it's out of your hands. You just have to wait.'

"This was the day before I was going to Italy to get married! I told him I wasn't sure what to do—whether I should stay and wait for any questions. Alvear-Reverte replied, 'Call the police officer who contacted you, answer any questions he may have, and tell him you'll be away. The machine will keep churning for a long time.' I called the police, but they didn't call me back before I left. Then I tried to get the coroner's report. I never got it."

I felt that Jan had switched from talking about Dr. Schwartz and his old patient who asked, 'Where's the body?' I wanted to go back to that hanging thread.

I asked Jan, "When you met him, did Dr. Schwartz tell you that he was upset when his elderly patient came to visit him at the ICU when Dr. Schwartz was himself hospitalized?"

"Yes, I thought he was upset because his patient was treating him more as a person and less as an analyst.

"I remember an outreach program at the VA Hospital for schizophrenic patients. It was a rotation where we tried to treat patients who didn't want to come for appointments. We often went to the homeless shelters and group homes, and I'd give them injections of Prolixin [a long-acting antipsychotic]. The social worker I worked with was a 72-year-old guy who had been a social worker most of his adult life. We spent a lot of time driving to the shelters, and we got to talk about many things. He was a Freemason. His father was also a Freemason. I learned a lot about Freemasonry in the United States and its many rituals. He told me that he had been in analysis for seven years. Before he began analysis, he was highly anxious. He wasn't functional; he couldn't do anything. Then he started to find out what was stopping him, and he began to be who he was. It changed his mind and his life. After his analysis, he laughed about the Freemason rituals.

"I wondered how he decided to stop the therapy, so I asked him, 'How did you know when to stop your analysis? Who decided—the therapist or you? How did it happen?'

"He said, 'I remember the exact moment it happened. I was in a session just like any of the other sessions I had been in. I saw him in this beautiful lake-view office. He was saying something, and suddenly, the phone rang, and he picked it up. He had *never* done that before. As he listened, he went pale. When he hung up, he looked at me and said, 'I'm sorry, I have to leave now. My son is in the hospital.'

"'I realized at that moment that these guys, these analysts, go to the bathroom just like I do. They dump and pee just like the rest of us. They do all this earthly stuff that I had never thought of before. I had put him on a pedestal like a divine being. At that moment, he became human. I felt equal to him. I knew I was finished with my analysis. I said goodbye, and that was the end of my analysis. I never came back, and I never looked back.'

"The social worker's story was a classic example of prolonged divine idealization followed by traumatic de-idealization leading to a patient terminating treatment. On discovering a common human element in the analyst—that the analyst interrupted the session to attend to his own son instead of the patient—the patient stopped treatment. Whether it was precipitous or not, the patient got a clear sense of the event, the time, and the cause for terminating treatment. It also gave the patient a sense of his own self-efficacy in making such a judgment. Right or wrong, I'd guess the patient was already feeling pretty ready to stop."

I decided to go back to the question Jan had asked. "You asked your friend about terminating his analysis. Why did you ask? How did you get that idea?"

Jan was amused. "Dr. Sripada, how do you get ideas? It just popped up in my mind." And then he trained his eyes on me and asked, "How do *you* get ideas?"

I laughed. Jan, realizing that it is not easy for anyone to locate the source of ideas, guffawed loudly. Although I had hoped for some insight from Jan and got none, I was pleasantly surprised by his roaring laughter. I wasn't expecting Jan to turn my question back on me.

"Well . . ." I began, searching for something worthwhile to say, "some ideas pop up, but some ideas are threaded." An image wafted briefly through my awareness: me threading sewing needles for my mother as her vision deteriorated.

I continued, "Ideally, any idea I convey to you must pass the test of reasonableness in timing, dosage, and tact. It must be meaningful to you at the moment that I say it. It must be proportionate—neither too much nor too little. And it must consider your sensitivities, so you are not offended. It's tricky to accomplish, like trying to pass a thread through the eyes of three needles. I can fail on one, two, or all three counts by your assessment or my own. My question to you is an example of a threaded idea. I asked you, 'How did you get that idea?' Earlier, you mentioned that the elderly patient's view of Dr. Schwartz shifted from seeing him as an analyst to seeing him as a person. Then you said there was a shift in the social worker, who stopped seeing his analyst as divine and started to see him as human. I was next going to ask if you were aware of any shift in the relationship between Amir and you."

"Well, yes. I experienced a transformation. My attitude toward Amir changed after he died."

"How so?"

"He became much closer to me than he was as my patient. Initially, there was something brotherly in the relationship. Still, I felt a distance: I gave him some friendly advice about dating, some common-sense guidance that might help him open his mouth with women. I tried to reach out to him to lessen the distance between us, because he tended to keep people at arm's length.

"When he died, it felt to me almost like he was a family member. My grieving for him was different from my grieving for my mom or my best friend, but it was still the loss of someone close. It was very intense. It was painful to think about his death. My sense of guilt was overwhelming. I blamed myself for not admitting him to the psych ward. He would have been safe if I had admitted him to the inpatient unit. I couldn't stop thinking about him.

"At the time, unless Maria asked me something specific, I was lost in thoughts of Amir. I participated in the wedding when Maria and I got married, but I couldn't get Amir out of my mind. While Maria's bridesmaids were helping her get ready for the wedding, I was waiting outside. I recall the exact street corner, and I remember I couldn't think about anything except Amir. I had stopped saying Catholic prayers when I was about 25. Suddenly, standing there on the street, I started to say them: the *Ojcze Nasz,* The Lord's Prayer, and *Zdrowas Maryja, Ave Maria.* I couldn't stop saying them. It was involuntary. And I went on saying them for three or four months after. In fact, it was only after I started seeing you that I stopped saying them.

"I'm not a practicing Catholic or a practicing Christian. Maria's not a churchgoer, either, but she appreciates the architecture of churches and likes to visit her favorite churches in Italy, especially in Rome. After Amir's death, something happened to me. We went to Florence to visit the Basilica di Santa Maria del Fiore. It's an amazing structure. I remember it from my trip to Italy in my twenties. I was overwhelmed by the size of the cathedral, feeling like a Lilliputian in the vast interior. The delicate ornamentation, sculptures, and paintings all made a strong impression on me, and going back there after many years triggered the same emotions. Still, there was one difference when we went this time: Once inside the church, I couldn't stop saying prayers. I felt compelled to say them. I was never compulsive before, but I became compulsive after Amir died and until I started seeing you. Maybe it was because I could make sense of what happened to my mom. She had lived a full life and died when she was 70. She had medical problems that prepared me for her death. She talked about her friends who had died and about her own impending death. She made Sofia and me ready for her death. I called my Mom every week. We talked about everything. I learned about her way of approaching the end. Although it was painful, she managed to prepare us for her death as much as she could.

"With Amir, I was totally unprepared. His death shocked me when it happened, and I'm still in the middle of that shock. He wasn't supposed to leave yet. He was young and just starting his life. Maybe I was using those compulsive prayers to try to undo the tragedy, or maybe I was just trying to keep my mind so busy that painful thoughts couldn't find a place to enter. He wasn't old, like the 95-year-old guy who was Schwartz's patient."

Jan appeared to be looking at me for some response, and I replied, "Yes."

Several themes in play seemed to speak to Jan's current emotional state. The most relevant one seemed to be Amir. I recalled that Jan had described two phases in his relationship with Amir. During the first phase, he saw Amir as a patient (although he did share some "brotherly" advice). After Amir's suicide, the relationship became incandescent. During this second phase, Jan saw Amir as a family member. This implied not only a new intensity but also a lifelong connection. You may or may not like your family members, but you're stuck with them. Amir was gone. That was sad, but I was concerned with Jan's ability to mourn the loss of Amir and get past it. In my view, Amir became enshrined as one of Jan's family members. A physician should learn his limits and maintain his boundaries. Jan needed to treat his patients only with what was possible.

I said, "You said that your attitude toward Amir changed. Initially, it was within the doctor-patient framework, and, later, you felt like he was a member of your family. What's your current attitude toward him?"

Jan thought for a moment. "Every culture has a way of saying 'Time heals all wounds.' I don't think about Amir's death as frequently anymore. Maybe it's because I decided to step into life: I'm no longer closeted in my apartment, and I've gone back to the university and started working. Most of my old patients have returned to me, and once again, I'm focused on becoming a doctor. And I have new patients, too. But I haven't forgotten Amir or how I let him down. I'm trying my best not to repeat my mistakes.

"I do think about other patients. I'm seeing this young Orthodox Jewish woman. I'll call her . . . Rachel. She's disturbed, but it's not easy to figure out what to do with her. When I met her, she carried the diagnosis of schizoaffective disorder and had had several psychiatric hospitalizations. She's paranoid, anxious, and dependent. Recently, homicidal ideas preoccupied her. She says she wants to kill her father and mother. She says it like it's her goal in life. She doesn't try to hide it, and she's told them that this is what she hopes to do. They've known it for about three years and aren't concerned. At first, I didn't realize that these thoughts weren't new. Rachel had repeated them so often that she had managed to desensitize her parents. I made it my priority to hear more details about her homicidal plans. I asked her, 'How are you going to kill your parents?'

"She said, 'I'll shave my dad's beard, and the drug dealers will do the rest.'

"I said, 'I'm sorry—I don't see the connection. I'm not sure how shaving your dad's beard will bring on drug dealers.'

"She then said, 'I'll get hooked on drugs. I'll run up a debt. The drug dealers are cruel and persistent. They'll come after me and, if I can't pay them, they'll kill members of my family.'

"When I expressed my doubts, Rachel simply changed her story. First, she said she would part the Red Sea, like Moses. Then, just when her mother and father got into the middle of the parted waters, she would un-part the sea and let the sea drown them. Nobody treated her seriously, and I didn't, either. She's never actually harmed them. Recently, she started to have suicidal thoughts. She said she would shoot herself to prevent herself from killing her father. She doesn't believe in killing herself but that killing herself is a lesser evil than killing her father. Sometimes, she also wants to kill her sister. She wants to kill her sister because she won't allow Rachel to visit her young children. Rachel is upset that her sister thinks she's crazy."

"What's her grievance against her parents?"

"That's another story. Her parents contacted a matchmaker who set her up with a guy in Los Angeles, and they clicked. His parents arranged for an elaborate wedding, and they got married. Two months after she was married, she ended up in a psychiatric hospital. She started to tell everybody that she was going to shoot her husband. The funny thing is that her husband was in love with her and wanted to stay with her. His father insisted on a divorce, though. He told his son, 'You're getting divorced. She's not good wife material.' So, her father-in-law talked to her father to resolve the matter. Her in-laws escorted her to the airport and sent her back to Chicago. All her belongings except the clothes she was wearing remained in Los Angeles. She talks fondly about her husband: 'He was a good husband. I was happy with him.'

"She also claims that five Mafia guys kidnapped her three years ago, before she was married, took her to a motel, and gang-raped her. She says that the police didn't believe her and arrested nobody. On the first anniversary of the alleged or real rape, she became depressed. To help her get over it, her father sent her to Israel. While taking a bus from Tel Aviv to a kibbutz, she 'fell in love with' the bus driver. She was convinced that he loved her, too. After all the passengers got off at the last stop, she came on to him, and he decided to take advantage of the opportunity. She changed her mind, but he continued and had sex with her anyway. Afterward, she worked on the kibbutz for a while. She kept 'falling in love' with guys who didn't want to have anything to do with her. Each time, she took the rejection hard. Now, even talking about it makes her tearful and upset.

"You asked me about the grudge Rachel was holding against her parents. She explained that she feels angry with her parents, especially her father, because they allowed all these traumatic events to happen and didn't protect her. She also felt that her parents and sister treated her as a lesser person because of her mental illness.

"Rachel started seeing me after Amir died. She was the first patient I accepted after returning from my 'exile.' The first time I saw her, we talked about safety and continued to do this for a few sessions. I asked her lots of questions, trying to understand how far she was from crossing the line. I was consumed with safety plans, rehearsing them until I felt satisfied.

"Rachel not only kept calling *me* as promised but, on one occasion, she called the on-call resident. He was Jewish, and she talked to him about her feelings toward me, a Polish doctor. She was preoccupied with Nazis, the

Holocaust, and the concentration camps, some of which, she knew, were in Poland. Knowing that, I've addressed what was happening between us in our sessions, understood her better, and helped her get somewhat better.

"Safety is still important, and we've had some crises. Her father recently called me and said that the family had gotten together at a restaurant. Rachel made a scene, so her parents had to take her home before they'd finished eating. He said that she was threatening to drink turpentine and that he couldn't figure out if she was making an empty threat or was really in danger.

"At the next session, we talked about her turpentine threat. She was playful and childishly manipulative. For example, she said, 'I could promise you that I won't drink turpentine, but I could be lying.'

"I answered, 'You confuse me, Rachel. I want you to be safe, but I can't read what's in your mind. I feel you want to tell me something that I'm not ready to understand. I need to spend more time with you to get to know you better. In the meantime, I don't want to take any chances. Would you agree to go to the hospital?'

"She agreed, but soon after admission, she started calling everybody on the unit 'a Nazi sympathizer' and complained that the food wasn't kosher. She didn't even keep kosher anymore! She told me that this was a way of punishing her parents.

"At the same time she was threatening to poison herself, she wrote a paper for a college course and got a B on it. I congratulated her and felt good for my role."

"Congratulations, Jan!" I said. "You're changing your attitude toward your patients. You seem to be managing suicidality more to your satisfaction."

"It's funny that you say that. I certainly hope I deal with suicide better, but the point is that Rachel and Amir are different. Their suicidal impulses are different. She had no problem going to the hospital. For Amir, psychiatric hospitalization was unthinkable. It was soul death. He knew someone or heard about someone who ended up in a psychiatric hospital in his country. It was a horror story. His view was that this person didn't just lose his freedom—he was stripped of his humanity."

"So, what was the change in your attitude in working with suicidal patients?"

"I had become vigilant when working with patients who had suicidal thoughts. My anxiety was clouding my view of the people themselves. Dr. Alvear-Reverte made me aware of this after hearing me interview one of the patients in the inpatient unit. I've struggled to change my approach, and I think I'm on the right path. This time, when I dealt with Rachel and the turpentine, I felt that I managed her based on her symptoms and needs and not based on my anxiety."

Jan paused a minute and then went on, "Somehow, this brings a Japanese patient to my mind. I'll call him Famuki. I always make up names for my patients when I talk to you . . . just in case. Of course, then I have to keep track of all those made-up names! I've worked with him for more than a year now. He's a complex patient, and different doctors have suggested several different diagnoses. After knowing him for a while, I can't really explain why he got stuck in his life. He's inattentive. He couldn't concentrate and finish any of his school assignments. He has a family history of schizophrenia. He's 40 years old and has never had a date with a woman. He's never even had a friendship with a woman. He said, 'Ever since I was a boy, I wanted to be in love with a woman. I want to have a female friend. I would love to have sex with a woman, but it never happened. I'm afraid that time is running out.'

Jan continued, "Famuki obsessively checks the political news from Japan, which takes up most of his day. With the help of a letter from me, his college dean gave him many academic accommodations, like extra time to complete assignments and during exams. But he still doesn't have time because he's preoccupied with the news cycle in Japan. Today, he told me that he joined a Christian church that also takes up his time. He feels that he's a sinner and that Christianity is the right religion for him.

"Famuki has become discouraged by online dating services. He said women always ask how tall he is. That question deflates him. He's about 5'2" and can't accept who he is. No woman so far has taken him for who he is. Famuki's father was a poor Japanese farmer. Famuki came to this country on some exchange program. He feels he's failed himself and his father. At the end of one session, he told me that he was feeling suicidal. We discussed his feelings, and, together, we came up with a plan that felt reasonable. I didn't hospitalize him."

"You seem to be taking better care of patients with suicidal ideation because you're addressing the specific facts of each case," I noted.

"I'm trying," he responded, "but I still have a keen awareness of, and I'm influenced by, Catholic strictures against suicide. In Poland, if you commit suicide, you can't be buried in a Catholic cemetery. My father was an Orthodox Catholic. He went to church regularly and never missed a mass. He often grilled me about facts or lessons from the Bible when I was a boy, but I always knew that he was a hypocrite. He displayed a lot of religious fervor, but he was a liar. I felt that his religious feelings were superficial, a façade. He was the main reason that being religious didn't appeal to me. I told you that I joined the group of reformed Catholics when I was a student. I tried to be more honest, and I wanted to find a sense of belonging, but it didn't happen."

"You mentioned that in Poland, if a Catholic person committed suicide, he can't expect to be buried in the Catholic cemetery. So he would be cut off from the Catholic community forever."

"Yes, this is a mortal sin. People who commit suicide are literally buried outside the fence of the cemetery. In Poland, I had a patient who had cancer on the floor of his mouth. He lived in the same town as my parents. One day, the guy missed his appointment. At the end of the day, I asked the secretary whether he had called, but he hadn't. So that weekend, I went to see my parents, and I asked my mom. She told me that she heard he had hanged himself.

"Then people started talking: 'How could he do this to his child?' 'How could he let his own child discover his body hanging?' 'What is his wife supposed to do now?' 'By committing suicide, he even deprived his wife of the insurance money.' 'It's completely irresponsible.' But no one said, 'Cancer must have made him depressed,' or 'Maybe he couldn't bear the pain.'

"I don't know what happened. Maybe he reached a point where he decided, 'I'm going to die anyway. I don't want any more suffering, and I don't want my breath to stink anymore. I don't want to impose my bad breath on my wife and my son.' He must have had some reason that he felt nobody could or would understand. Some said that he should have gone into the forest and killed himself there. For some reason, I found that argument persuasive. I felt it was better to commit suicide away from home, so someone else—not his son—would find his body. Now, I have more sympathy for the depressed person. Maybe he wanted to die in familiar surroundings. Any place is good when you're ready. The trick is not to need such a place!"

Jan laughed, hearing what he had just said. I don't know the proper place for sick jokes in life or treatment, but I felt that laughing at death was a good thing for Jan. It brought out a feeling other than dark depression, which had been his previous go-to. Instead, he had many thoughts and memories dealing with death because he was still working through his depression.

"There's no good way to deal with these kinds of deaths," I said. "Laughing is perhaps as good as getting depressed."

Jan responded, "I don't think depressed or suicidal people think about their effect on others. I told you I went to the funerals of many of my patients. It finally got me down, especially the deaths of my family friend and my former girlfriend. When I got depressed then, I would wake up ahead of my alarm clock. I would shave and get dressed . . . and then not go to work. Then, gradually, I stopped doing those things, one by one, and just stayed in bed. In fact, I intentionally overslept. Back then, I didn't know that it was depression. I didn't know what to call it. I felt it was simply me. I had no energy and didn't want to go to work. I didn't call it depression. I didn't call it anything. Sometimes, my alcoholic uncle, a war hero, would try to shake me out of my depression. He would insist that I take a bath and get out for some breakfast. Now I know how depression feels."

CHAPTER 10

JAN CAME IN, SMILING FROM EAR TO EAR. I had been pleased with the last session; I felt that Jan had gained some insight into his depression. I wouldn't have been surprised if he was less pained or even if he looked a little happy—but *beaming*? No. I was curious and eagerly awaited Jan's response as I greeted him with a noncommittal "How are you today?"

Jan responded joyfully, "I'm feeling great! It's a beautiful day, and I feel great. Really! I'm 43 years old, and I haven't felt like this in the past 40 years."

I was surprised by the specific time span Jan mentioned. I couldn't contain myself and exclaimed, "Given the recent past, that's a pretty big jump!"

"Yes, it is! It's personal: I'm going to be a father!"

"Congratulations!" I got up from my chair, walked over, and shook his hand.

Jan then pulled out a sonogram and showed it to me. As I looked at it, he pointed proudly to the spot of growing life.

"We just found out this morning. Of course, we expected it, but I also never thought that such a day would come for me. You never know if it will come. But, really, I feel great! I feel fantastic! We haven't told anybody yet. [I was so happy for Jan, I was fine with not counting as somebody.] Maria and I want to avoid the evil eye. We want to wait until we know for sure that everything is fine before telling anybody."

"Perhaps you feel that it's too good to be true."

Jan continued on his ebullient streak. "It's an incredible feeling. This is a day I've always dreamt about. All day, I couldn't think of anything else. I was thinking of the responsibility for Maria and me as parents, for me as a father. I was also thinking of financial planning, rearranging the

107

apartment to make a baby room. Then, during a session with a patient who talks chaotically, nonstop, I found myself drifting off into my own thoughts, thinking about how our life will change, about what I'm supposed to do. Not so professional, but I couldn't help myself. So many things to consider, so many questions to ask. I just can't believe what's happening. I'm hoping everything will be OK."

"You have doubts?"

"Yes," he replied, "I'm nervous because my first wife had two miscarriages. My treatment with you started with my depression, and everything has changed so rapidly that I still haven't told you about my previous marriage. After the first miscarriage, the doctor at the fertility clinic told us that my wife had early-pregnancy hormonal problems. Despite treatment, she had a second miscarriage. It's not easy being a doctor. It's not easy to know that so many things can go wrong. Maria is healthy, so even though I know better, I worry, and I can't think of anything else."

"Some things are necessary for the next generation to be born," I said. "There's no other way for you to be a father than for Maria and you to go through the hope and fears of pregnancy. As an expectant father, you're where you have to be, where you want to be. You and Maria are involved in restarting the adventure of life."

"It feels really good. It starts a new chapter in my life. Maria and I met by chance four years ago. It's a miracle that we even met. My boss, Dr. Mario Zazueta, was known for helping foreign medical graduates enter residency in psychiatry. So, one day, a nice girl came to his office with lots of anxiety and questions about the program. He said to her, 'I know this great guy who just went through all of this. Why don't we go to his office and see if he's there?'

"I wasn't supposed to be there that day. I was supposed to be at the VA grand rounds, but the rounds were canceled. So, entirely by chance, I was in my office. I heard a knock on my door, and Zazueta and Maria entered. Maria was in her late twenties and drop-dead gorgeous. I was immediately attracted to her, but I tried to be realistic. I didn't expect any romantic relationship. I tried to concentrate on doing my best to help her. Fortunately, it turned out that Maria was interested in me! The rest, as they say, is history. We used to talk about how fate brought us together.

"Maria told me about her visit to a Russian fortune-teller before coming to the U.S. He was her best friend, Tatiana's, relative, who was also a colorful and interesting Russian nobleman. His parents immigrated to Italy after escaping the Bolshevik revolution. He was born in Italy 12 years later and spoke both

Russian and Italian. As a young man, he studied everything from anthropology to physics, and, from Tatiana's stories, I assumed that he had visited every interesting place on Earth. Later in his life, he settled in Rome and worked as a freelance journalist. His side job was fortune-telling. According to Tatiana and all her family members, this was his real gift. So, anxious about her upcoming move, Maria asked him for a session. In the dim light, in a room full of paintings and memorabilia from Russia and the places he had visited, he read Tarot cards for her. First, he asked her, 'What's the question that you wish to be answered?' She replied that she wanted to know if moving to the U.S. would bring her happiness. He spread out the deck of Tarot cards and noted the overlapping influences of the Hierophant and the Chariot.

"Maria pointed at the Hierophant and said, 'He looks like a Pope.' He nodded and said, 'You'll find happiness if you meet someone touched by the Pope.'

"When Zazueta introduced me to Maria, he said, 'Please meet Jan. He's a great guy. Can you believe that he shook hands with the Pope?'"

"Is it true that you shook hands with the Pope?" I asked.

"Yes. The day before I met Maria, I showed Zazueta a picture of me shaking hands with Pope John Paul. When I went to Italy with my family years ago, we were lucky enough to visit the Pope in his summer residence in Castel Gandolfo.

"The beginning of my relationship with Maria was the happiest time in my life. Then Amir died right before we got married, and his death eclipsed any joy I felt. So when my friends would say that Maria getting pregnant was the next thing we should expect, I never felt it a real possibility. My future seemed to be obscured by a dark cloud. But it happened. The sun has started to shine again, and I can see the future."

"Future is fantastic. You were preoccupied with Amir and had time for little else for a long while. When you first saw me, you said that you were—"

"—detached from myself," Jan completed my sentence. "Not attached to anybody or anything, except Amir."

"Now that you're feeling better," I continued, "other priorities are emerging, and the detachment is melting away. Things are coming together."

"Yes," Jan said. "Until now, I had no idea what a top priority was. I've never been through such an experience. It brings out new problems, too."

"Like?"

"The responsibility for another human being feels overwhelming. I don't know what to do. How do you raise a baby in a foreign country? There are so many things I want to prevent, so many things I want to protect my baby from . . ."

I wanted to explain to him that such thoughts are common to all expectant parents and that, with time and experience, many of these concerns would dissipate. However, because Jan referred to himself as an immigrant, I felt that he might be missing his mom and family and regretting that his dad wasn't such a good influence on him, so I decided to co-opt his terminology: ". . . Yankee influences!"

"Yes, those, too. Since coming here, I've realized how much I miss the family closeness I grew up with. In both Poland and Italy, the family spirit surrounds you. Holidays like Christmas and Easter bring families closer. They're much less commercial. This is what I meant when I spoke about Yankee superficiality. Both Maria and I miss things about our families that we used to think were annoying, like everybody knowing everybody else's business. Here, life is a race. People don't seem to have time or energy to live a real family life. Days go by without you knowing how the rest of the family is doing. I've often felt that Americans are content to lead their own, separate lives, even though they claim to support strong families. I'm not saying this is a rule, but it's common enough for me to notice. I'm sure many Yankee families could prove me wrong, but this is how I feel. You need to meet other immigrants to get the family spirit.

"Maria and I also miss the sense of connection with friends back home. What is it to have a friend or be a friend? The answer is different here from home. After George W. Bush met with Vladimir Putin, he said he looked him in the eye and got a sense of his soul. But Bush didn't know what he was talking about! I remember countless conversations with my friends. After partying, singing, and drinking all night long, everything would slow down, and we would start to talk. Then I could say, 'I looked my friend in the eye, and I saw his soul.'

"All the crises Poland went through brought family and friends together. Sometimes, this was literally true. During martial law in Poland, there were often unexpected curfews. Sometimes, you couldn't return home afterward if you went to a party, which became an overnight event. Police roamed the streets, checking documents. Sometimes, you defied the law for fun, and they'd put you in jail for 48 hours. It happened to me twice. I didn't like the police, and I bristled at their meaningless restrictions. But the curfew taught us to look out for each other. In peacetime, we quarrel and don't get much done; our best comes out in a crisis. Maria sees the Italian family spirit similarly.

"I feel at home when I go to Italy. I feel at home in Latin America. I've gone to Mexico several times. There's a similarity in all Catholic countries. I even felt that way in Ireland. I spent three months there. As I told you, we radiologists got a lot of vacation time. An Irish friend in Poland gave me his parents' address in Ireland and invited me to visit them. They had a big house, and all the children were gone, so they were glad to have me. I felt truly at home. There was a Holy Mary at every street corner and in tiny chapels. Nasty pavements. Holes in the streets. These were all things I grew up with. So what's the difference between Poland and Ireland? Poles drink at home and speak Polish, and Irish drink in pubs and speak English. These days, Ireland is Yankeefied. In fact, so is Mexico, and so is Poland!

"Traditionally, the extended family is more involved in raising children in Poland and Italy. When relatives ask you questions about your child, they mean it. They're really trying to help. There's no sense of competition. No . . . I just can't explain it. Families in Poland take pride in their children's accomplishments, and there are jealousies, people saying, 'My son is smarter than your son.' But despite this, there's a greater family spirit. The whole family raises the child.

"In America, it seems that only the parents raise the child. Maria and I talked about this earlier today. Maria's grandmother is alive and healthy. She will take an extended vacation to come to be with our baby. We'll be glad to have her, not because we need the extra help, which we don't, but it will nurture the family spirit. So Maria and I will both take some time off after the baby is born. We also have a good family friend we hope will be our babysitter.

"A funny thing, though. Home for me now is America. When I'm outside America for more than two weeks, I feel it's time to get back home. I realized after my mom passed away how important family is.

"Since I was a little boy, I've always told people that I was going to travel far away. 'I'm going somewhere. I'm going somewhere.' Then my mom said, 'Wherever you are, you'll have a family. That will bring you close to Poland.'

"I'm talking a lot. The main idea is that family matters to me. When my mom passed away, it was important for me to talk to family members. Maria and I have lots of thinking and planning to do. Today, we had lunch together, and I was talking like this. She said, 'Let's enjoy lunch.' She's right, of course."

A story came to me about how an infant takes over the family. "Many years ago, at the Institute for Psychoanalysis, we had a Cuban psychoanalyst and teacher, Hugo Magrinat, who was teaching us about development. My friend and his wife were expecting their first child. He sensed that his life was changing, so he asked Magrinat, 'After my child is born, my wife and I want to spend two weeks in the Caribbean by ourselves while my parents take care of the baby. When would be the earliest time it would be safe to do so?'

"Magrinat hesitated and then replied in his thick Cuban accent, 'After your baby is born, if you still want to spend time away from him or her, you can ask me this question again.' Magrinat was saying what you said: When a child is born, the family spirit takes over, and such a question is moot. It's only before that such a question seems possible."

"To tell you the truth, such a question wouldn't even cross my mind."

"I understand. Most people wouldn't think of it."

"I would only think about going away for a short time after the child could talk. Sofia, my sister, and her husband went away for a couple of days after their baby was fully comfortable with my mom and when their daughter *wanted* to spend time with her. Earlier than that, no way! It's a huge challenge.

"I just thought about another patient who has 13 children. She would talk about her pregnancies with little emotion, like reciting a grocery list. She was pregnant almost every other year. She doesn't have clear memories of specific pregnancies, and she sometimes can't remember the birthdays of all her children. Now she has 14 grandchildren. It's all so complicated. Pregnancy is unique and special for some people, but it's ordinary and routine for others.

"Maria will take some time off after the baby is born; attachment is important, even though most families need two incomes. In other countries, the attitude toward children is different. When I was young, the paid leave for new mothers in Poland was one year, and women could take unpaid leave for up to three years. And they had a guarantee of returning to the same job or position if it still existed. That's how much motherhood was valued. On second thought, I might be exaggerating because this wasn't a Communist idea. It came from a time before the Communists took over."

"It must have reassured parents and contributed to the family spirit. Did your mom work after you were born?"

"She worked in a big factory as a bookkeeper. Sofia was born three years after me, so my mom was on leave for at least four years and then returned to work." Jan looked pensive, or maybe confused, for a moment.

"No, actually, it was a little more complicated. When I was about 1½, my mom was diagnosed with tuberculosis. The health policy mandated that she had to be isolated from the family, so she went to a sanatorium in the mountains, about 200 miles away."

"Who took care of you during that time?"

"My maternal grandmother. I was close to her. She died when I was 14 or 15. She was a warm and friendly woman, traditional and Catholic. I learned songs and prayers from her that I still remember. She was good to me. She tried her best to replace my mom. I remember her singing to wake me up every day. She would sing aloud while she was making breakfast or sweeping the kitchen, and sometimes she would stop working and sit by the window, humming under her breath while she turned her rosary beads."

"You said that, after Amir died, you found yourself reciting prayers."

"Yes! Those were the prayers and songs that she taught me."

As I looked at Jan, he seemed to be singing silently to himself. "It seems like it's a heartfelt song," I said.

"Yes. I'm struggling to remember it in Polish, but I want to translate it into English for you at the same time. Shall I send you the poem by e-mail?"

Jan struggled to navigate between the two languages, figuring out how to stay with the first while translating it. "Why don't you send me both versions?" I suggested.

"I'll do that."

Jan sent me an e-mail that evening, in both Polish and English. Here is the English version:

When the dawn awaking found me,
Hymns of glory rose around me—
From the heavens, earth, and ocean,
All creation sang devotion.

Should we humans, your creation,
Heirs in Jesus of salvation,
All alone sit out the chorus?
What a shame that would be for us!

Therefore I, your child a-borning
As I wake this glorious morning,

Sing your glory and your praises—
Hymns of thanks my spirit raises!

May all women know your glory,
May all children sing your story!
May we raise your praise with all men.

At the next session, I asked Jan about the lyrics. "The last verse in the Polish version has four lines, but the English version has only three lines. Why are they different?"

"I sent you a translation that I found online. I will now translate the last stanza, which *actually* says:

Many who yesterday fell asleep
Fell into a death dream
But we woke up this morning
To praise you, God."

The difference in the "translations" struck me, but I didn't say anything. Translating poetry requires taking some liberties, and I was in no position to judge. Yet I noted that when Amir fell into a final death dream, he left Jan unable to praise the Lord when he woke up in the morning. I could see the poignancy of this verse, for it had driven Jan to engage in a compulsive ritual to avoid thinking about Amir's death.

Our session continued with Jan discussing his grandmother.

"She wanted to make sure that I was a good Catholic. So she was the one who taught me prayers. I remember kneeling in front of a painting of Jesus, who held His own heart in His outstretched hands. A fluorescent aura surrounded him. The painting was brightly colored and, when I think about it right now, it was pretty kitschy. My grandma made me repeat the prayers until I could recite them perfectly. I didn't like it, but I did it because of the person she was."

"So, while your mother was in the sanatorium, your grandmother raised you and taught you prayers."

"Yes. My mom was gone for a few months. I don't know how long, exactly. I heard from one of my aunts that it may have been almost a year. I missed her very much. I remember seeing her in the passage."

It seemed a bit unusual for anyone to remember anything between the ages of one and two. Sometimes, fragmentary memories are fused with stories heard later. I was less concerned about the historicity of the report and more interested in the flow of associations that held the clue to the meanings behind such memories.

"In the passage?" I asked.

"In a hallway, through a window, or at a distance, but I couldn't touch her. The Polish government's health policy was strict regarding isolation procedures for patients with TB. Sanatoriums were isolated in the mountains, where TB patients could rest and breathe crystal-clear air. They ate well and tried to avoid any stress. Thomas Mann describes such places in *The Magic Mountain*. In addition to official policies and treatments, there were folkloric remedies, like eating the fat of dogs or mountain bears."

Jan made a grimace of disgust. "I hope my mom didn't eat those things, but she did gain weight. I think that Communist health policies almost eradicated TB, although it's coming back in some areas. They had a program of obligatory vaccinations and early detection. Buses with portable X-ray machines were everywhere. Chest X-rays were obligatory and helped identify many people in the early stages. Once a sputum test confirmed the diagnosis, you were placed in mandatory isolation, and family members had to be tested. The downside of these policies was that some kids—like me—had to spend many months without their mothers. At the time, nobody thought about early attachment issues. Nobody could predict how growing up without a mother could screw up a child's life."

"Having your mother in a sanatorium when you were so young was a heavy load," I said. "Your mother had to go away for treatment, but it's good that your grandmother was there to take care of you." I saw tears in Jan's eyes.

Jan nodded pensively and seemed comforted that I acknowledged his early pain. "My mother was so sick. I have just one clear memory of that time: I was so unhappy that my mother was gone that they bought me a little car to distract me. That's it."

Jan had come to the end of his memories or of his willingness to talk about them. Then, slowly, a memory of my childhood floated into my awareness. It started with the unforgettable sound of a toy that was like a bleating lamb. I must have been about three. Then, I walked into a room where my mom was breastfeeding my sister Padmini, who was a year and a half younger than I; in India at that time, most moms breastfed their children for up to two years. I approached my mom and rested my head on her shoulder, and she said, "Go play. I'll be with you after I finish feeding your sister."

Perhaps she said, "Play," and implied the rest. I didn't want to leave her, but reluctantly I did. I found a doll on a chair, and as I slowly picked it up, it made a sound like a lamb bleating for its mother: "*Maa-maa.*" It had brown hair, big black eyes, pink plastic limbs, and a soft cloth-covered belly from inside of which came the sound. If abruptly picked up, it bleated only a single syllable. Each time I picked it up, the bleat varied a little. Finally, I pulled myself away from the memory of the forced separation from my mom and came back to the present. I waited for Jan to speak.

"My two actual memories are of seeing my mom and not being able to touch her and of getting the little car. I remember so little of the separation, yet it must have had a lifelong effect on me. I like Erickson's ideas about the stages of identity development. For example, the time that my mom was in the sanatorium coincided with Erickson's stage of trust versus mistrust. I had that problem, but I don't think the ill effects were permanent. I'm not unduly suspicious or mistrusting." Jan fixed his gaze on me, eagerly awaiting my reaction.

Ideally, each person comes to develop their own metric for trust and suspicion, but others can shape the process. The best insight is self-reflection. The limitations on childhood memories are striking. Although we live intimately at every wakeful, dreaming, or sleepy moment, we are unaware of our infancy and early childhood. Early memories, by definition, are almost all forgotten. Perhaps there's a reason why we're incapable of remembering those times. Who wants to remember a time when you were at the mercy of the fates of hunger, discomfort, and abandonment?

This helpless time is also the time of giant, looming parents. A mother closing a door behind her might feel like eternal abandonment when all she needed was a few minutes of privacy in the bathroom. Yet, against the current of such universal forgetfulness, sometimes a strange piece of a remembered or imagined experience escapes. They are like a meteor shower in the night sky. These fragmentary reminiscences grab our attention and force us to ponder our past.

After taking a snaking road from the valley of infancy up into the mountains of adulthood, what does a man or woman see on looking back? We once traveled on a road obscured by mountains, trees, and low-lying clouds. There are breaks and disconnections in the ribbon of our intimate past and sections shrouded in mystery. Sometimes, however, a memory shines through as if reflected in a circus mirror, with times, places, or people appearing unduly elongated or foreshortened. These previously breathed moments and movements are totally unlike the subjects of current experience. They may reflect a time when a mother or father told stories and sang lullabies to quell the day's excitement and usher us to sleep.

Yet such fragments are all we can hope to recover about this time. We might dismiss these disjointed memories as false or meaningless, forcing them to dwell in the land of strange dreams or stranger imaginings. So, why dwell in the unknown land when we should be looking at the creaky, leaky house of the present? Why ponder on meteor showers raining down from the days of dim origins? The past is lost, yet we hope to find a way to make sense of this unruly court of our infancy and welcome whatever fragmentary memories we find. There must, after all, be some connection between an untouchable mother and an eminently touchable little car. We cannot expect a straight line connecting these two reminiscences. The most promising outcome is the emergence of another childhood memory or a link to some current or recent experience.

"Today, when you came in here, you said that you were 43 years old and that you hadn't felt so good in 40 years. Your mother left to go to the sanatorium when you were 1½ and may have been gone about a year. I imagine you were thrilled when your mom came home to take care of you, and that was the happiest time of your life, until now."

"Without a doubt," Jan said. "That's a good point. But when I said, 'in 40 years,' I was referring to the entire time period I can remember. I don't know exactly when all this happened."

"Do you mean to say that this is the happiest time of your conscious life?"

"Exactly."

"Whatever the timing, I'm glad that you were at least able to see your mother through the passage."

"That, I do remember . . . seeing her in the passageway when the door opened, but not being able to come closer. Just a glimpse, nothing more. I don't know what such memories are called."

"Freud called them *primal memories*. He attached great importance to them. He felt that, like dreams, they can reveal a lot about a person."

"I have one more primal memory. I don't know if this is an actual memory or if I made it up later, but it is very clear. I was young, less than 3 years old. There was a birthday party at my Aunt Gertruda's house. About 30 people were eating, drinking, and singing. I felt like an adult trapped in a child's body, and I wanted people to look at me. After someone made a toast, I saw that the excitement level had gone up and everyone was happy.

I wanted to make that happen, too, so I raised a pretend glass of alcohol and made a toast, and everyone sang and cheered.

"One time, I described this event to my mom. I remembered the house had wooden walls and a wooden roof. My mother said that the city council decided to build a new road, and they bulldozed the house before my fourth birthday. She was surprised at how much detail I could recall but suggested I'd incorporated some pictures of the house that I saw later. My mom said that they had many family parties there, but she didn't remember this specific incident. For me, it's an authentic memory."

"You may or may not have made a toast then, but today you're certainly toasting a great occasion in your new family's life!"

Jan became serious. "Now, toasting isn't enough. I have to be more responsible. I have to take better care of myself and start paying attention to money. My parents were considered middle class: "intelligentsia." In a Communist country, they weren't starving and were probably better off than 50% of Poles. Education, even medical education, was theoretically free, but the truth was that wealthy people could help their children get into college by paying sizable bribes.

"I was determined to be a doctor, and my parents didn't have money for a bribe, so my only way to get into medical school was by passing a competitive entrance exam. I could also improve my chances by earning extra points as a finalist in the National Science Olympics. So giving poor and working-class kids the opportunity to add extra points to their entry-exam scores was a kind of affirmative action. And I won second prize."

"Your plan worked out."

Jan continued, "Yes. I worked hard to get there. First, I had to pass local, regional, and national written tests. Then, I had to set up my own science project to demonstrate the effects of environmental pollution on habitats or organisms. I designed an experiment using a protozoan called *Colpidium colpoda*, easily visible in a light microscope.

"My bedroom was transformed into a lab with an incubator, dozens of test tubes, and other lab glassware. It smelled like a barn because the growing medium I used was hay soaked in water. There is a pulsating water vacuole within this organism. In my study, the pollutant was an anion detergent found in dishwasher liquids. I found a strict correlation between the rate of pulsation and the amount of detergent in the medium. Not very interesting science, but it got me an invitation to the national competition."

"So, Madame Curie can continue to rest in peace?"

Jan beamed with pride. "Most definitely. Actually, Marie was Polish; her name was Skłodowska. While working in France, she met the French scientist Pierre Curie. After they married, she used Skłodowska-Curie, but the French bastards have now fully claimed her by dropping her Polish surname!

"Back to my story. I did well on the written tests and my experiment. Then I took an oral exam conducted by Warsaw University professors, and that was it.

"Children should work to go to college, instead of having their parents provide everything. A few weeks ago, an article in the *Financial Times* dealt with brats getting angry if their parents don't buy them designer clothes. Until about 100 years ago, the article noted that child labor was widespread and accepted. Children worked in textile mills and even in coal mines. I'm not advocating that, but children on farms did chores, city kids sold news-papers, shined shoes, delivered flowers, etc. Then people's attitudes began to change. In my opinion, children need to learn the dignity of labor. As a teenager, I always worked in the summer to earn money.

"Maria and I live here, where education is expensive. We already had a conversation about putting our child through college. But, it feels good to think about the future of our baby. I want to give him or her everything I can.

"Our conversation today made me think of lots of things. You asked me about my mom being in the sanatorium. I still think about it. My psychiatry textbooks emphasize the importance of early-childhood interactions with the mother. I read it and can't help but wonder if being separated from my mom impacted my life.

"I knew the difference between my mom and my grandma. I liked my grandma, but I was happiest with my mom. I'm sure I missed her when she was gone, and I'm sure I was happy to see her again. She tried to compensate for the time she couldn't be with me. According to my aunt, my mom was so happy to be with me that she took me everywhere she went. She taught me many things and was proud to show me off. Then, a few decades later, as fate would have it, I left her to come here. After that, I didn't see her for almost four years.

"Right after I started my residency, my mom came to visit me. I wanted to show her what life in the U.S. was like, so we drove to California. We didn't listen to music; we just talked. We talked about my childhood, and I learned a lot about myself and my family, things that I somehow sensed, but had never confirmed, like conflicts between my father and her side of the family. I got to know about my grandmother on my father's side in a way I never knew before; I had few memories of her infrequent visits.

"My father didn't maintain contact with his side of the family, except his mother and sister, my Aunt Malgorzata. In Poland, first cousins are called brothers or sisters, but my father didn't keep in touch with his cousins. He never invited them, and we never visited them. I never knew why. This is in direct contrast to the closeness on my mom's side of the family. I miss that. America is a good country to live in, but I miss Poland. I spent lots of time talking to my family and friends on the phone, and the years when I couldn't visit them were painful.

"My mom and I took another trip to Florida. Again, no radio, just talking about everything: my sister, my childhood, my ex-wife, my divorce. I told my mom how I learned that my first wife was cheating on me and how we decided to divorce."

I had not known that Jan had been previously married and divorced. Jan was in the middle of his story.

"We talked about my father. She answered all my questions honestly and, for the first time, I felt that she was talking about things as they were, without trying to sugarcoat them. I wish she were still around, and I could ask her more, but it's too late. She's gone.

"My mom's older sister, who is now 81, is sharp for her age. Now that my mom is gone, I call my aunt more often than I used to. She's the last link to my mom and my childhood. They were best friends and knew intimate details about each other's life. My aunt is a wise person. Some things she tells me in detail. Other things she skims over for reasons I understand. She believes that some things are better left unsaid or unknown. For example, she doesn't talk about my father. I know she doesn't like him, but she won't say anything negative or unsettling. She doesn't want me to think less of him."

"You called today your happiest day," I said. "Do you feel that, instead of toasting that great news, I rained on it by talking about your sadness when your mother was at the sanatorium? Do you think my comments today would have been better left unsaid?"

"No. Those memories came to me and are important. Reading about early attachment, I realized that my mom going away to the sanatorium had a real impact on me, although I don't know to what extent. You started to see me when I was depressed. Maybe what happened in the first few years of my life made me prone to depression. The roots of my sadness should be explored and not left alone or shoved under the rug."

"You want to keep the good things you got from your mom and even your dad and to learn from the sad separation from your mom."

"These are the exact same words I recently said to a borderline patient. She hates her father and stepmother but loves her mother. She lives in a black-and-white world, not allowing herself to see any shades of gray. So it's hard to explain to her that the same person can be good and bad, and even good and bad at the same time.

"But let's close this session on the same note where we started. Today is a happy day. I can't wait to see Maria."

"All right, let's stop."

CHAPTER 11

In our first session, Jan was listless and depressed. Now, he was animated and alive. Although he still talked about depressing topics, he didn't seem depressed. I was glad about his more positive moods, but I also wanted to be sure that he learned everything his sadness could teach him. "Jan, your moods have improved dramatically. It's a big change, but change always holds mystery. Did this occur in a way that you understand?"

"Yes, my moods changed."

"You're a psychiatrist. You know how hard change is."

"It works both ways. Life events can trigger moods, and moods can trigger life events. When you're depressed, everything looks darker. You assume that whatever happens will be negative. There's no future, or if there is, it doesn't look good. In my case, it was my exam. Everybody expected me to pass it, but I didn't. Why was that? For a depressed person, it's natural to think, 'Whatever I do, it will turn out bad. I do my best, but it's not enough. The world is against me.' I don't mean this in a paranoid way. That's your outlook. The next question is, 'Why bother trying?' As I said, it can work both ways."

"You came to psychiatry with great hope."

"I came with hope and enthusiasm. I used to be a good listener."

"And Amir's suicide wasn't merely a setback; it changed your identity. Now, we can say that the change was temporary, but while you were in that depressed state, it seemed like it might be permanent."

"Yes. When I first came to see you, I doubted that I would ever again be a doctor. I thought I could never have the confidence to listen like a doctor. I didn't feel I deserved to be a psychiatrist."

"Now, when you see patients, you feel hope and excitement again. You believe that you are worthy of this job."

"I think it's helpful to feel the responsibility of messing with the delicate tissue of the human mind. If others expect you to be responsible, you find it easier to step into the role of a doctor. I'm doing a better job now. I allow myself to listen more carefully, more deeply. I'm more patient. I'm not jumping to conclusions so quickly, as I did before. I take my time to complete whatever I'm doing. I don't feel under pressure. I'm not taking shortcuts. My first meeting with Dr. Schwartz didn't go well because I took my time to give a patient what he needed. It wasn't that the patient was overtly suicidal. I just took my time to decide and act. So, Dr. Schwartz had to wait an extra 15 minutes.

"It's a good change, as I see it. Maybe I'm more balanced than I used to be."

"How did you first get interested in psychiatry?"

"I joined the Student Scientific Society in two areas, psychiatry and oncology. After I completed my study of the basic sciences, I tried to make up my mind. I read a psychiatry book on schizophrenia by Professor Tadeusz Kępiński, an important name in Polish psychiatry. His associates were friendly and charismatic and influenced many students to study psychiatry. They treated us like equals, and that was quite appealing. On the other hand, oncology was more practical, and I liked the science and physics behind cancer treatment. There was also some excitement because of the promising new immunological and genetic approaches. Plus, my grandmother had died of cancer. When I spoke to an influential mentor about my choices, he said, 'You don't really want to do psychiatry. You're too smart to do psychiatry.' Although I disagreed with him on that point, I saw other problems. Psychiatry can be abused. Communist countries used psychiatric diagnoses to discredit political dissidents and put them away. It had lost respect. So, this is how I chose oncology. I told you a lot about my experiences in oncology. I started my internship in a community hospital, but after a year, I moved to the Cancer Institute and started to work on the oncology wards. Soon, I lost contact with psychiatry as a discipline."

"A moment ago, you said you *used to be* a good listener, and then you said you're listening better. So, you feel you're connecting with people?"

"Yeah. I've always felt comfortable talking to people. I've also noticed that people like to talk to me. They see that I listen to them, and they unburden themselves. Once, I met a lady—probably in her sixties—on a train in

Poland. My sister lived in Warsaw, I studied in Krakow, and my parents lived halfway between, so I traveled a lot between Krakow and Warsaw. I don't know her name; I call her the Fossa Lady. We started with a casual conversation, but at some point—as if a switch had been flipped—she started talking about her experiences during World War II.

"She lived in Lublin, a town in eastern Poland. The Germans had carried out a mass killing and piled the bodies up outside the Lublin Castle. She went there to look for her husband's body, although she was still hoping he was alive. She was the only survivor in her family."

"Was she Jewish?"

"She didn't tell me. Maybe she was; maybe she wasn't. In the Second World War, the Germans killed so many people. They put Jews first in line because they wanted to exterminate the Jewish 'race,' but they killed many non-Jewish Poles. Sometimes, the Germans blocked a street and just killed everybody. Often, it was retribution for some action of the Polish Underground against the Germans, but sometimes they just did it to scare people and keep them under control. I'm sure that it was much more complicated than what I'm saying. Near the end of the war, the Germans went on rampages before they withdrew, killing many people in Lublin and elsewhere. I wasn't even born yet, so I can't describe what exactly happened.

"Anyway, this woman looked for her husband in the *fossa*, the moat that surrounded the city and the castle. That's why I call her the Fossa Lady. She said the bodies were piled face-down, so she had to turn them to see their faces; she had to touch many dead bodies. The bodies in the ditch were soaking in blood and water and rapidly decomposing. When she described how she had to turn over decomposing dead bodies to look for her husband's face, I was shaken. I had nightmares after that and started imagining such a thing happening to me. Here she was, telling this story to a stranger so many years after the war. It was horrible. You can never forget it; you can go mad.

"I think about this woman from time to time, although I don't remember her face that clearly. Sometimes, she comes to my mind when I'm watching the news, and they're talking about an atrocity somewhere and how many people were killed. Sometimes, they show the bloody limbs of wounded or dead people."

Jan's inability to remember the Fossa Lady's face made me think of his early childhood separation from his mom when she was ill with tuberculosis. I speculated that he displaced his feelings for his mother onto the Fossa

Lady. It undoubtedly would have helped Jan if his mother hadn't been ill and hadn't needed to be in a sanatorium. Recall that Jan was only one or two years old; at that age, he may have had the experience of forgetting his mother's face or being unable to conjure up her image when he felt abandoned. I thought that the separation from his mom was the most profound source of Jan's depression.

I recalled my own feelings and fears about separation. When I was about 11, I went to the Hussain Sagar Lake in Hyderabad with my friend Nagesh. Nagesh was a year older and a good swimmer. I was just learning how to swim. Knowing my swimming abilities were limited, my mother always warned me to swim only in a pool with a lifeguard. I thought she was overly cautious, so I disregarded her advice and went to the lake that day. It was hot, and the sky was clear blue with a few wisps of clouds far up in the atmosphere. Lots of kids—many of them younger than me—were swimming and playing in the water, having a great time. Kids were jumping off a granite boulder projecting about 10 feet into the lake. I sat on the boulder for a while. Then I decided to wade only in the shallow water close to the shore.

Nagesh helped build my confidence, and watching these fearless younger kids spurred me on. I felt great. Then Nagesh went out into deeper water with the more experienced swimmers. I waded into where the water was just a few inches above my head and noted that my feet had stirred up soil from the lakebed. I wanted to cool off, so I stuck my head underwater. I opened my eyes to see the blue-gray of the sandy water that had been kicked up by so many swimming feet. I spent about half an hour just cooling myself off and enjoying the scenery. I swam a few yards and then tried to rest by standing on the lakebed, but my feet couldn't touch the ground! I seemed to have forgotten everything I knew about swimming in an instant. I gasped for breath. I bobbed up and took a quick gulp of air but quickly sank. I could see many kids within a few feet of me, and I tried to scream for help, but I didn't have enough time above water to both gulp for air and scream. My arms were getting tired.

I recalled Amma's warning not to swim in the lake without lifeguards, and I wished she were there. I wanted to say, "I'm sorry," and felt sad that I wouldn't have the opportunity to tell her. I wished to undo this watery reality somehow and get out into the realm of air. I wished I would die somehow other than by going against Amma's warning. Realizing I might have only seconds more to live, I wanted at least to be able to see her once more.

Then I began to see a series of images of family members and friends. All the people who were important to me were lined up and saying good-bye to me. These images are still fresh and vivid. Amma's younger brother, Venkat, was one of my favorite uncles. He was a judge. He came up to me and asked, "Do you know why, when a judge decides to hang a guilty person, the judgment says 'hanged till death?'"

"I don't know," I replied.

"During the British days," Venkat said, "a guilty person was hanged, according to court procedures. Then, they took him down and removed the rope from his neck, but the person somehow survived the hanging. After that, they wanted to hang him again. His barrister objected. The State had already hanged his client, as per court orders. The State cannot punish a man again. After that, the order always said the prisoner should be 'hanged till death.'

"I once witnessed a hanging early in the morning," Venkat continued. "I was one of three officials who sat in front of a small wooden table in front of the gallows. The guards brought the condemned man in front of us. I asked him, 'Do you wish to say anything before being hanged?' He replied, 'Yes, Sir, I want to wish you a good morning,' and went smiling to the gallows."

This exchange came from old memory. Uncle Venkat was a district judge in a small town called Atmakur. One summer, we visited Uncle Venkat while the notorious Nanavati murder case, still undecided, was roiling the country. I was 10 years old.

Kawas Nanavati was a handsome Indian naval commander who had married an English beauty named Sylvia. Nanavati's duties kept him away at sea for extended periods. At some point, Sylvia became involved with his good friend Prem Ahuja, well known as a playboy. One day, Nanavati returned home and found Sylvia distant and aloof. He pressed for an explanation, and she confessed that she was having an affair with Ahuja and wished to marry him. Nanavati drove to his ship, docked in the Bombay harbor, and checked out a .38 Smith & Wesson from its armory. He then went to Ahuja's house and asked him if he intended to marry Sylvia. Ahuja replied, "Will I marry every woman I sleep with?" and Nanavati pumped three bullets into him. He then surrendered himself to the police and confessed.

When the court was closed on a Sunday, Venkat took my siblings and me to his courtroom. He showed us where the accused sat, where the witnesses sat, and the gallery for the spectators. He explained that the government pleader argued the State's case, and his own lawyer represented the defendant. We spent the morning acting out the roles of Nanavati, Sylvia, the government pleader, the defendant's lawyer, and the judge. There was no question about whether Nanavati had killed Ahuja. The question was whether it was a crime committed "in the heat of the moment" or whether it was premeditated.

When I was in the judge's chair, Uncle Venkat asked, "What would you do if Nanavati is declared guilty of cold-blooded murder?"

"Hang him!" I flippantly responded.

"And if by chance he doesn't die after you hang him, would you hang him a second time?"

I was baffled and froze for a moment. "That's a trick question. If hanged, people will always die," I replied, although I was bewildered by the idea.

"It's not a trick question," Uncle Venkat responded. "It happened once. Since then, the judge sentences a person who's guilty of premeditated murder to be 'hanged till death.'"

I thought a judge's job was easy until that moment, but when my uncle asked me to pronounce the verdict, I was paralyzed. Suddenly, I noticed an odd-looking curtain hanging over my head, with a rope leading to a hole in the wall. Amused at my sudden inability to speak and sudden interest in the curtain, Venkat informed me that the curtain was a big fan to help the judge keep a cool head as he pondered how to render justice. Next, he showed me how the rope went from the fan in the courtroom above the judge's head to the verandah outside, where a man manually operated the fan by pulling the rope back and forth, creating a gentle breeze above the judge's head.

The image of Venkat disappeared, and Amma appeared in my world of water. She didn't say anything; she simply looked at me. I could see deep sorrow on her face. Tears welled up in my eyes.

The water was only a little over my head. When I kicked the soft mud, I rose briefly—not enough to take a full breath, but enough to see and hear for a fraction of a second: The boulder from which the kids jumped off, the clear blue sky, the laughter of the children, and every other detail of life on Earth were particularly vivid. Then I watched a remarkable transformation. When my head bobbed *down* into the murky, gray-blue water, I could still see and hear: In a dreamlike state, I saw the rock, the sky, and the clouds, and I listened to the laughing children. It seemed that the world I perceived was merging with the world I imagined.

I wasn't dead. Although my thinking was muddled, I was still seeing and feeling. Just a few minutes earlier, I had had many choices. I could have stayed on the boulder. I could have stayed in the shallow water and not taken those fateful steps into the deeper water. Instead, I realized that all the possibilities in my life had now shrunk to fit the few remaining seconds I had left. Then, only one possibility was left—death—and it was now a certainty. My inner vision was destined to last only a short time, soon to be overtaken by the anticipation of losing consciousness. This anticipation was unbearable. Then the pain from the lack of air became even more painful. I realized that there were no miracles and that I would soon experience the reality of death. Death was staring me in the face, and I couldn't avoid its gaze.

I pondered life in a way I never had before. Although my parents acted to create me, I felt that I had come into being by chance. I didn't bring myself into being. Life consisted of an intention started and bounded by the chance of birth at one end and the certainty of death at the other.

But then I realized I wanted to live! The feeling was reflexive and barely conscious, but it was boundless. I wanted to live with every fiber of my being. Until that moment, I would have thrashed and protested and done my damnedest to continue to live and not accept death. Yes, I would die, but I would not accept its reality; at that moment, I realized that I could will my life for only so long. Right then, the reality of imminent death hit me, and I developed a new attitude toward it: I decided that, when the time came, I would not fight my fate. I would not struggle till my very last moment. I wanted to fight with all I had *as long as there was hope* for further existence, but I wanted to accept death with dignity when I felt that that possibility was gone.

And I decided that my moment had come! Somehow, the realization that I could choose to stand in the face of death gave me inner peace. I realized that this was my end, and I would die without ever seeing my mom again. I felt my tears merge with the water around me, the moment of resignation and the dawning of acceptance. But, death was just as real as life. I didn't want to thrash around anymore . . . so I stopped.

And then, suddenly I felt myself being yanked out of the water. Hooray for Nagesh! Water gurgled out from inside my chest. In a few seconds, I was surrounded by sweet air, feeling wobbly but on the firm ground of life once again.

When I got home, I told my mother how glad I was to see her and that I had nearly drowned. I told her how sorry I was that I hadn't heeded her warnings, about my imaginary conversation with Venkat, and how real the images seemed when I was drowning. She tried not to look alarmed and said something to the effect that I had learned a lesson. She was glad that I was alive to tell the tale and told me to thank Nagesh for her. That was mom: She wanted us to learn from life and didn't have to be heavy-handed about it. She knew just how to make her children feel loved and special with big or little actions, like bringing a glass of sweetened milk just when we were dreaming of it.

Jan was haunted by his mom's absence, especially when he was a child, and was running away from the fierce sadness he felt in response to it. Perhaps there was some unconscious anger at her, too, for what he had lost. However, those feelings were veiled, just as he could not call up the face of the Fossa Lady. I believed that Jan had been through a gut-wrenching loss as a toddler and hadn't mourned it sufficiently. If he had, he would have had a less-idealized image of his mom. However, and perhaps also when she returned from the sanatorium, Jan had decided she could do no wrong. It seemed he saw me, too, in a purely positive light.

This interpretation would be exceedingly hard to explain to Jan now. He needed to maintain his complete devotion to his mom and couldn't tolerate becoming aware of his disappointment or anger toward her for the time she was away from him. He had expressed little curiosity about trying to unravel the mystery of his depression. It afflicted him, but he now wanted no part of it. At any rate, the question was moot since he was talking freely. There was no occasion or need to re-inject sadness. Through the Fossa Lady's life—something far removed in space and time—he was dealing with the loss of his mother.

In World War II, the Germans took what they wanted from the Polish people, including their lives, without much thought. Poles must have burned with the wish for revenge. Did Amir's mom feel Jan killed her son? She must feel that, because of Jan, her live son became a dead son. Perhaps she wanted to see Jan suffer. Jan wanted to talk to Amir's mom. He seemed to have a magical hope of helping her overcome her grief. He wanted her to see him as a Good Samaritan. I saw that as utterly unrealistic. I knew that Jan wouldn't see my point of view now, and I didn't see any use in trying to get him to gain insight into his unrealistic hopes.

Jan brought me back from my internal musings. "When the Germans came, they took over many of the little castles and mansions and also a lot of houses, especially the nicer ones. They probably took over the Fossa Lady's house, just as they did my grandmother's. They would knock on the door and tell the occupant, 'You leave. Now. We need this house.' That's it. End of story. The house became a German officer's house.

"I know a lot about the war because one of my mom's cousins ended up in a concentration camp. My mom knew a lot about life in the camps from listening to people. The official Communist Polish propaganda was that the Germans had attacked Poland. They talked about the atrocities committed by the Germans, but they didn't like talking about the atrocities committed by the Soviet Union. The Germans invaded Poland from the west on September 1, 1939; the Russians invaded Poland from the east 16 days later. I heard many stories about people being gathered together and then killed. There was an incident where they put all the people from a village inside a church and set it on fire, burning them all alive. Wherever there was a Polish Underground, the Germans and Russians retaliated. They tried to keep control of Poland by killing people as an example."

I wanted to be sure I heard Jan correctly. "You said that your mom's cousin ended up in a concentration camp?"

"Yes. He died soon after the war ended. I've heard from my mom that the Auschwitz experience changed him. He became a recluse and seemed to be scared all the time. He never spoke about his experience. His siblings told me he was obsessed with food, hoarding and hiding it in his apartment. After he died, they discovered bags of sugar hidden in his sofa bed. He dug his own grave and had his gravestone made while still alive. Embedded in his grave is a picture of him wearing the striped uniform in the concentration camp. He had his birthdate inscribed on the stone; all the family had to do was add the date of his death. The Germans kept good records of everything they did. It is so characteristically German that they converted people into numbers by tattooing their arms."

Jan looked pensive and then asked, "Have you heard of *Sonderkommandos*?"

"No. Please tell me."

"The Germans killed most of the Jews who came to the camps by gassing them. Actually, they were so twisted that they made Jews—called *Sonderkommandos*—do their dirty work. Different *Sonderkommandos* had different assignments. Some would greet the new arrivals and lie to them, telling them that they would take showers and then be reunited with their families when they were really going to be killed. Some had to remove the bodies from the gas chambers and search them for valuables, like money or jewelry; they even extracted gold teeth. Some had to cremate them, and others threw the ashes into the river. The only part of the process the Nazis did themselves was the actual killing. If they refused to obey, the Germans shot the *Sonderkommando* on the spot. The only way to avoid this assignment was suicide.

"The *Sonderkommandos* got slightly better food and sleeping conditions and other small perks than the prisoners in the camp. Because they knew everything about the mass killings, though, they were marked for sure death. As a result, very few of the *Sonderkommandos* survived the war."

I winced at Jan's description of the lives of these men forced to choose between living with overwhelming guilt and dying a little sooner. And those little benefits must have only heightened their sense of guilt, as they came with the knowledge that they—and others—knew they were cogs in the machinery of evil. I wondered why Jan mentioned these doomed men, who must have become so completely alienated from themselves.

When I first started to see Jan, he was in a state of shock, alienation, and guilt. Now, the thought struck me that Jan may have felt he carried guilt similar to that of a *Sonderkommando*. Jan seemed to think that he knew or should have known that Amir was destined to kill himself, and he should and could have stopped it. Jan had done his best but felt that he hadn't done a good enough job protecting Amir. Although the connection made sense to me, I didn't think I could explain it to Jan in a way that would be useful to him. I understood the general idea behind my thinking, but perhaps it was irrelevant to Jan or Jan's relationship with Amir. Because I didn't know either Jewish or Polish cultures very well, the risk of inadvertently stirring up a hornets' nest was high. I did feel, however, that Jan had experienced profound wretchedness from which he was trying to emerge. I said, "The *Sonderkommandos* must have felt horrible guilt and lived a wretched life."

"Yes. Primo Levi said that the *Sonderkommandos* were collaborators whose word couldn't be trusted, but I think he was wrong. We can't imagine the choices they faced. The *Sonderkommandos* were recruited at gunpoint. The whole situation was perverse. The concentration-camp experience was a horrible nightmare for every inmate.

"The war affected my family in many other ways. I'm not sure why my mom's cousin was sent to Auschwitz. Often, there was no reason one was sent to a concentration camp. They just picked random people up and put them on the train.

"My Uncle Bozydar, my father's older brother, was a partisan fighter. The Germans tried to bribe Poles to supply information about their own countrymen. My uncle's job was to find those collaborators and hang them, to set an example for other Poles. They hanged them on street lanterns or windows—wherever. Sometimes, they simply slashed their throats or shot them. With women collaborators, they shaved their heads and let them go. If you were a woman with a shaved head, everybody knew that you were sleeping with Germans or spying for them. The few times my uncle would talk about the War, he would hold his hand like it was a gun and tell me, 'When you have life and death at the tip of your finger, you can go crazy!' What my uncle did was considered honorable because he was fighting for a free Poland, but he couldn't accept the killing, even of traitors, especially his role in it. He couldn't live with his guilt. I think he drank to try to drown his memories. One of my cousins felt Bozydar fought bravely against the Germans, but the rest of his family disparaged him as a common drunk. He would talk to my mom about the war because she understood. But the alcohol, the memories, and the guilt destroyed him."

This story reinforced my feeling that thoughts about guilt and killing intruded on Jan's awareness and identified with his Uncle Bozydar.

"My mom told me that she told Uncle Bozydar, 'It was necessary to kill collaborators.' She must have established a good rapport with him. This reminds me of my rapport with the Fossa Lady. I thought it would be nice to have a profession based on rapport. If you're a good listener, people talk and get cured. They open their hearts.

"I want to give another example of why I thought I was a good listener. I once met a guy who worked for ZOMO, *Zmechanizowane Oddziały Milicji Obywatelskiej,* the Motorized Reserves of the Citizens' Militia, a Polish paramilitary organization during the Communist era. The most qualified recruits in the army ended up in the ZOMO. They were like the police, but with more firepower: guns and longer sticks to beat people. The government sent them into critical and dangerous situations to suppress internal uprisings. Then, after 1980, when the Communist Polish government declared martial law, the ZOMO's role became important. Their job was to keep the country in fear. They used tanks and armored cars. They caught people who did anything related to the Underground and put them in jail.

"One day, I was on my way to see my parents. I got to the train early to get a good seat, and the train wasn't crowded. This guy showed up simultaneously and sat in the same compartment, so we were alone for about half an hour. We started to talk about a book I was carrying. Suddenly, he said that he wished he could be like me. He wished he didn't have his job and could get more education like me, so I asked him about his job. He said that people hated him just because of his uniform. 'My own family talks to me differently,' he said, 'even my mom. All my friends look at me suspiciously.' As with the Fossa Lady, he just started talking to me. I answered his questions and didn't judge him. He described going to some factory to beat up the workers. The people at the factory couldn't defend themselves, while he had a transparent shield and a long stick. He broke several people's bones. People called him and his platoon guys bad names, and he didn't like it. But, according to him, once he joined the ZOMO, he had no choice."

Jan went on, "Another time, my ex-wife and I went to a party in the mountains on New Year's Eve. I had a good friend from the Law Department at the Catholic University of Lublin; Pope John Paul II was a professor there. My friend had a new girlfriend at the time, who had had a child before they met. Everyone in his family disliked her because she already had a child and didn't want him raising someone else's kid. Everybody was drinking and dancing. Anyway, the girlfriend was standing near me, and I started to talk to her, just to be polite. Suddenly, she started to spill her guts. She felt that her boyfriend's mom didn't accept her. She said she didn't decide to get pregnant: The child just happened because she allowed herself to get pregnant. She wanted to be a good mother, and now it seemed impossible."

Like the woman who wanted to be a good mother, which was impossible, Jan wanted to be a good psychiatrist to Amir, but Amir was gone, so now it was impossible. From the associations of an analysand, the analyst may infer patient dynamics. When a patient talks of someone else's experience, they may indirectly refer to their own inner/unconscious feelings. Any interpretation of such a displacement has to be confirmed by the patient's subsequent associations and responses.

"She felt punished. She felt she would be punished for the rest of her life because she'd made the mistake of getting pregnant. That night, I didn't party much; I just listened. She was grateful, and I felt that I had made a difference. My ex-wife was pissed at me. She said, 'People talk to you, and you don't know when to stop them.'"

"Perhaps we should learn from your ex-wife and know how to stop," I suggested. "As a warning, we have only a few minutes before *we* need to stop. However, I want to ask: Did you have any further contact with the Fossa Lady or the ZOMO man?"

"No. I tried to contact the Fossa Lady but failed."

"You came to psychiatry with a lot of hope that your listening skills would help you cure people. You have good examples of how you've helped others. It must have been disheartening that your efforts didn't succeed with Amir."

Jan got pensive. "That's true. But I feel that some other memories of my life are now available to me. This wasn't true when I first started to see you."

"Yes," I said, "I agree."

CHAPTER 12

As SOON AS HE WALKED INTO THE SESSION, Jan announced, "I had a dream. The dream took place in our apartment. In my dreams, and I guess in everyone else's, the features from different places and times are sometimes fused. For example, you might go from your parents' bedroom in Poland to your own living room in Oak Brook. In this dream, it looked exactly like my real apartment.

"In the dream, I came into my home office, where we have the computer, and my father was hanging there! His face was blue and ugly and puffed up. I know what the faces of people who have hanged themselves look like. There must be a doctor on every ambulance run in Poland, and I worked in the Accident and Emergency Department for several years to make extra money. In addition to the doctor, there are two paramedics and the driver. This team goes to places where emergencies may have occurred and do whatever can be done on the spot. Sometimes, they just deal with the minor pains of a hypochondriac. Other times, they confirm deaths. I had a lot of cases like that. There's a horrible look on the faces of people who have killed themselves.

"What I saw on my father's face was a mixture of different memories of the dead people I've seen. When I saw people hanging for weeks before we found them, I could pronounce them dead from 20 meters. No need for a stethoscope; it was obvious. These are not pleasant memories. Anyway, in my dream, I saw my father like that. He had hanged himself and looked hideous.

"My emotions were mixed. One feeling was that I had to do something. So I grabbed him and tried to rescue him. But I also felt angry, furious! Maria

135

was going to come home, and normally she would go into that room to work on the computer. I felt that he could have hanged himself anywhere—why in my apartment? I didn't want Maria to have an unforgettable memory of him hanging there. It was inconsiderate, it was rude, and it was inappropriate. I was really angry with him! He had killed himself in my apartment. She could have stepped into a shocking situation and have this ghastly image in her mind, as I do."

Jan's anger was palpable. He was so emotionally overwrought, and then he burst out laughing. People sometimes do that, spontaneously to break extreme tension. I wondered if Jan's father was a stand-in for Amir. Jan was recovering from Amir's trauma; his suicide truly exploded into Jan's life just before Maria and Jan married. Although Amir probably didn't know about Jan's upcoming wedding, the timing of his death in Chicago had reverberated in Rome. Both Jan's father and Amir understandably made Jan angry, but it was Amir's suicide that led to Jan's own suicidal fear of flying through windows. At this juncture, many analysts recommend considering a patient's transference to the analyst in interpreting a dream. However, given Jan's prevailing trauma relating to Amir's suicide, I felt pressing my role in this dream would be premature.

"Did you laugh because it's hard to talk about such feelings, and only laughter could break the tension? Did you feel your father alone caused all those feelings? Is your anger connected to more than your father?"

"Yes. Every death has had some impact on me: my patients on the oncology ward, the accidents I saw in the Accident and Emergency Department, family members, my ex-girlfriend, my mom."

I noticed that Jan had left out Amir. Was this an unconscious omission? Would his associations continue freely?

Jan continued, "Each death stays with you forever. It never goes away. I just don't want Maria to accumulate this kind of garbage. For instance, there was a young boy who was drunk and suicidal. The story was that he jumped from the dormitory at Jagiellonian University. The building was 10 stories high, maybe more. He jumped or fell from one of the topmost floors. As he was falling, he hit the roof of the main entrance. A big chunk of his torso and a leg tore off from his body. He fell to the ground literally in two pieces.

"My horrific job was to take samples, so the authorities could make some sense of how he died—whether he was drunk, poisoned, drugged. People were everywhere. Crowds always gather around such scenes. The uglier the scene, the more people tend to collect there.

"I saw many lonely people who'd died alone in their apartments. I went with a paramedic to see a guy who had been dead for weeks, and the smell in the apartment was incredible. I had to cover my nose and mouth with a handkerchief before approaching the man's body. His body was not only fly-ridden but infested with fly eggs and fly larvae or maggots crawling under the skin. You could see these moving things on the exposed parts of his hands and face. As we were leaving the apartment, the paramedic was so upset that he wanted to light up a cigarette. As he was trying to light his cigarette, he dropped his lighter in his anxiety—and it *exploded*. I had never seen a lighter explode in my life, but it happened then. It shocked and spooked me. I felt like someone was shooting at me. The presence of death and this freaky accident messed with my mind. When I returned home, I couldn't wash the rotten smell of the dead body off. After taking a shower, I sat for a few minutes, but I still smelled it. That day, I showered four times. I couldn't figure out if the smell was real or imaginary.

"I saw another guy who was hanging in his attic among clothes his wife was drying. Because the attic was low, he was almost touching the ground.

"Oh, and I also saw drowned people. Once there was a party, and a young drunk girl decided to swim and drowned. The other students from the university continued to party and didn't notice. Then they went home. When her family started to make inquiries, someone remembered that she had gone swimming. They began to fear that she had drowned. The police called in the Accident and Emergency Department, and we, in turn, had to call a specialized team that had diving equipment. Each team member could be under the water for only a limited time, so I started to talk to one of the divers. I told him that his job wasn't very pleasant, and I wondered how he dealt with it. I told him about the ugly stuff in my job, but I thought this was probably worse. He disagreed. He said that after the initial shock, you get into a routine. He said that it was a job, and you didn't have to think a lot about it; you just did it. He said, 'I keep my emotions out of it.'

"I replied, 'Wow, I wish I could be that resistant to death and ugliness.'

"He said, 'They pay us by the hour. We found the girl three hours ago. We'll announce that we found her in maybe two days. Our supervisor doesn't like to get into the water. He trusts us and doesn't check on us, so waiting is just extra money. We've tied her up to a pole to make sure she doesn't drift. She's safe.'"

Jan continued, "I couldn't believe this is how he was treating it! I found him repulsive. Winking at me, he said, 'When we discover the body, I'll call you. Maybe after that, you want to go for a beer?'

"I made up some excuse that I had other plans. This guy was creepy."

As Jan indicated, pain accumulates with each death. Indeed, it could destroy one's life. Amir was only the last in a series of deaths. The burden Jan felt with Amir's suicide was like the weight of Amir's dead camel on his chest. So many casualties already weakened him that he couldn't get out from under such a heavy load. As a result, Jan's own personality had succumbed to Amir's suicidal depression. His *joie de vivre* and his ambitions had gotten lost, leaving a diminished self, tinged with severe depression, if not suicidality, that resembled Amir's. He wouldn't heal unless time, maturity, or someone else helped relieve him of these burdens.

"I have tons of memories like these. Why did I put my father in this situation?"

I thought, *Jan, my man! Now you're starting to work on your problem.* I wanted to acknowledge his curiosity. "That's a good question."

"My father once tried to overdose on medication."

This was news to me. So, the dream was also about working through his father's suicide attempt.

Jan continued, "Once, my father was sick, and I drove him to an emergency room in Krakow. He was out of it. Delirious. It didn't matter what pills his doctors prescribed to him; he deliberately overdosed. He felt that he would get better if he took more of them. In Polish, we have a word for it: *lekoman*. It means a person who likes to take medicine—anything and everything that's a pill, they put into their mouth. Unfortunately, my father was able to get more drugs than were prescribed to him. He volunteered to manage and distribute gifts sent to Catholic charities in Poland, including medications close to their expiration dates donated by Western countries. As a chemical engineer, he was somewhat qualified to sort them out. That was how he got access to a storehouse of medications. Initially, he just used vitamins and supplements, but later, he took sedatives—more and more, until he was stoned for many hours a day. When he became depressed, he didn't have to look far for stuff to overdose on. It was a disaster waiting to happen. In the ER, they pumped his stomach. Then I drove him to my university to be seen by a psychiatrist. He was delirious all the way. The psychiatrist decided to admit him to the hospital and kept him there for about two weeks. I've never talked about this."

Jan was slowly overcoming his resistance to talking about topics that he had previously kept bottled up.

"When he recovered, I told him that his overdose was hypocritical. 'You're an Orthodox Catholic pushing everybody to be religious. Your actions negate everything you believe in. Trying to kill yourself is a mortal sin. As a Catholic, you can't do this.' He didn't try to justify himself. Now I understand how depression affected him. Now I know that depression can erase core beliefs and negate the instinct for self-preservation. It doesn't matter how religious you are. It takes away any hope for help from anywhere. You don't see it. You *can't* see it. My father was just deeply depressed. That was the only time I saw him in such bad shape.

"This was the ugly part of what he tried to do in real life. My father in the dream looked like those dead people I had found hanging in my job. I was afraid Maria would come home and see him, but I couldn't do anything because I tried to support his body. I don't know if I was talking to him or screaming at him. In the dream, I was furious. I don't remember if he talked back. It was a horrible dream—a nightmare.

"Over the next few days, I called my father a few times. As you remember, I used to call my mom frequently. I try to call him at least once a week. He's in a nursing home now, completely demented. Sometimes he recognizes me; sometimes, he doesn't. Once, I called when Sofia was there. After initially muttering something to me, she said he put the phone on his pillow and didn't even try to listen. *I was trying to talk to him, and he wasn't listening.* It was just one more time when I couldn't communicate with my father."

Amir didn't communicate with Jan concerning his suicidal ideations when he had them; there was a communication gap there, too. I wondered if Jan felt similarities between his father and Amir. "So, when you called your father, you two weren't communicating."

"Right. He slept in the day and was awake at night. I would ask him what day it was and what he had had for breakfast or dinner. Regardless of when I called him, he would say, 'I just got up. It's morning. I'm going to have a big breakfast.' He would say this when I called him in the afternoon in Chicago when it was night in Poland. I would say, 'It can't be. It's nighttime in Poland.'

"I don't think he had a concept of me being in a different country. He would say in a slurred voice, 'You didn't come to see me last week. Why didn't you come?' I told him, 'For the past 10 years, I've been in the United States. I do come to visit, but not that often.'

"Right after my mom died, he was more energetic for a while. We had some arguments over the phone. He was trying to turn me against Sofia. He would say things like, 'They're forcing me to do exercises and forcibly drugging me. They're rude. They're trying to make me move, but I'm an old man. I can't move. I need to be left alone. They're forcing things on me. Nobody feeds me. I have no money to buy newspapers.'

"Sofia told me that she'd arranged to have part of her paycheck automatically go to my father. So I told him, 'Sofia told me that she gives you money and that you have food and all the newspapers you want.'

"My father would reply, 'She's lying. Your sister is a liar. Don't believe her.'

"My father also told Sofia, 'Jan hasn't called me in months.' He said this while ignoring me by putting the phone on the pillow. Sofia showed him the record of the calls he had received in his room, including several from me. She told him, 'These phone records are the reality; your complaints are made up. He calls you roughly every week.' He still didn't believe her.

"Then my father started to complain. His room was bugged. The staff was trying to eavesdrop on his conversations. I tried to make light of it. 'Tell me,' I said. 'What secrets do you have that they want to overhear?'

"Just as my sister's showing him the phone log had no impact, my joke had no effect. When you realize that you're an 80-year-old guy, it's hard. Maybe you don't want to accept that you're getting weaker. It's more animating to believe people are spying on you or stealing your money. He's like a child.

"I don't know why my father was hanging in my dream. I'd had deep anger toward him for most of my life. A few times, I had fleeting thoughts of poisoning him, shooting him, or killing him somehow. But, on the other hand, I certainly had moments in my life when I felt that I wouldn't mind if he died.

"I also recall a dream from my early teenage years when he came home from work intoxicated. My mom was watching TV, and she turned it off to go to sleep. He insisted on turning it back on. She turned it off again. They argued. I was upset, and when I went to bed, I slammed the door to my room. That night, I dreamt that I actually killed him with a poker."

A poker, I thought. *Oedipus, Polish-style.*

Jan continued, "I just remembered something. I resent people who try to put themselves above other people. My father was often a tyrant at home. One evening, Sofia came home really late, and he blew up at her. I heard him screaming and went to see what was going on. I saw him raise his hand to hit her and felt a sudden rush of feelings. I grabbed his wrist and told him really calmly, 'I don't want to fight you. I just want you to leave her alone.'

"He got angry at my calm tone and said, 'I can do whatever I want in my house.' He tried to hit me, but I twisted his wrist, forcing him to sit down. He was furious and tried again. I got behind him so he couldn't reach me. He became angrier and angrier, foaming at the mouth, but I held him down. Finally, I told him I would let him go when he calmed down.

"He realized that I was stronger than him and that I wouldn't let him go until he agreed not to hit Sofia. I knew he was vanquished when he said, 'Let me go,' He lost the physical part of the fight, but he still wanted to hurt me, so he said, 'You're not my son.'"

Realizing how hurtful it must have been for Jan to hear those words and to make sure he knew that I heard them clearly, I asked, "Your dad actually said, 'You're not my son?' Those are the words he used?"

"Yes. My father was dramatic, a real drama queen."

I realized now that Jan was working through feelings toward his father. These were even more crucial to address than his feelings for Amir in the long run. Initially, I felt that Amir had inserted himself between Jan and Maria to the extent that she had sought treatment for him. Earlier in the session, I had thought that, in Jan's dream, his father was a stand-in for Amir, that in Jan's unconscious, Amir was the ugly body that deserved to be blue and hanging for the crime of interfering with Jan and Maria. However, as the session progressed, and especially after Jan revealed his homicidal impulses toward his father, I saw it differently. Jan could probably learn from considering the dream to reflect his feelings for both Amir *and* his father. In any analysis, some aspect of the analyst gets connected with negative feelings stemming from disappointments the patient has with their own mother and father. Still, such feelings toward the analyst take time to build and are often masked by the usually friendly nature of their encounters. Jan had experienced mistrust with his previous analyst. Whether he would feel such negativity toward me remained to be seen. For now, such ideas were a stretch. This was, however, proving to be a significant session.

Usually, the Oedipus complex consists of homicidal feelings a boy or man has toward his father within the context of the love each has for the mother/wife. The boy resents sleeping in his room while the dad gets to sleep with his mom. There's a pervasive and emotionally charged jealousy, and when aggressive or homicidal thoughts occur, guilt often accompanies them. All this is from the framework of the family romance, as understood from the boy's point of view. There are innumerable variants of the Oedipus complex. In this case, although separately confirmed, Jan's love for his mom was not immediately manifest in this session. That came before and would come again. The part of the Oedipus complex visible now was Jan's homicidal feelings toward his father interfering with his love life.

My view was that this dream also reflected Jan's deep anger toward Amir for intruding in his and Maria's life—especially by committing suicide just before their wedding. Thus, Jan's feelings toward his father and Amir were valid, and there was no single, correct way to understand them.

Dreams and fresh memories have a way of pointing a patient toward additional possibilities as to their meaning. I considered Jan's associations to be the best gauge for the progress of his analysis, and they were flowing freely. He had opened areas of experience and feeling previously inaccessible to him. And he was approaching them without the sense of compulsion that drove the prayers he kept repeating on his wedding day. Instead, he was viewing his current feelings through the lens of human curiosity. In this session, he had asked, "Why did I place my father in the dream?" Such curiosity would lead Jan to better self-understanding. My speculative ideas about Amir, while not insignificant, couldn't match Jan's own associations in terms of dosage or timing. Although the areas explored by Jan were different than I had expected, I was pleased with his pursuit of self-awareness.

His last memory, about prevailing against his father in an actual fight, arrived as he was getting ready to leave. It was crucial and would need extra elaboration. I would wait for the right moment. In the meantime, we had to stop.

CHAPTER 13

JAN PICKED UP RIGHT WHERE HE HAD LEFT OFF. "Since the last session, I've remembered many incidents from my childhood. My father had this massive, solid-oak credenza with a door, which he had reinforced, replacing the original simple locks with Yale locks, used in entrance doors for houses and businesses. That's where he kept all his memorabilia: family photos, university transcripts, letters, gold coins, U.S. dollars. It was also where he hid smuggled vintage French wines and Swiss chocolates. He pointed to the credenza throughout my childhood and, with a severe look, admonished me to 'never touch it.'

"As a boy, I mostly cared about the chocolate, but later I started to obsess about the locked-up wine, the forbidden fruit. Remember, these were times when good wine wasn't available in the stores—only cheap wine made of apples and strawberries and reeking of sulfur. Also, you couldn't get real chocolate, only chocolate-like products made of rapeseed oil and chicory.

"Thinking about the special goods locked inside my father's safe stimulated my imagination. I pictured myself tasting heaven in my mouth, but I didn't know how to pick the lock. I'd poked the locks with a straightened paper clip many times, and nothing ever happened. Then I started to study Yale locks systematically. Using technical drawings, I took one apart and understood how they worked.

"So, the big day finally came. I got two pieces of steel wire to fit the lock. Thinking '*Open, Sesame*,' I twisted the wires, and the lock snapped open! I unwrapped and tasted the chocolate-covered cherries with cognac. They were delicious. I looked at the wine bottles and realized there was no easy way to taste the wine. They were corked. The winery seals on the tops of the bottles ensured that my father would instantly notice if someone had tampered with them, but I was driven to solve this problem.

"I was 14 at the time. I went through the toolbox, looking for inspiration. The idea came when I saw a big syringe with a 10 cm-long needle, which I used to fill the fuel tank of my remotely controlled model plane with ether. I remember the first bottle I breached: a 1974 Bordeaux from Baron Philippe de Rothschild Chateau Mouton. Carefully, I drew out enough wine to fill the wine glass. Then I brushed my teeth, sat in the armchair, and held the glass up to the light. I smelled it, celebrating the moment for a long while. Finally, I tasted it. It wasn't as good as I had expected."

Jan's recollection of picking the lock on his father's private credenza and draining his dad's wine bottles with a syringe and his dream about killing him with a poker are themes that are rich with possibilities for any number of analytic interpretations. I had been impressed by Jan's longstanding guilt-ridden personality and wondered if his guilt—unexpressed and hidden in this session—was something I should interpret. Pleased by the flow of Jan's new memories and eager to see where his associations and self-understanding would lead, I pondered whether to make some connection to his guilt or to let him go at his own pace.

I said, "You were naughty as a boy. You picked your dad's lock. You dreamt of killing him with a poker. It sounds like you were butting heads with him for a long time."

"Not only did I fight, but slowly I developed some feelings for him."

"Feelings?" I asked.

"Yes, pity and guilt. A few days later, I tried another wine and didn't like it at all. It was quite austere, with a bitter aftertaste. Over the next few months, I tried all of them until Christmas. The level got visibly lower in three or four bottles, and I had to inject water to correct the lost volume. Christmas came, and my father decided to impress the rest of the family with a special treat on Boxing Day. He opened a bottle and said proudly, 'You've never tried anything like this before.'

"This was the one I had diluted the most. One of my uncles gave a toast, and everybody tasted the wine. There was a long silence, probably because nobody wanted to sound ignorant, but then my Aunt Malgorzata spoke up. She said she could think of a few cheap fruit wines that tasted better. The rest of the family agreed, and each new comment was worse than my aunt's. They were joking and laughing for a long while. My father probably shared their opinion, but he wouldn't admit it. He just waved his hand and told them that it took a certain level of sophistication to appreciate good wine. I felt sorry for him.

"My father often traveled to work in France or Germany. Then, around the Polish Martial Law in 1980, my father left for about two years and lived in Germany. Sofia and I felt that that was the most beautiful time as a family: Sofia and me and Mom . . . and no father.

"Life was peaceful without him. We had fun every day, cooking fancy suppers with my mom, having parties for the extended family, and having conversations that didn't result in arguments. Sofia and I dreaded the day that my father would come back.

"My father, in his penny-pinching way, locked the car in the garage before he left. At the time, Poland rationed gas. Somehow, using his influence, my father had been able to purchase two 50-gallon barrels of gas before he left, but he didn't want us to use it. He measured the gas level with a long dipstick. He inserted it all the way into the barrel, and when he removed it, you could see the oil level. He carved a notch on the stick where the fluid level was, wrote the date, and put his signature next to it.

"On the day before he took the train to Berlin, he asked me to go to the garage with him. I was hoping that he would tell me I could use at least a little of the gas. Instead, he just showed me the stick and said he didn't want to see even one drop missing when he returned. I was angry for allowing myself to hope that he would have a change of heart. I had gotten screwed once again. The first weekend after his departure, I spoke with my mom about her friend from the sanatorium, with whom she corresponded regularly. She lived in a small town north of Warsaw, and they hadn't seen each other in many years. Sofia and I decided to take Mom on a road trip almost instantly.

"Mom smiled and told us that she would love to go but didn't know where the car keys were or how to fill the tank without using my father's stash. We called my cousin and a few family friends. Nobody could help. Gas was in short supply. Finally, my mom gave up, but we were determined. We went to the garage and searched methodically—no keys. We sat at the gate, looking around, trying to see everything with our father's eyes.

"Then Sofia got up and started to shake the paint cans. Bingo! The keys were rattling inside one of them. Now we just had to find some gas. Suddenly, an idea struck me. He hadn't measured the length of the dipstick submerged in the gas but only marked where the top of the fluid was on it. If I took some of the gas and then cut the dipstick from the bottom, the mark my father had made would still match the gas level in the barrel, and it would appear as if the amount of gas was unchanged. I did this many times when my father was gone. I probably cut one-third of the stick, taking plenty of gas from each barrel. After that, we went to visit my mom's friend. After that, we would sometimes just cruise around our town, visiting old castles, churches, and famous battle sites.

"I wouldn't have minded if my father had never come back at all, but immediately after having such a thought, or a homicidal thought, I would feel guilty. There was a time when I was still going to confession. It was hard to confess to homicidal fantasies and ideas against your own father. The priests were always sensitive to such confessions. It was unpleasant."

"What would they say?"

"'Killing your father is the worst thought that can cross your mind. It violates two of God's Ten Commandments: 'Thou shall honor thy father and thy mother' and 'Thou shalt not kill.' Therefore, you should be doubly ashamed of such thoughts.'

"When my father returned, he was rude and inconsiderate toward my mom. When he spoke in a certain way, I knew my mom was going to cry. There was no doubt about it. He was going to make her cry. If she had a suggestion about improving the house, he ridiculed the idea in front of Sofia and me. If she wanted a bathroom remodeled, he criticized her for not caring for the house. He wouldn't stop even when she had tears in her eyes. I hated him then. This happened many times over such an extended period, whether he was coming back from a long trip or just coming home from work.

"After our mom died, Sofia and I talked about our feelings about our childhood, probably the first conversation we'd ever had about it. She was relieved to talk; she said she couldn't tell anybody but me. She told me that she was afraid of our father. There were all these things she had to do as a daughter. She had to be nice and tell him that she loved him. If he said, 'I love you,' whether in person or on the phone, she felt obligated to say, 'I love you, too.' It wasn't easy for her to speak those words.

"When Sofia and I were busy with funeral arrangements for my mom, my father became obsessed with wanting a pedicure *right then*. He was in a nursing home at that point and suffering from dementia, but I think he understood the concept of my mom being dead. He insisted that he needed the pedicure *that day*. That was it. Sofia lost it.

"He was hypocritical in his justifications. When I was a child, he punished me with a belt. Many times, I deserved it, but often I didn't. Sometimes, after he beat me, I would cry. Then he would say, 'This is how my father made me who I am. This is how my father made me a decent person.' He told me how he greeted his father when he returned from the university and later when he was an adult. 'Whenever I saw my father, I always kissed his hand. I kissed his hand because it was this hand that made me a decent person.'

"When I was in my twenties and thirties, I made fun of my father, especially after he'd made a fool of himself. I would say, 'There's no consensus that you're a decent person. Sometimes, you act like an ass. Before you decide that you're a decent person, you should ask many other people whether you're a decent person. What you think about yourself isn't that relevant. You have to ask your wife. You have to ask your co-workers. You have to ask your children. They can tell you if you're a decent person. Otherwise, it's simply your own personal opinion.'

"I was much more eloquent in Polish than I am in English. Whatever angle he used, I would shoot his opinion down till he became angry and stunned. He finally stopped talking to me about his 'decent' upbringing. I told him, 'Your childhood stories seem pathological to me.' He was furious. After I confronted him and put him down when he was rude and intimidating to Sofia, he never touched me again. He used only his verbal skills.

"He was always fond of his mother, but I hated her. I would try to avoid seeing her by pretending to be sick. If I had to go, I would spend time with Uncle Bozydar, whom she disrespected as 'an alcoholic and a disgrace.' I thought Uncle Bozydar was the coolest guy ever. Oh, I wanted to get back to my dream and got carried away."

"That's the way self-understanding is. You can never know, beforehand, where it will go."

"I don't understand this dream. I don't wish that my father was dead now. I wish we could talk, but he's too demented to maintain a conversation. I don't even want to throw whatever I'm holding against him in his face. If only we could talk, and he could understand how I feel."

Although he couldn't talk to his dad, Jan's depiction of his family gave it a vivid quality that helped explain where his dream had come from. He had laid bare the strained connections between his father and the rest of the family. Now, Jan's thoughts seemed to roam more freely. Despite his angst over the estrangement from his father, I felt that Jan seemed to have found a new freedom. Therefore, I thought that it was a good session. I wanted Jan to leave with the feeling of accomplishment for having discovered this freedom that had allowed him to recover so many forgotten memories. Whether

Jan connected Amir to the dream or not seemed to be less important now than I had previously thought, mainly because Jan's emotional outpouring constituted a significant Oedipal working-through of his hostile feelings for his father. "One thing you mentioned about this dream was that your father should have known better than to subject Maria to such a shock. He should have spared her that pain."

Hesitatingly, Jan started, "Yes, it crossed my mind, but I didn't tell you. I felt that this dream primarily dealt with my not wanting to be like my father. My father used to scream. When I get heated, I feel like screaming. Whenever I so much as raise my voice, I feel ashamed because I don't want to be like my father. In the dream, I was screaming. So, in my dream, I hanged my father. I was killing whatever was in me that resembled my father. I don't want Maria to see it. I don't like this interpretation because it means that I'm like my father. It feels good to think that I don't share many personality traits with my father. He was stingy. He controlled money and deprived my mom and our family.

"My father was like his mother. She was a wealthy woman. She had a lot of money, but because she lived in times of great political strife and danger, she kept buying gold and jewelry and hiding it. Supposedly, she buried gold and other valuables in her backyard. When she died suddenly, no one knew where it was. My father combed her backyard with a metal detector, looking for the hidden treasure, but he never found anything!

"My mom and her older sister, Aunt Marta, were not only sisters; they were best friends. They talked about everything and shared secrets. More than I can even imagine, my aunt knows so many things about what happened between my father and mother. She's almost 80 now. After my mom died, I tried to talk to her, but she would go only so far. She probably doesn't want me to hate my father, and so she remains discreet. One exception was a letter my aunt showed me about my father. 'Physically, you're like your father,' she said, 'but you're so different as a person.' What she said was like music to my ears."

Jan was reliving and reassessing his earlier life from the vantage point of an adult. He expressed his hostility toward his father, understood his guilt, and explored the complex similarities and dissimilarities between him and his father. He was undeniably functioning better.

As an analyst, I felt that my initial success at helping his depression was significant. In contrast to his customary expectation of fatherly malevolence, Jan appreciated his progress and my attempt to help him.

An analyst hopes that a patient will eventually come to see him as he is, but also in ways reflecting his impressions of his parents. Indeed, during proper treatment, one expects such a development. If Jan experienced me only as a benevolent presence, somewhat as he felt toward his mother, that would be a limited analysis. I had helped him when he had walled off the world and feared jumping out a window. So I felt Jan would resist seeing me negatively, but his problems included a dose of negativity toward his father and dealing with the adversity of Amir's suicide. Initially, Jan's problem was conscious rage at his father and, perhaps later, unconscious anger at Amir. His current inclination was to protect me from such feelings. So I had to remain patient till he genuinely was upset at me for something. Jan had cycled through many connections the dream had to his father. I felt links to Amir might add still more. I eagerly anticipated looking into Amir's possibilities.

"Just because you're your father's son doesn't mean that you have to be like him," I began. "I'm glad that your aunt, who knew your father, could say that your character was different from his. You asked several times about the meaning of this dream. You've shared a powerful recounting of the amount of hammering you took from witnessing death, negative feelings for your father, and how it affected your life. The way I thought about the dream in one area was on a different track from the one you took. My idea may add to your thoughts; I don't intend for it to replace them. As you said, the theme of the dream is that your father, through his hanging, could hurt Maria. The best way for me to introduce my thoughts is through a question. Who else, other than your father, hurt Maria by his death?"

Jan seemed preoccupied and said, "Say that again. Sorry, I couldn't follow. I understand your question, but I don't know how to answer it."

Ah, I thought, *do I have to pay for my therapeutic ambition and overzealousness so soon?* I was struck by how concretely Jan had been in exploring his dream. He had followed thoughts about his father to the logical end that his memories, associations, and emotions would allow. Still, he couldn't see that his father might also represent somebody else. It became clear, to me, that the chain of thoughts that I was entertaining could represent a direction that Jan was unprepared to travel. That was why he couldn't understand my question; my principal goal was never to clarify a *single correct* meaning of a dream or symptom. There may be only one correct interpretation in religion or dogma, but the premise of psychoanalysis is that there often are other unconscious implications in addition to the conscious meaning.

I merely wanted to clarify my point of view, enable him to pick what made sense, and let the rest go.

Jan asked, "Whom do you have in mind, specifically?"

"Amir," I answered reluctantly.

Jan protested, "But when Amir committed suicide, he didn't hang himself!"

Then Jan looked like lightning had struck him. "I was thinking that I . . . Wow, I completely blocked this. I completely blocked out Amir. So when you started to speak, it made perfect sense to me. It did cross my mind before, but I was in a different mood and just couldn't go there."

"So, you may have been angry at Amir, too, the way you were angry at your father in the dream?"

"Yes, I was angry at Amir. I was furious. When I called the Cook County Hospital, I wasn't sure of his condition. I wanted to go there and be the first person he saw when he opened his eyes. I wanted to tell him how angry and pissed I was and how stupid he had been. Then I found out that he didn't make it, and everything changed."

"You were angry like the Polish priest who chided you for having the anti-Ten Commandments thoughts against your father . . . "

"It wasn't one priest; it was many priests. The thought crossed my mind on several occasions. Those confessions are . . ."

Brutal, I thought.

Jan veered. "Do you know the technical details of how confessions occur? Do you know how a confession happens?"

"Tell me."

"In the Catholic Church, you have a special place called a confessional."

"Yes."

"You enter the confessional. It's like a little booth with a dome. Instead of windows, there's a grate. You can't see the other person's face, just the silhouette. You can hear the voice, but you don't know who's sitting on the other side. You're supposed to talk to the priest about your sins. How do you know what sins are? They teach you! They teach you from the time you're in kindergarten. They teach you about sins in religion classes, so you know what to talk about when you're in the confessional. They tell you about the cardinal sins. And the creative priests interpret the Ten Commandments so that practically any action can be sinful. The basic message is, 'Whatever you do, be careful; it may be a sin.' You can become so anxious that you're paranoid. The question always playing on your conscience is whether you are sinning. Is this something I can do? Or is it something I can't?

"When you enter the confessional, there's a protocol. First, you initiate the confession with a sentence that you have to memorize."

"How does it go?"

"'The last time I was at confession was on such and such a date. Since then, I committed the following sins.' Then off you go. My list was always elaborate. I never liked it. I don't know how they made me go there. It just happened—especially the sins of a sexual nature, like sexual fantasies and masturbation. As a boy, they're impossible to say. They made you confess such sins anyway. I don't know how they managed it. No priest liked the kind of confessions I proffered. No one wanted to hear homicidal thoughts.

"After you finish your confession, the priest gives you a symbolic punishment. The punishment is to repeat the "Holy Mary, Mother of God" prayer a certain number of times. It may be a hundred prayers a day. It may be a hundred prayers each day for a week. Sometimes, they use rosaries to keep track of your punishments. It depends. It depends on their assessment of the nature of your sins. After confessions, the boys always met and asked each other, 'How much did you get?' Or 'How much did he hit you with?' You know, 'How much punishment did you get?'"

"*Bad boy!*" I scolded in jest.

"Yes, 'How much of a bad boy have you been?' Sometimes, the dorky guys, the nerds, exaggerated their punishment. To get a lot of punishment was 'cool.' I never liked to do this, but I felt compelled to do the punishment, so I came up with a genius method for dealing with the problem. Sometimes, I did penance in advance of a sin. I said extra prayers and held that excess in a surplus account, so the next time I went, I could deduct the extra penance I held in store if the priest levied a heavy punishment. I would calculate that I had three hours worth of prayers stored in my account, so why not put in six more hours to be free the next time I go to confession?

"I also have fun memories about this time. When I was young, the priests were an integral part of the neighborhood. They were like an older cousin or a remote family member. The rule of the parish was that the priest had to visit every house. He would survey the family to find out how religious it was. He would make notes and put them into the record. The family had to be good hosts and honor the priest when he came. It was customary to prepare a snack and offer him a shot of good alcohol. After they visited about six families, the priest was smashed drunk. Even at only one shot per family, that's six shots. Some priests were helpful. Sometimes, the priests acted as marriage counselors if a couple were having problems. Most were Good Samaritans; a few were arrogant assholes.

"There was a priest many suspected of liking young girls. No one caught him, but the suspicion persisted, so he never visited anybody: No family with young girls would invite him to their house. Finally, the church removed him from the parish. I can't remember his name. Many of the priests were in the Underground and fought the Communists. For this, they received universal praise. They didn't do anything extraordinary, but they kept a Catholic and anti-Communist spirit alive. For example, they assigned a priest to a small parish with no church near where I lived. The Communists said that there were too many churches, so they couldn't build a new one. This priest conspired with a lot of farmers who were Orthodox churchgoers. Almost overnight, they built a new church. One evening, there was no church, and the next morning, there was a new church. People from far-off villages came and prayed there. Of course, it wasn't finished, but it had a cross on top and people inside. That was an explosive combination. The Communists didn't dare say or do anything against it. There would have been a riot if they had tried to pull down the church, yank out the cross, or harm the people. There was no way to remove it."

We were at the close of the session. I thought, *How close to reality are our ghosts? The answer is, I suppose, it depends. Sometimes, they're closer than we imagine and seem very real. And other times, they're almost entirely only fears. For example, Jan feared getting angry and loud.* I now had the opportunity to comment on Jan's fear that, like his father, he was loud. "We should be stopping soon, but I want to say something before we do. You said that you were shouting at your father in the dream."

"Yes. I was furious and screaming at the same time."

I asked, "I wonder if you feared that the screaming in your dream might be like your father's everyday screaming?"

"I've always paid so much attention to not screaming because every time I raised my voice as a boy, my mom's family members said, 'You're like your father.' I felt that that was a slap in the face. So I was loud but rarely screaming or raging. My father, in contrast, often lost control of himself and screamed."

Today, Jan had been somewhat emotional, but he never raised his voice in my presence. "You've had a very trying time since Amir died. I feel that now you're finding it safer to be yourself. You feel you can explore your feelings of anger and homicide and the sense that Amir and others have injured you. I'm sure you wanted to scream when fate tortured you, like Munch's *The Scream*. You became emotional, as if you were a child or an adolescent, and didn't control your feelings. Although this is your fear, I don't see you as a screamer."

Jan smiled. "I'm sure that I was displaying my emotions today more than I normally do."

"So, it was uncharacteristic?" I asked.

"Whenever I spoke to my *mom*, I was always cheerful and definitely in control."

"With me, you are like you were with your mom."

"Yes."

CHAPTER 14

"Since I found out that Maria and I are having a baby, I've changed. It's a primal feeling. I'm not sure if you know what I'm talking about."

"Tell me."

"It's not a rational feeling. I'm participating in a miracle. I'm part of it, and I'm witnessing it."

"That's right."

"I know that I'll be the most important person for someone. Creating life is a gut feeling. When I spoke to Maria about having children, I didn't feel this. Having discussions or imagining being a dad never grabbed me in a way that I can compare to how I feel now. I am compelled to imagine this person. We don't know yet if it's a boy or a girl. I'm excited about this basic feeling. It's a nonverbal feeling. I can't express what I'm feeling. It . . . it . . . it . . ."

I wanted to share in this life moment and had a corny idea. So I added, "It connects you to the embryo! Or perhaps I should say *eukaryote*—the life force in all of us."

"Yes, yes—that's it! This is the first time I've felt that I'm in the presence of a life force. I'm part of it. I created it along with Maria. She feels it in her feminine way. So I enjoy every day."

Enjoyment! Good mood changes for Jan, I thought.

Jan continued, "I wake up with a good feeling. My main anxiety is about the kind of father I'm going to be. What kind of mistakes am I going to make? How do I avoid them? Am I doomed to be like my father? What kind of nurturing will we be able to give our baby?"

"I'm going to say something to you . . . in a humorous manner."

"OK."

As I spoke, I laughed. "As a physician, you know, 'First, do no harm.' We got that from Hippocrates. As a dad, I would say, 'First, do not shout.' In the dream that we talked about last time, you said that shouting was something you didn't want to do because it reminded you of your father."

"What you just said is also serious. I think every day about how not to be like my father. But I'm conflicted because I also feel that I owe my very existence to my father. It's because of him that I'm here. I should experience gratitude toward my father. I feel it toward my mother, but I don't feel it toward my father. He invested that one sperm in me. I should be grateful. Rationally, I appreciate it. I know that I'm here because of him. Have you heard the story of Salvador Dalí and his father?"

"Tell me."

"Salvador Dalí had a complicated relationship with his father. For many years, they didn't speak. Instead, they wrote bitter and nasty letters to each other. After one such exchange, Salvador Dalí masturbated into an envelope and sent it to his father. Dalí said that he was returning his father's investment. My confusion is that I feel guilty immediately after I have an opinion critical of my father.

"Yesterday, we talked about my dream of killing my father. I've had that kind of dream more than once. Every time, even if he dies from some other cause, I end up feeling guilty."

So, I thought, *my job is to help Jan understand and reduce his ferocious guilt.*

Jan continued, "I always felt guilty—as if *I* had killed him. Some of these dreams were vivid when I awoke, but they gradually faded. I have only a faint memory of the content now, but I know what my feelings were. I don't believe that dreams are some supernatural phenomenon. A dream is simply a way of processing experience. Dreams that include my father have a lot of violence. In that sense, they mirror my actual relationship with him. We had many verbal arguments and occasionally physical ones. I enjoyed disrespecting him. I knew that that was what hurt him most.

"Before he had dementia, I tried to do this many times. I told you about Uncle Bozydar, who was in the Polish Underground during World War II. When I was a kid, I saw Uncle Bozydar as a hero. I felt he risked his life and devoted his life to free Poland. He succeeded but became a wreck in the process. His father, my paternal grandfather, was also involved in the war. He, too, did his part in liberating Poland. He wasn't in the Underground, but he supported their members financially. He helped hide them when necessary and so on. I feel that both of them deserve respect.

"My father was born in 1928. After the war was over, he started to tell stories of his life as an Underground soldier. He was never a partisan, but he called himself a "courier." He said he passed information from one unit to a different team in the forest. He claimed that he was shot in the butt by Germans. If anyone questioned him, he showed them the scar. Then he changed the story and said he participated in meetings with some guys in the Underground.

"I had mixed feelings about his so-called exploits. I felt that he was an old man trying to make himself feel better. It was OK, but I didn't like it. He told so many people about it that he started to believe the stories himself. He became quiet when he realized that I was close enough to overhear his stories. I think he felt ashamed that he wanted to impress people so much that this need made him untruthful. That's why I never used it against him in our arguments. I simply dismissed his stories as a joke and made fun of them to my mom. She never said anything."

"From the history of Poland during World War II," I asked, "do you know the age of the youngest documented Underground partisan or courier?"

"There were several children; some of them even used guns. I know of a documented case of an eleven-year-old boy who participated in the Warsaw uprising in 1944."

"Your dad would have been sixteen in 1944?"

Jan calculated aloud, "Forty-four minus twenty-eight . . . yes, he was sixteen then. He claimed that the Germans shot him in the butt in 1940 or 1941, so he would have been twelve or thirteen. He could have been injured after the war, but he claimed it was during the war. I don't know what to think about it."

"You've seen the scar?"

"Oh, yes."

"That's how life is," I said half-jokingly. "Even paranoid people link their delusions to some kernel of truth. He had a scar that was real, which may or may not be linked to his story."

"That's true, but these small episodes mushroomed until he was linking himself to real heroes of the Underground. I was angry because he diminished the Underground by doing this. Every time he told a story, I felt that he was working a scam, but I also began to feel guilty for thinking so."

"If he wasn't a partisan, what do you think he was?"

"Maybe he was carrying messages and was a partisan, after all. Maybe he did it once. Maybe . . . Based on what I know about my father, I can't tell you. I'm not sure what he really was or is. I know who his brother was: He was a fighter for the Polish Underground Army. As a teenager, I glorified war. War stories and the biographies of war heroes were appealing to me. I spent sleepless nights reading books like *Krzyzacy: Knights of the Teutonic Order,* by Polish Nobel Prize winner Henryk Sienkiewicz. I idolized famous Polish knights. I learned about the famous Battle of Grunwald, which took place in 1410, and acted it out with lead toy soldiers; this was one of the most glorious battles in Polish military history, when the joint forces of the Polish Kingdom and the Lithuanian Duchy broke the power of the Teutonic Knights. The German knights were knights and also priests and . . . What's the male counterpart of nuns?"

"Monks?"

"Monks, yes," Jan continued. "They were knight-monks. They were powerful, especially in the north of Poland. But unfortunately, after the Battle of Grunwald, they were greatly weakened and never regained their previous influence. As a child, I loved to read stories about this part of Polish history and ran around with a wooden sword, eager to kill every Teutonic knight I found. Later, my fascination with history expanded and included other glorious eras of Polish history.

"At some point, I also had a taste for violence. When I was growing up, fighting was an accepted way to resolve conflicts. After school, the organized fights always took place under a pine tree just outside the school gate. Older boys served as referees, ensuring that the rules were followed: The rules prohibited the use of knives, legs, and teeth. After anyone drew the first blood, the referee called the winner. Fights determined the pecking order, and stories of these bouts circulated for weeks. Avoiding contests was considered dishonorable and shameful. My childhood heroes made me a person who wasn't afraid to pick fights with older and bigger boys. I became a popular fighter and known in my neighborhood for my fighting techniques.

"Then something changed. About halfway through high school, I lost interest in fighting. Gradually, I became a pacifist. Things that had fascinated me when I was a boy—wars, warfare, military tactics—lost their appeal. But in Communist Poland, after you graduated from high school, you had to complete two years of compulsory military training. If you were pursuing higher education, it was less. After medical school, I was supposed to be on military duty for two months. The training included target shooting with an AK-47, classes in military strategy and organization of battlefield military hospitals, and a brief course in Marxism and Leninism. I didn't want to waste my time doing any of this. With some help from my father, I found a doctor who gave me a certificate saying that physical exertion could cause me to have a potentially life-threatening arrhythmia. I got excused after less than two weeks! I had heard of people who wanted to be in the army, but I couldn't imagine myself being part of any military. I couldn't see myself killing people for any reason or getting killed for any cause. Fortunately, war never happened to me.

"The military training came hand-in-hand with propaganda. During a conversation with Dr. Schwartz, the topic moved to double-talk. He started to describe it to me, but I told him he could spare his efforts, as I grew up in a Communist country and know all about double-talk.

"It's hard to explain Polish propaganda to people who didn't live through it. The propaganda in Communist countries was deceptive, intrusive, and primitive. The Polish government erased any parts of history from the schoolbooks that contradicted the official claims of Soviet-Polish friendship. In 1940, almost 22,000 Polish officers and intellectuals were murdered in and around Katyn by the Soviets, but you'll never find it in Soviet history books. We knew about it, though. Everybody knew, but you couldn't talk about it openly. Families kept the truth about it alive by passing it down from generation to generation. Propaganda was incredibly destructive in the military. I think it could make a person believe that black is white. It's like American soldiers who go to Iraq and feel that they're fighting for freedom. They don't ask any questions. They go there and kill and maybe get injured or die, and they think that they're fighting for a noble cause.

"I'm not trying to demonize Communism. There were a few good things about growing up in a Communist country, like free education and more-or-less free universal healthcare. The dark times of Polish martial law, between December 1981 and July 1983, also had some positive aspects. If we were out after curfew, we stayed where we were, often in someone else's house. This built up my circle of friends and also my capacity to make friends. I developed deep relationships that continue to this day. We were only teenagers, but we didn't talk about trivial stuff; we talked about important stuff, like changing the course of history."

"Maybe your father, who was a young teenager during World War II, expanded his role in it to make himself feel better. There may or may not be some kernel of truth to his War; because of his dementia, it is almost impossible to tease it out. However, one thing that came up today is that he easily provoked your anger, which easily rolls into guilt."

"My question is whether my guilt is my own or whether it was the result of manipulation by my father. I've asked this question so many times, but I can't answer it. He was masterful at making me feel guilty, especially if I did something against him.

"There was a Polish TV theatre play called *Wooden Plate*. It's about a kind old man who lived with his family. He wasn't ambulatory, so when a huge flood came, they left him in his room on the top floor with some food on a wooden plate; the plate was made of wood, not porcelain, because he was clumsy and dropped stuff. They all escaped, but he died.

"My father repeatedly used the metaphor of the wooden plate to try to make Sofia, my sister, and me feel guilty, but over the years, we grew immune to it. Whenever he mentioned the wooden plate, we laughed because we knew that he was manipulating us to make us feel guilty: as if he were good, like the man in the play, and we, his children, were abandoning him."

"When you interact with another person, they could put a guilt trip on you. What about the guilt you have in a dream or after a dream? I ask because you said something before like, 'Every time I imagine killing my father, or he dies in my dreams, I feel guilty.'"

Jan was silent for a long time. "I feel guilty. I feel guilty. That's all there is to it. Every time my father is killed by me or dies in my dreams . . . In a dream I had some time ago and only vaguely remember, I had to decide who was to die: my father, my sister, or Maria. Of course, I picked my father. When I woke up from the dream, I felt very guilty. I didn't try to come up with an idea to rescue all of them. I didn't do anything heroic. I accepted that I had to make this decision and chose my father. Whenever I don't call him for more than a week, I feel guilty.

"Not long ago, we had a busy weekend when the 19-year-old son of one of my best friends came to the United States from Poland to stay with us. I had to pick him up at the airport and make various arrangements. Bottom line: I was so busy, I didn't call my father. For one whole week afterward, I didn't call my father, and I felt so guilty. When I call, my father usually doesn't know who's talking to him for the first few minutes. He doesn't listen. I told you, Sofia says that sometimes he just puts the phone down while I'm talking."

I thought of Sofia and Jan laughing when their father mentioned the wooden plate. I felt a slight twinge of empathy for Jan's dad and also some guilt, as a line from a Beatles song wafted through my memory: 'How can you laugh when you know I'm down?'

"When did you start experiencing the guilt?" I asked. "Is there any connection to the onset of his dementia?"

"He has evoked guilt in me all my life; it has nothing to do with him being out of it. Every time my thoughts went too far, I felt it. I would think that it would be nice if my father didn't come back home, and then I would feel guilty. Finally, I was compelled to confess it in my religious period, and it caused me further embarrassment and more guilt—you know, the Ten Commandments. I had no problem respecting my mother, but the rule includes your father. Because every day I had disrespectful thoughts toward my father—my guilt really impaired me.

"I wanted my family to be picture-perfect. From the outside, it looked nice: two educated parents and two children with bright futures. I dreamt that my family would feel as good on the inside as it looked from the outside. It was like that briefly, when my father came back from Germany. There was an evening when I felt connected to him and felt that our family was whole. He finally got it! He had changed: He had grown a beard. He wore not-so-conservative clothes. He looked like a cool guy. That day, my dad watched me fight a guy on the street just below his window, establishing my street cred, and he cheered me on from his window."

I noted that Jan, on this occasion, felt connected to his "dad" when he, from a window, cheered Jan on during a regular fight to establish his street cred. At that time, Jan even saw his dad as a cool guy. Previously, Jan had always used the word "father," with hostile or antagonistic connotations. I understood his feelings because once his father disowned him after a fight. Although the two words, "father" and "dad," described the same person, only one stood out in Jan's heart. Jan mainly experienced the hostile "father" from his childhood to this day. The "dad" was a rare and precious entity that peeked out today. Although a singular event, I believe, the word "dad," with positive connotations, may have the potential for further links. In the future, if Jan could remember more instances of his dad's encouragement, a dad might become a more significant entity. Coming to better terms with his past could also decrease the darkness associated with his father and result in a more textured and non-split combined father-dad.

I pondered how best to draw Jan's attention to and clarify this single time he used the word "dad" without overblowing its significance. Jan always had displayed a ferocious and persistent resentment toward his father. Till now, I had used the term "father" as Jan did. But, now, I resolved to use "dad." However, my use of the word "dad" would be appropriate when some affection was attached to a situation; it would not be a credible term if associated with hostility in that context. However, for a dad to become meaningful, Jan had to bridge the gap between his attitudes of hatred and affection; this may simultaneously reduce the distance between "father" and "dad." However, moving from "father" to "dad" and merging them was not a linguistic proposition; it required a change in Jan's heart. Jan didn't need to stay hostage to the idea of having only a "father"; maybe he could construct a "dad." Whenever I used it, I wanted the dad's quotient to be significant, plausible, and tolerable for Jan. My overzealous "dad" interpretation could easily result in Jan rejecting the notion that his *father* could also be an occasionally affectionate *dad*.

I said, "When he encouraged you, in your fight, from his window, you saw him as a dad. He even appeared *cool*."

"The feeling lasted one day. The next day, he started to fight with my mom, which was the end of the dream. He accused her of wanting to spend too much money. Then he gave a massive donation to a church, but he didn't want to tell my mom. He hoped that this donation would influence the church to appoint him a deacon. My father was friends with a corrupt priest, so the offering paid off, and my father became a deacon. I don't know how much money was involved. I never spoke to him about it. This is only one example of his shadiness and hypocrisy.

"My father was obsessed with saving and hiding, but I couldn't save. I was more of a 'live in the moment' guy. Once, when I was about twelve, a money wire transfer came by mail. I signed it on behalf of my father and took the money. My mom knew the money was supposed to come, and somehow, she figured out I had taken it. She said loudly, 'I have to go to the post office and tell them that the money is missing.' She made me feel guilty in a way that I couldn't tolerate, and I immediately confessed. Then she made me admit it to my father and apologize.

"My father's first question when I got a job as a doctor was, 'How much are you making?' Money was his primary concern. Even now, when he has dementia and doesn't understand much, he asks money-related questions. For the past twenty years, I've had the same answer: 'I make enough.' That was my answer regardless of my actual financial status. I never gave him numbers. That would have given him too much pleasure.

"Even saying that makes me feel guilty. I can't stop myself."

I assigned great importance to that one good interaction between Jan and his father when his father watched the street fight and cheered him on. When Jan talked about it, he called him his *dad*—but it was an isolated memory. In general, his *father* remained *only* a bad guy. For Jan to progress, that label had to change. Similarly, Jan saw me as *only* a good guy. That, too, would need to change.

I had identified a goal, but getting there was something else. I said, "Well, you know, your father gave you many reasons to be disappointed and angry at him and . . ." I briefly paused as I struggled to find words to complete the sentence as I wished.

"I want to say I agree," Jan interjected, "but that would make me feel even guiltier."

I continued, "The thing is that you went beyond a tipping point with your anger, so it's been hard for you to recover from your corresponding guilt. You didn't have a chance to work it through. He wasn't home. Then he came home and was good for just one day. And then he developed dementia. You didn't have the time and opportunity to smooth down the jagged edges of your guilt, so it cuts deep whenever you encounter it. Your guilt has an eternal quality: Old incidents don't become part of the past. They remain bleeding wounds rather than scarring over. Although he gave you enough reasons for the anger that induced your guilt, the continuation of the guilt is your contribution. There were a few good interactions, but not enough to sustain good memories or feelings. You did form a good relationship with your Uncle Bozydar, your father's substitute, though. You were involved with the Church, but it seems to have lost its meaning. You also have this idea of pure heroes. You ended up with obvious good guys and equally clear bad guys. It's a little like *Star Wars*: The good guys are your mom, your sister, and Uncle Bozydar, and the bad guy is your father. You see me as incorrigibly good, too."

"That's true: You helped me when nobody else did! And two other things in my life also helped flip the switch away from depression and toward hope: passing the exam and knowing that I'm going to become a father. Still, when my life is going well, I tend to do something to change it for the worse. It's like I invite bad events."

"Like forging your father's name on the money-transfer receipt? Did you really think you could get away with it? Then your mother figured it out, and you had to go to your dad and apologize. Maybe you needed that periodic slapping around to feel that your father was still involved with you. You and he couldn't allow each other to have a benign connection, but guilt kept you connected."

"When my mom said that she would go to the post office, I knew the postman would have gotten into trouble, and I could no longer keep it secret. I felt guilty that my cowardice in avoiding the consequences of my actions could cause the postman harm. That's when I confessed. It was a good lesson."

I felt free to comment on his jerky self-regulation of guilt and his need to provoke situations and get others involved to bring him into line. "Your mom made you confess at home, confront your demons, and do some penance. She helped to regulate the situation. But you had to provoke the correction from her. It wasn't smooth or automatic."

"An interesting thing was what my father said on that occasion and how it changed me. He gave me a speech about how disappointed he was, that he didn't expect me to do something like that. He made me feel like crap. Afterward, if there were a situation where he suspected hanky-panky, he would bring it up: 'I know you're capable of doing stuff like this. Remember the time you forged my name to steal my money?' Even though I never did anything like that again, he was nasty and never let up."

"Do you feel like I've been carping too much about your guilt today?"

"No, not really. We explored it, and you asked valid questions. Is this *my* guilt or guilt manipulated in me by my father? My father's favorite line was, 'Never talk to anybody about what's happening at home.' In Polish, it rhymes and goes like this:

Nie mow nikomu
co sie dzieje w domu.

He wanted to keep it within the family."

"So others would have a good image of you?"

"Yes, that was his only concern. He had another Polish proverb: *Swoje brudy pierze sie w domu*, 'You shouldn't let anybody look at your dirty laundry.' Actually, a better translation would be 'Do all your dirty laundry at home.' Today, I say so many things against him. I feel guilty and feel I should apologize to him. But because of his dementia, he can't understand my apologies or anything else."

"As I said earlier, you didn't have the opportunity to work this stuff out with him. He wasn't at home and wasn't very generous to you. You didn't have the friction of everyday experiences that smooth out the rough edges of excessive guilt. Instead, there's a dance of anger and hurt followed by

'I'm sorry' and 'It's all right.' These routines dull the white heat of excessive anger and guilt."

Jan nodded. "I shared this very idea with Sofia; she feels the same way. She's a good Catholic and wanted to make peace with my dad but couldn't. But the reality is that even today, I have so much stored-up anger and ill will that I can't bring myself to apologize to him. Frankly, I don't feel much for him nowadays."

"Also," I added, "he's not the man that he used to be. He's not the man you were angry at when you were growing up."

"That's mostly true, but Sofia feels that he still retains a high degree of nastiness and manipulates the nursing-home staff. He rings his bell for small things that he can do himself, like adjusting his pillow. People come to hate demanding and whiny people like my father. He peed on the floor on purpose when he was angry with a staff person and made more work for them. Now, he's in diapers."

I sensed that Jan was more frustrated than angry right now but that his anger was more habitual. "It's true, but I feel from your tone today that you don't get as worked up by your anger as you used to."

"True, I don't get seduced by my dark side as much as I used to."

"We have to stop soon, but I want to note that you said two sentences in Polish. As a person born in a different country, I appreciate that using your native language feels more genuine."

"Yes, it carries more weight. The prayer songs my grandmother taught me when my mom was in the sanatorium were in Polish."

Dear reader, this is the everyday spadework of healing. Perhaps reading it is like watching paint dry. Ideally, it provides at least as much emotional protection as a coat of paint.

CHAPTER 15

"I'M NOT GOING TO WHINE TODAY."

"What do you mean?"

"I'm not sure. I'm not changing anything I said last time, but I'm thinking about life changes. Sometimes, you change other people, and sometimes they change you. You feel an influence from other people. Dr. Alvear-Reverte tried to teach me that there's a point in someone's life when there's no way out. It could be your own fault, the result of unforeseen circumstances, or a combination of the two. I have to process how Amir got to where he got and the pearls of wisdom that my teachers have tried to impart to me to understand these situations. It was a cop-out when I thought I shouldn't be a psychiatrist. You can't run away from problems like this. The intensity of stress and impact on my life of my mom, uncle, and best friend's deaths is comparable to Amir's suicide.

"I'm sure that my conversations with my mom before she died helped me deal with her loss better. She prepared me, while Amir shocked me. My mom and I had conversations about end-of-life issues. Reassuring and comforting a person makes sense to some extent. She had cancer in her gall bladder and underwent surgery. Later, she wanted me to explain another procedure that might relieve the blockage of her biliary tract. After I finished, she said, 'If this procedure doesn't help more than the last one did, I'm not interested.'

"I felt the urge to say, 'Oh, no. You shouldn't say that. There's always hope,' and so on, but I knew that she knew that we were talking about heroic measures. Nothing was going to change her outcome significantly. She had come to terms with what was happening and the fact that her life was ebbing away. After that conversation, I knew that my mom understood that she had a short time to live. I knew her and decided not to push anymore; it was time to accept reality. But you can be supportive in other ways. I understood it then but didn't put it into words. Now I'm able to talk about it. This was the turning point, and, in my opinion, it helped my mom die peacefully.

"After she died, we notified the family. I had been gone for ten years, but Sofia knew Warsaw and had a vast network of people to help, so she made most of the funeral arrangements. I took it on myself to do the least pleasant thing: take care of my father. After he made the scene about getting a pedicure, my sister just couldn't stand him, so I took him out to different places. We didn't talk a lot since he seemed focused on an issue I had no interest in: He wanted me to make peace with my Aunt Malgorzata.

"I had always felt that she was anxious and disturbed. When I was growing up, I knew she existed, and she sent cards from time to time, but she appeared in person only a few times. She was there for my baptism, and she showed up one year for Christmas. It was one of the most uptight Christmases I ever experienced!

"I don't know if I told you this story about my Aunt Malgorzata. My paternal grandparents first had Uncle Bozydar, then Aunt Malgorzata, and then my father. All of them were disturbed in some way. My aunt's son died when he was seventeen. He abruptly lost consciousness and died of bacterial encephalitis. From that point on, she was certifiably ill. She was depressed and had panic attacks daily. She became hypercritical, judgmental, and intrusive. My mom tried to take care of her and invited her to stay with us. She rarely even visited. Because of her, my father's side of the family remained estranged from my family, except for Uncle Bozydar.

"Aunt Malgorzata claimed to be an Orthodox Catholic, but she was a hypocrite. After getting divorced from my first wife, I had many uninvited conversations with Aunt Malgorzata. She would call me out of nowhere and say that my divorce was wrong in the eyes of God, and so forth. I asked her, 'How do you know how things look in God's eyes? How did you get this information? How dare you call me and tell me that this is wrong in God's eyes? This divorce is something between two people you don't know.'

"She would say, 'Then why don't you explain?'

"I said, 'I don't want to explain to you what happened and how it happened.' I got angry at her for injecting herself into a situation that was none of her business. At a time like that, you want someone friendly and supportive, not someone hostile and judgmental.

"I hated to visit my grandmother on my father's side. I made myself sick to avoid it. Sometimes, I would eat a raw potato, which would make me puke. My feelings toward my grandmother bled into my feelings toward Aunt Malgorzata. They were similar-looking and had the same nasty personality.

"When my mom was going through treatment, she spoke to my aunt. She told my aunt, 'I'm going through these medical treatments, with doctors coming in and out. My husband isn't very helpful. So if he can stay with you for a few days while they're doing these procedures, I'd be very grateful.'

"Aunt Malgorzata exploded, 'So, this is how it's going to be? He's a piece of garbage that you're going to throw out? You've never felt that he was one of you. You've always been against him. You always wanted to isolate him, even turning his own children against him!'

"I wasn't there, but I got reports of the conversation from Sofia. Sofia said, at some point, my mom's face changed, and she began to cry. Sofia took the phone from her and asked Aunt Malgorzata what she had said, and my aunt told her.

"Now, you don't want to be the target of my sister's anger! She doesn't scream, she doesn't yell, and she doesn't swear. But she talks in a steely manner that you can't escape. Sofia continued the conversation with my aunt. She described my mom's condition, her request for help, and the impact of my aunt's response.

"Then she said, 'My mom is dying, and we need help. I have a four-year-old daughter who doesn't understand what's happening. Jan is thousands of miles away. Almost every day, we must either go to the hospital or have medical assistants visit us at home. My mom asks for help because my father wets himself and needs supervision. She isn't getting rid of him; she wants to be sure that someone takes care of him. Mom gets maybe two or three hours of sleep a night and can't be taking care of her husband while she's dying. This is a time that you could show compassion for her, but you've chosen to behave like a stranger. Your behavior is almost bizarre.'

"Aunt Malgorzata shut up after that. Mom died two weeks later. The funeral took place in the town where she was born, so I got a chance to see her extended family. They talked about the good times and their conversations with her. Everyone agreed that she had lived a full life.

"Aunt Malgorzata was also invited. She arrived at 4 a.m. and went straight to the church. We heard that she planned to pray for six hours. In Poland, there's a wake after a funeral called a *stypa*, but Aunt Malgorzata wanted to stay in the church. So we specifically invited her to the *stypa*.

We told her that we had arranged a place for her to stay overnight. After some initial hesitation, she finally relented and ended up at the house of one of my cousins.

"During the *stypa*, I was sitting at a table talking to my mom's sister when Aunt Malgorzata started signaling that she wanted to talk to me. Of course, she was the last person I wanted to talk to, but I remembered what my mom had once said: 'Your Aunt Malgorzata is a part of our family, and you must be respectful to her.'

"So, we stepped out to a quiet place, and she started up, 'You'll hear many bad things about your father now. They've been waiting for this moment when your mom is no longer with us. This is a golden opportunity for everybody to tell you that your father is unnecessary, that you should forget about him, and that he should be disposed of. I want you to know that these people are not your friends.' She had an intense look and repeated, 'Remember, these people are not your friends.'

"I was seething, but I didn't say anything. I wanted to go, but she insisted on talking to me, repeating what she had said. Then I lost it. I said, 'This time is for my mother. If you were looking for the *least* appropriate time to have a conversation like this, you've hit the bullseye. First of all, you're not a part of my life. If I have any problems with anybody in my family, I won't discuss them with you. Whatever we decide about our father, it will be our decision. You weren't a part of my family in the past, and for future decision-making, I will not consult you. You're welcome to visit my father, but he won't spend even one day with you. When my mom asked you for help with him, you decided otherwise. You missed your chance.' She didn't respond.

"So, my father moved in with Sofia, her husband Marek, and their daughter, Kasia. When I visited, Sofia started to cry, 'I can't take it. I don't sleep a wink all night. Dad is impossible on purpose.'

"'Maybe you and I are biased against him,' I said.

"'No,' she replied, 'he's ten times worse than he used to be. He sleeps all day and is awake at night.' She felt he did it on purpose to upset the routines of the house. When I was with him, I also concluded that he stayed awake at night intentionally to disturb everyone else's sleep. You can wake up and sip water without much commotion, but he turned on all the lights, banged the refrigerator, and rattled the dishes in the sink when he got up. When I explained that it disturbed others, he would curb his behavior for maybe a day or two.

"While my father was staying with Sofia, she gave him Kasia's room, rearranging it for his convenience, but Kasia got upset. She didn't understand why she couldn't have her room and was afraid she'd never get it back. She saw my father as an intruder, and sometimes she let him know it: 'This is *my* room,' she'd say, or 'I'm coming to take a teddy bear from *my* room.'

"Sofia smiled at the drama and hoped that my father would get it, but she never said anything to him directly. Then Kasia became depressed, especially when my sister was at work, and something had to give. Kasia cried inconsolably and didn't want to leave the house.

"When Sofia asked why she was crying, Kasia replied, 'Grandpa scared me. He said bad things will happen to me if I come into *his* room.' She became afraid of her own room and worried about the bad things that might happen to her. She became petrified of him. She was hysterical in his presence.

"Because we expected the situation to continue, we tried to explain to my father that Kasia was only four, but talking to my eighty-year-old father was like talking to a four-year-old. We couldn't work the situation out, so Sofia sent Kasia to live in a residential school run by Catholic nuns. Fortunately, the school encourages parents to be involved with their children, and they talk with them about how their child is doing. The teacher told my sister Kasia should see a psychologist.'

"So, Sofia made an appointment with a psychologist. Kasia told the psychologist in between her sobs, 'My mom gave my room to Grandpa. My parents are going to get rid of me. No one loves me. No one wants me because I'm adopted.' She *is* adopted, but she is very loved."

Jan was sensitive to the importance of acceptance. It occurred to me that Jan was particularly tuned in to Kasia because he had experienced the agony of being separated from his mother for a long time when she was in the TB sanatorium. Although he was with a loving grandmother, Jan suffered from being away from his mother. So he could understand how his niece felt that no one loved her.

"My sister tried her best to make it up to Kasia, but Kasia was too suspicious for it to work. I told my sister that I felt horrible because I couldn't do anything to help. I could bring my father to the United States, but he had so many medical problems, and you know how hard it is to get insurance here. It was better for him to stay in Poland, so we looked for a nursing home. Sofia toured many places. Finally, she found him an excellent assisted-living facility run by nuns, through her church connections. It has physical therapy, access to doctors, and church-based religious services.

"Initially, we put him in a room for two, but he beat the other patient with his cane. He never told me what the problem was. I think it was about cookies or something. So, now he's in a single room. I admit that I don't call him as often as I called my mom. My purpose in calling my mom was to *talk* to her, and we had a lot to talk about. I did so religiously, every weekend and sometimes more often. With my father, the purpose of the call is to avoid the guilt that I would feel if I *didn't* call him. I call to let him know I exist.

"At some point after we put him in the nursing home, Aunt Malgorzata called. She was furious. She felt that Sofia and I had gotten rid of him. She was rude and unpleasant. Sofia finally said to her, 'This is what Jan and I arranged. He has rehabilitation and regular visits by general doctors and specialists. If we made a mistake, I apologize. I understand that you want the best for him. You're welcome to suggest any changes in his care or even to take him home. If you think that's the best solution, that's fine with us. You can take him, but if you can't take care of him, or if we *feel* that you can't, then we'll bring him back.' Aunt Malgorzata said that she wanted him to stay at her place.

"I told my father that his sister wanted him to come to live at her house. As we drove there, we talked, and he said he didn't want to go to her house. I said, 'If you don't want to stay there, tell your sister, and I'll arrange to bring you back to the nursing home.'"

"Aunt Malgorzata lasted two weeks. She called us every day about getting prescriptions and arranging appointments. Because of where she lived, it was difficult to arrange for his medical care. It quickly exhausted her. She began to cry on the phone because everything was impossible. 'I don't know what to do with him. He's making my life into a living hell,' she said. 'He peed on the carpet. He acts like he's seeing things that aren't there. And he doesn't want to eat. I'm sorry. You were right. The best place for him is the nursing home. Please, please, take him back.'

"By then, I was back in the United States, so my brother-in-law made arrangements to bring him back to the nursing home. After only two weeks at Aunt Malgorzata's, Sofia said that he looked like a homeless person. He was smelly and unshaven. Sofia had sent him with a suitcase, and when she opened it, she saw that everything was just as she'd packed it. It hadn't been opened once! And he'd been wearing the same clothes all that time! He required so much prodding to overcome his inertia that Aunt Malgorzata didn't even try. Now, she's stopped complaining. It's over."

"So, your behavior modification worked!"

"Yes, it was a great success. Shortly before last Christmas, we asked her if she wanted my father to visit her for a week or so. Yeah, right! She said that she was busy with her church, making arrangements to feed some homeless people, so it wouldn't work out."

"Well," I said, "I think you are juggling many difficult feelings. Also, as you mentioned, you have negative feelings about your father's mother that you apply to your Aunt Malgorzata and others."

"Yes, she's a traumatic memory from my childhood."

"These memories are gushing out, as I think they should. You needed the opportunity for your thoughts about your family drama to come out."

"You see, the problem is that I feel—"

I completed his sentence, "—guilty?"

Jan nodded vigorously. "Yes. I feel bad about it. Aunt Malgorzata went through one of the worst things you can imagine: the death of a child. When I talk to her, I maintain a degree of control and don't go too far. I know she would have been a different person if her son hadn't died young. She made a shrine for her son in her house and kept it for a long time as if he were still alive. I had a patient like that who also lost her son. The thing is, I feel a great deal of compassion for my patient but very little for my own aunt. Some people with losses are more open with their feelings; others become closed. Some people become absorbed in themselves when hurt, but some can still care for others. My aunt kept it all in and created crappy situations. Maybe the fact that she came only at Christmas and to my wedding and to my sister's wedding turned me against her."

"You mean your wedding in Rome?"

"No, my first wedding. Maria and I sent her an invitation, but she didn't even acknowledge it. Remember, she told me how evil I was to remarry. Then, after Maria and I were married, she called me around Christmas. We wished each other 'Merry Christmas,' and then immediately after, she said, 'In the eyes of God, your marriage to Maria is illegal. The Church doesn't accept your wedding as valid.'

"I didn't respond, but she persisted in seeking a reply. We had already been over some of this. Finally, I said, 'In my opinion, when two people are happy with each other, that's good enough. One of my friends is a lawyer-priest for the Notre Dame church. He told me the procedure for getting a marriage annulled. It takes time. Because my first wife and I didn't have children, the Vatican would probably grant the annulment. I may or may not do it.' She didn't bring the topic up again."

Jan knew he could go only so far with Aunt Malgorzata and had to limit the damage she could impose on him; so, too, with Amir's mom. Jan could help Amir's mother deal with her son's suicide only so much; beyond that, his efforts would be futile. Therefore, I felt that there was no gain in introducing the topic of Amir's mom till I had more explicit indications that Jan was on that wavelength himself.

"You realized that you can reason only so much with your aunt," I said. "Beyond that, a further conversation isn't likely to move her. So you created a fence or a moat to keep her noxiousness at bay."

"The conversation I had with her during Mom's funeral proves the point."

Notwithstanding what I had thought only moments before, his emphatic agreement emboldened me. Finally, I felt it might be possible to explore his associations and feelings about Amir. "I would add that, although you experienced guilt after you spoke to your Aunt Malgorzata, you had the relief of having talked to her directly. With Amir, you didn't have such an opportunity. With Amir's mother, you may not get such a chance."

Jan thought a moment. "My biggest life lesson was working with Amir. He was my school of psychiatry, although there were no lectures. My divorce was another lesson. My wife was with a guy for three years, and I didn't know about it. The divorce was nasty, but I don't hate her. She came to my mom's funeral; we hugged and then said goodbye. If she ever needed help, I would help her."

CHAPTER 16

JAN ARRIVED EAGER TO TALK. "I'm so glad that I'm getting back into psychiatry," he began. "It's been good to return to seeing my patients, and they were all glad to see me." He paused. "My life has been unusual. I was an attending physician in Poland and had junior physicians and students working for me. Then I gave it all up to come here. Most people go through their education and career stages without a break. They don't leave their country and go to another one. It must have looked crazy to them for an established attending to put himself in the position of a resident again. I didn't care; I thought it was a great idea. The situation with Amir and what happened afterward was unfortunate but just a consequence of this choice. Depressed people need treatment, and people do kill themselves.

"I don't think I ever told you this: Wherever I've been, I've always imagined a better place for myself. Good change always seemed to be possible. I just got an itch for something new after being in the same place for a few years."

"I thought you left because so many people died, and that got you down."

"Yes, although at the time, I didn't know it was depression. My job was stable, and I could have continued there for as long as I wanted, up to retirement. I realize many things now that we have a baby coming. The fact that we'll be raising our baby without family closeness hurts a lot. During my childhood, I remember that there were always family members around. There was always someone. My mom often took me to her sister's place. My aunts and cousins visited us almost every day. Maria's family was also close. She told me that there wasn't one day she spent just with her parents in her life. There was always someone coming to hang out or pick up Maria and her siblings to do something with their own children. Now, Maria and I feel isolated. We're worried about our baby. Somehow, we have to create a substitute family."

"There's no question that, when you leave your country and go far away, you need to create a substitute home," I agreed, "but you still have to understand the itch that made you move in the first place."

"Yes, of course, there's an excitement in moving from place to place, but looking back, I also see I needed to escape from situations causing pain. When I started as a physician, I established myself quite quickly. Many of my patients liked me, and some were even impressed with me. I think I can say the same about my colleagues. But, despite that, I started to have doubts.

"I was afraid that people would discover that I wasn't that good or that I wasn't what they thought I was. I had stability—a wife, a good job, good money—but I felt that something was broken. I lost the sense and meaning of what I was doing. I didn't want to continue like that. My confidence as a physician diminished with each patient's death. After coming to the U.S. and working as a doctor again, I thought I had gotten it back, but my confidence completely shattered when Amir killed himself. I thought that something irreversible had happened that undermined my identity as a psychiatrist. I could only think of myself as a psychiatrist-whose-patient-killed-himself. You witnessed it: I told you I couldn't be a physician. I thought that maybe I should find something else to do, but I didn't know what. If I hadn't passed the exam, I would have been forced to be something other than a doctor."

"You were concerned that people would label you a suicide-doctor, a doctor whose patients commit suicide, a doctor who's an impostor. You came to psychiatry with raw confidence that you understood people, and Amir's suicide undermined that. Since then, you've had patients you've diagnosed and treated appropriately, and you're in the process of finding a balance in your self-assessment. You've had serious failures and also significant successes. When you first came to me, you felt you were only a bad psychiatrist; now, you feel that you're a good-bad or bad-good psychiatrist. Like any other physician, you're a mixed bag. But, as you said today, after Amir killed himself, you changed; you felt you could not continue to be a physician."

"I didn't see it then," Jan continued, "but dying people always surrounded me. After I finished medical school, I imagined being a slave to an attending physician, doing scut work every day, and being on call every other day. Then I had a vision of the promised land of being an attending physician myself, with a house, a car, and a wife, and everything would be cool. But when I got there, I realized it was no utopia. In fact, I didn't want to be there."

Jan's father moved around a lot, so I wondered how much Jan identified with him in that respect. On the other hand, I mused, his father's very unavailability made his mother's presence all the more critical, and it was her love and stability that enabled him to dream. And as the dream of paradise gave way to the reality of death and dying people, the utopia he had imagined with his mother was supplanted by sadness and loss when she became ill. My initial sense was that Jan's identification with his dad motivated the change. However, this understanding was off the mark; the pivotal element was the death and loss of his mother. Although there was some truth in both approaches, I weighed which understanding would be more in tune with Jan's. Once I decided, I used my imagination to reformat all the information I had about Jan. This was my construction:

"You mentioned earlier that, when you were a child, your mother managed your life very well. When she left to go to the sanatorium, she was able to get her sister to be with you." I thought I saw a look of pain on Jan's face and wondered if it was because I mentioned that his mother left to be at the sanatorium.

"It wasn't her sister; it was her mother, my grandmother," he said.

"Right, and although your grandmother immersed you in religious songs and prayers, your spirit was broken during this time. You were upset when your mom left and very glad when she came back."

"It's so interesting that you bring it up. I spoke to Maria about my grandma's visit to Mom in the sanatorium just yesterday. Maria is studying the attachment theory of Bowlby. He did a study of children who were abandoned, like me.[41] They experienced *severe* emotional loss as children.

"Maria said, 'You're lucky that you turned out as well as you did. You had a strong likelihood of being seriously screwed up.' When I took classes on development as a third-year resident, I, too, felt that I should have been more messed up. I do see that my unhappiness can be explained in many ways, but the most important factor was that my mom had to leave me when I was a child."

41 Bowlby, J. (1969). *Attachment and Loss: Vol. I: Attachment*. London: Hogarth Press and the Institute of Psycho-Analysis.

I said, "Despite it feeling like abandonment when she was away for treatment, you were in good hands. I think what made you more resilient was that you always knew that your mother loved and cared for you deeply. She was ill, but she made arrangements for you to be taken care of by another loving person, her own mother. So, your trauma was deep, but if you hadn't had such a loving mother substitute, it could have been more serious. It may have left you with the feeling that, if you become too dependent on one place or thing, like your mom, you would be at risk for a devastating loss, so you avoided that deep attachment by leaving. You could compare it to a football team that always has a second-string quarterback in case the starting quarterback gets injured or leaves. This also relates to your sense of having choices, for example, between oncology and psychiatry, Poland and the United States."

"I just remembered, when my mom came home, I avoided my grandma and wasn't affectionate to her. I felt she was behind my mom's disappearance. Maybe I was punishing her. Now about your comment: I'm not sure if that's the case. I don't know that choosing two different specialties, oncology and then psychiatry, is related to my mother's illness. My choices were logical: I sought a higher position, better money, and fewer work hours. There was always a reason."

My last interpretation, including the example of oncology and psychiatry, was incorrect because it was too specific, without any justification for being so. A patient's resistance often attaches itself to an analyst's inadvertent and careless comments, so it is wise to use brief, simple, and sustainable statements when offering interpretations. Sometimes, an analyst may succumb to the spontaneity of real conversation in treatment and talk too loosely. I was keenly aware that disagreements with his father generally came with a lifetime warranty for Jan. I also noted that he was usually too quick to agree with my views. Jan didn't know much about mixing agreement and disagreement. His gray areas were sparse, and the contrast between the areas of white and black was stark. For this reason, I was glad to hear him voice disagreement and divergent ideas. He had to grow into more uncertainty, which required clarification of the importance of uncertainty.

"Right," I said.

Jan continued, "But the last example, of coming to the United States without knowing anybody and hoping that I would reestablish myself, that is a different situation. Unlike my professional choices, I have no idea where the motivation for that change came from."

"That is what I was trying to address," I said. "When your mom was in the sanatorium, you knew that your life had changed. You had to learn to get along in a strange new world. You cried when your mom was gone, but you adjusted to your grandmother."

"My mom told me that, when she came back, it was like she had never left me and that my grandma virtually ceased to exist for me immediately. My grandma gave me what I needed to survive, but deep inside, I knew that she wasn't that special person in my life."

Jan was distraught when his mom left him with his grandmother, but that deep pain of separation was denied and forgotten instantly. His grandmother became his attachment figure during his mom's absence, but she lost that status when his mother returned.

"By and large," I said, "I think you treated the pain of her leaving as a challenge and overcame it. But when a succession of people close to you died, you experienced hopelessness and became periodically depressed and vulnerable. Amir was the straw that broke the camel's back. Not only did your mood collapse, but you felt you couldn't be a physician."

Jan protested, "Well, but . . . You're saying that this is out of the ordinary. You're saying that this isn't a reaction that everybody has to death and dying, especially when close members of the family or their patients are involved."

Jan's response puzzled me. Since the beginning of his treatment, he had freely acknowledged his intense depression, but he suddenly seemed to be arguing that his depression was ordinary and reasonable. Was this a repeat of his flight to health? Was he minimizing his previous depression or merely describing his current status? Jan's current view that his response to Amir's suicide was not out of the ordinary provoked a few thoughts in me:

Normal narcissism is that buoyant, self-righting spirit that helps us feel good about ourselves and those we love and present ourselves in the best light. It generates the built-in, rose-tinted glasses that help us feel uplifted despite our imperfections and the slights and misfortunes with which we contend. We look in the mirror and are pleased with the image of our embellished lives and selves. While people are aware of such spontaneous enhancements, they don't take them too seriously. They are like the pleasant exaggerations in daydreams. They are harmless and leave reality intact.

On the other hand, pathological narcissism demands a sense of perfection (or normalcy) when things are far from perfect (or normal). In this case, we paint over reality with a coat of false perfection (or normalcy), exaggerating accomplishments or denying problems. This emotional Teflon hides hard-to-acknowledge vulnerabilities and may skew reality testing, obscuring even significant flaws; it is not easy to remove. The pathological narcissist may bestow excessive adoration onto others to shine in their reflected glory, but that glow stays for only so long. Eventually, it will fade, and a negative image will emerge, allowing blaming, recriminations, or rage to enter. Disillusionment is cold, just as the previous adoration was warm but just as strong. Thus, an excess of pathological narcissism creates a world of stark contrasts: well-being and fear, security and vulnerability, connection and disconnection. Under its reign, small but actual accomplishments recede unseen.

Many psychiatrists and therapists have treated patients who commit suicide. It's a devastating experience and increases the risk for suicide for themselves. And some do commit suicide. Jan had come dangerously close to the brink of that abyss.

Amir's suicide hit Jan like a personal earthquake, unsettling his moods, functioning, identity, and very will to live. In the aftermath, Jan had entertained the thought of flying through his previous analyst's window. Still, here he was, back to his job as a resident, with improved moods and an attitude toward the future imbued with the excitement and (appropriate) worries of parenting. Jan had moved to a place of life and vitality.

From his current vantage point, he seemed to view his previous melancholy as a form of ordinary misery, almost unaware of how Amir's suicide had nearly consumed him. Now, he saw himself as normal, a view that helped him overcome feelings of isolation and loneliness. This would explain his irritation when I reminded him of his previous depression.

Although I rejoiced in his progress, I felt he needed to remember his past. He should not forget and have to relearn his history lessons. If he forgot his pain or couldn't bear to acknowledge it, I feared his depression might return. Of course, most people would be distressed by the death of someone close to them, but he needed to be aware of the extra layer of distress added by his unique emotional past without dismissing it. This understanding would give him the best chance of continued success in the future. As I mused, I realized that my distinction between normal and pathological narcissism was too rigid. Jan fit partly into one and partly into the other, and I wanted to share that.

"Your feelings were completely understandable. Most people would feel similarly, but in your case, it really got you down."

Jan was firmly set in his new mode.

He said, "I don't think my reaction was unusual. But, this was a wake-up call. Everybody gets it when they face death. This is going to happen to you, too, if it hasn't already. This feeling is even more intense if you don't have enough emotional balance; obviously, I didn't."

Jan's last sentence indicated he was thinking about the time right after Amir killed himself. I was glad to hear this because, despite his current sense of normalcy, it revealed the self-awareness that, at one time, he was not emotionally balanced.

Jan continued, "I felt, 'What's the point of anything?'"

I felt that Jan was becoming philosophical to distract himself from his depression. He was still experiencing some degree of ambivalence and uncertainty. Maturity exacts a steep price. Given Jan's changing position, I wasn't sure what he was trying to communicate.

"What's your point, if I may ask?"

"My Uncle Hektor was a friendly person. He was fun to have around, and I remember him being the center of attention at any gathering. He liked to joke a lot. He had a charming way with the ladies, and they all loved him. He was about my age when he died of lung cancer. He never smoked cigarettes, never drank too much. One day he started to cough, and a few months later, he was dead. I was sad. Before I forget, my point is that the culture of denying suffering is alive and well. People don't like to talk about it."

True, I thought.

Jan continued, "You may not mind watching some stupid made-up stories of suffering on reality TV, but when it's real, you want to run, like the suffering of Hurricane Katrina. People usually don't want to acknowledge that suffering is part of life."

"Yes," I said, "drivers often slow down to look at roadside accidents. Part of that is the relief that the accident didn't happen to them, and then they speed away."

Jan continued, "We strive to have a happy family and a good life, but life also comes with sadness, suffering, and death. We try not to see that side. Knowing how to accept and deal with the two sides of life comes with age. When Uncle Hektor died, I was six or seven. They placed him in an open casket in the middle of his living room during the wake. Flowers and candles surrounded the coffin. My grandma brought me closer and told me to touch his finger. 'Say goodbye to your Uncle Hektor,' she said, 'and he won't come to visit you in your dreams.'

"It was hard for me to touch his lifeless finger. I remember the feeling as if it were happening now; it's so imprinted in my mind. When I touched it, it felt cold. It kind of felt like a thing, like a piece of wood, but I also felt that it belonged to a person. Then my grandma said, 'Now you know that his body is an empty vessel. When the soul is gone, this is what becomes of a person.'

"So, I listened to my grandmother and said goodbye to him. Then there was the funeral. I felt like crying, perhaps because everybody else was crying, but there were no actual tears in my eyes. They didn't come until the pallbearers began to lower the coffin into the grave. That was when I burst into tears and felt overwhelming sadness. At that moment, I knew I had lost him forever. I told Maria this story. She said that it was unlikely that I was really that sad because, at that age, I couldn't have had a concept of the permanence of death. I disagree.

"I grew up with the Grimm Brothers and Hans Christian Andersen books, and some of them are sad, and some are horrific! One of Andersen's stories, *The Little Match Girl*, is tragic. This little girl sold matches on the street. On a cold night, when she was out trying to sell her matches, she was freezing but was afraid to go home because her father would beat her for not having sold any. So she found a nook and tried to warm herself up by lighting the matches. She had a beautiful vision with each one: a Christmas tree, a family gathering with lots of food on the table, a comet in the sky. And then she saw a vision of her grandmother, who told her that a comet crosses the sky when a person dies. So the girl died, and her grandmother took her to heaven. People passing by the next day saw this little girl frozen to death, but with a big smile."

"It makes sense that you had such reactions to encountering death as a child and then repeatedly confronting it again as an adult," I said. "When we talked about your previous depressions before you saw me, your moods dipped very low and remained there for a long time. For example, after suffering from cancer, Nina, your girlfriend, died. You got depressed and stopped doing everyday things like getting up out of your bed in the morning, showering, and shaving. When you stirred, you had to tear off a month's page from your calendar. You did not register the sunlight of the daytimes; you felt the darkness."

"I was suffering from clinical depression, then."

Now I knew that Jan's earlier protest that his depressive reactions were normal had not erased his memories of being depressed. The time had come for me to address his narcissism and depression together. "For much of your life, you weren't sad or depressed. You overcame your traumas generally quite well, and you were the way you are now. You felt good and wanted to maintain that good feeling by overlooking some negative ones and as a way of maintaining a positive self-image. On a few occasions, though, you went to that other place and experienced deep pain from the past. You haven't forgotten it. You know it in your bones. And at those times, you get overwhelmed."

"I was about to say it happened only once," Jan added, "but that's not true. I was depressed in Poland, and I was seriously depressed this year. I didn't know it was a depression the first time, so I sank deeper and deeper and couldn't help myself. This time, I started taking antidepressants, saw the other analyst, and then saw you. I'm taking care of myself."

"Those who cannot remember the past are condemned to repeat it, but this time you had new tools, and you *didn't* repeat it."

I felt that the first time Jan was depressed was when his mom went to the sanatorium. The other times he was depressed in Poland, he couldn't help himself; he had no word for *depression* and thought it was just life. After Amir died, Jan got depressed again, but he started treatment and averted a catastrophe because he was more aware. I felt satisfied that Jan gained critical insight into his depression and managed it better.

Jan continued, "In Poland, my depression deepened, and I didn't talk to anybody. I didn't know what to talk about. In my eyes, the depression was a fact, a reality of life. It doesn't matter who you are or what kind of person you are. It's something you can't avoid. It doesn't feel good, but that's irrelevant. It's reality. It's going to happen."

A sense of passivity had overcome Jan in the face of misfortune. He felt that his actions were futile. So, I said, "Your sense of the future was clouded over. A fact of life was staring you in the face, and there was no purpose in trying to change it. You were bound to fail. Maybe you thought, 'I can't change things. There's no point in my actions. There's no purpose in trying to change it.'"

Jan agreed, "Yes, exactly. I couldn't describe my feelings coherently at the time. It was just, 'That's how life is sometimes.' Perhaps my friends saw me get down and then slowly shake it off and become myself again, but no one tried to do anything about it. There was no purpose in doing anything."

From my point of view, the focus of Jan's early treatment had been to address depression and any possible suicidal behavior. I also hoped Jan would come to understand the sources of his melancholic grief in response to Amir's death, which filled him with so much guilt, self-remorse, and self-loathing. In addition, he needed to enjoy the everyday humdrum of marriage and the return to work and function in society. These goals were accomplished mainly or were on their way to being completed, but no achievement is so stable that it can guarantee future good health.

Deeper changes in Jan's personality had to occur for a truly meaningful transformation. I felt that this would require a deeper dive into his relationship with his mother. This would be hard because, although—or because?—his positive feelings for his mother were intense. At present, he had a limited capacity to separate from her enough to acknowledge, recognize, and critically work through this idealization of his mom. Of course, if his mother had to leave for an extended period, any child would experience feelings of abandonment, anger, and rage. But, just as he saw his mother as an ideal, he saw me in such a purely positive light that he couldn't recognize or overlooked my lapses.

Jan was deeply attached to his mother. She was truly generous and giving. She reminded me of Amma, my mom. I, too, had a good mother, and I would have a hard time criticizing her. Thanks to her, I didn't have to be well-schooled in the art of conflict and strife. Amma managed to run a household—cooking, cleaning, and tackling all the problems of everyday life—and tend to her five children. She ensured that we did our homework, including tutoring us, when necessary; she was a good tutor, especially in math and English. We knew she could always help us, whatever we needed. And she made sure we visited all our relatives regularly to develop a broader sense of family belonging. She was a confidante to a great many relatives and neighbors. Even when I was in medical school, she kept up with my friends and conversed with adolescent boys and girls with ease. She helped the neighborhood girls and women with family-planning education and, for many years, was part of a community of elders in charge of women's issues. She even put out saucers filled with milk for stray cats!

If the description of my mom seems idealized, it is. Jan's looking up to his mom reflected her intrinsic goodness, but it reverberated with my own feelings for Amma. Although Amma didn't develop tuberculosis and didn't leave me to go to a sanatorium, she gave birth to my sister Padmini when I was seventeen months old. Both the birth of a sibling and the sickness of a mother are stressful. I felt displaced by my sister and abandoned by my mom in a way that words cannot express. Yet, I needed my mom and wanted her love. Many families had five or more children in my neighborhood, some less. We did not grouse much about emotional hurts, like the birth of a sibling close to one's age; we simply chalked it up to fate. It gave us a chance to observe the cycle of birth, copulation, and death.

To what should I attribute my choice to emigrate and create a 10,000-mile physical distance between my mom and me? To the birth of my sister soon after I was born? Perhaps. My mom's chosen goddess was Saraswati, whose ministry was knowledge, and my mother cherished education and encouraged my leaving India and going to the U.S. for further studies. Generally, I did not feel much strain in my relationships with my mom or dad, either as a child or as a grown-up. As an adult and living far away from them, I visited them often—and more so after my dad died. Amma came to the U.S. many times and insisted on coming to a family wedding when she was ninety. My younger brother, an attorney, Prabhakar, accompanied Amma and brought her. Our meetings were joyous occasions after inevitable prolonged separations due to my emigration. However, soon the time came for her to leave.

Since her ninetieth birthday, Amma has repeatedly asked family members a question. So finally, when she had to return, and we were at the airport, she chuckled and said, "Should I ask you *the* question?"

Knowing what she was going to say, I still asked earnestly, "What question?"

As expected, she asked, "How long will I live?"

I said, "Amma, only time will tell. I think you wonder if we will ever meet again; I, too, wonder the same thing."

Tears welled in Amma's eyes, and I could not hold back my tears. I hugged her frail body. After a few moments, Amma collected herself and said, "I'm glad I came to see you."

"I am glad, too. On another topic, not many 90-year-old people travel 10,000 miles; you are bold. But, I have a question for you. For you, nowadays, what is life like?"

"Nanna died about 20 years ago, and many of the people I grew up with are dead. I should be with them and not belong to life. But, I still look forward to each morning. If I am alive, I feel good."

"Soon, one of these mornings, I plan to surprise you with a visit. I hope fate allows it." It was a good ending for her visit. I felt our brief, frank talk helped my mom and me. I watched her walk through the security line till I could no longer see her head. I saw that she mingled with everyone else through my wet eyes and became part of my memory. I did see her one more time. A few months later, after a brief illness, Amma died.

In coming to the U.S., I did not feel that I was acting out some deep rage against my mom and dad for having my sister so soon after; however, I felt the sting. However, I believe that I lived out my mom's and dad's dreams of higher education, freedom, and economic security. Still, I pondered my childhood.

Amma stood by Nanna's side all the time because she was a good-enough[42] wife and because, most of the time, he was a good-enough husband

---

42 In Winnicott's (1953) theory, "good-enough mothering" refers to a mother's ability to adequately adapt to her infant so the child can form a relationship with the world. In addition, Winnicott's (1958) concept of the maternal preoccupation with an infant's needs, Kohut's (1982) emphasis on the mother's (analyst's) empathy for a child (patient), and Stern's (1985) descriptions of maternal attunement with an infant relate to similar early developmental themes. These ideas have gained wide acceptance in the analyst community. Moreover, they have expanded an analyst's focus on conflict interpretation to include the mutual relations and active interactions that promote an analysand's growth and development in all areas. Considering these contributions, I summarize my ideas of mothering and the mother.

Assuring her child's safety, comfort, and well-being is always a good-enough mother's priority. She organizes her child's timely feeding, toileting, playing, bathing, and sleeping routines on time and without excessive conflict, stress, or distress. A mother's preoccupation, empathy, and attunement with their children facilitate the child's joyous or resilient progress through life. Of course, a caregiver, father, siblings, grandparents, babysitters, or childcare workers can also perform these mothering functions. But because of the child's unique attachment to the mother, she is the best example of this function.

However, no mother can spend as much time with a child or be immediately available as the child wishes. As a result, frustration is inevitable in any child's life. When a mother spreads her attention to another sibling, is inattentive, or is busy with another task, the child must cope with the unavailable mother. Infants soothe themselves by sucking their thumbs, holding onto a blanket, or playing with a toy associated with their mother to cope with frustrating times. Such transitional objects may temporarily relieve a child burdened by their mother's absence. Whether viewed as substitutes for the mother or symbols of the relationship she shared with the child, they can help a child deal with his longing and tension.

If a mother's absence stresses an infant, he cannot calm himself. Children can become irritable, angry, or lowkey if their mothers fail to respond to their repeated cries for attention. A good mother provides emotional and physical comfort by communicating her understanding of his moods and does so without getting unduly annoyed, overwhelmed, or retaliating against the child. Yet, she teaches the child to talk or play rather than vent his frustrations. She manages and clams a child's excessive passion through acceptance and compassion. The mother praises the child for safe play, but she does not insist that the child do things that give her pleasure. Instead, she teaches her child to take the initiative and learn from their successes and failures. By doing so, she contributes to the well-being of each child and the entire family. A good-enough mother can help a child work around the imperfections in a mother, Self, and world, and even help others in distress. A good-enough mother, father, caregiver, or analyst within their respective domains helps through love, caring, understanding, healing, and fair criticism.

While psychoanalysis has provided a workable clinical framework for understanding factors facilitating and inhibiting a child's development, it may have unintentionally prioritized mothering and reduced the rest of a mother's life to the background. For example, a mother takes care of her child; but she may also be a spouse, a mother to her child's other siblings, a caregiver for her parents, and a provider for her family. If these moments of ideal fit between mother and infant or "mothering" establish maternal care expectations that caregivers must continually meet, they may lead to unrealistic expectations. Just as the common earth's dirt, water, and sunlight are necessary for a plant to blossom and bear fruit, a mother's entire life (and a child's predispositions) contribute to the wonders of mothering and her ability child to learn from experience. Sometimes, analysts compare the analytic situation to the idealized relationship between a parent and child, thus burdening psychoanalysis with ideal expectations of therapeutic interaction between analyst and patient. Both mothers and analysts make mistakes and learn from them; they will never be perfect – they only need to be good enough.

The mothering function is different from a mother's life. Therefore, inferences drawn from considering mothering alone will necessarily be different from those drawn from considering both mothering and the mother's entire life. I have worked with several thousand mothers for almost thirty years, many of whom struggled with homelessness, poverty, domestic violence, and hunger while seeking safety and sustenance. Although a spouse and resources do not guarantee a good-enough mother, their absence can make a mother's job even harder. Yet, these women have attempted mightily to be good mothers and care for their children despite the challenges and impediments. So, my interest in the mother and her mothering shaped my ideas of the *good enough mother.*

In addition to providing therapeutic services, our team helped the distressed mother find housing, encouraged her to at least complete her high school education, and helped her find a job and entitlements. If the mother was pregnant, breastfeeding, or had special nutritional needs, we helped her access the Women Infant Children program. Whenever she took steps toward sobriety, we praised her. Through our conversations, we encouraged her to reduce street drug use, move towards less destructive relationships, and prioritize safety. However, understanding her life meant appreciating the slim pickings that often ground her dreams into dust and turned them into sleepless nightmares. Her adversity taught her the annoying virtue of making do with less. Here I draw a thumbnail sketch of a session with a patient in which she described her typical mother's day.

Since childhood, she dreamed of having her own family; a family with a father, a mother, and children - something she had never experienced before. Instead, the state removed her from her neglectful parents and placed her with her grandparents, who eventually adopted her. She looked up to her grandparents, who had been married for over forty years. She has three young children. The last two are from her current baby daddy. Unfortunately, they often argue because he is preoccupied with sex while she is looking for love. She isn't an angel and cannot resist reading his messages occasionally. So, she knows he is two-timing her and spending time with another woman. She was furious because he continued to gaslight her and acted innocent when she confronted him about his affair.

Additionally, he accuses her of cheating on him, which she says is false. He does not buy diapers for their children and does not pay any child support. Nevertheless, he does not fail to show up on her payday or when she gets her tax refund-- he is hanging around her, waiting for his cut of her income. She spends the entire shift on the floor of the candy factory, except for lunch and a brief break. She commented that her feet were "hurting like hell" when she left her job.

Tired, she picks up her kids from daycare and goes home. She tries to distribute the inner pizza rectangles and the outer pieces with crusts to her children. They claim that she favors another child and is unfair. Patiently she hopes they will come to appreciate that she is doing her level best. While each child clamors for her full individual exclusive attention and affection, she wants all of them to share her love, creating an inevitable conflict. There is also tension when she catches one in the cookie jar with her hand and must dish out the consequences. Occasionally, she and her children have beautiful times while enjoying home cooking or eating out at McDonald's, watching Disney's Lion King, drawing, singing, playing, and storytelling before sleeping. Unfortunately, she lives in her skin all day and has only a fraction of time to devote to any single child. Because a mother's job is impossible, she only lives up to these ideal moments for short periods. I listened to her day's account in that session and had nothing more to add. However, as my patient prepared to leave the session, the words from the first line of Donna Summer's "She works hard for money" escaped my lips. Initially surprised, she quickly brightened, smiled, and sang, "You better treat her right."

and father. Sometimes, though, she seemed to belittle him for not being as intelligent or accomplished as her brothers. I realized, only as an adult, that I resented this. However, she *did* disagree with him when she felt that disagreement was necessary. There is only one time I can remember my parents having a serious argument. I was about three or four years old; we lived in Chilkalguda (Parrot-town) in Secunderabad. As we sat for dinner, Nanna informed us that he had received orders transferring him to a railway hospital approximately 80 miles away in Kazipet. Amma knew what that meant. She said, "My only concern is the children's education. Are there English medium schools for the children?"

Nanna replied, "Yes, the Railway School, Saint Gabriel's, and St. Fatima."

A mother's priority is her child's life. However, mothers must balance their children's lives with their callings and those of their work and the intimacy they desire. She has to stock her baby bag with food, diapers, clothes that fit seasonally, a rattle, and other child necessities. In addition to ensuring that she gets adequate sleep and toileting, she must also plan time for her makeup, nails, hair, and other beauty concerns. Given so much to do, she has to choose between her own needs and those of her child, setting up the conditions for her child's disappointment and self-doubt. Generally, mothers are sufficiently loving and caring towards their children. Still, mothers and children have different interests, which leads to miscues, miscommunications, and misunderstandings. Children and mothers will not always share the same interests. Since a mother needs to live her life, provide for the family, struggle to survive, ensure the family's safety, and take care of other sibs, a mother's life and a specific child's wishes will inevitably conflict. As a result of conflict between mother and child, both have their own perspectives on the situation. Even if such differences are unpleasant, they do not necessarily hinder or harm a child's growth. Providing the injury is not beyond the child's ability to cope. Such situations can also stimulate previously unknown capacities in the child. Resilient children can play creatively and manage their mother's absence or the prevailing disagreement. A mother taking care of herself may be able to demonstrate to her child that a mother loves her child and herself, even though it involves some frustration tolerance and waiting.

Consequently, a minor injury from a mother may become an opportunity for growth. Conversely, a mother who always sacrifices her interests and life to be available to her child encourages unrealistic expectations and reduces her ability to become independent. Therefore, a mother need not feel excessive guilt for not living up to the same standards as her child.

When a child lacks the resilience to cope with some injury, the damage could cause stress, personality weakness, symptom, anxiety, or inhibition. Further development or treatment may be able to overcome this weakness. In addition, if the conflict results in child abuse or neglect, the state may terminate a mother's parental rights and appoint an alternative guardian. As a child and mother mature, both learn from their own experiences, often yielding mutually beneficial accommodations, a hallmark of progress. Nevertheless, children, mothers, and analysts will always encounter challenges.

Winnicott, D. W. (1953) Transitional Objects and Transitional Phenomena—A Study of the First Not-Me Possession. International Journal of Psychoanalysis 34:89-97

Winnicott, D. W. 1956 Primary Maternal Preoccupation. *Collected Papers* New York: Basic Books, 1958 pp. 300-305

Kohut, H. (1982) Introspection, Empathy, and the Semi-Circle of Mental Health. International Journal of Psychoanalysis 63:395-407

Stern, D. N. (1985) The Interpersonal World of the Infant: A View from Psychoanalysis and Developmental Psychology. The Interpersonal World of the Infant: A View from Psychoanalysis and Developmental Psychology. Basic Books. New York

"Is there electricity?"

"No."

"It's hard for children to read by the flickering light of kerosene lanterns," Amma said, "and teachers in small towns like Kazipet are probably not as good as teachers in Secunderabad. Can you try to get the posting canceled?"

Nanna was irritated. "No, an order is an order. You can't fight with the Indian Railways. I can't disobey or try to undo the government."

Amma became more upset, and Nanna got more indignant. And then he got up from the table and walked away. I became afraid and worried; I had never before seen my mom or dad become *so* emotional.

I agreed with my mom because we had always had electricity, and I, too, wasn't sure how life would be with lamps. At that time, I was under the impression that electricity defined a city because the word *electricity* contained the word *city*. A city was electric, and a town was coal. Although I did not know much about them, I agreed with Dad that the Indian Railways was a world unto itself. I didn't know how one could fight the world in which one lives. Amma came to the bedside of each of us children that night and reassured us that she would enroll us in good schools, help us study hard; we would be fine. The railway-transfer disagreement between my parents was one of their few significant conflicts. The dust settled quickly, and we moved. The few years we spent in Kazipet were the most memorable years of my life. Yes, we had to do without electricity and read by the flickering light of kerosene hurricane lanterns. But, we lived up close to steam locomotives, which, to me, were even more miraculous than electricity.

That my mom wanted English as our medium of instruction impressed me. In her high school, she won the entire works of William Shakespeare for being the class valedictorian; she especially enjoyed *The Merchant of Venice*, *The Tempest*, and *As You Like It*. She felt that English was the gateway to our future worlds. However, for our family, our vernacular mother tongue best represented our hearts, souls. I appreciated her wisdom in blending Indian culture with Western education. My dad was a physician, and my sister became one, so the idea of me going into medicine myself felt natural. But my father's episodic tales of his experiences during World War II, especially his descriptions of amputations and dramatic renderings of *hara-kiri*, turned me off to the blood-and-guts surgical specialties. Then, as a young medical student, I won a copy of Freud's *Interpretation of Dreams* as a debating prize. I was fascinated by Freud's magnum opus, which so wonderfully elucidated the smoke and mirrors of the human mind that hid emotions and conflicts in plain sight. There and then, I decided to dedicate my future medical career to the study and practice of psychoanalysis.

My thoughts returned to Jan.

Jan was understandably reluctant or unable to fully explore the implications of the loss he suffered when his mother became sick and had to leave him when he was a toddler. Jan covered over his grief about this time by idealizing his mother; this enabled him to overlook the effect of her illness on his emotional stability. Jan idealized me since I had helped him during his more recent dark days, and he may not have been aware of any frustration he might have felt with me. I believed that I was standing in for his good mother. As a *good* son to my own mother, I understood that I was a good mother for Jan.

I resumed the conversation. "Today, we talked about many things, but I want to draw your attention to a few of them. When you and Maria talked about your mother leaving to go to the sanatorium and about Bowlby and attachment, she said, 'You're lucky that you turned out the way you did.'"

"She was joking."

"Do you think Maria was also making you more aware of the times when you missed your mother?"

"Yeah, there's a grain of truth in that."

Although hard to put into words, the memories of my own childhood anguish and the feeling that my mother abandoned me when my sister was born came back to me.

"I think your pain was profound when your mother left, and Amir's suicide reignited that feeling. Maybe because your mom left you at a critical time, you had a feeling that, if you become dependent on one person, like your mother, or on one place or thing, you would risk a serious loss, so you avoided that deep attachment by leaving. I'm not saying that I'm necessarily correct, but I'm interested in your thoughts."

Jan looked pained and irritated. "About this period in my life when my mom went to the sanatorium?"

"Yes."

"I feel like correcting the record, but I also feel like I have no right to make corrections. I was told stories, like how I behaved when my mom came back: that I was always around her, that she couldn't even go to the bathroom by herself."

(Note to my reader: Jan's accounts concerning the separation between him and his mother were not direct recollections but hearsay. Yet, he had faith in such reports. Additionally, in his bones and beyond words, Jan continued to harbor a fear of loss.)

Jan continued, "I heard this story many times, but I don't remember much of it. I remember a few scenes, but they're irrelevant. I remember burning myself. My grandma had this fireplace, and I loved playing near it. I don't remember anything else."

I wanted to clarify whether Jan chalked up this burning incident entirely to chance or if he had any further associations related to his mom or grandmom.

"The burn happened by accident?"

"Yes, but that's what I mean: I don't remember. My mom told me I wouldn't leave her and didn't want her to leave me. I believe it, but I myself can't confirm or deny it. I want to know the facts, but I have no way to know them directly. It's hard to explain. You can imagine those events so clearly that you're not sure if they're memories or memories of reports. I do have direct memories of my grandmother. For example, if I got sick on a school day when my mom was working, I would spend the day at my grandmother's. However, I have only a few isolated memories of my mom's time in the sanatorium. I never meditated on that period.

"Once, I was playing a game with a group of people, where you had to recollect your earliest memory. My earliest memory was the time when we lived in a certain house, and I felt like I was an adult trapped in a child's body, and I made a toast, and everybody was laughing. Have I told you this? It was like they were saying, 'Look how smart this kid is!' I felt like I was an adult with a long past and many experiences. I had a little body and couldn't do much, but I wanted to get their attention. I knew they would find it amusing.

"I asked my mom if she had any recollection of such an event and whether such a memory was possible. She didn't remember it, but when I described the house, she said that we lived in a house like that until I was about three years old."

"How old were you at the time of this memory?"

"Two or three, so that fits."

"Is it correct to say that your parents entertained when you were a child?"

"Yes."

"So, can it be said that their marriage, when you were small, had a social component and was better than it was later on—that their marriage deteriorated in later years?"

"Yes, that's how it was."

"When did your parents' marriage sour?"

"What I remember was that my father had conflicts with various family members. For example, if my father was offended by my grandma's statement, he wouldn't show up for family gatherings. I remember feeling ashamed that he acted like this. 'Everybody is here, except my father. What's happening?'

"A bunch of families used to do things together: have picnics, go for rides on a little train, organize games and competitions, visit old towns with castles, or just get ice cream. My father didn't understand the spirit of fun involved in such activities, and the times he *did* come, he was so serious. On one occasion, when I was maybe nine or ten years old—I don't remember if I challenged my father or if he challenged me—but we had a swimming race . . . and he didn't let me win! I was devastated. I thought I was the best swimmer on Earth. I was sure that I could beat anybody, including my father."

So, Jan's father *did* spend some time with him. "You and your father challenged each other in a swimming competition?"

"Yes. I was always losing and always being criticized by my father. I cleaned and vacuumed the apartment on Saturday mornings, but he was never satisfied. He would show me the dust on the tip of his finger from some obscure corner and say, 'What's this?'"

"It's clear you didn't care for his guidance," I said. "I want to go back to something you mentioned earlier about your toasting memory. Who normally proposed the toast at social gatherings?"

"Anybody, but usually, the hosts went first."

"So, it would be the role of your parents to offer a toast. As you said, you wanted to be in the limelight, even when you were young."

"If my memory is correct."

"This may be a real or fabricated memory, but my question is the same. Would it be accurate to say that you wanted to act like one of the adults of the hosting family?"

"Yes. I don't remember if I ever told you about levitating or floating in the air."

"No, I don't recall."

"I liked to climb on furniture. I was sitting on a chair like this," Jan said, pointing to the chair he was sitting on. "I was watching the annual cyclists' competition, *Wyscig Pokoju*, Peace Tour, on TV; it's like a Polish Tour de France. So many bicycles were going really fast. I got excited and fell and banged my head. I have a vivid memory of floating in the air before I landed. The memory is vivid, but, of course, I didn't really levitate.

"I don't know how other people's memories work. Maria's recollections of her childhood are much more precise. Maybe that's because she had two sisters close to her age. There were lots of everyday interactions among them, so their memories were fixed and sharpened. Her parents also took many pictures and movies of them singing and dancing. They are like documents of their childhood. In Maria's house, the images in the movies, which the family watched often, reinforced her natural memories.

"I don't have such evidence for my childhood memories. There are only about forty or fifty pictures from my childhood. That's all. I asked my mom many questions after discovering that she was dying. Mostly, I wanted to hear her understanding of how my father acted after I was born. She answered all my questions. It was a painful experience having these conversations with my mom because I knew that time was running out. Sofia did the same thing, and she had the same feeling."

"No matter how much time you have, your curiosity can never be fully satisfied," I said. "New questions keep cropping up, but the relationship must eventually come to an end. The other thing is that you'll never have that opportunity with your father. First, he may not be willing, and second, he may not be able to respond. Even though he's alive, your paths with him are severely restricted or blocked. You cannot work through anger and disappointment with him. He might talk, but he does not listen or understand how you want him to. Goodness, he was preoccupied with his pedicure when your mom died! He might put the phone down again and frustrate your efforts."

Jan replied with deep sadness, "I know what you're saying. I haven't called him for two weeks now. I've been busy."

"So, it's time to rev up the guilt?"

"Yes, I feel guilty. It's a problem: Due to my father's dementia and personality, my questions to him will remain unanswered; perhaps, I'll never even ask them. Once, when I was in my twenties, I was at my parents' home, and the phone rang. I answered it. There was a woman on the other end of the phone, and I could tell she thought I was my father—my voice *is* very much like his—and she said something that only men and women having affairs would say to each other. That phone call told me my dad was cheating on my mom. After that, I engaged in a systematic investigation to prove that he was an asshole, that he wasn't the person he proclaimed himself to be.

"He always prided himself on being a churchgoing moralist and Orthodox Catholic, but he was an adulterer. I challenged everything he said. He told stories of his time at the university and stories of what he did when he was my age. He claimed to be a great student. He wasn't. I discovered the box where he kept his secret things: There were old yellow and white daguerreotypes and pictures. Some of them were from the fifties, before he was married. On the back were inscribed words like 'to my lovely Max.' When Maria and I were in Poland, she looked for pictures of me as a baby, and she flipped through his stash. She discovered a few pictures of me, but we found more recent pictures of women, with notes written on the back. All of them had something irresistibly whorish in their faces. I had to conclude that my dad was a liar and that whatever he said, there was an 80% chance that it was false. I've never spoken about anybody as negatively as I've spoken about my father.

"My father was the only person I felt like thoroughly investigating. After I caught him in a few lies, I tried to verify everything he said. Because of this, I know a lot about my father. I found a yearbook of his and read all the entries. I spied on him even before discovering that he was cheating on my mom. I found the hard evidence for his cheating when we moved my parents to a place near my sister. He was already demented by then, and we had to pack their stuff. Sofia became upset and outraged; it was such a shock to her. For me, it was something I had been putting together for many years."

"Well, Jan, this was an interesting session, but it must come to an end like all things, both good and bad. And we're almost there."

Jan responded abruptly, "It *doesn't* end here, actually. What we do here triggers lots of memories in me. Some of them come to me when I'm driving. It's a perfect time for something new to surface. Where nothing existed, suddenly there's a new angle, and it happens more and more. Last week, we talked about my Aunt Malgorzata. It was an interesting session because she caused many problems and pain when I didn't need it. She had disappeared from my life, and then last week, she came alive again in the session. After I left, I called my sister, and we talked about how Aunt Malgorzata reacted to the death of her son and how upset she became when my mom asked her to come live with us for a while. As I remember her, she was a religious fanatic preaching love and not knowing anything about it. Now I can see her other side."

"She was deeply hurt when her son died," I said.

"Yes, so deeply hurt."

CHAPTER 17

THIS SESSION MARKS THE START of the fifth month of Jan's treatment. Jan came in eager to engage. "Remember how I told you how everything we talk about here triggers more memories and emotions? More and more details are surfacing in my consciousness. It's like a strange archeological dig. When I dust off these forgotten fossils, they come alive again. I call it 'an awakening of memories.'"

"So, what new demons are surfacing?"

"Unpleasant ones. Some I hadn't touched for so long that they were quite petrified until we started to talk. The excavated memories come with strong negative emotions, so I tend to go for clarity and extremes when I first describe them to you. The subtleties and details emerge slowly, later. I realize, for example, that maybe the portrayal of my aunt was too biased and skewed."

"You mean your father's sister, Aunt Malgorzata?"

"Yes. After seeing you for almost five months, it's only now that I'm able to see her as a grieving mother, mourning for her son. I was young, but I remember my parents and my mom's sisters trying to console Aunt Malgorzata. That doesn't fit her picture as a selfish, hateful religious fanatic. Now that we're expecting a baby, I have a hint of what it means to lose a child. Instead of seeing Aunt Malgorzata as a one-dimensional person, I see her as someone more complex. I don't see things as they are right away. I first see them in black-and-white and then slowly notice the more subtle points and begin to see shades of gray. Some people see the whole complexity of another person almost immediately. Their views of the person are nuanced from the beginning. This black-or-white, all-good-or-all-bad bias probably

193

has to do with, among other things, my father's harsh lessons. I'm trying to change it now."

"I agree. I said something last time, which I'll repeat in a minute. I want you to know that when I say something, I say it with the full understanding that I'm lucky if I'm even in the ballpark of what's relevant to you. I'm not saying something because it's the only right way of looking at a situation. I am just giving you my opinion at that moment. You may take all of it or part of it, or you can reject it entirely."

"But your examples really stick in my mind," Jan insisted.

"Maybe you're still looking at me through rose-tinted glasses or . . . goodness-tinted glasses. Everything I say seems good to you. Last time, I said to you, 'You made a remarkable recovery in terms of your accomplishments and personality, but perhaps because your mother went into the sanatorium, you're prone to occasional bouts of feeling abandoned, left alone, not knowing what's happening. At those times, you suddenly experience a loss of belonging or being. You can call it whatever you want. When I said that she *left* you with her sister, I made a mistake. You corrected me and clarified that she left you with her *mother*, that is, your grandmother. Given the way your face looked at that moment, I felt like I had said something really off. I then thought about your recollections of your mother, who was so devoted to her children. There's an aura of goodness that emanates from her. I suggested that your wanting to move periodically may be connected to your mother's stay in the sanatorium, that you'd rather leave others before someone leaves you. But in saying that, I felt that I brought something extraneous into the way you like to think about your mother. The memory of her availability stays with you, but this was when she wasn't available. From the look on your face, I felt that something I said didn't sit right with you."

Jan responded with relief. "Maybe I was reacting to the word *left*. That didn't agree with me because—"

Jan stopped mid-sentence, perhaps because he was trying to figure out how to avoid criticizing what I said. I completed the sentence, "—she didn't leave or abandon you. She *had* to leave you. She was ill, and she went to get medical treatment."

"Exactly. My mother had no choice. I reacted to your idea that my mom 'left me' and not leaving me *with my grandma*. It was the standard of care at the time."

"I understand. I'm glad you clarified from where your pained look came. It was a reaction to my incorrect and careless choice of words."

Jan's correction reassured me. My saying that Jan's mom "left" him when he was a toddler expressed only a part of my intention but unfortunately neglected a key component. Although her absence affected him, she did not intentionally abandon him. Therefore, saying she "left" was an incomplete statement of my understanding—therefore, offensive to Jan. A patient's correction of an analyst's interpretation is, in my opinion, a precious contribution to the analysis, but only if the analyst is capable of accepting corrections from his patient.

"I'm not sure if it was a wrong choice of words," said Jan. "I also wanted to correct you and clarify that it was my grandma and not my aunt who took care of me. It's not that I'm so attached to details; I'm often sloppy myself. I think we're delving into an area that reflects a deficiency in my upbringing. The schedule of my day changed when my mom left. With my grandmother, I could do whatever I wanted. She wanted to spoil me. She knew that I was missing my mom. Whatever I wanted, I asked for, and she gave it.

"I'm not sure what my father did at that time. He was busy with work. He had to travel for weeks at a time. He was a chemical engineer, and he had to analyze coal samples from strip-mining facilities in different parts of the country. I remember him telling me about strip mining and black coal and brown coal. Even if a facility wasn't very far away, he had to be there for a week or so at a time. It was the sixties, and there were no private cars in Poland. Only party *apparatchiks* had personal vehicles. The higher up you were in the Communist party, the higher the probability of being assigned a government car. Public transportation was the only way everyone else could get around. When he was on-site, he would stay in a nearby hotel. I discovered this just before my mom died when I was trying to find out from her as much as possible, and this information popped up.

"I also had some memories of my father talking about his achievements. As a boy, I was impressed with his life. He would scold me for not doing my best and talk about always being the best student and getting awards. When I became a teenager, I started to suspect that he was exaggerating. He told me once that he was in a graduate program and was close to getting a Ph.D. I told you I learned how to open his safe, and I checked his papers. He applied to the program, but I saw the letter of rejection in response to his application. So, I found out he had never started when he was saying that he was almost finished. This discovery affected me because he always put himself out there as a role model. Still, I learned not to confront him directly because he would become even more nasty than usual. This is how he ruined quite a few Sunday dinners."

"Sunday dinners?"

"It was a big tradition in our family. We used the good china and real silver, and my mom would spend all morning cooking. She would get up early and put food in a slow cooker, so that we could come back home after mass and have dinner. Then, we would sit around the table, eating and talking. I behaved myself most of the time, but sometimes I just couldn't take it and had an argument with my father. Once, the argument became louder and more and more heated until my father was about to explode. Everyone sensed it. At that point, my mom, my sister, and I exchanged knowing looks, and all conversation stopped. Over time, we learned to avoid certain topics and never to criticize him. Often, I wanted to say something but decided it just wasn't worth it.

"I especially remember Christmas, the most beautiful of all holidays. My mom and her family put their hearts into celebrating Christmas. The house looked beautiful, cleaner, and nicer than at any other time of the year. My mom and aunts spent many days cooking and preparing traditional dishes. Polish cuisine is elaborate and time-consuming, and the women in my family made everything from scratch. Slow cooking was an essential part of celebrating Christmas. Of course, everything had to be perfect. I remember a few situations, though, when my father screwed things up and spoiled the atmosphere right before Christmas.

"One year, Mom had discovered that the grout was missing between a few tiles in the bathroom and asked my father if he would fix it before Christmas. Suddenly, *just* before Christmas, he decided to do it. My mom went shopping, and when she came back [Jan laughed], he had not only started to work on the grout, but he was also remodeling the apartment! The house was a mess. My mom got upset, but all she said was that maybe another time, rather than just before Christmas, would have been better. He said he underestimated how long it would take.

"Another example, also right before Christmas: There was a party at my father's work, and some of the partygoers had had a few too many drinks; he brought them home without telling my mom. So in the middle of the night, she was completely surprised—and really upset—to find more than a dozen guests in her house!

"At Christmas dinner, you're supposed to forgive others for all the wrongdoing they may have committed in the past year. You stand up at the table and break off a piece of flatbread. In the Christian tradition, it symbolizes the body of Christ. I don't know what it's called in English."

"The host?"

"Yes, we call it *hostia*, from Latin, or *oplatek*, in Polish. Anyway, you must forgive the transgressions of your loved ones, and it can't be just an act; it has to be done from your heart. But even if you don't *feel* like doing it, you pretend to do it. I remember one Christmas when I was holding a huge grudge against my father. I didn't even feel like pretending that I forgave him, so I refused. When my maternal grandmother was alive, she was the matriarch, arbitrating family disputes and discord. After she died, Aunt Marta took over this role. Aunt Marta took me aside and said, 'Remember: This is the only night that you absolutely have to do what's right. If you have problems with your father, take them up some other time, not tonight. Your whole family has to be together this one night. It's important.'

"I was upset. I don't even remember what the fight was about. I thought she was letting my father win, but I had to obey her."

"It's so important that you forgot!" I responded. I had no idea what may have been responsible for Jan's forgetting. Still, I wanted to impress on him that, for our purposes, sometimes an alternative to the forgotten thought can be valuable for understanding.

Jan continued, "A son expects protection, education, and love from his father. Unfortunately, mine didn't have the heart of a father. He put me down so many times. He was never satisfied with anything I did. Until I left home, I had to deal with his constant disapproval. I needed validation, but my father was incapable of giving it to me.

"After I left home to attend medical school, he would try to test my knowledge of various medicines. He was a chemical engineer, and he also took many medications, so he knew something about them. He would ask me about their chemical composition or their side effects. Sometimes I just didn't want to talk to him. I started to ignore him and distanced myself from him by stonewalling. This gave me some comfort because I felt that I could control our interaction.

"I believe that, deep in his heart, he was actually proud of me. That's what I heard from others, especially after my mom died. My father had a friend from work whom I met after my mom's funeral. He told me how proud my father was of me, but I never felt it directly. He always focused on what I wasn't doing right, often contrasting them with made-up stories of what *he* did right. I considered him a hypocrite.

"I never could let go of the idea that he cheated on my mom, even though I couldn't tell anyone. I certainly couldn't tell my mom. I didn't want her to be upset. Now I feel that she knew but didn't want to confront him. She was that kind of person. Maria thinks my mom stayed there, unhappy, for the children's sake.

"Mom wanted us to have an intact family. At some point, though, my father's presence in the family didn't make any sense. On one of my visits home, my mom and I were standing on the balcony, and I remember telling her, 'You're unhappy. Maybe it's time to consider it. Let him go. Get divorced. We're grown. There's no reason to continue to suffer. We can take care of ourselves.' She didn't reply. She stayed with him. Then he started to lose his memory, and she *couldn't* leave him.

"His dementia got worse, and he abused medications. Sometimes, he would hallucinate, and he became bitchier and more impossible. To cope with this added stress, my mother would go for a walk or visit one of her friends. When she came back, she often found him watching TV or simply sitting on a chair. The storm had passed.

"She came to see me here, in Chicago, a few years ago for an extended visit, and she asked some relatives to take care of him while she was gone. He didn't cooperate. Our relatives said that he would say he had just taken a shower and was naked and couldn't open the door whenever they came. Actually, he *never* took a shower during those weeks! He did always answer the phone, though. He would say, 'I'm OK. Don't worry about me.' He basically became a recluse. They didn't see that he was such a goner.

"My mom realized it when she came home. She said she wanted to cry. The house was a total mess and smelled awful. There were dirty dishes everywhere. Each time he ate, he left the dirty dishes wherever. And when he wanted to eat again, he took out a new one. The bathroom stank. And he had dropped clothes all over the house. It was like a mad person's house. He had utterly deteriorated.

"Sofia called him every week from Warsaw to check on him. Often his speech was slurred because he was abusing medications for anxiety. When my mom had tried to control his medications, he became agitated and hostile, so she gave up and left him alone; when she stopped interfering, she had peace again, if you can call it peace."

"What do you mean?"

"He was stoned all the time and slept sixteen hours a day. My mom cooked him whatever he wanted; she enjoyed cooking. He got up and watched TV from time to time, but they rarely spoke.

"Then he started to spend tons of money on ridiculous items. When he retired, he was the head of the research unit in a factory, so he had a pretty good pension, more than anybody else in his town. For weeks before his check came, he was tired and lethargic and wouldn't do anything. Then it came, and he was full of energy, running to doctors to get prescriptions and then going to the pharmacy and buying all sorts of vitamin supplements. And then he would leave for a few days. Maybe he was depressed and anxious and used all those pills to self-medicate. He took mouthfuls of them, overdosing to the point that he didn't care what he took or how much.

"Unfortunately, he'd been prescribed L-DOPA for his Parkinson's disease. It helped him temporarily, but it suppressed his body's production of L-DOPA. He would buy a month's supply, and it would run out before the month was out. He denied taking more than he was prescribed, but he liked to overdose on it because it gave him energy. In fact, it made him *crazy* with energy, and he didn't care about the consequences. When we were packing his stuff to move him to the nursing home, we discovered a big stash of medications in a hidden compartment in a cabinet. And on top of that, he took many snake-oil supplements that were supposed to make him young again. There were bottles of *tonicum* containing lecithin, Gingko biloba, ginseng . . . He spent so much money on this stuff.

"One day, my mom served him just pasta and nothing else, and he complained, 'What is this? This isn't food. You can't live on this.' 'Well,' she said, 'if you give me money, I can buy groceries, and we can eat better, but this is all we have for now.' He was blowing so much money on drugs!

"After my mom died and I began talking to friends and relatives, I came to realize what a difficult situation she had endured. My father got so agitated and incoherent from overdoses of L-DOPA that my mom thought he might kill himself. One of my cousins is a psychiatrist, and my mom asked him for help. He came to the house to talk to my father. It didn't take long for him to decide he needed to be hospitalized. Somehow, my dad agreed and signed the necessary papers. I don't know why it bothers me. I suppose that I'm concerned about my own genetic predisposition. Maybe I'm prone to similar depressions."

"When you spoke earlier," I said, "you clarified that your Aunt Malgorzata was nasty, and you felt that it might be that she became bitter after her son died."

"Yes."

"Concerning your father, most of your memories have been about his nastiness, but there are a few good memories, too. At the same time, you seem convinced that his depression and dementia were self-induced by his abuse of medications. Either way, it's important to consider the degree to which he is or is not, now, the father that you knew. He's not real because he's demented. Is he deliberately nasty or demented nasty? Is his current nastiness different from his nastiness when you were growing up?"

"He started developing dementia in his sixties. Now he's almost eighty, so he's been getting progressively more demented for the past fifteen years or so. He functioned well enough to hide it for a long time, but he can't anymore. We started to notice dementia when he pretended that he knew people when he actually didn't. He would say, with conviction, 'How are you?' without saying the person's name, and then, 'How's your family?' If the person looked young, he would ask, 'How's work?'"

"Yes, that can work for a while. In 1984, Ronald Reagan debated Walter Mondale and blanked out in the middle of a sentence; he subsequently developed Alzheimer's disease. In my opinion, his advisors put him in a closet for much of his second term and allowed him to appear only for public occasions or when he was delivering written speeches. He was still disciplined and could deliver excellent speeches when he wasn't under a lot of stress. Just as Reagan's advisors came up with a strategy to deal with him, you're also trying to figure out what happened to your dad and how to deal with him."

"Although he's demented, he engages in drug-seeking behavior that makes his condition worse. And he uses his toilet accidents to be nasty to others."

"You seem to feel that there's a vein of his original nastiness continuing in his demented behavior?"

Jan readily agreed, "Oh, yes. His nastiness is alive and well, and he's manipulative. However, years ago, when he was with a new group of people, he was always nice and pleasant. He had no problems handling social interactions, and people liked him."

"Especially strangers."

"Yes, that was often amusing to me. How was it possible that he could behave so well?"

I wanted to be sure Jan knew I heard what he said concerning his dad's reaction to close family members. "When your dad became impossible, such as when he insisted on a pedicure while you were planning your mother's funeral, your sister's attitude was one of disgust. She was just fed up."

"Yes."

"It seems to me that, although you are also disgusted, you have more curiosity about his functioning. Is that true?"

"For Sofia, his nastiness shines so brightly that everything else about him fades away. His senility enhances his nastiness, and his personality hasn't changed."

I spoke mockingly, as if from his sister's point of view, "Old age has deepened his personality!"

"Yes, he's uninhibited, but the same old guy. He can't sugarcoat his real self now. I do try to understand his situation, but I live far away. I have to deal with him much less than my sister. It's a big problem for me that I'll never be able to understand why he was the way he was. I wish I could talk with him, appreciate him better, and know why he behaved like he did when I was growing up. I'd like to have asked him questions about his upbringing. He told me some stories about his childhood, but I tuned him out. I felt that they must all be lies, like his participation in the Polish Underground. He claimed he didn't party or do anything stupid. I think those are also lies.

"I don't know much about his childhood. He had a rough life. I know a little about his father and only slightly more about his mother. His mother could have made anybody sick. I heard from my mom that his father was strict but fair: an old-fashioned Orthodox Catholic. Everybody had to follow his rules. My father said that he kissed his father's hands, the same hands that punished him. I don't know. I don't understand my father. Why was he so insecure? Why was he not able to invest in his family more? Why was he so selfish? Why did he make my mom cry so much? Sofia's resentment toward him stems primarily from his mistreatment of our mom. She feels that he poisoned her life. Sofia and my mom were close and shared their problems and worries.

"I grew up under the influence of the traditional Polish image of a man. A man's job was to be a breadwinner. Therefore, a man should always be a man and should never cry. I can see how hard it is for Polish men to admit to any weakness. Words like *depression* or *anxiety* were never used. Such 'nonsense' was reserved for women."

"Because your sister and your father live in Poland, she has to respond to him at close quarters. You're far away, and you're also using psychology to try to understand him. His dementia makes it hard for both of you, but it's perhaps easier for you than for your sister to show some understanding. You and she agree that he poisoned your mother's life. And you feel that he poisoned your life, too."

"Yes. To ward off his poison, I started to stay away from home as much as I could. I started to travel for longer periods. At the age of fifteen, I started to hitchhike—in Polish, it's called *autostop*—first just in Poland and later throughout Europe. I'd work hard for a few days in construction or on a farm and make some money during the summer. Then I'd travel until the money was gone. I was away the whole summer break."

"I think the work and travel were valuable experiences for you. As far as dealing with your nitpicking father, I don't know what to say except that he is elderly, and he will die one day. In the meantime, you struggle with being a decent guy to a demented and helpless dad. You call him on the phone and visit him. You try to look after his welfare."

"Yes, but although he has dementia and can't understand me, I'm often sarcastic. For example, I made fun of him when he told me that the nuns were stealing money from him. He's so suspicious."

"You told me that he came from a family that had lost wealth."

"Concern about money was a big part of his mother's life. She never stopped complaining about it. Supposedly, she would use whatever spare money she had to buy gold coins and then put them away somewhere. After she died, my father tried to find out where she hid the family 'treasure.' In desperation, he even bought a metal detector and spent days searching her property, but he never found anything."

"So, he feels robbed of his inheritance, and he transfers his suspicions to the nuns?"

"Yes. There was another issue with Marek, my sister's husband. Marek is a chemical engineer and works with synthetic polymers, my father's area of specialization. My father patented a few things in his life, and he told me Marek was stealing his ideas. I told him that the field has probably changed in the 30 years since he got his patents, but his mind was made up, and I couldn't change it. So I stopped trying because I was afraid he would explode.

"When my father talks about Kasia, Sofia's daughter, he says, 'What if her biological parents had bad genes, and she turns out to be a monster?' He told me that my niece is suspicious and maybe a sociopath. I told him, 'Of all the nasty thoughts you have, keep this one to yourself,' and he became defensive."

"In that conversation, your father seemed to be aware of the themes of suspiciousness and sociopathy, but he saw them as characteristics of others and not as features that others saw in him. A little projection?"

"My father has clear sociopathic traits. I wish I knew more of what he went through, but that wish will never be satisfied."

"True."

"I saw a picture of my father when he was in grammar school. Some of the other people are still around. One of the guys wrote a book about the Polish Underground from my father's area. He visited us one time, and I wanted to ask him some questions, but I didn't. I wanted to ask him what my father was like when he was young and whether he ever had a role in the Polish Underground. It's important to me."

"Curiosity about where we come from and about our parents is natural, but there are limits beyond which we can't go. One major limit is when they die, they can't speak for themselves. Perhaps your father has already reached that point. Dementia may have robbed him of his ability to communicate. And even if he could talk, you think he often lies."

"When Sofia talks about my dad, she makes me feel uncomfortable. His brain has shrunk, and she doesn't make accommodations for his real dementia. I think both of us should ease up about him."

"It's important for you to be able to talk to your dad, if you can, and understand him, because he can still influence your judgment about other people."

"For example?"

"You felt, maybe too readily, that Amir's dad was similar to yours. The funny thing is that your dad's personality didn't overwhelm you, as Amir's father appeared to have done to him."

"I told you, I grew up with one thought: I don't want to grow up to be like my father. Sometimes, Sofia would say, 'You're raising your voice like Dad. You think that the louder you are, the more you're right.' That cut deep. I was offended to be compared to my father. Even to be told that I looked like him was deeply wounding. I felt jealous when someone wanted to be like his father. I thought that was so beautiful."

"At least you're working on creating a thermostat for your loudness. I can attest that I've never heard you shout."

"A second ago, I said that when people say I look like my dad, I feel hurt. I felt guilty after I said that."

"You're being disloyal to your genes!"

Both of us laughed, and we ended the session.

I indicated that Jan laughed when describing his father's wild behaviors in this session. The laugh, in this instance, was a combination of annoyance and resignation at how incorrigible his father was. In addition, the laughter indicated to me how Jan accepted, with humor, the slings and arrows of having the father he had, even though he did fight his father when he was younger.

Because of the predominance of the themes of death (in many forms) and Jan's heartfelt anger, you should not conclude that a heavy cloud hung over our sessions. On the contrary, a lighthearted tone imbued many sessions, although certainly not the earliest ones. Jan sometimes tickled my funny bone, and we often joked about the lives and times of two shrinks practicing the impossible profession. Jan did, however, become somber when talking about the deaths of his mother and Amir.

I tried to convey to him my sense of good fortune for the experience of every breath of my life. A jesting awareness of life's many absurdities and treatment gradually infused the therapy, sometimes a joke or laugh, but often in our tone of voice. Both Jan and I found ways to address such absurdities with, by turns, hilarity and irony. However, it is difficult to adequately convey here the lightheartedness that poked through Jan's profound pain.

CHAPTER 18

By now, I had been seeing Jan for almost five months.

Jan started the session. "I called my father after our last session. It was about 9 a.m. in Chicago, so it was 4 p.m. in Poland. He didn't pick up the phone for a while, and then a nurse did. She told me that he'd been sleeping most of the day and was still drowsy.

"She put him on, and I went into my routine. I told him who I was and asked if he knew who I was. As the nurse had just woken him up, I thought he was still drowsy and disoriented. I said, 'Maybe you were just awakened from sleep and didn't recognize me right away.'

"He felt that I was testing his orientation, and that touched a raw nerve. He was upset. 'I wasn't asleep. I was just lying down.'

"I had intended to let him talk and just listen to him. Instead, the conversation got started on the wrong foot. After talking a while, I still doubted whether he knew he was talking to his son. He made generic comments and didn't say anything specific that indicated that he recognized me. That was the worst part. I don't know if he knows that he can't recognize me, his own son. He didn't say 'Jan' or 'son,' and he didn't even utter a generic greeting for a relative like 'my dear.' That's connected with what we talked about last time. I have no sense that I can communicate with my father. Whatever I make of all this is for myself alone. He's not there. He doesn't have any periods of lucidity. He can't participate in any meaningful conversation. My sister says that, from time to time, she feels that he does understand. My feeling is that he's responding to the cookies and treats that she brings him—he *does* recognize food. She seems to feel that this positive reaction is a significant social interaction. I don't know."

"Does he recognize her?"

"She said that sometimes he does, and sometimes he calls her by the name of some other family member. So, the family names are in his mind; he just doesn't connect them to the right people. I think he did some of this to himself. He was popping pills and fried his brain. Once, he complained of fatigue and was depressed. Finally, his doctor prescribed *Cardiamid-Coffein,* which had caffeine and some neuro-stimulant. Soon after, he was out of it and taken to the hospital. My sister and I visited him, and then we went to his house and found two buckets full of empty bottles of this drug! I was stunned. I was surprised he wasn't dead!

"Once, he went on a health kick, exercising every day, eating only sprouts and seeds, and drinking only *Zuber* spring water, which smelled and tasted like rotten eggs. He cultivated some Chinese or Mongolian organic fungi. He grew the fungi buds in milk for two or three days and then ate them. It looked like mucus but tasted like yogurt.

"He punished anyone who wasn't living a 'healthy' lifestyle like his. He criticized my mom for being overweight. He criticized my sister for not being active. Many relatives in the family got tired of his health talk. His main point was that they were killing themselves. He left me alone, since I was on the university swim team. I woke up before 5 a.m. and swam for two hours; then, I went to the weight room. After a few years of his 'health' kick, he returned to his old habits. He even started smoking again. Everybody was relieved. We call people like my father *słomiany ogień,* "straw fire," in Polish. They're inconsistent people who get overexcited about something for brief periods, and then, like straw fires, they burn out quickly.

"The one thing he did consistently was to go to church. He was an aggressive believer in what he thought the Bible said. For example, he thought Jews would go to hell for what they did to Jesus. When my sister pointed out that the Bible doesn't say the Jews did anything so wrong, he was surprised and upset and refused to believe her. He followed the Polish Catholic tradition as practiced by the Church, which had a good dose of bigotry, and mistook it for the teachings of the Bible.

"I was just thinking, what triggered this chain of thought? I think it was when we started to talk about father-and-son issues in the last session and whether he gave me a predisposition for depression."

Jan was pensive as he continued, "The trigger was when we asked the wider question: How much is my life similar to his?"

I was glad that Jan was thinking about the similarities between his father and himself. Previously, I had felt that he was more invested in denying any similarities between them. I didn't think that I had a real understanding of his dad, so I was in no position to judge Jan's distortions. I didn't particularly care that he felt he and his father were similar. The important thing was for him to develop a multifaceted view of his dad and others. The fact that he was comparing his father with himself was a sign of analytic progress. My job now was to sit back, relax, and watch this bud of self-understanding grow.

Jan continued, "This week, I got two e-mails. One said that a friend of mine, a psychiatrist, had died of pancreatic cancer. The other said that a patient killed his psychiatrist in North Carolina. I got them confused, though, and told my residency classmate that my psychiatrist friend was killed by his patient. I don't know how I merged these two events and made this story up. I realized that my brain sometimes short-circuits, like my father's. All of a sudden, I felt a need to call my father and talk to him. That got me thinking of other similarities between my father and me. I don't know why."

Forgetfulness and confusion relating to dementia are different from forgetfulness and confusion related to events in everyday life. Jan's father produced confabulations, the made-up statements of a demented man. On the other hand, Jan's misstatements stemmed from unconscious conflicts that were amenable to correction through self-understanding. I felt that narrowing the gap he had opened between his father and himself would foster greater emotional maturity. We could explore Jan's problems to the degree that his insight, the focus and timing of my treatment technique, and the quality of our relationship would allow. Any similarities between Jan and his father could serve this purpose. Still, I felt stuck because the differences in the causes of the two incidents were the worst examples from which to derive meaningful comparisons. Without much confidence, I made a halfhearted link between them. "Were you concerned that you were similar to your dad because you, too, made up a story? He confabulates, filling memory gaps with—"

"—normal-sounding sentences that cover up missing chunks of the brain," Jan completed my sentence. "Yes. I'm wondering if this is what sometimes happens to me."

After exploring the futility of this comparison, I hoped that Jan would look for better examples. "Tell me more."

"I don't think that, at my age, I'm missing any brain tissue. My problem was more of whooshing through things without thinking them through so that they merge awkwardly from time to time. I read a lot, and I read fast, even when I have plenty of time. I see a few letters or parts of letters, and a word pops into my head. I'm looking for the gist of the story. I do not look at the specific words or terms and put them together in sentences. I've always sought out the essence of what I was reading. I think this was how my father approached reading, too, but I'll never know: He liked to read bigoted, religious pamphlets, including anti-Semitic stuff like *The Protocols of the Elders of Zion*. They weren't interesting to me. My father believed these religious conspiracy theories like they were coming from verified historical sources, and he railed against anyone who dared to question them. As a result, almost all of our conversations on such topics ended up as arguments. Now, I can see it wasn't all his fault. I also had a role in creating this pattern because I started with a closed mind, dismissing everything he had to say before he even opened his mouth. And he did exactly the same with me. I used to think that we argued because we were so different. Now, I wonder if we argued because we were so similar.

"Another philosophical question that I have has to do with genetics. I have my father's genes, so how different from him can I be? Am I doomed from the very beginning? Am I destined to be an anxious, irritable, and compulsive conspiracy theorist like my father? Can your treatment help me change? In general, how much can treatment change a person's basic predispositions? Besides, I'm past forty. How much can I really change? I don't think human beings maintain the ability to make profound changes in their lives indefinitely. I do believe, though, that as long as my heart is beating, I can still learn. It's not as easy as when I was younger, but I want to change because I'm unhappy with some parts of myself.

"My psychiatry training has helped me identify what's healthy and what's pathological in a person. I see this in myself *and* my father. I don't know if having this knowledge and perspective will give me a leg up and change me to be different from my father. I wanted to be the exact opposite of my father at one time. I had concrete notions of good and evil; he represented evil, and I wanted to be good. He went to church, so I avoided it. He told me stories about how hard he studied, so I got the dean to approve years of leave from school and went traveling. Then my father told me that he would cut me off, and I was on my own financially. I was passive-aggressive. I never actually confronted him. I never told him, 'I want to travel to experience what life has to offer. Someday, I'll marry and settle down, but I want to get to know the world first, and now is the perfect time to do it. If I don't, I'll get bored and boring, going to the same places and doing the same stuff every day.' I never had such a conversation with him. I took a leave from my studies, and he found out later. I got some twisted pleasure from doing things he didn't like and couldn't stop.

"But there's another side to the story. My father never knew exactly where I was, who my friends were, or what I did at school because I excluded him. But I still did allow him to influence my life. For example, when he said he would no longer support me financially, he insisted that I acknowledge that I was ready to accept adult responsibilities. He said that I had to go to the next level and support myself. I agreed; it was time for me to grow up. And we didn't have any arguments about it.

"As I look back at those times, I see that my views on life and the way the world works were black-and-white. Life was simple—no shades of gray. *Them* meant Communists, and *us* was pretty much everybody else. Communists deprived people of freedom, and people fought against them. A common enemy unified members of the opposition, who had many different ideas of what Poland should and would look like when the Communists were gone. After the Communists lost power in 1989, the opposition broke into warring parties. No one knew who the good guys and bad guys were anymore. Life got complicated.

"I would like to know how I'm similar to my father, but I had no one to talk to until I started seeing you. I'm not sure if my sister is a good source because of her fixed, negative view of him. And maybe I don't want her to think about the similarities between him and me. I would ask my mom if I had the chance. Before she died of cancer, I asked her opinion and advice on everything I could think of in a desperate attempt to get as much from her as I could to guide me for the rest of my life. When she passed away, I felt that so many questions were still unanswered. As my father is preparing to say goodbye, I fear that this might be much harder. In my experience, if the relationship between a child and a parent was troubled, grieving is more difficult."

Jan had a historically troubled and hostile relationship with his father. Now, his father was demented and helpless. Jan was thinking of possible similarities and differences between his perceived *evil* dad and himself. Taking stock of their relationship might constitute anticipatory grieving and possibly help lessen Jan's pain upon his father's death.

Jan's father's actions were irritating and provocative. Given that Jan was guilt-prone, I feared that Jan might, in the future and after his father's death, regret any current angry interactions with his father. So, I thought it would help Jan if he appreciated that his father was demented and helpless and treated him with as much compassion as possible. Analysts differ on the best time to offer interpretations to patients. At that time, I could not think of a way to convert my thoughts about anticipatory grieving into any meaningful intervention. Even if I did, I tend not to provide interpretations when a patient is freely associating. I felt Jan was freely associating, so I said nothing at that time.

Jan continued, "One of my patients said that she didn't care if her father lived or died. After he died, she had a horrible time. Maybe there's a rule: The more unresolved conflicts a person has with their parent, the more confusion and pain there is after the parent dies. I know that, in my case, there are so many unresolved issues that the likelihood of this happening is high. And yet, in another sense, I think maybe I won't have much of a reaction when my father passes away. I guess we will see."

"Well," I said, "it's hard to predict how you would [I was careful not to say *will*] react to your father's death. It may be easier to speculate about your current attitude toward him. You said that you wanted to be different from him, better. You want to be an excellent psychiatrist. There may also be an 'Amir angle' to this situation. Both your father and Amir's father were demanding. Both were rarely satisfied with their son's accomplishments and felt their best wasn't good enough. A lack of basic recognition breeds anger. I think Amir's hostile feelings toward his father were similar to your feelings for your father. Amir couldn't express his frustration toward his father. Maybe, based on his feelings for his father, Amir developed a negative transference toward you and unconsciously needed to frustrate you, so he kept his depression a secret. Finally, he killed himself, shortly after maintaining that he was fine, right when you were going to get married."

"I see the similarities between Amir's upbringing and mine and our fathers' consistent attempts to invalidate what we did," Jan responded. "Both of our fathers discounted our accomplishments. Although I realized this even then, I never told Amir about the similarities between his dad and my dad. [*Dad*, I thought.] He didn't even know if my father was alive. In this area, I never crossed the line. There was no self-disclosure from my side. For example, one of the Critical Incident Review Committee members, Dr. Shastri, asked if Amir knew that I was getting married. *I* never told him that the purpose of my vacation was to get married, but in a university community, people often hear things through the grapevine. For example, a woman in the waiting room once asked me, 'Is Maria your wife?' Later, I found out that this woman was Maria's patient. Maria hadn't told her, but somehow, she found out. Maybe Amir overheard someone talking about my marriage in the hallway, but he wasn't curious like this woman was. He didn't snoop around or ask questions."

I noticed that Jan pondered the similarities between Amir's dad and his own and used the word *dad*.

"The similarities between our fathers were clear to me from the start, and he didn't know anything about it. Hence, the way I engaged in this case. . . . Because he was so attached to my life, I started to use words, methods, and ideas from my life from before I started to train in psychiatry. I cared about what he said, and we had what I think was a brotherly relationship, although I don't have a brother in real life. This was particularly true regarding his attempts at dating. Although there's no such diagnosis, he had a sort of intermittent body dysmorphic disorder. Sometimes, he felt he was a handsome guy. Other times, he thought he was unattractive and got depressed. My own experiences guided the way I tried to help him. I gave him advice about dating and women based on the experiences I had had."

I wondered if a person can give any advice outside the range of one's experience, thinking, imagination or feeling.

"You and I discussed some of the guidance that I gave him," Jan continued. "It worked, but the results terrified him."

When Ms. Chen tried to kiss him, I remembered that Amir called one of his friends in a panic, and she left.

Jan and I were on the same wavelength. "I'm sure you remember. When Ms. Chen kissed him—"

I completed his sentence, "—he called his friend."

Jan continued, "It worked, in that he got a kiss, although it wasn't in the proper context of what he was struggling with. You *can* make a depressed person smile. For a moment, it makes them feel better, but it doesn't cure the depression because you aren't making any meaningful change. That requires a coherent approach that the patient can consistently use. I know what I gave him; I gave him my dedication. I accommodated him when he was late and always tried to be available. We worked it out alternate times, if he had a class or a seminar or had to leave town. Amir did convey that he felt supported by me. The time and support you give to a patient are a significant part of the treatment. It can help change someone's life. I thought I had great intuition about him and understood the events and things in his life, although, ultimately, I was wrong. Like, sometimes he would bring something up, and I would decide that the time wasn't right to dig into it."

"Like?"

"There was one situation when he went back to India to visit his family, and they tried to fix him up with a girl. He was petrified. He didn't want it. He didn't want them to look for a bride for him, but he never confronted anybody. He never said, 'I'm not interested.' He just said, 'I like women in the United States.' But he was scared of women here, like Ms. Chen. Somehow, he found women wrong for him, like Natasha, the Russian lesbian. Ultimately he found it impossible to bring the Muslim and Western cultures together. He couldn't decide how he should be with women. Although he was attracted to and fascinated by American women, in the back of his mind, he still felt that women were inferior to men, that women had to follow the rules that men set for them. He was almost like Dr. Jekyll and Mr. Hyde. He shifted frequently, and different attitudes floated up at different times."

"Attitudes toward himself or women?" I asked.

"When he was twenty-one years old, his parents set up meetings with prospective brides. Amir felt trapped and became depressed. When his mother came to visit him here, she was preoccupied with getting him married. She became frustrated and seemed to have doubts about his sexual orientation."

"Did Amir say that, or are you saying that?"

"He said it. He said that even suggesting someone has a different sexual orientation raises alarms within his culture. He said that his family did everything humanly possible to fix him up with a woman and show everyone that he was 'normal.'

"He said, 'I'm not sure if I have any confusion about my sexual preferences,' but they put him in a bad situation by insisting on looking for a wife for him. Maybe he felt like an American soldier fighting in Iraq, who wants to get out, but has to keep on fighting because the military continues to send him back. He felt that he couldn't escape his family's wishes; he felt that they would trap him with a woman."

"I want to be sure that we understand the implications of what you've just said. Do you think *Amir* felt he was gay or that his *parents* were concerned that he was gay?"

"He never used that word. I'm sorry. Did I use the word *gay* when I described him?"

"No, you didn't. That's why I want to be clear about your thinking."

"He didn't use the word *gay*. He told me that his parents insisted on fixing him up with women, right now, right away. They said, 'Let's get the wedding invitations, so we can show everybody that you have a wife.' They didn't say, 'You're twenty-five, and you still are not with a woman; this looks bad in the eyes of culture.'"

"*culture* being—?"

"Indian Muslim culture."

"Did he go through the motions of looking for a wife?"

"They forced him to. He became depressed after that. He told me that was when he was closest to committing suicide. Several times, he told me that he felt attracted to women. As you know, one of them was a beautiful and feminine Russian girl, but she was a hard-core lesbian. She was active in the gay and lesbian community and was very open about her sexual preference. It was with this woman with whom he fell in love! He was hoping to change her sexual orientation through his love. He believed he could 'straighten her out' by putting his heart and soul into her.

"And there was Ms. Chen. His most significant sexual encounter was with her. She reciprocated his feelings. She kissed him. They petted. They even lay in bed together for a while. Then he panicked and invited his friend over, so she left.

"There was another girl with whom he was involved. From the way he described her, she probably had some character pathology. She would go from suicidal depressions to states of ecstasy. He told her that what he wanted was her happiness. When she was in a good mood, she would declare her love by e-mail. When she was in a bad mood, she would 'officially' break up, also by e-mail, and would even copy all of their friends! Then, the next day, she would show up at his apartment and apologize and then cry all day.

"Amir wanted to contact his dream woman. However, meeting the American Woman made him anxious, for he had to deal with women's lib, lesbianism, immodesty, craziness, or sex."

Jan laughed. "I told him that it's not really like that. I said, 'Who knows? The next one might be better. Having relationships with these women was impossible. Maybe they have more problems than you. Some women like drama.' He and Ms. Chen finally broke up for good. She did it the way borderlines do: She started to date his best friend and roommate and rubbed his face in it. She wanted him to know that she and his best friend were in love and happy together, so she sent him postcards from Michigan or wherever they went and told him they had sex all day long. It tortured him, and she knew it; that's what she appeared to want.

"Oh, and there was another woman. She was submissive and boring, but she showed interest in him. He didn't say it, but I sensed that he thought he would keep her for the time being until something better showed up. He wasn't interested, but he struggled with her for four or five months, trying to figure out if he could live with someone he had no feelings for. She would show up at his door, and he would try to hide. He started to feel that she was stalking him. Then, all of a sudden, *she* dropped *him*. He found out that she was using *him* as a backup. She had found her man, a married man, and started an affair. Although Amir had used her as a backup and thought he had no interest in her, their breakup crushed him. Then, he started to blame his problems with her on the medications I had prescribed."

"How did he blame the medications?"

"He thought she found out that he was taking medications and concluded that he was abnormal. He wanted to stop the medications so that he would feel normal. He suffered a lot because he couldn't attract a woman he could admire. It looked to him like everyone else around him was dating, having sex, and playing games, and he felt alone. He felt like an outsider. The psychotherapy I tried to do with him was mostly supportive and problem-solving, but my life experiences likely biased it."

"I think a psychiatrist has to base his practice on what he learns in his psychiatry residency *and also* on what he has learned from his own life," I opined. "No one can ignore life experiences and practice in a vacuum. No one should pretend that they operate without memory or desire. Although you shouldn't overburden a patient with personal details, there's no way *not* to bring them into your life. It's revealed in your actions and inactions, whether you want it to be or not. Objectivity is, to some degree, a pretense. Its strengths and limits have to be acknowledged. If you feel a similarity between your dad and Amir's dad, that's a thought. If you get a thought, you get that thought. You can't strike it out or erase it like they try to do in court proceedings. You can't separate your life from your self. The trick is how to combine your schooling and your life experiences in treating patients. You try to take from that well of yourself and give each patient what they need to thrive. With Amir, as you said, you were consistent, and you were dedicated. You gave him brotherly affection while maintaining boundaries in that you didn't burden him with details of your life. There were similarities between your lives and your relationships with your fathers. You tried your best. That is important to acknowledge. No one can fully control the final result, but you can control your effort."

"You're saying I'm still preoccupied and wondering what I missed. As you were speaking, a possibility occurred to me: Maybe the mistake I made was wrongly assessing Amir's depression. I looked at Amir's life through my eyes and assumed that he was similar to me. Now I know what depression is, but before, I didn't. I was just depressed. I explained this to you—feeling like it was always night, not wanting to get up, not leaving my room for months at a stretch.

"When Amir said, 'I'm feeling very depressed,' I remembered my own depression. But I never felt like committing suicide. That was the main difference between Amir and me."

I felt like a light bulb lit up in my understanding of Jan. "Yes, you felt depressed when people around you were dying. Your depression trapped you, but you never wanted to kill yourself. Amir also felt trapped when his parents tried to match him with women in an arranged marriage. He felt trapped in his depression, but he *did* want to kill himself."

The similarity between Jan and Amir went only so far and then stopped. When the severe depression came, Jan didn't feel like killing himself, but Amir not only felt like killing himself, but he kept it a secret and then actually did it. I added, "We started with the similarity between your fathers. You extended that similarity to depression. Until there, you were right. But you overextended the similarity when you considered your depression as a model for his depression."

"Yes."

"Today, you asked a question, 'What did I miss?' I think this reveals a new level of your self-understanding. Also, the reflection you did today isn't something you could have done previously. You didn't have this depth of understanding before. It's an important understanding for you to have now, about what you did then and what you couldn't have done then. I would like to say another thing about you that may apply in this case. You said that when you criticize your father, you feel guilty, right?"

"Yes, it always comes. Guilt always follows my criticism."

"Right. About Amir, there are many emotions, including guilt. Something like, 'I should have done something, but I didn't,' or 'I shouldn't have done something, but I did it.' You know: shoulda, woulda, coulda. I could say to you, 'Don't feel it' or 'Don't blame yourself,' but, as you said, that would be like forcing a depressed person to smile. So there are connections between you and Amir. Today, your insight offers a deeper and more subtle explanation of that connection; it clarified the areas of similarity and areas of dissimilarity between Amir and you."

There was a long, deep silence, during which Jan heaved a sigh of relief, perhaps comforted by my acknowledgment of his self-understanding. Our task was to bury a dead man, not battle his ghosts emotionally. Jan remained silent but looked at me as if he wanted me to say more. I continued, "There may be cultural factors at play, too. You remember you said that acting out suicidal impulses is taboo in Poland. You don't go there unless you're willing to be excommunicated and deprive yourself of happiness for eternity. So, if you want to commit suicide in Poland, you have to be ready to subject your soul to an eternity of unrest."

"True," Jan said, "but there's more to it. It's not an individual act. You're disgracing the whole family that's left behind. You know what I mean?"

"Tell me."

"The suicide will always mark the family. 'She's the one whose husband committed suicide' or 'She's the one who drove her husband to suicide.'"

I wanted to be sure I understood. "So, in Poland, suicide could be imagined, but there's a steep barrier between suicidal thinking or feeling and a suicidal act."

"Yes, for everybody in Poland and every other Catholic country in Europe, suicide is a big no-no."

"Do you have any information on Amir's view or his family's?"

"I asked him about views on mental illness and psychiatry in his country among Muslim Indians. On many occasions, he told me, 'Being a *pagal*—a crazy man was unacceptable. If you're in a nuthouse, it means that you're no longer a person. It's the end of your life. It's shameful for you and your family. Going to a psychiatric hospital is so shameful that it's worse than killing yourself. You're worthless.'

"I'm quoting his words, so you know how strongly he felt about this. I tried to get him to see a psychiatric hospital as a safe house, a place where his privacy would be protected. I tried to reassure him that nobody would know about it, but the idea of a safe house didn't click with him. He rejected it vehemently."

I caught a glimpse of the clock. "We don't have much more time today," I said, "but I wanted to be sure to follow up with something you said earlier. You said that Amir's mother's visit was interesting. . . ."

"Yes, I was going to say something about his attitude toward women. His mother was an important person in his life. She supported and comforted him, but he never said, 'My mom was the only person I felt at ease with.'

"My feeling was that, when he was a boy, he was taken from his mom and had to join the company of men. In some cultures, a boy goes through rituals, and from that point on, you're 'a man,' and you can't turn back. For Amir, it was something like that. From that point on, his mother was just a woman. He struggled with it and didn't fully accept it. He told me before his mom came that she was coming. Anticipating her visit made him happy and excited. When she arrived, we talked about his relationship with her in more detail.

"He mentioned that there was a time in his life when he tried to be a religious person. That reminded me of my own life. He became a strict practicing Muslim. He was so religious that he started criticizing his mother for not being religious enough. He preached so much that she started to listen, and he turned her into a more religious person. Later, he lost his faith, but she continued to be religious. When she came here, she recited his own words back to him. She would say, 'If you have a problem or don't feel right, pray. Praying does miracles.' He laughed at her when she quoted his own arguments back to him.

"And he became very critical. He wasn't rude or disrespectful, but he was dismissive. He treated his mom the way women in his culture are treated—like a child. You're attached to a child, you care for a child, but you don't take the child seriously. You're superior to the child. That's how he felt about women. I got that feeling from the way he talked about his mom. She was a physician, a highly educated woman who had spent many years in England. Yet, he only allowed her to talk when he felt like listening. As a man, he could stop her if he wanted to."

"So, it was like he was turning the tables on her," I said. "She wasn't treating him like a dim-witted child; he was treating her like one."

"Yes."

"So, he didn't think that his mother or any woman—"

Jan completed my sentence, "—was equal to him. Yes. He said a woman was a weaker vessel. Meanwhile, he was attracted to liberated and free Western women who wouldn't put up with his notions of a woman. And he was also overwhelmed by them."

"Did he think that the liberated women he met here were also inherently second class?"

"Yes, that was the contradiction. There was sexual attraction and also the feeling that women weren't his equals."

"Coming from a Muslim culture, Amir was familiar with men and women having separate and unequal identities," I said. "Women there accepted that difference as a fact of life. If he saw a woman here, he may have felt similar to his mother and the other Indian women because they were all females. He may have felt that all women, having similar bodies, must have similar feelings, but here, he had to deal with women who insisted on having the same privileges as men. The women in America were different from those he knew, including his mother, who may have accepted their 'inferior' role. Just as judging suicidality was difficult for you, Amir found it difficult, if not impossible, to deal with the way women strive to achieve equality with men. It must have been difficult for Amir. . . ."

"And confusing," Jan added. "He wanted to adapt, but he didn't want to accept social equality between men and women. It was impossible to resolve. Several times, he tried to have relationships with free-thinking women. He was open to the possibility of dating one, but he didn't meet the woman of his dreams—a free-thinking subservient woman."

"That seems to be a problem many men share," I laughingly added. "And many women, too, feel that the pickings are slim when you're looking for a good guy!"

"Maybe if he had lived a few more years, he could have realized that the striving for freedom and equality can be just as strong as any other feeling. Then, maybe he could have found a compatible partner. But unfortunately, whatever he was taught or learned about women in India was wrong for this country. At least, *I* feel it was wrong, but he felt it was the 'right' way to treat women. According to him, women have to obey men."

"He wanted that, and he struggled mightily to find such a woman."

"He wanted a woman who was both Muslim *and* Western."

"He didn't want the type of Muslim woman his family was willing to find for him," I said. "He also felt that the attitudes of Western women were wrong, and he wanted them to be like Indian Muslim women. As you say, he wanted a combination: freedom-loving and obedient. That's hard to find."

"The woman who was interested in him was a Pakistani Muslim, but he wasn't interested in her. That shows his confusion and contradiction."

"Before we stop, what's your sense of what transpired today?"

"I think that my misunderstanding about the deep similarities between Amir and me was critical. Our fathers were similar in being unkind and in not trying to understand us, but I don't know the true extent of the similarities. Now, my father's dementia makes it impossible for me to communicate with him. I know I'm wordy and repetitive when we talk about my father. Whatever it may be, I couldn't have discussed these matters with Amir earlier; I didn't understand these conflicts. I understand the similarities and conflicts better now, but now it's too late."

"You thought that Amir's suicide eradicated *his* problems," I said, "but created huge problems for you. Amir's father subjected him to watching a camel sacrifice, which he could not tolerate. This irreparably damaged Amir's relationship with his dad. Your father, too, ran through your life like a tornado. Once, he even disowned you. Because of his dementia, he's emotionally gone now, so you can't discuss anything meaningful with him. He can't help you pick up the pieces. All you have left are your feelings. You've come to understand a lot about Amir, and, slowly, you'll come to terms with your dad, too."

CHAPTER 19

JAN STARTED THE SESSION. "I haven't had much sleep lately. I've been spending a lot of time helping a big shot organize a conference. I like what I'm doing, but I can't get away with sleepless nights now the way I could when I was younger. Poor sleep changes my personality.

"For about three years, I've been seeing a Black lady with thirteen children. I'll call her 'Laticia.' When she's in a crisis, she always pages me, and we talk. There's some scene from time to time, and she ends up in the hospital's psychiatric ward. The latest one was last Friday. She woke up with an electric cord around her neck and a suicide note next to her. The letter is coherent and straightforward, but she doesn't remember writing it. The staff in the emergency room paged me since they knew she was my patient. At first, she didn't tell me about the letter. Then, after her discharge, she mentioned it and said it was in the garbage, and she found it when she got home. It's hard to describe what happened because each sentence—on its own—is clear, but some of what she says is not believable.

"Laticia is pleasant and easy to work with. She comes for her appointments consistently, but she frustrates me because I don't know what I'm doing with her. She lives on the South Side, and most of her problems stem from being just poor. Her children aren't doing well in school and regularly get into trouble. Some use drugs. Some sell drugs. One of them is working for a cell-phone company. But she has a hard time accepting this one daughter because she's a lesbian, and Laticia thinks that abnormal. She also has a son who's gay, so we've spent a lot of time talking about sexual orientation. And one of her daughters is a successful psychologist. Unfortunately, that daughter was born with webbed fingers. Laticia blames herself because she was drinking and doing drugs during that pregnancy.

"After I had been working with her for about a year, I got thoroughly frustrated because I felt I wasn't getting to the heart of the matter. Her problems were real problems, but I doubted whether I was helping her change anything. I expressed my frustration to Dr. Alvear-Reverte. He told me, 'You don't realize the important role you play in her life. You're the only person in the world who's validating her. You listen to her and don't dismiss her, like much of her family.'

"To get to the bottom of Laticia's story about the suicidal letter, I had a family session. Laticia said that she must have been crazy to write such a letter *if she wrote it*, and, because it was crazy, there was no sense going into it. I told her that the letter was well written, but in my opinion, the writer sounded depressed, not crazy. Laticia always tries to escape. She maintained that she didn't remember writing the letter and probably was crazy. I noted that the letter followed all the rules of a suicide note and said to her, 'If it is you, you said why you felt like killing yourself. You said you were sorry. And you described a plan.'

"Laticia started to cry and mentioned her oldest daughter, Mary, with whom she had a conflict: 'I feel responsible. My children will learn to get along better when I'm taken from this world. I'm breaking up the family.'

"One of her other daughters said, 'Mom, nobody gets along with Mary. She's moody. She doesn't listen. She starts fights. Nobody likes her. That's why no one talks to her. You have nothing to do with why no one talks to Mary.'

"I thanked the daughter for making clear that her mother was not to blame. Then it came out that everyone was mad at Mary because she didn't want to contribute to the rent. So, at times, I can reach Laticia, even though I can't really change anything in her life.

"Amir kept his suicidality a secret and refused to let me assure his safety. I know that Laticia has lied to me on many occasions. She tries to keep her suicidality a mystery and insists on her so-called craziness. Sometimes, she talks in a different voice, as if she has a different personality. But unlike Amir, she *did* come into the hospital when things became overwhelming; she protected herself from death. I learned a lot from her. She's taught me the beauty of psychiatry by letting me see interesting things through her. I'm not treating her mental illness. I just try to validate her, even when she lies to me. Sometimes, she pages me or calls me with phony complaints, always trying to be 'an interesting case.' I've probably read more psychiatry because of her than any other patient. I listen and relate to what she says. I'm the only person who treats her this way to the best of my knowledge. As Alvear-Reverte says, I feel that I'm doing my job, even if the only thing I do is validate her as a person."

I appreciated that Jan felt confident, but the situation wasn't hypothetical: Laticia had indeed woken up with an electric cord around her neck and a suicide note next to her. Sometimes, overconfidence presents itself as confidence. However, overconfidence can also be a bridge to *real* confidence. Jan has supervisors helping him manage the case, so I decided to let it pass to avoid the risk of destroying a fragile sense of growth.

Jan continued, "The very notions of suicidal intentions, suicidal plans, suicide notes, which used to drive me crazy after Amir died, are more tolerable now. After Amir killed himself, I saw a complicated Russian guy with severe problems. Every few months, he tried to kill himself. He threw me out of balance. I couldn't see all the facts, but luckily, I got good supervision from Alvear-Reverte. He told me that I wasn't asking the right questions or understanding what happened.

"Since I started seeing you, I'm more competent in dealing with suicidal patients *and* non-suicidal patients. Even though I just learned about Laticia's letter, I expect to sleep well tonight. After Amir killed himself, I couldn't sleep for weeks.

"Laticia doesn't have a real urge to kill herself. She's suffered physical abuse. She's suffered sexual abuse. She married a guy who prostituted her, selling her to different business partners. And when Laticia found out that he was having concurrent relationships with many other women, she started to drink. She was an alcoholic for many years. At her worst, Laticia drank half a bottle of gin before she went to her job as a cook, but she was still able to work. She frequently drank so much and went out with so many guys that she couldn't account for all of her pregnancies. As a result, she doesn't know who many of her children's fathers are. She would wake up naked and assume that she had had sex, but she didn't know with whom. After living like this for many years, she decided to stop drinking, and she stopped. When Laticia says she's weak, I bring up this fact to show her how strong she is.

"A year and a half ago, she paged me early in the morning and said, 'I'm on the balcony of my apartment, and I'm thinking of jumping.' I said, 'Why don't you come to the hospital instead. I'll meet you there.' And she came. Maybe I prevented suicide that day. This time, with the electric cord and the suicide note, she actually did attempt suicide. I must talk to her and find out why she's doing this, and maybe her family members can help.

"I just don't feel as much panic as I did after Amir killed himself. In his case, I knew that, if he attempted to kill himself, he would succeed. It was real. I still don't know if there's a way to tell those who've reached their breaking point from those who are still willing to fight their demons. The good thing is that now I don't feel any irritation or anger. I feel like I'm hunting for the truth. You have to corner the beast and expose it. Maybe this is a change, my trying to understand her and reach her at a deeper level. Today, she was emotional, crying and feeling guilty. 'From now on,' she said, 'I'll never forget to page you. You're such a good doctor.'

"I told her, 'If you don't know what you're doing, how will you remember to page me or call me? We need a better plan.'

"I don't know if there's a bottom to her problems. It seems there are always false bottoms. I don't think I can change her living conditions. If she moves to another apartment but can't afford it, there will be problems. She has thirteen children, and she says she blames herself that they are difficult, but I'm not sure whether saying that is just a way of getting them to do what she wants."

Jan then changed the topic by posing a question. "Did you see the movie *Analyze This*?"

"No."

"In the movie, Robert De Niro plays a *mafioso* with a panic disorder; Billy Crystal is his psychiatrist. There's a scene of a psychiatrist and his patient. The psychiatrist is seated like you are now and listening to a patient talk about her life. She's anxious and talkative, going on about how she can't get any relationship going, how she feels lonely and ugly. She's talking in a somewhat superficial manner when you suddenly see the psychiatrist put his hands down, and he says, 'Let's cut the bullshit. Get a life. What are you doing here? Why are you coming here? You're paying me $200 a session and wasting your time. You're fine. Get a job. Go out with someone. Have fun. Go dance. You're going backward, wasting your time talking to me.'"

"Wait," I asked, "Billy Crystal tells her, 'Go dance. Don't waste time talking to me'?"

"No, it's his internal monologue. The camera then focuses on Billy Crystal's face and stays there as the scene fades into reality. The dialogue continues, 'Our time is up. OK. I'll see you next week.'"

"Oh, he thought it and *imagined* saying it."

"Yup. Sometimes, I smell bullshit." Jan laughed. "But I don't always confront it. That's probably good. I've never pushed so far that a patient just quit on me, but I have learned to use gentle confrontation from time to time. A good example is addiction. The main point is that I feel more comfortable treating patients now compared to when I first saw you."

"I think that's true," I said. "You're less anxious. You're doing your best and taking reasonable actions, but no one can guarantee the end result. You remember to use tact as you approach patients and family members. You wondered before whether it's possible to distinguish who's truly suicidal from who's falsely suicidal. You know that most situations are exceedingly complex. As psychiatrists, we do many things we can't be sure about.

"A good example is judging levels of danger. Society wants us to predict danger. That's what others believe our job is, but it's impossible. No one can predict the future. All the algorithms and guidelines for assessing suicidal risk are statistically OK, but for any individual patient, they're pretty useless. It's genuinely impossible to predict suicidality with certainty. A patient can look perfectly fine in the morning and be acutely suicidal in the evening. Sometimes, suicide succeeds almost accidentally. People count on different outcomes, but they just go too far, and even though they don't mean to kill themselves, they make a misjudgment, and it happens anyway. Some people, on the other hand, really mean it. It's scary. How can you stop people from killing themselves if they're hell-bent on doing it? In Amir's case, the general thought of ending his life was there for years—he felt so inadequate and damaged inside—but there was some temporary stability to the suicidal impulse. And then, it just exploded.

"Victor Frankl said that, in the concentration camps, those people who could find meaning in their lives survived better than those who could not.[43] Even if it entailed imaginary companions, fantasies, or hallucinations, that meaning was useful. In other words, anything—even craziness—can have survival value: Write a diary, do anything, but don't give up. That's the message. In your case, Amir died. In his death, he established for you, or you established for yourself, a one-person concentration camp. It needed no barbed wire because it had no boundaries; it was limitless. You were the prisoner, and you were also the SS man. You were trapped in that state and couldn't get out. Later, you thought about following Amir and feared that

---

43 Frankl, V. (2006). *Man's Search for Meaning*, New York: Beacon Press. (Original work published 1946.)

you would jump out a window, but you weren't crazy enough to do it. You learned to give yourself a pass to leave that personal prison and get a glimpse of freedom. You're experimenting more and more with your freedom. Now, except for periodic regressions, you generally feel free. You're even free enough to help patients, even depressed, suicidal patients."

I continued, "Today, you gave a clear example of a suicidal patient you helped. I'm sure you remember that when you took the USMLE, questions about depression in suicidal patients paralyzed you and set off the intrusive thoughts of Amir. Now, with actual suicidal patients, you figure out what to do. Not only are you helping Laticia, but you're doing it without undue anxiety. You predicted that you would sleep well tonight. We'll see how that prediction works out. All of this is the change that you've achieved. You feel it with conviction. You validate yourself. You don't need much validation from me; I'm just giving you acknowledgment."

"I see the change," Jan responded. "The depression hasn't fully disappeared. I don't have a healthy perspective toward suicidality yet, but it's much better. I can manage and do my job."

I was pleased to hear that Jan's depression wasn't as intense as it had been. In giving a sense of the direction of progress in the treatment of hysterics who suffer from a sense of tragic wretchedness, Freud said that much would be gained in analysis "if we succeed in transforming . . . hysterical misery into common unhappiness."[44]

"No one can write a manual on how to prevent all future suicides," I said. "To prevent all suicides, you'd have to convert the entire country into a mental institution. Everyone may have a touch of the madness that killed Romeo and Juliet, but most of us can find enough reason to live and find the next love. Periodic wars clarify that men and women will willingly sign up to become cannon fodder. Mercifully, for reasons that are hard to fathom, most people are spared this fate. You're learning how to help patients, manage your practice, make a living, and sleep. With Amir, you had no ally, as you have with Laticia's daughter. Amir kept you in the dark about his suicidal feelings until afterward, and when he gave you a stale confession, you didn't know what to do with it. Without information, what *could* you do?"

"You have to reward the patient for gathering the courage to tell you that he felt suicidal," Jan responded. "You should say, 'Thank you for telling

44 Freud, S. (1893). "The psychotherapy of hysteria from Studies on Hysteria." J. Strachey (Ed. and Trans.), *The Standard Edition of the Complete Psychological Works of Sigmund Freud* (Vol. 2, pp. 253–305). London: Hogarth Press.

me how you felt.' You should do this even if you feel like saying, 'What good can come out of telling me this, three weeks after the fact?'

"You can't always say what you want to say, and sometimes you have to say what you *don't* feel like saying. Maybe such a discussion can change a patient for next time. Can there be *any* usefulness in delayed communications?"

This was a touchy question. I thought for a moment. "Maybe. Consider a patient talking about suicidal thoughts that occurred three weeks ago. The patient could be displacing suicidal thoughts to the past how he's feeling now."

Jan was silent, and his brow furrowed. Perhaps he felt that I was criticizing him for not seeing this in Amir, so I added, "I'm not saying that's what happened. I'm just saying it's a possibility."

"I don't think I was ready then to conceive of such a possibility," Jan responded. "When I spoke to Dr. Amiss, my supervisor, he told me that he had had a similar situation with a patient. He told her, 'If you continue this pattern of delayed reporting of suicidal thoughts or actions, I can't be your doctor. I'll have to stop treating you. This isn't safe for you or me. You have to tell me what's happening when it's happening, or there's no relationship.' 'Tell your patient that this is not how the game is played, that the treatment won't work.' I told him I didn't think I could do that. Still, maybe that was the way to go with Amir."

"Namely?"

"Maybe I should have confronted him about his delay in suicidal reporting. 'It's not acceptable for you to tell me that you felt suicidal three weeks ago. I have to have a real relationship with you in real-time, not a delayed relationship with a three-week lag. This is the way it has to be. If you don't like it, find another doctor.' I don't even know if this is the right technique. I don't think I could have said that to Amir because of the similarities in our lives. I couldn't give up on him this way or even suggest to him that I was capable of it. I thought I was giving him consistency, validation, and hope for the future. He felt he could never change, and I was trying to tell him he could. I felt that was more important than setting rules and limits. I still do."

"Earlier, we talked about certainty," I said. "All of us would like to have certainty. We would like to say, 'This patient is suicidal, and that patient is not suicidal.' Similarly, we would all like to have certainty about what constitutes a good therapeutic technique. Saying you'll end treatment if the patient delays giving you information is a risky strategy. You don't know how your patient will react to that kind of intervention. There are no simple answers. Some patients may start to provide current information; others may conceal that they're hiding information and simply not talk about suicidal thoughts, past or present.

"I had a patient who had a bad marriage and couldn't decide if she wanted to continue it. She also said that she was prone to procrastination. At work, her supervisors constantly reprimanded her for putting things off. After seeing me regularly for some time, she started to miss sessions. I scheduled to see her four times a week, but she started missing about half the sessions. My supervisor felt that this was unacceptable. I was frustrated and tried many interventions to encourage her to come regularly, but they didn't work. Finally, my supervisor decided that the case was unsalvageable. Like your supervisor, he said to me, 'Dismiss the patient. Tell her you can't see her anymore because her noncompliance made her untreatable.' I agreed with my supervisor that the patient's noncompliance compromised the treatment, but I didn't want to fire her. Despite my reservations, I spoke to her, telling her that her noncompliance made analysis impossible and that we should consider stopping the treatment.

"My patient said, 'I can't believe what I hear you say! This is not the kind of speech that a doctor should make or even be able to think! But, mainly because of your treatment, I've changed. I decided that my marriage was no good, and I got divorced. And, as you well know, rather than getting depressed and withdrawn after the divorce, I started dating, and now I'm engaged to a man I love. And I've become a model worker: I used to be delinquent and late, and now I'm on time and efficient, and I was promoted *twice* for my good performance. So, I made the right decision to get divorced because of the analysis. But I'm not going to stop. Your plan is unethical.' So, we continued.

"You can't terminate a physician-patient relationship just like that!" I laughed. "She said that it was her view that I was a good analyst but was acting on bad advice. I agree. Abandoning a patient is serious business. A physician might feel that a clean break would bring a measure of certainty or, at least, that he would no longer have an exasperating patient. Still, you could unleash a series of events even more complicated than the original ones by doing that. If you tell a patient you want to stop, you've rejected her, and both of you could become trapped in a crazier situation. You can start having nightmares of making your case to the American Psychiatric Association's ethics committee or the American Psychoanalytic Association. A patient could engulf you in a mindless mess that could consume you for years with a simple letter of complaint. We all want certainty, but uncertainty is often inevitable, and many times it's not so bad.

"Going back to Amiss, you told him you could not tell the patient that you would stop treatment unless he spoke about suicidal thoughts immediately. What did Amiss say?"

Jan had a sardonic expression on his face. "I found my supervisor's solution to be perfect but impossible to implement," he said.

"What stopped you?" I asked.

"My patient was already dead."

"Oh," I said, drawing in a deep breath. "I'm sorry. I misunderstood the timing of Amiss's comment. I thought Amiss had spoken to you about this delayed communication while the patient was alive."

"No, we spoke right after Amir killed himself," Jan said. "The only thing I could talk about was Amir. At the time, I was craving a clear solution. I thought I didn't deserve to be a physician and that I deserved punishment for my poor judgment. So when they told me that I couldn't return until I passed the exam, I was glad. In almost every way, my life was in a catastrophic tailspin."

Jan continued, "One thing I learned was that it's impossible to reach the bottom. You think you've found the bottom, but it's a false bottom. Underneath is another false bottom and so on—an infinite regress. One thing I can't figure out is how you terminate an analysis. How do you know that you've come to the bottom, or the end, of anything?"

Jan paused and then continued, "I recently spoke with Dr. Schwartz, my star supervisor. He said that the Institute teachers showed him the so-called right way. They'd say, 'This is how an analysis should be done.' However, Schwartz said he always had his own opinion and felt that their way wasn't the only right way. He felt that you had to unlearn what they indoctrinated into you to purge what didn't apply to you. Making it fit your personality was a necessary component of completing your training, so you could figure out how to understand and treat your patients."

"Yes . . . ," I said.

"As an analyst, I think, you try to witness more and speculate less. You see health and sickness in action as dynamic imaging of someone's psychopathology. You see it so often and so intensely that you have a good idea of the person. I can imagine that. Seven years later, there's a new person. I met a guy who was a caseworker at the VA Hospital. He told me that analysis changed his life, that it was the best money he'd ever spent.

"As an analyst, you participate in someone else's life and then say, 'My job is done.' By what criteria do you decide to say, 'You're a changed person. Go and live your life'?"

"Let me respond," I began. "I provide space, time, and my opinions for a price. What you do with my opinions is your business. You're responsible for your choices unless you're a minor or dangerous or can't take care of yourself. Each person is the prime mover in their own life. A physician prescribes medications, but the patient has to swallow them. Both parts are important. The physician can't force the patient to swallow them unless there's a court order, an emergent danger, or some safety issue involved. Do you remember you said that your mood now is different from when you first came here? You can't get back into that mood now. It's almost impossible. You can find words to describe it, but you can't re-create the feeling. A no-longer-existing mood is hard to recapture."

"Yes," Jan said, "you mean the subjective feeling. I can describe it with words, but the feelings are in a world of their own."

"Right. Where you are now, you feel that it would be impossible for you to decide when it's time to stop. It may be hard to imagine, but a time comes when the patient says, 'It's time.' Many years ago, I had an anxious patient whose parents had had a messy divorce when she was a child. It was confusing for her because, like many kids, she felt it was her fault. She desperately wanted to be in a relationship, but she thought *I* wanted her to be in a relationship. From time to time, she would say to me, 'All you want is for me to get laid.' We did a lot of work in the treatment, and then she said, 'I'm finished,' and we stopped. A few years later, she sent me a letter with a picture of herself with a beautiful son. On the back, she wrote, 'I could not have done this without you.' It's not Billy Crystal telling a woman to stop treatment. *She* wanted to stop. Although the therapist may see clues that a patient is ready to stop, it becomes a real possibility when the patient brings it up. When both parties feel it, the decision is not hard. It's unavoidable. It's obvious that now is not the right time for you. You can't imagine it. Think about other decisions you've made: How did Maria and you decide to get married? How did Maria and you decide to have a baby? Until the time is right, it's a mystery. When the time is right, reality emerges, and the ability to see it emerges, too. Then, you cannot avoid reality."

"That's how it happens?"

"Yes. Except for the time, almost twenty-five years ago, when my supervisor insisted that I terminate a patient, I've never started such a discussion!"

"Do you have any patients with you now who started with you when you were a trainee?"

"I started almost thirty years ago. No one has continued that long. My longest analytic case was seven years. For the kind of analysis you're referring to, I would need a Woody Allen!"

"Oh, I forgot to tell you: Maria and I are going to Rome next week to meet her family and share the good news."

In analytic practice, vacations are part of essential analytic rituals. We try to plan for them, discuss them, and understand how the patient reacts to them. Analysts try to inform patients about any sessions they plan to cancel, and patients learn to give sufficient notice about any sessions they plan to cancel. A patient who drops news about a vacation abruptly misses out on opportunities to learn from anticipated events. Although this was short notice, I decided to ignore the issue. I felt, instead, that the occasion demanded a clear recognition of how far Jan had come. I extended my hand and, shaking his, said, "*Bon voyage* to Maria and you. Have a great trip."

CHAPTER 20

Jan returned from Rome, eager to jump back in.

"During our trip to Rome, Maria had a high-resolution sonogram. Despite the early stage of the pregnancy, they could determine the sex. We're having a boy!"

I got up and shook his hand. Jan was deeply joyful, and I joined in his rejoicing.

"I knew from the beginning that we would have a boy."

"Beginning, meaning . . . ?"

"Maria, too. Every time she spoke about the baby, she said 'he.' Even before they could tell from the sonogram, she asked the doctor, 'So, how old is he?' Now we know for sure it's a 'he.' We had them give us pictures, and we showed them to everybody. When Maria's sister saw them, she started to cry. Her grandma almost fainted when Maria told her that those were the first pictures of our baby. She thought that it was some piece of modern art. She told us later that she would congratulate Maria for making this piece of art, even though she didn't like it! Everyone is talking about making plans to visit us.

"Also, Maria and I became godparents, for Maria's best friend, Gina's, first baby. So we're trying to deal with this new reality. While we were in Rome, I didn't think about anything else really, except that I had some 'Amir moments' when we went to some of the same places that we went when we got married."

"When was the last time you were in Rome?" I asked.

"Soon after Amir died."

It was what I expected Jan to say. If he had said, 'when we got married,' I would have been a little surprised. "So, this visit was like a soft echo of Amir memories."

"Yes. During our wedding, I had many intense Amir moments; he had just killed himself. Now, at happy times, I think of Amir and how he missed out on the experience of love. And when I saw our son on the screen in the obstetrician's office, I felt the same: Amir will never be a father. If he had lived a few more years, maybe he would have been in my shoes. I feel that he would have been happy, too, but it's over for him—finished. And my thoughts of him are dispersing and dissolving. Now, my other patients are the ones occupying my thoughts.

"I have this twenty-one-year-old guy who has schizophrenia. I'll call him Tom. He's psychotic. He suffers from hallucinations and delusions. He hears voices that don't exist, and firmly believes in ideas that no one else does. He doesn't want to be schizophrenic, but the odds are against him: He has a strong family history of schizophrenia. He's educated; in fact, he's overeducated. He takes his medication but keeps asking me what the medication is supposed to do.

"I told him that it was supposed to take away his voices. Then he asked, 'How do you know the reason for my voices?'

"I told him, 'Everybody who hears hallucinations has a similar set of neurochemical changes in the brain. I'm assuming that, because you're hallucinating, the same thing is happening to you, and the medication that you're taking has helped other people with hallucinations and delusions.' He knows the concepts of hallucinations and delusions. He challenges my 'assumptions' and doesn't like to be labeled 'schizophrenic.'"

I felt Jan was drifting too far away from talking about the pictures of his son. If he continued on this path, there was a chance that he would lose the thread that started there. So, I decided to ask about Maria's pregnancy at the risk of interrupting him. Besides, I thought Jan could gainfully mix emotions, so I decided to be bolder in my expressions. "A few minutes ago, you said that, when you were looking at the pictures of the sonogram of your son, you had an Amir moment. . . ."

"It was actually not a still picture. It was during the sonogram, more like a live movie."

"OK. You showed me a picture of a sonogram."

"Yes, there are two. A few sessions ago, I showed you Maria's sonogram in Chicago. In that one, they couldn't tell the sex. The more recent one we did in Rome was much better quality, and he was older. This time they could see everything clearly, even the facial features. And you could see that it was a boy."

"You said that if Amir had survived a few more years, such an experience could have been his."

"Yes."

"Then you said, ' . . . for him, it's finished.'"

"Yes. It's over for him."

"Now, I think you said, a long time ago, that the first time you had an Amir moment in Rome, soon after he died, you felt jealous. You were jealous because he solved his problems with suicide and left you with the overwhelming problems of living. It's taken some time for us to grasp what happened: how you felt then and how you feel now. Today, you said that Amir's time was finished because of what he did. Perhaps today's realization was hard for you to acknowledge then. There was a life, Amir's life. Amir snuffed it out. It's not easy to accept. It was a loss. It was a waste. So, soon after he died, when you felt that he solved his problems by committing suicide and you were jealous of him, it was true in the sense that it was how you felt. But underneath that feeling was today's realization that . . . "

"It was a shocking thought, and I tried to push it away almost immediately after it crossed my mind."

"What thought?"

"That Amir's problems were over, and mine had just started. I didn't like that idea. That sort of thought doesn't agree with me, but it just popped up. I tried to push it away, but it was pretty intrusive, and I couldn't. All these things were happening simultaneously, and I couldn't push them away. After a few weeks, it didn't get better; it got worse."

I thought Jan's previous jealousy-without-acceptance-of-death was a defense against guilt-with-acceptance-of-death. "So, you felt jealous of his solution. It was a powerful thought that you couldn't shake. But the thought that you were jealous of his solution spared you from the dark realization that he was gone for all time. Finished. That feeling of *jealousy* reduced the burden of grieving over his death. Today's statement that, for Amir, 'it's finished' means that now you fully accept his death. Indeed, he did lose the opportunity to have sex, feel love, and be a father. I'm sure you're sad that he missed out on life, but right after he died, your jealousy pushed out that sadness, which would have been unbearable then."

"Yes," said Jan, "there was no thought like that then."

"That's what I mean."

"When I was in Rome getting married, I wasn't enjoying much of what was happening."

"How aware is your dad of what's happening in your life?"

"I called and told him that Maria is pregnant, and we're having a boy. He didn't say, 'I'm very happy.' He said, in Polish, '*To bardzo milo.*' It means 'That's nice.'"

"And?"

"It's not what most people would say. For example, if someone says, 'I'm going to have a baby,' you say, 'Congratulations, I'm very happy for you' or something like that."

"Yes."

"My father used these very words: 'That's nice.'"

"What's the difference between 'nice,' which he said, and 'happy,' which he didn't?"

"I actually asked him, 'Why did you say that this is nice and not that you're happy?' He couldn't explain. I told him people usually say this when a couple says they're having a baby. Then I didn't want to go any further. Maybe he had some deep thoughts about our relationship or how he'd performed as a father . . . I don't know. I'm probably ascribing too much meaning to his words. I have to remember: He's demented."

"From your point of view, 'nice' is not good enough. Is that true?"

"Well, . . . your mother tongue is . . . ?"

"Telugu."

Jan pronounced it out loud, "Telugu. I'm sure that, if your sister . . . no, if you were announcing that your wife is pregnant to your father . . . Let's imagine it."

"OK." I imagined possible responses in Telugu from an imaginary dad to a son. For example, he might say, "The news that you will be having a baby brings *chala santosham*, great happiness." Or he might say, "The news that you will be having a baby is *paravaledu*, OK." I clearly understood what Jan was trying to convey, although I didn't verbalize these alternative responses.

Jan was animated. "Let's imagine that he's speaking in Telugu. If he says, 'That's nice,' and it's not what everybody would say . . ."

In his disappointment, Jan seemed unaware of his unreal expectations of his demented dad. Despite their apparent conversations, Jan often suspected his father often could not recognize him. Here was a clash between Jan's natural desire for understanding from his dad, at a momentous time in Jan's life, and the improbability of empathy from a demented person at this critical time in his life.

"'That's nice' indicates that he was missing the significance of the moment," I agreed.

Left to himself, Jan would continue to be disappointed by his father's unresponsiveness. However, his father was no longer his previous hostile self; he was in a nursing home. Thus, Jan could continue in his current path and be angry when his father died. Or, Jan could change himself and show compassion and care for his enfeebled father. Perhaps Jan would be prouder if he could become a generous son, despite his father's meanness.

Then I thought Jan's dad was nuts enough to immediately demand a pedicure on the day of his deceased wife's funeral. So Jan could cut him some slack. I channeled Jan's dad, and a laugh escaped me. I said, "But 'That's nice.' Perhaps it means he knows or pretends to know who you and Maria are and what pregnancy is. What he said was different from, 'I'm upset that you and Maria are going to have a child!' Jan's expectation was perfectly understandable, but his father had dementia. My response was a bit of psychodrama with Jan to revivify what his father was. At that moment, I empathized with Jan's father; I simultaneously displayed anti-empathy to Jan! Was I mean to Jan, like his father, or did Jan need to be awakened to reality? I could not decide.

My thoughts went to some consequences of extreme or unusual attitudes held by people. I once worked as a consultant for a clinic that mostly saw homeless women, all of whom had experienced much degradation and domestic violence. One had a partner who wanted her to sleep naked next to the bed on the floor. She reported that he told her, "so I can roll over and screw her like a bitch" without bothering to undress her. Another had a partner who prostituted her to pay for his drug habit. One woman, the girlfriend of a powerful drug dealer, discovered him in bed, actively engaged in sex with a man. She was stunned! "You're gay!" she exclaimed. He got mad and promised to kill her by the end of the month. Even though she was terrified of dying, she didn't want to give him the pleasure of killing her. So, she immediately contracted with a hitman to kill her, before her boyfriend could make arrangements. The fee was $1,000! She called the sum "1K." But she gave herself a few days to love. When she came to see me, she discussed her predicament. We talked, and she changed her mind. I helped her move and stay at a domestic-violence shelter. All domestic-violence shelters are anonymous and do not have a label. So her whereabouts would not be public knowledge. The next time she came to see me, she reported contacting her intended hitman and calling off the hit. He was upset, since he counted on that money. So, to avoid hard feelings, she did not insist on a refund! Although she was sorry to say goodbye to the 1K, she was glad to be alive. What craziness there is in this world!

"I've met many women with a history of abuse who were initially unable to leave an abusive relationship and find a non-abusive mate. Validating an abused woman's experience and empathizing with her helps you establish an immediate connection. It provides some emotional relief when you provide a safe place for a traumatized patient to vent about her abuse, but it doesn't always lead to change. Excessive empathy may entrench one in victim hood, and prevent them from taking advantage of an opportunity to change. It's like with a physical injury: Rest and sympathy are good. But healing requires pushing through the pain of rehabilitation and acknowledging new realities. You need empathy to get started, but you also need to commit to a plan for change and then actually change. Empathy alone won't do it. My understanding is different from your change. Do you want to be an angry man forever? How long do you want to be pissed-off at your father?"

Now, Jan laughed. "Oh, I know. I *know!*"

Jan agreed with me, but I realized he disagreed with me, as well. He continued in a loud voice.

"Please don't think I'm making a big deal of this, but I don't know anybody who would say, 'That's nice.'"

"I agree. No normal person would say it."

We both continued to laugh and relish this moment of crazy emotions amidst Jan's simultaneous *understanding* of what I was trying to say and his protestations *against* what I was saying. Jan's change gratified me. He now could both agree and disagree with me at the same time. Ambivalence like this is the gateway to complexity. It accommodates uncertainty and doubts while avoiding excessive simplicity. It makes practical both known and unknown aspects of living with others in this world. It is an invaluable tool for psychiatrists who wish to help their patients better understand.

Jan reflected for some time and then said, "He could have given me a formal response, 'I'm positively surprised,' like when you have an official meeting at a high diplomatic level, and you say, 'I'm so glad to meet you.'

"Here's what you say," Jan persisted. "'I'm happy.' 'I'm very happy.' 'I'm very happy for you.' That is what friends say!"

"That reminds me of Billy Crystal's many versions of 'Dahling, you look marvelous!'" I added. "I understand. You have a point. You have a very good point, maybe a very, very good or even a perfect point. But let's take a moment to acknowledge what you accomplished: You concentrated your dad's focus enough for him to have the thought, 'My boy, Jan, is having a child,' or 'My boy, Jan, is having a boy.' He got it!"

"Yes, he got it, for that moment. The next time, he may forget that I'm having a boy. The next time he may forget that he, himself, had a boy . . . me."

"Yes, but for one lucid moment, *you* were able to convey to him that you and your wife, Maria, were expecting a baby." But, again, I wanted to emphasize *Jan's* accomplishment. "That's an accomplishment, even though his reaction was lukewarm."

"Right."

Although Jan was grateful for that moment of awareness, I thought he felt that I assigned more significance to it than he did. To me, it signified Jan's singular achievement of having communicated to his demented dad the idea that Jan would be the *father* of a boy and maybe the idea that he would be the *grandfather* of a boy. Jan's dad had had a moment of clarity. Still, even in that instant, his callous attitude remained: He was unable to manage an appropriate response to his son's monumental announcement of the continuation of his own bloodline. Jan also appreciated that he had had a succession of playfully contradictory and delicious exchanges with me. Perhaps, because I played the devil's advocate by speaking for his dad, Jan experienced vicarious friendly combat in the father transference. "Here, I played his role, but in your interchange, his mind may have been clear for a moment," I said, "but he also showed that he was still a son of a bitch."

"Yes, that's the way I would describe it," Jan agreed.

I was glad for this confirmation.

Jan continued, "At one point, he was able to converse with people, like his old friends from work, even though he had no idea who they were. They would greet him affectionately with, 'Hi, Max. How're you doing?' And he would say, 'I'm *so* happy to see you.'"

Because Jan could remember social occasions when his dad expressed being *so happy,* I appreciated Jan's pain occasioned by his father's lukewarm response to his proud pregnancy announcement.

"He would ask, 'How's your family?' He was good at small talk. You know what I mean?"

"Yes."

"He made people feel like he was really responding to them personally. And then, after they left, he would ask me, 'Who *was* that?'"

"But when he asked you who those people were, he knew who *you* were, right? And he knew you could give him the right answer."

"Yes. Until now, my father recognized my voice. He recognized *me*."

I nodded approvingly, infusing significance to Jan's embeddedness somewhere in his dad's rapidly disappearing self. "It could be better, no doubt, but I think he got the idea, 'My boy is having a son.'"

"Yes."

"I'm glad that it happened because you're talking to somebody who's half in and half out of reality."

Jan continued, "The next day, though, we couldn't have a conversation. He couldn't recall our conversation. If a person is unaware of time and place or cannot recognize people, even close people, it's hard to feel that he retains an event in his mind. For my father, there is no yesterday and no tomorrow. In fact, for him, there's no today. He doesn't know what the date is. He doesn't know where he is. Sometimes, he says he was born in Niepokalanow. That's where he is right now, but he was born in Terespol. I don't feel that he got the message about my son at such times. It's hard to understand or predict what's happening in the mind of somebody who's losing touch with reality. I started talking to you about this guy with schizophrenia. Hallucinations and delusions make his world disjointed. In dementia, too, the world becomes disjointed."

A vision of the melting watches in Dalí's painting *The Persistence of Memory* flickered into my awareness.

Jan continued, "It's scary for a person to lose their memory. Losing touch with reality is frightening. You feel yourself drifting away from everyone and everything. Even if you can adapt and cover it up, I'm sure you know what's happening to you. I wish I could talk to him about it and validate how scary it must be for him. I hope he knew that I wanted to talk to him. I didn't know whether he would see it as good news or bad news. I would like to tell him that there are other people with the same disease he has, that this is how dementia progresses, slowly and unrelentingly. That's what I would like to tell him.

"What I started to tell you was that my previous focus on Amir is now dissolving into a focus on many people. As a result, I talk and work differently with people. I can see it myself."

"How so?"

"One, I don't talk as much. I ask questions," Jan chuckled. "Pretty much what you're doing. I listen. If they're unclear, I take time and ask questions until I understand what they're trying to say and what's happening. It doesn't work with everybody. Some people *like* to confuse you. I have borderline patients who deliberately use vague language to talk about dangerous thoughts or plans. They sneak in ideas that are like thought bombs. You assume the best-case scenario and move forward, and, later, you pay the price. I've learned that you have to expend the effort to understand what's going on. You have to try to figure out what people mean."

"I had a thought when you were talking," I said. "When you were explaining to me what you did before becoming a psychiatrist, you dealt with something inherently dangerous: radioactivity. So, let's look at the case of patients with cancer who need radiation therapy. If you don't understand radioactivity, radiation treatment could be deadly for the doctor *and* the patient. On the other hand, if you know radioactivity and know when and how to use radioactive substances, you could help patients with cancer and protect yourself.

"Similarly, your reaction to Amir's death was toxic: very severe and too hot to handle. You had intrusive thoughts, either of jealousy focused on Amir or guilt focused on you. Now you're finding ways to defuse this rigid and excessive focus and use a more flexible and adaptive approach. You're taking the lessons you learned from Amir's suicide and applying them, in proper doses, to specific aspects of other patients. Working through your grief is transforming you into a better psychiatrist. You have more tools in your bag. You listen to patients and put in the effort to understand and figure out what they mean. You clarify unnecessary or dangerous ambiguity and try to implement useful approaches. You're also on the lookout for patients' thought bombs so that you can defuse them. I think you're making a good comeback."

"I was thinking about an astrophysics metaphor," Jan responded. "There are big, heavy stars that are collapsing under their own gravity . . ."

"Black holes?"

"Yes, black holes. Amir became a black hole in my universe. For a while, for a *long* while, he was my only gravitational force, grabbing all my attention. Now I feel different. I can interact with other gravitational forces in my life. I feel better than I did even a few months ago."

"The black hole is a good symbol to describe your illness after Amir's suicide and now your progress," I said.

Jan went on, "When I saw my son's image on the screen in the obstetrician's office, I had an anti-Amir moment, and the metaphor came to me.

Right then, my son drew all my attention, and my obsessions with Amir began to drift away."

He paused and then went on, "I'm really unhappy that our wedding happened so soon after he died. I couldn't enjoy it. Of course, I see much better now how important the wedding was for me during the event itself, but I couldn't enjoy it because Amir had hijacked so much of my attention. I tried hard to forget about Amir then, but the harder I tried, the more intrusive he became."

CHAPTER 21

In the last emotion-laden session, Jan talked about finding out that he would be the father to a boy, his dad, his wedding to Maria, and Amir. I wanted to find out if any positive feelings or memories from that time could be resurrected or reanimated. So I asked, "Is Maria from Rome?"

"Yes."

"When you were there this time, did you go back to the church where you got married?"

"No, our friend's son's baptism was in a different church."

"Did you see any people or places that were associated with your wedding?"

"Yes, but it was very different. I have pretty stable good moods now. But, then . . . well, there's just no comparison."

"I'm sure that Maria was glad to see you in a good mood."

"Yes, our focus was and is the baby. It's all we talk about now: our plans for him, how we need to modify the apartment, how to arrange for babysitting."

"It's like building the nest."

"Yes. I spoke with some friends who have a 7½-month-old. They said that all their planning did not prepare them for how much their baby changed their lives. But they emphasized that an infant is a powerful director. He guides his parents in figuring out what changes are needed and in making them. They said that no book or studying is necessary; the baby automatically teaches you. We picked up a lot of good ideas about the baby's room, cribs, toys, car seats, safety, bathing, feeding, diapering . . . They gave us some excellent tips.

"I used to have this thought that life is a strong force, but now I'm equally impressed by how fragile it is. You know, sudden infant death syndrome . . . And when the baby begins to crawl and walk, you have to baby-proof the apartment: no sharp stuff, no exposed electric sockets. So it's all a big challenge, but I think we'll be prepared."

"I think so. I know that both of you are doing your best. You know more than most people. Your outlook has improved, and your different moods help you to see different things."

"That's for sure. Now I have the luxury of allowing myself to be preoccupied with my son and to care more. Depressed people don't care about themselves or others or anything. Do you agree?"

I completely agreed, but I was thinking about the hurricane-like disruption that Amir's suicide and Jan's depression had wrought on his wedding and the opportunities Jan and Maria had lost—a genuinely celebratory launch of their marriage. A sense of sadness clouded my thoughts for Jan, and I didn't respond when he spoke of his depression. Perhaps Jan noticed that I was quieter than usual, or maybe he just wanted some validation. Perhaps, even in his joyful life, Jan still needed some reassuring sense of residual vitality from me, which I hadn't provided. His vivacity stilled. Because I fully agreed with Jan, his question had surprised me.

"I *completely agree!*" I said emphatically. "You and Maria are doing everything you can to make a *home*. No question about it. You mentioned that you were only going through the motions when you were in Rome and were emotionally detached. Because of Amir's suicide, your heart was too heavy for you to participate in your wedding fully."

"Right."

"When things happen on time, they're in sync. For example, a birthday card that arrives before the actual birthday is on time. But a 'belated birthday card' is not the same, although it's still better than a greeting that never arrives. Unlike the happiness of a timely greeting, one can be somewhat glad for a late greeting. Do you—"

"—understand? That's what happened exactly!" Jan completed my sentence as both of us laughed.

"So, in addition to your timely joyful preoccupation with the baby, there are belated wedding and wedding-related emotions that you may be experiencing now. Perhaps you're also trying to express your love for Maria as a bride. Even if the timing isn't right, your previously unexpressed or under-expressed joy and gratitude toward Maria for standing by you are still there. I know that you're glad, and I'm sure Maria feels it."

"Yes, she says so. Some time back, I made a bitter statement about the lack of closeness of relationships in the United States compared to Poland or Italy."

"Yankeelandia!"

"Friendship here is more superficial. It's very different from what Maria and I understand it to be. A friend is someone who becomes a permanent part of our lives, like a family member. When I went to Italy for our wedding, I felt supported by Maria's family. Maria's grandma speaks *only* Italian, and I don't speak *any* Italian, but I could feel her support. She knew that my patient had killed himself, and she cared. In Italian, she said, 'My poor boy, I wish I could make you happy.' Such words don't change anything directly, but they're reassuring. What she said helped me survive as well as I could, considering . . . *This* visit, though, wasn't tainted by tragedy. I was happy, Maria was happy, and there was happy news. It was a great visit. Everything about my life is changing.

"I'm completely preoccupied with images of my son, imagining how he'll look, based on the sonogram. And I have very strong emotions. I can't even describe my feelings. He's changed the order of my world completely. When you look at a sonogram, the doctor has to tell you what's what. She pointed to the screen at what looked like black and white stains. And, in those shadows, she pointed to his head, his arms, his penis. As she was doing it, I realized that I was looking at *my son*. I had tears in my eyes."

"It's great that these feelings are coming to you. The feelings speak for themselves. You know you belong to the chain of life in moments like these. If you're an evolutionist, as I am, the chain began in the days of the first living organisms. If you're a believer, then it began at the first moment of creation. The repeating pattern of life has happened for millions of years, and suddenly you're a part of it. You're the living link between the previous generation and the next. It's a tremendous feeling."

"It's a primal feeling. It goes beyond words like *being happy*." Jan laughed and said, "Or *nice* as my father said. It goes *way* beyond that. It's amazing. It's so visceral. Things are starting to make sense and fall into place. I think about how I've led my life, getting into situations without thinking about the dangers, without knowing all the angles. Now, I realize that you have to be aware of all the scenarios, and if one of them says that you might die, you should step back and think again.

"I used to drive go-karts. They're small, but they can be pretty powerful. With a big-enough engine, they can go 120 kilometers per hour; that's 70 or 80 miles per hour. A go-kart is a collection of steel pipes with an engine and a seat for the driver. That's it—no shields or protection. When I was 15, I was in a go-kart accident. I was driving recklessly, but the other driver was *crazy*! He bumped me off the track, and the shoulder was icy so that I couldn't steer. I ended up wrapped around a pole, with my helmet cracked. I probably lost consciousness on contact. I regained it for a few seconds a couple of times, but mostly, everything seemed dark and silent. Then someone flashed a light in my eye, I got stuck with a needle, and I heard the piercing scream of a siren. I woke up in the hospital. I spent two weeks there with a concussion, broken ribs, and a broken right arm. That was just one of many accidents.

"And then there were the fights. Oh, my God. Sometimes, I got into fights with people who just didn't care, who had no warning system in their heads to tell them when to stop, but I did it anyway. Somehow, I was always in the wrong place at the wrong time with one of those guys. I still remember the horrible chill, realizing that they wouldn't hesitate to take my life."

"You were talking about your dad, who doesn't know what day it is now," I interjected. "Because of your concussion, you have a good sense of what it means to lose your bearings and not know what time it is. I'm sure you experienced a loss of orientation."

"Yes, briefly. When I woke up in the hospital, I opened my eyes and stared at all these strange things around me, and then slowly, I realized who I was, where I was, and how I got there.

"Later, I saw the outcome of other's people's accidents when I worked for the Accident and Emergency Department. It paid well—much better than my day job. And there was always lots of action, which I really liked. At the same time, it was exhausting. I would spend all night on my feet, shower in the station locker room, and then do a full day of regular work. There were times I did ambulance shifts fourteen nights in a month. One day, I felt sick, with a fever and a cough, but I still went to work. I ended up with pneumonia, and my own ambulance had to take me to the hospital! When I woke up, I was hallucinating. That was stupid. I should have stayed home when I started to feel sick. Instead, I didn't take care of myself. Part of me believed I was immortal like many twentysomethings do, but thinking about it now, I think I was pushing it much further.

"The reason I started to think about all this is that we're going to have a boy and, unfortunately, he's going to have 50% of my genetic material. I wonder what I'll say to him when he's being stupid and careless. 'Don't be like me. Be more like my sister!' Just joking . . . but maybe not joking. Can I avoid being a hypocrite? That's a real question for me. What am I supposed to say? 'This is stupid; take care of yourself!' You can imagine how effective that would be!

"Fortunately, I didn't die despite my stupidity," Jan continued. "There was a medical student from the town where my father was born. Some moron friend stored acid for a car battery in a bottle on a balcony. The bottle looked like a bottle of alcohol. This medical student was drunk in the middle of the night and discovered the bottle. Before he realized what it was, he had drunk a fair amount of acid; it ruined his life. They tried to graft part of his gut onto his gullet. Ugh! People mainly focused on the moron who put acid in the bottle and not on the guy who drank from a bottle without checking it out.

"There was another guy who was drunk and trying to show off. He was walking on the fence of a bridge above the water. The wind was blowing. Maybe he was suicidal or just wanted to amuse other people. You can be gone in a moment. It's crazy. I'm going to try to make my son wiser than I was. I'll explain to him how to make good choices. I'll try not to lie. My father used to say, 'When I was your age, I studied 10 hours a day. When everyone else was partying, I was doing my homework.' I know that 90% of that was a lie.

"But it scares me, the responsibility of being a father. When I was younger, I bought a motorcycle. It was a 900cc Honda RR-Race Ready with a maximum speed of 240 kilometers per hour. Eight years ago, I took it to its max on a straight highway. It gives you a ride! Balancing between life and death gives you a thrill. Young people like that. Driving fast or on one wheel is a way to show off, to be seen as brave. Well, I don't think of it as brave anymore. It scares me. It really scares me. I know that I'll be facing this when my son grows up. How will I keep a balance and prevent these things from happening? My father gave me lies, and I took false freedom. Children want dangerous things, and I know, from experience, that it's fun. It gives you a nice rush of adrenaline, riding a fast motorcycle, racing in a go-kart, or free-fall skydiving . . . I don't know."

Jan became pensive.

"My mom would have been amazed to hear me saying all this. I guess I can't believe how everything changed because I saw my son on a screen. I always found some way of explaining why what I was doing was right: how unique the experience was, how much courage the experience demanded, how much my coordination improved, how many new skills I developed, how much it widened my world. The string of justifications was endless. But, the bottom line was the adrenaline."

I asked myself whether Jan's adrenaline-seeking was an attempt at restoring a prior dip in self-esteem. I asked, "Do you feel that there was any pattern in terms of what was happening right before you did those kinds of things?"

"For example?"

"I can't say because that's the question. But, for example, a guy's girlfriend leaves him, and then he goes skydiving. Was there some precipitating event?"

Jan remained silent for a while, so I asked, "Do you understand my question?"

"I know what you're saying and the purpose of the question. The answer is 'no.' Really. It wasn't only the driving; I built the go-karts, too. I built it from scratch, under the supervision of a good mechanic, the scout leader. Making it was as much fun as driving it.

"I always wanted to fly. It wasn't an idea that I had out of the blue or a reaction to some bad event. It was my life's ambition. That's how I discovered skydiving. I first heard some guy talking about it on TV. He said lots of romantic things about it, and then he said, 'This is the closest you can feel to flying. You're all by yourself in this perfect silence. You see the houses, roads, and cars—they're like toys—but you don't hear anything. It's beautiful.' I always wanted to do it. So the first opportunity I had, I went for it. The place is called Chicago Skydive in Ottawa, off Interstate I-80.

"After you land, the parachutes are folded, by high school students paid maybe $5 an hour. Knowing that a high school kid folded your parachute adds to the rush. It's additional risk . . . I mean, extra adrenaline!

"The first jumps are with a trainer. When you've completed enough jumps, you can go by yourself. Every time you want to jump, you must sign a stack of legal documents.

"If the parachute doesn't open or if there is an equipment malfunction, the place doesn't take any responsibility. They mention that the risks may include broken bones, evisceration, and death. You sign the agreement with the full awareness that you might die, and no one else is responsible if you actually read every word. You sign that you're aware of it, and you're cool with it. They ask you again before you jump, and you have to sign again that you want to jump. Many people change their minds at the last minute. When you look down from the plane, it's scary—really scary. But I always wanted to jump and fly. When my son wants to jump, I may go up again for him. I have to make sure that everything is all right. I have to make sure that everything is perfectly safe. That's probably my future role. I'll pretend I'm doing it for fun, but I'll actually be making sure that he's safe. Accidents happen. One of the trainers I knew died three years ago, even though it's supposed to be almost impossible. You're protected by so much electronic and safety equipment, even if you lose consciousness. If you jump and bang your head against the plane and become unconscious, the parachute will deploy at 2,500 feet without any human action. If that happens, many of your bones will break—because there are certain things you have to do before you land—but you're still alive."

After a pause, Jan spoke again.

"That's ambivalence: the dream of flying and the fear of dying. In the end, it's an enjoyable experience. I can't say I regret it, but I'm glad to be alive to say that. The role of experience shouldn't be overrated, though. The guy who died was an experienced instructor. He was an expert, but his parachute didn't open, and he dropped to the ground. The danger is random. I'm not sure how people do it. Can you be a father and also jump? What's the proper balance? You have to allow your son to make his own mistakes. On the other hand, you have to be a father. Safety is number one. Extremes in any direction have costs. Over-protective parents aren't helpful, and under-protective parents are neglectful. Finding the balance is hard. Do you agree?"

"It's always a struggle, figuring out what to do," I said. "I do think an actual disagreement, say, between a father and a son, provides a point of focus. What you say is true but abstract; your son isn't even born yet, and he's not challenging you yet, so these conflicts are hypothetical. When he disagrees, you have an opportunity. For example, you and your father had a problem in this area. If you and he had worked things out . . . You feel that he lectured or lied to you and wasn't genuinely available. You feel that he could have done better. Perhaps if he had been more available or if you had been more direct with him when you were growing up, maybe you would have taken fewer risks. Also, you didn't allow him to influence you in certain areas, and in other areas, you fought his influence."

"When I was in high school, I decided to stay at a party one night rather than go home. So I came home early the next morning. My mom had gone to work already, but my father was still home. I knocked on the door. My father answered, 'Who's there?'

"'It's me,' I said. 'I'm home.'

"He was upset and said, 'Go back to wherever you came from.'

"I was tired and feeling the effects of the alcohol, and I didn't want to deal with him, so I said, 'OK,' and crashed at my friend's house next door. My dad was angry but didn't express it. He didn't say, 'When I was your age, I would never do this.' He never said that."

"He sure didn't act like the father of the Biblical prodigal son," I noted. "He didn't open the door and make you breakfast. But, of course, had he followed the Bible, you might have acted differently. But that's something you may be able to do for *your* son."

"I came home expecting an argument from him. I sort of did it on purpose. I wanted to feel independent. I wanted to be free and say, 'You don't have power over me anymore!' Although he physically punished me, I no longer feared that."

"How so?" I asked.

"There was this one day when my father was seething with his own frustration. Some guy in the lab where he worked had started a campaign against him, pointing out inefficiencies and poor results of my father's team. Things were getting out of control. My father displaced it immediately. He tried to be in charge of everything *at home*, barking orders at everyone. When we questioned him, he answered, 'You do what I tell you to do! End of story!'

"I resisted, and that only made things worse. One day, when he was crazy with anger, I got mad myself. He had been beating me, and suddenly, I felt he had crossed the line. I asked him to stop, and then he started to threaten me. He challenged me to a fight. I agreed, and we had a physical fight. I quickly realized that he was an old man with no real strength. I held him from behind and put a hold on him in a way that he couldn't hit me, and he couldn't escape. He kept trying to hit me, but his fists couldn't reach me. I held him for about 10 minutes as he tried more and more ineffectually to hit me. When he became tired, I would release my grip a little, and then he would try to fight again. HE BECAME ANGRIER when I tightened my grip, but he was powerless to do anything. Then he ordered me to release him. I said, 'I'll let you go if you behave.' He didn't say anything; he just nodded in agreement. He didn't give up the passive-aggressive stuff, though, like, 'Go back to wherever you came from.'"

"There are things that have to be addressed and negotiated between human beings: father and son, mother and son, husband and wife, friend and friend, patient and doctor."

"Constantly."

Waiting for Jan to expand, I said, "Yes."

"Constantly, because people are always changing their minds. So, one agreement is replaced by another. I missed that part. I never tried it with my father. I made so many mistakes."

"Let's say that we hope you learn from your mistakes. Children are good teachers. Young ones are better than older ones, and the real experts are the newborns."

"A newborn can *only* be honest," Jan said. "I heard this from many people. Now, I'll experience it myself. It's exciting, but I have many fears. I've thought for so many years that I didn't want to be like my father. I want to be more involved and interested. For some reason, I think of my father more now, much more than before. It's a painful feeling, the feeling of a lost chance. I don't think I have any more chances with my father. We don't and can't communicate. I still have the hopeful fantasy that I'll somehow reach him, knowing what I know now. I also want to make more sense of our relationship, for his sake. Now, it's going to be my turn to see if I can be a better father."

"Yes, and you have the choice: to drive fast or to drive within the posted speed limits."

"Now, you couldn't *pay* me to drive fast!"

CHAPTER 22

"I'M SORRY I'M LATE. I got delayed taking care of a patient, an Orthodox Jewish girl. Did I ever talk about her?"

"Is she the one who's psychotic and homicidal?"

"Yes, she's the one. I think I called her 'Rachel.' It used to be that every time she came in for treatment, she said she wanted to kill her parents. If the resident didn't know her, she got admitted to the hospital. It was a knee-jerk reaction. She would go into the hospital, quickly get discharged, and then promptly get readmitted again. This vicious cycle started two years ago.

"I first met her four months ago. In the six months before, she needed psychiatric hospitalizations seven times. My goal was to prevent these frequent hospitalizations. I hospitalized her only twice, which is pretty good. The last admission just occurred. She called a younger resident, Lopez. Do you know him?"

"Yes."

"When she called Lopez and told him that she wanted to kill her parents, he called 911, so firefighters and police went to her house. Her landlady was stunned, upset, and angry, so they first restrained the landlady, and then they took Rachel to the hospital. I called the hospital and explained the situation to the doctor, and they quickly discharged her. But, unfortunately, because of her threats, she lost her apartment and ended up in a nursing home. Her parents are frustrated and angry. They want to take care of her, but at the same time, they're afraid of her. So today, they allowed her to come and see me.

"She apologized for the drama before her hospitalization. 'I should listen to you,' she said. 'People are overreacting to me.'

250

"I told her, 'You can't blame Dr. Lopez. He did what was safe and legally required. He wanted to prevent something bad from happening, so he called your parents and warned them. And he called 911 and got you hospitalized. He was right on target and did a good job.'

That's what a doctor has to do, according to the *Tarasoff* ruling.[45]

"At the end of the session, she asked, 'Do you think I'll survive till next Wednesday?'

"I see her twice a week, and she asks me this often. I always tell her, 'I can't answer this question. I don't know. You have to tell me. You can walk out this door and do whatever you want. Tell me. Are you safe? Can you go home? Will you be back here on Wednesday? Will you kill yourself or someone else?'

"She always plays games like this: 'I don't know,' she says. 'I think I'll be here next week, but I can't promise you.'

"There's a Jewish holiday coming. As she was leaving, I again asked her, 'Are you safe? Are your parents safe?'

"She said, 'Yes, I'm seeing them on Monday.'

"She grew up in an Orthodox Jewish home, and her father is a rabbi at a local synagogue, so religious observance was an important part of her upbringing. Many times, though, especially during her excited mood swings, she broke the strict commandments of her religion and felt guilty while sinning."

I reflected on Jan's subtle point about Rachel feeling "guilty while sinning." I was a little surprised as I expected her to say she felt guilty *about* sinning. A person who is guilty *while* committing a "sin" may not suffer any guilt before or after sinning. The purpose of guilt is often to inhibit future transgressions. Consequently, the guilt while sinning doesn't prevent future sinning, so such a pang of guilt is an ineffective brake. A person who feels guilty *about* sin may feel guilty in anticipation of sinning while sinning or after sinning or some combination of them. If it includes all of them, we can call this *generalized guilt* because it persists, allowing a person to reflect on the tendency toward sin, feel remorse, learn, and refrain from sinning again. On the other hand, of course, excessive guilt may be paralyzing.

---

45 In *Tarasoff v. Regents of the University of California*, 17 Cal. 3d 425, 551 P.2d 334, 131 Cal. Rptr. 14 (Cal. 1976), the University of California in 1974 held that mental-health professionals had a duty to warn targets of potentially violent patients. This was broadened in 1976 to include a duty to protect them, as well.

An overzealous doctor may attempt to react to a person "guilty while sinning" with excessive exhortation or admonishment. It will produce little change because there is little remorse. Even a cautious, levelheaded therapist can hit an impasse. In setting up treatment expectations for a person who feels "guilty while sinning," the best advice to the doctor would be to proceed with caution. So, to Jan, I said, "These situations are tricky."

Jan replied, "I said, 'I need a serious promise from you that things will be safe.' So, I made her swear by God Almighty that she wouldn't kill her parents."

I felt that Jan's description of the nature of Rachel's guilt was accurate, but I questioned how he addressed her accompanying dangerous behavior. He seemed to think that he could magically change the situation by having her swear by "God Almighty."

Priests, rabbis, and imams concern themselves with their believers' spirits and the afterlife. They can always appeal to God in their ministrations because God is everywhere and eternally present. Keeping the lines of communication with God open for the flock is a weighty responsibility. However, it is impossible to know if someone's soul reached heaven or hell because they are ethereal entities. Therefore, it is impossible to tell if a priest has succeeded or failed to get a soul into heaven. Whether a cleric has delivered on the promise to have the believer's soul pass through the heavenly gates can only be known with certainty on Judgment Day. Till then, or at least till the afterlife begins, spiritual ministrations are safe from being proven wrong. Even if someone suspects a priest of spiritual misdirection of a soul, the cleric can, till judgment day, challenge and continue to debate the issue. However, assuming that there is evidence, any person, including the clergy, may be charged with embezzlement of church funds or pederasty and found guilty. At any rate, the State doesn't obligate a cleric to protect a patient's physical safety and life or to protect society from the danger a patient poses. However, state laws bind a psychiatrist to protect patients from self-harm and protect the community from dangerous people.

A physician has fiduciary responsibilities for the actions of the corpus, the body, of a patient: They should minimize suffering and enhance wellbeing. Hurt to a body is easy to prove; there is blood and guts, perhaps an accompanying knife, gun, or pill bottle. So, what is the medical value of invoking "God Almighty" in these circumstances? God may be beside the point. As a medical proposition, God may work but doesn't always. A doctor looks for potential failure areas, especially in medical ministrations, and must institute actions to mitigate such an event. Following the Hippocratic Oath, a physician first seeks to "do no harm."

Many people swear by beliefs in the divine, which are fundamental guiding principles in the conduct of their life. Prayers are effective and reassure the devotee of acting in the face of adversity. Such a self-initiated call to God can steal one's motivation and nerves. Still, when a *therapist* suggests God in the face of danger, we must consider the legal question of God's role in preventing or limiting harm.

God's glorification may occur if a therapeutic appeal to the Divine is successful. But, what if such an appeal fails? What if a patient, after swearing an oath to God, kills himself or someone else? No judge would accept "swearing by God Almighty" as an acceptable psychiatric or mental-health intervention. The psychiatrist would be liable for loss of life or limb. It is not a doctor's job to be a preacher or a crusader. At the end of each day, the doctor hopes to return home alive and free, with the means to support himself and his family. He has no wish to squander his chances for a livelihood.

Consider a lifeguard on duty who notices a swimmer flailing in the water. If the lifeguard's exhortation, "Pray to God and keep trying!" encouraged the swimmer to make it ashore, the encouragement would be a success. However, if the swimmer drowned, the lifeguard would be legitimately accused of negligence and suffer agonizing self-blame. When life is at risk, a lifeguard must guard life and take actual measures *on this Earth* to protect life, that is, jump in the water and pull the swimmer to safety! Similarly, the therapist's responsibility is to protect the patient and society. He cannot waive his corporal duty by invoking God; at the very least, he must honor the separation of Church and State.

I needed to understand Jan's assumptions. Jan was just recovering from a miscalculation in which he thought Amir's personality structure dealing with depression was like his own. Jan grew up within the Catholic tradition, which forbade suicide, even though he knew Poles killed themselves. Therefore, he presumed that Amir had suicide barriers like his own. Did Jan consciously ponder the implications for Amir's treatment of such contrary examples, namely, Polish people who committed suicide? With Amir, Jan clearly didn't understand the risk of naively injecting his personality and Catholic cultural beliefs into his therapeutic work. Now, he needed to be more self-conscious and careful about any actions invoking divine intervention and consider the implications of Church-State separation for psychotherapy. These ideas were helping me understand the source of Jan's misunderstanding, but now I needed to communicate to Jan the repercussions of his assumptions. I was not sure I knew how to do it.

Jan continued, "Rachel hesitated. I told her, 'We aren't leaving this office till I hear you swear by God Almighty that you and the others will be safe. The only way out of this office is through the emergency room or by saying that you swear by God Almighty that you and others will be safe. Say it even if you don't mean it. Just say it. Just pronounce those words.'

"It took 15 minutes before she would do this. In the meantime, I checked my messages and answered my mail. Then, periodically, I would say, 'Just say it' and go back to my tasks.

"She said, 'It wouldn't be fair to say something if I don't mean it.'"

I agreed with the patient. I felt that putting a patient in a position where she had to say something she didn't mean was coercion.

Jan continued, "I said, 'I don't care. Just pronounce these words.'

"Rachel said, 'I swear to God Almighty that my parents and I will be safe,' and suddenly looked stunned. She knew something important had happened. Then she asked, 'Are you going to hospitalize me?'

"I said, 'No. I feel safe. My role has ended. You promised by God Almighty; now it's God's business. I know for sure that you won't kill your parents.'

"Then she protested and said, 'Did I *really* say that I swear by God Almighty that my parents and I will be safe, or did I just repeat what you said?'

"I replied, 'You said it, so I feel sure everyone will be safe.'

Jan smiled, pleased with what he considered an undeniable therapeutic success.

Rachel's comment that she just might be repeating what Jan said was an example of the dangers of patient compliance with the therapist. People agree with others sometimes to avoid conflict. Because of this comment, I felt that Jan's intervention was an instance of his belief in the power of sacred words. I understood that Jan consciously resorted to those words based on goodwill and his deeply held understanding of how religious beliefs worked. Nevertheless, the differences between Jan and me regarding the expression *God Almighty* struck me as significant.

People's perspectives and practices are rooted in their systems of belief. Whatever their origin or form, beliefs influence day-to-day actions, sometimes consciously, but often unconsciously. Therefore, doctors making treatment decisions for others must be aware of and account for the effect of their belief systems on the patient.

I wasn't very optimistic that discussing this topic with Jan would be fruitful, yet it was necessary. I was concerned that Jan might feel that I misunderstood the context of his practice, coercing him to change his beliefs or methods, or demeaning his notions of God, although I had no intention of doing any of those things. Accordingly, I set myself three goals: one, to communicate to Jan my point of view; two, to help Jan distinguish between the religious beliefs he was free to have and the extent to which his faith impacted his psychiatric practice; and three, to make Jan aware of the risks and benefits of his psychiatric interventions, so that he could make any changes that he felt improved his practice.

In the meantime, Jan continued to describe Rachel's case. "I said again, 'I don't care. I feel safe. I know you're safe. I know your parents are safe. Your holidays are going to be good.'

"I know that God is now involved. I spoke to my supervisor, Dr. Schwartz, about this. Schwartz is Jewish, and I like his perspective. He thought that part of my trouble forming a therapeutic relationship with Rachel was that I'm Polish.

"There has been a lot of animosity between Poles and Jews for a long time. You can see it in Poland and any Jewish community, including those in the United States. Initially, Rachel had a big problem with me being Polish. When Rachel's previous therapist graduated, she needed a new therapist. It was hard to reassign her because she was so difficult that no other resident wanted to see her. Finally, I was the only one willing, and I *wanted* to see her. Unfortunately, she had an extensive history of suicidal gestures. She was also manipulative and noncompliant: a truly challenging patient. So, when I started to see her, we had a problem: Rachel couldn't accept that I was her therapist, and she would frequently miss her weekly sessions. She wanted to talk to me about the Holocaust and Polish anti-Semitism when she came. Once, she asked, 'Why were most of the concentration camps in Poland?'

"As it happens, I know a lot about these matters because I lived in Krakow, which is only 50 kilometers from Auschwitz. Whenever guests from Western Europe or the United States came to conferences or seminars, I drove them there. Understandably, everyone wanted to see Auschwitz. It was always a depressing experience. During the guided tours, I learned a lot about the history of the concentration camps. I learned about their organization and how legendary German precision played a role in keeping them functioning.

"The Nazis didn't intend to produce or build anything. They just wanted an efficient way to kill what they called *Untermenschen*, unworthy people, and get rid of any trace of them. That was the only goal. I've seen other concentration camps. Some are in Germany, like Dachau. Another is near the village of Stutthof in Gdansk [Danzig], a free city before the war but became part of Poland in 1945. One of the first battles of World War II took place in Westerplatte, near Gdansk, when Germany attacked Poland. During World War II, Germany expanded to occupy many areas of Europe, including Poland. The Germans built concentration camps inside Germany and also seized land. For example, Auschwitz was a German-controlled concentration camp in occupied Poland. Therefore, it is wrong to call a German concentration camp a Polish concentration camp. They killed Jews and Poles in the camps. Germany and the Soviet Union occupied Poland, and it ceased to exist as a nation. During World War II, Poland vanished as a nation. In fact, Poland became free—from the Soviet Union—only in 1991.

"Anyway, these discussions made our relationship stronger. At some point, Rachel started to come twice a week, although she was sometimes half an hour late. I felt that I needed to accommodate her. So I rescheduled some of my other patients to make it convenient for her to see me whenever she could. This phase of resistance lasted a couple of months. Then I started to become stricter, and Rachel began to be more regular and punctual. This stuff about wanting to kill her parents started two years ago. She said she didn't know why she wanted to kill them but that the thoughts were intrusive and that she couldn't stop them. She said that she didn't agree with these thoughts and that they were painful. Sometimes, they disturbed her so much that she thought of killing *herself* so she wouldn't kill her parents.

"Her plan for killing her parents was psychotic. Once, she told me, 'I'll kill my father by shaving his beard. I'll shave his beard, and the drug dealers will do the rest.'

"I said, 'I'm sure that you see some connection between shaving off your father's beard, killing him, and drug dealers, but I don't see it. Will you please explain?'

"Her explanation was crazy. She expected someone on the train to offer to sell her drugs. So, she would buy them and get hooked on them. Then, when she couldn't pay for them, the drug dealers would go after her family and kill her father. She would shave his beard beforehand so they wouldn't hesitate to kill him—not very realistic, as you can see. Every time she came to see me, she talked about different ways of killing her parents.

"I remember a few of the recent stories. According to the Bible, the Egyptian army pursued the just-liberated Jews. Moses parted the waters when the Jews came to the Red Sea, and the Jews went through, with the Egyptian army in hot pursuit. After the Jews crossed safely, God made the water rush back and drown the Egyptian army. She said that she would part the waters just like Moses and, when her parents were in the middle of the seabed, she would close the seas again and drown them.

"I said, 'It sounds like you have a plan, but how will you part the waters? Have you ever tried it before?' She agreed that she couldn't part any waters. She knows it. She's an educated woman. She goes to a community college and is close to graduating. Yet, at the same time, she keeps creating these scenarios. She could easily challenge them herself, but for some reason, she doesn't.

"For a long time, she didn't tell me *why* she wanted to kill her parents. Then a month ago, she told me that she'd been raped twice. She was subject to frequent mood swings, and during one of these episodes, she went to a Greyhound Bus station when she was very agitated. There, she met two guys and got into a car with them, and there were two other guys in the car, too. They asked her if she wanted to go to a motel with them. She said 'yes.' They asked if she wanted to drink some alcohol. She said 'yes.' They got her drunk, and then all four guys raped her. She was shocked. She says she believes that they belonged to the Russian Mafia. I wondered if she wanted to punish her parents because they didn't protect her.

"The other one happened when she was in Israel, traveling to a kibbutz by bus. She was the last person on the bus, and she started talking to the driver. She was friendly and smiled at him and then hugged him. He probably thought she wanted to have sex, so he had sex with her. She felt violated. Although she initiated the physical contact, she thought she was raped. She gradually became more open to telling me about her traumas—and there were so many—but it still didn't click. I still didn't know why she wanted to kill her parents.

"Then, out of nowhere, she said, 'My father broke my arm when I was seven years old.' 'Why?' I asked. She said, 'I don't know. He was upset with me and pulled my arm violently, and it broke. That made him even more upset. He cried afterward.'

"Suddenly, things started to make sense to me. I felt I had an idea of why she acted the way she did. She has ambivalent feelings toward her parents because she felt they didn't protect her, but she doesn't want to let go.

Recently, she visited the Millennium Park in Chicago and told strangers, 'I'm going to kill my parents.' One guy replied, 'Why don't you kill some Arabs instead?'

"Today, she was able to acknowledge that she doesn't want to leave her family. Instead, she said, 'I want my parents to be around me. I want them to take care of me.'

"Now Rachel has her older sister on her hit list because her sister doesn't want her around her children. Rachel said, 'I can't believe it. She's my sister, and she pushes me away,' and she became tearful."

Jan smiled. "I told you all this to explain why I was 20 minutes late."

"You said that you spoke to Schwartz about Rachel."

"Yes, we are both curious about this Polish–Jewish thing. I know the stereotypes Poles have about Jews. Some narrow-minded Poles, especially in the countryside, think that Jews are preoccupied with money. The farther from the big city, the more Orthodox Catholicism and anti-Semitism you see. The stereotype is that the Jew is greedy and money hungry, that they gladly lie, break the rules, and betray friendships and loyalties to get rich. Where money is involved, an answer from a Jew is never definitive. There's always a second meaning or a third. In other words, there's always something crooked behind their communications. Another example . . . it's hard to say it in English, is that offering you something in a 'Jewish way' means you'll have to pay a lot more for it later. But I never knew much about what Jews in the United States think about Poles, so I asked Schwartz.

"He said that Jews think of Poles as drunk, lazy, not very smart, and unable to follow the rules. There's a joke about Jews, Russians, and Poles trying to escape from a concentration camp. The Jews constructed a trampoline near a fence; they jumped on it and escaped. A Russian tried just to jump the fence, but he didn't jump far enough and landed on top of the fence, and the Germans killed him. Then the other Russians managed to escape by jumping on him and then over the fence since his body protected them from the barbed wire. But every time a Pole tried to jump the fence, the other Poles clung to his leg, and he fell back into the camp, so none of them escaped. Exchanging such jokes made me feel closer to Schwartz."

"I get it," I said. "The Jews used their smarts to escape, the Russians used ruthless sacrifice, and the Poles were stupid and got stuck."

"Yes. At first, Rachel blamed me for all the atrocities against the Jews. When she said that the concentration camps were in Poland, I told her I knew about the concentration camps because I had lived near one. And I tried to clarify that the camps were a German project, that Germany set them up after Germany occupied Poland, so, at that time, there was no Poland. The Germans forced Polish prisoners to construct the camps and then killed them after the project's completion. None of the Poles knew what they were building. Rachel didn't know these historical details. That discussion put our relationship on a different footing. She felt relieved that I wasn't offended by her comments and was willing to talk about them. At some point, I may have wanted to talk more about the concentration camps than she did! I think she appreciated my consistency. Our relationship grew in stages. After talking about the camps, she told me about her father breaking her arm. We reached another stage when she swore to God Almighty. Whether Jewish or Christian, it was a big step for a strict believer. I know what I did was blackmail, but I felt that it would be a good lesson and therapeutic. She knew she shouldn't take the name of God in vain.

"She has great potential, but she's profoundly damaged. Schwartz felt that she had invited some of her own troubles and that, in a sense, she was at fault. I don't think so. I feel that she's screaming for attention when she puts herself in harm's way. Her family wants to send her to a nursing home for Orthodox Jews in California. Orthodox Jews differ from other Jews because they have special rules, and they feel they should be in a place that understands and can accommodate their beliefs and customs. The application form requires input from a psychiatrist. On the one hand, I understand that she's a great burden to her family, but I also feel that they want to dump her in this place."

"So, what did you say in the application form?"

"Well, Rachel has nowhere to live now because she lost her place after this last episode. Rachel's family often hosts religious gatherings and family parties where children are present. Dreading that Rachel might do something embarrassing, they didn't want her to live with them, so they rented an apartment. Her landlady asked her to leave the apartment after the last episode. Her family decided they wanted to send her to this faraway place. I spoke to her parents and told them that I wish I had had more time to work with her. They said that more time with me was impossible. Rachel is fine with the move. Once she heard that the place was for Orthodox Jews, she was eager to go."

I now wanted to explicitly draw some parallels between Jan's previous treatment of Amir and his current treatment of Rachel. However, I wasn't sure how he would respond, so I spoke with some hesitation.

"Recently, when we spoke about Amir, you said that the key problem was that you thought he was more like you than he really was. In *your* depression, you may have had suicidal thoughts, but you never ventured into the actual suicidal territory; *his* depression included suicide. In your *depression*, you were similar, but you were different in your attitudes toward suicide. You remember that, right?"

Jan nodded.

"Your attitudes were based on your Catholic upbringing and the Catholic proscription of suicide. In Poland, there are religious and customary barriers to suicide. For example, you cannot bury the body of a person who committed suicide inside the sacred grounds of a church cemetery."

"Yes. Also, there are negative consequences for the family, even after you're dead."

I continued, speaking slowly, "In this case, do you think there's any personal or cultural element that's significant?"

"Yes. It's paradoxical. Christians and Jews share the Ten Commandments."

"Yes . . ."

"We have the same set of basic rules regulating our lives."

"Yes . . ."

"Rachel leads her life as she thinks the Bible commands, to the comma, so it's blasphemy for her to say, 'I'll kill my parents.' As a rabbi, her father guides other Jews in the neighborhood. His goal is to convey a certain vision of the Bible to them, yet he has a daughter who wants to kill her parents. It's a horrible thing to say, and it has consequences for Rachel and her family. I don't know if she does it consciously, but she does it purposely. She says it openly to her friends and to the people who went to high school with her. She's been saying it for two years, and it has spread to the entire Jewish community. It's very hurtful. It's one of the worst things you can do if you're a Jew or a Christian.

"You know how they find a mate in the Jewish community? It's probably like in India. There's a lady matchmaker; they call her a *yenta*. She matches up a Jewish boy and a Jewish girl after considering what they're like, how much money their parents have, their standing in the Jewish community, and local politics. A *yenta* introduced Rachel to a nice Jewish boy in Los Angeles. He's a jeweler. His family is wealthy; her family is well off but not wealthy. Rachel's family is, however, highly respected in the community. Anyway, they got married, even though they hadn't spent that much time together beforehand. She left for Los Angeles and began living with her husband. She liked him. She said, 'He was good to me,' and 'He never screamed at me.' She also said, 'He never forbade me to do things like many other guys who try to rule their wives. He allowed me to take the car and go out by myself. Some guys don't allow that.' He even allowed her to talk to other men. She loved him.

"Unfortunately, after they were married for two weeks, Rachel started to talk about killing him. In this case, she had a clear plan: She was going to drown her husband in the bathtub. As before, she talked to her friends, her family, and even his cousins about it. His cousins ratted on her to his parents. His father contacted her father, and they agreed to dissolve the marriage. Then she went into a hospital and spent two weeks there.

"I didn't understand her. I asked her, 'You said your husband was a nice guy and was nice to you. You said that you loved him so much. You compared your life to the lives of other Orthodox Jewish wives and felt that yours was good. Why did you threaten to kill him?'

"For many sessions, we talked about her marriage and divorce. Finally, she told me, 'Here, I was going to school. I had friends. I was a free person, and I could do whatever I wanted. Then I got married, and I had to quit school. My job was to get pregnant as soon as possible and have as many children as possible. Everyone was open about it. They were waiting for me to get pregnant. I didn't like it, so this is what I did. As an Orthodox woman, I couldn't ask for a divorce, so I got a divorce my own way.'

"According to Rachel, there was a difference between talking about killing her husband and talking about killing her parents. Rachel insisted that she had 'real' thoughts about killing her parents. These homicidal thoughts of killing her parents scared her, so she started talking about suicide, so killing them would be moot.

"Dr. Schwartz liked this case very much because it was interesting for him to see a Polish doctor treating an Orthodox Jewish woman. He pointed out the weight of her saying, 'I'm going to kill my parents.' He said that for Jews, threatening to kill your parents is a big taboo; it's a definite no-no. So you don't say it. You don't even think it.'

"I agree with Schwartz. If any thought of killing crosses your mind or pops out of your mouth, it's not a good sign. As Schwartz said earlier, this is the ultimate blasphemy. It's sinning against God. I know it was hard for her. But, I must tell you a story. I'll explain why in a moment.

"When I worked in oncology, many patients suffered from pain. Sometimes, it was unbearable to the point that high doses of painkillers weren't sufficient, and they had to have surgery to cut the nerves transmitting the pain. But some patients didn't want any medications or invasive interventions. Instead, they wanted to try the 'natural' way and hired healers called *znachor* in Polish. They're shamans or witches, who treat people with herbs and magic.

"I remember this one patient. She was anxious and hysterical. She suffered from severe back pain due to cancer metastases. She despised medicine and doctors. Finally, she resigned herself to me but specifically requested that I not oversee her pain control. I saw her suffering from severe pain, but she wouldn't agree to radiation or any surgical procedure to relieve it. Then she hired this witch. The witch came and mixed up some bogus herbs and drops of honey. Then she boiled it and splashed the hot liquid over the woman's legs! The lady started to cry about the pain in her legs. While she was screaming about the pain in her legs, she forgot about the pain in her back. For me, this was nothing but a silly distraction. All it did was shift her attention from her back to her legs, but she acted like it was a miracle.

"I think this story can serve as a metaphor for what happened to Rachel. Talking about killing her parents was burdensome and caused her many problems, but doing anything against God was worse. Because of my insistence, she swore by God that she wouldn't kill her parents or herself. Breaking such an oath is one of the worst things you can do as an Orthodox Jew, so guarding against *this* sin is her new burden. Her oath today is like the treatment given by the Polish healer who burned my cancer patient's legs to get her to forget about her back pain."

I agreed with Jan's summary. He understood the diversionary shifting of attention from one situation to another. Although he may not have intended it, Jan had just compared his introduction of breaking a divine oath with the witch's burning of the cancer patient's legs. Both the lady and the witch treated the event as a miracle. Earlier in this session, I outlined my thinking on these issues, but conveying this thought and its implications to Jan, who felt that he had just performed a miracle, was a different matter.

"First," I said, "I want to acknowledge that bringing God in made you feel good. When she used the phrase *God Almighty*, you felt great satisfaction and relief about her safety."

"At least, I said that. I know she believed in it very much, but I don't think my religious beliefs had much to do with bringing God into the picture. But, I told *her* it makes me feel much better and much safer."

"I understand that this woman is an Orthodox Jew. She was already at war with the Ten Commandments and the Jewish tradition before you brought God in."

"Yeah . . ."

"She wanted to kill her parents, which is against the Bible and the Ten Commandments. You're a physician specializing in the practice of psychiatry."

"OK."

"The government gives different powers to different people. As a psychiatrist, you can temporarily deprive patients of their rights if you feel they're dangerous to themselves or others by committing them to a mental institution for a short time, whether they agree or not. You're depriving them of their constitutional rights to freedom of movement and association during that time. You're telling them that you're going to deprive them of the full enjoyment of these rights, so what you're doing is a big thing. You're taking away what Washington, Jefferson, and the Founding Fathers labored mightily to give every American. Within a few days of your certification, a judge in the mental health court will rule on the matter. If the judge concludes that there is danger, he will allow continued hospitalization of the patient for a certain time; if he concludes the patient is not dangerous, he will let the patient go. Your power to restrict the patient's rights is only temporary."

"I'm with you."

"If you stay within what the State says are your powers, you're operating on safe ground. You're in no legal jeopardy. But suppose you're practicing witchcraft. Suppose you diagnose blasphemy and enforce anti-blasphemy treatment by invoking the magic of the Ten Commandments or God Almighty. Are you on safe and legal grounds?"

Jan grasped what I was trying to say and took a moment to respond. "OK, that's a good question, but before I answer it, I'd like to point out that this wasn't the first time that Rachel made dangerous statements. She had made a few suicidal attempts already."

"Yes."

Jan continued, "During every session, she threatens to kill her parents or herself. She asks, 'Do you think I'll be back here for our next appointment?' In the beginning, when she couldn't convincingly deny having an intention or plan to do herself in, I would walk her to the emergency room and get her admitted. Then, only days after being discharged from the hospital, she would again say, 'I'm going to kill my parents' or 'I'll kill myself to avoid killing my parents.' After a few months of seeing her twice a week, I've seen changes in many areas, but these declarations never change."

Laughingly, Jan continued, "So this time, I asked Almighty God for help. God and I are going to make Rachel safe for a weekend. I don't want to sound pompous, but I would do whatever it takes. I don't think it's a breach of the Mental Health Code to use someone's beliefs to prevent bad things from happening. I did this with a patient whose teenage son died in a car accident. She was despondent and chronically suicidal. Since she was a Polish woman who happened to be an Orthodox Catholic, I felt comfortable pointing out that suicide is a mortal sin. We—I mean Polish people—don't feel right about it."

I said, "If it works, it works. That's wonderful. No problem. We can invoke all the world's spirits to do some good for a patient. If you prevent bad outcomes, there's no problem. My question doesn't arise when she *doesn't* kill herself or somebody else. Suppose that after such an intervention, she kills herself. Then what?"

"Did you see the movie *One Flew Over the Cuckoo's Nest*?"

"Yes."

"Do you remember the scene in the day room by the drinking water-fountain? Guys are shooting breeze. Jack Nicholson, as McMurphy, says, 'I'm going to lift this huge drinking-water fountain, throw it at the window, and escape.' It was a solid few hundred pounds of marble and metal. As the veins on his neck bulge, all these nuts are looking and laughing at him. He tries to lift it, and, of course, he can't move it an inch. Then he turns to them and, after a suspenseful moment, says, 'At least I tried.' This is my answer. Even if she kills herself, I'll say, 'At least I tried.'"

"Right. There's an upside to the invocation of God. However, she has her own rabbi for religious counseling and didn't come to you for divine guidance. If your approach fails, the risk that you take is that all you can say is 'I tried.'"

"I would say I used everything divinely possible to prevent it."

But you are not divine, I thought. "I understand. Now, to follow up on a previous topic, I asked earlier if Schwartz had some ideas about what to pursue during your sessions with Rachel."

"He wants me to dig into her past. For example, she said that her father broke her arm when she was seven. Schwartz felt that her telling me this was a turning point in the therapy and that we should understand it further. He wanted more information about her childhood to identify her risk factors thoroughly. What would you say?"

I replied, "I might say, 'Your father broke your arm, and your mother didn't protect you. I understand that you are angry at both of them and feel like you want to kill your parents. However, your husband was more interested in his babies than the fact that your world changed after marriage, and you missed your friends. You feel that people are taking advantage of you and using you. And now, you can't believe people; you can't believe in love, etc. But do you want to spend the rest of your life in a jail cell?'

"This chain of thought shows empathy to Rachel but doesn't invoke God. My thoughts are perhaps like what Schwartz is saying. If you decide to go this route, you can note in the chart that such homicidal statements have been made regularly without any previous harm to her parents. You could say that because her plans to kill her parents involve a Moses-like parting of the sea, it's your clinical judgment that, despite such threats, she's not a danger. You discharge her and will continue medication and outpatient therapy.

"The emphasis is on your *clinical judgment*, which is part of the professional performance for any psychiatrist. Despite her statements, you don't find her to be homicidal. A lawyer can easily question any extra-psychiatric, God-based measures but has to grant you clinical judgment. God can be a spear, but not your shield. Anyway, I think I'm having trouble letting go of the topic of God and therapy, but you know there's that saying, 'Render unto Caesar the things that are Caesar's, and unto God the things that are God's.'"

"Yes."

"Did the Pope appoint you to this position?"

"You mean the position of treating Orthodox Jews?"

"Yes."

"As a psychiatrist?"

"Yes. The President of the University hired the Chairman of the Department of Psychiatry, and he hired the Residency Training Director, and he hired you. What do you think of what I said?"

"Since I started seeing you, I've learned to be careful about what I think, say, and document. I don't document what I *thought* happened. If a patient says it, I put it in the record. I don't make interpretations for which I have insufficient evidence. I don't speculate unnecessarily. It's easy to put a diagnostic label on a patient. In the past, I would diagnose quickly, but now I take my time."

"In one area, you must indicate your judgment: Is she dangerous, either suicidal or homicidal?"

"I understand. In Rachel's case, there's been no serious homicidal attempt. Another way she wants to kill her parents is with a gun she hopes a stranger will give her on the train. I told her, 'Guns cost money. No one is going to give you a gun for free. How much money do you have?' She said, 'My mom just gave me $5.' I asked, 'Why did your mother give you the money?' She said, 'For the train ticket from home to here and back.'"

"So, is your conclusion that Rachel is dangerous or not dangerous?"

"Not dangerous."

"OK, that's what you put in her chart. But, in my opinion, a note that says that she wasn't dangerous in your clinical judgment will help you more if she kills herself or somebody else, not a statement about God Almighty. People swear to God and on the Bible in Court. Yet, nobody has heard from Him as a witness in a court of law."

Jan was exasperated but also laughing. "Of course, this is the Caesar stuff, but to prevent bad things from happening, in the case of this unpredictable patient, I think God Almighty will do the job."

I repeated myself, "That's fine, but be sure also to say in your note that it's your clinical judgment that you didn't think she was dangerous at that time."

"Yes, I understand what you're saying."

"We don't disagree, at least as far as the note is concerned."

"That's correct. I hate my last note about Amir. Emotionally, I couldn't read it for months and months. Then, his mother applied for his records, and I had to sign to have them released. Then I looked at my last note. It looks decent. Everything that was supposed to be there was there. What we talked about and what I tried to do. It's a bad note."

"Why?"

"He killed himself. I feel that I should have talked about him trying to kill himself. I didn't talk about it. What we talked about was that he wanted to go to a party. He bought some new clothes. He was on his way to buy flowers and a gift for a girl. It's like I completely missed the point. The problem was somewhere else entirely."

"The main thing is what you said. You tried, and you continue to try." I deliberately and pointedly inhaled deeply. Then, I looked at Jan and said, "Take a breath." He was surprised but took a deep breath. I continued, "Feels good to breathe. Do you like the taste of air? It's life!"

Jan nodded.

"From the moment of birth," I said, "you need that feeling to live. No one else can give it to you. If a patient refuses it, no psychiatrist can give it to him."

As Jan left, I sensed a deep sorrowfulness in him.

CHAPTER 23

THE PREVIOUS SESSION ENDED with Jan talking about his last session with Amir. As this next session began, a sense of poignancy filled the air. I opened the discussion by raising those feelings obliquely. "After the last session, I started to think more about the Fossa Lady, the woman whose husband the Germans killed. She turned over body after body in the castle *fossa* to find his remains."

"In occupied Poland during the War, you didn't have to be guilty of anything to be killed. If some Underground action killed a German, the Germans retaliated. They picked people up off the street. They would close a road at both ends and seize all the people there. The Polish people called it *lapanka* or "catching." Sometimes, they took people to the forest, killed them, and buried them in a mass grave. Other times, they would send them to the concentration camps. Polish collaborators, called *volksdeutsche,* applied for German citizenship and had German allegiances. The collaborators often served as Polish-German transla-tors, but they were mostly just paid informants who tried to infiltrate the Polish Underground.

"Sometimes, the Germans knocked on doors, and sometimes they entered houses without any warning. They took people suspected of illegal activity in for questioning. The family got no explanation. They told the family where they should go later to inquire about what happened. If you lived in a city like Lublin, where the Fossa Lady came from, they took you to the castle, where the Nazis had set up a prison.

"If you killed a German officer, they would kill you and your entire family: parents, grandparents, children. This was a message to anyone who

268

might be thinking of retaliation: If you kill a German officer, they will wipe out all three generations of your family.

"When the Germans came to a Polish town, they would decide where they wanted to live and just take over the house. Sometimes they said, 'Pack your stuff and get out,' but they let you stay if they wanted services like cooking and cleaning."

"What happened to the Fossa Lady's house?"

"They didn't take her house. They did take my grandma's house, and she had to cook for them. I learned about the difference between German and Russian invaders from her and my Uncle Bozydar.

"On September 1, 1939, Germany invaded Poland from the west, and on September 17, the Soviet Union moved in from the east. Poland was divided up in a secret annex to the Molotov-Ribbentrop Pact, with the Vistula River as the border. Then, of course, Hitler later invaded Russia.

"My grandma's hometown, Tarnopol, was closer to the Soviet Union. Tarnopol was Polish before the war and now belongs to Ukraine. When the Soviets came, they picked her house for their living quarters and stayed there for two or three years. Then, in 1943, Hitler decided to invade the Soviet Union. The Germans crossed the Vistula River and started to walk eastward toward Moscow. They *also* picked her house for a short stay.

"According to my grandma, the Soviets were less civilized than the Germans. The Soviet foot soldiers stank. They didn't know what a bathtub was for and used it as a urinal. They even shat in the middle of the room. They didn't have regular uniforms. They stole clothes wherever they could. Their shoes were made of straw rather than leather. Instead of water flasks made of aluminum, they had glass bottles hung on their belts with a string or a rope.

"She said they ate onions like other people eat apples. One time, she told me, Soviet officers came in with a bag of mushrooms they had picked in the forest, and they wanted her to cook them. She recognized some poisonous ones in a pile and balked, but they forced her to cook them at gunpoint. The Soviets guzzled *spirytus,* almost pure alcohol, along with the poisoned food, while she prayed for her safety. None of them suffered any serious negative consequences from the poisonous mushrooms or the *spirytus.* Later, I also found out that the Soviets would rape any woman, regardless of her age.

"In contrast, the German soldiers who stayed in her house were squeaky clean. They shaved regularly, smelled of cologne, and dressed in matching uniforms. The designer Hugo Boss produced the black SS uniforms. They used silverware when they ate. OK, so they stole jewelry and artwork from wealthy Jews, but they didn't steal clothes and stuff like that from ordinary people."

Here, Jan laughed with irony and said, "You can even have a preference about which invaders you want to be invaded by!"

"But both the Russians and the Germans were killers," I said.

"Do you know how they trained the SS to be killers?" Jan went on. "When a young recruit to *Hitler Jugend,* the Hitler Youth, came to boot camp, he was given a German Shepherd puppy to train and take care of. Over the months of training, each boy naturally grew to love his dog. Then, when he was about to graduate, a final test ordered the boy to shoot and kill the dog. If you hesitated, you failed."

"Would you say that, after the invasions, the Polish people wanted to kill Germans and Russians in revenge?"

"Yes, that's what my Uncle Bozydar did, but his desire for revenge was even worse. He killed not only Germans; he killed Polish collaborators who had helped the Germans, and he gave orders to others to kill Polish collaborators."

"When you are driven from your house or country, it's natural and normal to want to kill the invaders. But, I just had a thought about your patient, Rachel. When you all decided to admit her, she may have felt like she was being evicted from her home by enemies."

"It's a pretty funny story. Do you remember that Rachel paged my fellow resident in the middle of the night? She told him about her thoughts of killing her parents and sounded pretty determined, so he decided to bring her in. When the police and the ambulance arrived, they saw the landlady screaming and yelling. Thinking that she was the crazy and dangerous person and the reason for their presence, they wanted to take the landlady to the hospital. So after some screaming, yelling, and talking, they took Rachel to the psych ward. However, when she was ready for discharge, neither her parents nor her landlady wanted to take her back. Back to the issue of revenge. I know a lot of people who suffered horrible things during the war but didn't want to kill others."

I replied, "I understand. I'm talking about the difference between feelings and thoughts about killing, which are understandable if people are deeply hurt, and the *actions* they undertake in such situations. We must try to understand the patients' feelings, to make sense of their demons, and then intervene before they are manifest in homicidal actions."

Jan responded, "Rachel realizes that some of what she wants to do is wrong and struggles with her feelings. We processed this incident when she came to see me: While walking to my office, she overheard a conversation between a doctor and a receptionist. She recognized this doctor as the resident who admitted her against her will; he has a distinctive accent. She said he had apologized. He later told me that he had also spoken to her parents. They were rude to him and called him an asshole. They felt that he had no business calling 911, that he should have called me before doing anything. When I met her parents, I told them that the resident acted appropriately and in Rachel's best interest.

"But now, I'd like to change the topic. I want to tell you that I like talking to you about my patients. It always gives me new ideas, reduces my anxiety, and decreases my insecurity in dealing with them. In this sense, you're different from Schwartz. Schwartz is less practical. I would say he's less immediately helpful. When things get stalled with a patient, I raise it with you, and you do your best to advise me. For example, when I was working with you in the inpatient unit, you told me about a woman in a homeless shelter. You and a psychiatry resident had interviewed her together, and the resident concluded that she was depressed because she couldn't communicate with her son, who had been in prison for a long time. After the resident finished, you continued the interview to figure out how to help her. Soon after you began talking, she told you that her son's birthday was coming up, and she couldn't afford a postage stamp to send him a card. You took a stamp from your wallet and gave it to her. Suddenly, there was a big smile on her face. It worked better and faster than Prozac. You need to know that I've often felt like that homeless woman.

"Usually, Schwartz cares more about historical backgrounds and uses a wider perspective to understand cases, so I asked for his thoughts about my situation: a Jewish girl having a Polish therapist. But in this case, he said that the specific transference-countertransference is more important than historical context. So I'm not sure if this will help me move forward in Rachel's case. That's why it's good to talk to you."

"I get two things from this session. First, in Amir's case, your anxiety overwhelmed you. The anxiety around treating Rachel gives you different ideas about assessing and handling therapeutic risk. This is like a yellow light at an intersection: It gives you time to come to a gradual stop. This kind of anxiety is called *signal anxiety* and is barely perceptible. However, there is no warning light when an accident is imminent: If a runaway car is heading for you, all you can do is slam on your brakes and twist the steering wheel in panic and fear. That's what happened with Amir. So, with Amir, you suffered from severe symptomatic anxiety and other feelings that devastated you. With Rachel, you're anxious because she's a difficult person to treat and because you have more signal anxiety. Here, though, the anxiety helps you choose the best course of treatment and regulate it."

"What you're saying is true, but with one clarification. In Amir's case, I was anxious *after* he killed himself. Before that, I falsely assumed that he would never kill himself, like me. I had felt a growing self-confidence, maybe even arrogance, regarding my ability to heal him. In the case of Rachel, there's a constant switching in her personality when it comes to her parents. Love and hate happen almost at the same time. This is true for most situations and for many topics we touch on. She doesn't want anything bad to happen to her parents, but she wants to kill them! Love and hate seem to coexist in her head. This is confusing for me, and I don't try to pretend I get it. Sometimes, the feelings appear to alternate but also to coexist simultaneously. Such constant swings in emotion are puzzling and hard to describe."

I said, "Rachel's parents see her actions as incoherent: They give her love, and she wants to kill them. And, every session, you are also trying to make sense of what she tells you. I view the case like this: Because her dad broke her arm, and her mom didn't protect her, she wants to kill them. At the same time, she knows she can't take care of herself and needs them. She wants to be close to them and feels hurt when they don't accept her in their house. She might or might not accept such an explanation. I'm sure she wants you to understand her anger. Maybe she can come up with a better explanation. You can also bring to her attention that her landlady, parents, or psychiatrist will stop her if she tries to act on those feelings. Even if the explanation is wrong, you've introduced the notion of cause and effect: The cause is her threats, and the effect is hospitalization or losing her apartment. You can clarify that her anger is understandable, but her threats are dangerous and will put her in the hospital."

"Giving up on people is not easy. After Amir killed himself, and before I started to see you, sometimes it seemed that people were just giving up on me. Every psychiatrist has moments when their own problems are no different from the problems of the patients they're treating. You must know that about yourself. You could easily put yourself above the patient. You could say, 'I'm sitting here in a bigger chair as a doctor, and you're sitting in the patient's chair.'"

"You've gone through a lot. We have to stop for now. We will continue next time."

My memory wandered to the beginning of my medical training. Like many other aspiring physicians in India, I began my training when I was seventeen. Like many college students, I joined the National Cadet Corps (NCC). This government-run volunteer organization seeks to inculcate in young adults a secular outlook as it builds character, courage, camaraderie, and other leadership qualities. NCC also acquaints cadets with first aid, map-reading, and camping skills, and offers basic military training in small arms. Like my father, I had briefly considered joining the Indian Armed Forces as an army doctor, but being in the NCC doesn't obligate you to join. Instead, many students joined the NCC for camping trips and other activities.

As a medical student, I attended the NCC camp in Guntur, about 55 miles from the Bay of Bengal, in the State of Andhra Pradesh. We began with lessons in first aid. Next, the instructors taught the theory of the structure and composition of advanced dressing stations and field hospitals. Then we play-acted an advanced dressing station, constructing makeshift stretchers, and carrying or being carried on them on an imaginary battlefield.

Soon, the training moved to small arms, primarily the .303 caliber Lee-Enfield bolt-action repeating rifle. Between 1895 and 1957, the British Army's standard firearm played a considerable role in the First and Second World Wars. We learned about each part and how to assemble, disassemble, clean, and use it. An essential part of our training was learning how to estimate how far away an imaginary soldier was, based on identifiable features—the outline of the human form, the head, a beret, the whites of the eyes, etc.—so that we could set the rifle sight appropriately. Then, we practiced shooting at such targets. About forty-two inches long and weighing eight pounds, the Enfield was an effective instrument of death and destruction.

When we went to the firing range, I picked up the ammunition clip and rammed it into the magazine. I worked the bolt with a flick of my right wrist and loaded the chamber. Even without previous experience, I did it right; there was no way to make mistakes. I marveled at the genius of the rifle's design, which ensured that the killer instrument functioned efficiently. I fired several rounds. With many cadets firing away, the session ended with the pleasant smell of what I presumed to be smokeless Cordite in the air.

I read that Cordite was discontinued soon after World War II, so it must have been surplus. For a while afterward, I would experience ringing in my ears and sore shoulders from the rifle's recoil.

In the beginning, our targets were stationary concentric circular patterns. These were then replaced by moving cardboard cutouts of men, with an X marking the heart's location. From an abstract design to the outline of a person, I noticed that this changed and evoked a vague unease. However, the queasy feeling was easy to hide.

Sergeant Baldev Singh was a typical middle-aged Sikh who wore *kesh* (unshorn hair) covered by a *pagadi* (a turban) and a *kara* (pronounced *kada)*, an iron bracelet. He was pockmarked and spoke with a nasal accent. During a break in the drill, when one of the cadets asked him about soldiering, he discussed the importance of *ahimsa* (non-violence) and explained that it includes the duty to prevent violence. "A good man cannot stand by when someone attacks a defenseless person; he must act." He paused for what seemed a long time and then added softly, "He must act, and if necessary, kill the attacker."

While the big black crows of coastal Andhra cawed loudly one hot afternoon, Sergeant Singh announced that we would practice the bayonet charge. He would start by giving a demonstration. He raised a bayonet and yelled, "*Yeh bayonet ka ladai hai!*" (This is battling with a bayonet!). He described the bayonet's parts and their functions and showed us how to affix the blade to the rifle. His expression then changed from distant to fierce to steely. He proceeded with the demonstration, screaming in a fiery guttural voice as he approached the gunnysack as though it were a *dushman* (an enemy soldier). His words were almost undecipherable, but the look on his face and the drumbeat of curses made me think that he was screaming, "*Oy teri maa dar chod!*" as he wildly attacked and furiously jabbed the dummy enemy soldier. That loosely translates as "motherf__er." It literally translates as "your mother's c..t," but implies, "[I'll f___] your mother's c..t."

He then lined us up in front of a post with a large gunnysack filled with sawdust or straw hanging from it. When it was my turn, he asked me, like every cadet before me, to affix the bayonet and then inspect it to ensure it was attached correctly. As I advanced toward the bag, the *dushman*, the Sergeant, urged me to approach menacingly, scream, and invoke a killer spirit in me "*Josh se dabow!*" *Stab with vigor!*

I could do none of these with any level of conviction. Nanna's emotion-laden voice talking of Japanese soldiers doing bayonet practice on Allied soldiers in the War reverberated in my memory, causing revulsion. Even a straw- or sawdust-filled sack effigy looked too close to human. As I prayed for my turn to be over, I meekly took a jab at the gunnysack. The Sergeant screamed into my ear, "*Twist, twist* the bayonet! Destroy him!" I found myself being angrier at the yelling Sergeant than at the gunnysack. I was willing to believe that the sack was a soldier, and I felt a force in me that I couldn't overcome. Before this, I had considered joining the Indian Army, like my father, but as I twisted the bayonet, I knew I couldn't.

CHAPTER 24

"I HAVE A NEW HISPANIC PATIENT. I'll call her Isabel. She divorced her husband because he was beating her, and she couldn't take it anymore. She has an aggressive and irritable child and won't listen to anyone. So the doctor prescribed Risperdal for him. Then she heard on TV that Risperdal has many dangerous side effects. So she asked the doctor, 'Why are you giving my son Risperdal? What is his diagnosis?'

"The doctor yelled at her, 'Are you a doctor? Do I have to tell you his diagnosis? What do you understand about mental illness? You're coming to a doctor for a reason. The doctor knows best. If I tell you something, you'll misunderstand and misinterpret it. There's no point in talking to you about these matters. Either you trust me, or you don't, and if you don't, find someone else.' What a prick.

"Isabel never found out the answer to either question. Now, she's lost her job, and she's lost her apartment. She and her son live with her brother, but he told her that he would go back to Mexico, so, soon, they'll have no place to live. And her ex is way late with child-support payments. She cries and cries. She is so full of pain.

"She reminds me of a Polish patient I have; I'll call her Zuzanna. After her son died, she said, 'There's no purpose for my existence. I have no reason to live anymore.'

"I told her, 'You have lots of love to give,' but the reality is that she doesn't have anybody to give it to. So she's thinking about volunteering in a children's hospital. She says she's living day to day.

"She went to Poland and felt fine there. She enjoyed going to the forest and picking mushrooms. When she came back, she went to the parking lot

276

of her apartment building and saw two cars, hers and her son's. One look at his car, and she was overwhelmed with sadness. She visits her son's grave almost every day and then gets even more depressed.

"She said, '*życie nie ma dla mnie sensu*' ("Life makes no sense to me.")

"Now that Maria is pregnant, I feel like I can relate to her. I don't know my son yet, but I can imagine her feelings. This is a big question. How can one lose a child and want to continue to live?

"Have I told you about my brilliant 21-year-old schizophrenic patient? I have been seeing him for several years. He has clear-cut symptoms. He's intelligent and has read up on schizophrenia. His grandmother on his father's side and his grandfather on his mother's side had schizophrenia, so he knows how the disease progresses. A research program for people with schizophrenia accepted him, but he still doesn't want to accept the diagnosis.

"As is typical with people with schizophrenia, his face doesn't show any feelings. He has the characteristic intense stare of schizophrenia: When he looks at you, you feel like he's burning a hole in your head. Sometimes, you can make the diagnosis based on the look alone. His parents say, 'Talk to your family more and show your feelings.' They keep trying to teach him how to look more emotional. 'When someone says something to you and laughs, you should laugh, too, because it's probably funny.' Often, they comment, 'You don't look normal *today*.'

"As much as he's not able to express his emotions, he feels bothered by their comments. He's a bright student at the university, but he's isolated and has no friends. Then, one day, he had to come to the hospital because he had become frozen: He had sat in a chair for a couple of days, almost motionless. He didn't talk or eat; he peed and shat in the chair.

"After being discharged from the hospital, he wanted to stop taking his medication. He asked me, with some feeling, 'Do you think I should tell my parents that I'm taking medication, even if I'm actually not?' I told him, 'The medication seems to be working. You came to the hospital because you were frozen, and now you're not. It helps you express yourself better and allows me to understand your feelings better. I think you should take it.'"

Jan's emotions rose. "I told him, 'Whatever you do, just tell me. If you decide against medication, just let me know. We can talk about it. I'll always tell you what I think you should do, but the decision is ultimately yours.'

"Well, that was quick. He told me today that he hates the medication and is going to stop taking it. Medications change the course of schizophrenia in the acute phase, when a patient is hearing voices and is crazy, but they don't change the long-term course of the disease. And they're of limited value between flare-ups of psychosis. So I wondered why I told him he should take the medication."

"That's a good question to ask yourself," I said. "Also, you said you told him, 'I think your symptoms are relieved by the medication. I think you should take it, but it's your choice. *The most important thing for us is that you tell me what you're actually doing.*' You're telling the patient, 'Keep me in the loop. I can help you more if you tell me what you're doing as you're doing it.' You're engineering a conversation with this patient by telling him, 'I want today's information today, not two weeks from now.' I think you're establishing a structure for dialogue that increases the possibility of more honest and timely interactions. Do you agree?"

"Yes, absolutely. That's why I'm changing my approach. I'm asking questions about what's happening in real-time."

"We doctors don't have to pretend we make all decisions about treatment. You can explain to the patient that his communications and the timing of those communications are important for the treatment. If a patient feels that he has some skin in the treatment game, it increases his engagement. Still, if he feels the treatment is being imposed on him, he may resort to resentful compliance, secrecy, negativism, or rebellion."

"This guy's parents want to know what we talk about. With his permission, I let his parents sit in for the first ten minutes of each session. After today's session, his mother said, 'Because he lives in our house, he has to follow certain rules. We have a right to set a time for curfew. Coming home at 4 a.m. is not acceptable. We also have a right to know what he's doing in therapy. Is he taking medications, or is he not taking medications?'

"I told her, 'Legally, I can't tell you what your son tells me. He is allowing you the opportunity to join our sessions for those ten minutes. I don't have permission to talk to you about what we discuss outside of that. I must respect his confidentiality and limit what I tell you. If he permits me, I can tell you. And you can always ask him.'

"She looked stunned and just walked out. Later, she called and said she was trying to understand where I was coming from. I told her to bring up her concerns during the first ten minutes of the next session. My patient likes my attitude and method of treatment, but he's still in denial about his diagnosis and feels that I'm wrong to say he has schizophrenia. He feels that I'm calling him 'sick' and resents it.

"In addition to his obvious illness, this constant negative feedback from his parents prevents him from doing even what he *is* still able to do. He has learned to put on a fake smile when they need him to smile, like when one makes a joke. We talked about it today. He says that his parents forced him to smile. If he doesn't smile, they get mad. They say, 'You don't look normal,' and he tells them, 'My smile is an act.'

"He's very smart and knowledgeable. Like many people with schizophrenia, he has an interest in esoteric subjects. He's reading Maslow and Nietzsche. He likes to talk to other similarly minded intellectuals. He says his parents aren't in his league, and he has nothing in common with them. He says they force him to be 'normal' and to smile, and he takes revenge by refusing to interact with them."

Jan paused and then went on, "A lot of things came to mind when we found out that we are going to have a son."

"Yes?"

"Every time I see a young, sick guy, I wonder, what if something like this happens to us? What if Maria and I have to struggle with a child who has schizophrenia or some other serious diagnosis, for that matter? What if he has an accident? This is a completely different dimension of life. I don't talk about this with Maria; she's already anxious. But questions keep coming into my mind. The most persistent one is, 'What is the connection between Amir and the birth of my son?' Amir is missing this vital part of life. He can't be a father and have a family. He's dead. But he was *part* of a family. They miss him, and nothing can bring him back. I'll soon become a father. My son is not yet born, and I feel so much responsibility already. For the first few years of my son's life, I'm going to be the highest authority, a godlike person. Whatever I say will be the most important thing in the world to him. So I guess I'd better say important things!" Jan spoke with emphasis as he sat there, imagining his son.

"It's true," I responded, "but an infant has real power and lots of resources to get what he wants. Nobody can tolerate a screaming baby, and nobody can resist a smiling baby. So, whatever he does, you should pick him up and cuddle him till he learns to soothe himself. There's so much power in a so-called helpless infant! Maybe you had an insight into the beginnings of the psychology of religion, a god person, and the power of infantile dependency."

Jan mused for a while, looking pensive, and asked, "Why did you mention religion and infantile dependency at the same time?"

"Because you said that, for your son, you will be 'a godlike person.' There's another aspect of this godlikeness, and it has to do with your perspective. It's implied in your getting ready for your job as a parent, saying, 'I'd better learn to be godlike.' When your helpless baby calls, he's calling for godlike help, and you are godlike in your capacity to respond as a parent. There's this power in you to be so because you provide food, clothing, shelter—everything. To your baby, you're on call 24/7. In that way, you're just like God, always on the job, always on call."

"Yes, that's true."

"I'm a physician, and I believe in psychology," I continued. "Previously, you and I discussed the desirability of a psychiatrist invoking the Ten Commandments."

"Yes, I used religion in dealing with Rachel."

"There is a psychology of religion. Why are human beings attracted to exceptional people? Why do human beings seek superior powers? Why do human beings seek God or godlike people? Where does this hunger come from? You used the term *godlike person,* as you were considering the job of parenting. Birds build nests in preparation for offspring, and humans speculate about the phenomenon of godlike people when they prepare for childrearing. As a parent, you assume the mantle of God. You and your wife will be everything in your baby's life and his ticket to the future. You'll give everything you possibly can to your son; that's the psychological nest that you're preparing."

"Definitely."

"Most people, when they talk of parenting, talk about feeding, diapering, attachment, bonding, and love. Your statement was very profound. It went way beyond such considerations."

"I certainly meant it as a profound comment—about responsibility. It's a big challenge. It's a big responsibility on my shoulders."

"Yes, you're thinking about how to be and act and reciprocate when the time comes. But the greatness of what you said was that you put it into one word—*godlike*—that said it all," I responded.

"Anyone who has had children can relate well to what I said. I once saw your daughter after work, so I know you know. You have . . ."

Laughingly, I interjected, "I have three children. I'm now most concerned with college tuition, but unlike you and Maria, who are pondering the godlike power of parenting, I'm dealing with the *limits* to power in parenting. That phase will come for you, too, but not for a while."

"That's true. When that time comes, I will have to figure out how to act. There was an interview on one of the morning news shows with parents and children talking about college admissions. Bright kids. One of them was trying to get into Brown University, one into Northwestern, and one into Chicago. The kids have been working for many years to prepare themselves for college, racking up both academic and extracurricular accomplishments. That time will come for us, too, but not just yet."

"I want to ask you a question or, actually, two questions at once," I said. "They're parallel, so if you answer one, you may have answered both. That's my psychology of complexity." I laughed as I pondered the craziness of what I was thinking. "Question 1: When would a parent want a child to smile? Question 2: When would God want a human to smile?"

"All the time. Constantly. Happiness is the highest point of existence. I think that is what God would want. And, as a parent, I would want my child to smile all the time, too."

"Then what is a child to do when he is hungry or scrapes his knee or feels sad and is *not feeling* happy?"

Jan didn't seem to have expected this question and hesitated before responding, "That's tricky. I want him to be happy, but smiling all the time . . . ?"

"I was thinking, particularly, about your patient with schizophrenia. So I'll add one more question: When does a psychiatrist want his patient to smile? And consider what your patient would say about smiling."

"He doesn't feel like smiling. He doesn't want to smile. Nietzsche said that human existence is a sad thing. I also had painful and dark periods in my life. I remember reading Sartre and Nietzsche without real understanding. The goal was to be worthy of belonging to a 'club' of dark thinkers. 'Members' were expected to display their understanding of existentialism and nihilism and, also, to look the part: black sweater, dark glasses, and an expression like you don't care and have no reason to smile."

"What do your patient's parents want him to do?"

"To smile. To respond."

"Do they want him to smile and respond even when he doesn't feel like smiling or responding, or only when he does?"

"They joke to trigger the emotion and a smile."

"So, their thinking is, 'You should smile when we crack a joke, so whether you feel like smiling or not, give us a smile anyway.'"

"In a way, yes. His mother specifically said she wanted him to smile and say, 'Good morning!' and 'Have a nice day!' But, unfortunately, from time to time, even people without schizophrenia don't feel like smiling."

"So, the question is, as a parent, a psychiatrist, or a god, do you want people to smile to get genuine communication going, or do you want to force them to smile, which may shut it down? All three questions have the same answer!"

"The ideal situation is for people to be happy and to smile because they're happy."

"Of course," I agreed. "That's what you try to do as a psychiatrist, by improving the patient's moods. But when a patient isn't happy and doesn't feel like smiling, what should the psychiatrist's attitude be? Earlier, you described a good attitude for a psychiatrist: You told your patient, 'I'm going to tell you what I think is good for you, but it's your choice. The main thing is to communicate authentically. If you take medicine, tell me; if you don't take it, tell me. If you feel better, smile at me; if you feel crabby, give me a frown. Then I'll know the way you feel.' That's my understanding of what you did. It happens to coincide with my philosophy of treatment. I'm not sure how it compares with the philosophy of Maslow, Nietzsche, or Sartre. Nothing, however, compares to being a parent."

"I'm looking forward to it. But I'm scared because it's happening so quickly. We're almost halfway through the pregnancy. At first, the baby will mostly be a body and have many reflexes, but emotions and thoughts will come before long. We have friends who had a son six months ago. I like to hang out with little Florian and try to understand how it all works. He mainly explores the world by putting stuff in his mouth, touching and hitting things, and making noises. He throws stuff and experiments with gravity. His grandma says she sometimes feels that he's out to destroy the house. But what he's doing is learning and testing all the time.

"I came across a great metaphor from *The Teaching Company* lectures on human development: A teacher brought a Christmas tree into the classroom, and the lights seemed to be flashing on and off haphazardly. The seemingly random pattern was annoying and even unpleasant to some students. On the other hand, humans like order and sense. Then he put on some Mozart, and suddenly, everyone realized the synchronization lights and music were. Life sometimes seems like random lights blinking. Even when you look at developmental theories, it's hard to make sense of it. But when you're the parent of a particular child, you have a scheme that applies to him, and things start to make sense.

"It's important for us to try to facilitate understanding. First, you want to foster a greater sense of self-understanding *in your patient* to improve his knowledge of himself and his situation. Second, you want to cultivate *your own* understanding of the patient and communicate your ideas. Third, you want to foster the patient's ability to recognize his areas of agreement and disagreement with you and share that. Fourth, you want to promote the patient's ability to act unless their contemplated actions are dangerous. You have to intervene and override his wishes to protect him and others. Fifth, you want to facilitate changes in yourself in response to each patient that will help you to become a better therapist to all your patients and a better human being.

"It's often impossible to achieve these overlapping goals. Mozart may bring order to the lights for some patients, but not for others, and even for the same patient, at different times or under different conditions. It's not easy to always know what to say to a person sitting in front of you and depends on your expertise and wisdom. You should be so genuine with your patients that you can say, 'I don't know.' And you must vary your music from session to session. I think you're doing more good for your patients than you were earlier. I also think you may be doing more good for your patients than you realize. By constantly fine-tuning the music—that is, the therapy—you can improvise from moment to moment. And you'll continue to get better. What do you think?"

"I think that's right, but, sometimes, I do too much. I overplay the music and stretch some sessions when I feel it will help. Some therapists are strict about ending a session on time, but I like to decide the right moment to stop. On days when I'm supposed to have supervision, I've told Schwartz, 'When you come to my office, you don't have to knock; just open the door. I'll wrap up whatever I'm doing. I'm usually writing notes, but if I have a patient, I'll end the session in a minute or so.'"

I was surprised and dismayed that Jan was still doing this. A therapy session should never be interrupted so cavalierly. But I kept my counsel as he continued.

"This last Wednesday, the receptionist stepped out while I was with a patient. Some patients like to drop bombs, atomic bombs, when there are five minutes left in the session, and that's what had happened. I was with this patient and had to spend extra time with her. Then the receptionist knocked on my door. She said, 'I'm sorry. I had to go on an errand. The guy you see every week is in the waiting room. He looks like he's pissed off.'

"Then my patient said, 'I'm so sorry. I didn't mean to overstay and cause problems for you.' So I told her, 'It's OK. Don't worry,' and we finished up quickly.

"Schwartz didn't open my door as I had asked him to, so I thought he hadn't come yet. But, instead, he had been sitting in the waiting area for fifteen minutes, and he was clearly annoyed.

"He came in and started talking, jumping from one topic to another. First, he talked about my patient, Rachel. Then he talked about therapy. And then he talked about a paper he'd given me last time I saw him. He asked if I'd read it. I had made some comments, but he seemed to be unhappy with my responses. Finally, he said, 'Not exactly, not precisely.'

"When we had ten minutes left in supervision, I said, 'I'm so sorry about this morning. You were waiting for no reason. I really apologize, but I've told you, please don't wait outside. Come in, and we can start supervision as soon as you arrive.'

"Clearly, he was uncomfortable with the arrangement, but I explained, 'It works for me. I'm usually seeing a patient or writing notes. You're the only person who will be knocking at the door and interrupting the session. I can always blame my ending the session on you. This way, the patient can stay longer. I feel good about it, though you might be a little uncomfortable.'"

Jan smirked about having placed Dr. Schwartz in such a predicament. I was glad that Jan was aware that he had put Dr. Schwartz in the bad-guy role, but his apparent glee concerned me. And I respected Dr. Schwartz for his reluctance, indeed unwillingness, to be compelled to play the part of the interrupter. So either Jan was unaware of the norms of psychiatric practice and the routines of such professional comings and goings or didn't care.

Jan continued, "Schwartz said, 'Let's talk about it,' referring to setting time limits for sessions, 'so that everyone knows when a session starts and ends. It's important to keep to the schedule.' I agreed with him and told him what I told you about my routine. I specifically added, 'In certain situations, I don't mind spending extra time with a patient.'

Jan's wish to have a scapegoat, blame somebody else for ending the session hinted at his immaturity. The psychiatrist's job is to establish the routine for starting and ending sessions. Patients who are overly dependent or have anxiety about separating may resist leaving on time. The psychiatrist's job is to manage this challenge with tact and discipline. Establishing predictable routines ultimately promotes both the patient's growth and the therapist's professional development. Jan had resisted taking this step on his own or addressing it with Dr. Schwartz. Instead, he seemed to like casting Dr. Schwartz as the bad guy.

Jan's father had played this role throughout Jan's childhood and adolescence and into adulthood. Something in Jan's father's personality tolerated or fostered this bad-cop role. Schwartz was trying, unsuccessfully, to bring this dynamic to Jan's notice. Jan needed to learn how to be both the therapeutic good guy *and* the therapeutic bad guy. He needed to be prepared to end therapy sessions himself and deal with any attendant patient frustration. However, needing to be primarily good was deeply embedded in Jan, and he resisted changes that would make him look bad in the patients' eyes.

"Then I talked about a patient who was chronically late," Jan continued. "Early on, she was sometimes four hours late. I would have an appointment with her at 9 a.m., and she would come at 1:00 p.m. If I had a cancellation or could squeeze her into my schedule, I would tell her I'd see her later in the afternoon. If not, I might see her for half an hour or even ten minutes. She never minded. I was pleased that she came at all and praised her for her effort. She gradually started to improve. It's important to be flexible. You should accommodate patients who know they need help but can't keep to all the rules. After a while, I said to her, 'If you know someone is waiting for you, it's not polite to be late. Why do you come late?'

"She said, 'The medicine you gave me makes me drowsy, and it's hard to get up. Your medicine is the reason I'm late.' I told her, 'I know how powerful some medicines are.' It's important to find the best balance between being flexible and enforcing rules; it's not the same for everyone.

"She's special . . . but every patient is special. My Japanese medical student is special. This guy can talk your ear off. He knows a lot about water purification and the science and politics of water. When he starts to talk, it's hard to have a conversation because he doesn't pause. It's hard to interrupt him, but what he says is interesting."

I wasn't ready to let go of the issue of forcing Dr. Schwartz to interrupt. "Before we move on to this other patient, I'm curious about whether Dr. Schwartz said anything else about what happened."

Jan responded, "I felt that he was, metaphorically, bringing a stick to punish me for keeping him waiting that morning. I somehow took the stick out of his hand when I asked him to knock, but then he brought another stick. He was trying to make a point, but I said, 'I'm going to be an independent physician in a month or so.' Then I said that I feel about what is important to patients, and I have to go with that feeling. I'll modify my sessions based on what I feel is useful to each patient. Polish patients are peculiar, and I understand them. My Polish women patients, for example, always sit on the edge of the chair, waiting for me to give them a signal to leave—I mean, a sign that the session is over. They're on the lookout for your body language that says the time is up. The one I saw today was apologetic for being two minutes late!"

Two things struck me, one related to ending sessions and the other with Dr. Schwartz. First, all patients should leave at the end of a session, and it's the psychiatrist's job to establish this routine, yet ending a session may entail a slightly painful adjustment for the patient. It's like a mother breastfeeding her baby. After feeding her infant, she sometimes has to actively slide the nipple out of the baby's mouth. That may be easy if the child is satiated, but sometimes the child resists. A mother provides a child with opportunities to self-manage some frustration. Family life builds this in, especially if a mother is taking care of other children, attending to other duties, or has to attend to the calls of nature. In the context of providing manageable opportunities to help a child learn to tolerate frustration, a "mother" could well be a father or any caretaker.

In the same way, ending the session is part of the treatment process. A psychiatrist needs to learn how to do it and use it to provide opportunities for the patient to understand the world's ways. It cannot and should not be waived or displaced to some external agent.

Jan's passive-aggressiveness toward Dr. Schwartz mirrored the hostility he showed his father. It was a specific manifestation of Jan's negative father transference onto Dr. Schwartz. Recall how Jan said that Schwartz was "bringing a stick to punish me" and "I was somehow able to take it away." Taking away Schwartz's metaphorical stick reminded me of Jan's physical fight with his father when he pinned his father down in a martial-arts hold.

Earlier, I commented on Jan's difficulty in expressing negative feelings toward me. Perhaps, because he got out of his deep depression so quickly after he started to see me, it was difficult, if not impossible, for Jan to have negative feelings about me. There had been only two occasions when Jan seemed to experience a twinge of tension with me. One was when I said that his mother had "left" him when she went to the TB sanatorium. He had objected to the idea that his mother had "left" him because she had to do it to get necessary medical treatment. The other was when he called his dad and told him that Maria was pregnant and that they would have a boy. His father had said, "That's nice," and not "I'm very happy." Because of his father's entrenched dementia, loss of orientation to time and person, and helplessness, I played devil's advocate and took his dad's side.

I felt that Jan was a fine fellow, but he sometimes pigeonholed himself and others. Just as no one can expect an overweight person to lose weight just because he's told to do so, I couldn't expect Jan to change his attitude toward me, his mom, his father, Schwartz, or anyone else. The process of change is complicated. (I've tried to chronicle my views of Jan as they've developed. So the reader is free to decide if Jan changed, how he changed, and whether my intervention had anything to do with his changes.)

I felt that I had to clarify Jan's negativity toward Schwartz. Was it displaced from me? It could well be that Jan's gratitude toward me for helping him out of a hole prevented any hostility toward me from emerging. What was now in focus was his hostility toward Schwartz.

"I have a couple of comments," I said.

"All right."

"I believe in a flexible approach to patients," I began.

"I know that."

"You said that when somebody knocks on your office door, the knock is a signal to the patient that it's time to end the session. It's as if some intruder knocked on the door and ended the session. When you watch a crime show on television, there are usually two kinds of cops, the good cop and the—"

"—bad cop," Jan completed my sentence.

"Right. To the extent that it's a pattern—and I'm not saying that it's a pattern—you've created a setting in which a bad cop triggers the end of a session. That's one comment."

"Yes."

Now it was time to focus on Jan's anger, hostility, and concern about an attack from Schwartz. I needed to bring his attention to the connection between his image of Schwartz approaching him with a stick and his longstanding hostile feelings toward his dad. I decided to take a dramatic approach. I stood up and mimed grabbing a stick away from an attacker. I wanted to convey to Jan that his taking a stick away from a male authority figure had symbolic significance beyond its current application to Schwartz or its historical connections to his dad. It was a loud statement about his own personality.

"You've spoken about having physical fights with your father, like when he tried to hit your sister," I said. "I remember you said that after you overpowered your dad, he said, 'You're no longer my son.'"

"He said, 'You're not my son.' Remember, my father was dramatic. He was a drama queen."

"You know the anger when people give up on you. The Jewish patient felt it, and you know it, too. You also had a feeling that Dr. Schwartz came at you with a stick, and you took the stick away from him."

"Yeah, that *was* my feeling. He wanted to make a point. He was angry. For most of that supervision, I saw him boiling with anger, but he didn't say a word until right before the end of the session, when he chastised me for keeping him waiting and for suggesting he should knock on my door and interrupt my session. In a way, I felt that it would be disrespectful if I didn't tell him to come directly to my office. I respect the guy. I wouldn't want him to feel bad."

I interpreted Schwartz's motive for him. "Schwartz's view was, 'I don't want to come to the office and interrupt you. You end your session. That's your job. Then we'll meet.' In other words, Schwartz was telling you, 'I won't play the bad cop.'"

"You felt that Schwartz's clarification that he wouldn't play the bad cop was tantamount to bringing a stick, and, in response, you took the stick away from him."

"Yes."

I couldn't read Jan's face. Was he just being polite? Did he disagree with me? I went on, "Every family has a unique culture. You feel that, in your family, there were many good people and one bad person. You felt that your dad was bad, and you experienced him as an intrusion."

Jan nodded.

"And when he came home, the mood of the family changed."

"Yes, absolutely."

I continued, "In that sense, he was a good model for a bad cop. He destroyed the good mood your mom, your sister, and you struggled to create and maintain. Finally, when you physically encountered him and held him down, we could say that you took his stick away from him."

"Yes."

"So, for you, the music that goes with the Christmas tree lights is the music of the good and the bad, maybe of the good mom and the bad dad. The lights and music appropriate for you are in the opening scene of *Star*

Wars, with the exploding speed and disappearing stars. Just as in your own family, it's easy to identify the good and bad guys. However, as the *Star Wars* series progresses, the good and the bad mix and become interrelated. Good and bad meet each other as we grow. Do you need a bad cop in your life forever? I think something in Schwartz may have reconnected you to your original bad cop, your father."

"I'm a *Star Wars* guy, so I get what you're saying. It fits the way I feel. Regarding Schwartz, yes. The first time one of my patients started to talk about suicide, I felt that I needed to explore it further. So I told Schwartz about it, and he was fine with it. So this episode was the second time."

"The time with the suicidal patient was the first time you'd put Schwartz on hold?"

"Yes."

"So, this was the second time you put him on hold when he came to meet with you. Maybe he wants to teach you how to set limits and boundaries with patients. I can see that the waiting put him off, but that may be beside the point. He may have been trying to teach you to end sessions on time."

"We made peace before the end of the supervisory session. Schwartz knows that I wouldn't do this frivolously. I wanted to give my patient more time because of the suicidality; I tried to be as flexible as possible. Schwartz didn't comment when I told him this. Sometimes, he's been late himself when he came to see me right after another supervision. I told him, 'Relax. Take it easy. Whenever you're here, you're here. Just come in. We'll take it from there.'"

"I think he's more formal than you. For example, you expect the waiter to clean the table before he seats you when you go to a restaurant. Similarly, Schwartz expects you to finish with your previous patient before inviting him to come in. You can learn from his expectations, too."

"I've learned a lot from him. He's not an orthodox psychoanalyst. He's not an old-fashioned analyst. He's a rebel and an innovator. He's implementing different treatment techniques. He's a flexible person, too. He told me toward the end of today's supervision that he, too, sometimes goes beyond the time of the session. So maybe I should tell my patients that we've reached the end of the session and that now I'm giving them some of my private time."

I feel that an analyst (even a student analyst) should educate a patient concerning analysis and, sometimes, standard patient etiquette. "I have to say something as we wrap up today's session," I said. "I believe Schwartz wants to give you the best possible supervision."

"He's very good."

"His comments are intended to advance your development as a psychotherapist. When you have someone like Schwartz, you can learn from your perception that he's carrying a stick and learn about the proper role of boundaries and formality."

"Yes. I'm not going to do that again. From now on, I'm going to do it the way he wants."

"To some degree, that's like smiling when he cracks a joke," I noted, smiling to myself, "but it's the process of compromise at its heart. You give a little; he gives a little, and you both learn about boundaries. However, at another level, your own family background, especially with your father, makes you see good cops and bad cops everywhere. Everyone experiences conflicts. Its successful outcome is a reasonable compromise; however, it ends up as a split if you cannot bridge it. With Schwartz, some of your past life, with your father, was being projected onto the Schwartz in the present."

"What you say is interesting because what crossed my mind as a reaction to our entire session is that my view of human behavior is simplistic because of my home situation with my mom and father. There was a lot of action and reaction, especially in my early teenage years. There were strict rules I had to follow, and the explanation was always 'Because I said so.' I feel freer now. I see how complicated things really are. On many occasions when I thought I had a solid, well-formed view, I found a second bottom, a third bottom, and even more beyond that."

"Yes, there are always new depths to plumb. And with Maria and your son, they will be infinite. This remains so as long as we're alive, when we join the great tradition of our ancestors."

"Yes," Jan responded. "Yes, it does."

CHAPTER 25

"Maria's father is coming to visit tomorrow."

"He's coming from Italy for Thanksgiving?"

"Yes, he comes quite often. We get along well. Sometimes, he comes with his girlfriend. She's somewhat anxious and makes everyone else tense, too. Maria isn't crazy about her, but she wants her father's visits with us to be pleasant."

"What about you?"

"I want my wife to be happy. What makes her happy makes me happy. So I just do what she wants and never talk about how guarded I feel around this woman. I think Maria expects me to comment, but I don't. Giving advice can be tricky."

"You're talking about advice from whom and to whom?"

"I mean, a husband advising his wife about her family. For example, when she talked to her dad on the phone, she said to him, 'Why don't *you* come?' She meant that she would like *him* to come, but not his girlfriend.

"His girlfriend is intrusive and seems to be trying to become part of the family. She's pathologically jealous of Maria. It seems like every minute Maria's father spends with his daughter kicks the girlfriend's jealousy up a notch. Maria resents her. I'm sure you know the type: classically neurotic. Maria and her sisters wonder if she can be helped. If someone is fifty and has been insecure, anxious, and rigid all her life, is there much anyone can do? Do you think people can change later on in life? I'm talking about core-character change. I wonder if my father could have benefited from therapy in his fifties or later. Do you think he would have been able to change? Or

291

are the habitual ways of being so imprinted by that time that nothing can change them?"

"My inclination is not to ask those kinds of questions, for which there is only a 'yes' or 'no' answer. Instead, I would ask, 'What kind of help are people hoping for?' 'Can you help them where they want help?' This may result in various possible strategies, including saying, 'I can't help you,' when you can't. Thus, the answer may be many 'yeses' and also a 'no.' I got the idea of using this functional approach from Dr. Williams."

"I know him! He's a great guy. He was my psychodynamic psycho-therapy supervisor."

"I'm glad you got to know him. He and I are close friends. Let's go back to the functional approach. Here's an example: Suppose two people become blind due to some structural problem. One person might become so anxious about the dangers inherent in being blind that he never leaves his house. The other might get a Seeing Eye dog or a cane and gain access to a range of activities outside the house. In both cases, the structural problem—the blindness—remains, but one person is more functional. To be effective, I think a therapist of any patient, old or young, needs to be able to see a brighter future for the patient than the patient can see for himself."

"I see. In close relationships, you want to offer protection and advice simultaneously. For example, you may give them unsolicited advice if you feel a person will make a mistake. It may not even really be advice, but just a reaction conveyed in body language, phrasing, or tone that registers your disagreement. Maria is good at this. For example, without confrontation, she communicated to her father that he should come *alone*, sneaking it into a normal conversation."

I chuckled at Jan's phrasing in describing this benign, universal cunning.

Jan continued, "My mother did it a lot, saying something just short of advice. She didn't like my first wife. When I told her I was planning to marry her, my mom never said, 'Don't do that.' She said, 'Well, you're an adult, and you'll do what you think is right. You have to ask yourself if this is a person you can trust and be completely at ease with, and then make a decision.' She was suggesting that I ask myself these questions, but at the time, I didn't stop to think about what she meant."

Imagining how he might have rejected her concerns, I said, "She tried to sneak it in, but you would have none of it."

"Her bottom line was: 'Do what you want, and I hope it will be the right decision, and you won't regret it.'"

"I had a patient whose mother thought she was headstrong. The mother often said, 'Do what you wish; you will anyway!' In other words, the mother didn't have much hope of influencing her daughter. In contrast, your mother tried softer techniques to try to influence you. What was her objection to your first wife?"

"After we got divorced, she told me, 'Your ex-wife was always happy and smiling, but she didn't have a real range of emotions. She always appeared sweet—too sweet.' My ex-wife's parents lived in the same town as my parents. She wanted us to spend more time with her family than with mine whenever we went there. Finally, my mom said to me, 'You don't spend time with us—only an hour or two.' It was true.

"And then there was the time I had an accident. Sofia and my mom came to visit me at the hospital, and during the visit, they said they wanted to stay at our place. My ex-wife said, 'Of course, you're welcome.' But she said it in a way that meant they were not truly welcome. So they stayed in a hotel. I didn't find out about this till after I got divorced. My mom said that my ex-wife was 'not open.' In Poland, that's important. She was too reserved and too conscious of what she was saying. She never talked about her problems. She was always cheerful and always smiling. But that's what I liked about her.

"Before my mom died, she met Maria. They couldn't communicate much because of the language barrier, but somehow, they connected. My mom said, 'I like her. She's a great girl. I wish I could talk to her more. I hope you'll be happy with her and that you won't screw it up.'

"When Sofia met Maria, she said, 'She's great. *Trafiło Ci sie jak ślepej kurze ziarno.*' It means, *It happened to you like grain to a blind hen.* That is, *I'm lucky.*

"When my mom visited me here in the U.S., we took a road trip from Chicago to Florida. I enjoyed the many hours of conversation we had during the two days in the car. Certain funny things are expressed well in Polish but are hard to translate into English. For example, one Polish saying in loose translation is that a short woman is more likely to be ill-tempered because her heart is closer to her gut and sinks close to shit. Yet, it somehow makes sense when you say it in Polish.

"In my family, all the women are tall and big, like Maria. They had a way of looking down on petite women. At the time of my mom's visit, I hadn't yet gotten over the divorce. So my mom made fun of my ex-wife to cheer me up."

Jan was silent for a while.

"How long are your father-in-law and his girlfriend going to stay?" I asked.

"We don't yet know if *she's* coming. Maria spoke with her father yesterday, and all we know is that *he's* coming for the week of Thanksgiving. Thanksgiving isn't much of a holiday for either of us. I doubt Native Americans are so thankful for Thanksgiving; it's a celebration of genocide if you think about it. There was a lot of looting, killing, and raping done by the crooks from Europe to North America. Indians were treated as subhuman and systematically killed. So Thanksgiving is hypocritical and doesn't make sense, although Europeans didn't exactly invent genocide.

"There's a new Mel Gibson movie called *Apocalypto*. It deals with the times before the *Conquistadors*, during the decline of the Mayan civilization in Central America, when there was a planned genocide of Indians by Indians."

Reflecting on the deceptions of history, I said, "People put smiley faces on many holidays and histories."

"I don't know that you have to. It's good to know what happened and see the whole picture."

I didn't know if Jan grasped that I didn't condone genocides but merely reflected on the fact that it's usually the victors who write history. The task of a psychoanalyst is to introduce an adaptive interpretation into the flow of the conversation. The idea is to offer pertinent and new possibilities of thought or action for the patient's consideration, which the patient is free to accept or reject. I felt that this discussion was still on a sociological plane and hadn't reached the transference junction that would permit us to explore its personal implications.

Jan went on, "People get killed by people who believe that they are saving the world or spreading freedom and democracy. It's good to know a little more than what you've been told."

"Have you heard of Lamaze?"

"No."

"Lamaze is a breathing and relaxation technique that helps a woman, with her partner's support, to lessen the pain of labor and delivery."

"Oh, we're planning to do that; I didn't know it was called Lamaze."

"What do you automatically do if you bump your knee against a table?" I asked.

"You massage it or near it."

"Right. The massage doesn't eliminate the pain; it just draws your attention away from it. In Lamaze, the father-to-be learns to massage the woman's abdomen to shift her consciousness away from her pain. Human neurology has prepared us with mechanisms to do this. Unfortunately, history is also a compendium of massaged painful facts. We try to deny, suppress, or displace pain. I'm not saying that shifting our attention away from pain is always good; I'm merely describing what usually happens. As we discussed, your father caused you so much pain that you had to distance yourself from him or label him as mostly bad. In this process, the few good deeds he actually did, like applauding you from the upstairs window, went missing from your memory. We want to try to see the whole picture of your dad."

"I know there's plenty of hypocrisy. We can start by calling things what they were. It's best to look at what a person did."

"That's why, in treatment, we try to bring out the connection between the massage and the original pain. Have you already seen *Apocalypto*?"

"No, I read about it, and I'm looking forward to seeing it. A genocide was taking place in South America just 15 years ago. A girl from Colombia was a research assistant in our department. She was part of a social movement trying to expose the facts of this genocide; many tribes in the Amazon were killed off recently. Some companies have no problem invading a clan, shooting everybody, and helping themselves, whether cutting down the trees for timber or taking the land for mining. If they don't exterminate the tribes, they have to pay them. That's the rule. But if they annihilate everybody, there's no one to make a claim.

"The *Conquistadors* who invaded South America killed an astounding number of native people. It was just horrible. They killed people for their land. If the people had any gold, The *Conquistadors* would kill them. As in some other places, they didn't try to make them 'civilized.' They wanted them gone. They wanted them out. They wanted them to disappear. The same thing happened in Brazil and Bolivia just 10 or 15 years ago. I found this out on a visit to South America.

"I found out about another genocide of indigenous peoples in the latter half of the 20th century in the region of Parana, where Argentina, Brazil, and Paraguay come together. Mercenaries came and just shot everyone. The people were voiceless. Some were tribes in the remote parts of the jungle that nobody outside even knew existed. Nobody cared if all of them died. So I'm looking forward to seeing the movie, not because I like to torture myself, but because I want to know the truth.

"Speaking of Thanksgiving, there's a made-up Communist Polish 'Thanksgiving.' On July 22, 1944, the Soviets kicked the Germans out and gave us our country back. The border of Poland was shifted to the west because the Soviets annexed Poland's eastern part, but they gave us our country. According to the rationale of this Polish Thanksgiving, the Soviet Union helped establish the best government ever in Poland.

"I remember having this Thanksgiving when I was in school, but anybody alive during World War II—like my grandma and grandpa—knew that it was pure bullshit. The Soviets were partners with Germany in the invasion of Poland in 1939. Germany and Russia shook hands in 1939 and divided Poland; Poland, as a country, disappeared. There was no Poland when the Germans committed atrocities in German-occupied Poland against the Polish people, including Polish Jews. Then later, Germany and Russia fought each other.

"All the Poles were going to be extinguished. The Germans had a term, *Drang Nach Osten*—"thrust toward the east"—which meant they should kill all the Poles and make space for the Germans. Many Poles were sent to Soviet concentration camps. The inmates of the camps, particularly ones with military experience, were given an ultimatum, 'Stay here and die, or join the New Polish Army in the USSR—the *Soviet*-Polish Army—and go back to Poland.' Many Poles agreed to join. They felt, 'Why not? Better to go back to Poland and die than to stay and die in Siberia.'

"The Soviets allowed one unit of the Polish army to go toward what is now Iran. That army eventually ended up in England. Then, the Soviets allowed them to form another army called *Pierwsza Armia Ludowego Wojska Polskiego,* the First People's Army of Poland, and used them most horribly; the expression means 'meat for cannons.' Is there a similar English expression?"

"Cannon fodder."

"What does 'fodder' mean?"

"Fodder is cattle food. So, cannon fodder is food or meat for the cannons."

"Oh, I see. It's a similar expression, but I think meat carries a more truthful message than grass. They were dying by the thousands marching through Poland on their way to Berlin. The Poles attempted to liberate Warsaw before the Russians did. The Polish Underground Army, *Armia Krajowa,* the Country's Army, organized an uprising in August and September 1944. They wanted to liberate Warsaw before the Soviets, but they overestimated what they could do. The Germans destroyed Warsaw; the city was flattened.

Soviet tanks were waiting on the other side of the Vistula River. They could have helped the Poles, but they didn't. Their actions seemed to say, 'You wanted to do it yourself? Then, do it yourself.'

"Many of the Poles involved in this uprising lost their lives. After 1948, the Soviet Union established the Communist Polish government and created the phony Thanksgiving. That's not where the truth is. The truth is awful: The Soviet Union was responsible for a lot of preventable bloodshed."

An image of the macabre sign outside the Auschwitz death camp, *Arbeit Macht Frei*, "Work will make you free," flashed in my thoughts. It was a prime example of depraved human deception. It would have been more honest to say, "Abandon all hope, all ye who enter," but the lie served the Nazis' purposes better. Dishonesty is a tactic used by a long list of killers. All humans are at risk of feeling hate, and any individual or group considered an alien or rival is in danger of becoming a target of that hate. Humans can camouflage themselves and set upon unsuspecting prey like beasts and insects. And almost everyone who perpetrates killing or causes pain denies or minimizes it. Some who have survived brutality are so traumatized that they withdraw from the world. And there are others—victims or their offspring—who respond by becoming killers.

"Your father hurt you. You could massage the situation to try to decrease the pain. And sometimes, you need to avoid him."

I felt that I misspoke. I meant that to say that Jan's tendency to avoid his dad was related to the pain his dad had inflicted on him. The session started referencing biological adaptation to pain. Now, it had become embroiled in the hypocrisy practiced by the perpetrators of genocide. I now had to deal with the consequences of my loose talk with spurious comments about Lamaze and killing.

"I didn't mean that one should be a hypocrite," I said. "I didn't mean you *should* massage it; all I meant to say was that massaging—coping with pain—happens."

"Yes, I know. Anger and frustration last for generations, and there needs to be a safe place to put it in our historical narratives. I think hypocrisy is worse than . . . anything. Living a lie for generations and generations is confusing and demoralizing."

I thought we could draw something good from this session by making the notion of identification explicit, which is critical to understanding identity formation. In this instance, Jan's identification wasn't with his fellow Europeans who settled America but with the Native American Indian tribes. "It seems to me that, due to your knowledge of the history of Poland, your sympathies lie not with the English or European settlers but with the American Indian tribes, who—like the Poles—suffered greatly, and you identify with them."

"Absolutely."

"So, you feel that the Germans and—"

"—the Russians treated the Poles the way Europeans treated the American Indian tribes. Yes, they wanted to exterminate the whole nation."

I agreed with Jan's opinion that one should, at least, express anger and frustration. So, too, the feeling of victimhood and its attendant passivity. Such emotional states, if unexpressed, are a drag on efficient functioning. Living with powerful and unexpressed feelings is like driving a car in an inefficient first gear when the road is clear and straight.

All victims feel grieved. However, a person's map of deprivation and loss changes across a lifespan. I felt that Jan saw his dad as a *Conquistador* who had tried to snuff him out. He felt robbed and angry and wanted to retaliate. Jan's anger was as intense as it had been for a long time; it was as if he were driving his life in first gear. I hoped to explore how he could decrease the intensity of that anger from a boil to a simmer.

Children sometimes feel they are victims of their parents' whims or evil intentions. They may make up romantic stories that imagine being born to more benign parents or some faraway royals. An unkind or busy parent may overlook a child's demands. The child may deny and project his anger onto the parent, setting up a vicious cycle of further misunderstanding. Of course, parents busy with work and other children may overlook a particular child's need for exclusive attention; the child may feel this to be wanton neglect or abuse. Parents loom large, whether as powerful gods or as formidable evildoers; this is the nub of the Oedipus Complex. Everyone has a perspective on the evolution of his personality. The details of his parents' actual benevolent or destructive contributions add another layer of understanding.

Jan's perception of his father's evil deeds remained relatively static, mostly unaffected by his growing awareness of his father's occasional good deeds. Thus, in his relationship with his dad, Jan was stuck in the first gear of human functioning. I hoped that, when his awareness of his dad's rare goodness increased, the degree of hatred toward him would diminish, giving him access to a more efficient second or third gear. Perhaps the experience of trying to be a good dad to his son, yet having his son be angry at him despite his best intentions, would modify Jan's uncompromising stance toward his father. I did not intend to diminish the impact of his father's inconsiderate actions, of which Jan was a competent chronicler. Jan was excited about being a father to his unborn son. Becoming a father would allow Jan to reassess his negative feelings about his father. Gaining a new understanding of his father was a good goal for the future, but not one that I could approach now.

Jan continued his history lesson, "The Germans carried out war and killing in a precise, systematic way. The Russians were different. My grandma saw this up close. The Russians were wild, primitive people, uneducated, uncivilized barbarians. The Germans were more sophisticated and efficient killers. But cultured or not, killing and genocide happen all the time, even now. Mass killings have occurred in Nicaragua, Guatemala, El Salvador, and East Timor. And the U.S. has orchestrated some of it.

"I saw a BBC documentary about Hugo Chávez, the supposedly crazy guy from Venezuela. Based on stories from people who lived there and CNN, I imagined this wacky, grandiose guy who has bipolar disorder and wants to irritate the United States. This documentary showed when Chávez was arrested in a coup led by Pedro Carmona. Carmona was the pro-U.S. interim head of state. All the government members holed up in the parliament building and requested that Chávez be released; it took three or four days. They released him because crowds, sympathetic to Chávez, flooded the streets, threatening an uprising, and demanded his release. The country started to hate Carmona, and this poor guy ruled the country for only 36 hours. The documentary showed a few interviews with Chávez. He didn't look crazy at all. He appeared to be a skilled, moderate politician. He didn't say, 'Let's burn the American embassy because they're behind the coup.' He said things like, 'The crisis is over now. We have to take care of Venezuela. All oil-producing fields have to be protected. We have to be disciplined and vigilant and work together.'

"I saw another show on the BBC about Iraq. We did something evil in Iraq. Donald Rumsfeld had gone to Iraq right after the Iran-Iraq war started, around 1983, while Saddam Hussein was gassing his own people in Northern Iraq. At that time, the U.S. gave Hussein weapons, advisers, and tons of money. Even after the first Iraq war started, I heard that some U.S. companies were supplying weapons to Iraq. I don't know why I like this kind of stuff, but I spend time discovering that things never look quite the way the media describes them. I try not to become a conspiracy theorist, although some of the things that I discover are scary."

Jan's history lessons sounded to me like a way to avoid his own history. I wanted to bring him back. "Let's consider a couple who decides to start a family," I said. "To some degree, they can be compared to two people starting a colony. The first child is their chosen love. Initially, the child is utterly helpless. Let's say it's a boy. As he grows, he will feel that his dad is a *Conquistador* and his mom is a *Conquistadora*. The parents do their best, but he may think that he's a victim of their way of life. Sometimes, the wishes of one or both parents *are* inimical to the child's wishes, but sometimes that is only the child's perception. When he wants something, they try to teach him to wait and learn that things happen at their proper time.

"What is the child to do? All he can do is cry for help. He might command a parent to stay with him; sometimes, that works. He can smile, be cute, and drop hints: 'I'm inviting you to come to play with me.' Parents can do damage if they don't or can't listen to their children adequately. That's why we have child-welfare agencies that take children away from parents proven to be abusive or neglectful. If we were to act only on children's complaints, almost all parents would live in penal colonies!

"But I agree with you in this critical regard: Every story has another side or many other sides. Take the brain. It has two sides connected by the corpus callosum. Its main job is to keep the right side of the brain informed of happenings on the left side and the left side informed of happenings on the right. In your case, Jan, I feel that your moods and thoughts are lodged more on one side, and I try to give a contrary example to increase the integration between the two sides of yourself. The neurological metaphor is just that, but it intends to create more grays in you. Perhaps you feel that I'm eroding your previous clarity. I try to give my thoughts in bite-sized pieces, but sometimes what I say may be too much to swallow. What is an old man to do when he feels lonely? He has grown children. He wants another partner and finally finds someone who loves him. Is your mother-in-law alive?"

"No. NO. They got divorced just before she died. That's another sore point. He decided to divorce her just before she died. His daughters have many problems with the way it happened. Maria's mom had cancer. Issues between her parents had been piling up for many years, but he just dropped the divorce on her before she died."

I regretted my flippant "What's an old man to do?" and said, "Yes, children at any age have a strong wish for their parents to be together. It's painful even if you're in your forties or fifties."

"It never happens overnight. The relationship between the parents deteriorates gradually, and the child doesn't know it. It comes as a shock and surprise to him *as if* it happened overnight. You said that my moods tend to shift suddenly. I go into one mode of thinking and have a hard time getting out of it. I do have peripheral awareness, though. I know that there's another side."

"I agree with you. You could almost say that each mood has a focus and a periphery, where other moods emerge. Some people are focused and don't have any peripheral awareness. Others are focused but are aware of other moods. Still others are so scattered that they're confused. You're between the first and second categories. For a period, you're passionately attached to a given mood but still aware of other moods. Switching moods is a challenge, like changing direction when you're pushing a barge. The original mood has a lot of momentum, so switching to a new one takes great effort. Your focus is strong. For example, you're not depressed now, and it's hard to imagine the depression you focused on before. I think you may want to understand the changes in your mood. Did you feel that I was critical of you or your fixed-mood style?"

"I didn't feel criticized. Sometimes, my inner emotions are more in control than my appearance would suggest, especially when I look angry. When I was fighting a lot as a teenager, I learned it was useful to look like you might be crazy-mad. Then nobody knew where it was going. Deep inside, I wasn't that mad. I always had a red light inside and knew if my anger was close to getting out of hand."

"So, you didn't want your anger to go beyond a certain point?"

"Right—it was tactical intimidation. Now that I think about it, I could win by seeming emotional. There was a pine tree in front of my school. Every day after school, you went out there to challenge others. Everybody was watching. You invited people to fight. Whoever won was the hero of the school. Of course, anyone could challenge the reigning hero, but sometimes that didn't happen for a day, a month, a year."

"In birds and animals, males often challenge each other to impress potential mates. The battle is serious and can be deadly in some species, but it may be a display of plumage, or a little sparring, or just a skirmish in others. They don't fight until one of them dies, but only until it's clear who the winner is. Once the loser acknowledges his loss and slinks away, it's over. The fight is heartfelt but not deadly. It's a controlled battle. Is this what you mean?"

"Yes, the idea is to overpower through intimidation. That was how you established your status in the group. I've traveled a lot, but I haven't seen this exact thing elsewhere. Boys in other countries compete in sports or race motorbikes. Those things weren't available in small-town grammar schools when I was growing up. Poland was poor. We had hands, energy, and anger, so that's what we used to establish our standing. We had a tournament or a series of fights, and the winner was decided. The kids kept track of it. Everyone knew who you had to face in the next fight. I was pretty good at it."

"As you said, one of the components of this was having anger. I think your family dynamics fed off your anger. For example, it makes children mad when their father disrespects their mom by asking for a divorce when she's down, as in Maria's case, or by seeking another partner. Similarly, they feel anger if their parents are physically abusive."

"I got married when I was 24 years old. My first wife had two miscarriages. They were horrible experiences. The first one occurred six weeks into the pregnancy when I was 28. The second occurred eight weeks into the pregnancy when I was 31. I couldn't imagine what it meant to be a father then. I was immature. I didn't make sense of many things. I didn't know whether I would repeat the same patterns as my father because there was still so much negative energy in me.

"So many negative things happened: I started to work in oncology and saw patients suffer and die, and that made me sick. The more I worked, the more depressed I got. And I liked to socialize and party, which meant drinking too much. My first wife and I didn't sleep much; we weren't home much! I don't think I was very self-aware then. I'm not sure that I could have been a good father."

I wanted to acknowledge that Jan had made changes in his life. "You've had a chance to reflect on your life," I said. "You've made a lot of early late-life changes. You asked if older people can change. I don't know about that, but I think you changed after you were 31 . . . significantly. Do you agree?"

"Yes. It was mid-life."

Human pride is so natural! I noted that, whereas I called the stage when he made changes *early late-life*, Jan called it *mid-life*. I said, "I apologize—" but Jan cut me off in a friendly manner, so I didn't clarify for what I was apologizing. So often, it's after uttering a sentence that you establish its meaning. Perhaps I wanted to apologize for not treating him as a young man.

"It's OK. When I turned 30, I reflected on what I had done and what I was supposed to do and became sad. I had initially been excited about my job and finding a cure for cancer. Everybody would be happy. I visited my mom and told her I was sad because half of my life was over. I remember she started to laugh."

I reflected on the passage of time in my own life and its gentle slipping away while we raised three kids. Then, imagining the scene between Jan and his mom, I laughed, too.

Jan continued, "So, I thought 30 was the beginning of being old. I was dissatisfied. I had a mid-life crisis when I was 30. Who knows? Maybe I was right about half of my life is over. You never know what's going to happen. I have good genes, but there's cancer in the family. It's an interesting time for me. Maria says that the baby is active. She'll be watching TV and suddenly groan because the baby started kicking a lot. We talk about her childhood, and she asks about lots of things I've told you. And, of course, we have religious and cultural disputes and discussions. How should we relate to an American son? He'll speak English with no accent whatsoever and hopefully Polish and Italian, too."

I've found that asking about details concerning an upcoming event helps communicate that I pay attention to small events in a patient's life. So I asked, "Who's going to the airport to pick up Maria's father?"

"I'll go. It's early in the morning, and Maria sometimes doesn't feel so well in the morning."

"I ask because there was a question about a possible mystery guest."

"I'll find out soon enough. It's not like she's a bad person. I don't think she knows that I find her tiring. I can relate to her, but if I had a choice, I wouldn't spend time with her."

"Well, she's not a central person in your life."

"No, she's not a central person, but she's pushy and tiresome. She desperately tries to be involved because she has a feeling that she's being rejected. All three sisters, including Maria, reject her. They can't hide it. So as much as possible, I try to be a bridge between them and her."

"There's that old saying, 'This, too, shall pass.' So if she comes, it will be temporary."

"Yes, but she does so many intrusive things. When we were in Italy, we talked with Maria's family about what to name our son. Some people jokingly said that a good choice would be the name of Maria's grandpa, whose name is the same as Maria's father. He's called 'Junior,' and so our son would be 'the third.' I didn't want my son to be a 'third,' but I didn't say anything. Maria and her sisters mumbled something, and the topic died.

Then Maria suggested 'Ludovico.' Her sisters shot it down, so we dropped it. I don't remember what the objection was. One of her sisters suggested 'Armand.' Maria rejected it. Then Maria's father's girlfriend suggested another name, and there was dead silence."

"So, she got the silent treatment."

"Yes, the message was like, 'We didn't invite you into this discussion. Just shut up and listen.' She looked like she'd been slapped. I felt terrible for her.

"Then Maria said, 'David,' and everybody nodded."

"'David' is a great name," I said.

CHAPTER 26

NOT LONG AFTER THE SESSION DESCRIBED ABOVE, I made plans to go to India to visit my family, whom I had not seen for some time. Therefore, I needed to let Jan know sometime in advance that I would be gone.

Analyst vacations may also stimulate intense feelings to surface and stir up old memories of past losses, deep hurts, or abandonment. From this can emerge a motherlode of material to process in the analysis. So, when an analyst goes on vacation, particularly a long one, it is crucial to optimize the time spent after the announcement and before he leaves in helping the patient process his thoughts and feelings about the separation. I felt it was vital with Jan because of the losses he had suffered, his mother, his homeland, and the loss of Amir to suicide.

I also had noted that Jan left on vacation to Europe without telling me he was going until the very last session before he left. I surmised that this was his way of not facing my temporary loss and represented a defense against loss. There had been no time to process what the separation had aroused in him. I hoped my bringing it up would help us better understand his feelings about abandonment, both his of me and mine of him. So, three weeks before I was to leave, I brought up my intentions early in a session.

Analysts work by processing treatment events such as unplanned irregularities or absences such as the analyst's lateness, restlessness during a session, or unconscious enactment like ending a session early. For example, if he forgets a session or is absent for unplanned personal reasons like accidents or sudden illness, these behaviors invariably produce valuable information.

"I need to tell you that, starting in three weeks, I'll be off for a month," I said.

"Wow, that's a long vacation. Are you going to India?"

"Yes, I'll be visiting my family."

"We're hoping to go to Poland around then. Pregnancy seems to make Maria emotional and irritable sometimes, and I always try to figure out why she's upset. The other day, she said that her life is changing for the better, but she regrets that she didn't travel much, as I did. I promised her that we would travel together as much as possible. We'll have to ask the doctor to give us the OK."

"It'll be good for her to see your dad and family in Poland," I said. "How do you feel about seeing him?"

"Sofia told me that my dad accidentally hit his head recently and is in the hospital. My concern for him now is different, but I can only tell you what I *think* it's about because I'm not clear on it yet. You know that, in the past, I've had strong negative feelings about my father, especially about the selfish stunts he pulled right after my mother died. At one point, Sofia lost it, but I was also very upset and harbored dark images of him for a long time. Even considering his dementia, I've had a bad opinion of my father since childhood. Now, though, I feel this growing concern about him. There are all these negative memories about him that I've felt so—"

"—passionately?" I reflexively completed the sentence.

"Yes, passionately. But those feelings aren't so important now, probably because I'm going to be a father myself. There's just one big question: How do I do a better job than my father did? Do you remember how my father said, 'You're not my son' after I managed to overpower him? I never forgot this. I kept rejecting him. As a son, I now understand that there's a space for forgiveness."

I wondered just what Jan meant. "In this space, who's forgiving whom? Are you thinking he, the prodigal dad, is the one who has to secure your forgiveness, or are you thinking that you, the typical son, need to seek his?"

"I thought he was the one who needed *my* forgiveness, although now I don't despise him so passionately. He's nothing but an empty vessel with random thoughts in his hollowed-out mind. Until I started to talk to you, I thought I would never change my mind about my father. I've been stuck in one negative way of thinking about him and believed with all my heart that he was the one who needed to ask me for forgiveness."

"I can see that."

"But I feel sorry for him that he banged his head. I feel for him as a helpless old man, and the anger and disgust I always felt for him seem to be slowly dissipating."

Jan had just made a personality leap. He now saw just a feeble old man in the father he hated for so long. "You're changing," I said. "You're less depressed. The prospect of becoming a dad has made you nervous, excited, joyful. Your father probably deserves hate, but compassion and thoughts of forgiveness are creeping in."

"You see, I feel that my father's end is closer than I ever imagined. When he felt powerful and in charge, I wished he were dead. Now his death might happen any day. It might happen when I'm in Poland. I don't know how well my sister is describing the situation. In her eyes, he never really changed. He can't understand anymore, but I need to understand. I lived with a person, such as he was, an asshole most of the time. I tend to forget the positive stuff. I tried to repress it and push it away because it didn't fit the image. Now, I'd like to get a clearer picture of who he was. Hatred makes things simple, but I know that's not the way to be. You have to see all the shades of gray to see the whole picture."

"As I see it, you may be struggling with two important strands. One strand is that you want to treat people based not only on what they deserve but also on who *you* are. You've changed, so now you're reassessing the way you treat your father. If you're a compassionate person, you'll treat every-body with some degree of compassion, regardless of who they are or how they act. That's one strand."

"You've put what I think is happening into nice words. I wouldn't feel good about myself if my father died tomorrow and I continued hating him. I wouldn't feel good about myself if this shift in thinking about him didn't take place."

I continued, "The second strand is that you want to see things clearly. Anger makes things clear but not always accurate. When you're angry, you tend to forget the shades of gray in your father. In earlier sessions, you mentioned that, when you were young and got into fights, your dad sometimes watched from his window and cheered you on."

"Yes, it happened often. I remember it clearly. But I also remember him comparing me to some of my friends or colleagues and saying, 'Why can't you be like him?' I told him, 'Because I'm *me*.' I never felt validated by him."

I wasn't sure that Jan had heard what I said, so I repeated it. "You gave an example of fighting in front of your house and him watching from the window, encouraging you. He was backing you."

"Yes. I tend not to remember such incidents."

"We agree on that point. That's what I mean. You tend to forget or discount the few good things your dad did. It keeps him well-defined and dark."

An aside here: I'd spoken to a Biblical scholar friend in the preceding week. She cited 1 Corinthians 13:12 from the King James Version: "For now we see through a glass, darkly; but then face to face: now I know in part; but then shall I know even as also I am known." I felt this verse had some implications for understanding Jan.

The verse distinguishes between what we can see and know *now*, through earthly light, and what will become visible *then*, in the light of heavenly knowledge. First, she clarified the terms *glass* and *darkly*. Seeing through a glass refers to seeing one's image in a mirror. In Biblical times, imperfectly shaped and polished metal surfaces served as mirrors. They were crude, often like funhouse mirrors that create distortions, making one look excessively tall, short, thin, or fat. In addition, those ancient images tended to be dull due to the oxidation of the metal, causing the object in the mirror to appear obscure, unclear, and dark. Thus, because of the limitations of the instruments humans make, we can gain only partial knowledge of ourselves. Likewise, we can only see darkly here and now because what we know of ourselves is based on imprecise reflections.

Whereas *now* refers to a human's life on earth, *then* refers to his life in heaven. Then, in heaven, darkness will not exist. His knowledge will be complete. He will see face to face, that is, directly. Just as God knows all about man, so, too, man will know himself. The wisdom of 1 Corinthians 13:12, like that of other great religious writings, is universal. We all start with imperfect knowledge based on dark, unclear, distorted, and partial reflections, but we can progress toward bright, complete (or fuller) understanding. The meaning of such ideas and progress toward better understanding depends on the unique circumstances of each person's life.

However, Jan suffered from years of excessively clear and grim visions of his father. Jan could see no redeeming features in his father. Considering the verse in 1 Corinthians, we can interpret this negative view as an example of jumping to conclusions based on distorted information. A more compassionate Jan was amending his impressions, which yielded a more nuanced and measured understanding of his father as bad, but with some good features. Sometimes, we latch onto one element and overlook the rest in perceiving a complex or variegated image. When we are young, we may think we see the whole picture clearly, but we may gradually come to see its many subtle shades as we mature.

Back to Jan. "Although you want to push them aside, you still have those rare memories of times your dad did something good. They're hidden or veiled, but you can recover them. I am merely reminding you of something you once said to me, but I still tend to forget. You're feeling ambivalence toward him, not just hostility. You're becoming more compassionate, even toward him, and, reluctantly, you're factoring in the memories of his few good deeds."

"Yes, but I wouldn't be too enthusiastic about it because I don't remember feeling absolutely at ease with my father, ever. For example, I never felt comfortable, like I am with you here and now. I was always on the lookout for some plan or trick or manipulation with him."

"Your wariness was justified. However, this train of thought is important. Now you're thinking about the kind of father you want to be. The bad parts of your dad form a template for what you want to avoid. And the good parts, if there are any, will serve as a model for what you want to enhance."

"Maria and I had an argument when we were driving home from work the other day. It started with a program on NPR. After a recent conference about gay people, the commentator said that the Vatican issued a paper stating that it opposed homosexuals in the Church. Maria was furious. She said, 'Who gave them the right to say anything about gay people in the Church? Why is what they think or say so important that everybody has to listen to it on the radio or see it on TV? I don't think we need the Pope or even the whole Vatican. I don't think we need them for anything!'

"Then I asked her, 'What should we do with David?' Maria thought for a moment and said, 'When David is old enough, I'll tell him what I just told you!'

"And I said, 'Will you really?'

"She said, 'Yes, I'm going to tell him my opinions like they're giving their opinions. I'm not going to hide anything.'

"I didn't like Maria's approach. I do believe that religion has a purpose. So I said, 'Not everybody is as smart and brave as you. I see a role for religion. Some people need guidance. Religion prevents people from doing bad things and acting on their raw instincts. You shouldn't deprive a child of the experience of religion. And I'm not talking about Orthodox Catholicism. Both of us grew up in almost uniformly Catholic countries. Exposing a child to religion and some transcendent force helps society implement good rules. I don't have any problem with it. In fact, I feel it's necessary.'

"Maria said, 'Absolutely not! It's not necessary. You don't even go to church yourself. You're not a practicing Catholic. So why impose it on him?'

"I answered, 'There were periods in my life when I needed the Church. I wanted to believe that there was a good, almighty Father up in heaven. It didn't work for me, but that doesn't mean religion is meaningless. I wish I could become a believer. Now, I have neither the need nor the time for it, but maybe when I get old and face my own death, I'll find the time and space for religion.' I laughed afterward and thought, 'The baby isn't even born, and we're already fighting about him!'"

CHAPTER 27

"I spoke to Maria recently about the differences between the United States and the countries we come from. Every time I travel back to Poland, I feel it. I don't feel truly at home here. When I spent some time in Italy with a good friend, I felt at home, even though I didn't speak Italian. They start parties at 10 p.m. and don't finish till early morning. In Poland, we start a little earlier and end a little earlier, but it's a custom I'm familiar with."

"So, Italy is worse than Poland?" I asked jokingly.

"In this regard. I felt at home in Ireland, too, when I spent a few months there. It's hard to say why I don't feel at home here. Maybe it's the way people relate to each other. When people ask questions, do they want to hear the answer? This is probably the most striking difference. They ask questions, but they don't give a flying f___ about anything. 'How are you?' seems to create distance in the U.S. And the answer, 'I'm fine,' is equally superficial. In Poland, Italy, and Ireland, people seem genuinely interested in what others say and want to make emotional connections. Even the body language is different. People aren't threatened by physical closeness, so personal space is much smaller.

"But I also realize how Americanized I've become. Here's a good example: I'm in line at the movie theater. When I first came to the U.S., the space between people felt excessive, and I missed the closeness with which I grew up. I have been in the U.S. for more than a decade. Yet, when I go to Poland for a visit, it pisses me off when someone is breathing down my neck in a line."

"I, too, have had this experience. When I was growing up, it was common for customers who didn't come into a restaurant together to sit at the same table. Now, I feel that my space is being invaded when I re-experience this Indian-style restaurant seating. Also, when Indians nod in agreement, the head nods side to side at an oblique angle. Compared to the vertical nod of many in the U.S., it's ambiguous. Many Indian immigrants who stay in the U.S. for a long time lose this oblique/side-to-side nod and acquire the vertical nod."

We both laughed intuitively at the implications of these adaptations that most immigrants undergo when they live for a long time in a different country.

"I learned English in England," Jan said. "When I first came to the U.S., I couldn't understand what anyone was saying because Americans pronounce words differently. TV helped me adjust to American English. I watched *a lot* of TV back then. Once I started to understand what people were saying, I realized how alien this country was. One of the first shows I could follow was the stupidest program on TV: *The Jerry Springer Show.*

"One episode was about people having sex with animals. Jerry Springer was interviewing a woman who had sex with her dog. He did this in front of a huge television audience, and she was embarrassed. Then he leaned toward her and said, in a concerned voice, 'I hope it will help you to know that you're not the only one.' Then a screen opened and in came a bunch of people, and he said, 'These people are doing the same thing.' I was stunned. Who allowed this? Who thought that this was a good topic for a TV show? How could anyone say, 'You should be happy because you're not the only one having sex with a dog'? I couldn't believe it.

"TV commercials also felt strange. I felt that they were intrusive, offensive, and crude. Like, if you want people to look at you with envy and respect, you ought to drive a BMW. Then, recently, there was an ad for Macintosh computers. One guy is obese and balding and looks boring—and he uses a PC. The other is handsome and hip and looks smart, and *he's* using a Mac. The ads tell you how to live and what's good and bad in a catchy and seductive way, but it's all bullshit, even if you think about it for only a second."

"Maria and I have a lot of concerns about raising David. We'll be the most important people for him for the first 10 years or so. How can we help him make sense of everything around him? Did you know that they released a new PlayStation yesterday?"

"Yes."

"There were lines of people waiting overnight."

"I heard on the news that somebody killed somebody else in line, too," I added.

"I wouldn't be surprised. I passed by an electronics store yesterday and saw the preparations. People were lining up with blankets and polar fleece jackets, waiting for the store to open the next day. I can't imagine such a frenzy about a gadget in any other country. The only mass excitement that I can compare it to from my younger years was when the Pope was about to visit Poland."

"Well, the Pope is different from PlayStation!"

"He sure is! He came to Poland a few times, and people lined up, giving up sleep and the comfort of their beds just to see him. I grew up waiting in lines, but it was exactly the *opposite* of consumerism. It was an everyday struggle to get basics, like meat, butter, rice, laundry detergent, and even toilet paper. The government rationed all of these things. You got a coupon for, say, one kilogram of meat per week. If you wanted more, you had to wait in a long line. The alternative, the black market, was much more expensive. This is probably difficult for many Americans to understand. I remember when my friend and I stood in line overnight just before my mom's birthday. I wanted to be sure that I would be the first in the line when the store opened to buy meat without coupons. We made it fun by turning it into a party: playing music, drinking, singing. But I can't imagine myself camping overnight outside a store for some stupid toy.

"What is a progressive civilization? I know that the U.S. is a leading force in the world in many areas. But the rules of society are poorly defined, and the values are quite different from those I learned during the first 30 years of my life. It's so easy to become controlled by seductive Yankee advertising. How do I keep my children sane? I don't want David to spend his life being manipulated without even knowing it."

I laughed at his perfectly understandable concern, which he could do little about at this point. "Yes, you pour your love and attention—not to mention lots of money—into child-rearing, but it's too late to become a monk once the baby arrives."

"Did you ever see video games for youngsters?" Jan asked.

"Yes, I know there are many. . . ."

"You have to play them to understand what they are. They're unbelievable. Have you seen *Grand Theft Auto*?"

"Yes, it's horrible!"

"My God, it's beyond horrible! It's shocking. Its language, weapons, people—pimps, prostitutes, and thieves glorify the underground elements.

Because of the technological generation gap between parents and children, the parents don't know what their children are playing. A patient told me about an even worse game. It takes place in a concentration camp. You're a guard finding Jews in the camp and putting them into an oven. This is the 'game.' Nothing more needs to be said.

"Look at all the people who are role models for teenagers. Take idiot Paris Hilton, the woman with some looks and no skills whatsoever, no education, and no talent. She just *is*. She's made a big deal out of it. When I turn on the TV and go to any channel, she'll be there in five minutes. Children look up to Paris and her kind. Growing up, I learned to value God, honor, and Fatherland. My heroes were different from those my son would grow up with. In Poland, there were also a lot of restrictions. At the same time, I'm missing European-style music.

"I feel there's more balance in Europe than in the United States. If I were one of my anxious patients, the world would look crazy to me, too. I was in the Houston airport, and there was an Orange Alert. The airport went crazy. There were flashing lights everywhere: 'Be hyper-vigilant! Be hyper-vigilant! Be hyper-vigilant!'"

During this time, the Iraq War continued for a while. The frequent Bush-Cheney orange and red alerts jacked up the country. There was no question that the country was on edge, and Jan was just one of the millions moved by the flood of orchestrated war news. But, right here and now, how did Jan's concern for God and honor and the restrictions of his Fatherland morph into talking about European music, and then the Houston airport with its "hyper-vigilant" signs flashing everywhere? Jan's train of thought seemed to be jumping tracks. This wasn't his usual style of talking; he was usually more sedate. Did the crazy flashing alerts have something to do with Jan's personal anxiety? What could it be? Jan had lived with a father he despised, and now he wanted to be a loving father to David. Did he wonder whether he had it in him to be a good dad or whether he would, himself, in time, repeat the mistakes of his father? Was this making him agitated?

"A lot of thoughts are going off in you like alarm bells," I said. "This is how I see your situation. Although it's impossible to separate the two, we're all confronted with a mixture of two information streams. One comes from the external world, and the other comes from our memories, desires, and expectations. You're giving me a good demonstration of this now, in your anticipation regarding David. You want him to have a good world. What is a good world? What are the pernicious temptations that he may come across?

What is good parenting? For you? For Maria? You and Maria have different opinions. On gayness, for example. How will Maria and you resolve who an expert on gayness is? Is the Church the only one able to talk, or can Maria express her thoughts, too? Is anyone unqualified to talk on certain topics?"

"Yes, yes, yes."

"We can call these anticipations that you and Maria have *pre-parental preoccupations*. They are emotional nutrition for David because your conversations will help you prepare for and nurture him, but he will be a brand-new being. Autonomy is going to happen. He'll explore the world by himself. I know it's important that you give him as solid a foundation of love and support as you can, but, just like you, at some point, he'll begin to explore and go his own way. In an imaginary conversation, you referred to a parent insisting that a child do what the parent says. When the child questions the parent, sometimes the parent says, 'Because I said so.'"

"Yes. I don't want that."

"Given what happened between your father and you, maybe you're nervous about what will happen between you and David. Perhaps you fear that you may tell David, 'Because I said so.' Fear of that happening is the red alert that's keeping you vigilant. Maybe this worry made you anxious when you saw the flashing alerts at the airport. Fortunately, you have a deep awareness of the consequences of such a destructive parenting style, where others wanted you to change against your will. What to do when your wife, patient, or kid asks, 'Why?' You want to be prepared for a long conversation. That's not what the U.S. did in Iraq. The U.S. dictated to them what to do. Perhaps our attitude was that the Iraq War was like a video game: We press a button, and a building blows up. Now that the caskets are returning, we realize that it's not a game. As you say, David's strivings to be autonomous will eventually come, and he'll want to go against your advice and desires. The question is how to nurture him until then . . . and beyond."

Jan said, "The atmosphere that you breathe here gets to you. I'm not looking suspiciously at everybody to see if they're planting a dirty bomb or something. I don't do that, but some people have a predisposition to paranoia. They're suffering a lot. They would benefit from traveling outside the United States. The atmosphere is different when you go to Poland, Italy, or many other countries. You hang out with people for a while, and you feel yourself relaxing. I observe it in myself. The pace of life is different, and there's more nurturing. This is true even if there are political problems, and they're unhappy with who's ruling the country."

Jan's love and longing for his country seemed so natural, but he'd left Poland willingly. Nevertheless, his vivid, nostalgic imagination dwelled in Poland, and his muddied reality was here. Jan needed the shades of gray, as much as the bright light, of his love for Poland.

I said, "Aside from what you've talked about, going to Poland reminds you of your younger days and the time when your mother was alive. Most immigrants are nostalgic for their country of origin unless they leave because of persecution. When Americans go abroad, even to Europe, many of them miss something of home: maybe McDonald's or Jerry Springer, just as you miss speaking in Polish to your family and friends back home."

"I don't know about that. I know Americans who move permanently to Europe."

"That's true," I acknowledged.

"Many Americans live in Holland. I even know some Americans who moved to Poland. One went Polish, and she's more critical about the U.S. than I am!"

"Well, it's a free world."

CHAPTER 28

THIS SESSION MARKS THE START of the sixth month of Jan's treatment.

As Jan parked his briefcase in the corner and settled in, I remembered that we had recently talked about his uncertainty about who was coming for Thanksgiving. "So, did you have one guest for Thanksgiving or two?" I asked.

"Oh, it was just my father-in-law."

"So, he heard Maria," I smiled.

"Yes, he came alone, and we invited a few friends. Maria has a Thai friend who came with her brother. It was a really nice evening, with lots of good cooking. We made everything by the Yankee book: turkey, cranberry sauce, the works. Her dad brought some fine Italian wine that's not generally available in the U.S."

"In matters like this, it's better to have a non-event rather than turbulence," I said. "It looks like you had the makings of a normal American Thanksgiving."

"Yes, but it made me think of Italy and how my life has changed since Amir killed himself. I realized that I had just passed the anniversary of Amir's suicide. I'm completely different now from how I was right after he died and for quite a few months after."

"How did that realization come to you?"

"I looked at my father-in-law's plane ticket, and the date on it struck me. It was Amir's suicide anniversary. A year ago, I felt lost. I was out of work and trying to pass the USMLE. And then I wondered: *Is this a lot of time or a little? Everything is different now.*"

"This is just a speculative thought: They say that melatonin helps us keep track of day and night. Similarly, maybe there's a mechanism to keep track of anniversaries."

"You mean a biological mechanism?"

"Yes, for tracking solar events. You looked at his ticket, and it popped up. Leaving the biological stuff aside, though, I do think that anniversaries are important opportunities to take stock of life."

"The good thing is that I was looking at it from a different perspective. I'll be getting my physician's license soon. There's always some bureaucratic crap to go through, but I want to be a doctor. I *will* be a doctor. In fact, I've never stopped being a doctor. I still have a few formalities from the licensing board, but they're not a big deal. I'm finishing my residency soon, and I have a job lined up. I've been in the process of saying goodbye to patients and making referrals to other residents.

"When Maria and I went to Italy a few months ago, it evoked memories of Amir. You may remember that when I was there immediately after his death, I said Catholic prayers compulsively."

"Yes."

"Every place where I had said prayers reminded me of how I was then. Along a little street in Rome, Via Lombardia, I had paced back and forth, waiting for Maria as she tried on her wedding dress. Finally, at the Domine Quo Vadis Chapel, we received our blessings. Our reception was at a nearby restaurant on the bank of the River Tiber.

"My emotions were still strong in each of these places, but not as intense as they were soon after my wedding, that is, soon after Amir's suicide. Then, I couldn't sleep; now, I have no problems sleeping. I'm being more thoughtful about planning for patients when I leave. Saying goodbye to medication-management patients is important. Even though I see them for 15 minutes once every few months, I'm always surprised to see how strong the connection can be."

CHAPTER 29

JAN CAME IN LOOKING BEATEN. The spring in his step was gone, and instead, he seemed to be dragging his tail.

"I first wrote to Amir's mom nine months ago, and then again three months later. She didn't respond, so I didn't know if she even got my letters. I just received a response."

Jan read aloud: "I am an obstetrician. I have delivered thousands of babies and have also seen many die. I have gone to funerals and consoled the bereaved families. Although they suffered the loss of life, they thanked me for my services. Normally, that is what a patient wants—to thank their doctor.

"I am still in shock. I tried to accept Amir's death. After all, everybody must die. But I am still in shock. I mourn every day and can't live without him. I cannot understand what happened. I have recurring thoughts of what happened and frequent thoughts of what could have been. I blame myself for not preventing his death.

"I do not know what kind of doctor you are. You treated my son, and I should be thankful to you. I want to thank you, but I find that such thoughts do not occur to me. My son died while in your care. Initially, I felt that you were sympathetic and tried your best. But now, I think that you are a cold American. You do not care. Now, I doubt if you cared for him while he was alive. I even doubt that you can do a competent job of caring. Was his suicide an actual suicide or a so-called suicide?

"I was perhaps neglectful in letting you treat him. I trusted your judgment, and that was my fault. I wish you had known what you were doing. I was sure you would have contacted us, his friends, or his school if there was any danger. I was wrong. I cannot believe that a doctor cannot make his patient take his medication. I cannot believe that a patient can do whatever he chooses. This seems insane. He is a patient, and you are a doctor. Are you not there to protect him? Could you not have hospitalized him?

"I cannot turn the clock back. Amir is gone. There is nothing that can be done. I still want to scream at you. For me, your explanations will always ring hollow. They will always be excuses. You did wrong. Your hospital did wrong. Is it only incompetence? Or was it also ill will?

"Although I wish to blame you, I cannot do so entirely because there is a family history of depression and suicide in my side of the family. Perhaps it was inevitable. Maybe Amir should not have left India. I wish that we had communicated earlier so that I could have found some other doctor.

"I did not respond to your letter because I could not do anything. I do not know if I can open your letters. I do not know if I have the strength to deal with you anymore. Goodbye."

After Jan finished reading the letter, he sat silent. Both Jan and Amir's mother had strong emotional reactions to the anniversary of Amir's death. The letter changed his mood. I wanted to process the shock Jan felt receiving such a letter, considering his discovery that Amir's mother was still in a state of shock. So I said, "Were you expecting a letter?"

"No. I asked if she had gotten my first one in my second letter. I wanted to find out what was happening. I wanted to find out why she wasn't answering. I feared that she hadn't gotten my letters. But, instead, she's repeating all the questions I've repeatedly asked myself."

Although this was certainly not a moment to point it out, I felt—in their identical questions—the overlapping feelings and connection between Jan and Amir's mother. Understanding emotional and relational patterns is the work of psychoanalysis. The analyst can bring the patient into this pursuit once the patient has achieved sufficiently improved self-understanding. Jan was, once again, so close to his emotional vulnerabilities that I doubted he would be able to hear much that I might say. I wondered what I might offer him.

"Could I have hospitalized Amir and managed him differently?" Jan asked. "I was worried and asked him to come in, and he said said 'No.' In his last e-mail, he'd said, 'I don't feel like coming. I feel depressed.'

"I had written back, 'What's happening? You didn't answer my call. Let's set up an appointment.'

"He didn't write back. So I called and asked him to come to see me before I left, and he did. So all his mother's questions are valid. They're what I felt exactly.

"She asks, 'Why didn't you contact family members or friends?' That's a great question. I could have done these things, but I didn't. His family was in India, and his friends were immature young adults. I described them to you.

"When his mother came to visit, he didn't want me to see her, and since he's an adult, I couldn't involve her without his permission. People from other countries sometimes have a hard time grasping and accepting this. He was his mother's son, but he treated her as someone who had less to say or, at least, as having fewer rights to say anything. He felt her opinions as a woman were less valuable. When he was a practicing Muslim, he thought he was superior to her because he was a man. She wasn't very religious then. He thought she was lost and tried to engage her in the practice of Islam. After coming here, he lost religion, and she found it. She kept reminding him of his own lessons. In return, he was sarcastic and dismissive.

"I've been thinking about which of his friends I could have contacted. Amir was shy but likable. Many people liked him, but he wasn't close to anyone. His roommate was into animal porn: He liked to watch women having sex with animals. He even tried to interest Amir in it! Amir was grossed out and nauseated and considered him a deviant. They didn't trust each other after that. The other person he mentioned was the Russian girl. He had a romantic interest in her, but she was interested in women. He kept obsessing about how to change her sexual orientation.

"I didn't feel that there were any suitable friends who could help guard his safety. His mom is right: There should have been people watching and assisting him as much as possible, but Amir just didn't feel comfortable around anyone. As for his medications, I don't believe treatment works well if patients are *forced* to participate.

"I have to answer this letter, but I don't know what to write. And I know that she may not even open it. I need to be professional. Should I tell her how Amir affected me? His suicide changed my life; it was also a big loss for me. After this letter, I feel she deserves a real response.

"Amir's father sent me two angry letters. First, he said that the evil United States killed Amir. I don't know where to start with this guy and have little hope or interest in dealing with him. Then, he requested that I print out and send him Amir's medical records. I explained that he should request directly from the medical-records office and gave him their address.

At first, he wouldn't contact them and insisted that he was being denied access to Amir's records."

I felt that Jan's negative father transference was now being displaced toward Amir's father.

"I wanted to tell him that if he read my notes, he would suffer more, because Amir was critical of his father. I think he finally got the records and read them. After that, he never wrote to me again. I believe his son's words came as a shock to him. Amir blamed his father for all his misery."

"Whatever response you make to Amir's mother, do you feel that she would communicate with—"

"—I wish she could be my advocate to her husband," Jan interjected, finishing my sentence a bit differently than I would have.

That's a tall order, I thought. "We don't know if she could or would be your advocate. But in formulating your response, you might write it one way if you think that only she will read it herself, and somewhat differently if you think she may share it with her husband or a lawyer. Regardless of the truth. . . ."

"What is the truth? In this case, I don't know what the truth is. She's absolutely right. I could have involved other people in Amir's case. But his family was halfway across the globe, and I didn't see any suitable candidates nearby. So I felt that he was pretty isolated, and I was trying to connect him more to the world, especially to help him with his romantic life. The problem was that Amir was pursuing futile relationships.

"And she's right that I could have put him in the hospital. I regret that I wasn't jumpier and more vigilant. Sometimes, he would write me an e-mail and say that he was depressed. I would answer and tell him that maybe it was time to find safety in the hospital. But I couldn't find the right time or a good enough reason to do it because he would say, 'Yeah, but I thought of killing myself two weeks ago, too. I don't think I would do it right now.'"

Going over Jan's painful memories that preceded Amir's death was essential. Given that Jan had announced that he would respond to Amir's mom, I felt that his immediate task was to compose the most appropriate reply he could muster. So I said, "The way you write to her may depend on whether you think she'll communicate with you or not."

"You're right. I don't know how I'm supposed to write this letter."

"So, the challenge is how to hedge your bets."

"I'll write it and send it off. I may show it to you before I do. I want to send it as soon as possible, maybe by Friday. I don't know. It doesn't matter if she answers me. I owe it to her. I want her to know what I think and what I feel. As I told you, Amir felt that his father never truly accepted him. His father's letter put all the blame for Amir's death on me, which I resented. He also blamed American discrimination against people from India. I couldn't relate to him, but I believe I can relate to the mother. Based on how she wrote her letter, I feel what his mother is feeling. She's blaming herself as much as—"

"—you blamed yourself," I finished his sentence.

"Yes, as much as I blamed myself."

"I think you're trying to manage an impossible situation," I said. "Any possible rapprochement with her runs the risk of being overwhelmed by her husband's anger and hostility. Because Amir died young, her grief and mourning can never be complete. She needs to come to terms with his death and also have thoughts unrelated to him, but there will always be anniversary reactions and regressions. Hopefully, her interest and dedication to her work will return. She needs to express her feelings and accept the reality of her loss. I think you feel that this is possible with her, and you're trying to facilitate that. The danger is that you might reactivate the initial raw feelings and unleash a new round of uncontrollable emotional storms. This is what happened with Amir's father. Because his mother and father are together, you must figure out how to express yourself without risking another eruption from one or both. So, let's ask: What is your goal in writing to her? What is the outcome that you most desire?"

"I want her to find peace. I want her to feel better."

These goals were understandable and laudable. But Jan wanted to write to someone with whom he had no real relationship. So I tried to clarify Jan's aims and help him think about how realistic they were.

"So, your goal is to improve the feelings of the surviving non-patient. Do you think this is possible?"

Any letter Jan wrote had to be for her benefit, not his. Jan couldn't use a letter to discharge his own guilt. For this letter, how he felt was irrelevant; the question was how *she* (and, perhaps, Amir's father) would feel. Because the matter was incendiary, it was easy for me to imagine a half-cocked message provoking an unprecedented and unwelcome reaction. Whether she would feel better after reading it was an open question. I hoped that Jan would also consider that an ambitious goal, such as change at a distance, might simply be impossible. I wanted to know the connection between Jan's understanding of Amir's problem and his current wish to help Amir's mom.

"What was Amir's main problem?" I asked.

"His relationship with his father. He felt that his father never acknowledged his accomplishments. I felt similarly about my father."

Earlier, Jan had been burned by assuming that his depression, with no suicidal impulse, was like Amir's depression, which did have a suicidal component. Could some different danger lurk behind Jan's felt similarity between his father and Amir's? Today, Jan referred to his lack of anxiety when dealing with Amir's suicidality before he killed himself. "Today, you said that you weren't nervous enough at that time."

"I said 'jumpy.'"

"Why were you not jumpy?"

"I believed in my own strength and ability to translate it into the way Amir was feeling."

What was this strength? What was the link between Jan's strength and Amir's feelings? Did he mean Amir's suicidal feelings? I felt that Jan's statement was a crucial new thread and needed further explication. I thought that a clarification based on Jan's understanding of his own depression might be a good starting point.

"You, too, had depressed feelings at some times in your life," I said.

"Deep."

I felt that Jan should be the first to broach the topic of his own suicidality. He shouldn't have to react to *my* injecting the topic into the conversation, but I realized that this was a good opportunity to spell out a thought that had just occurred to me.

"*Deep*," I said. "You didn't work for a month or more. During that time, you don't remember seeing daylight. But even in the depth of your deep depression and in the presence of significant losses, you never felt that you were going to harm yourself or kill yourself?"

"I thought about it."

It was still ambiguous. Jan and Amir were similar, in that they had suffered from depression. I thought it might be useful to determine the depth of their resemblance.

"Did you ever plan it?"

"No, I never felt close to crossing the line."

Jan had thought about suicide but was never close to acting it out. He would never succumb to the impulse, even though suicide thoughts occasionally tempted him. This was my understanding of Jan, and I felt Jan was ready to hear it. Perhaps, it would help him gain some self-understanding about the source of his fatal mistake with Amir: *Jan wrongly assumed that Amir, like him, would never go through with suicide.*

"Perhaps you felt that, just like you, Amir would never be able to pull the trigger," I said.

"Yes, I felt that he was comforted by the *idea* of suicide. I thought he would play with it, but that he could never, never pull the trigger."

"At some deep human level, you felt that he was like you and wouldn't cross the line. Right?"

The word "right" may be gratuitous, but I needed Jan's confirming response to proceed. If Jan said, "No," I would have had to rework my notion of his central problem.

"Yes."

I was relieved.

"You had suffered from depression, but you would not have considered suicide. You thought Amir had this guardrail, too, but he didn't."

"Yes, that's right."

This understanding was old ground by now, but Jan had to relive the wounds of Amir's death—the sounds, sights, feelings, and memories of the final moments they spent together—to process his grief further. I was deeply aware of Jan's progress. Both Jan and Amir had had suicidal ideas, but Jan had a safety net that protected him, and Amir didn't.

"Thinking that you were similar when you were different was the mistake that permitted the suicide to unfold. You thought there was no actual risk of suicide. Because of this assumption, you weren't 'jumpy.' Right?"

Jan nodded.

What was the source of Jan's safety net? Probably his Polish Catholic upbringing and his desire to be buried with his family in a community graveyard.

Jan elaborated on his affirmation. "It could be. Yes, it could be. That very day, when he came to my office, his face was less than enthusiastic, but he always had such a face. Then he said, 'Can you give me a prescription? This time I'm going to take it.' What could I have said?"

"Jan, in this kind of a situation, there are many questions, but no answers, so I have a question: Let us assume, for the time being, that what we just talked about was the crux of the problem. You weren't nervous or jumpy at that time because you believed Amir would not violate the cardinal rule about suicide: 'Thou shalt not commit suicide.' So let us imagine that your belief that Amir had internalized this rule was one of the main problems."

"OK."

"I'm asking this question because Amir's mom has touched your heart, and you feel a sense of urgency to respond to her letter. You said that she still feels the same grief that you felt when Amir died. So, you want to write a letter that might somehow make her feel better. For now, we've assumed that you weren't jumpy because you knew *you* would obey the no-suicide rule and assumed that *Amir* would obey it, too. So, is this rule relevant or not relevant to her feelings?"

There was a long pause. "Not relevant. She doesn't need to know how I feel about Amir. Nor does she need to know how Amir felt toward his father. Nor does his father need to know how Amir felt about him."

"Why?"

"She's alive, and he's alive, and they're both mourning."

"Right."

"I'm afraid she'll always need a person to hate. She tried to hate me. She wanted to shout and scream at me until she read my letter and realized that I didn't want Amir to die."

I felt that Jan wanted Amir's mother to understand that he meant to help her son, but I felt Jan didn't appreciate the anger component of her grief.

"You said that she doesn't need to know how you feel about Amir or how Amir felt toward his father. I think you're suggesting that this information could exacerbate her pain rather than lessen it."

"Yes."

"It could fuel anger, self-blame, or blaming others."

"I don't know much about their relationship, but I'm afraid that such feelings could turn her against her husband."

I wanted to clarify to Jan that, if he was going to communicate with Amir's mother, his message had to be focused and disciplined. It couldn't include gratuitous or unnecessary allusions that could be counterproductive. The risk was not so much that he would cause a rift between Amir's parents, as that they would direct their anger at him. "I think that, to the degree that you consciously or unconsciously communicate the problems that existed between Amir and his father, she may turn against him. Similarly, if you consciously or unconsciously communicate problems between Amir and you, she might turn against you. Either of these could complicate her mourning. You don't want to rekindle unnecessary, unmanageable feelings in her."

"In her letter, she asked why Amir wasn't hospitalized. I was afraid of . . ." Jan responded haltingly. "There were a few statements . . . I was afraid she would find out about his previous attempts to hurt himself, for which he was hospitalized and later followed at another clinic . . . I had a moment of anxiety when I heard about those but still believed that he wouldn't go further than that."

"I realize that Amir sabotaged you by not communicating with you promptly."

"Yeah. He didn't give me real-time information."

"He told you about his suicidal thoughts three weeks after he had them, so you couldn't develop a plan to help him. Then, a short while ago, you mentioned therapy for Amir's family members. What exactly were you thinking about?"

"I want to reach her on a more personal level, to let her know that I understand how she feels."

This was precisely the well-meaning but dangerous response to Amir's mother that I feared most. Jan had little understanding of Amir's mom's pain or fury. The idea that he would appreciate the pain of a mother who had lost her son, especially to suicide, was naïve. Instead, Jan saw himself as a Good Samaritan, and she saw him as Satan incarnate, her son's killer. "That's my point—" I began when Jan interrupted me.

"I don't know if I should keep it professional, which was Dr. Alvear-Reverte's advice," Jan said. "I called him when Amir died, and he said, 'I won't tell you much, but I will tell you that, from this point on, the machine is in control. You can't influence what's happening and what's going to happen. It's out of your hands. This will go through the technicalities of the Incident Review Committee. If the machine asks you a question, do your best to answer it. If you're planning to fly to Rome to get married, you should get on that plane.' He told me that the process was soulless and that administrators were concerned about hospital policies and whether I had followed them. Later, I realized that he was right, but I wanted to talk about what happened back then. I *wanted* to be grilled and be asked difficult questions."

Grilled! Such masochism! I thought Jan could easily slip into a self-blaming regression or provoke others to interrogate him, beat him up, and satisfy his dangerous need to be punished.

Jan continued, "In the Incident Review Committee meeting, Dr. Balint, who had just started his psychoanalytic training, was surprisingly understanding. He said that relationships like Amir's with his father are extremely difficult. He noted that a demanding father always causes serious problems. I understood what he was talking about perfectly, although he didn't know that.

"Dr. Shastri was politically correct. He said, 'I don't see anything that you did wrong. Some things just happen. Some things can't be prevented. Sometimes, people just get to the end of their rope.'

"Alvear-Reverte said the same thing: 'At this time, there's no point in thinking about it. You must wait for the machine to stop. Whatever you tell anybody should be professional and balanced.' I followed this advice until I met you. After you and I began to meet, I started to talk about similarities in Amir's life and mine, my assumptions about him, and my feelings toward him."

"I thought of it today because you said you weren't jumpy enough. When I mentioned therapy for the non-patient survivor, I wasn't clear. I meant to ask if a psychiatrist of the patient who committed suicide should help his mourning and angry family members? Or are all such efforts doomed to failure?"

"You misunderstood me," Jan responded. "This is how I heard what you were saying: When you said, 'psychotherapy for the survivor,' I thought you meant that I should keep it professional and treat her like I would any other patient. The problem is that I don't want to relate to her as a patient. I know what she's going through. Not only do I understand her, I feel what she's feeling."

No, he doesn't! I thought. I was glad that Jan felt that I misunderstood him. There might be some chance to correct a misunderstanding like this or, at least, acknowledge it. But what of Jan's false sense of empathy for Amir's mother?

That would have to wait. Jan was talking. "On my way here, I tried to imagine what letter I would like someone to write to me if it happened to me. That is pretty much what I want to write."

As I noted earlier, an interesting dynamic was developing between Jan and me when I missed the mark in an interpretation. In psychoanalysis, expressions of patient dissonance are critical. They open the door to further rectifying the misunderstanding and repairing errors. Unfortunately, at times, despite the best efforts of the analyst, misunderstanding persists and cannot be fixed.

However, Jan was expressing himself freely and seemed comfortable addressing our misunderstandings. Now, I felt that we were working through the critical event that had brought Jan to see me. I suspected that he conflated me slightly with Dr. Alvear-Reverte. I had questioned Jan's approach to the letter—I had my style, and he had his—but I wasn't writing it. Of course, he would write it, but I wanted him to consider the emotional and legal consequences that his letter might engender. I didn't question the desirability of what Jan was attempting, just the likelihood of his accomplishing his stated goal.

"Amir's mom wrote you a letter. If your son committed suicide, do you think you would write the same kind of letter to his treating psychiatrist?"

"Yes, I would blame myself. I would blame others, including the doctor, who could have done more but didn't. In this case, I feel there was a deep misunderstanding between who she thought I was and who I really am. She thought I was some kind of national expert on depression. I wasn't, but I *was* able to get closer to Amir than anybody else here. I could relate to many things Amir was going through. There were similarities between our personal stories. He transplanted himself from his country to the U.S. So did I. He had conflicted feelings about many aspects of life here. So do I. There were striking similarities regarding our relationships with our fathers. Did I tell you about his experience when he entered the national math competition? He came in second, and his father asked, 'Why not first?' When I came in second in the national biology Olympics, my father asked me the exact same question! I maintained a strictly professional relationship with Amir, but he wasn't just a case or just a patient. Although I didn't care much about policies, I never held sessions with him in Starbucks. I didn't divulge personal information about myself. He didn't know much about me.

"In the Incident Review Committee, Dr. Balint asked, 'Did he know that you were about to get married?' I explained that *I* had never told him. If he found out, it was from overhearing someone else's conversation."

"Did Dr. Balint say what was behind that question?"

"I thought it was obvious, so I didn't ask him to clarify: Amir was getting more depressed, but I was getting happier. He might have felt that everybody had reasons to be happy but him and treated it as a final confirmation that his life wasn't worth living. It was a good question that Balint asked, but based on what I knew, I replied, 'Not to my knowledge. I didn't tell him anything.'"

Jan continued, "I know Amir's dad read the medical records. But, I wonder if his mom did, especially about Amir's difficult relationship with his father."

"In general, you know that I don't advise you about what actions you should take. Today, I asked you what you wanted to achieve in responding to Amir's mother's letter."

"I can't tell you because I don't know. I just feel she deserves an answer on a personal level."

"I also believe she deserves a response, but the question is, what kind of response? I asked because she told you that she might not open any future letters from you."

"But her reference to my letter is itself an invitation to respond. So she's expecting a response from me."

I never questioned Jan's good intentions, but I was concerned about his efforts backfiring. "Rudyard Kipling was my dad's favorite poet, and he read many of his poems to me. I recently read his biography."

"I read *The Jungle Book* when I was a boy. It was one of my favorites."

"After World War I, Kipling had a job with the Imperial War Graves Commission. Until I read his biography, I didn't know that such a job even existed. Kipling composed or selected inscriptions for headstones for soldiers who died in the war. Separately, he also wrote the poem 'Epitaphs of the War.' But Kipling's hardest job was composing the inscription for his son's headstone. John, also called Jack, was Kipling's 18-year-old son, a lieutenant in the Irish Guards, and died in the Battle of Loos. Jack was on the 'missing believed wounded' list for two years before his death was confirmed. The Kiplings were devastated.

"In writing your letter, my sense is that you are concerned about making her feel better, but not so much about feeling Amir's loss yourself. So, I can tell you it won't be easy to write. But, if you write it, it will be one of the most important things you'll ever write."

"You're right. The *most* difficult letter I wrote was the first one. Right now, I have some distance and a sense of balance. Back then, I wasn't at all ready to address Amir's family members. My emotions were strong, and my mind was scattered. I couldn't understand why his mother wrote demanding, accusatory letters. It was difficult. I didn't know how to reply in a way that wouldn't hurt her more. This letter is different. Now, I want her to feel better. I want her to understand that she shouldn't blame herself.

"I do smell some conspiracy. You know the circumstances of death. But I must tell you, that day when Amir left my office for the last time, no red lights were flashing in my head. I wasn't lazy. If the idea had occurred to me, I would have stopped him. He told me he was going to a girl's housewarming party. He had down-to-earth concerns: what gift to buy, what to wear. A few hours later, I found out that he had killed himself violently and brutally. If you point a gun to your head and pull the trigger, there's no way out. This shows that he had a lot of determination and felt he was at the end of his rope. But I didn't have a clue."

Amir didn't wait for the rope's end; he finished himself off. He took charge of ending his life, and Jan was still dealing with the repercussions. Now, the echoes were from Amir's mom. "Her letter changed you. The distance you thought you had put between yourself and Amir's death has suddenly vanished. Your old feelings are back and are still—"

"—strong," Jan said. "I went through this before when I first replied to her and her husband. But it's different now."

"This will be the second most difficult letter," I said.

"Yes, now it's not about Amir; it's about her. I'm able to see beyond him. It's easy to be irrational when you're under so much pressure. In my case, the wish to quit medicine altogether was an irrational and easy solution."

"Today, when you were driving to see me, you knew that you would be dealing with the unwritten letter. What was your hope, anticipation, or expectation?"

Jan chuckled. "In the back of my mind, I was hoping that a miracle would happen, and I would know what to write. But, no, I need to struggle with it myself. I don't know what I'll write, but our talk has significantly lessened my anxiety. I'm glad that I showed you the letter. But, unfortunately, there are only a few people I could show it to."

CHAPTER 30

"Last session, I referred to Rudyard Kipling and his son, Jack, who died in World War I. In 1915, after finally getting confirmation of Jack's death, Kipling wrote the poem, 'My Boy Jack,' in his memory."

I handed a book, opened to the page with the poem, to Jan. He read it to himself.

My Boy Jack[46]

"Have you news of my boy Jack?"
Not this tide.
"When d'you think that he'll come back?"
Not with this wind blowing, and this tide.

"Has any one else had word of him?"
Not this tide.
For what is sunk will hardly swim,
Not with this wind blowing, and this tide.

"Oh, dear, what comfort can I find?"
None this tide,
Nor any tide,
Except he did not shame his kind—
Not even with that wind blowing, and that tide.

---

46 Smith, F. (1978). *Rudyard Kipling.* New York: Random House.

Then hold your head up all the more,
This tide,
And every tide;
Because he was the son you bore,
And gave to that wind blowing and that tide!

Jan handed the book back and said, "I have a patient who just returned from Iraq. He was an inner-city gangster. Nice guy. I like him. He said that he had seen two people shot and killed before going to Iraq. 'Shooting was no big deal. Dying was no big deal,' he said, so he thought that he would be good for the job. He got recruited right after high school. Two recruiters dazzled him with 'exotic travel' and the 'fun of being in war.' He signed up and was shipped to Iraq. With a big gun in his hand, he felt powerful. He thought he was the toughest tough guy. He served two tours. Then he got a raging case of PTSD and got discharged. He was shaken by what he saw and the conditions he had to live in. He told me that his tough-guy self-image disappeared in a few weeks. He was never so scared in his entire life. He felt paranoid and mistrusted everybody: local food suppliers, drivers, translators. He didn't know whose side the Iraqi helpers were really on. Sometimes, insurgents killed American soldiers and these helpers, and sometimes the helpers turned out to be insurgents themselves. He never knew who was a friend and who would turn out to be an enemy.

"He specialized in disarming roadside bombs, IEDs. Once, when he was defusing one, it went off. The blast threw him into the air and roughed him up. He lost consciousness briefly. When he regained consciousness, he saw that half of his buddy's body had disappeared. And then he realized that that could have been him if he had been one inch closer. After that, he couldn't do his job anymore. He barely spoke to anyone and considered himself lucky if he slept one hour a day. The next step was booze. He drank whenever he could. He was finished.

"This is what the military does to people. I truly believe that if you want to be successful in the military sense, you must be anti-social. You should want to kill but not be a freewheeling sociopath. You also need to follow orders."

I thought Jan was displacing his anxiety about writing the letter to Amir's mom onto his soldier patient. "Following up on what we discussed last time, you're familiar with tough situations," I said. "You had a tough childhood and tough adolescence, and now you have a tough letter to write.

In responding to Amir's mom, you want to be bold, but writing this letter is like experiencing your own personal Iraq. Every word has the potential to be a friend or an enemy. She may perceive any particular word or phrase as an IED. I assume that you're still struggling with—"

"Yeah. I tried to write but couldn't get it going. I wrote a few sentences and immediately deleted them." Jan paused, visibly struggling with what to say next. He seemed to want me to say something.

"Using your soldier as a symbol," I said, "let's imagine the situation from the perspective of Amir's mom. Her son was killed. She could see you as the insurgent who killed him or as her son's buddy, who was also injured. Not knowing how she sees you or how she will react is why it's so hard to write to her."

"Amir's death is different. It was unjustified. It was useless. It served no purpose. Amir was trying to catch the train of life. When he realized he couldn't, he gave up. Amir's death went unnoticed by society, and now he's just a statistic."

"I wasn't thinking of Amir; he's gone. I was thinking of his mother, who is still alive. Her moods change easily, based on her anger at you and her efforts to understand you, and that uncertainty makes it so hard to know what to write. There may be only a millimeter separating her anger and her empathy, and you aren't sure how to stay on the right side of the divide."

"Amir's mom said it. She said that she wanted to scream and yell at me and accuse me of things, but after she read my letter, she decided not to. Her situation is similar to the one I was in. She doesn't know who's guilty. What happened? Why did it happen? What should I have done? Why didn't I do it? Self-blame; then blaming others.

"I know what I want to say. I want to tell her that if there were any divine intervention I could conjure or any means to make her feel better, I would do it."

"Yes, I understand your intention. I think you did everything for Amir that you were *consciously* aware that you could do." There was a long silence. "I don't know if that makes sense to you."

"It does. It makes perfect sense with the emphasis on *consciously*. After you and I dug deeper, though, we discovered unconscious things that prevented me from taking certain actions."

I didn't feel it necessary to reiterate the safety-net metaphor we had explored in detail in the last session. "Yes. That sentence was . . . unclear. I knew what I wanted to say. I'm glad you understood it in the way I intended. I believe you understand what I meant."

"I think so."

I continued, "It's harder when there's no heroism associated with an action. It's a personal agony." I hesitated. "The most reasonable thing you can hope for is the passage of time and the healing that time often facilitates. Unfortunately, you can't undo her loss. It's a fact that will remain, regardless of any other change."

"That is something I want to tell her. After my mom died, it was an open wound for a long time. At first, I couldn't cope without an emotional flood. It still hurts, but I can manage it."

"There's one difference between our last meeting and today. Two days ago, it was clear that you wanted to respond, but what you wanted to say was unclear to me. Today, it seems that you have an emotional sense of what you want to say, but you don't yet have the language with which to say it. You still have to fashion the words and sentences to match your intention. Nevertheless, you're moving in the direction you need to. I'll see you next week, and then I'll be away for a month."

CHAPTER 31

Our last meeting before my month-long vacation was, on the surface, polite and uneventful. Jan was proud to take his pregnant wife to see his family in Poland and wondered how they would interact and manage the language differences between Italian and Polish. His vacation and my vacation overlapped, and we went over details of our next session's specific date and time. In several sessions leading up to my vacation, Jan had dealt with Amir's mom's accusative "letter" that hurt him deeply, but Jan hadn't mentioned it in the last session. Neither did I. I felt Jan was trying to keep the session on an even keel and not get emotional. After some polite banter, we wished each other bon voyage. However, I told Jan that my vacation came at the wrong time as we left.

What transpired interpersonally, described above, and what I thought of the session contribute to an analytic perspective. I appreciate that I let slip away the opportunity to manage our respective vacations analytically. The letter from Amir's mother came after my vacation announcement. Her note overwhelmed Jan, and we had spent a great deal of time processing his emotional collapse in response. Despite this recent upheaval, Jan maintained composure in the main, which I felt was necessary during some times of stress, especially if I was absent. Although I gave Jan a three-week notice about my vacation, brought it up during the last session before my holiday, and was consciously aware of the month-long treatment interruption, I did not interpret the transference implications of our separation. His reactions were evident in his associations. My vacation may have precipitated angst, helplessness, disorganization, and anger, which was, to some extent, displaced to Amir's mom. I appreciated how his mother must have felt going

336

away to a sanatorium when he was a year-and-a-half-old infant. But, I was glad to be going on an extended vacation to visit my family and leaving him to his own devices.

I was afraid that interpreting the significance of the break in the treatment or mentioning the letter could trigger, in Jan, an explosive turmoil when I was away. I felt guilty that while I was away, Jan, while being overwhelmed, had to deal with Amir's mom's harsh criticisms. I could not bring myself to offer an interpretation that my leaving might be similar to his mom's going to the sanatorium. Perhaps not mentioning the letter and emotional reactions to the break kept him away from his dread of my vacation and me from my guilt. I believe in transference interpretations and am generally confident of my tactfulness. However well-timed and well-intended it may be from an analyst's perspective, sometimes a patient can experience an interpretation as a burden, if not an impingement. This was my concern. Jan was raw and had barely managed the "letter." His reserves were low, but he still had planned his family vacation in Poland. He was proud to take his wife to his family. I felt an interpretation that my vacation was similar to when his mother needed treatment at the sanatorium could reawaken difficult memories and upset his composure. Therefore, I decided the transference interpretation could wait. I recognize that my assessment of Jan's fragility could have been wrong and might have had a self-serving quality.

On the other hand, Jan was a proud husband and father-to-be returning home ready to face the world. At any rate, I did not offer any interpretations regarding my upcoming vacation. If a candidate analyst or analyst reads this chapter, they could have a field day detailing how they would better manage such a situation.

I was away for about a month. During that time, Jan and Maria visited his family in Poland. Their vacation was, appropriately, our first topic of conversation.

"The trip was great for Maria and not so great for me," Jan began. "My father developed aspiration pneumonia and was in a hospital on Christmas, so Sofia and I were back and forth taking care of him. It's good that I was there, first, because medical care around Christmas is lousy, and second, because, as a physician, I could communicate directly with the doctors, which meant he got extra attention."

"Did your dad recognize you?"

"Yes, surprisingly! Initially, he was delirious, but his mind cleared up after the antibiotics kicked in, and he started to recognize me. Of course, he was exhausted and thinking slowly, so normal communication wasn't possible, but he did recognize me."

"I'm glad," I said.

"He was clearly grateful I was there. He understood that we had made sure that he had good care. He even said, 'Thank you' a few times."

"That was meaningful," I said.

"It was. Overall, the trip was good. Maria tolerated it well. She likes Christmas in Poland. We were a little scared to travel a month and a half before her due date, but it was uneventful. Even though we're anxious to meet our baby finally, we're fine to wait until he's ready. We had some discussions about raising him. Maria said, 'You'll teach David about manly stuff, like fishing, shooting, and picking mushrooms. I'll teach him about literature.'"

"David—only one name?"

Jan looked confused, "What do you mean, 'Only one name'?"

"What if it's a girl?"

"We already know— . . ."

"Oh, I'm sorry. I forgot. I come from a time when parents didn't know the sex of the baby beforehand. I don't have the proper expectations for the modern world. I forgot that we'd talked about it."

Jan *had* told me that the ultrasound indicated it was a boy. My forgetting I knew the gender of the baby is an example of the effect of our not meeting regularly. I had lost a sense of continuity. As Jan's analyst, I lost a key piece of information which had evaporated. But, of course, such a memory lapse could have other meanings, too. At least, I acknowledged it immediately. We both laughed, Jan with gracious kindness, and I with self-conscious embarrassment at my forgetfulness. Perhaps I was a bit like his father?

"We knew the sex of the baby at about fourteen weeks. The decision about the name came after long family arguments. Finally, everybody agreed that 'David' was a good name. Maria and I are happy, imagining and getting ready for David. Maria will be a great mother. Just a reminder: Maria is nine months pregnant and is due any time."

CHAPTER 32

Jan called to announce that he would be gone about a week—Maria was going to the hospital! A week later, Jan walked in with an uncharacteristic spring in his step, beaming from ear to ear.

"I'm so happy. I wanted to call you the next day, but David is waking us up every hour."

I roared with laughter, imagining the warm, wet, magnetic greeting David gave his parents. An infant's cry is a delightful alarm signaling some pressing and immediate need that irresistibly draws a parent to their job. I remembered that the fatigue resulting from lack of sleep for a new parent is also peculiarly delightful, at least for a while.

"I haven't slept at all. Is today Wednesday? I've gotten a little confused about the days. I'm so tired. Yesterday, David slept for three hours straight. I took care of him after Maria fed him, so she had a chance to rest a bit. But now, I'm back to work. I wish I could take a few months off. It's so hard to go to work when I can see that he's changing every day. This opportunity will never come again, and I don't want to miss a thing. I'm sure it will be even more challenging as David becomes more interactive, although he's already responsive. He settles down when Maria or I pick him up and nestles in our arms. I know we have a bond already. Maria seems more tuned in to him, and I'm a little jealous. It will be difficult when Maria goes back to work. It's hard to imagine leaving David with someone else. I wish we had the means just to stop working for a while. I told her today to go for a walk and buy a lottery ticket. After all, we're lucky people: We have David. Maybe we'll get lucky again. I know it's silly, wishful thinking.

"You remember when I was on leave of absence. I had more time, but I didn't feel any joy. Now, I feel happy, but I don't have the time to be with my son. Peering into the future would be so helpful in making the right decisions now, but nobody can do that. I couldn't have predicted that I would be capable of so much happiness. It's an amazing feeling!

"Yesterday, as the day progressed, I just wanted to leave it all and go home. But, at the same time, my patients were terrific. It was like the best of psychiatry in one day. I saw a genuine case of PTSD, not like some patients I remember from the VA, who just go there to milk the system. They're high on cocaine and heroin and try to pass themselves off as war heroes, but facts back up nothing in their stories.

"The guy who came yesterday told me his wife made him schedule an appointment. She had seen stuff on TV and in newspapers about PTSD and realized that was what was happening with him. But, she told him, 'You never told anybody what you went through that got you that Purple Heart.'

"The guy brought me an album with wartime photos from Vietnam. My heart was pounding just looking at them, but he showed no emotion. He was the commander of the Medical Battalion's Air Ambulance Platoon. They flew the Bell UH-1 Huey airborne ambulances responsible for aerial medical evacuation of casualties. They were called *medevacs*, or *Dustoffs*. He was once called to rescue casualties from tanks blown to pieces by landmines and enemy fire. Most of the soldiers had died instantly. He pulled bodies and body parts from these wrecks, looking for survivors. One picture showed four charred corpses next to the metal scraps that were all that remained of the tank. He got through the war without a physical scratch, but since his discharge 40 years ago, he hasn't had one good night's sleep.

"My heart was pleading for me to go home to my son, but I wanted to honor this soldier, so I listened: While trying to evacuate the surviving soldiers, his team was attacked. He showed me a picture of three or four Vietcong soldiers who were kneeling. He said, 'We called additional helicopters to pick them up and take them for interrogation. The helicopters didn't come. I had to tell my buddies, 'We have to kill them. We gotta move. We have work to do.' We captured them while they were guarding some underground hideout,' he continued. 'We couldn't take them with us. Too much risk. We had to shoot them.'

"His tone was flat and emotionless, like 'I went to a cafeteria for lunch and decided to get some Pepsi . . .'

"He showed me a picture of a fellow soldier. 'He tried to sneak through Vietnam without doing any work,' he said, 'but a sniper got him.' Then he showed me his Purple Heart, with a commendation attached, describing why he got it. First, his helicopter was shot down. Then, of the six people on board, he was the only one who could still walk. So he brought back his buddies.

"Sometimes, he had to carry a guy. Sometimes, he brought a leg, all wrapped up. It was ripped from the rest of the body. He said he stayed in touch with one of the soldiers for a year, then they lost touch. In the 40 years since he came back, he buried his sister, brother, mother, and father—a soldier—and never shed a tear. Two weeks ago, his dog died, and he hasn't been able to stop crying. He said he was surprised by his own reaction. 'I wake up, and I cry. I sit on the porch, and I cry. I cry when I go to bed. I don't understand it. Finally, my wife asked me to get some help. I'm so happy that I came to someone who can understand me.'

"But the fact is, I said almost nothing! I was acting like you or Dr. Alvear-Reverte. After he showed me his album, I may have said something like, 'It's hard to even look at these photos,' and then I just listened. I had strong emotions about what I heard and saw, but I tried hard not to show it. After his comment, I suddenly realized the importance of listening. Till that moment, like many other residents, I felt compelled to react immediately, to try to say something smart.

"After listening for most of the session, I told him, 'I have to be honest with you—I don't understand it, either. I don't know why you didn't real-ize that you had a problem all these years.' I told him it would take time to find out what happened to him and, when I understood it, I would share it with him.

"He shared some pretty crazy stuff with me. Once, he went on a vaca-tion with his family. A young guy in a loose T-shirt was hanging around, trying to pick up his daughter. My patient thought that he had a gun under his shirt and, before anybody could react, he started to beat him up. His wife had to stop him. He had mistaken a bottle of beer hidden under the guy's T-shirt for a gun. For many years after the war, he felt he could turn into a killer in a split second. He was ashamed of the demon that lurked in him. He thanked God for his wife; she brought him back to his senses."

Jan got up suddenly and, seeing the surprise on my face, said, "I need to go."

CHAPTER 33

"I'M SORRY. Last time, I ran out without saying goodbye. I was eager to see David. He's fine now, but he had developed jaundice. There's a cool device called a Bili blanket. It's made of optic fibers that emit UV light to break down the bilirubin. It's like a big spoon. You put the naked baby on it before putting on his diaper. The only inconvenience is a 1 1/2-centimeter-wide pipe going to the machine that produces the light. We used it continuously for two days, and his bilirubin went down. Now he's fine, so the pediatrician told us we could discontinue it. We have an excellent doctor for him, Dr. Patel. She's calm but also decisive. That's important because Maria is anxious and always has lots of questions. Dr. Patel is patient and reassuring and answers all her questions.

"Before, Maria was anxious about the pregnancy, and now she's anxious about protecting David, sometimes overly anxious. For example, David sleeps on a small bed attached to our bed. No matter how we placed it, there was little space between the two beds. I thought I could insert some foam there with the same consistency as the mattress to close the gap, but Maria was concerned that he would get into the gap and suffocate. She has a great imagination. We plugged in a baby monitor next to his bed to hear him cry from another room. Maria was afraid that he might bite the cord and get electrocuted. I won't even discuss it with her. I just say, 'Yes, yes, yes. Whatever you want to do is OK.' On the one hand, these things she thinks up are highly improbable, but on the other hand, accidents happen. I could have reminded her that he doesn't have any teeth yet, but instead, I bit my tongue. It's better if I do what

342

she wants and don't voice my opinions. She's a great mom. You can see on his face that she's taking such good care of him. He cries only when he's hungry or wet."

CHAPTER 34

THIS SESSION MARKS THE START of the ninth month of Jan's treatment. Unfortunately, the session with my previous patient had run over by a few minutes. Welcoming Jan, I apologized for being late.

"Don't mention it. You remember, once I completely forgot about our appointment. I still feel guilty about it."

"How long do you plan to feel guilty about it?"

"For a long time!" Jan exclaimed, laughing heartily. "In the first year of my residency, I rotated with Dr. Alvear-Reverte, my attending. We saw patients together. One day, because of an emergency on the unit, he and I were late for an appointment with a patient. When we got there, she was upset and scolded us. She said, 'You were supposed to be here half an hour ago.' I immediately apologized for both of us. Dr. Alvear-Reverte said nothing. Later, he said that explaining yourself to a patient is unnecessary. 'Your job as a psychiatrist is to acknowledge how the patient feels. The psychiatrist must act confident even if he feels unsure.' That was before I met Amir. Back then, I was prone to act confident anyway.

"He said that the psychiatrist is the person designated to resolve a crisis or problem; his anxiety is irrelevant. So, apologizing for the side effects of a medication, like dizziness or dry mouth, isn't very useful. And excessive apologies by a psychiatrist can even paralyze the treating team. I think that was a good lesson, though perhaps a little exaggerated because there are always exceptions. Admit to yourself that you're human and have doubts, but your demeanor and actions should convey that you know what you're doing concerning the patient.

"As I just said, this was before Amir. Often, I tried to cover up my insecurity as a psychiatry resident with overconfidence. Then, regardless of its impact on a patient, I would do or say something based on my impulses. I was more friendly and pleasing than I was a good therapist. I didn't understand that many of the actions intended to be in my patient's best interest maybe weren't.

"Right now, Maria and I are anxiously trying to arrange child care for when Maria returns to work. The maternal instinct is such a powerful force that I'm sure that she thinks about not returning to work at all. So, knowing how important closeness to the baby is, Maria worries that going back to work after just three months will create problems. She said, 'I don't want to create a patient for someone else.'

"I started seeing a new patient and asked her what was happening in her life. She said that she feels bad but can't pinpoint a cause. 'My husband doesn't beat me, but he doesn't understand me,' she said. 'He's, well, you know, just a regular husband. Nobody's fired me. Nobody called me names. I didn't lose any money. Nothing bad has happened. I just feel bad.'

"During her second visit, I saw that she noticed a scrap of light blue wrapping paper with little teddy bears in the trash and was staring at it. I saw that her eyes narrowed with curiosity. I said, 'Something in my office seems to have grabbed your attention.' She didn't respond. I acknowledged that I hadn't gotten a chance to clean up my office before she came in and said, 'I see that you're looking at that piece of wrapping paper.'

"She still didn't say anything, but she started to cry. I asked her what had happened that changed her mood. 'I should apologize,' she said.

"'What should you apologize for?'" I asked.

"'Seven years ago, I had an abortion,' she replied. 'My husband made me do it. It was near the end of the third month. After the abortion, I felt guilty and nervous. I tried to drown myself in alcohol and partying, but nothing helped. The pain in my heart weighed me down. Whenever I see a pregnant woman, an infant, or any maternity or baby items, I'm overcome with sadness and can't help crying. I actually feel the same pain in my belly I felt after the abortion.' Finally, I just looked at her and listened. At the end of the session, she thanked me for letting her speak from her heart.

"I feel like I've made a discovery: I understand more about how to talk to people who come into my office. I rely less on medications because I learned that short encounters could also be meaningful to the patient *and* me. Some therapists say that we shouldn't touch memories that are too painful. I feel the opposite is true, especially if the patient can talk about them. Every detail of the trauma should be uncovered: what happened, how it happened, what feelings she had. If she's ready and willing to talk, it may help her. If she doesn't want to, then I don't force her. She may have to go through this process repeatedly, and each time, a little more work gets done.

"So I asked her, 'What do you mean, your husband made you have an abortion?' She said, 'When he's satisfied with me and is in a good mood, he's sweet and brings me flowers, and we plan and go on vacations together. But when I disagree with him, he's cold and angry. He doesn't even acknowledge me when he comes home from work. I feel that I'm not doing something right. When I became pregnant, I was so happy; I felt my dreams had come true. He had children from a previous marriage and told me that he didn't want this child. We had a big conflict: I wanted to have the baby, and he didn't. He stopped talking to me and became distant. Finally, I couldn't take it any longer and had the abortion.' I don't yet know the full extent of their conflict before she decided to get the abortion."

"As psychiatrists, we have to be careful," I said. "When the patient expects confident advice from us, we may feel an impulse to give it. In fact, by reflexively responding to a patient's need for a self-assured psychiatrist, the doctor can develop a false sense of self-confidence. This confident attitude is not always a reliable guide. If you don't know the extent of a conflict, it may be useful to wait until you have a better sense. Even though his facts are half-baked, a psychiatrist can sound convincing without this. For example, you might think to advise your patient to divorce her husband in this case. By being aware of your doubt, you bought yourself time to get more information and think."

I continued, "The situation, in this case, took on a transference layering after she figured out you'd just had a baby. By *transference layering*, I mean an interpersonal layering between her and you. She was not talking about her mother or father; she was talking about you. She reacted to seeing the remnants of wrapping paper with a teddy bear design. You knew she was responding to you and your life. When you realized that, the incident took on a specific patient–psychiatrist meaning. She inferred that you had had a baby, and it rekindled the painful memory of her abortion and the strain in her relationship with her husband. Thus, something coming from you during the treatment became linked with something with which she struggles. Many therapists may feel that this reaction is unrelated to her treatment, and they don't need to try to understand it. However, you realize that discussing her response to you may be the best way to understand her life's realities.

"Psychoanalysts feel that talking about such relationships between events in life and therapy is important. But, as you can see, there's a degree of unpredictability in the analytic framework. We can't tell in advance what aspect of your life, what intervention, or what attitude will be meaningful to her, which you can go on to interpret in a manner that will help her."

"Yes, she saw that I had what she dreamt about, and we had a moment of connection. If I had been too rule-bound or too dry, I might have missed it altogether."

CHAPTER 35

JAN WALKED IN, discouraged and downcast.

"Remember the letter I got from Amir's mom? She said, 'I blame myself for placing Amir in your care. I blame myself for letting him come to America. I can't stop thinking about the so-called suicide of my son. I am not sure where I will go with my feelings. I am not sure if I will ever contact you again.' She was blaming herself for what happened to Amir."

"It's easy to say, 'Don't blame yourself,'" I replied, "but hard to implement."

Jan looked at me for a long while before he spoke again. "I know this from my own experience. People keep telling me, 'Don't blame yourself.' 'Fate is inevitable.' 'He was at the end of his rope.' 'Things happen, and you have to accept it.' So, based on my own experience, I'd like to tell her, 'Don't take it personally, and don't blame yourself.'

"I read the letter over and over again. She said that she wasn't sure if she would communicate with me in the future. She appears to be getting more suspicious: She referred to Amir's death as a 'so-called suicide.'

"I feel bad for her because her questions are legitimate. What if she wants to come here to pursue them? It won't be easy. She's 10,000 miles away and will have a hard time negotiating the American administrative and legal systems. It's not simply the problem of obtaining a visa. The cultures and laws are so different that this would become a major and uncertain mission. In America, psychiatrists think it's important to understand her and her husband's contribution to Amir's problems. Their self-understanding is also critical. I don't know if she's interested in these issues or if she's more interested in blaming me. I'm not the person to help her develop her self-understanding, though; I failed to do that with her son."

Earlier, I had felt that Jan expected to influence her grief positively. Now, it was clear that he understood he was ill-equipped to help her—a more painful, but indeed a more realistic, stance.

Jan continued, "As I said, I don't know if she wants to come here, but just thinking about it, I started having some paranoid thoughts of her, or them, coming and trying to get revenge."

Jan was now aware of Amir's mom's suspicions and his own paranoia. He couldn't change her, but I thought he could gain a better self-understanding of his new fear. Unfortunately, the situation seemed to have taken a turn for the worse.

I've worked with hundreds of homeless women over the years. Many of them carry numerous Biblical verses in their memory and quote them with ease. As a result, occasionally, Biblical references just come to me. For example, I paraphrased this quote and said, "Why do you look at the speck of sawdust in your brother's eye and pay no attention to the plank in your own eye?" [Matthew 7:3].

Jan continued, "I think the American media's drumbeat about Muslim terrorists is getting into my head. Because Amir's family is Muslim, I fear they're capable of deeply felt acts of personal courage or craziness. So even though I know that they're a highly refined family, I feel the fear.

"I spoke with Dr. Williams soon after Amir killed himself. He told me, 'I know you feel horrible about your patient committing suicide, but worse things could happen. Who knows? This guy could have blown himself up with a bomb in a crowded place for the glory of Allah.'"

Jan laughed nervously.

"There's always some way to think positively," Jan continued. "I found Dr. Williams's statement funny and crazy, and I told him so, but he said, 'No, no, no. Desperate people with chronic depression can experience a loss of purpose in life and find refuge in an apocalyptic cause and give their lives for it.' I understand he said that to make me feel better. But, as you well know, I was in a zombie-like state at that time. So maybe he wanted to perk me up with this crazy idea."

"I have a thought that may or may not be crazy," I said. "It's not necessarily related to what Dr. Williams said, and it's not intended to cheer you up. Otto Kernberg, the psychoanalyst of *Borderline Disorder* fame, had the notion of micro-paranoia experienced by the therapist as a form of countertransference. In treating borderline anxious, hostile, and maddeningly demanding patients, the boundaries between the patient and the therapist sometimes become blurred. It's hard to say, for example, whether your guilt is your own or whether the patient has set you up for a guilt trip.

"Many borderline patients are suspicious. In response, a therapist can have a micro-paranoid episode. He doesn't go fully crazy, but he may mistake a stranger in the mall for the patient. In your case, Amir's mother's anger at you and your sense of guilt is so intense and reciprocally reinforcing that there's some blurring between her and you, which resulted in your particular paranoia."

Jan looked stunned. "Such things *can* happen!"

"I think the paranoia isn't part of your normal personality," I went on. "It's being triggered in response to this exchange with Amir's mother."

"Yes, and I can see something else that contributes to my paranoia. My son is the center of my universe, and I must protect him from harm. I don't want any connection whatsoever between David and Amir."

"You worry that she's capable of changing from blaming herself to blaming you?"

"I feel like she's talking about a conspiracy because she used the phrase 'so-called suicide.' What is she thinking? She's moving toward feeling that someone killed her son and maybe that there's some conspiracy to cover up his murder.

"In India, especially in the Muslim community, maybe people believe that Americans wouldn't mind if a Muslim person dies. I can't speak for everybody in the U.S., but I didn't want him to die. I probably would never be able to convince her of that, though. The harder I would try, the more suspicious she would get. I can't even go there with her because that would be professional suicide. I don't want to touch it. But such thoughts do cross my mind. I continuously replay different scenarios of what a conversation with Amir's mom might be like, and they all go wrong. Sometimes, I ruminate about it half the night. Maybe it's not paranoia, just high anxiety. I imagine bad things without any evidence from anywhere. After she wrote that she suspected ill will and implied foul play, it got worse.

"In fact, I recently talked to the administration. I told them that Amir's mom had communicated with me. I also wanted to ensure they wouldn't give her my home address or phone number. They told me that the case may end up in court and that University lawyers will handle all future communications."

"Indeed, you can't control what she feels or says," I said. "What's your take on having lawyers handle all future communications with her?"

"I wish she would rise above her suspicions about what happened and see it as reasonably as possible. Everybody tried their best, and Amir's death was a tragedy. The whole situation was complex. Now she seems to think that Amir didn't commit suicide but that he was murdered. She'll have to get past her conspiracy theories if she wants a dialogue."

"This is how I understand what you're saying: You want better communication with her. However, that can happen only if she can get past her accusatory and conspiratorial mindset."

I thought Jan was now closer to accepting the adversarial framework of the American legal system, and I wanted to underscore this.

I continued, "Let me give you an example. I have a patient who's been married for more than 20 years. She feels she and her husband may be incompatible. Her husband is a well-to-do financier, and they are well off, but when she bought a copy of the *Chicago Tribune*, he resented her spending the 50 cents. He said, 'You're wasting *my* money.' He also complained that she treated him like an abandoned street dog. She decided to seek a divorce because he started to call her a bitch, screamed at her, and threatened to beat her up. They both hired lawyers. Because of the steep drop in real estate values, they couldn't sell their fancy condo and had to continue living together under the same roof. How do you think they communicated during this time?"

"Writing notes?"

"No, through their lawyers! Although they were in the same apartment and even in the same room, they used their lawyers. So if she had to say something, she would contact her lawyer, and her lawyer would contact his lawyer, and then his lawyer would contact him."

"This reminds me of a story my mom told me," Jan said. "A couple was getting divorced, but they continued to live together during the process. They didn't talk to each other, either, but instead of using lawyers, they communicated through notes. One night, the husband wrote on a piece of paper, 'Wake me up at 7.' He woke up at 11 and got angry. Then he noticed a piece of paper with his wife's handwriting: 'Wake up. It's 7:00.'"

Both of us laughed.

"Why do things like that happen?" I asked. "The story from your mom and the example I gave are alike. Both couples—one in Poland and the other in the U.S.—lived together during a divorce but wouldn't communicate directly. Why?"

"There may be lots of things behind it." Jan paused. "Maybe they don't want their discussions to become too heated, or they don't want to say things they will regret."

"Yes," I agreed, "this may help them avoid inadvertent, unnecessary, or inflammatory communications."

"It's like communicating through a filter that screens out all negative emotions."

"Maybe communication between Amir's mom and the University will become formal, and legal. For your own good, your lawyer told you not to communicate with her directly."

"I've heard from other psychiatrists about patient suicides. Sometimes, families have lawyers go through the chart trying to find irrefutable physician mistakes so that they can sue the doctor."

"And who communicates about what they find?"

"The lawyers."

"Yes, the grieving family and the doctor are not involved in direct discussions."

"It's different in my case because a lawyer for Amir's family hasn't contacted me. Instead, his mom is sending accusatory letters directly to me. What she probably wants is to sit with me and ask me the questions that keep her up all night. What happened? Why did it happen? What could you have done to prevent it? Why didn't you do this or that? The problem is that I don't feel like I could answer any of her questions."

Despite his understanding that sometimes indirect, lawyerly communication is best, Jan could easily succumb and communicate with Amir's mom again, against the advice of his lawyers. I wanted to find out whether Jan would accept that advice. "Let me ask you a hypothetical question," I said. "Let's say she writes a similar letter to each of the supervisors of this case, accusing them of negligence. What would they do?"

"They might try to answer her formally, stating that a review committee concluded that, despite Amir's tragic death, the treatment had been conducted professionally . . . But, honestly, I don't know how they would respond. So I think maybe I'm not answering your question as you imagine I should."

"Your answer is fine. First, we have to go through a process to get a sense of the direction of each action and then calculate the risk each one carries. After that, we should think about how to think. At this point, there's no legal case. Is that right?"

"Yes."

"But if and when there is a legal case, what should you say?"

Both of us spoke in unison, "Contact my lawyer!"

"Right," I said. "Based on the direction in which the situation is proceeding, no one except the University lawyers should communicate with her if she files a lawsuit. She can send you all the letters she wants. You would be obligated only to forward them to your lawyer. The lawyer would presumably ask her to stop communicating directly with you or anyone else in the department. That would give you some distance from her, like the distance between the Polish man who wanted to be woken up and his wife who left him a note to wake up. Do you agree?"

"Yes, but I understand where she's coming from, and I'm still willing to try to answer her. I want to validate her feelings. I don't want to give her the impression that I'm a person getting away with murder by hiding behind a legal wall. Truly, I don't know what happened that day, and that is the only thing that she wants to know."

"Given that you want to respond compassionately and rationally, can you imagine some trigger point when you would say, 'I need an emotional filter'?"

"During our last session, I felt that I could, and want to, talk to her. But the answer to her main question, 'What happened?' is 'I don't know,' and I'm sure that would be frustrating to her.

"When you and I started to meet, I talked to you only about Amir. After I passed the exam and Maria got pregnant, that changed. Talking to you gave me some distance from Amir. Since my obsessive way of thinking about his death gradually faded, I've been able to talk about other topics. Now I'm more rational than emotional when I think about him, but I haven't forgotten him. Thoughts about Amir still cross my mind quite often, but they don't overshadow everything else. I'm able to see the brighter side of my life, too."

"I think you've matured as a therapist," I said. "You're in touch with Amir's mom's turmoil and would like to help her, but you are limited by what's possible."

"She feels I participated in a hate crime. I think she's breathing an atmosphere that makes her think this way. She watches the news, listens to her spiritual leaders, and believes that her son died because he was a Muslim. Popular beliefs can make people irrational. For example, during World War II, the U.S. government interned all Japanese-Americans because they thought they were enemy sympathizers. Suppose Amir was a Japanese-American during that time and committed suicide. His family might claim that everyone hates the Japanese, that there was a master plan to eradicate them all, and that the doctor was part of it."

"Today, we talked about distancing mechanisms or emotional filters to help people deal with fraught situations. Lawyers come in when people can't communicate any longer. In your case, I'm sure your own lawyers would recommend that you cease all contact with Amir's mom. How do you feel about that?"

"You mean, with assuming my communication with her would go bad? Well, if someone on the street became nasty and belligerent, I would say, 'You're not supposed to talk to me like this. If you continue, this conversation is over!' But in her case, as a psychiatrist, I should say, 'Tell me more. Tell me why you feel this way.'

"I would try to understand why she's acting this way and what I could do to calm her down. Then, if I was lucky or more experienced, I might see some solution right away. It could be one word, it could be one expression, it could be one reminder, or it could be one idea that could help her. Putting my own emotions aside helps me think of such possibilities. The problem is that I'm not yet that skilled.

"Today, I saw an out-of-control hypersexual Polish man. He was in restraints after attacking a nurse, grabbing her, and pulling down her panties. No one understood him. There was a huge commotion, and everyone was screaming. I started speaking Polish and immediately caught his attention. I spoke softly, almost whispering, so the patient had to move his head toward me to hear. I felt confident that I'd be able to calm him down, and it was surprisingly easy. After listening to me for a minute, he started to address me how Poles address their priests, as *prosze ksiedza,* monsignor. Despite intense staff pressure to shoot him up with some horse tranquilizer, I just listened to him. Then he started to cry and asked my forgiveness. I don't have a style as a psychiatrist yet, but I hope I'm developing one. I'm still baking!"

CHAPTER 36

LIKE KEATS'S TRAGIC, NOBLE KNIGHT in *La Belle Dame sans Merci,* abandoned by the beautiful and merciless Lady, Jan walked in pale and woebegone. Today's session was going to be heavy.

"I feel like I felt a few months ago. I want to tell Amir's mother I have many thoughts that mirror hers. She accuses me of things for which I blame myself. For example, I wonder if I should have put him in the hospital against his will, even though I thought it would destroy his soul. He told me that being in a psychiatric hospital was worse than death, but now I think it would have been worth it.

"I told him it would be a safe place where changes in medication could be better managed. Although he communicated a general sense of being depressed, he never told me about suicidal plans *when* he had them, only weeks later. The day he died, I wouldn't have thought to put him in the hospital."

"Did you get another letter from Amir's mom?" I asked.

Jan sighed. "Yes, since we spoke last time, she sent me another letter. I'd like you to take a look at it."

I accepted the letter, but before I could read it, Jan continued, "Basically, she said that I was negligent and, therefore, fully responsible for Amir's death. Reading it, I had a horrible feeling of being trapped, with no way out. Even before getting the letter, I've felt responsible for Amir's death. I've endlessly ruminated about the signs of his suicidality that I missed and the rescue options I overlooked. She just substantiated and fixed my guilty conscience. Again, the day he died, the day he committed suicide, I

355

had no reason to put him in the hospital. He talked of going to some party, for God's sake. I can't even tell her this, that he was talking about buying a new suit for a party he intended to go to, that he wanted to buy flowers and a gift for a girl he had a crush on."

Jan felt, sequentially, irredeemably guilty and then genuinely blameless. When he felt responsible for Amir's death, he wanted to be punished, and Amir's mother did a good job of it. Still, he was also beginning to disclaim responsibility for the unpredictable loss of Amir's life. He couldn't bring himself to have these two opposing feelings at once, but that was what he needed to do to come to terms with what happened. When circumstances reawakened those feelings, like receiving a letter from Amir's mother, his agony would return once again. Nothing could take away the reality of the tragedy, but reflecting on *all* of his feelings simultaneously, as he was starting to do, would slowly give him some measure of relief. He had to do it at his own pace, however, preferably by starting to reconcile his guilt and his blamelessness, so I held my tongue.

Jan's emotions shifted, for now, to the non-guilty mode. "Amir's love interests were peculiar and hard to figure out. One girl was unstable, clearly borderline. Two others were lesbians. After they broke off the relationship, he continued to communicate with them. He asked me if he was doing the right thing. I said, 'I can't tell.' After a while, the Russian lesbian got mad and told him, 'I only like girls. Get that into your head!' He didn't give up because he believed he could transform her into a heterosexual. It was crazy.

"The last time I saw him, he was on his way to a party. It was confusing for him. A lesbian girl who had rejected him previously invited him to a party. Because she had rejected him, it confused him that she asked him to come to the party. He, now, felt hopeful that he could win her back. So, he wanted to look great and had difficulty deciding what to wear. He tried to impress her with a gift but had no idea what to buy her.

"I was satisfied that he wasn't suicidal. I asked him specific questions, and he said he was OK. We discussed my upcoming vacation. He knew I would be gone for two weeks, but I didn't tell him I was going to get married, and I don't believe he heard it from anywhere else. He asked for some samples of an antidepressant, and I gave them to him."

"Amir's mother's feelings are understandable," I said. "She's saying that Amir's death is your fault and that she can never forgive you." I handed the letter back, unread. I felt Jan had already described its contents.

"Amir's death *is* all my fault, and I can never forgive myself. She'll never know that right after he died, I blamed myself. If she had asked me then, I would have agreed with her. With your help, I've understood that I had a share in his death, but other factors played a role, too. All of this changed yesterday. Amir's mother doesn't know that Amir communicated his suicidal thoughts to me only two weeks after he had them, and she doesn't know about his feelings about psychiatric hospitalization. She thought that, as a doctor, I could do anything I wanted at any time, including locking him up in a psychiatric unit against his will. Because of that fundamental misunderstanding, she thinks his suicide is my fault.

"Just as you helped me lessen my excessive self-blame, I have tried to reduce her self-blame. In this last letter, though, she flung all the blame back on me.

"There was something peculiar about Amir's attitude toward women. I never pinpointed it till the very end: painful ambivalence. He was both condescending and loving toward women, so he didn't know how to deal with them. This was an underlying cause for his sexual inhibitions. His roommate tried to help him by encouraging him to watch porn on the Internet. Ohhh, there's a ton of information Amir's mom isn't aware of . . . and never will be! Or, at least I hope not. I don't remember how much I wrote about his hostility and negative feelings toward his father in my notes. As I told you, I haven't been able to bring myself to read his record. It's probably a good thing you can't put down everything a patient says, verbatim, into progress notes. I certainly wouldn't tell them anything that isn't there."

"How do you intend to respond to her letter?" I asked. Notwithstanding the earlier discussion, I had a hunch he had already responded rather than turning the letter over to the department lawyers.

"I already did. I said, 'I'm sorry that you feel the way you do. I worked closely with your son. I respected him. I don't believe I was negligent in treating him.' But because the tone of her letter clearly suggested that she felt I was negligent, I just acknowledged it. I said that she had a right to pursue legal options if she wished. I signed it and sent it.

"I thought of calling you to ask your opinion but decided against it. So I have to start making decisions on my own."

I appreciated that Jan felt that he should make autonomous decisions. Still, Jan had already made numerous good critical decisions: becoming an oncologist, taking decisive actions while treating his cancer patients, choosing to leave his home country, getting married, deciding to become a father.

Jan continued, "I considered writing that maybe I was lacking experience as a psychiatrist but decided against it. By now, she knows that I'm a resident. I was upset by the suicide, and I know that she's devastated. I wanted to tell her to keep an open mind because she didn't know all the facts. For instance, I don't think he communicated his previous suicidal preoccupations to her. Caring for him was complicated. It's hard to describe the psychiatric treatment of another human being. Amir was far worse off than I imagined. We shared some similarities, and I kept assigning my strengths to him. He was a confusing person because, in some areas, he was extremely competent, and in others, he was surprisingly impaired. She couldn't see his sickness and perceived him as successful and accomplished. Therefore, she feels I was negligent."

"How fixed do you think her opinion is that he died due to your negligence?" I asked.

"I don't know. I really don't know. In our first communication after his death, she said she wanted to scream at me, but she acknowledged that I really cared for him after exchanging a few letters. Then she became bitter and said that, as a Christian doctor, I would soon forget him and move on with my life. That couldn't be further from the truth. Amir isn't gone from my mind. I can't forget him."

"I have three questions for you: Is dialogue with Amir's mom possible? Is dialogue with her desirable? And do you want to engage her in dialogue? Let's look at the first question: Is it possible for you to talk to her?"

"I don't know. You once said that if she decides to sue at some point, it becomes a legal matter. If that happens, it's out of my hands, and the lawyers will lead the process. A dialogue is possible, but the American court system will conduct it. When I think of India and the Muslim culture, I see suicide bombers, kidnappings, and other violent events. I see fanatical killers with no respect for human life. I know it's bigoted and unrealistic, but this is what I irrationally and intrusively think."

Everything Jan feared could well come to pass, but I was glad to note that Jan was aware of his own irrationality, what he called his *paranoia*.

"When she thinks of me, she probably sees someone who participated in the killing of her son for being a Muslim. She refers to his 'alleged suicide.' Evil visions of America influence her. Maybe she feels that there was a conspiracy, and I'm involved in a cover-up."

Jan paused a moment and then asked himself my question. "Do I *want* to talk to her? Yes, I want to talk to her. She should be able to come here. I'd like her to get to know me. At the same time, I'm afraid that she's stuck in her thinking about Amir's death and wouldn't accept any of my explanations. It would open a Pandora's Box of fear and suspicion. What if she's already plotting revenge and isn't interested in what I have to say? My mind creates awful scenarios, and even knowing how crazy they are doesn't seem to help. I would rather be safe than sorry.

"So, I guess my answer to your question is 'I don't know.' I don't want her near my home. I don't want her to know about my wife and my son. I don't want to talk to her in this frame of mind. Then again, I realize I'm a parent just like her. I'd want to know if I were in her shoes, so she has a right to know.

"I want to tell her that I made the mistake of not realizing that Amir was going to kill himself. I had no idea. I invited him to my office for an additional visit because, in his e-mail, he seemed more depressed, but when I saw him, I didn't feel that he was suicidal. So I asked him, and he said, 'No. No. No. Not now. I'm going to a party. Thoughts of suicide cross my mind from time to time, but not now. I've had those thoughts for years, but not now.' I'd seen him in worse condition in the past, and I'd talked to him about hospitalization."

"For discussion's sake," I said, "there are three possible outcomes to your communication efforts: The first, most positive, outcome is that, together, you and Amir's mother come to some terms with Amir's death, she with her loss and you with your sense of guilt and responsibility. In this scenario, she continues to feel that you were responsible but not negligent. The endpoint is a shared sense of grief and the feeling that the dialogue was meaningful.

"The second is a standoff, where she thinks you were responsible *and* negligent. You accept partial responsibility but deny negligence. Finally, you both agree there is no purpose in further communication.

"The third, and worst, the possibility is that she insists that Amir died because of your negligence, and you accept your responsibility but deny negligence, but—unlike in the second scenario—you remain tethered because you continue to communicate. She periodically sends you heartfelt, hurtful letters that crush you and make you suffer for extended periods, creating a crazy situation where she is being sadistic, and you are being masochistic.

"The first outcome is adaptive and optimal, the second reflects a realistic possibility, and the third is pathological. What do you think of the scenarios I've described?"

"You have a gift for creating examples that help me think. Until I got this last letter, I felt that she and I could help each other. I hoped that we could have the first and most optimistic outcome. Now, I don't know if that's possible. When I read her last letter, I thought it was over. A court is the only place to establish if I was negligent. My response to her was that I respected her son and didn't feel that I was neglectful. I hope that she will write to me again."

"Having reflected on the situation, how do you feel about your response?"

"It took six hours to write a twenty-word reply. I was upset because I couldn't answer her promptly. I kept deleting what I wrote and trying again. Finally, I wrote, 'You don't have sufficient information to make certain judgments' and then deleted it. I felt disappointed and resigned. If I couldn't engage her, the next step would probably be going to court."

"I realize it was agonizing for you to figure out how to respond and have an informal interaction. But, by the time you wrote the last sentence to her, did you think that future communications with her would be formal or informal?"

"I was afraid that she would misinterpret whatever I said. She has a lot to learn about the system. For instance, when she requested the medical records, I told her that she should send her request to the medical records office, that I wasn't authorized to release them, and I gave her all the contact numbers. If she chooses the formal route, she could be deciding to go to court. From that point on, her lawyer will speak for her. The University lawyers will speak for the University and me."

"I think you're working toward an optimal solution," I said, "while still preparing to deal with all possible outcomes."

"I'm becoming more paranoid. I'm not sure of the extent of her anger, so I fear for my family. I imagine horror-movie outcomes. I'll just have to wait and see what happens."

I became concerned that our discussion had made things worse for Jan. I began to feel that there was a fate worse than the three scenarios I had outlined. I felt that Jan had become paralyzed writing his response, was becoming unhinged, and that we needed to focus on his well-being. Could I do anything to alleviate the negative impact of this session? "What is your sense of the value of our discussion today?" I asked.

"I can't talk to anybody else. It's frustrating. Holding it back and trying to bottle it up affects my mood, sleep, anxiety level, enjoyment of my work, and personal life. After the letter came, I didn't feel like talking to

Maria because I didn't want to infect her with my paranoia about David and Muslim suicide bombers."

"I think it's important that you want to protect Maria from your fears."

"Even if I weren't seeing you, I would never impose such fears on her. I do immensely appreciate you and the haven you provide. You give me a sense of safety that I can't find anywhere else, a time and place where I can talk about my fears without worrying about overburdening my wife. If I didn't have our discussions, my fears would never disappear. I'd be stuck in the state of mind I was in before I started seeing you. I'm better now than I was then, but images of suicide bombers still haunt me."

I felt that Jan was emotionally stirred up and might take actions that could be harmful. I said, "If and when you communicate with Amir's mother, there's a risk that you may provoke her, so—"

Jan interrupted, "—I know what you're talking about. You said it once, and you don't have to explain any further. That's what was on my mind, exactly. It's why I sat in front of the computer screen for so long and produced twenty words! I don't want to create an unnecessary storm."

"I think you've concluded that, although you may experience a strong urge to counter her assertions, it's futile. Besides, you told me that you weren't negligent, but she is fixed on the idea that you were. It will be hard, if not impossible, for her to give it up, so—"

Jan interrupted again, "—defending myself was wrong."

"I think she's in an angry phase of mourning," I said. "She wants to lash out at somebody, and right now, that's you. You may say you weren't negligent, but her view is that you were. What's more, she wants to whip you into submission so that you'll crawl back to her and whimper, 'Yes, I'm guilty. Yes, I was negligent.' She'll continue to whip you as long as you allow it. It's difficult to present a minimal target in this situation. Let me try to put myself in your shoes. I think you can say to her, 'I appreciate how hard it was for you to lose your son, and . . . and . . . I appreciate your letter.' Or perhaps, 'I received your letter. I don't have the words to respond to you meaningfully, but I thank you for this communication.'"

"You're trying to say that less is more, yes? Maybe I should have waited a few days before I responded."

"Jan, your response was your response. The purpose of this discussion is to clarify certain principles of communication. This discussion can serve as an exercise in minimalism. The case, as a clinical matter, is closed. You and Amir's mother can't come to a private agreement about whether you were negligent. Only a court of law can establish negligence. She by herself cannot establish it, nor can you. It takes two opposing parties, their respective lawyers, a jury, and a legal process. In the meantime, it's important not to inadvertently say anything that might compromise your position in court if it ever came to that. I think the main thing is not to make her angrier or more sadistic." I noticed that Jan had become pensive. "You reacted to me. What I said made your eyebrows furrow."

"No. No. No. I wanted my response to be balanced, and I think that—after hours of trying—I pretty much hit the right note. Now, with a few days having transpired and today's session, I see that I could have written a leaner and better response. If she writes again, I need to keep our discussion in mind. There's no proper way to describe how I feel toward her. I'm glad I told her, 'I'm sorry that you feel this way.' I don't know . . ."

Jan's voice trailed off, and then he fell silent.

After a while, I said, "No one truly knows how to respond in such situations. I know that you have the honesty, strength, dignity, and will to deal with Amir's mother as a human being. The fact is that it's not entirely up to you. Whether she has the willingness and ability to reciprocate in a like fashion is now the question. Is she willing to make some peace with the tragedy? Can you both let this gaping wound heal over into a scar? That remains to be seen. If she communicates again, you may have some indication."

"*If* there is another letter! If not, this letter will remain on my mind as long as I live . . ."

After a long pause, Jan spoke in a softer, more reflective tone, "I wish she would answer. You're probably right. As much as I tried not to trigger a storm in her mind, I may have done just that. Things are so twisted."

After a long silence, I said, "She has a right to be angry, but you have a right to get on with your life."

"Our thoughts are overlapping. I thought I was an irresponsible and neglectful doctor and wondered if I should continue to be a doctor . . . a psychiatrist. She pushed exactly those buttons. Just so you don't think I'm totally unreasonable, let me make one thing clear: I hope that some closure with Amir's mom is possible, but I don't plan to try to achieve any closure with Amir's father."

"It's been a difficult week for you," I said, "but I'm glad that we had a chance to talk. You're leaving the door open, and we have to see what she does. You have to recognize that she wants to be angry; in fact, she *needs* to be angry. Communication between her and you has the potential to heal or to make things worse. Your response was a good one. Now, it's up to her."

"I can't contain myself. I'm so impulsive."

"You said that you experienced an impulse to call me but didn't. Why?"

"I'm old enough to make decisions on my own. After all, I'm a freaking attending! I *do* make my own decisions regularly, and I think most of them are good."

"Yes," I said.

"Maybe the impulse was there because you're the only person who knows all the details."

"You make your own decisions. This is true. I have my own opinions, and they don't bind you in any way. We see how another human thinks and access alternative explanations in our conversations. That's all. But I want you to know that, please do, if you ever want to call me. I'm always available."

"Actually, I just realized something: I didn't want you to know about this letter. I was ashamed to show you what she wrote about me. I didn't want anybody to see or know about it. She read my mind, and I didn't want you to do the same. Amir is dead, but *my* life is going on. I had difficulties because of his death, and, mostly thanks to you, I overcame them. I'm not always going to be unhappy because of Amir. I love Maria and David, and nothing can spoil that. Nothing can take my love away.

"Amir is a life- and career-defining patient. I love and respect him, but his mother will never understand how important he was and still is to me."

"Jan, these are my concluding thoughts for today, and I want you to respond to them. You just said that you live simultaneously as a spouse, a parent, and a professional, each identity representing a sphere of your life. When you first came to see me, the professional—in the form of Amir—overshadowed the others. Yet, you have worked to create balance in yourself. You have reclaimed the role of a spouse with Maria. You have created the role of a parent for yourself with David. And in this last hour, you transformed yourself."

"This is true. It is true of today. Amir's mother's letter sent me back in time, and I regressed. I had a consult this morning and lost my confidence in making a simple diagnosis."

"Your self-doubts had increased," I said, affirming the cause.

"I had to keep pushing the '3' button on the phone. It's the one for rewinding during dictation. I just wasn't sure of anything I said. Now, after our talk, I feel less restless. Do you have any other thoughts or advice before we stop?"

"Yes, see the movie *Becket*," I blurted out, almost involuntarily. I was rather surprised by Jan's question. Upon reflection, I felt that this had been a gut-wrenching session for him. However, as I had already signaled that the session was ending, perhaps his question was intended to get me to say something that would allow him to linger a little longer by prolonging the conversation.

"Shall I tell you why?" I asked.

"No," Jan replied. "Let me see if I can figure it out myself."

"You're on," I said, smiling. Then, hoping to cushion his departure after such a difficult session, I added, "We'll meet again, *soon*."

CHAPTER 37

Jan arrived, somewhat flustered. "I was afraid I was going to be late. The traffic is so unpredictable. Even when it rains only a little, Yankees slow to a crawl. With all due respect to my adopted country, they don't do this in Europe. Europeans slow down when it rains, but not like this."

Calmer now, Jan continued, "I haven't gotten an answer from Amir's mom. I was looking for it, checking my mailbox every day. So that you know, *Becket* will be out on DVD in a few weeks. I read about it, and it has a great cast: Peter O'Toole, Richard Burton. I moved it to the #1 position on my Netflix queue. I saw it in Poland a long time ago, when it was first released, but I'd forgotten. So I read the reviews and refreshed my memory."

"And?"

"They say that King Henry II and Thomas Becket had a beautiful relationship; they were party boys, drinking buddies. When Henry became King of England, he appointed his friend Becket to become the Archbishop of Canterbury, the highest position in the Anglican Church. The King was primarily interested in his royal powers, while the Archbishop had responsibilities to the Church and felt loyalty only to God. Their friendship changed, as a result, into something cruel and ugly. I want to see the movie again and figure out why you said I should."

"Yes, Becket, the Archbishop, and Henry II, King of England, battled over the conflicting rights and privileges of Church and State. Finally, Henry declared, 'Will no one rid me of this troublesome priest?' Four knights, the King's henchmen, heard him, and on December 29, 1170, they killed Becket in Canterbury Cathedral. T. S. Eliot called it *Death in the Cathedral*. Maybe the title *Murder in the Cathedral* would have been more apt."

365

I knew at once that I had misspoken, misremembering the play's title as *Death in the Cathedral,* when it *was Murder in the Cathedral.* (The word *death* came from a false connection with Arthur Miller's play, *Death of a Salesman.* In that play, Willy Loman, an aging salesman, is guilt-ridden for cheating on his wife. Whereas Loman couldn't bear the pain of his guilt and killed *himself* by crashing his car, Henry II "drove" his henchmen to the church and had *them* kill Becket. But, of course, the King preferred killing Becket, the guilt of ordering the murder of Thomas Becket, and then receiving lashes across his back, rather than the continued presence of his meddlesome old friend.)

I found that the *death/murder* error was interesting to *me* but seemed irrelevant to Jan. I wasn't sure if he had read Miller's play but felt confident that this was not the time to go into it. So I let my error drop. "I want you to see the opening scene, which is completed only at the end of the movie."

"Tell me."

"The scene starts with the face of Peter O'Toole, playing the King. You hear the crack of a whip and see him wince. You know, Peter O'Toole is good at wincing. In the beginning, all you see is his face. Then, as the camera zooms out, you hear the order, 'Harder.' As the sound of the whip keeps getting louder, it becomes almost unbearable to watch. And then you realize that he's being whipped *at his own command,* as he tries to deal with the guilt he feels for ordering the killing of his friend. The story is about the King's unbearable guilt and his need to be punished."

"So, this was self-punishment."

"Yes."

"Henry wants redemption."

"Yes, this is a masochistic way of relieving himself of guilt."

"I see. Do you remember the woman I told you about who had an abortion? She doesn't whip herself, but she often starves herself. She deprives herself of everyday necessities and does her best to look unattractive. She thinks that if she looks pretty, she may attract a man who will have sex with her and get her pregnant. She believes that, because of the abortion, she doesn't deserve to have a child. This is how I understand her behavior."

"Do you remember the context in which I asked you to see this movie?" I asked.

Jan laughed anxiously. "I remember that you wanted to tell me, and I told you not to. I told you I wanted to see the movie first, and then I would try to guess why you thought it was relevant to me."

"Regarding the movie, the horse has left the stable: I've already summarized it for you. But you can still make a guess. I suggested you see the movie toward the end of an extraordinary session when we discussed three possible communication outcomes between Amir's mom and you.

"The first was productive: Communication would result in you and her working through your respective losses regarding Amir. After some discussion, she would appreciate your view that you were responsible but not negligent.

"The second was a stalemate: She would continue to insist that you were responsible *and* negligent, while you would stand firm that you were accountable but not negligent. Your positions remained unchanged. Since Amir's mother and you would not be in direct contact, only the lawyers would have the headaches and also get rich.

"The third would be malignant: She would insist that you were responsible and negligent, *and* she would continue to punish you with letters telling you so. By reading them, you would be colluding in her efforts to punish you, and by responding, you would be encouraging her to provoke still more guilt."

"The assumption that Amir's mom is inducing guilt in me is wrong," Jan protested. "I already felt guilty."

"That's true. What I mean is that she whips up your guilt and, like Henry II, you are asking for more punishment. After a good licking, I'm sure that even Henry asked for the whipping to stop at some point. I wonder how much more punishment you will take before you say 'Stop.'"

"I went through such emotional turmoil in the past week. It took a long time to write a short reply denying I was negligent. It would have been better not to answer her than to send what I wrote, even though I thought a lot about what she said. I didn't want you to get involved. I wanted to do it myself. Amir's mom blamed herself for letting Amir come to the U.S. and for letting me treat him. I know a lot about self-blame and tried to address hers. Then I got defensive. In fact, she didn't put Amir in my hands. He did.

"Amir was ambivalent about his mother. As a teenager, he became religious and insisted that she do so, too. Later on, when he lost his faith, his mother used his own words to bring him back, and he got mad at her. Amir and I talked a lot about his father, too. He mentioned him in every session.

"Amir was chronically broken-hearted. He talked a lot about his students and teaching assistants. There were several students he tutored in math. Some were young, and some were much older. He wasn't picky. He fantasized about them all! He tended to fall in love with either unstable women or lesbians, so his love life was never successful. I knew almost everything about his circle of friends, both Indian and Western. I felt I knew him well, but his mother didn't know much about his life in the U.S.

"In her last letter, Amir's mother tried to place the entire blame for his suicide on me, and it made me angry. So I asked myself, 'Why does she do it?' My answer is that she's in pain.

"After receiving her letter, I realized that he wasn't my only depressed and suicidal patient. There's an older German woman I'll call . . . Greta, who came here after World War II, and she still speaks with a heavy German accent. She touches a spot in me that I don't understand. She had a son who was 52 when his first wife died, leaving him with a baby daughter. He had a hard time taking care of the child and, in desperation, remarried quickly. The new wife avoided Greta and kept her from seeing her son and her granddaughter. And, the new wife didn't even seem to care about him.

"Greta's son had diabetes, and his new wife was always baking cakes he liked. But, of course, eating them made his condition worse. And she would let him go for days without taking insulin. When the first wife was alive, the son listened to Greta when she encouraged him to take his medicine and go to the doctor. Still, after he remarried, he became apathetic about his health, even after he ended up in the hospital a few times. Greta urged the new wife to be more proactive and encourage him to be more responsible, but the wife said her husband was an adult and could decide for himself whether to follow his doctor's recommendations. Then, one day, he had a heart attack. His young daughter found him on the bathroom floor and screamed, but the stepmother watched TV and didn't respond for a long time. It was too late by the time she decided to find out why the girl was calling her.

"I saw Greta this week. She is furious at her daughter-in-law. Throughout the session, she kept saying, 'My son is dead. She killed him. She's totally responsible for his death.' My first temptation was to remind her that she instructed her daughter-in-law to get him to go to the doctor and had never insisted herself, but I resisted. Greta was so sure that her daughter-in-law killed her son that there was no other option but to agree with her.

"At that moment, I saw Amir's mother in Greta. I was glad that I didn't say, 'You should reconsider.' I realized that it wasn't the right time for me to talk. The best intervention was to shut my mouth, so I kept quiet and listened. I saw that, just as Greta brands the second wife as a 'killer,' Amir's mother brands me as a 'killer.'"

Bravo, I thought, and I, too, kept my mouth shut.

After a while, Jan added, "I doubt I'll ever be able to make a dent in Greta's belief. Finally, I said to her, 'I understand how hard it is for you. You want to maintain contact with your granddaughter. She's all you have of your son. Figuring out how to remain part of her life is hard. What are you planning to do?'

"Greta appreciated what I said, but her relief was short-lived. She regretfully announced, 'Doctor, I know you want to help me, but I don't want to talk to that bitch.' It was funny to hear an old woman in her seventies saying *bytsch*, with a German accent. However, it's been 14 months since her son's death, and Greta's strong opinion concerning her daughter-in-law is unchanged.

"I feel that the same vicious energy that exists between Greta and her daughter-in-law is what exists between Amir's mom and me."

Amir paused for a moment. "But I was in a bind," he continued. "Amir felt that psychiatric hospitalization—being admitted to a 'cuckoo's nest'— would be worse than death. That's how I feel, too. And he felt the same about being forced to take psychotropic medications. I could have gone to the mental health court and told the judge that Amir was suicidal and imminently in danger of killing himself, and he would have been forced to take medications by a court order. But, because of the similarities between our lives, I assumed that he wouldn't take things so far."

"Right."

"I knew that Amir was gambling with suicidal ideas, and that scared me. I knew he was finding pleasure in thinking about suicide. And even though I knew about his deep angst and dark side, I was convinced that, because I would never kill myself, he wouldn't, either. But he was who he was."

Jan's thinking swerved. "I was neglectful. I didn't do what was right. I should have put him in the hospital. But I thought that we had a good relationship, and I knew how he felt about hospitalization. I never thought he would kill himself, and I didn't see any warning signs even in the last session. So my conclusion was that he wasn't suicidal, so I didn't see any reason to hospitalize him."

"Do you feel that Greta and her daughter-in-law can have a dialogue?"

"No. Referring to her daughter-in-law, she said, 'I don't want to know her.'"

"You told me that you feel there are similarities between Greta and her daughter-in-law, on the one hand, and Amir's mom and yourself, on the other. Given that you specifically feel that Greta can't have a dialogue with her daughter-in-law, how do you gauge the chances that you can have a dialogue with Amir's mom?"

"Hopefully, she's gone through some of the stages of mourning and grief. After Amir's death, when we spoke on the phone, she said to me, 'You made mistakes, but I know you cared for him.' So, at some point, she believed that. In Greta's case, she never liked her daughter-in-law and always saw her as no good. Greta wants to have a relationship with her granddaughter, and she needs her daughter-in-law to do this, but Amir's mom has no use for me. So, I'm going to continue trying to dialogue with her."

"I think you're saying that the only intervention that has any chance of succeeding is acknowledging the main areas of agreement and disagreement between Amir's mom and you. Currently, she disagrees with you and feels that you were neglectful and responsible for her son's death. In the past, she was more charitable, and because of that, your hope may be rational. However, hoping for more than what the facts allow is masochistic. It's also a false hope. Is this a reasonable summary?"

"Yes."

"Your German lady is ambivalent because she wants to continue seeing her granddaughter. There's nothing for the daughter-in-law to do until Greta makes the request. Likewise, there's no opening for therapeutic action in the case of Amir's mom and you. You just have to stay where you are and wait for a sign from her. I'm not saying I'm right but merely stating my point of view. Any thoughts?"

"Despite all the risks and despite advice from the legal department, I'm tempted to reopen communication with Amir's mom. I feel that I owe it to Amir. I wrote a lot in my notes about him—detailed accounts of events and relationships in his childhood, especially with his parents. He resented his father deeply, his mother, less so. I haven't had the guts to read what I wrote since his death, but his family has a copy, and they have to live with what I wrote. I feel that, after they're done blaming me, they'll begin to torture themselves, so I owe them complete transparency."

"What do you mean?"

"Amir's parents' pain was and is a million times more intense than mine. They watched him grow up. They put their hopes and ambitions in him. They may not be able to make any sense of my notes. If I could have a conversation with Amir's mom, I could explain them. I think the fact that she bottled up her feelings for a long time triggered this angry communication.

In one of her letters, she wrote, 'Your explanations are not satisfactory to us.' But I hadn't given her any explanations! I told her, 'I don't know why it happened.' I felt that his depression was getting worse, which was why I met with him before I left. I had gone on vacation before, and he had done fine. And he knew who was covering for me."

"What do you want to tell Amir's mom now?"

Jan shifted gears. "I want to tell her, 'Your suggestion of negligence will have some legal consequences. The lawyers of the University will speak for me. The legal machinery has started, and the situation may already be out of my hands. You'll face the wall of the American system, which will be very hard to scale. You'll feel that nobody cared about Amir.' I want to tell her that that is not the case and that I don't want to hide behind that wall. Then, I'd like to have a direct conversation with her, although such a conversation would be difficult for her . . . and me.

"The administrative, legal process can be aggravating. For example, the University will first have to establish that she is the mother of a deceased patient. Then, she'll have to go through lawyers to get information and can't expect to receive informal communications with people involved in his care.

"I'm afraid that the University lawyer would say to me, 'If your patient's parents have a legal problem, let them engage a lawyer. The Court will settle all legal issues. If I need your testimony, I'll contact you.'"

I said, "You want to talk to her and be available to her, and you want to initiate a conversation with her, correct?"

"I want her to know that a legal wall will be facing her. But behind it, I am willing to talk to her. I want to validate her feelings. I know she's angry with me, and I want to acknowledge that she has reason to be angry with me. I don't think I'll tell her that I agree with her and that she's merely repeating my own thoughts. If she gets lawyers involved, though, it will fortify the wall and prevent any further communication."

"I want to clarify one point: In an angry letter, she blamed you and said that she may or may not contact you again. I know you want to have a conversation with her. Does it matter to you if *she* wants to have that conversation?"

"Of course, it does. Of the many options she has, she could decide to forget that I ever existed. She did say that she wasn't sure if she could communicate with me anymore. That's the possibility you've just raised. Maybe she said that in the heat of the moment, but she keeps searching for an answer. I want our communication to continue being personal. I don't want to be restrained by lawyers."

Jan hesitated a moment.

"There are some things I would never tell her—like Amir's elaborate, unfulfilled sexual fantasies. I don't want to talk to her about the intimate details of his life. She said, 'After all these months, you've probably forgotten about Amir.' I want her to know that, quite to the contrary, I think about him every day."

"The essence of what you want to say is that you think about Amir every moment and that you're willing to talk to her. Now, my question to you is, 'Why do you dwell on the legal smokescreens, not of your making, that she'll have to face'?"

Jan chuckled. "I didn't want to mention this to her. But I know that if she pursues a legal route, that's what she'll be facing from now on."

I wondered why Jan laughed at that moment. I felt that he was caught between two conflicting impulses. His conscious, benevolent impulse was to bend over backward to understand and support Amir's mom. But I felt that he also harbored an unconscious, hostile impulse to get back at her for torturing him. In other words, Jan's laugh was a manifestation of his *schadenfreude* at her potential misfortune at the hands of the lawyers. I concluded, though, that he was too deeply rooted in his conscious impulse to be able to consider this idea, so I sat tight and kept my mouth shut.

"Is it your job or the lawyer's job to explain the walls of legal rules and regulations?" I asked. "Who should tell her that lawyer-to-lawyer contact is necessary for legal communications and that direct contact between litigants is inappropriate?"

"The point is that that's what she would be facing from now on."

I noted that Jan hadn't answered my question and was still preoccupied with the legal wall. "Presumably, she would have her lawyer clarify why such legal procedures exist. Still, I think it's important for you to consider how you treat her, but it is also important to consider how you treat yourself. So, to be blunt, are you acting in your best interests? I ask because you are communicating with Amir's mom against your lawyers' instructions."

"I see. I see. The problem is that it's already too late for her to avoid getting involved with the lawyers. I don't know if she realizes that she started a legal process by making these inquiries."

I noticed that, yet again, Jan hadn't answered my question. Perhaps he felt cornered by my asking whether he was taking care of Number One. I did feel a little pang of remorse for suggesting that he first take care of himself: Psychoanalysts don't like to be caught making suggestions. Right now, Jan and I were having a failure to communicate.

Jan mumbled something that I didn't understand, and then he went silent. Finally, after a while, he spoke: "You're right. There's a strong need for humans who have suffered a loss to blame someone. Acceptance is never the first stage of grieving, right?"

"Yes. I want to stipulate that, as far as I'm concerned, you're 100% free to do what you want, to use or discard any of my ideas. I'm just responding to what you're saying."

"Amir's mom sees me as part of a conspiracy that killed her son. At this point, she's focused on me and the hospital system protecting me. But, unfortunately, she may yet expand her suspicions to the whole United States! I took a course a few years ago, and the essence of the professor's message was, 'If you have to jump on a live grenade to protect a patient, jump. Whatever you do as a practicing physician should be done for the good of the patient.' I took this lesson to heart, so it's hard for me to think of any other way to act, even if I hurt myself. I know this sounds counter-intuitive to you."

Throughout Jan's treatment, I noticed that his generosity sometimes veered into a tendency to jeopardize himself. However, he was improving in that he was more aware of it. I saw that Jan was letting me know that he was now conscious of his tendency to help others, even at the risk of his own welfare. My job was to move his unconscious or preconscious masochism into the conscious arena so that he could examine it and decide whether to sustain it or change it. Jan would be able to improve it only after becoming more aware of his own best interests. Masochism is very sticky, though, and ideally, the patient himself must address it. If someone else tries to explore it, it can become even stickier and retreat, once again, into the unconscious. So I decided to wait for him to speak and clearly indicate that he wanted to change it.

"Amir's mom knows about me only from our limited but important communications. Because she knows that I was in training until recently, she may think that I am young. I'd like to sit with her and tell her about my relationship with her son, but I still feel obligated to protect his confidentiality. I have many doubts about whether she would understand that limitation. Initially, she believed that I cared about Amir. Later, she changed her mind and attacked me. If I had a chance to talk to her, I'm confident that she would end up concluding that I'd made wrong decisions but that I wasn't negligent. I'm sure that she wouldn't accuse me of not caring or not being compassionate."

"I understand how sincerely you feel this," I said. "Although she sees you as the bad guy, you want her to see you as a good guy. It could be that she wants to bury you, but you want to shake her hand."

"I'd like to talk to her like I'm talking to you. She'd be sitting where you are. I would love to be able to do that. I want to tell her what I thought of Amir as a person. He never gave himself credit for all the goodness that was in him. What a shame that a guy in his twenties killed himself. Now she hates me because she thinks I caused it and that I belong to this evil system, that, I'm hiding the truth and giving her the runaround. I wish she knew that after Amir died, I was devastated, too. I felt that nobody really cared."

"Jan, you're one of a kind," I said tenderly. "You do really care."

"But I need to tell you something else. If she came, I would meet her on some neutral ground."

"Neutral ground?"

"I would never invite her to my home."

"Why not?"

"I'm afraid that she would kidnap or kill my son!"

I laughed. "That's the start of good and healthy paranoia!" I looked at the clock on the wall, and so did Jan. Our time was up.

Jan stood to leave but then turned toward me with a surprised expression. "What do you mean?"

"Good paranoia?"

He nodded.

I said, "By *good paranoia*, I mean the measures you will take to protect Maria, David, and your family from any real or imaginary enemies. *Good paranoia* makes you a better husband and father, and protects your family against excessive guilt and masochism!"

Jan didn't respond, but I think he seemed genuinely surprised and intrigued by what I said. Then he smiled. I hoped the smile indicated that he was starting to realize that he had to give up some of his guilt to get well.

I raised my hands as if toasting and said, "If paranoia could be a path to health, three cheers for good paranoia!"

CHAPTER 38

I HAD A DREAM. I was a guest at a traditional Muslim wedding reception in Hyderabad, India. Because of *purdah* (the convention of women wearing a veil), women were secluded and separated from the men. I was in a long procession of men arriving for the night function to greet the groom. I heard the beating of drums. Men carrying brightly lit Petromax lamps guided the guests toward a *shamiana*, a colorful ceremonial tent. One of the lamp carriers walked close to me. Looking directly through the pane of the glass lamp, I saw the filament's white-blue glow and felt temporarily blinded.

Once inside the tent, I noticed geometric motifs of arches and domes of an idealized Middle Eastern royal palace. A caravan of camels stood against a brown desert background and a blue sky outside the palace. The painted sides also had a repeating complex rosette pattern. The tent was held in place by a series of bamboo poles that held fluorescent tube lights, tied to the bars, and bathed the space in light. One of the tubes was blinking, and part of one side had turned black. Repairers were eyeing it and discussing the best way to fix it.

At one end of the space, the groom sat on a dais at the end of a long carpet, receiving guests and well-wishers. He was a handsome young man in a green silk *sherwani*, a calf-length coat, and a red *sehra,* a head garment tied to several strings of white flowers that hung down over his face. One by one, the guests greeted him, shook his hand, wished him a happy marriage, hugged him, and moved away to mingle with the others. From the way they approached the groom, it was clear that he was a beloved member of the family. He was self-assured and comfortable around his family and friends.

I walked toward him, and he smiled warmly. I noticed that his eyes were prominently lined with *kajal*-mascara. As I walked closer, under the streams of flowers, I spotted a prominent flaming boil on his nose, which I had not seen earlier from a distance. He extended his hand, and as I reached to shake it, he abruptly withdrew it, reaching into his pocket and retrieving a pistol, which he pointed at me. He had looked gracious and friendly until that moment, but his expression was now menacing, indicating an iron-willed determination to shoot me. I had the impulse to run away, but, to my surprise, I reached out and grabbed his outstretched arm, wrenched the gun away, and pointed it at him, ready to shoot. I was about to say something when my alarm clock startled me awake.

I woke up. I immediately realized that the groom in the dream was Amir. I recognized him because *I* was not myself; I was *Jan*, and Jan knew Amir from personal experience, not just from hearing about him. I had identified Amir based on experience in the dream, *just as Jan would have*. I felt in the grips of an infective killing spirit. At that moment, I felt the killing had started with the sacrifice of a camel. His father forced Amir to watch the blood-letting sacrifice.

The killing spirit Amir had was aimed at his father, but it took his own life instead. The spirit transferred its aim, maimed Jan, and now ricocheted into my subconscious. The feel of a pistol in my hand was novel, as I had never held one, but it reminded me of the Royal Enfield .303 rifle I used when I was in the National Cadet Corps at the camp Guntur. I loathed the idea of weapons or any act of killing in my waking life, but as Jan's surrogate, I was ready to squeeze the trigger in my dream.

I hoped it was only a brief and attenuated affliction and would help me develop some ideas about treating Jan. I suspected Jan himself had had that homicidal impulse I briefly sensed in my dream. It was a tiny but powerful feeling located in my right index finger. I believed that the desire to kill that I tasted was something Jan had also felt briefly but denied. Although so far, Jan had denied having this feeling toward Amir. I could speak to Jan about his killer *spirit*, in general, but it wasn't clear that he could understand what I meant regarding Amir. Things take time. I would get more ideas in my later discussions with Jan, and I hoped to convey some of these ideas into conversations from which he could benefit. I would wait for the moment when some path of interpretation opened up.

I pondered the other ways Amir's life might have gone. His mother loved him, and only if he were the best would his father love him. Amir's father dismissed him only because Amir did not conform to his father's image of an ideal son. It wasn't a lack of love; Amir's father wanted to be proud of him, but Amir didn't fit the mold. His parents could have married him off to some maiden had he allowed them to do so, and they all would have felt the joys and pain of so many other families. Instead, he was taught and learned how to pray to Allah as a growing child and adolescent. He knew the customs of his community, how to greet friends and reciprocate their love. Had he stayed put, he could have known where he belonged. He could have been one of the many and fit in.

But Amir had chosen to leave his land and come to America. The challenge of creating a new self in a land with few discernible culturally familiar landmarks proved too daunting. In his privacy, Amir had conjured the shape of a mate. His yearning drew him to several women. Yet, she evaporated when he tried to fit her into his dreams. Their independence and decisiveness blinded him, and he blinked. The flaming cauldron of the American melting pot consumed him. As I reflected on the actual course of his life, I felt the pain of Amir, his mother, and his father. The dream I had, Amir the Groom—the fulfillment of his parents' wish—was never to be.

CHAPTER 39

JAN LOOKED DOWNCAST.

"How are you?" I asked.

"I'm OK," he responded, not very convincingly. "I still haven't gotten a response from Amir's mom. Every day when the mail comes, I look to see if there's a letter from her. Maybe I should write again. I can't decide. I've been expecting a letter, even though there's always a delay before she writes. Maybe I need to be more patient."

"What's the relevance of your patience to this situation?"

"I'd like her to reply and continue the conversation. After talking to you and being helped by you, I know that I need to see what my words have triggered in her before I say anything else. That's where I need to be patient."

"Your situation is difficult. You want her to communicate with you, but you also dread it. The fact is that she will communicate—"

"—only at her pace."

I realized that Jan still thought that their communication would inevitably continue. I wanted to clarify that this was not the case. "Yes. If she chooses to communicate, the conversation can continue. If she chooses not to communicate, it's over. The ball is in her court."

"I understand what you're saying. Unfortunately, I'm too focused on this problem."

He paused. "It left me with a bad feeling. The lack of closure bothers me. She said all these things in her letter. My response was . . . Instead of listening to her, I said too much."

"A smooth ending is always desirable, but no one has a *right* to such a closure," I said.

"Yes."

"I want to tell you a story, a true story," I said. "There was a woman married to a violent man. One day, her husband smacked her. She was furious, so she hit him back. He picked up a vacuum cleaner and swung it at her but missed. She fought back, hands poised like a boxer's, punching him. She was white-hot with anger, adrenaline making her blood boil. She was so enraged that she had zero capacity to listen to anything or anybody. After she punched him, he took another swing at her with the vacuum cleaner. The blade at the bottom of the vacuum cleaner met her punching hand and chopped off a finger."

"Oww!"

"She had no idea what was happening. By now, her sister had heard the commotion and rushed in. She saw the blood dripping and ran to get a towel. The woman had no pain on the way to the emergency room—just anger. It's hard to stop when anger, fear, or hormones get you going.

"Amir's mom is like this woman. Her son is dead, and she needs to be furious. A John Donne poem ends ' . . . therefore send not to know for whom the bell tolls; It tolls for thee.'[47] You've heard it?"

"Yes."

"To me, it means that the moment Amir put that bullet through his skull, a good part of her died, too."

"I've observed changes in her," Jan said. "Earlier, she was just devastated and shocked. But now, she is suspicious and angry."

"Amir was her only son. Just like you, she went through a stage of deep mourning. Perhaps she's still in it and feels mostly dead. Now, she has only one emotion that makes her feel alive, and that feeling is—"

"—blame and anger toward me."

I nodded. "Right—anger allows her to feel alive. Blaming you gives her a sense of purpose. If she lets go of it, she'll feel dead again. She'll have to go back to her deep funk."

"You're right."

"I know you want her to say that you were responsible but not negligent, but attaching negligence to your responsibility keeps her together. She can't give it up."

---

47 Donne, J. (1624). "For whom the bell tolls," from Meditation XVII, *Devotions Upon Emergent Occasions.*

"Yes, it probably makes the most sense for her," Jan said softly. "She doesn't want to look at Amir's life, his experiences as a child, and his serious problems with adjusting to life in the U.S. She can't understand how he got so desperate. *She only wants to find the guilty one, the murderer.* I hoped she would apportion her anger to all the parties involved in the tragedy. But for her, my face is the face of the killer. She has no idea how the mental-healthcare system works. It works for many, but some feel mistreated or even abused by it. I can think of patients who were angry that they were committed against their will or forced to take tranquilizers because they can't remember that, at the time, they were dangerous, and the treatment was for their own good."

I responded by saying, "Amir's mother hasn't communicated with you for a long time, and in her last communication, she unleashed her understandable anger and blame. Since then, you've had the opportunity to reflect on the situation. You've felt and worked through your guilt. In the past, guilt drowned you. Now, you have David and Maria, who bring joy to your life."

"Yes," Jan said, "I worked through overwhelming guilt, and I think I've progressed. Now, there are new challenges in my life as a psychiatrist. I'm more cautious around suicidal patients without being too anxious, although I'm worried right now about one particular patient. I'll call her Alice. Alice is depressed, and all the medications we've tried have been useless. I talked to her about ECT—what people call electric shock—and she agreed to try. It worked wonders on most of my previous patients, but there was no benefit for her at all. She's as depressed as she was before. She sleeps 20 hours a day and doesn't leave her house for days. She doesn't think about suicide, but her melancholia has drained out all of her life force. I'm worried that something may set her off. She missed an appointment yesterday. When I called, I could hear intensified depression in her voice, just as I sensed the growing depression in Amir's last e-mail to me. Amir's e-mail had alarmed me, and I told him I had to see him again before leaving. He came, but I still didn't see the storm coming. I had a chance to do something, and I missed it. It's hard to push the fear out of my head that this might happen again. It's taking over my thoughts, and I'm having difficulty balancing my other work and home life. I usually call Maria several times a day, just to keep in touch. Today, I had a tough time remembering to call. I was just too preoccupied with Alice. A minute ago, I said I'm less anxious around suicidal patients, but what I said just now suggests I'm not. I guess I'm not sure how I feel."

I realized I hadn't been listening correctly to Jan. I was preoccupied with the conversation we had had a while back about how, sometimes, feelings can be communicated directly, without the use of words. So rather than responding to Jan, I chose to follow my own thinking. "Some time back, you spoke about certain smells or hormones that communicate . . ."

"Pheromones. They convey emotions that you can't consciously or specifically pinpoint. It's like you smell the feelings of the other person. It leaves you with a distinct sense that something either good or bad may happen."

"Since receiving the letter from Amir's mom, you see threats everywhere. Now, because of Alice, you smell danger everywhere. Just like in the months after 9/11, everything looks like a terrorist plot."

"Especially for us. Watching the U.S. news, the wholesale manipulation of fear was evident. That's why I watch BBC news. It allows me to relax."

"Now, in your case," I continued, "it's hard to distinguish between your patient's signaling of danger and your own increased *awareness* of danger."

"True. I don't know how much of it is my hangover from Amir, how much is from Alice, and how much is coming from my own fears, unrelated to Amir."

I thought that anchoring Jan's distress to a specific event might be more productive than sending him into a tailspin over those three possibilities, so I said, "Receiving that last letter from Amir's mom shook you up."

"I wanted to hear from her and was glad that she communicated with me. It's also true that my mood is in the pits right now. I've been in a state of high alert with other patients, too. One patient wrote a suicide note to her brother, saying, 'I love you. I know my suicide will hurt you, but I have no other option. I want you to know that I will always love you.' Then she took an overdose and came to the hospital. I asked her brother to come, and he brought the note with him. The patient claimed that she had no memory of writing it. When I first heard that she had attempted suicide, I felt like she had punched me. Yet again, I hadn't seen it coming. I thought I knew her. I thought she didn't hate herself enough, and she didn't have a history of acting impulsively. When I talked to her and realized that she was somewhat manipulative and not as depressed as Amir, the feeling of being punched suddenly disappeared."

Regardless of whether Jan's conclusion was correct, I could see that his self-awareness had increased. He had felt a knot in the pit of his stomach, discovered a way to understand it, and then managed the feeling.

"Because Amir thought that being admitted to the 'cuckoo's nest' would kill his soul, he downplayed his depression to prevent it," Jan said. "Now I feel that things might have been different if I had been firm with him and said, 'Amir, this is what needs to happen. You have to go to the hospital.' I should have told him, 'If you won't get admitted, I can't treat you anymore.' But I couldn't say anything like that to him."

It's consoling to imagine being firm.

"Your Monday-morning quarterbacking about being firmer with Amir is understandable," I acknowledged. "Sometimes, we wish that we had acted differently with patients, and sometimes that wish is hard to acknowledge. D. W. Winnicott, a great analyst, spoke of the hate that therapists sometimes feel toward patients." I had interrupted Jan's flow of associations. He continued addressing Amir directly as if he were alive, and I hadn't spoken.

"'Right now, you believe that killing yourself will solve all of your problems, but this feeling will pass if you give yourself a little time. You don't really want to kill yourself. Nobody does. I know you think that being in the hospital is a horrible thing, but in the hospital, we can watch you and make sure that you're safe during this critical time.'"

Jan looked at me and continued, "I could have manipulated him and insisted on hospitalization. Instead, I thought of taking him on a tour of the hospital to show him that it isn't like the hospital in *One Flew Over the Cuckoo's Nest*. I hate myself for not trying, and sometimes I hate him for being so obstinate. Now, I'm much quicker to assume the role of an authority figure with patients who are suicidal or dangerous. I just tell them we're going to the psychiatric ward. It doesn't give me any comfort that I learned my lesson the hard way and that the price of that lesson was someone's life. When I started to see you, I was involved in continuous self-torture with such thoughts. I did it every day, from the time I woke up until I finally fell asleep."

"You can choose what to do now," I said, "and you can choose what to do in the future, but you cannot choose what you already did in the past. You are working through your trauma and learning the lessons of a tragedy that happened, recognizing you cannot undo it. Hopefully, what you learn will enable you to do your job and prevent possible future suicides."

"You know what I think?"

"What?"

"This week, Alice didn't show up. I saw some patients, did chart dictations, and then sat in on the nurses' morning report. Then I remembered that it was my birthday. Because I'm at the age that I am, more than 40—"

"Belated Happy Birthday!" I interrupted.

"Thank you. So, I wondered if I'll ever be able to say things like what I've heard from you and Alvear-Reverte. He once said, 'The patient may be near the end of his or her rope, and all we can do is delay the moment.' I see so many opportunities that I missed. I wonder if someday I'll be able to accept, without feeling guilty about it, the fact that people do just kill themselves.

"I don't know why Amir killed himself that day. He left no suicide note. I don't know what he thought after he left my office. I had already told him that I would be away. During this session, I believed it would be the last before I left, we said goodbye, and I reminded him that I would return in two weeks. He seemed OK with it, but later, he sent me that e-mail indicating that he was depressed. I was concerned enough that I arranged to see him again before I left. When he came in, I asked him about the tone of the e-mail. He explained that he was obsessing about this girl who had previously rejected him. She had invited him to her party, and he didn't know what it meant. At the end of the session, he asked me for some medication samples and seemed to be looking forward to the party. I sensed he was depressed, but he also had plans. I didn't think to put him in the hospital.

"In the past, we've talked about similarities between Amir's life and mine. For sure, this clouded my view of Amir. I've been depressed in my life, and I wouldn't have wanted to be locked in a psychiatric hospital. I'm sure I would resent the person who put me there, even if he did it to save my life."

"I think you're right. Amir and you are similar in some ways. Heinz Kohut described the situation when a patient feels that the therapist and the patient are alternates for each other as an *alter-ego transference*.[48] I'm not sure if Amir felt this."

I continued, "Regardless of what Amir thought, *you* felt that he and you were similar. The feeling of similarity was *your* feeling. Therefore, we don't know if there was an alter-ego transference, but there was an alter-ego *countertransference*. As we've discussed, in your own depression, you never came to the point of true suicidality. There was a Polish Catholic wall that separated your depression from the act of suicide. Amir had no such

---

48 Kohut, H. (1968). "The psychoanalytic treatment of narcissistic personality disorders: Outline of a systematic approach." *Psychoanalytic Study of the Child, 23,* 86–113.

wall. Because of this alter-ego countertransference, you thought that your depression, lacking the danger of suicidal acting out, was like Amir's, so you concluded that, even though he was depressed, he wasn't suicidal and, therefore, and you could manage him on an outpatient basis. You two were also similar in rejecting inpatient psychiatric treatment. I'm not sure, but I think this is a new thought that you expressed today. In the past, I don't believe I've heard you say that you felt the way Amir did about refusing to be admitted for inpatient psychiatric treatment."

"That's correct. Last Wednesday, I saw a patient who gave me a sense of being at the end of her rope. I hospitalized her."

"With Amir, you didn't have the sense of impending suicide. It would have been incumbent on you to take follow-up action if you had. But here's another question: How do you measure the degree to which you and a patient are similar or different in a particular way? As you just said, in Amir's case, the question was whether he had the same kind of wall between depression and suicide that you had. I think we agree now that the answer is 'no,' but that wasn't obvious then.

"It's not easy. There's a lot you can't know. You may get a sense of a patient. You may have an intimation of danger. Some of it is intuition, but a good bit of it is luck. Despite having suicidal thoughts, most people want to live, which also shades your thinking.

"What's Alice's current status?"

"She didn't show up today. She said she's afraid to go under anesthesia again. It doesn't make any sense. She was so hopeful about this treatment, and her hope fueled its success, but now she's going down. I told her that this was one of many options. I changed her medication to something more activating, but it didn't work, and I know she takes her medications religiously. Maybe I could try an MAO [monoamine oxidase] inhibitor, this new Selegiline patch. I've tried everything on her that's worked for my other patients, but she seems resistant. I wanted her to feel some new hope with a new approach, but it's all going nowhere. I don't have any hunches about what will help her.

"In one of the letters I wrote to Amir's mom, I said that he had no sense of his future and no hope. Alice is like that, too. As for other similarities, she looks a little like my mom. I'm careful not to cross any lines professionally. Still, I have an uneasy feeling about Alice—but it has nothing to do with any similarity to my mother. The fact is that my mom is dead, and I wish she were alive. Alice has melancholia in her voice. I heard that same melancholia in Amir's e-mail, although he sounded more hopeful when he came in that last session.

"There was a patient of Alvear-Reverte's who was admitted for depression at least four times in a year, and he actually attempted suicide a couple of times. Each time he came into the hospital, he felt hopeless and responsible for all the tragedies in the world. Under Alvear-Reverte's care, he was always able to absorb some hope, but it was short-lived. All the residents knew him. I was one of those residents, but I didn't know Alvear-Reverte very well back then. Even though the change was temporary each time, I knew something momentous happened between the doctor and the patient. I felt it was magic. At that time, though, my focus was on finding the right mix among the many extraordinary combinations of medications.

"When I was an oncologist, I used to work with some surgeons who were radical and heroic. They would take all cases, even the almost-impossible ones. I felt that they harbored messianic rescue fantasies. In the 'successful' cases, the surviving patients had miserable lives because of the nature of the salvage surgeries. For example, a surgeon would take out almost the entire lower part of the face of a patient with advanced oral cancer. The patient was alive, but he would question the value of his life. Reasonable surgeons would say that the tumor was inoperable and move on to palliative measures, but these surgeons weren't like that. They wanted to do the impossible.

"Going back to my own experiences, sometimes I was a little uneasy with the dosages of medicines that Alvear-Reverte prescribed. It may sound like I thought Alvear-Reverte was a foolish hero, but he just knew a lot about how to use the medications and understood what was possible. He really knew his patients. After Amir died, I spoke with Alvear-Reverte again. His patient, who I mentioned earlier, had committed suicide around the same time. Alvear-Reverte said, 'I tried my best to keep him alive. He knew that he had this place where everybody would do anything and everything to keep him alive. He'd just reached the end of his rope.'"

"I think your premise is that heroic measures are suspect, and reasonable measures are preferable," I said. "What can you reasonably do with Alice that you aren't doing?"

"I called her the day she missed her appointment. Her son picked up the phone, and I asked how she was. He said that she was bad but not as bad as when she came to the hospital. So I asked him to put her on the phone. She promised to come for the next appointment today, but she didn't show up. The same thing happened in the hospital: She would improve when I spoke to her and then slump. She's slowing down. She speaks one word every two minutes. It feels awkward, but that's her speed now. And she's slowing down more and more. It's bad."

For a long while, Jan seemed preoccupied. Just as Jan waited for his patient, I waited for him. One never knows the next thing a person is going to say. There is always the potential for a surprise. So I waited, wondering what was coming next.

"I had a patient who was kidnapped in her own car when she was a teenager. The carjacker told her, 'I'm gonna take you to a quiet place, get some head, and kill you. I'm sorry. It's not personal.' She managed to jump out of the moving car. She was hurt, but she escaped. She couldn't sleep during the weeks following the event; she couldn't sleep and had terrible anxiety. Over time, she made an excellent recovery. She met a nice man, got married, and had a few children, including a daughter who is now a teenager. Recently, my patient saw a movie where a man put a knife to a woman's throat and asked her to look at him, and suddenly, my patient began having nightmares, replaying the scene of her own assault. She couldn't snap out of the terror when she woke up. Sometimes, she'd be in a trance for ten or twenty minutes. I suggested that perhaps the old trauma had lain dormant in her, and the movie had re-activated it. For me, it was an obvious inference, but she hadn't thought of it. Finally, she agreed and said there *was* a connection . . . and . . . I'm sorry, I just lost my chain of thought."

As Jan's own flow of thoughts derailed, I continued to wonder what would come next. The loss of a train of thought through forgetfulness or an unexpected shift to a new thought reveals the working of our consciousness and leads to new knowledge. "Your experiences are always in the background," I said. "Your memories of Amir and his mother's letter are now mingling with new stuff."

"I agree, but it isn't something I can control."

"Have you ever seen pointillist paintings? When you get too close to such a painting—"

"—you lose the picture," Jan interjected. "Yes, you need a sufficient distance."

"Right. The letter from Amir's mom has made you lose the reasonable distance you need to have from people who suffer from depression. You had gained some distance from Amir, but his mother and her letter reawakened the old anxieties and disturbed you. This is like the patient with the teenage daughter who started re-experiencing her abduction after watching a movie with a woman-slasher scene. Suffering isn't the only experience there is in the world, however, and you know it. You now . . ."

" . . . can go home and play with David and rest my head on Maria's shoulder," Jan said, smiling.

"Yes."

CHAPTER 40

JAN FLEW INTO MY OFFICE, a little breathless. "Sorry, I'm late. Traffic!"

"I'm glad you were able to come."

"I'm glad you waited."

"Did you have any doubt that I would?"

"No, but it's not polite to be late. We're stressed out right now, especially Maria. She's scared to leave David with a babysitter, but she needs to go back to work. There's a woman we had met with a few times, and Maria was comfortable enough to hire her, and then suddenly, the woman backed out, and now we have to start over. The whole thing seems unnatural: mothers under pressure to return to work leave their babies with paid strangers. The U.S. isn't a child-friendly country. For us, the problem is temporary, because Maria and I can coordinate our schedules once she finishes her training, but for so many others, it isn't.

"There's a guy named Dr. Malhotra where I work. Wherever you go, he's there. I see his name as the treating physician next to an insane number of patients. Actually, there are three Indian psychiatrists; everyone calls them the 'Indian Mafia' ... affectionately, I must add. [*I smiled to myself: I never thought of myself as Mafia material.*] Everyone likes them. Sometimes, a Polish patient switches from one of the Indian Mafia to me because I speak Polish.

"I have one such patient I'll call ... Elena. She's been depressed since her son died in a car accident two years ago. Who wouldn't be? I imagine some of her feelings are like Amir's mother's, and some are different ..."

Jan's voice trailed off, and his eyes went blank. "I still haven't heard from her," he said quietly. For a moment, time stopped, and then Jan perked up and continued, "Elena is so polite and respectful. She never

388

interrupts me, and she answers most of my questions, 'Yes, Doctor. No, Doctor.' She seems to sit on the edge of the chair, waiting for the slightest sign from me that the session is over. She's always ready to jump up and leave.

"A few weeks ago, she overheard my secretary talking about cute pictures of David I had shown her. My secretary confirmed this when I asked her later. Just before the session was over, Elena said, 'I heard you have a son.'

"'Yes, I do,' I said and showed her a small album of pictures I have on my desk. She said something nice about him and left.

"The following week, Elena was in Poland, and she wrote me an e-mail. She said she was so grateful that I'd showed her the pictures, even though she is only a patient, that it was like a gift and helped her feel healthier and more normal. I told her that we had known each other for a long time and that the relationship goes both ways, so I was glad to show her the pictures.

"She mentioned it again after she came back. The small things you do are important to the patient. Sometimes, you reap more than you sow. How do you understand these things in treatment? Can you give me some ideas?"[49]

How should I respond to Jan? How, in general, should an analyst respond when a patient makes a request or asks a question? Many analysts are reluctant to accede to patient requests or answer such questions. The rationale has been that there are risks to gratifying the patient and, therefore, the analyst should abstain: If I give my own answer, will the patient continue to search for his own? Others feel that the patient should not be frustrated, and the analyst should be optimally responsive. Still other analysts, including me, think that rigid rules on this should not bind us. We should be free to use our judgment based on the history of the patient, our relationship, and the circumstances prevailing at that moment. The important thing is to be aware of the patient's reactions to our response or our reticence.

Analysis doesn't require the analyst to be *right*; it requires that the analyst be willing to be *wrong*. That means that the analyst welcomes equally a patient's acceptance *or* rejection of his ideas. If a patient rejects an interpretation, the analyst asks, "Where and how am I wrong?" and keeps the

---

49 My response to Jan was an abbreviated version of what I elaborate here. This section contained ideas about the history of psychoanalysis, intended for the lay reader. Analysts are familiar with this history. Because of the length of this elaboration, I divide the chapter into two parts. The continuation of this chapter also details the interactions between Jan and me.

treatment dialogue open. The analyst should not impose his views on the patient because of his own narcissism or pride. The patient must be free to form their own opinions and even be critical of the analyst. The patient's ability to disagree with an analyst reinforces that freedom, just like a child's ability to disagree with a parent.

I continued, noting that Jan had asked me for my *ideas* (plural).

"I think this situation offers me a chance to clarify some psychoanalytic ideas and my own beliefs. Humans have always suffered from emotional problems. Freud discovered that suffering is often associated with contradictory or conflicting impulses. His discoveries brought much initial excitement. Psychoanalysis enabled patients who were previously unable to find relief to experience improvement and feel more in control of their lives. Analysts and patients were pioneers in advancing the new psychoanalytic discipline.

"Before long, psychoanalysts began to realize that there were dangers to this intimate form of treatment, like sex between doctors and patients. Today, we call such actions *boundary violations*, inappropriate behavior that grows out of the analytic setting, the helping nature of the psychiatrist's role and ministrations, and the patient's vulnerability. For example, a patient who has had a difficult relationship with a parent, spouse, or boss often discovers something ideal or magical in the therapist. These emotions are byproducts of the treatment to be harnessed to benefit the patient. Sometimes, the patient's interest in the analyst, namely the patient's transference, stemming mostly from the patient's childhood, can be misunderstood by the analyst as being personally or uniquely directed to them. Such an analyst's misreading of the patient can lead to the analyst's inappropriate collaboration with the patient; if so, this is an example of the analyst's pathological *countertransference*. The patient's feelings or actions may be sexually suggestive, over-idealizing, or involve gift-giving. The countertransference-ridden analyst may respond by manipulating the patient and engaging in sexual acting out, taking advantage rather than interpreting the over-idealization, or exploiting the patient's financial generosity. Such a course of events turns the professional relationship into a personal one that no longer serves the patient's therapeutic interests. The analyst's job is to maintain boundaries and act professionally, so psychoanalysts and psychotherapists established firm rules that support emotionally intimate treatment but prevent countertherapeutic complications."

"Yes, I see," Jan said. "This applies to all medical practice, not just psychoanalysis. The Hippocratic Oath warns the physician to *do no harm* and refers specifically to avoiding sex with 'men or women, free men or slaves.'" Jan recited the last few words with a flourish.

"Yes," I continued, "and in psychoanalysis and psychiatry, the patient and the therapist are more likely to be tempted because of their private, frequent, and often intense encounters. Early in the history of psychoanalysis, after instances of sexual activity between patients and analysts became known, it was necessary to figure out how to manage the intensity of feelings treatment aroused. Freud and others established and practiced the rule of abstinence, that is, non-gratification of *all* patient wishes in the treatment.

"I believe that the main *countertransference* danger for psychoanalysts is suggestion. Sex, for example, is more obvious than a suggestion, so it's easier for an analyst to fixate on than his suggestions. Therefore, Freud developed the free-association method for psychoanalysis, which occurs when the patient is awake, in contrast to the then-current use of hypnosis, which is susceptible to suggestion or manipulation. He thought that free association prevented suggestion and, thus, that analysis could be objective. However, in the era of modern science, we know that analysts and patients mutually influence each other and that total objectivity is an illusion.

"Furthermore, we acknowledge that the analyst's job changes the analyst himself so that even the task of describing what he observes is exceedingly subtle, complex, and uncertain. Stripped of the fiction of objectivity or the privilege of power, the analyst cannot overrule alternative views of the patient. Influencing others requires endless persuasion based on evidence and error correction.

"Still, because boundary violations like sex between patient and analyst are possible, psychoanalysts became fearful of *all* boundary violations. The rule of abstinence set out rough guidelines for avoiding patient gratification. It came in handy for managing temptation, but it's possible to throw the baby out with the bathwater. Understanding where and how temptations arise in the patient and/or the analyst is just as important as avoiding acting them out. At the same time, the patient needs to feel connected to the doctor, and the doctor must show enough human sensitivity that the patient never feels the doctor is an automaton.

"Your patient felt better due to your responsiveness and common courtesy. Showing her pictures of your son is the Polish cultural norm. *If* she had felt it was a violation on your part, you would have to have taken that into account. Although some may question your action, I see little that is objectionable. You reaped a lot from sowing the seed of decency. Understanding why she felt better can now be part of further understanding and treatment." (Ultimately, the proper judge of your actions is your patient, who should always have the freedom to express agreement, disagreement, gratitude, or criticism. Boundary violations are a potential danger to a viable therapeutic relationship, but not all non-interpretive behavior of the analyst should be considered a boundary violation. Behaving in socially mandated ways, like shaking hands, giving a patient bus fare home when a patient's purse or billfold is lost, or, like Jan's sharing of his son's picture, do not fall under that rubric. Likewise, the label *boundary violation* would lose significance if applied to all informal interactions between patient and therapist. Analysts have to harvest these ordinary encounters for therapeutic value.)

"Was it Freud who realized these boundary violations were a danger?"

"To answer that correctly, I have to start at the beginning. Joseph Breuer, Freud's contemporary, may be called the first psychoanalyst. Breuer treated Fräulein Anna O in Vienna between 1880 and 1882."

"I read about Anna O! She suffered from many symptoms: a cough, paralysis of her limbs, anesthesia, disturbances in vision and speech, confusion, loss of consciousness. She and her mother took care of her sick father, who had a sub-pleural abscess. One day when she was alone with her father, she had a frightening hallucination of a snake approaching her father's sickbed, and she became paralyzed. She couldn't move or shake off the hallucination. The train whistle bringing her father's doctor broke the spell finally. She chatted with Breuer about her many experiences, memories, and fantasies that she called 'chimney sweeping' in a freewheeling manner. Her symptoms diminished after her talks with Breuer, and she felt better. She called it *the talking cure!*"

Jan was pleased that he could remember all this, and I wanted to acknowledge it.

"Exactly. Breuer was a mentor of Freud, and they discussed this case. Breuer diagnosed her as an hysteric and was impressed by the role of fantasies in her hysteria. He used the term *catharsis* to describe her improvement following her emotional sessions. So, together, Anna O and Breuer devised this new talk-therapy method, which may be called the start of psychoanalysis proper. Breuer became so involved with Anna's treatment that his wife became jealous, and Breuer himself became troubled by his feelings for Anna. You are not the first analyst to react strongly to a patient![50]

"Breuer didn't have a specific theory about hysteria and was eclectic in his approach. But, Breuer thought various kinds of sexual *and* non-sexual trauma could cause hysteria. In contrast, Freud initially believed that neurotics suffered from various symptoms, inhibitions, or anxieties because they had experienced traumatic *sexual* events in their childhood. Freud went on to formulate an elaborate theory and method of psychoanalytic treatment. According to Freud, patients' traumatic experiences contained toxic memories that strangled growth and development, but they resisted or were totally incapable of remembering their childhood seductions during treatment.

"Initially, Freud thought that the cure for such neurotic problems lay in helping patients overcome their infantile amnesia using hypnotic suggestion. During hypnosis, patients *abreacted*, meaning they emotionally recalled and re-lived such repressed events. Abreaction allowed the channeling of pent-up experiences into consciousness, where they would no longer be toxic. The healing effect of hypnosis was like the relief brought about by lancing a boil to drain out infected pus. Unfortunately, the *analyst* witnessed the patient's recovered memories, but the *patient*, who was under a hypnotic spell, did not and, therefore, couldn't recover them after the hypnotic session. As a result, the relief was only temporary, and the symptoms connected to the unconscious memories returned, sometimes in a disguised manner."

Jan was listening closely.

"Hypnotic suggestion required that the patient surrender some portion of their will. Freud became ambivalent about the use of suggestion required by hypnosis, though, because he didn't want to impose his will on his patients, so he searched for alternative strategies. Freud never treated Anna O, but through Breuer's reports, he was familiar with Breuer's method of listening and to Anna O's 'chimney sweeping.' Finally, Freud decided that this was a good way around suggestion and termed the patient's waking, ongoing description of their experiences during the analytic session *free associations*. He trusted them so much that the fundamental rule was the

---

50 There are many questions concerning the treatment of Anna O. Some question Anna O's pseudocyesis (false pregnancy) and Breuer's second honeymoon. Some have argued that it was Anna O who initiated the termination of treatment. Still others opine that Anna O did not suffer from hysteria/neurosis, but rather from some organic illness—possibly temporal lobe epilepsy.

only instructions he gave to his patients. It instructed patients to say whatever came into their mind, to verbalize their thoughts as freely as possible.

"Although free-associating eliminated the problems with hypnosis, it turned out that even when they were awake, patients were still subject to the workings of the unconscious. In the process of uncovering the patient's forgotten, pathogenic childhood, Freud discovered what he called *transference*, which occurs through what he called a *false connection*. For example, one of Freud's patient had a symptom whose origin was associated with a wish she had had years earlier that now lay dormant in her unconscious. She wished that the man she was talking with would suddenly decide to kiss her! At the end of a session with Freud, the same wish emerged in her about Freud.[51]

"Freud found he would encounter patient feelings directed toward him. He realized, for example, that a patient could be seduced and enthralled by her curiosity about his cigar. She might talk about its aromatic smoke yet be disinclined to talk about the sights or smells of the traumatic seductions of her childhood. Initially, Freud was annoyed by patients' incidental preoccupations with him, which seemed to hinder the exploration of their actual neuroses, and saw their investment in him as a *mésalliance*, a false connection.

"Then, wisdom dawned: Patients often resisted considering the pathogenic areas of their lives because they were not conscious of them! Unable to call up memories or feelings connected to conflict-ridden events, they would fall silent when such topics arose. And if they *did* remember and talk about them, they either saw the events as unrelated to their problems or dismissed them. When these unconscious feelings from the past emerged, they were often displaced from their original objects onto Freud so that he became a stand-in for the experienced or imagined parent; this is what Freud called *transference*. To complicate matters, features that combined the past-significant-person and the now-analyst might take a disguised, displaced, or condensed form in dreams or people or objects outside the treatment, like a member of the royal family, a hero, a person of higher social standing, or an idealized character or neighbor.

"The task of the analysis was to draw lines connecting the *current* transference emotions toward the analyst and similar *past* feelings toward parents

---

51 Freud, S. (1893). "The psychotherapy of hysteria," from *Studies on Hysteria*. In J. Strachey (Ed. and Trans.), *The Standard Edition of the Complete Psychological Works of Sigmund Freud* (Vol. 2, pp. 302–303). London: Hogarth Press.

or other important people. Thus, understanding the patient's transference feelings was critical for the analysis. It was an emotionally meaningful crossroads that joined the *here-and-now* of the present in the analysis to the *there-and-then* childhood neurosis that was still unconsciously active. Working through such revivified conflicts increased the patient's ability to love and work."

"It fits like a puzzle," Jan said.

I chuckled. "That's the main complaint *against* Freud! He made the pieces fit so well that it was probably too good to be true. Karl Popper said that made it more like a myth.[52] According to him, whatever the field, a scientific hypothesis should be an idea that *could* be proven wrong; otherwise, it's not science. But that's going off course from your question. Patients' free associations during treatment sessions revealed both their immediate concerns and the content of their transference feelings. Because the analyst wasn't directing the process and patients could speak with minimal social constraint, the patients' free associations were relatively unguided. Still, the analyst's physical presence, attitude, tone of voice, mannerisms, interpretations, actions, and even office décor inevitably influence the patient's associations. They would tend to tiptoe around the heart of a matter without directly addressing it, so the connection between any given free association and the corresponding unconscious issue required the analyst's interpretation.

"Freud viewed interpretation as different from, and superior to, hypnotic suggestion because any construction by the analyst could be actively accepted or rejected by the conscious, engaged patient. And, whereas hypnosis was short-term and analyst-dependent, psychoanalysis was primarily guided by the patient's own insights and had the potential for long-lasting effects.

"Freud's discovery complicated the analyst-patient interaction that the unconscious was a characteristic of human *psychology*, not only a manifestation of patient *pathology*. Therefore, even if analysis using free association wasn't at risk from the analyst's conscious suggestions, it *was* subject to the analyst's unconscious countertransference, that is, the analyst's normal or pathological reactions to the patient."

Jan nodded vigorously.

"In short," I went on, "according to Freud, free associations may seem like random, silly thoughts, but—understood through the lens of unconscious and preconscious motivations—they are often quite meaningful.

---

52 Popper, K. (1959). *The Logic of Scientific Discovery.* New York, NY: Basic Books.

Your thoughts sometimes meander that way here." I went to the bookcase and pulled out Volume 14 of Strachey's classic translation of the Standard Edition of Freud's works. A dirty dog-eared page marked one of my favorite passages. I read aloud Freud's 1914 definition of psychoanalysis: "'It may thus be said that the theory of psycho-analysis is an attempt to account for two striking and unexpected facts of observation which emerge whenever an attempt is made to trace the symptoms of a neurotic back to their sources in his past life: the facts of transference and of resistance. Any line of investigation which recognizes these two facts and takes them as the starting-point of its work has a right to call itself psycho-analysis, even though it arrives at results other than my own.'[53]

"As you can see, this is a broad and flexible definition. Psychoanalysis is a time-consuming process of indefinite duration, . . . but Freud was a patient man. He was also resourceful. In Freud's view, the ongoing task of the psychoanalyst was to alloy the gold of analysis with the copper of direct suggestion. Finding the proper proportions for a therapeutic mixture is the emotional alchemy that has kept psychoanalysts busy; it is still a work in progress.

"Sándor Ferenczi, one of Freud's early disciples, broke with Freud, the master-builder of psychoanalysis, over issues of the analyst-patient relationship. Freud jealously guarded the forms of its permissible expression and held two ideas sacrosanct: the principle of abstinence—that the analyst should assume a passive role, and the theory of infantile sexuality—that the child's feelings toward their parents were and are sexual.

"Ferenczi advocated for a more active and affectionate technique in psychoanalysis. He felt that there might be confusion between how children and parents (or parent substitutes) communicated and how patients and analysts did. So, a girl might innocently play being her father's wife and seek tenderness and snuggling without any of her words or actions being sexual. However, if the father were emotionally sick, he might misinterpret the girl's role-playing and act out sexually. Ferenczi claimed that misunderstandings between generations could result in children's exposure to violence, sexual or otherwise.[54]

---

53 Freud, S. (1914). "On the history of the Psycho-analytic movement, Papers on Metapsychology and other works." In J. Strachey (Ed. and Trans.), *The Standard Edition of the Complete Psychological Works of Sigmund Freud* (Vol. 14, p. 16). London: Hogarth Press.

54 Ferenczi, S. (1949). "Confusion of the tongues between the adults and the child: The language of tenderness and of passion," *International Journal of Psycho-Analysis, 30*, 225–230.

"In Ferenczi's view, the analyst, through his or her behavior, should counterbalance the emotional deprivations and misunderstandings the patient suffered in childhood, perhaps acting like an affectionate mother or father, providing warmth and acceptance. For him, the main risk in the analysis was repeating the original trauma and re-traumatizing the patient. During childhood, a patient may have been reluctant to criticize his parent. In the treatment, that patient, in a similar manner, may also be disinclined to criticize the analyst. Ferenczi felt that both analysts and patients were prone to resisting knowing the patient's repressed or suppressed criticisms of the analyst.

"Ferenczi recommended that analysts help patients overcome early emotional deprivation by gratifying their craving for love and affection, including hugging and kissing them. Freud was concerned that this *kissing technique* would lead to further erotic escalation.[55] In a nutshell, are the child's emotions toward his parents sensual, as per Ferenczi, or sexual, as per Freud?

"In 1932, Ferenczi planned to present a paper summarizing his ideas on this issue at the International Psycho-Analytical Congress in Wiesbaden, Germany.[56] Freud read the paper before it was presented and asked Ferenczi to withdraw it. Ferenczi was shocked by Freud's disapproval but presented it anyway. When they next met, Ferenczi, seeking rapprochement, greeted Freud with an extended hand. But, unfortunately, Freud was still so pissed off that he refused to shake it!"

I wondered if Jan could imagine me ever refusing to shake his hand. I couldn't.

I continued, "Ferenczi confronted what he most feared: a reenactment of the lack of tenderness he had experienced with his cold and rejecting mother. Freud never forgave Ferenczi, and Ferenczi died of pernicious anemia the following year. Some have speculated that his death was a psychosomatic reaction to Freud's rejection.[57]

"Franz Alexander coined the term *corrective emotional experience* to describe a therapeutic experience that 'healed' disturbances caused by early

55 Freud, S. (1931). "Letter from Sigmund Freud to Sándor Ferenczi, December 13, 1931." In E. Falzeder & E. Brabant (Eds.), P. T. Hoffer (Trans.), *The Correspondence of Sigmund Freud and Sándor Ferenczi* (Vol. 3, pp. 421–424). Cambridge, MA / London: The Belknap Press of Harvard University Press.

56 Ferenczi, S. (1949). "Confusion of tongues between adults and the child: The language of tenderness and of passion." *International Journal of Psycho-Analysis, 30*, 225–230.

57 Rentoul, W. R. (2010). *Ferenczi's Language of Tenderness: Working with Disturbances from the Earliest Years*. Lanham, MD: Jason Aronson.

trauma.[58] He suggested that the analyst remedy the patient's trauma by re-exposing him to it within the supportive interpersonal climate of analysis.

"In the corrective emotional experience, the analyst creates or takes advantage of a scenario that resembles one the patient associates with trauma. As the action unfolds, the patient expects the usual rejecting response he has experienced in the past. However, the analyst counters the patient's expectation by responding positively, thereby beginning to erase the attitude and actions of the patient's parents or whoever caused the original trauma and neurosis.

"The archetype of Alexander's principle of corrective emotional experience was the conversion of Jean Valjean, the thief on the run in Victor Hugo's *Les Misérables*. Bishop Myriel, a kindhearted clergyman, took Valjean into his house, fed him, and gave him a place to sleep. True to form, Valjean woke up in the middle of the night and made off with the bishop's silver. When the police arrested him and brought him to the bishop, he was expecting to be accused by the bishop and punished again, but the bishop told the policeman that Valjean had not stolen the silver; rather, he had given it to Valjean as a gift. And, further, the bishop handed him a pair of silver candlesticks he said Valjean had 'accidentally' left behind. This unexpectedly positive act converted Valjean from a thief to an honest man.

"Alexander's use of active manipulation in creating corrective emotional experiences introduces the danger of *wild analysis*. Most analysts stuck to rigid, rule-bound analytic techniques to curtail the risk of recklessness or the label of kissing or wild analysts. An analyst being wild *is* a real danger, but being excessively tame is, too.

"Gradually, the classical analyst came to be identified as an anonymous, silent, restrained, objective, blank-screen presence whose central aim was to avoid 'contaminating' the patient's associative process—and an inspiration for many a great *New Yorker* cartoon! It portrayed the psychoanalyst as serving the rich—sometimes called *the worried well*—oblivious to the looming challenge of contemporary scientific methods. But disregarding the masses and the scientific method was not the only problem threatening psychoanalysis.

"It was also being battered by the efficacy of psychotropic drugs, the practicality of Cognitive Behavioral Therapy, and limitations on insurance

---

58 Alexander. F. (1950). "Analysis of the therapeutic factors in treatment." *Psychoanalytic Quarterly*, *19*, 482–500.

coverage. The first came from advances in medicine and biology, the second from innovations in pragmatic and time-limited therapy, and the third from economic necessity. The net result was that psychoanalysis got outgunned and outsmarted and found itself priced out of the market. However, the primary injury was self-inflicted: Psychoanalysts didn't listen to the call of modern philosophers of science like Popper, who insisted that analysts had to be willing to be proven scientifically wrong before they could make scientific claims. Many analysts who believed in the universality of the Oedipus Complex, or that women suffered from penis envy, or that empathy was curative held these views to be self-evident. Inconsistency, the lack of evidence, or failure did not shake the believers. They rarely conducted experiments and thereby lost out in the game of psychological treatment. Psychoanalysis, which began with Freud as a discipline of inquiry, became rigid, turning into a system of beliefs, if not an outright religion. However, some voices along the way called for more self-scrutiny.

"Samuel Lipton distinguished between Freud's flexible personal technique and what he called *standard* or *modern* technique.[59] Lipton notes, for example, that on a cold winter day, Freud fed a meal to a hungry patient. Lipton called attention to Elizabeth Zetzel, a prominent analyst, who considered the event shocking and unanalytic.[60] Lipton's view was that Freud fed his hungry patient only as a component of his non-technical personal relationship. It was part of the unobjectionable element of the transference and not part of the analytic technique. Lipton's view was that the standard psychoanalytic technique had become hardened and inflexible contrary to Freud's flexible approach.[61]

"Psychoanalysis today is seriously wounded, but perhaps not mortally. There have been calls for investing in the basic methods of modern science, increasing flexibility, and putting our efforts into identifying the essence of psychoanalysis so that it can regenerate when the time is right. We now have the job of discovering what can be salvaged and at what cost. I view

---

59 Lipton, S. D. (1977). "The advantages of Freud's technique as shown in his analysis of the Rat Man." *International Journal of Psycho-Analysis*, *58*, 255–273.

60 Zetzel, E. (1976). "Additional notes upon a case of obsessional neurosis: Freud 1909 (1966)." In M. S. Bergmann & F. R. Hartman (Eds.), *The Evolution of Psychoanalytic Technique*. New York: Columbia University Press, p. 164.

61 "Paradoxically, modern technique can produce just what it may have been designed to avoid, a corrective emotional experience, by exposing the patient to a hypothetically ideally correct, ideally unobtrusive, ideally silent, encompassing technical instrumentality rather than the presence of the analyst as a person with whom the patient can establish a personal relationship." Lipton, 1977, p. 272.

that psychoanalysts try to help their patients as best they can, using various theories and techniques, and I acknowledge their earnest efforts. I don't believe in a single formula. Treatment should fit the patient. Depending on how psychoanalysts respond to current challenges, some forms will survive, albeit in a modified state; others will die, even those beloved to their adherents.

"There you have it, my timeline for how psychoanalysis evolved and, perhaps, lost its way. It began as an open theory with some 'give,' and then it entered a classical period during which rules and rigidities became established, followed by attempts to revive its original flexibility. Such a lecture from an analyst to a patient is frowned upon in classical analytic circles. I could have sat tight, but I laid it all out. If you feel I wasted your time, I apologize. I was answering your question in my own fashion. You're in the best position to assess my monologue."

"This is the best short lecture I've ever heard about the essence of psychoanalysis: how it evolved, its excesses, and its efforts to self-correct! I assume that my first analyst was a classicist, and we didn't click. Without further knowledge of how the psychoanalytic process should look, my choice is now clear and easy to make. I like what you do. You've helped me. Because the orthodoxy will judge you, I feel pressured to say something wise and relevant, but on second thought, I think that whatever I say won't matter. You're screwed. If my response is positive, they'll say you elicited it, and if it's negative, it proves their point. Either way, your effort will be discredited. Isn't that so?"

"That's one way of looking at it, but appropriate praise and criticism are at the heart of improvement. I welcome them from patients and peers, and I hope to offer some myself. I am willing to be proven wrong. If I were unwilling to be proven wrong, I could only practice the *religion* of psychoanalysis. I want to practice the *science* of psychoanalysis.

"Was this history lesson on the evolution of the practice of psychoanalysis useful or proper? Was it appropriate to respond to a psychiatrist-patient with psychoeducation, even if it is not directly therapeutic? Or was it a boundary violation? Classical analysts adopted a long list of don'ts. Maybe they overreacted. The problem is that it's hard to know when you're wrong. Science helps one evaluate, but there's plenty of added uncertainty because psychoanalysts haven't adopted scientific methods sufficiently. Some ideas may be dead wrong, but there is no easy way to know. Therefore, every analyst has to figure out what does and doesn't work for them. Analysts who want adoring patients should adhere to the 'rules.' Analysts who are susceptible to the temptation to want adoring patients will foster idealization. Analysts who can tolerate criticism may encourage criticism. Flexible analysts will learn how to be more effective from their successes and mistakes. Bottom line: If you want to drive 100 miles per hour and are often drunk, get a cab. On the other hand, if you're a good driver, put your seat belt on. Your guide should be your own sense of what is best for a patient, not what might sound best to a judge in a malpractice case or to the members of an ethics committee.

"The question of why you shared pictures of David with your patient is part of the joy of being a psychoanalyst. At the same time, psychoanalysis requires both order and reasonable technical and ethical guidelines. So, I'm like a jailbird. Although I want to be free, I go back to what Arnold Goldberg called *The Prisonhouse of Psychoanalysis*.[62] My pleasure in being a psychoanalyst is not only in helping patients but in the process itself. But I want to get back to this very proper patient who asked to see pictures of David. I want to be sure that you complete your thoughts about her."

---

62 Goldberg, A. (1990). *The Prisonhouse of Psychoanalysis*. Hillsdale, NJ: The Analytic Press.

CHAPTER 41

THIS CHAPTER IS A CONTINUATION of chapter 40.

"It seems to be characteristic of Polish women that they try to conform to what they perceive as the expectations of the doctor," Jan began. "I noticed it back in Poland, where most of my patients were women. A physician is a respected person in Poland. Just as you would nicely dress when you go to church, you nicely dress when you go to the doctor. The Polish women I see here are similar. Elena always sits at the edge of the chair, paying attention to everything I do or say—." Jan moved forward in his chair to demonstrate.

"—waiting for the signal that the session is over, lest she overstays her time," I said and realized it recalled my description of the classical psychoanalyst. "They're classical Polish women."

Jan laughed. "You could say that . . . rigid and proper."

"Anybody can see what motivates Elena, this respectful Polish woman," I said. "I'd guess it becomes more pronounced as the end of the session approaches. She wants to be ready to comply and leave quickly, as soon as you give the signal. Her musculature and posture convey this attitude."

"True," Jan said slowly. "Where are you going with this?"

"Elena asked you a question about your personal life just before the end of the session, right?"

"Yes, but I'm positive she wanted to ask as soon as she came in, and she struggled with it until almost the last moment. Then, with lots of hesitation and excessive apologies, she finally said, 'I'm sorry that I even ask. I know you're busy, and I hate to waste your time, but . . . is it true you have a son?'"

I asked, "Do you think she was afraid she was being disrespectful by asking?"

"Absolutely. She acted like she was about to commit blasphemy."

I continued, "So, I have a hypothetical question for you: If you had frowned just before she spoke, what do you imagine would have happened?"

"She wouldn't have asked the question."

"Perhaps. Now, I'm talking about her flow of thoughts and expressions. Your manner of receiving and treating her influences Elena's associations. This influence is inevitable and not confused with a conscious suggestion or manipulation, such as advising a patient to get a divorce, etc."

"Yes, the therapist's manner affects the patient's thoughts and emotions. I've seen how your manner influences patients. For example, I observed you when I rotated through the Children's Hospital. There was a gypsy girl who her parents sold for $2,000. Do you remember her?"

"No, but continue."

"She was just one of the many patients I've seen you with on the inpatient unit. And there was a boy whose uncle was selling him into prostitution and collecting money from gay Johns. And there was a psychotic boy who was sexually active with other boys in an orphanage. I tried to speak with them before we did rounds and couldn't get them to talk. I used all the clichéd psychiatric approaches, like 'I know it's difficult to talk about it, but can you tell me more?' and never got the answers that you got. Maybe it was because I was uncomfortable asking the questions, and they could sense it. Then I saw how your manner influenced the patients. When you spoke to them, I thought that you became one of them by using their language, goofing around, and making them laugh. Then you asked these difficult questions, and they answered without even noticing.

"For example, that last boy was hypersexual toward his male peers. When they teased him for being gay, he became aggressive and hostile. He was candid about his actions and wanted to clear up his sexual confusion. He asked you, 'Am I gay? Is there a test you can use to check it out?'

"And you simply asked, 'What picture do you get when you masturbate?' One might see it as an inconvenient question, but he didn't mind, and you got an answer. He said, 'I think of boys.' After he was stabilized on anti-psychotics, you asked, 'Do you give to others or receive from others?' He said that he gave dick to the other boys. But he added that when he jerked off, he thought of women."

"I try to put into practice what I learn from my supervisors: respect and sympathy. You like your patients. You don't hurry them. You wait patiently and listen. In your presence, even silence is comfortable. Alvear-Reverte taught me how to tune in to patients. I saw him talking to a depressed patient who didn't say a word for days after her admission. Alvear-Reverte sat in silence next to her for a while and then started to talk to her in whispers. Slowly, the patient began whispering back. Later on, I mimicked these techniques like a monkey with my own patients, even though I knew nothing of any underlying theory, and it worked!

"Today, I saw a 14-year-old girl who had always behaved perfectly and gotten A's and B's in school. Then, one night, she came home late. In the days and weeks that followed, she became almost mute. She would start to talk, but she would become incomprehensible after the first few words.

"So, I talked to her like I saw you talk to patients. I told her, 'I got the first part of your sentence, but I couldn't understand anything after that.' She didn't say anything, didn't even blink. I said, 'You know, English is my second language, but it's your first. I should be able to understand you better than you can understand me.' And she smiled. I failed in getting her to talk, but I established a connection.

"Her mother suspects that something sexual happened. So I asked the girl, 'Did something bad happen to you?' She didn't say 'Yes,' but she nodded. There are different kinds of patients, and it's tricky to choose how to act with each of them."

"Yes," I said. "Patients, just like non-patients, are all different. Some are buttoned up to the neck, while others expose a sequined bra. Some can listen to words or music, others listen to the music of words, and still, others are tone-deaf and don't want to listen to anything or anybody. An analyst might use humor, a whisper, or a song to reach a patient. You cannot know in advance which technique or interpretation will work. You can only evaluate its usefulness afterward, based on each case's results."

"You make every patient feel special. You also give immediate feedback. Dr. Williams does it, too. Dr. Williams's ideas are often startling. For example, he said that what Amir did was generous: 'He went out by himself and didn't take others out with him by strapping some bombs onto himself and becoming a suicide bomber.' When I think of that example, I chuckle more from anxiety than from any humor in the situation. Do you remember?"

"I remember exactly. He has a creative way of seeing the positive element that most people miss. I'll give you another example. Freud had oral cancer for 17 years before he died; he suffered terribly. His physician, Max Schur, came to see him periodically. Toward the end of his life, when he was in great physical discomfort, Freud told him words to this effect: 'Max, all my life I've tried to understand the human condition. You know more than anyone else that I've worked despite much adversity and pain. When the time comes, when the pain is too much, will you be there for me?' Max replied, 'Yes.' Sometime later, when Freud's condition had deteriorated, he said to Schur, perhaps in a whisper, 'Max, it's now.' Perhaps Schur nodded in understanding. Maybe they shared one last look of recognition and trust before Schur gave him the lethal dose of morphine. This is detailed in Schur's book, *Freud: Living and Dying.*[63]

"So, from this tragic story and its intimate details, we see something positive: the amazing relationship between Freud and Schur and the courage it must have taken Schur to give Freud that lethal dose and then to write about it! He must have had unbelievable trust that Freud's daughter, Anna, would understand his motivations and that British society wouldn't charge him with murder. Schur was a great and courageous man."

"That's what friendship means," Jan said. "Your word to your friend is paramount. If I gave my word to my best friend, I would do the same, regardless of the consequences."

"When the patient has hit the wall of his conscious capacities, he will unconsciously change the topic, become vague, or tell you he can't go further. Your responsibility, as an analyst, is to stay with him as he pursues a thought or a feeling, however embarrassing or inconvenient it is to either of you. This is the essence of the psychoanalytic endeavor."

"That's true. A depressed patient avoids talking or talks only softly. I can say that because I've been there. When you're depressed, it takes a long time to put words together. And when you can't get a response out fast enough, people—even psychiatrists—get impatient, so you stop talking and withdraw totally. When you're depressed, it becomes so painful and futile to do *anything* that you stop trying. That's why depressives often just don't get out of bed. When I was at my worst, I was almost paralyzed. And then you helped me begin to move.

"A psychiatrist has to tune in to the patient. That seems obvious now, but it was a revelation for me. I learned from Alvear-Reverte not to pressure patients and allow them as much time as they need to formulate a response. If you have to wait a few minutes for even a simple answer, so be it; that's

---

63 Schur, M. (1972). *Freud: Living and Dying.* Madison, CT: International Universities Press.

the pace of the depressed mind. As I say it now, it sounds easy, but it takes time to appreciate it and to make it part of your practice."

"True," I said. "Many psychotherapy training programs understandably concentrate on teaching you how to avoid errors: 'Thou shalt not this.' 'Thou shalt not that.' And when the residency is over, you know what *not* to do, but you don't know what *to* do, because no one has clearly said, 'Try to do this.' 'Try to do that.' 'Try to tune in to the patient!' 'Be yourself!' You talked before about mimicking Alvear-Reverte like a monkey because you hoped what worked for him might also work for you. But I think you're selling yourself short; I would call it learning."

"Yes, it is learning, but you feel like you're learning magic when you have a good teacher. When you do the same thing your teacher did, you're still surprised and excited when you get the same result. It's amazing—quite different and more powerful than learning to do other stuff, like repairing a car."

"Yes, the process is creative. For example, a child first learning numbers sees each number as an independent entity, like each word is different. Then, he learns to count from 1 to 10 to 20 and beyond. Next, he begins to understand how those number words are related. Finally, he leaps to discover that those numbers that go on forever enable him to understand and manipulate the world in infinite ways! I think you did the same thing: You learned the fundamentals, you generalized from them, and then you made a leap in your understanding and practice . . . all under the guidance of Alvear-Reverte, Williams, and others."

"And you," Jan said.

"Yes," I acknowledged, "and also me."

There was a heavy pause, and then Jan said, "Amir's mother hasn't responded yet," his words sucking the air out of the room.

I cringed and felt my whole body slump. "My discourse on the history of psychoanalysis was *bullshit*," I said. "It sidetracked us from talking about how you were feeling. You mentioned not hearing from her early in the session. I should have followed up on it, but instead, I conspired in avoiding the subject, giving you a long-winded dissertation on psychoanalysis. Your idealizing talk about Drs. Alvear-Reverte, Williams, and me also helped lift you and me defensively and away from your emotional turmoil.

"I have said before that your expectation that a mother in the middle of anger and mourning over the loss of her son can have a dialogue with the person whom she holds responsible is unrealistic and masochistic. By saying nothing, Amir's mom can stir up quite a storm in you. You were keeping those bad feelings away till this last minute."

"Every time I think of Amir or his mom, my mood drops. I need to learn to live with it better. I have more of a sense now of what can happen, and I'm trying to be more proactive, but every depressed patient reminds me of Amir. I think I'm doing a better job, but somehow I feel worse!"

As the reader can see, I spent much of the hour discussing the development of psychoanalysis before I realized I'd done so because of my *countertransference*. It was an ongoing challenge to understand and appreciate the depth of Jan's compulsive guilt and masochism associated with Amir's mother's communications. Nevertheless, I caught myself at the end of the session. After Jan left, I quietly berated myself for my careless collusion.

CHAPTER 42

THIS SESSION MARKS THE START of the twelfth month of Jan's treatment. "I could never work in the same place for long," said Jan. "The longest I worked in one place was back in Poland at St. Bernard Hospital. As soon as I had an itch to go somewhere else, I left. Some people can work in the same place, with the same people and the same daily schedule, for decades and be unable to even *think* about a change. Routines give a person a sense of security. I started my medical career in oncology and sometimes wonder what would have happened if I had stayed with it. If I had stayed there, it would now be 17 years. I don't think people are designed to stay in the same place for a long time. I used to find it fascinating to move around, but now, not as much. Now, I want stability: a home with a backyard with grass and trees where David can play. Becoming a father was a major change for me; sometimes, I think I waited too long."

"You've also talked about your change from oncology to psychiatry. Are these two things related?"

"The itch mainly was due to being young and wanting to experience new things. So I went to England to do a fellowship in oncology. That would have been a hard decision for married people who had children. For me, it was easy because my then-wife and I had no children. I also spent five months in Germany learning new techniques, hanging out with experts, and asking many questions. More important, there was an exciting life outside the hospital. I loved exploring new cities and making new friends. I still have the urge sometimes. Like, I've always wanted to go to New Zealand. But it's not so strong now. It's more like a nice thought.

"Giving up oncology wasn't about the excitement of trying something different. I saw too much pain and death, and that's what made me want to find a new specialty. Some people were harder to lose than others. I couldn't get them out of my head."

I wondered if there was yet another tributary feeding this desire for change. "You've mentioned that your dad moved around, too."

"Yes, he moved to France for a year, and then a few years later, he went back for two more years. Then, starting in 1981, during Martial Law in Poland, he lived in Germany for two years. However, he has been in the same place for the last thirty years. So maybe he was more adventurous when he was younger, but it disappeared as he grew older. So I don't see this as an essential characteristic of my father.

"It was one of my mom's, though. She loved to read books about traveling and constantly desired to go to places she read about. She traveled a lot in her imagination, but she actually visited only a few countries in Europe, and six years ago, she came to see me here. I wanted her to really see the country, so instead of flying, we drove everywhere. I remember that we made it down to Florida in two days, talking all the way. She was a great companion, never complaining about being tired.

"When I was about twelve or thirteen, my father happened to be in a good mood one day and promised to send me to France for a vacation, but when the time came, he forgot about it. I was disappointed and angry; I felt deceived, but I didn't say a word. I didn't tell him about my feelings until about ten years later. After that, I took every opportunity to travel; I even postponed graduating from medical school for two years. On the few occasions when my travel plans fell through, I was disappointed. I didn't tolerate it well.

"What was fascinating for me about travel was making new friends, not just seeing new places. For example, in England, the people I worked with accepted me as a friend. They even asked to join the hospital's rugby team. That was quite unusual, as they typically kept their distance from foreigners. But they always invited me to parties at their homes, and I made special efforts to meet everyone there.

"Life in England was different from life in Poland. There was less closeness among friends and even among family members in England. For example, in England, an older couple might send a written dinner invitation to their own adult children. That would be considered absurd in Poland. Words like *friendship* and *family* had different meanings back home. The other side of this story is that leaving Poland gave me a break from too much closeness with *my* family. They seemed to have a get-together for a birthday or anniversary every other day, which gave me very little time for myself.

"So, I went to England, where there was none of this. Even when people invited you into their homes, there was a sense of formality. But almost immediately, I began to miss the Polish family spirit and my friends. Saying this, I realize that I feel the same way here. Maria grew up in a close, traditional family. She and I intend to keep up our Polish and Italian ways of celebrating Catholic holidays, like Easter and Christmas. We want David to know what a family is—not just our nuclear family, but a sense of being part of something bigger and deeper."

Jan paused for a moment. "And then there's Germany: It's clean, beautiful, and organized, but I would never want to live there. There's too much distance between people. Germans are so formal, and most Germans require lots of personal space. So it was hard to make friends, to feel really connected to people. I don't think it was just a language barrier. After almost a year in Munich, working in the hospital and being invited to people's homes and going to parties, that feeling didn't change.

"My all-time favorite country, after Poland, was Ireland. I loved Ireland with all my heart. It felt like home. Everything felt familiar, including Orthodox Catholicism and heavy drinking, although Poles drink at home, while Irish drink in pubs."

"Where were you in Ireland?"

"Everywhere. My home base was in Cork, a university town south of Dublin, at the home of a friend's parents. I visited natural wonders nearby, including the Ring of Kerry and the Cliffs of Moher, which rise about 700 feet from the sea. I couldn't look down because I was acrophobic, but the feeling was incredible. It was a strange mixture of awe and fear. There are vast stretches of flat terrain covered with grass and a few bushes here and there, and they suddenly end. Literally, the end of the world. Amazing! I was there for a couple of weeks and then went to Limerick, where I spent another week. After that, I went to Londonderry, back to Belfast, the Isle of Man, and finally to Scotland.

"Traveling in Scotland was different. The landscape was beautiful but had a harsh, alien feel to it. In Ireland, I had a sense of familiarity. In contrast, I had no feeling of familiarity here; but I loved Scotland, too. The English spoken in Scotland sounded Germanic to me. There are islands on the west coast: the Inner and Outer Hebrides. I visited two islands in the Outer Hebrides, Lewis and Harris. I left my car on the Isle of Skye, boarded a ferry, and rented a bicycle when I arrived on the island. Peculiar people live there. Most don't speak English; they speak Scottish Gaelic. Those I could talk with never had traveled, even to England. They had little exposure to the ways of other people and other cultures. Generations of people live in the Hebrides and rarely move. Because I spent lots of time thinking about traveling, it was hard to understand. Any travel is exciting and makes life richer. I enjoy meeting people and learning how they live and feel while far away from civilization. One day in the Scottish Highlands, I remember driving from dusk till dawn, and no one passed me. It added to the mystery.

"I could travel more than most of my colleagues in other specialties because of the strict limits on radiation exposure. I had six-hour workdays and eight weeks of paid vacation a year. Learning about different countries and meeting people helped me overcome some typical Polish prejudices. For instance, after World War II, hatred of Germans was understandably almost universal in Poland. Even though I was born more than 20 years after the War, I also learned to distrust and dislike Germans. If not for my visits to Germany, I might still feel that way. Prejudice based on ignorance spreads until people meet each other and form relationships. During a war, you have to brainwash soldiers and demonize the enemy to overcome the resistance to killing, and it takes time to undo this when the war is over. Hatred continues until people start to mingle and realize that they're not so different. Travel exposes people to different ways of thinking and other cultures.

"It's surprising how different life can be just over a border. From Poland to Slovakia, it's a different world! At the beginning of the 20th century, the two countries were so similar that there was an idea to unify them. There are still striking similarities between Poland and Slovakia, but small things—little tweaks of tradition and linguistic variations—reveal differences in their cultures. For example, *Dziwka* means 'young girl' in Slovakia. Still, in Poland, the same word means 'slut.' The cadence of the Slovakian language sounds funny to Poles, like adults talking baby talk, and Slovaks think Polish sounds like crinkling cellophane. Still, the languages are so close that I understand spoken and written Slovakian. They are probably closer than Portuguese and Spanish.

"These discoveries make travel so interesting to me. If I changed careers, I would look for a traveling job, a journalist, or a travel consultant. The husband of a high school friend worked as a supervisor for a big German corporation, and he was always visiting new places to establish more branches for his company. What a great job! Learning new languages is much easier when you travel, especially at a young age. You can sit in a classroom for years studying a new language and still struggle, but if you go to a country where that language is spoken, you can speak it in a few months."

"You draw attention to the stages of your life and your comfort levels," I said. "You're thinking about stability now—a house with a backyard—which was not the case in the past. The background and foreground of your life change with each stage of development. You see how a change in feeling can transform everything."

"Yes, becoming a father was a major change for me. I want to be a good father and a role model of a good person and a good husband. I don't think my father was good at any of these. I waited a long time to become a father, maybe too long. I hope I'll be around to see what kind of adult David becomes.

"In Poland, when you're middle-aged or maybe slightly older, you start to think about where you'll be buried. In addition to having a house, you're on the lookout for your cemetery plot. Some rich people go overboard, building mausoleums that look like palaces. Poor people have to make do with a cheaper place. Many people in their fifties have not only picked out their gravesite, but the headstone already has their picture and their date of birth inscribed on it, ready for the date of death to be added. On All Saints' Day, you go to the cemetery to respect your departed relatives. You light a candle on an unattended grave and place flowers there out of the goodness of your heart. My mom always felt sorry for these poor souls who nobody remembered. When we were walking together by an unattended grave, my mom lit a candle and prayed for a moment. Suddenly, a woman came out of nowhere and said, 'Thank you.' We looked at the picture on the stone, and it was her! She had erected her stone and stood by it every year to see who would visit her!"

We both shook with laughter.

"I joked about it for many years," Jan went on. "I felt that anyone who did such things was ridiculous, and then my mom started to talk about *her* burial, planning it in every detail. When she got sick but was still in reasonable shape, we discussed remodeling the family grave plot. It had been almost 100 years since the last remodeling, and it had become crowded, so adding a new 'resident' would require destroying the old gravestones, digging out remains, and building a whole new gravesite. Of course, such plans need to be approved by the cemetery administration. After their approval, we had to pick a *kamieniarz*, a headstone engraver. He then hired gravediggers to dig out the old foundations, bones, and pieces of coffins. These guys, invariably, are alcoholics and hard to deal with. They lived in a shed next to the graveyard and looked like zombies—like *they* were already dead. People shun them like they're Polish untouchables, probably because of people's fears about death and dying. After I sealed the deal with them, I had to shake hands with the lead guy. I recoiled from the contact and immediately became obsessed with this touch of death. I went home and washed my hands compulsively, over and over, and even used alcohol prep pads to try to remove it.

"My mom had several discussions and planned how our family names were to appear on the gravestone. I couldn't imagine how she could do that. I felt creeped out and impressed at the same time. But now, I'm starting to think about it, too."

Laughing, I asked, "So, what do *you* want?"

"I don't know. If I plant myself here for my eternal rest, I'm afraid I'd be cold and lonely forever. No one in the U.S. visits family graves, and if they do, it's a quick in-and-out drive right through the cemetery. In my experience, people in England, France, and the U.S. seem to feel burdened when they visit family graves.

"That's not how it is in Poland. Every time I'm there, I visit my family graves. I did it even before my mother passed away. Now, with my mother in a grave, I most certainly go to visit. In the same way I always visit family members who are alive, I also visit deceased ones. These visits remind me of where I come from. It's a feeling that I'm a link in the long chain of my family. The first two days in November, All Saints' Day followed by All Souls' Day, are emotionally and visually stunning; they're really a time for the living. At night, the cemeteries look like big lakes of heavenly light. Your nose and face turn black from the soot of the candles. It's a time and place to run into people you haven't seen in years. Being reminded of death brings people closer. The chant for this time is *memento mori*, 'remember that you will die.' Therefore, don't waste your remaining time pushing people away. People resume friendships after years of not communicating. Old feuds get resolved. It's a special time. For some time afterward, I'm more aware of my mortality."

"I think you need an address where you can live and take care of your wife and child before you worry about an address for your headstone," I said.

"In Poland, a family house for living and a family grave for memorializing the dead go together. It's a package deal. A cemetery keeps memories of our loved ones alive and reminds us of the family 'chain of being.'

"Let me tell you a story about Comrade Rossa, who was an idealistic Communist, a true believer. Unlike those comrades who had one foot in Communism and the other in Catholicism, he was the real deal. He memorized Marx and Engels and truly believed that religion was the opium of the masses; he never set foot in a church. The next generation of Communists, who came to power after World War II with Red Army help, were opportunistic rather than idealistic, a different breed from Rossa. He was buried next to my grandmother. His moss-ridden, concrete gravestone proclaimed that a comrade was buried there. This was a one-of-a-kind headstone in a sea of crosses. I heard stories about him growing up, and, as much as I didn't like Communists, I respected him.

"One cold All Saints' Day, my mom and I noticed that Comrade Rossa had a new marble gravestone, a shiny, white cross with S and P letters inscribed next to his name. S and P mean 'Świętej Pamięci,' which indicates that the inscription was made in the 'holy memory' of the person. So he was no longer a comrade!? My mom said that his family maintains the pretense that he had always been a Catholic deep in his heart. They made up a story that he went to church at dawn so that nobody would see him and continued to receive Holy Communion even while he was a comrade. None of this was true: His wife paid for the new marker.

"Polish customs are interesting in the way they approach death and dying. I remember seeing a movie that showed Hindu funeral rites, with piles of wood and bodies burning. Those with money added some butter to help the wood burn better. And there were pictures of body parts floating in the water. I was told that these belonged to poorer people who couldn't afford a full funeral. I don't know if this is true. Sometimes, people who travel make up stories or misinterpret customs."

"It's true that Hindus burn their dead, except Sadhus, holy mendicants who have relinquished their caste. The idea is to shatter any illusions that one may have about the nature of the body. They want the finality of the death of the person and his body to be beyond question. Most Hindus believe that the soul lives on reincarnated in another body after the body's death. I'm an agnostic: I've seen many people, but not a single soul."

"In Catholicism, we believe that at the End of Days, the dead are physically resurrected. Then everyone will go through a final judgment and spend eternity in heaven or hell. That's why people are buried rather than burned and scattered. It's hard to make sense of religious fairy tales. I see atoms and molecules of dying people getting recycled thinking of reincarnation. Those that once constituted another person's body may now be in mine.

"Telling you this awakened some memories. For some reason, I thought about my mom and aunt talking about what they had heard from the gravediggers who open old graves, including my family plot. Over time, the plots get too crowded. With each new death in the family, the grave cover has to be opened and the oldest remains re-interred respectfully in a paper or plastic bag. Family members don't directly oversee this process, but the gravediggers tell them what they see inside the tomb and consult with them throughout the process. I remember my aunt sharing such stories after the death of my grandma. My family tomb was made of concrete slabs and had six previously occupied niches. The oldest niches were those of my great-grandparents. After the grave was opened, the gravediggers' messenger described their condition, and my aunt decided that we should re-use my great-grandmother's niche, as the coffin was more decomposed. After some time, the messenger returned and said that tree roots had grown into the skull and trapped many large bones. He asked for permission to use force to remove them. My aunt allowed it but instructed them to do this reverentially. Maybe half an hour later, he came back asking where to place the remains. My great-grandmother's bones were placed at the head of my grandmother's coffin. The rest of her had found its way into the leaves of the tree above, rustling in the wind. Do you get any ideas from what I'm talking about?"

I remembered a movie that I had recently seen. It was an adaptation of a book by one of my favorite authors, W. Somerset Maugham. I said, "Yes, she became part of the leaves. As you were talking, I thought of a movie called *The Painted Veil.*"

"Who's in it?"

"The male lead is Edward Norton, who plays Walter Fane. Naomi Watts, the female lead, plays his wife, Kitty Fane. I feel this movie is relevant to what we're talking about."

"Don't tell me. I finally saw *Becket,* and I'd like to see *The Painted Veil* without knowing anything about it. Instead, I can tell you about a documentary of Sigmund Freud I just saw. Freud had cancer in the floor of his mouth; his surgeon operated, and he was fine for a while. Then the cancer recurred, and he had many surgeries, one after the other. After the *Anschluss* and his daughter Anna's brief arrest by the Gestapo, Freud was persuaded to move to England. He left for Britain in 1938. His sisters were killed later in concentration camps.

"One of the things the movie focused on was the Austrian anti-Semitism that Freud grew up with. The movie described an incident where some Viennese hoodlums knocked Freud's father's hat onto the pavement, one of them saying something like, 'You can't walk on the same sidewalk as us.' His father picked up his hat and didn't respond. Freud was furious that his father just took the abuse and humiliation. The movie also dwelt on his self-analysis. And it said that he constantly smoked, maybe 20 or 30 cigars a day and that he avoided analyzing his cigar-smoking, which, of course, is what killed him.

"Another interesting theme was his relationship with Carl Jung. Initially, it was close and fulfilling. Freud was almost in love with Jung, partly because he wasn't a Jew. Freud felt that psychoanalysis was in danger of being viewed as a Jewish science, and he thought that, as a non-Jew, Jung could widen its scope of influence and take the idea of psychoanalysis out into the world. Eventually, though, Jung and Freud came to disagree about the nature of the libido and the unconscious. Jung rejected what he saw as Freud's over-emphasis on sexuality, which ruptured the relationship. It's sad. Freud's life was interesting, but the way they teach about him is boring. They idealize him too much and make him into a cartoon guru. But, unfortunately, he was human and didn't quickly admit to his mistakes.

"I went to a meeting about Freud at the Psychoanalytic Institute. Most of the people were over 65, and their attitude toward Freud was reverential. There was a hushed mention of Freud spending one night with Minna Bernays, his sister-in-law, in a hotel. The hotel register indicates that they were signed in as husband and wife. Maybe something happened, or maybe not. The elders of the psychoanalytic tribe dropped it like a hot potato. I feel a realistic portrait of any leader is more credible than an idealized view."

"I agree with you," I said. "John Gay wrote a book called *Freud: A Life for Our Time*,[64] and he devotes a chapter titled 'The Dog that Didn't Bark' to this so-called affair. Gay is skeptical that there was an affair, but we don't know. I also find Freud's life interesting, but I'm more interested in his therapeutic ideas and how they help treat our patients. I highly regard Freud's definition of psychoanalysis as a science concerned with transference and

---

64 Gay, M. (1988). *Freud: A Life for Our Time*. New York: W. W. Norton.

resistance. I'm impressed by the flexibility inherent in that statement and have fashioned my practice on this understanding. Freud demonstrated this flexibility, too: Freud's treatment of Miss Dora, Ida Bauer, an 18-year-old hysteric who lost her voice, lasted only three months. He also had a four-hour psychoanalytic walk-talk session to help the famous composer Gustav Mahler, who became stricken with fear that his wife would leave him. And he treated Little Hans, Herbert Graf, a five-year-old boy who was afraid of horses. Freud primarily helped Han's father, Max Graf, to understand that the arrival of his younger sister and his curiosity about the origin of babies caused Hans's anxiety about horses. Although Freud formulated formal rules about psychoanalytic techniques, he treated them as rules of thumb. And even when Freud didn't follow his own recommendations, he still called his work psychoanalysis! Despite being aware of the particulars of Freud's cases, many psychoanalysts seem to be guided by the restrictive and formal technical requirements more than *he* was, such as frequency of sessions, use of the couch, and minimum duration of treatment."

"That's why Freud is closer to you than he is to the orthodox psychoanalysts."

I was pleasantly surprised by Jan's comment that Freud was closer to me than to some orthodoxy but wanted to clarify that I was not making any comparisons to Freud. "I didn't say that. I just find Freud useful."

An analyst can easily criticize my work from their point of view. In addition to speaking openly and in everyday language with my patients, I try to write about what I do transparently. I show others what happens in my treatments: helpful things I did, mistakes I made, and the specific way things unfolded in an analysis. (Hence, this book.) Psychoanalysis needs detailed descriptions, in addition to traditional case reports and presentations. I welcome all critiques, and I try to respond to patients' criticisms promptly, with clarifications, explanations, or interpretations. Like all analysts, my primary concern is to help my patients.

"It's hard to define what is or isn't Freudian," Jan said.

"For me, the patient drives the treatment more than any teacher or theory. Because you are not these people, you cannot directly apply Freud, Kohut, or Kernberg to help your patient. You can't blindly follow what some famous person did; what you do depends on the patient and your talents. You have to use *yourself.* There is no other possibility. The contribution of your personality is inevitable. I'm practical. I don't see myself as being closer to Freud than anybody else. I want to be close and available *to my patients.*"

"I think what happened to Freud and psychoanalysis is similar to what happened to Jesus and Christianity," Jan said. "Both started with great ideas that—over time—have been continuously reinterpreted. Churches were built to continue these ideas, but priests and rituals have become more important than the original ideas."

"It's my impression," I replied, "that some American Christians became overzealous in their concerns about the politics of abortion, same-sex marriage, school prayer, and the teaching of creationism as a science. Now, maybe in response to the recent hurricanes and other disasters, some are revisiting the traditional values and putting their efforts into feeding the poor, taking care of the helpless, and being Good Samaritans."

"I think I know the answer, but to which group do you belong?"

I was somewhat puzzled by Jan's question. I had previously told him that I was agnostic, so the question of what kind of Christian I was was moot. However, I assumed he was referring to the divide between politically active people and practically oriented people, so I answered generally. "I'm of the latter kind: I spend some time each week trying to help women in homeless shelters deal with their emotional problems."

"That's exactly what Jesus did . . ."

Oh, my. First, Jan compared me to Freud. Now he was promoting me to Jesus! Jan seemed hellbent on looking up to me. Such are the pearls, or perils, of over-idealization. Earlier, when Jan compared me highly favorably to his dim estimate of his previous analyst, I had unsuccessfully tried to address this idealizing-disparaging tendency in him. I wondered whether his second comparison, to Jesus—because of my work with the homeless— was any more amenable to my interpretations. Although I wanted to reply, Jan's statement was sufficiently surprising that I could not construct even a lame response, let alone a clever one.

"Helping people who are suffering isn't a high priority in Vatican circles," Jan went on. "When you do a good deed, you know it, and others feel it. You also know it when the dark side seduces you, and others suffer your harm."

I responded, "For you, the dark side is getting stuck in a whirlpool of guilt for being negligent in your patient's death. You feel that you alone are responsible. Today, we talked about life and death without Amir once crossing our path. This is a personal change for you."

"Yes, this conversation wouldn't have been possible before I met you."

CHAPTER 43

"Maria and I watched *The Painted Veil*. It starts with infidelity and how people hurt each other, and Maria kept asking, 'Why did Dr. Sripada recommend this movie? What did you *say* to him?' And I kept saying, 'I don't know. I've never had, let alone voiced, any thoughts about cheating. So he must have had something else in mind.'"

Oh, dear, I thought. *I had wanted Jan to see the movie, but it hadn't occurred to me that he would see it with Maria. It should have.* I deeply regretted that my action had put Jan in such an uncomfortable position and that I had caused Maria pain and uncertainty. Maria had already been burned by how Amir's suicide had impacted Jan. Now it was her misfortune to be hurt a second time by me. I had suggested the movie instinctively. I hoped to explore my dream-based understandings of links among Amir's father's initiated traumatic camel sacrifice, Amir, Jan, and me. In my eagerness, it hadn't occurred to me that Jan might see it with Maria and that they would see infidelity as its most salient feature.

Patients may talk about analytic events with their spouses or friends early in the analysis. However, later on, most patients don't tell their spouses about treatment conversations because therapeutic discussions are often too detailed and complicated to explain, even to a spouse. Nevertheless, an analyst must consider the possibility and accept responsibility for unusual interventions' actual or potential consequences. Still, it would be most inappropriate for me to call Maria to apologize. The most I could do to salvage the situation would be to explain to Jan how I thought the movie applied to Amir and him.

419

"So, I'll give you my summary of the movie and my take on it," Jan began, "and then you'll tell me why you wanted me to see it." It heartened me that Jan was both curious and surprised.

Jan continued, "It's the 1920s. On a trip to London, Walter Fane, a British bacteriologist working in China, meets a self-centered young woman named Kitty Garstin and falls in love with her. She doesn't love him but agrees to marry him to escape her cold family in England. Soon after they arrive in Hong Kong, Kitty begins an affair with Charles Townsend, the British vice-consul.

"Walter learns of the affair and is deeply hurt. He tells her, 'I knew when I married you that you were selfish and spoiled and that you only married me to get as far away from your mother as possible, but I loved you and hoped that there'd be something more between us one day. I was wrong. You don't have it in you.'

"There's a cholera outbreak in the interior of China, and Walter volunteers to go as a medical worker. He gives Kitty a choice: He will forego shaming her in public over her adultery by divorcing her *if* Charles will marry her, but if not, she will have to accompany him, as his wife, to the cholera-plagued zone. Charles, who had only wanted a fling, refuses to divorce his wife to marry Kitty. While Kitty and Walter prepare to leave for China, Kitty accuses Walter of putting her life in danger. While they discuss getting vaccinated, neither of them does so. However, Kitty is transformed once in China, surrounded by death and disease. As she sees Walter selflessly devoting himself to people who are suffering and dying, she begins to love him. It's too late, though. Walter contracts cholera, and with his now-loving wife at his side, he dwindles and dies."

In Jan's life-chilling connection to Amir, I saw a resemblance to the dangerous relationship between Walter and Kitty Fane as they ventured into the epidemic, unprotected by available vaccinations. In my view, Amir's death had pulled Jan into a malignant homicidal-suicidal *pas de deux* that Jan was unable to escape. I hoped that, with time and work, I could help Jan understand what happened. That would require further exploring the implications of Jan's ongoing struggle with Amir. It also meant understanding his reaction to *The Painted Veil*, because I recommended it.

"What do you remember about what we talked about last time?"

Jan thought for a moment. "We talked about my attitude toward change and stability, about changes in my life, and life and death. I didn't give much thought to becoming a father for a long time, and now David is the center of my life. I understood my mission from the first moment I saw him. I knew that I had to protect him, and I wanted to teach him by being a good example. And I wondered if I would live long enough to do it. So, then I began thinking about death and dying and finding a place to rest for eternity, whether to be buried in a place where people will come to visit on birthdays, anniversaries and, for sure, on All Saints' Day. Or whether I should find a place in a Yankee cemetery with fields of grass, where people would drive past me or even walk over my head. Or maybe be cremated and have my ashes tossed into the ocean."

I nodded, confirming his recollection.

Jan continued, "A year ago, Amir's death was at the center of my universe. The conversation you and I had at our last session couldn't have taken place then, or it would have taken place with completely different emotions."

"Yes, feelings—primarily guilt connected to Amir's suicide—are now becoming associated with other emotions and other elements of your life, including your own mortality. So we need to understand and come to terms with the most egregious type of death, like Amir's suicide, and with ordinary kinds of natural death. So, back to the movie.

"*The Painted Veil* movie is based on W. Somerset Maugham's book by the same name. It is, not surprisingly, somewhat soupier than the book. That's Hollywood. We'll get to that in a moment. Maugham took the title from a sonnet by Percy Bysshe Shelley." I handed Jan a copy of the poem.

"Lift not the Painted Veil"

Lift not the painted veil which those who live
Call Life: though unreal shapes be pictured there,
And it but mimic all we would believe
With colours idly spread,—behind, lurk Fear
And Hope, twin Destinies; who ever weave
Their shadows, o'er the chasm, sightless and drear.
I knew one who had lifted it—he sought,
For his lost heart was tender, things to love,
But found them not, alas! nor was there aught
The world contains, the which he could approve.
Through the unheeding many he did move,
A splendour among shadows, a bright blot
Upon this gloomy scene, a Spirit that strove
For truth, and like the Preacher found it not.

Jan read it silently and then looked up expectantly.

"Shelley's veil is both a covering and a canvas," I said. "Life—or reality—is forever shrouded in mystery because a veil covers it, and then it is further obscured by a painting *on* the veil. Shelley's view is that we don't have access to the truth; we have access only to people's façades, their veils. The veil obscures what lies beneath and is also a canvas we continuously paint and re-paint our lives. The sonnet is a poetic intimation of the layering of human personality and human relationships. It's a warning not to take the most obvious thing to be the final thing. You may, in fact, never know the final thing, but you have to live in the meantime with both fear and hope, that is, with complexity.

"In the preface to the novel, Maugham says that a vignette from the *Purgatorio* section of Dante's *The Divine Comedy* also inspired the story. Pia's husband, Nello, suspects her of adultery, but is afraid her family will seek revenge if he kills her. So, he takes her to a castle in Maremma, surrounded by 'noxious vapors' that he believes will kill her. But she doesn't die fast enough, so he has her thrown out the window."

"Maugham clarifies that, in contemplating the murder of his wife, Nello was desecrating the marriage just as Pia would have done by committing adultery. Walter, like Nello, has murder, or at least manslaughter, in his heart. *Walter doesn't care for his own life; he just wants to punish, that is, kill Kitty*, so he arranges for them to go to the cholera-infested area unvaccinated. Walter thought he was engaging Kitty in a suicide–homicide pact, but Maugham adds a twist: Walter, not Kitty, contracts cholera. As Walter is dying, Kitty, who has come to love him and regrets the pain she had caused him, says, 'I'm sorry. Forgive me.' But here's the kicker: Walter dies in her arms, a touching and tragic scene at that point in the movie. *In the book*, though, he says faintly, 'The dog it was that died.' *That* metaphor comes from Oliver Goldsmith's 'An Elegy on the Death of a Mad Dog.'"[65] I handed Jan a copy.

"An Elegy on the Death of a Mad Dog"

Good people all, of every sort,
Give ear unto my song;
And if you find it wondrous short,
It cannot hold you long.

In Islington there was a man,
Of whom the world might say
That still a godly race he ran,
Whene'er he went to pray.

A kind and gentle heart he had,
To comfort friends and foes;
The naked every day he clad,
When he put on his clothes.

And in that town a dog was found,
As many dogs there be,
Both mongrel, puppy, whelp and hound,
And curs of low degree.

This dog and man at first were friends;
But when a pique began,
The dog, to gain some private ends,
Went mad and bit the man.

Around from all the neighbouring streets
The wondering neighbours ran,
And swore the dog had lost his wits,
To bite so good a man.

The wound it seemed both sore and sad
To every Christian eye;
And while they swore the dog was mad,
They swore the man would die.

But soon a wonder came to light,
That showed the rogues they lied:
The man recovered of the bite,
The dog it was that died.

Jan finished reading and looked up.

"The man in the poem appears to be upstanding, even exemplary," I said. "He comforts everyone, takes care of the poor, and even befriends a pitiful dog. Then the dog seemingly goes mad and bites him, and the townspeople, believing the dog must be rabid, expect the man to die. But when the dog dies, they conclude that there must have been something toxic about the man and that his apparent kindness was all a sham.

"Maugham is a genius. His metaphors are complex and can yield different meanings depending on the reader. For example, Walter wanted to kill Kitty because she rejected his love and had an affair. Kitty's betrayal is so toxic to Walter that it breaks his heart.

"When Walter says, 'The dog it was that died,' he communicates to Kitty that he intended to kill her. In making this declaration, he tells her that she should not attribute only heroic good intentions to him and that he is unworthy of her grief. Walter's dying statement offers Kitty the chance to appreciate his true intentions toward her and understand why he brought her to the epicenter of the cholera epidemic. Though veiled and figurative, Walter's message could have helped Kitty realize the nature of their complex relationship. After his death, she could work through her guilt over her affair; most importantly, she could live a good life both as a woman and a mother.

"Walter wanted to kill her through cholera because she rejected him by her infidelity. Since he did not get himself vaccinated, either, Walter was probably suicidal. So his death, by cholera, would be an instance of covert suicide. In my opinion, the story of *The Painted Veil* has parallels to your situation with Amir. It is not easy to unpack because there are so many players: Maugham, Shelley, Goldsmith, Dante, Walter, and Kitty; and Amir, Amir's mother, Amir's father, Maria, you, . . . and me.

"I recommended it because, as I see it, the relationship that evolved between Amir and you paralleled the relationship between Walter and Kitty. Just as Walter went to the cholera-infested area on a homicide-suicide mission, Amir also took you on a deadly mission. By failing to communicate to you, on time, about the depth of his depression and especially of his final intention to kill himself, Amir induced ferocious guilt in you that influenced you to identify with him and become suicidal, like him. According to this understanding, Amir, most probably unconsciously, wanted to go . . . and take you with him. That Amir was suicidal is apparent from his actions. I only infer Amir's homicidal trajectory from the resulting depressive, suicidal preoccupations in you. Your problem is not entirely attributable to Amir because your past has a melancholy blue vein.

"However, unlike Walter, Amir didn't give you any indirect tips. Amir did not offer a clarifying communication or a dying declaration. He killed himself and sent you into a depressive-suicidal funk. Amir burdened you with a deadly surprise, a gigantic load of guilt, with no clues about his motivation. The gun with which he played Russian roulette was pointed as much at you as it was at him. *You* felt that both of you were on a proper therapeutic path. You felt he was a good patient since he seemed motivated and kept his appointments, but he enticed you into a confusing and poisonous relationship. His conscious or unconscious plans uniquely fit into your personality. Did he know his intentions? Did he deceive you intentionally? I do not think he knew himself that well, beyond feeling he'd failed his father. The therapy was dangerous because you did not *perceive* any suicidal-homicidal danger, so you did not feel that such a situation existed or needed management. The camel of Amir's childhood, whose sacrifice he could not bear to watch, also represented his father's rejection of Amir; it symbolized the problem that finally consumed him. From Amir's life, that camel stuck its nose into the therapeutic tent and almost pushed you out of the tent of your life. If I were a psychoneurobiochemist, I would say that you could not metabolize Amir and his suicide. He was toxic for you."

Jan did not say anything.

I continued and now spoke very slowly and deliberately, "Jan, as psychiatrists, sometimes we're so burdened by our patients that we don't want them. Sometimes we hate them. Sometimes we wish them gone. Sometimes we even wish them dead."

Jan did not respond for a while. Then, when he did, he started slowly. "I'm stunned. I wouldn't have known what you meant if you had told me this just three months ago. I wouldn't have understood it. I think I'm ready to start thinking about Amir's suicide completely differently by thinking less about how it affected me and more about why and how it happened. My thinking is still largely guided by my emotions. I still can't isolate myself from the horror when I think about Amir actually doing it—committing suicide. My chest becomes so tight when I think about it that I can hardly breathe."

At this point in the analysis, Jan clarifies that his understanding of Amir's suicide has changed from looking at it in terms of his own personal reactions to appreciating Amir's dynamics. He attributes this change to the treatment process over the last three months. One of Jan's presenting complaints was overpowering guilt because he felt responsible for Amir's death. In addition, the reader will remember that Jan felt bludgeoned by Amir's mother, who attributed Amir's suicide to Jan's negligence.

An interpretation is the spear-tip of the treatment process, and so this analytic juncture offers a good opportunity to review my explanations. Most analysts agree that any interpretation should be timely, tactful, and dosed appropriately to effectuate patient change. In addition, the current scientific method does not allow infallible hypotheses and limits the scope of science to provisional knowledge that a better explanation may improve. So interpretations are like hypotheses to be tested by the patient, which the analyst cannot hold as absolute. Because most contemporary analysts view the analytic relationship as mutually influencing, an interpretation must also reflect a shared reality.

Currently, my interpretation that sometimes therapists may even wish a patient's death was not about who was responsible for Amir's suicide but alluded to and hinted at Jan's unconscious death wish toward Amir. My generalizing interpretation referred to many overburdened therapists who may wish their impossible patients dead. I did not refer to Jan in particular, but my sentence included him. Although there is a difference between being responsible for someone's death and wishing someone dead, I did not want to risk Jan confusing the two and exacerbating Jan's guilt for Amir's actual suicide. Previously, I acknowledged Jan's difficulty with Amir because Amir did not concurrently communicate his suicidal thoughts. Now, I introduced the idea that whether Jan was responsible for Amir's suicide, Jan may have unconsciously wished it. That was the essence of the interpretation even though it relied on Jan's dynamics transferred to the displacements afforded by *The Painted Veil*. In this instance, my understanding was informal and offered within the flow of our conversation. Because I gave it in such a casual manner, some analysts may not even consider it an interpretation.

However, it is possible to frame a formal interpretation that makes a direct and explicit connection between Jan's ideas or emotions, Amir, and me. For example, I could have said, "I asked you to watch *The Painted Veil*. Knowing what I know about you and based on your thoughts in response to the movie, my interpretation is that you unconsciously did not want to treat Amir and wanted him dead." Such an interpretation forcefully expresses the same idea I brought up to Jan. However, in my opinion, Jan could perceive this direct, formal interpretation as an attack on him, as the attack by Amir's mom.

All analytic activity considers the patient's living conditions—stresses, defenses, self-esteem, and the benefits of the patient's sense of self-discovery. Thus, the main goal of any interpretation, formal or informal, is to produce adaptive patient insight or enhance the patient's existing self-understanding to enable the patient to change. In addition, any interpretation aims to uncover and restructure maladaptive defenses and bolster effective and necessary defenses in the process. The interpretative process starts with the analyst's personality, takes shape in explicit or implied analyst's statements, and ends with the patient's insight and change; ideally, it also results in effective patient feedback to the analyst. Finally, the patient's self-interpretation add to the analytic understanding.

An analyst's interpretation is only a plausible explanation. Because the analyst has an ongoing relationship and a vast reservoir of information about the patient, an analyst's interpretation can be correct. Still, it is also possible for it to be mistaken. The analyst may offer an interpretation with confidence but explicitly tell the patient that the patient is free to reject it and submit an alternate one. The ambiguity, doubt, or distance held in an interpretation may imply its amenability to rejection. The patient-analyst relationship may contain the history of the analyst's tolerance toward the patient's disagreement, which carries over to subsequent interpretations, even formal and direct ones.

For example, suppose an analyst makes no allowance for the possibility that his interpretation may be wrong. In that case, he is offering an infallible interpretation, which is not conducive to the inquiring method of psychoanalysis. In some instances, the analyst's explicit and direct statement is most effective. In other situations, a veiled interpretation may best suit the purpose.

The patient reworks all that analyst's interpretations, generalized or specific, and further fine-tunes acceptable aspects to fit the patient's personality and circumstances. Second, the patient then transforms inexact, approximate, generalized, or implied elements of the analyst's interpretation into relevant particulars to fit the patient's current circumstances to facilitate self-understanding, change, or action. Third, the patient rejects unsuitable interpretations and ideally provides feedback to the analyst.

Assessing an interpretation requires the patient's input; the analyst cannot independently claim his interpretation to be correct before the patient completes his response. Finally, knowing that the interpretation is only the initiation of the interpretative and change process and that the patient will revise, correct, or improve upon his efforts, the analyst should feel freer to offer his interpretations. If a patient validates the analyst, this can help confirm that they are on the right track. However, a rejected understanding is also of great importance, for this starts an error-correction and learning process that is crucial for growth.

The analyst's tact is crucial if the patient feels bruised, on guard, has shaky self-esteem, or fears impingement. All interpretations reveal new connections and subject the patient to some degree of novelty. The patient often recognizes an interpretation's utility and intent and accepts such therapeutic novelty. However, the analyst's job is to limit the surprise to within the patient's tolerance levels. Otherwise, the very analyst's interpretations could traumatize the patient or impair a fundamental and necessary sense of pride in being a subject. Especially in such circumstances, the analyst chooses to employ interventions that the patient can easily accept and finds plausible. The patient may be more willing to consider the generalizing interpretation I offered, with some built-in distance or ambiguity offered by displacements of play, toys, art, or history.

In my view, the active participant analytic transference-countertransference imprint is discernible in this entire sequence of conversations regarding *The Painted Veil*. Based on my previous awareness of Jan's pathology, concerns, free associations, and relationship, I asked Jan to watch the movie. Thus, the evolving transference-countertransference matrix underlies all our analytic conversations, even those with displaced contents. While in some interpretations, the analyst chooses to make the transference elements of the matrix explicit, in other interpretations, the analyst may choose to let them remain implicit.

Today's discussions shook up Jan and provided a pivotal moment of personal insight for him. Our long, slow discussions, the reworking of ideas and emotions were bearing fruit. He was having an uncharacteristic difficulty finding words and breathing. It would take time for him to think through what he had said. I would have to carry a more significant share of the burden of conversation for the rest of the session. It was essential for us to explore this insight, but the conversation would have to be limited to what Jan could tolerate. I would need to monitor his tolerance of deadly insight from moment to moment.

I thought of D. W. Winnicott. He was an extraordinary analyst who wrote about hate as a form of countertransference in an analyst. Winnicott was simply acknowledging that no one person (including an analyst) can be the repository of all good, since man has both good and bad qualities. Is it possible Jan was too much of a good-focus Catholic to be able to hear my imputation of suicidal homicidality to Amir and Jan's unconscious homicidal hostility towards Amir? Whereas Jan's hostile impulses were unconscious and blocked by guilt, Amir's hatred, probably originally directed toward his rejecting father, had turned inward, where it became conscious and deadly. It struck and killed Amir, then ricocheted toward Jan, and almost killed him. Indeed, I felt that Jan had dodged a metaphoric bullet. But, although heartfelt, I feared that Jan might see my interpretation as an attack on himself or Amir. I wondered if I had overburdened Jan with literary metaphors and weighty interpretations. I needed to assess more of Jan's reactions to decide for sure.

"Therapists are often just as unaware of their own feelings as patients are, and our motivations can be hidden from us by a veil. And as psychiatrists, we have a persona to maintain, which is also a veil. From a human perspective, an ethicist could say, patients as humans in an interpersonal sense should owe us an explanation, especially if they're putting us through hell. But things are not as they should be. Both patients and psychiatrists share responsibility, whether things go right or wrong. It is often not entirely one person's fault or wholly to another person's credit. I think you blamed yourself, and that's where you needed the most help. You thought Amir's suicide was almost entirely your fault.

"Do you remember what Dr. Williams said to you? 'Amir did the best he could. He killed himself alone. He didn't strap on a bomb and blow up a lot of other people, too.' That's a strong statement, but it may give us a clue about Amir's motivations. In his inimitable manner, Williams was suggesting that Amir's anger was directed only at himself. However, my view is that some of the anger was other-aggressive, directed toward you. He didn't leave any clues to his motivations, but he knew you; he was aware of your personality. He knew that you would suffer deeply and perhaps permanently be hurt if he killed himself. We can only speculate that the original target of his hostility was his father, and he displaced those hostile feelings from his father onto you.

"We know that he didn't express anger overtly. Perhaps it was unconscious, or he could express it only through disagreement about inpatient treatment and delaying reporting of his suicidal thoughts. Maybe he was angry at his father for demanding that he witness something he was unable and unprepared to see. The sacrificial killing of the camel, no matter how his culture sanctioned it, was beyond what Amir could tolerate as a boy. He expressed that original anger toward his father in the treatment but then directed it against you when he killed himself. More than a year later, you are still feeling its after-effects.

"Perhaps Amir was so much in awe of his father that he had to remain unaware of his anger. He painted his father as a hero who deserved admiration and couldn't allow his anger to surface. He acted out his unconscious hostility toward his father by turning it inward onto himself—hence, his suicide. Amir's anger toward his father was also translated into anger at you in the transference and almost destroyed you.

"As for your role, perhaps he wanted some other human being to understand and share his unbearable pain. He succeeded, but at the cost of his life. Your two selves became mirror images of each other. When you take on a suicidal patient, you take on a world of mighty powerful forces."

I could have been more succinct, but since Jan had said he was stunned, I felt that I had to regulate the aftermath of that shock. I overdid this perhaps by being unusually speculative and waxing eloquent about anger turned inward.

In a half-joking manner, I added, "Considering *The Painted Veil*, perhaps you could say that every patient is inviting us to go on a humanitarian mission or a mission to the 'heart of darkness.' When you're a young doctor, you are bright-eyed, bushy-tailed, and eager to sign up for the journey. The residency programs train you to ask the patient for his insurance, but the patient may secretly be signing you up for something else."

"In my case," Jan said, "I signed up for a challenge from the very beginning."

Since Jan had not spoken for a while, I was glad to hear Jan say anything! I replied, "Yes, it was the ultimate challenge."

"It's horrible to say, but it's been a life-changing experience for me. I'm not the same person I was when I deal with people now."

"Why is that horrible to say?"

"Because Amir had to die for me to have this experience."

"Absolutely. Because Amir is dead, all we can do is speculate about him, and after a while, speculations can turn into rationalizations. But you're still around. You said earlier that today's discussion would have been impossible even three months ago. Can you explain that?"

"Initially, all I could do was describe my reactions to Amir's suicide. There was no room for constructive analysis of any kind. When I got the letter from his mom, she confirmed, in my mind, that his death was my responsibility. Even after she found out that I was in training and had supervisors, she blamed only me."

I quietly rejoiced that Jan had given me an opening to talk about Amir's mom. "I've mentioned before the dangers I see with your relationship with Amir's mom. Continuing it could take you on another dangerous, choleric journey in the movie's terms. I think you can see that now.

"So, back to where we started this session, I recommended the movie because I thought it might help you process your professional but deadly relationship with Amir. Obviously, it has nothing to do with your personal life with Maria, and I'm sorry for the unnecessary anxiety I caused her on that score."

"I understand," Jan said. "Our therapeutic relationship is so self-contained, it was easy for you not to think I might see the movie with Maria. So the first thing I will do when I get home is to clarify to her that the movie was a recommendation for me, not for us, and that it pertained to Amir's relationship with me and not to my relationship with her.

"And other than that, we liked it very much."

I laughed, relieved.

Thinking movies, Jan continued, "The climate and pace of the movie reminded me of *Indochine*. Have you seen it?"

"No."

"*Indochine* is what the French called Vietnam when they were there from the 1930s to the 1950s. Catherine Deneuve is Éliane, a stylish rubber-plantation owner, businesslike during work hours—and an opium addict in off-hours. She lives a satisfying life with her adopted Indochine daughter, Camille. And then the political situation changes beyond her gates. As the Communists are trying to gain power, France loses its footing in the region. This doesn't affect Éliane until a French officer suddenly arrives on the scene and disturbs the cozy world of mother and daughter. Both are attracted to him, and he reciprocates their affections, but ultimately, he chooses Camille. Éliane is hurt and arranges his transfer to the frontlines . . . and danger. There are lots of complications in the story, but eventually, Camille becomes a Communist sympathizer. However, as much as Éliane is immersed in her own world and wishes to keep it that way, the world outside penetrates it. Because of the vividly painted landscapes, you can almost smell Asia in both movies.

"The scenes in the hospital in *The Painted Veil* are vivid. Maria and I joked that there was a lot of information there for the first step of the USMLE (United States Medical Licensing Examination). For example, stuff dealing with the bacteriology part of infectious diseases. We both remembered the watery rice stools, like grains of rice in water."

CHAPTER 44

"I've talked before about how reckless I was when I was younger," Jan began. "I tried to test the limits of everything. As a result, I was admitted to the hospital several times with wounds and broken bones and had three close brushes with death. Once, I had an accident racing go-karts and lay unconscious for close to two weeks with a fracture at the base of my skull. After that, I was no stranger to the local hospital!

"This racing accident happened suddenly and unexpectedly, like the stingray that killed Steve Irwin, the great Australian showman. He wrestled with alligators and crocodiles and was famous as 'The Crocodile Hunter.' Then, while his crew was filming him approaching a stingray fearlessly, it pierced his chest and lodged its stinger in his heart. He died instantly."

As Jan talked about the sudden death of Steve Irwin, it reminded me of a recent incident in my life. "For many years, I've had a bird feeder in my backyard," I began. "I keep it full of seeds, and it regularly attracts chickadees, cardinals, woodpeckers, finches—you name it. I had heard that some birds—like doves, robins, and sparrows—feel safer eating off the ground than from a bird feeder, so I fed those birds by sprinkling seeds on the ground. But the squirrels helped themselves, too. And because I was so diligent about stocking the feeder and the ground, the number of squirrels and birds in my backyard kept increasing. Unfortunately, the abundance of food didn't make them more content. Despite, or maybe because of it, they became more greedy and more aggressive.

"Yesterday, I witnessed an unusual encounter between a squirrel and a sparrow. Usually, sparrows fly away when a squirrel is nearby, but this sparrow was so engrossed in getting food that it didn't notice the squirrel moving toward it. Instead, the squirrel lunged at the sparrow and snapped at its throat as I watched. The stunned sparrow went limp and, after struggling a bit, oozed a few drops of blood and died. The squirrel looked surprised—I'm guessing he had expected the bird to fly away in time—and came closer to inspect the dead bird. It was almost like the squirrel was asking himself, 'Is it that easy to kill?'

"I was shocked and hurt and disgusted. I intended to bring more life to my backyard, but there lay a dead bird and the stunned squirrel that had killed it. My caring and feeding had the opposite effect from what I had intended. I felt that I had lured the unsuspecting sparrow to its death and considered ending my hobby. It hurts to see a dead bird, especially one that perhaps wouldn't have been, but for me."

"It's hard to deal with death," Jan agreed, "even that of a bird. I didn't know that squirrels were predators."

"In general, they're not. I think it was an accidental killing since the squirrel and the sparrow seemed equally surprised."

"What you described can happen to humans, too. I once mentioned a patient of mine, a Vietnam vet who had been a medevac helicopter pilot. He told me that they got orders to transfer some wounded soldiers one day, but they had captured a bunch of Vietcong that morning. They couldn't bring them on board, and they couldn't let them go, so he gave the order to kill them. He said he didn't think about whether he was doing the right thing, and even thinking about it later, he didn't think there was anything wrong with what he did. 'We had to go somewhere, and they couldn't go with us.'

"That happened after he had been in Vietnam a few months. He said that he was shocked the first time he saw people being killed, but it stopped bothering him after seeing killing for a year. War demands that you stop pondering and act. He just became part of the killing machine. 'It was my job,' he said. 'I had to follow orders. What had to happen had to happen! It would be treason to refuse to kill. Wrongs and rights are for priests.'"

"Last weekend, I saw a movie called *The Good German*. Have you seen it?"

"I loved it! I don't understand why it got bad reviews. I thought it was great."

"What was great about it?" I probed.

"I like the genre and the style. I like to watch movies from the thirties and forties. They're in black and white, so you see more of the interplay between light and shadows. This movie shows what people do in times of war and how they behave when human life is cheap. You pray that the cheapening doesn't happen to you and to the people you love."

"Who was the good German?"

"Where the title comes from?"

"Yes. What's your view?"

"I think it was Emil Brandt, although he wasn't good. Unfortunately, he was the one who got killed in the end."

"Why was he the good German?"

"Well, he was an SS officer working at the V-2 rocket-production plant at the Mittelbau-Dora Mittelwerk concentration camp. He was part of the Nazi killing machine, tallying food rations for the prisoners used as slave laborers. He fed them just enough to keep them productive. The Germans killed the prisoners after they extracted the last joule of energy from them. He excelled at his job and was proud of it. He was a good German."

"OK. What do you think of Lena Brandt, Emil's wife? What about her?"

"Let me think. Lena Brandt was a German Jew who survived the war because she was the wife of an SS officer. At the end of the war, when Emil had to go into hiding, it's implied that she became a prostitute. Then she encountered her pre-war lover, Jake Geismer, an American journalist investigating the murder of his soldier-driver and the deaths of slave workers at the Dora camp. Jake was searching for Emil Brandt because of his value as a witness to atrocities involving Franz Bettman, a Nazi engineer who had worked at Dora. To go back to your question, . . . I have no answer."

I responded, "In the last scene, after Jake has obtained an American visa for her, Lena is saying goodbye to him. She's about to board the plane to take her to safety when she refers to the challenges Jews faced in Germany. That's an understatement! And she tells Jake that because of her actions, some Jews lost their lives."

"Yes. She says, 'I did it to survive.'"

"Right. Although all Germans were good Germans from the German point of view, here, *good* is ironic. In this movie, *good* from the SS point of view means a good killer. From a non-German point of view, a good German might also refer to those Germans who opposed Hitler. Lena rationalizes that she played a part in the killing only to survive. But she lost her soul in the process. So, although she was a Jew, she was also a good German."

"We have a saying in Polish, and I'm sure it exists in other languages, that it's the winners who write history. If such a movie were to be made, *The*

Good American would cause as much confusion in the United States. Do you know the name of the tribe that lived in what is now the State of Illinois?"

"No."

"They were called Sauk. They still exist, but few people have heard about them. I had never heard about them until I read about the history of Illinois. What happened to them was that they got into trouble with several presidents; they called them the 'Big Fathers from Washington.' The government initiated the Indian Removal Act in 1830 when they decided the settlers needed more space. First, they demanded that the Sauk move *toward* the Mississippi River. Then they told them to move even farther west *to the other side of* the Mississippi. At some point, the Sauk fought back and won a small battle. This victory was followed by another battle, in which the U.S. used more professional soldiers and won decisively. The Sauk survivors who wanted land had to buy back their own land! Gradually, most of the Sauk suffered extermination.

"I remember growing up in Poland and watching Western movies. Everybody wanted to be a cowboy so they could shoot Indians. Nobody wanted to be an Indian; Indians were always losers."

"So, like the good Germans, the settlers were all good cowboys. Now, back to the movie. In the last scene, Jake and Lena are standing in the rain near the plane that will take her to the U.S. Lena tells him she turned twelve Jews over to the Gestapo. 'What could I do?' she says. 'I did it to survive. Everything was to survive. Now you know. That's the last piece of the puzzle.' And what does Jake say?"

"Oh, yes—I remember the scene. It's an homage to *Casablanca*!"

"Yes. It's raining. The plane is waiting. What does Jake say?"

"I don't remember."

"Right! You don't remember because he doesn't say anything. He just looks at her. Then she kisses him on his— . . ."

". . . —cheek?"

"More like his jaw. And then she walks to the waiting plane. George Clooney, who played Jake, has the reputation of being an *Ocean's Eleven*-type of superficial actor, but I believe he can be deep, too. So, let me ask you a question: Were you convinced that Jake was in love with Lena?"

"Oh, yes."

"In that last scene, before she speaks, you can see his love for her in his face, but after she tells him what she did, the camera closes in on him, and you can see, in an instant, without him saying anything, that his love for her has evaporated. At that moment, his feelings change, and he knows he can't be with her. He conveys that change simply by looking—hard and cold—and she obviously sees it; she knows he can't love her anymore. That's why she doesn't kiss him on his lips. The kiss on his jaw is more a token of their past passion than any current feeling or hope of future love. And he doesn't reciprocate with even a token pucker. So, to belabor my view on this once again, she's a good German like the good cowboys.

"If my version of the story is plausible, Jake, in the end, was the ethical character. He didn't say, 'You had to do what you had to do,' or 'You were a Jew in Nazi Germany, and you did what you did to survive.'"

"I feel he didn't judge her for her role in the extermination machine," Jan said. "He just decided that he couldn't love her anymore."

"Yes . . . In my opinion, that decision came at a great cost to him personally—the loss of his love for Lena."

"I'll have to watch it again."

"Please do. You have to decide if what he's communicating is the extinction of his love for her in one moment."

"When I saw the movie, I recognized the parallels between *The Good German* and *Casablanca*, the position of the man and the woman, the plane, the rain, and the play of light and shadows. One big difference is that in *Casablanca*, love continues; in *The Good German,* love comes to an end."

"She was a good German, her husband was a good German, and maybe all of Germany was a good Germany, but Jake didn't go along with such rationalizations. His judgment was visceral and immediate and had little to do with being a winner or loser. I repeat this point because it's not easy for us when we, as psychiatrists, deal with borderline, psychotic, suicidal, or antisocial patients. In the case of your Vietnam veteran, we have to take a stance. If we completely agree that the Vietnamese prisoners had to be shot, we risk becoming 'good psychiatrists.' To your credit, you struggled and still struggle with doubts and memories of Amir and your other patients. That's why you've suffered so deeply. So, considering the inverted metaphor of the good German, you're not a good psychiatrist!"

We sat looking at each other silently for a minute, knowing the session was nearing its end. Then, as he got up to leave, Jan said, "I felt the same way you felt when the sparrow's life drained out. It's a shame. It shouldn't have happened."

"I think this is your current feeling. What you felt before you saw me was not only 'It's a shame that Amir killed himself,' but also, 'I am the guilty one; I alone am responsible.' We live our lives, but we don't set the terms of life and death. We should consider the hard existence of birds and squirrels and the amount of energy they have to spend just to survive. Should we stop giving because there are tragic events? I decided that all I control is feeding or not feeding. I relinquish control once I put out the food. The birds and beasts do whatever they do. Should we feel responsible? Who can answer? How much time do we have to dwell on these questions?

"You invested your heart and soul in Amir and, despite your best efforts, you had to deal with a tragic outcome. Your treatment of Amir is a great professional and personal misfortune, and you'll bear its burden for the rest of your life. Life can be so unpredictable. Ultimately unexpected things can happen. By following simple guidelines, some psychiatrists manage these situations without much angst. You immersed yourself in Amir's life and can never completely let go. Hopefully, your pain will become less of an open wound and turn into a reasonable scar without becoming a keloid. David and Maria have given you a taste for life, and every day you keep wanting more. Where there is love, there is life.

"You did a great job with the woman who made a shrine for her son, the Japanese man, the Vietnam veteran, and the Jewish woman who wanted to kill her father. Your contributions to your patients have been valuable. Your Polish patients only want to see *you*. They come to you because you give them something precious. But the negative outcomes, like Amir's, are in your memory, too. It's an ongoing challenge to maintain a reasonable balance among your experiences and continue to deliver for your patients."

CHAPTER 45

"MARIA AND I JUST RETURNED from taking the Psychiatry Boards. If I pass, it means I am a certified psychiatrist."

"How was it?" I asked.

"It was so different from the previous exam, when I felt completely paralyzed. This time, I was pretty relaxed. When we were studying, we had the babysitter take care of David. We realized we couldn't study at home; he's too powerful a magnet. We just can't resist him, so we prepared for the exam at the library nearby, and the babysitter brought him in a few times a day so we could play with him. We're happy to have it over with so now we can focus on David.

"I can't predict the results, but I feel confident. They're supposed to test your knowledge of psychiatry and neurology. The neurology questions were about rare forms of brain diseases, like Jakob-Creutzfeldt disease. The psychiatry questions covered psychiatry's biological, metabolic, and genetic bases, but there were very few on psychotherapy, in general, and hardly any on dynamic psychotherapy."

"That's understandable. The medicalization of psychiatry is proceeding at a rapid clip. The exam that you took is for certification in The American Board of Psychiatry and Neurology. Given the developments in neuroimaging and genetics, the star of biological psychiatry is on the rise. It's true that Freud and psychotherapy once made up the lion's share of the exam, but Freud and his tribe are on the wane. You're good with the biological stuff, right?"

"I hope I am, since that's what we needed to know to pass. But it makes me sad that Freud and dynamic psychotherapy, which are the basis of

439

most talk therapies, are slowly being forgotten. On the other hand, many questions in neurology were typical of 19th-century neurology, things like locating the lesion in the brain based on clinical examination. Anyway, this exam didn't paralyze me nearly the way the exam that brought me to you did."

"It's funny to hear you say that you were relaxed while preparing for this exam, even with David. It seems that when you're less anxious, you can do more."

"True. Except for that previous exam, I've always been more relaxed about tests than Maria. Since childhood, she's been anxious to be the best in the class. But, this time, we were both at ease because David is far more important than any exam."

"I think you're saying that you're reverting to your personality before Amir died."

"That's true," Jan confirmed and then became pensive. "I became somebody other than myself. I thought about Amir a few times during the exam because there were some questions about suicide. Actually, this time, thinking about Amir was helpful. I knew what to look for. I had no problem identifying the focus of the questions and felt pretty confident with my answers. For example, there was a question about a young girl who attempted suicide by taking five aspirins. The specific question was whether the doctor should address the fact that she thought aspirin would kill her or dismiss the seriousness of the attempt because five aspirins weren't lethal."

"How did you answer?"

"I said that the girl's expectation is more important. I do not doubt that this is the right answer."

"That's what you mean about Amir being helpful."

"Yes. If she was planning to die, her suicide attempt should be taken seriously."

"It was a trick question," I said, "but you knew the trick."

"Well, . . . yes."

"After Amir died, when you were in the middle of unresolved grief, even a straightforward question looked like a trick to you."

"Yes, I think that I would have doubted myself even a few months ago. I would have looked for hidden clues, some mysterious second bottom. Now I know what's important: It's not what *I* think, but what the *patient* thinks. If you're thinking normally, it seems pretty obvious."

Jan's cell phone rang. He apologized and answered it. Maria was calling to let him know that she had just completed her analytic session. Jan's train of thought veered.

"It turns out that Maria and Dr. Mario Zazueta share the same analyst. After years of analysis, I recently joked about it, telling her that I was worried about her because Dr. Zazueta is still an asshole. Maria laughed and asked me how my treatment was going. I said that I was more hopeful because I wasn't aware of any of your failed cases. I know analysis works. I *feel* it. I *believe* it. Also, I can think of a few other people who helped. Do you remember Dr. Balint, my old attending? He's a great example. He started analysis and really changed. He used to use the royal *we*, but now he's like everybody else. To quote Dr. Schwartz, 'I don't need any stinking fMRI [functional Magnetic Resonance Imaging] to prove it works. I know!'"

"You're throwing Copernicus, Galileo, and the whole of scientific tradition out the window! And your bacteriological studies! And your *second* position in the Biology Olympiad in Poland!"

"Yes, I'm throwing it all out. I'm a believer. After a few years of analysis, Balint is a different person. A few years ago, he would never greet you with a simple 'How are you?' He was a psychiatrist with no apparent concern for others. I just saw him, and he *sincerely* asked how I was. We chatted about my career, and he gave me some good advice. I felt empathy, care, even compassion from him. We also spoke about a patient he wants to transfer to my hospital. He gave me a good history and asked for my thoughts about it. Then he patiently listened to my answer. I was amazed."

"Change! That's what you mean by 'It works.'"

"Yes, I've changed personally, and I've observed changes in Balint—positive and undeniable changes in both of us. Now I understand Schwartz's fury when he said, 'I know I'm helping, and I don't need any proof.' He acted like seeking proof for psychoanalysis was violating some holy rule. It's like asking for proof that God exists. You don't do that. It's meaningless, senseless, and wrong. You believe it, or you don't, so today I'm telling you that I'm a believer."

This unexpected turn of events struck me. It was as if a believer in God had become a believer in godless psychoanalysis. It was a big leap, indeed. But, being a believer in skepticism myself, I didn't wish to quickly acquiesce to a religion of psychoanalysis, so I asked, "How do you think it works?"

Perhaps Jan picked up my skepticism.

"I don't mean that psychoanalysis always works. In Zazueta's case, it didn't work. I think Balint built up a shell in his childhood or adolescence.

He was a sensitive and insecure person inside and created this shiny, narcissistic armor to prevent people from seeing who he really was.

"I sometimes saw Balint as an adolescent—I mean, the old pre-analytic Balint I knew when I began the residency program. I can easily imagine his family: His mother must have set high standards; I think he brought a sparkle to her eye. His father may have wanted a meaningful relationship with him, but he was distant. I don't know who his analyst was, but he or she was good! The treatment softened Balint's tough exterior and healed some of the damage caused by his mother's impossible standards. His analyst also rekindled his wish for true closeness. After his analysis took hold, he was able to be a more secure person."

"I think you detected positive change in him some time ago, when he was on the Morbidity and Mortality Committee that met after Amir's suicide. I remember you saying that both Balint and Shastri were evenhanded and understanding."

"Yes, Shastri was supportive, too. He made many general comments that acknowledged the sense of shock I felt and the tragedy of the loss of a young life, but his comments weren't directed to understanding the case. Balint was different. He went beyond what Shastri did and tried to understand what had happened. He said that it was important to manage the event and to learn from it. He talked about a possible father-son dynamic and wondered if Amir's suicide was acting out of a father transference with me. He cautioned me not to assume too much blame by feeling that I was the prime mover of this tragedy. He said powerful individual and family forces were at play that overwhelmed the treatment process, that I was a tiny element in the situation. I found his assessment helpful, but my sense of personal guilt was so powerful that the relief was short-lived."

"So, you felt that Balint was both supportive and understanding."

"Yes. At the time, I wasn't sure if his comments revealed only his intellectual understanding of the situation or reflected a genuine concern for me, too. Now, I feel it was real. He'd been in analysis for a year, and change was already taking place."

"In your case, why do you think it works?" Although the need for such a question was obvious to me and one I frequently asked, Jan seemed surprised by it. He took a long time to answer.

"When I first saw you, I felt guilty and had poor judgment. But, most importantly, I felt I *had* to be guilty; no other feeling was possible. I couldn't see any other option. Alvear-Reverte said that some people are at the end of their rope and try to manage and sustain their lives. Sometimes we succeed, and sometimes we don't.

"Once, we talked about a patient that I had had at the Veterans' Hospital. In the depths of winter, he got a pass and jumped into the cold Chicago River. He was at the end of his rope. He was depressed but didn't know it. Depression was his reality. Why did analysis work in my case? I knew I was depressed and thought of depression as an illness, so I must have had some hope."

"You said you assigned all the guilt to yourself. That's a grandiose position: You, and you alone, were responsible. Perhaps you had an unreasonable expectation of how much you could control. Your position was that you should have been able to prevent it, but at the same time, you felt that you were worthless and shouldn't be a doctor. You were simultaneously occupying both ends of the spectrum. Now you've moved to the middle, and you see other possibilities, less black-and-white, more gray."

"And even colors! I see more possibilities. I'm in a much healthier place. Now I don't allow dark feelings to go too far. But, as I said, it works."

I laughed, a quiet self-congratulatory laugh. I was pleased that my efforts to help Jan seemed to have paid off and that his depression had limits he could identify. "Now you tell me you're a believer in psychoanalysis. It's hard to take stock once you have a firm conviction. Residency programs today put much emphasis on the scientific method, not to mention neurology, biology, psychopharmacology, and Cognitive-Behavioral psychology."

"Yes, and the Board exam didn't have a single question about defense mechanisms. And they didn't ask much about psychoanalytic contributions to the clinical practice of psychiatry. They used to ask such questions just a few years ago.

"There was a question about a gay guy and his partner. The gay patient says, 'I have HIV, but I'm not telling him. This is because I love him so much, and if I tell him, we won't be together.' There were a few answers to choose from. I remember just two: 'If you love him so much, you should tell him because it involves his life and health,' and 'I'm not going to listen to you anymore; I'll call the police and tell them that you intend to kill your boyfriend.'

"In the whole exam, this was the closest they came to a question about psychodynamics, though it was, in fact, related to the Tarasoff decision and a psychiatrist's duty to warn a potential victim."

"I see. It looks like one of the elements in the relationship between these two guys is selfish, reckless love coupled with possible deadly consequences. Killing oneself involves killing one person; killing someone else involves the death of only one person. But if a person kills himself and kills another in the process, it's a double killing. If a person who commits suicide induces another person to kill himself in response, that also involves the death of two people. In the case of Amir, both he *and* you came under a killing spell. He succumbed, but you survived."

I continued, "Remember when you and Maria saw *The Painted Veil*? There are many dimensions to understanding a homicidal-suicidal situation. The homicidal undertones in the exam question dealt with gayness. For now, let us set aside adultery and gayness and stick primarily to the killing aspect. I want to go back to the conflict between Walter and Kitty. He wants to kill himself *and* her. Thus, she's the intended victim of his homicidal impulses, and he's the intended object of his suicidal impulses, and, ironically, he plans to accomplish these goals through a so-called humanitarian mission. His plan is premeditated: He deliberately fails to have either of them vaccinated. You can kill directly, with a knife or a gun, but you can also do it indirectly, through a distant instrument, like a bacterium, or even by inducing a feeling, such as guilt.

"Just as Walter formulated a homicidal-suicidal plan to take his wife to a cholera-infested place, Amir trapped you in his directly suicidal and indirectly homicidal plans. In my opinion, his suicidal thrust was overwhelming him, but he kept it a secret from you. It culminated when he pulled the trigger of a loaded gun. I only infer Amir's homicidal trajectory from the resulting depressive, suicidal preoccupations in you. But, of course, your own past contains a melancholy flavor.

"The two main characters in any therapy are the patient and the therapist. You were the therapist of a patient like Walter Fane. The relationship was dangerous. As psychiatrists, we need simple terms to identify, describe, and understand such situations.

"Killers kill—often others and sometimes themselves. Our shared reverence for life usually hides the urge to kill, but it can make an appearance under certain conditions. In general, a sense of life-preservation; love of self, other, or family; empathy for others keeps us from unbridled killing, but all humans have the potential to experience the impulse, and some succumb to it. We may go through life being barely aware of this tendency. Anger or desire for revenge, which we all experience, may bring up expressions like

'Go to hell' and sometimes a conscious desire for killing. Extreme jealousy in love, war, and hurt pride are situations when anyone may become aware of this predisposition. In melancholy, we can turn this feeling on ourselves. An unseen wall usually holds such emotions in check, but there's death and certain suffering for those left behind if they break through.

"We encounter dangerous patients who want to kill themselves or others. They need special attention. A killer is someone who has lost that basic love or respect for life and acted on it; on the other hand, a *potential* killer experiences that impulse but hasn't acted on it. For our purposes, any psychiatrist or mental health professional—whose job it is to try to heal a patient who may be a 'killer' in either sense—can be designated an angel. In this context, an 'angel' doesn't mean that the physician has sprouted wings, but that he has assumed a healing role, and society has bestowed the mantle of the guardian spirit on him. It also grants him professional privileges to act to protect life. You were the therapist, the anointed 'angel.' Amir, who experienced the spirit of killing, was a potential killer who became an actual killer, of himself, when he committed suicide. In general, the ministrations of an angel may heal the sickness of wanting to kill oneself, the suicidal impulse, or another, the homicidal impulse, but sometimes the opposite may happen. Treatment poses risks for the patient *and* the healer.

"Amir kept you from knowing when and how deeply the killer possessed him. This was his resistance to treatment. Amir not only killed himself, but the killer spirit in him got to you and made you, the angel and the protector of life, doubt the value of your own life. In this way, you became infected by Amir's macabre sickness. You became enamored with or felt strangely jealous of his suicidal problem-solving and almost identified with the killer in him. You wanted to hurt yourself and hence became a killer angel.

"I use the term *killer angel* to describe the killing-infected disorder of a therapist who is not only unable to heal the killer in a patient but is unable to protect or preserve himself. This is more likely to occur after a patient successfully commits suicide. If the killer angel is active, the healing angel in the therapist has become paralyzed. This was your situation. The killer angel could also, in theory, be manifest in a doctor who is dangerously hostile to a patient. Again, this was *not* your situation. In either case, when a killer angel is at large, there is a severe problem. Sometimes, a discomfited angel can turn back from the killing impulse and return to his benign self through proper understanding of self and others. Understanding this doesn't muzzle or deny the killer spirit dormant in each of us, but it sheds light on the darkest areas of our minds. The best way for a doctor to inoculate himself against this possibility is to be self-aware of the entire range of feelings he may have toward the patient, from caring to hostility.

"Your *killer angel* is not isolated; your personal history feeds into it. Between 1½ and 3 years old, I'm sure you cried for your mom many times, but she couldn't answer you. It wasn't her fault; she was sick and recovering in the TB sanatorium. But no one can satisfactorily explain a mother's absence to a toddler; it's beyond his comprehension. Fortunately, your mom was an extraordinarily kind and caring person, and she showered you with love all her life. Still, her physical absence in the sanatorium left you vulnerable, which fed into the *killer angel*. You experienced your dad as mean and rejecting for most of your life. You have difficulty remembering and holding onto the occasional fragments of positive recognition from him; now, he has dementia. Also, you felt he was similar to Amir's father. These personal aspects of your life contributed to your *killer angel*.

"Therapists shouldn't be so naïve as to believe that the killer spirit is active only in the patient. The killing impulse is universal. Every therapist needs at least a workable awareness of the killer spirit to deal with it and not be overwhelmed by it.

"The lesson is that life is precious. Each person is a unique variant of existence. Sometimes, we feel that life is unlimited, but that is an illusion for children and immature adults. So, while we have life within us, we must safeguard it. Even if we grow someone's cells in a petri dish after they have died, the person, the life, is gone. When we are children, the responsibility to protect life falls to our parents, but as we grow, it is up to us to assert a will to live and a desire to exercise it. Doctors can *support* our patients' efforts—with chemicals, procedures, and artificial joints and organs that improve their quality of life—but we can't transfer our *will* to them. And always, in the process of helping others, doctors must protect themselves from self-destruction.

"Jan, you encountered the killer when dealing with Amir, first in him and later in yourself. Amir encountered the killer when he was forced to see the slaughter of a camel. That event shook his capacity to live. *He* developed a fault line, even though most of the kids in his neighborhood somehow continued to cherish their own lives. On a lighter note, maybe it's like how kids here come to terms with eating a hamburger: They know it comes from an animal, but it doesn't really register since they don't witness the killing.

As David grows, I'm sure you'll come to watch many cartoons with him and see a lot of violence in them—not only the violence required for acquiring and producing food but also gratuitous violence."

"I'm familiar with many such cartoons. For example, Hanna-Barbera cartoons were allowed on TV in Poland when I was growing up. I loved her cartoons."

"Hanna-Barbera isn't a woman; it's a composite of William Hanna and Joseph Barbera."

"Really?! I grew up imagining Hanna Barbera and wondering what kind of woman she was!"

"As you can see, you can spend many years of your life chasing an elusive woman! *The Painted Veil* is a story of violence expressed as a fatal embrace between two people.

"Cartoons are made by people who are nothing short of geniuses. Consider *The Tortoise and the Hare.* You know the story: The hare challenges the tortoise to a race and is so confident of victory that he preens and whiles away time playing games and impressing the girls, while the tortoise plods along. Then the hare sees the tortoise approaching the finish line and hurries to catch up, but he can't, and the tortoise wins. There's a striking look of surprise on the hare's face in the cartoon. We study medicine and become physicians, and we become confident that we will triumph over disease, but we all meet patients who surprise us. A patient may suddenly say, 'I felt suicidal three weeks ago.' This is where new learning occurs. No amount of biological, neurological, chemical, radiological, or genetic theory or analysis can take the place of a serious discussion about why the patient decided to communicate this *now.* You can't reduce the chronological frame of reference to any other frame of reference. If you do, you run the risk of being as surprised as Hanna-Barbera's hare."

"Well, my everyday practice is full of surprises. The surprises are not only related to suicidality. My hospital is the trauma center for the south side of Chicago. I'm still surprised by how much senseless violence there is."

"Violence in a family and violence in a community may be connected. For example, when a parent or other adult slaps a kid around, they get the desired 'good' behavior from the child . . . but only for a while. Then the good-docile behavior evaporates, leaving a residue of intensifying rage from the slap's pain and shame. It's an expensive lesson for the parent because it takes progressively more energy to discipline a hardened child and causes growing frustration. But violence isn't just slapping people around. It can take an even deadlier turn, like the Nazis killing hundreds of people and leaving them in the fossa to rot.

"I've worked with homeless mothers who were physically abused as children. Unfortunately, such early stress clouds their lives as adults. Overwhelmed by their experience, a few are at risk of abusing or neglecting their children, and they may be more vulnerable to violence from their partners. But I have also treated some remarkable women. Family members or partners physically or sexually brutalized them, but they transformed themselves. They grieved the loss of a normal, humane childhood, purged the bitterness that usually follows trauma, and somehow broke the cycle of senseless violence and abuse. They hadn't experienced safety and caring but somehow taught themselves to protect and love their children. These brave, often homeless, women are generous beyond reason, risking their lives to nurture their children. They have taught me hope, patience, and compassion and made me a better person. I'm sure you know of people who suffered as children but escaped their family's pattern to become good and kind people. If not for the possibility of such transformations, violence would only keep repeating itself and there would be no hope.

"Just like those amazing resilient mothers, killers can change. A killer angel whom a killer has infected can recover. Killer angels can learn from hopelessness—their patients' and their own—and transform themselves into better healers. To do this, they must shed their naïve illusion that depression is only for patients."

"Where did you get the idea of a killer angel?" Jan asked.

My eyes unconsciously went to the Kali painting, and I remembered that Maria had shuddered when she first saw it. Although Jan had seen it—or, at least, been in its presence—many times, he had never commented about it.

"The idea of a killer angel is everywhere and in every culture. For me, the idea springs from Kali, a Hindu goddess who is the slayer of illusions. That's her," I said, pointing to the painting. "Most illusions seek to veil the inevitability of death or change. We all imagine ways to hang on to youth or dodge death. On the surface, Kali looks like the centerfold of our nightmares: a dark, bloodthirsty, howling she-devil. She's dancing in jubilation, having conquered an evil monster whose cut-off head she holds in one hand. At a deeper level, though, she represents hope and motherly love, for she can hear an infant's cry in the middle of chaos. Kali teaches the necessity of shedding illusions and acknowledging the truth. Her message is that permanence is an illusion, change is inevitable, and death is inescapable. When a person realizes and accepts these self-evident but disagreeable truths, they are on the way to being liberated.

"Michael Shaara's book, *The Killer Angels*, used this phrase in describing the American Civil War. My son read the book and recommended it to me. It's a great book. Slavery was a killer of the American spirit. Freedom-loving Americans abolished it, but at the cost of so much precious blood. And the U.S. is still a work in progress. When my family visited the Gettysburg Civil War site, my son misidentified the bronze 21-foot-tall statue of the Goddess of Victory and Peace atop the Pennsylvania Monument as the 'killer angel.' Based on the sheer power of the statue, I also instinctively thought the same at first. The raised sword in her right hand and the palm leaf in her left hand signify war and peace. Although she suggests America is a country dedicated to victory and peace, subsequent American tradition seems to embody more of the sword of war and less of the palm of peace. The killer angel I envision includes both the notions of victory and peace, but in addition it involves appreciating the illusions we have about eternal life and permanence."

"This reminds me of another killer angel, the Christian Archangel Michael, often portrayed with a flaming sword," said Jan. "He is second only to God, and his name means 'who is like God.' He's a *Capo di tutti capi*—the boss of all bosses among God's lieutenants. Like the Goddess of Victory and Peace, Archangel Michael was an impossible combination of *sacrum* and *profanum*. He spread the divine message among people, but he served as a hitman for God when necessary.

"Talking about hitmen makes me think of the traditional honor killings among Polish Highlanders: If someone in the family was killed, the person responsible for the death had to die; it's an accepted kind of extra-judicial justice. There's no reason for a judge or a courtroom or a lawyer. No one would report the crime, and no one would testify in such a case. And, somehow, there were never any witnesses! Only a dead body and a secret carried by the whole community. It's not senseless violence. It comes from a deep belief that, in some situations, you deserve to die. Everybody is on the same page except for the person who's about to be killed. There's a kind of moral code."

"Oh? The Highlanders seem to have made quite an impression on you. Tell me more."

"The Highlanders I got to know are from the Podhale and Tatra Mountains in the south of Poland. I spent many winters there. They speak a characteristic Polish slang. They have unique music and customs. Many of my friends and former patients were Highlanders. I liked to spend time with them. That is how I learned about the moral code passed from generation to generation, like the Sicilian *vendetta*. In the 1980s, I went skiing in Zakopane, the Polish winter capital. We rented a house from an alcoholic who didn't drink during Lent and other religious holidays.

"A drunk driver hit his teenage nephew as he was crossing a street. A few bystanders saw the accident. One of them took a piece of wood from the fence of a nearby house and bludgeoned the driver to death. Then the boy woke up. He had only lost consciousness. The drunk driver's family took revenge and killed the guy who murdered the driver. When the police came to investigate both the accident and the murder, they could find no witnesses. Nobody saw anything, but the whole village knew everything.

"There seems to be a lot of senseless violence on the south side of Chicago—just random, unprovoked drive-by shootings. If you cross an invisible line in gang territory, you can be hurt or killed. Or some strung-out guy can kill you for a few bucks or even for your sneakers. This is what I mean by 'senseless violence.' Maybe you heard of this recent shocking example: A boy with an artificial leg was attacked and killed with his own leg."

"We should be stopping soon," I said. "At the beginning of the session, we talked about helpful treatments, and now we find ourselves talking about senseless violence. Concerning your treatment, I'm glad you feel that psychoanalysis works for you."

"I'm not sure when I will see you next. My dad recently started having trouble breathing, and Sofia called to say he'd gotten worse. I was about to call you to cancel this session when she called again and said that he had stabilized, so things are in flux."

"OK. We'll plan to meet, but you'll keep me posted."

CHAPTER 46

When I was about 3½ years old, my mother enrolled me in a pre-kindergarten class less than half a mile from our house. Our trip started with a bus to the Secunderabad railway station; you could tell you were near the station from the sounds of steam engines and the sulfurous smell of the engines burning bituminous coal ("devil's coal" in Telugu). I was fascinated by the ticket collector's leather bag and the ticket machine with a dial to calculate the fare and a lever he turned to print a ticket. To let the driver know you wanted to get off the bus, you would push one of the buttons on the ceiling, which made a *ting* sound. Amma would lift me so I could press the button. After getting off the bus, we walked the short distance to the school, often taking different routes to make the journey interesting. The first school day was short, so Amma and I went to the beautiful Secunderabad Clock Tower garden, where Amma treated me to peanuts from a street vendor. She showed me the clock hands and tried to teach me to tell time, but it made no sense. After taking me to school every day for a few months, Amma asked our nanny, Lakshmamma, to take me to school. Lakshmamma's name means "the goddess of money," but she was poor. When she took me, we usually walked to the school.

I remember being very excited about crossing the Oliphant Bridge for the first time. Trains ran above the stone bridge, buses, cars, rickshaws, *tongas* (horse-drawn carriages covered with small canopies to protect the occupants from sun and rain), and pedestrians using the road below. As we neared the bridge, Lakshmamma suddenly stopped in front of a small shrine, so small that no person could enter. She clasped both hands in front of her, bowed, and paid obeisance to the colorful picture drawn on the outer wall that was at

451

an adult's eye level. She mumbling something I couldn't hear. When I looked up, I saw that it was a woman, with many hands, seated on a lion. With a spear in one of her right hands, she was piercing a demon, and she held the cut-off head of another demon with one of her left hands. And her tongue was sticking out, red with blood. This was my shocking introduction to Kali.

Hindus pray to whatever gods they choose; they may choose one, or several, at any particular time. Most people pray to and venerate a god during festivals celebrating a particular god. Unlike the many magical Greek and Roman gods and goddesses in the West, who no longer attract divine worship by the peoples of Europe, the Hindus actively worship their gods and goddesses today just as they did thousands of years ago. Hindus immerse themselves in the lives and legends of their gods, who are intimately known to the imagination. They are part of everyday conversations, like how contemporary American children and adolescents follow the fictitious Wonder Woman, Princess Leia, Sarah Connor, Lara Craft, Buffy, Sheena, Superman, Spider-man, Luke Skywalker, Obi-Wan Kenobi, Darth Vader, Neo (Matrix), Tarzan, Simba, Power Rangers, and others.

Amma's chosen gods were the goddesses Parvati and Saraswati. Amma prayed at home to the goddess Parvati and her husband, Shiva, often depicted with the snow-capped peaks of the Himalayas in the background. Similar idealized, mass-produced pictures hung in the prayer room at home, along with images and idols of other gods and goddesses. There was no blood or gore, at least on the surface.

Parvati and Shiva were initially childless. Shiva's wanderlust often drove him to all parts of the universe, so he was often away. One day, Parvati wanted to take a bath. She magically created a son, Ganesha, and instructed him to make sure no one entered the house to guard her privacy. As fate would have it, as Ganesha stood guard, Shiva returned home, and Ganesha would not let him in. Shiva didn't take kindly to being blocked from entering his own house and promptly beheaded the boy. When Parvati heard Shiva, she anxiously inquired about Ganesha, and Shiva confessed that he had killed the boy. Parvati flew into a rage. Shiva then instructed his lackeys to get the head of the first living thing they saw. They found a hapless elephant sleeping nearby and severed its head. Shiva arranged for transplanting the elephant head onto Ganesha's headless body. From then on, Ganesha was the elephant god. He became very fond of food and grew fat as he grew up, yet he chose to ride around on a mouse!

Another picture in my parents' house was of Saraswati, the goddess of knowledge, dressed in white and seated on a white lotus near flowing water.

Saraswati has four arms: Her lower-right and upper-left arms play the *veena*, an ancient musical instrument; her upper-right arm holds a rosary; and her lower-left arm carries the *Vedas*, the inspired books of wisdom. Amma hoped to inspire us to be studious, and Saraswati was her ploy.

Due to my familiarity with these and other pictures, as a child, I simply accepted that heavenly beings could be endowed with whatever special features and as many pairs of arms as they desired or needed. The curbs that earthly reality put on human imagination did not apply to the celestial world. Common to these gods and goddesses in the prayer room was a core of serenity and beauty and a capacity to get rid of demons. To me, they were also inspirations for love and learning.

As I mentioned earlier, I stood with Lakshmamma in front of the Kali shrine almost at the age of four. She looked like an ogress and opposite all the goddesses I knew. To me, she was a demon, yet she instilled no fear in Lakshmamma. I shuddered and asked her what shrine it was. She replied that the figure was Kali Amma (Mother), whose job was to protect people. Terrified, I asked her whose head Kali had cut off. Lakshmamma replied that Kali beheaded Rakshas, evil demons.

Lakshmamma prayed silently for just a few seconds, and then we walked on. This quick, simple procedure was another surprise. In contrast, a priest came to our home on special occasions and held long, elaborate ceremonies in which they recited hymns in Sanskrit, a language I didn't understand. Not only were the rituals meaningless to me, but they meant a delayed lunch. After the prayer, my mom fed the priest first, before the family ate. So, I was pleased that Lakshmamma's prayer was short and sweet. Curious, I asked her how people pray at the Kali temple and what ceremonies they hold on special occasions. She replied that Kali *puja* destroys evil. People pray to Kali for health, wealth, happiness, and wisdom. If Kali is angry, she may rain down *Ammavaru* (smallpox or other illness). Killing a sacrificial animal keeps Kali at peace. Lakshmamma said that she prayed whenever she wanted and had the time. She described the *Mahakali puja*, the ritual festival of Kali, the Great Mother. As a witness to the sacrifice, my friend Kanti became obsessed with it, often reenacting the beheading himself. Growing up, I saw many street *Mahakali* processions, but not the sacrifice.

Celebrants decorate a male water buffalo with paint, garlands, and bells during this annual festival and parade it around the town. Women walk behind the animal carrying stacks of earthen pots on their heads. Neem leaves decorate the jars on all sides, and a lighted lamp sits on top of the uppermost pot. There is a lot of excitement on the way to the temple. Men dance to the rhythmic sounds of many frenzied drummers. Finally, in front of the temple, the revelers witness the sacrifice of the male water buffalo. Ideally, a *jhatka*, a single powerful decapitating blow with a ceremonial axe or sword, instantly kills the sacrificial beast.[66] According to Hindu tradition, it is bad omen if the sacrificial animal unduly groans, gurgles, or shows excessive distress or suffers before its death. Mercifully, many years ago, the Animal Welfare Board of India banned such sacrifices. So, now, ceremonially smashing pumpkins has replaced beast or fowl sacrifices!

As we walked on, my legs grew heavy. Then, I noticed that Lakshmamma chewed *paan*, betel leaf with areca nut, making her tongue and mouth red, just like Kali's. Suddenly, I understood just how different Lakshmamma's world was from mine. I was frightened, realizing that my mom was nowhere near me.

Lakshmamma and I left the path, and she guided me to school through the byways of the Regimental Bazaar, where I had never been before. As I reluctantly moved along, I saw a huge banyan tree with multiple trunks, its branches crawling through the nearby temple's walls and its roots eroding the curb and surrounding grounds. Big brown branches grew in every direction around the monstrous trunk, making a thick canopy and giving it an eerie look. As I walked closer, I saw that the lower part of the trunk was colored red ochre. The roots parted to create a shadowy dark cleavage, and installed inside that cave was a small image of Kali. I suddenly felt lost and yearning—even more—for my mother in fear of the demon tree.

When I returned home, I asked Amma about Kali. Why was she so ugly and fearful, while Parvati was beautiful, peaceful, and calming? Amma replied, "It only looks that way. Parvati and Kali are the same. Parvati is

---

66 Like the *Mahakali puja* ritual described by Lakshmamma, the movie *Apocalypse Now* captured a ritual water buffalo sacrifice, with a machete, in the Philippines in progress; reportedly, the director, Francis Ford Coppola, did not direct such an enactment but merely recorded one in progress. As the orgiastic music crescendos, the movie simultaneously intersplices Benjamin Willard (Martin Sheen) hacking off the head of Colonel Walter Kurz (Marlon Brando), who had become an evil, deranged ruler of the jungle. Inspired by James Frazer's *The Golden Bough* and Joseph Conrad's *The Heart of Darkness*, Coppola shows the persistence of ancient beliefs and practices in the heart of the modern world. He was attempting to answer an eternal question: Why do we periodically kill our kings (presidents and prime ministers) that we previously adored? In a democracy, anointed leaders wield extraordinary powers. But after their term in office is finished, they are evicted from their pedestal by the same people. Democratic term limits may well be a modern version of the ancient ritual of beheading a dethroned king and installing a new king.

the goddess in a calm mood, and Kali is the same goddess when killing evil demons. Both are different forms of the same goddess married to Shiva."

Seeing how afraid I was of the Kali shrines, Amma transferred me to another school to not have to walk past them and had me enrolled in a school-bus pickup. So the blue St. Ann's school bus, with a friendly golden-toothed driver, was my childhood path to salvation from Kali! Lakshmamma, with her Kali-like tongue, remained part of our household, as if to illustrate the close relationship between Parvati and Kali. When I was 10 or 11, I deliberately went past the Kali temple, curious but proud that I was no longer afraid. These experiences left a lasting impression on me. As an adult, I appreciated the directness with which Lakshmamma approached Kali. Her short, unmediated prayer, said in public at a humble street temple, came from her heart. It was very different from the formal ritual worship practiced by my family. My mom said informal prayers in our in-home prayer room. However, on important religious festivals, a *purohit* (a formal priest), while offering commentary in Telugu, my mother tongue, recited the central prayer in Sanskrit, an ancient language that no one in my family understood.

However, on important religious festivals, a *purohit* (a formal priest), while offering commentary in Telugu, my mother tongue, recited the central prayer in Sanskrit, an ancient language that no one in my family understood. (Start of new addition) Despite my curiosity, the gap between my known mother tongue Telugu and the unknown language of Sanskrit proved too much to bridge. Language barriers blocked me, and some Hindu customs relating to menstruating women directly affecting women and their children and families also seemed destructive and meaningless. From ancient times, Hindus linked spirituality and physical cleanliness and feared that pollution would destroy their purity. So, avoiding contaminants such as blood, feces, wastes, dirt, dead people, and people dealing with animals and bodily wastes became a priority. If a corrupting touch occurred, a bath and a prayer became necessary to remedy the stain of the taint.

Hindu traditions surrounding menstruating women are based more on ancient mythology, superstition, and animistic beliefs than modern reproductive science. They support the belief and custom that one should shun a menstruating woman because she is impure. Touching her contaminates a person's purity. Although I refer to the terms applicable to Telugu-speaking people, there are many variations to such customs based on location, language, and caste.

Hindu women isolate themselves during their menstrual periods, and family members and others avoid making contact and segregate them. Depending on the context, the Telugu word *muttu* means "to touch" or "touch." Paradoxically, the same word *muttu* refers to this period when a menstruating woman becomes temporarily untouchable. Other terms refer to similar practices depending on the language, region, and caste. From as far back as I remember, my close, caring, affectionate, and touchable mom became a distant, unreachable, periodic monthly mystery. So I assume every child asks, 'How can a mom regularly become untouchable?' At these times, she occupied a corner of the house away from the foot traffic patterns. Because her menstrual presence would defile the space, she did not go into the *puja*-prayer room located within the home or go to the temple. Additionally, she did not enter the kitchen and cook food for us. As a result, my siblings and I separated from our mom and felt strangely alienated in our own home.

While we separated from our mother during her periods, my father took care of household duties and comforted us. Usually, my mom's cooking involved rice, lentils, curry, sambar, buttermilk, or yogurts with pickles. He cooked differently, quick-simple-slop but with more noise and fanfare. We got his supervision with our homework, teeth brushing, card games, bedtime stories, bath time, etc. During our childhood, although we bathed daily, we shampooed less often. There were no ready-made shampoos when I was a kid, so all families used a homemade concoction. Ground Shikakai nuts (Acacia concinna, often translated as "fruit for the hair") soaked in water produced a foamy, irritating, soapy solution. However, if it accidentally went into the eyes, it caused them to itch and tear for quite some time. Usually, my mom or dad (during her periods) started the bath, first shampooing hair safely and rinsing off the head with water so no shampoo remained. They then left me or my sibs alone to finish bathing. Thus, from my scalp memories, I remember my mother's soft, slow touch covering the entire scalp and my dad's rough contact mainly surrounding the head's crown. While she asked me to tilt my head backward and gently sponged away the Shikakai shampoo to prevent it from entering my eyes, he asked me to close my eyes, dunked water on my head from a big bucket, and instantly washed off the shampoo. While helping us, she wanted us still to minimize the chance of water accidentally spilling on her; he did not care if he got a little wet. Both got the job done in different ways. The *muttu* period necessitated action-empathy from my dad and all fathers;

it regularly occasioned him to walk in her slippers and carry her burdens for a few days every month.

However, the customs surrounding *muttu* burdened young children with the regular but mysterious separations from their mothers. Of course, no mother wishes separation from her children desiring her touch. Fortunately, custom allowed an exception to the no-touch rule--breastfeeding infants. My family was relatively progressive. If one of my siblings or I were in distress and reached out and touched our mom, she soothed us with a word of encouragement or a hug, and my dad helped reestablish the separation with some distraction. It was a no-no but not a capital offense. My dad being an atheist, perhaps would not have cared if my mom abandoned the custom. So in our family, the *muttu* practice had the force only of tradition but not of deep conviction. However, in orthodox families, the convention took on the tone of prohibition and taboo. A touching violation would call for immediate admonishment and atonement and require an immediate cleansing bath.

During this isolation, my mother did not wear her vermilion dot on her forehead. Usually, a woman with such a dot is married or unmarried; one without such a dot is a widow. So, my mother's face looked strange without the red dot, and I couldn't bear to look at her directly. She took a purifying bath after the isolation, and the first thing she did was approach the mirror outside and apply her forehead dot. I often watched this change with relief and fascination and was glad she was back to her usual self.

CHAPTER 47

"I RECENTLY READMITTED A TEENAGER, just weeks before he turned 18," Jan began. "I'll call him John. John used to be a skinny, fragile boy, but after using a whole lot of anabolic steroids and working out every day for almost a year, he had bulked up and gotten over-confident.

"The shit hit the fan when John's parents found out that he had stolen $15,000 from them. John's family is not rich, its just an average middle-class family that owns a small business. Whatever they could save each week, they put in a chest in their bedroom. Over time, their 'deposits' of $50 at a time grew to $15,000. And then John stole it and spent every single penny on steroids. They were furious. John's father is an angry man, and his mother is very anxious. When they realized that the money was gone, they yelled at John and threatened to call the police and take him to the Juvenile Detention Center. John told them about having suicidal thoughts, so instead, they brought him to the hospital for an evaluation. He spent less than a week in the inpatient unit and was discharged and transferred to the day hospital for three weeks. I was his treating psychiatrist when he was an inpatient and during his stay at the day hospital."

"Was he attending day hospital regularly?"

"Yes, he came every day, Monday through Friday, for 6 hours of intensive therapy; I saw him for half an hour each day. It was like being in the inpatient unit, except he slept at home. The staff gave him great reviews while he was at the day hospital. They were planning to discharge him when the family gun disappeared. His father had gone to clean it and discovered that it was missing. He started to panic that his son was about to kill someone. He called the police and John's school. Police officers picked him up at school

458

and brought him home for interrogation. It took about 15 minutes for him to admit that he had stolen the gun. So, he went back to the inpatient unit.

"I didn't understand why John did so well in the program and suddenly behaved so erratically. Maybe it was because of his steroid abuse or withdrawal, but John claimed he hadn't used any steroids for three months. When I spoke with him, I had a gut feeling that something wasn't right. He was polite but superficial. He had a way of saying, 'F___ off' in a polite and non-offensive way. I didn't mind his style, but I wanted to know the real story, so I kept probing.

"I asked him why he had started using steroids. He claimed that he'd always been a small, wimpy kid and felt terrible about himself. So he took steroids to bulk up; he also got engaged in many sports, especially martial arts. Steroids made him feel euphoric. He felt super-good when he looked at himself in the mirror and saw growing muscles.

"Then he told me that his best friend, who had also used steroids, had committed suicide a year ago during withdrawal. I felt like we were getting somewhere. I said, 'That must have made you feel horrible.'

"John replied, 'Yes. He used steroids for about as long as I did. When he stopped, he got depressed and then killed himself. As you said, it was horrible.' Then John said, 'I was close to my uncle, and he also died a year ago.'

"I said, 'I'm sorry. Two important people died, one of them likely because of the drug you were also taking. You may have been scared when you finally decided to quit. Please tell me how you felt.'

"John told me that he was fine. His goal in life was to become an FBI agent, and he worried a little that his school grades had deteriorated. But overall, he felt all right. There was a problem with the money he stole, but he and his parents had created a payback plan. First, he would work part-time and eventually pay the whole sum back. He said he appreciated my help. He was grateful for my interest and all the time I had spent with him. Certainly, this was something I wanted to hear, such a positive response to my healing presence. He kept saying, 'I understand my mistake. I'm going to make amends.' It seemed like a real success story, but I felt a growing fear inside. He seemed too eager to wrap things up.

"I said, 'That sounds good, John, but before we decide what to do next, I need to meet with your parents and, together, we'll create a solid safety plan. Also, after I discharge you, I'd like to meet you in my office from time to time and see how you're doing. Eventually, if there are no reasons to worry, we'll shake hands and say goodbye. What do you think?' He agreed.

"I set up a family meeting for the very next day. When John and his parents came in, I looked at them and asked, right off, 'Was the gun found?' They said they couldn't find the gun. After they searched his room, they looked at his computer and found some scary Internet searches. He had done thorough research and constructed two homemade silencers. And his parents got really scared when they discovered a ski mask in his room. John never went skiing.

"I asked myself: silencers, a ski mask . . . what's going on? What is John hiding?

"All this just added to the uneasy feeling I already had. So I asked John's parents about any recent event that could have upset him. I asked about his friend who committed suicide. At first, his parents didn't know what I was talking about. Then they remembered that the so-called best friend was a kid at school who was on steroids and had committed suicide, but he wasn't John's friend. They didn't spend time together outside of school.

"Then I asked about the uncle. The parents said that John had rarely spoken to his uncle. They weren't close by any means. When his uncle died of cancer, John didn't want to go to the funeral, and they had to make him. As they spoke, I looked at John, but he was impassive. He didn't utter a word. The session ended without much progress, but all agreed to continue family sessions over the next few days.

"I asked the parents to bring a printout of John's Internet searches to the next session. The keywords that John had used were gruesome and unmistakable. For example, John had been looking for answers to 'How to commit a perfect murder.' He also looked up 'How to hide a murder.' Another one was 'Police procedures during murder investigations.' I asked the parents what John had to say about the silencers and these Internet searches. They told me that he just ignored their questions.

"During the session, John said, 'So I have a ski mask. What's the big deal?' and 'All kids search the Internet.' Again, for the rest of the session, he just listened."

As Jan spoke, he chuckled with understanding and self-assurance. When Jan was initially treating Amir, he was relatively confident, under the false belief that Amir would never act out his suicidal ideation. After Amir's death, however, Jan had become paralyzed by anxiety and guilt. Like Goldilocks and the three bears, a psychiatrist must have neither too much anxiety nor too little. Dear reader, you may recall my unease as I started to treat Jan; I think it's human nature to want to avoid anxiety.

Jan got serious again and conveyed his determination to manage the evolving situation as well as possible. He was trying to plan a course of treatment, with his primary motive being the safety of everyone involved.

"All this creepy and disturbing stuff: silencers, a ski mask, a stolen gun, and Internet searches for information about how to commit the perfect crime. It scared me," he said. "I felt bad that, so far, all I had spoken to John about was his depression. So, with the permission of John and his parents, I called the school counselor to find out what he thought about John. I also wanted to know if there were threats of violence in his school.

"The counselor said, 'The more I talked to John, the more scared I got. I felt that something was alarming about this boy and that he might be dangerous. The school takes the potential for violence seriously, but there was nothing I could prove.'

"I decided to ask John about the gun with both of his parents in the office. He agreed. When everybody came for the meeting, I asked him point-blank, 'Did you take the gun from the chest in your parents' bedroom?'

"John said, 'I took it from their bedroom, but I have no idea how it ended up in my room.' I knew this wasn't true because, during the police interrogation, he told the officer that he had hidden the gun in his parents' room.

"John continued, 'My parents are making a big deal out of it, but it's nothing.' After he spoke, his father pulled out a paper and showed it to me. It was an organized checklist that John had made while searching for his father's gun. In addition, he had made notes of all the places he had already checked.

"I asked John an obvious question: 'Why did you steal your father's gun in the first place? What did you plan to do with it?'

John hesitated. He lowered his head and looked sad and serious at the same time. Then, finally, he said, 'OK, I'm going to tell you.' He continued talking for a few minutes, without answering the question, but finally said, 'I was scared. My parents told me they were going to call the police. It meant that I would be arrested and have to go to jail. If the SWAT team showed up, I wanted to be ready to blow my brains out.'

"I said, 'Wow. That's a scary thought.' He nodded, and we just looked at each other. Then I asked him, 'What was the silencer for?' He hesitated for 5 or 10 minutes."

I exclaimed, "He didn't answer for 5 or 10 minutes?!"

"OK, I should have said 'a long while.' It felt long and uncomfortable. Sometimes, I talk too much, but I bit my tongue this time and didn't say anything. I wanted to hear what he had to say. So I waited for a response that didn't come.

"His mother cleared her throat, obviously wanting to say something. I put out my hand to stop her and waited a few more minutes. Then it was time for me to speak. I said, 'I don't know if you realize it, but this is serious. I want to make one thing clear. After the recent school shootings, everybody has a zero-tolerance policy for violence. If anybody fears that you're dangerous . . . I consider you a dangerous person because of the stolen gun, the silencer, and the ski mask. If a judge agrees with me, your life may change forever if you actually cross the line. You'll never get a government job. You'll never fulfill your wish of becoming a police officer or an FBI agent. So I'd like you to cut the crap right now. Tell me everything you have on your mind, and I'll try to help you. I'll do everything I can to help you. To do my job as a psychiatrist, I need to know your thoughts. If you're not communicating honestly with me, your case will become a police matter. I'll notify the authorities and let them find out what the heck you're up to.'

"After thinking a while, John said, 'I wanted a silencer so that if I shot myself in the head but didn't die instantly, no one would come and rescue me. I wanted to make sure that I would die.' I didn't believe him and wanted to find out the depth of his deception.

"'John, I understand your answer,' I said. 'You wanted to use a silencer so you would die before anybody found you, but explain why you searched the Internet extensively to find out how to commit murder and hide it. Why were there no searches for the perfect suicide?'

"He didn't hesitate. 'Some time back, I searched for suicide, too.'

"'OK, so what was the purpose of your searches for murder investigations?' 'That's easy,' John said, 'I didn't want my parents to be charged for murder when it was, in fact, a suicide. I didn't want to cause any problems for them.'

"I commented, 'I know a few people who committed suicide. They did it when they couldn't take the pain anymore. I don't think they cared about the noise the gun would make when they fired it. Most likely, they didn't care about the possible legal consequences of their decision, either. They just got a gun and blew their brains out. You told me that your parents were the reason you wanted to commit suicide, that they caused you lots of trouble by calling your school and the police, that it's because of them that you felt trapped. Your parents wanted to lock you up, and you were steaming mad at them. So, I don't understand why you're expending so much effort to protect your parents.'

"He had a ready answer. 'It's not like that. We're a family. There are three of us. They have their problems, and I have mine. Your parents are your parents, even if they're not so nice to you. My parents love me, and I love them.'

"I had a medical student with me at the time. Nice and shy. Until that point, she hadn't said a word. So I said to John, 'This is the first day this medical student and I have worked together. She doesn't know you, and she doesn't know me. Do you mind if we ask her what she thinks about our conversation?' He immediately agreed.

"The student was great because she gave a heartfelt response. Looking straight into his eyes, she said, 'I was scared hearing what you said today. I felt that you had a plan to kill somebody. That's how it sounds to me. I'm sorry. I don't know much about you, but based on what I heard, I feel that you had some bad thoughts in your head, and you wanted to kill somebody.'

"As soon as she spoke, he became nervous. He got fidgety and kicked his legs a few times. He was shaking and had lost his cool, which he'd been able to maintain till then. I told him, 'You just reacted. We don't want to make you nervous, but we have to understand what's bothering you to help you. We have to make sure that everyone is safe. Before you get discharged, you have to convince me that you and others are safe. At this point, I don't feel it's safe to discharge you. I'll talk to your parents and solve some problems, but I will not discharge you until I feel it's safe.'

"While he was in the hospital, he wrote a few letters to his parents. In one of them, he said, 'I've thought things over. One of my main problems was that both of you were often drunk. Mom, you would have six glasses of wine at dinner and get smashed. Father, you would have four or five Scotches. I thought having so much wine or Scotch was normal, but now I realize it's abnormal. You're not social drinkers; you're alcoholics. My problems started because you didn't pay enough attention to me. What I did was wrong, but you are responsible for me. You made me the way I am. As a result, I have self-esteem issues and abused drugs, which messed up my personality. I love you, but don't blame me for everything.'

"He gave me this letter and said, 'I want you to read it before I give it to my parents.' Then, he asked what I thought of it.

"I said, 'I don't have any comments, but it makes my job easier because you've provided topics for us to discuss in our family meeting. So we'll see how your parents respond.'

"After John's parents had a chance to read the letter, we all met. His mother didn't say anything; she just cried. Finally, his father said, 'Your mom got upset with your letter. I didn't know that you felt this way about me.'

"I was concerned that we would descend into guilt-tripping or a blame game, so I interrupted and said, 'While John is here, there's a lot of information we need to help him. However, we need to focus on healing, not for John alone, but the whole family. John made an important point. He doesn't want to be the only person held responsible for the current situation. Do you think the three of you can work on this problem together? Can you try to work as a family?'

"John's mother and father agreed. His mother was willing to enroll in an addiction program, but his father was reluctant to acknowledge his contribution to the problem. He said, 'When I found out about the stolen gun, I was afraid that my son would end up on the front page of the newspapers. I'm still scared and feel that he's lying, but I want him to get better. He's angry and irritable and blames others easily. One day, he's one person, and the next day, he's a different one. Maybe he needs a steroid-addiction program.'

"I explained that steroid addiction is medically and psychiatrically dangerous, but it's not treated the same way as other addictions. Programs like Alcoholics Anonymous and Narcotics Anonymous are not helpful to people abusing steroids. Very likely, he wouldn't be able to relate to other, typical addicts. He might feel rejected by them because his problem was steroids.

"I consulted an expert in violence and conduct disorders. She immediately recognized the difficulty of the case and was pessimistic about the outcome. She thought the made-up relationships were telling: John's so-called best friend was only an acquaintance, and he had no real connection with his uncle. It's like the Virginia Tech mass killer. Remember him? When he touched a girl's hand two months before the killings, she became his girlfriend in his mind. There were no signs of interest, affection, or intimacy on her part.

"In John's case, I recognized a pattern of manipulation, lying, and disregard for other people's feelings, but there was no history of fire setting, torturing animals, anything like that. I'm not even sure if he meets all the required criteria for a conduct disorder. Also, his abuse of steroids may make the case look worse. The expert advised me to do all the relevant psychological tests. I ordered them. The psychologist felt that he was really depressed and had many other problems, but he didn't feel that John was dangerous, implying that outpatient treatment might be more appropriate. Between us, I think it's the psychologist who's dangerous. I still feel uneasy about John. That's the story of my week."

I waited while Jan collected his thoughts before wrapping up the session. After a pause, Jan continued, "I wish I could finish here and end this session, but I can't. Something keeps bothering me. I think that he genuinely planned to kill someone. I'm not buying anything he said. I thought his parents might be the target. Remember the Menéndez brothers? They used a shotgun and brutally murdered their parents. They claimed they did it because their parents had emotionally and sexually abused them for many years. Eventually, the court convicted them for the murders. On a *Saturday Night Live* skit, the Menéndez brothers pleaded for clemency because they were orphans. John is like one of the Menéndez brothers, except he doesn't have a brother.

"I wondered if his father felt the same way I did, so I asked him, 'What do you think your son's plan was?' He answered, 'Listen, $15,000 is a lot of cash. Maybe he still owed some money to the guys selling him the steroids. Maybe they started to threaten him, so he wanted to gun them down. He must have had some plan.'"

Jan now looked at me directly.

"Today, John told me, 'Thank you. I'm so glad that I met you. You helped me.' I felt John had exhausted his bag of tricks. The last one was an expression of gratitude, perhaps hoping to change the topic. What do you think of this case?"

I felt that Jan's approach to John was different than his approach to Amir. If Jan had felt that Amir was dangerous, his treatment plan wasn't commensurate with his sense of the situation. In contrast, Jan felt John was dangerous. Therefore, he insisted on hospitalizing John and keeping him there until there was a safety plan and a reasonable follow-up plan.

I said, "Well, I feel one thing. No, two things. No, three things. First, your index of suspicion in John's case is focused and, in my opinion, appropriate and based on the facts of the case. Second, neither your index of suspicion of John's dangerousness nor your fears and worries are dominating your decision-making process. You had your opinions, and, in addition, you sought consultations. You're thinking and acting professionally. Third, I agree with you that steroid-abuse treatment is different from alcohol- or cocaine-abuse treatment. Patients need to feel that the treatment applies to them and that they're in an appropriate setting. Putting a guy who isn't an alcoholic or a heroin addict in such a group is likely to make him feel out of place."

I continued, "This is obviously a complicated case, and deciding whether he's clinically dangerous is certainly within your jurisdiction, but there may be other useful angles. For example, maybe an expert in endocrinology could put a different light on this case. This would be in addition to the appropriate actions you've already taken. Perhaps you've already explored such avenues."

"Yes, I have, and I gave John relevant feedback. As a result, we agreed that he'd be tested periodically, without warning, to ensure that he doesn't continue to abuse steroids. I'll decide on the frequency of those tests. His parents agreed. If he doesn't comply and becomes dangerous again, I'll hospitalize him."

"This is where you come to the end of the road in rule-based psychiatry and psychology. In simple cases, your personality may remain in the background, but it can become a crucial part of the treatment process in difficult cases. Just as crooked businesspeople keep two sets of books, 'crooked' patients can co-opt and corrupt the treatment by hiding the gap between what they declare and what they think, feel, and do. You are gradually peeling back the layers of John's deception. So far, you've done a good job, but I acknowledge that John is a tough case. He can put on a good show and will resist any true change; treatment needs to address that."

We discussed some of the forensic-psychiatric, legal, and administrative aspects of the case in greater detail, and I gave Jan the name of an excellent expert in adolescent and forensic medicine. He was grateful for the referral. We also discussed the problems related to the fact that John was about to turn 18. Till now, his parents have been able to authorize treatment. However, as soon as he was nominally an adult, he could torpedo the treatment by refusing consent.

Jan asked again, "Based on everything I told you, what's your feeling?"

"I feel that this is a difficult case, and you're managing it reasonably well. Unfortunately, there are no good options in this case; nothing can guarantee you a rosy outcome. No one can predict the future, let alone guarantee a positive one, but you seem more at peace with your actions. Although John has no overt delusions, maybe he has a steroid-influenced paranoid process. The paranoia may be the last thing to respond to treatment in steroid abuse and may persist. If you agree, you have another avenue of treatment: antipsychotic medications for paranoia till the critical period is over."

"I have a problem with that. I often admit out-of-control adolescents with parental requests to medicate them. It doesn't take long to realize that you're medicating a child for parental screw-ups. So whenever I can, I refuse."

"I didn't mean that you should medicate him immediately. It's just another avenue of treatment to consider, but not necessarily to use. The last option is a second opinion, a consultation with a different expert, like Dr. Goodbar."

"Why? Why not the previous one you recommended?"

"For two reasons: one, you get the opinion of the most renowned forensic child psychiatrist in town. He's famous for being famous. He's regularly on TV."

"Is that your proof of someone's expertise?"

"No, but do you have something against TV personalities?"

I said this jokingly, and Jan laughed, too.

I continued, "Seriously, the second and real reason is that it covers your ass. Goodbar's credentials are different from yours. He's a well-known child psychiatrist, and you're not. He's a forensics expert, and you're not. Remember, in any court, the attorney first establishes who you are and your credentials and areas of certified competence."

"So Goodbar protects me?"

"Yes. You're sometimes rebelliously proud. If you prefer, I'll say it differently: Everyone has vulnerabilities and needs to act to protect themselves. I know court routines. When I ran an adolescent program, I never kept people against their wishes if they were not dangerous, but some were, and I took a lot of violent kids to court. As their court date approached, the kids would become influenced by discussions with their lawyers and use legal jargon. They talked a little like your patient. Although these kids were violent, threatened, or destroyed property, they felt that I violated their rights, and their attorneys wanted them discharged. But when I took dangerous adolescents to mental-health court, I was very successful. I often had the judge commit them to the hospital against their wishes for further treatment, if that was what they needed. Nobody can predict the future, and you should consider the possibility of a negative outcome. Imagine a scene where an attorney in court asks you why you did or didn't give antipsychotic medications to a delusional teenager. Your credentials will work against you. If you have Goodbar's imprimatur, you're better protected."

"Fair enough. A consultation is reasonable."

"This boy is playing a dangerous game," I said, "and you've made a good connection. He's talking to you. You're willing to help him to the extent that he wants to help himself. That much is clear. He is very sick, and your ability to manage the situation will benefit from whatever help you can get from anywhere."

CHAPTER 48

JAN CAME IN A LITTLE OUT OF BREATH and seemed distraught. "I'm sorry I'm late."

The situation with his patient, John, was explosive. We had discussed it in the last session, and I was thinking about it before Jan came. "No problem. Catch your breath. While I was waiting for you, I was thinking about John; his case is truly tricky."

"It's not over. That's why I'm late."

From the look on Jan's face, I could see that he was curious about what I was thinking, too. "So, what are your thoughts on the case?" he asked.

"Have you heard of the term *bookends*?"

"I don't know. Like the ends of a book?"

"I use *bookends* as a metaphor for change. You can see the change from the *before and after* or *then and now* perspective. Assessments made at two critical times indicate change and constitute bookends. In your case, the bookends have to do with your attitude toward two of your patients, Amir and John. They reflect how much you've changed. Amir was a dangerous case, and you dealt with it in one way; that's the *before*-bookend. John is another difficult case, perhaps as dangerous as Amir. I see him as the *after*-bookend. The difference in your management of these two cases reflects your change. In John's case, you're asking questions like, 'Is John dangerous?' 'Who is in danger?' 'How can I safeguard everyone?' In the past, you asked these questions more theoretically and with less focus, but there is an urgency to focus your thinking and actions with him. For us, psychiatry is not theory but real life. Of course, no one can predict the future. You couldn't do it before, and now you can't do it. But you are

469

looking at reasonable options. Something happened that made you keep him in the hospital. What was it?

"John signed a contract with his parents that included a plan to repay the money he stole. He agreed to follow a reasonable safety plan and continue seeing me in my office. I transferred him from the inpatient unit to the day hospital program. Unfortunately, a big part of the transfer was pressure from his parents' insurance company. The insurance reviewer was disappointed that John wasn't more medicated and denied my request to keep him in the hospital longer because 'he didn't do anything dangerous.'

"John presents an image of the perfect patient. He says all the things a good patient is expected to say: 'I enjoyed being in the groups.' 'I find them to be helpful.' 'I have more and more insight into my problems.' 'I know that my parents are only a part of my problem. They drank and probably overlooked critical incidents in my life, but this doesn't justify what I did.' This is how he talks, something between psychobabble and legal jargon. He's pleasant and always smiles, but I'm not convinced. I want to know what's behind the smile."

"There are many times when your eyes can deceive you," I said. "Dr. Williams gives an example of an experience everyone has had: You're in the supermarket, and you see a friend. You start to walk toward him and raise your hand to wave. Then, suddenly you realize that he's not the person you thought he was; he's a stranger. It's like a momentary hallucination. In a split second, realizing you made a misidentification, you stifle your greeting."

"I look at John's smile as I walk him to the therapy room for each session. I use every Sripadism I've learned."

I raised my eyebrows, inviting Jan to explain this further.

Jan noticed and said, "What I mean by *Sripadism* is challenging to describe. For me, it's connected to the fundamental question of how you become a good psychiatrist. Books and lectures are essential, but they don't really tell you what's important. There are psychiatrists with different styles, and you try to learn from them. You soon realize that you don't know what you're looking for because patients and psychiatrists are often like two ships crossing in the night: There's not much meaningful connection. Then, suddenly you see a doctor who says or does something that builds a relationship with a patient. It's a gift; it sets an example for you. It shows you what being a psychiatrist really means. You're one of these teachers."

"How so?"

"I remember an adolescent girl you treated when I rotated through the inpatient unit. She was aggressive and hostile and utterly silent. She would viciously attack other patients and staff with no warning or pretext. I remember that she spent most of her hospitalization in seclusion, and she was often zonked out by emergency medications the nurses administered when she was agitated. The first time she saw you, she said nothing. She just sat and watched you talk. You didn't seem bothered by her silence, and you didn't put her on the spot with any questions. After that, we saw her every day, and with each visit, she showed small, but increasing, signs of receptivity. First, she smiled a few times, then she laughed. Gradually, she started to talk, and, slowly, she revealed the source of her rage: 'I don't trust anybody because my mother sold me for $2,000 as a toy to a mentally retarded rich boy.' Do you remember this girl?"

"I have a vague recollection of the case."

"Yeah, sometimes you make an impact on others without being aware of it. Anyway, I saw that you tune in first to see whether a patient is ready to accept anything you have to say. This, in itself, slows time and makes patients less anxious. You taught me the importance of tuning in and developing a sense of the *right moment*. These are what I call *Sripadisms*.

"Now, let me go back to John. He's a dodger and won't allow anyone to tune in to him. For example, I asked him, 'What do you think of this program?' He said, 'I think it's a good program. I feel productive. I feel changed. I realized that my father's social drinking isn't social drinking.' These were good observations. I may say, 'How come?' or 'Why did you say that?' I got that from you. When he says something funny, I laugh. When he says something I don't understand, I tell him, 'I'm not sure if I understood that. Can we go back so I can be sure that I understand you correctly?' I repeat my understanding and ask him to correct me. I look forward to experiencing this thread of empathy, this sense of connection that usually happens after one or two sessions with most patients. But so far, with John, I haven't felt anything. Every time I see this guy, I feel more uneasy. I don't feel good about anything he does, even his smile. I feel that he's very deceitful. Even when he praises therapy, I feel like he treats it as a joke. He knows how to play everybody."

Jan hesitated for a short while and asked, "Do I sound paranoid?"

"I don't know, but earlier, you said that the story continues. What happened?"

"Here comes the bomb. Today, we planned the last family meeting and discharge from the day hospital. Most of the staff was convinced that John was ready to go, but I couldn't shake my suspicion about the stolen gun, the silencer, the ski mask."

"OK, where's the bomb?"

"This morning, I got a phone call from his mother. She sounded freaked out. As hard as she tried to sound normal, she was obviously terrified. She said, 'I need to talk to you immediately, before our family meeting. You need to know something.'

"I said, 'Go ahead. What's on your mind?' She was sobbing, and for a few minutes, she could barely speak.

"Finally, she sputtered, 'I found something in his room.' Again, she tried unsuccessfully to compose herself. Despite several tries, she couldn't tell me what she found.

"I said, 'Bring whatever you found and come 15 minutes before our family meeting. We can talk about it then.'

"John's mother kept repeating, 'Thank you. Thank you. Thank you.' I knew that whatever she'd found, it was horrible. In addition to the gun, the silencer, and the ski mask, which were real, not imaginary, I had a record of John's dubious suicidal plans and a frantic phone call from his mother about some new evidence. Yet, I still didn't know how dangerous John was. How, by the way, can you assess dangerousness when someone hasn't hurt anybody yet?"

I said, "I once treated a young adolescent who lived with his grandmother in a third-floor apartment in a gang-infested neighborhood. He had a toy rifle that he pointed at people walking on the street below. His grandmother got word from some friendly neighbors that they had noticed his rifle. They thought some gang member on the street would confuse his toy rifle for a real one and shoot him. She tried to get him to stop, but she couldn't change his behavior. Then a bullet from the street broke her window. Even then, he said he wouldn't stop.

"She brought him to the hospital, and the emergency room admitted him, but he immediately signed a form saying he wanted to be discharged. A guardian can admit an adolescent into such a unit, but the adolescent has the right to sign out. To continue to treat him against his wishes, two physicians have to certify that he needs inpatient treatment. The case goes to mental-health court, and there is a hearing within a stipulated period. If the judge agrees with the kid, he gets discharged. If the judge decides the kid is dangerous to himself or others, he can be kept against his will and get further inpatient treatment. We could keep him on the unit for only a limited period without a court order, so we had to get the process going.

"I felt this kid needed to have his day in court. I assigned my inpatient-unit resident to complete the first certificate and planned to complete the second myself. When the resident found out that the rifle was a toy, he strongly protested the boy's hospitalization and didn't want to do the first certificate. I spent hours explaining the grandmother's concern that the boy was a danger, and the views of both the emergency room resident and me, as an attending, that the boy was a danger. But for the inpatient resident, the issue revolved around a single question: How could a toy gun be dangerous? I tried to explain that while the toy gun couldn't shoot, the people on the street didn't know that. If someone on the street thought it was real and shot at the boy, *that* bullet would be real. The boy didn't understand the danger he was putting himself and his grandmother in. I wasn't convincing the resident, so I reassigned the case to another resident, and we completed the certificates in time. Afterward, I spoke to the residency training director and voiced my criticism of his performance, attitude, and inflexibility; the director insisted on educational remediation for the resident. So, even if the rifle is a toy, the situation may be dangerous; when the gun is real, as in John's case, the danger is looming."

Jan replied, "I've tried to separate my gut feeling of John being a danger from any suggestions of danger his parents have made. I'm sure you'd agree that it's very hard to make this separation."

"Yes, it may even be impossible. Your job is to take reasonable actions in the presence of the danger you perceive."

"The problem I had was that, because of the masterful way John complied with the treatment, I was at the point where I had to let him go, even though I had a feeling he wanted to kill someone."

"What happened next?" I asked.

Jan took a deep breath. "So, John's mom and dad came to the hospital two hours before the scheduled family meeting. I had some free time and took them into my office. They gave me this piece of paper John had hidden in his room this morning." Jan started to read:

1. Take my bike and leave it in the abandoned ACME factory
2. Steal a car for a getaway
3. Time: after dark when they're drunk
4. Wear different-sized shoes and walk backward to enter the house through the side door. Make it look like someone was leaving the house

5. DO IT
6. Put rubber gloves on and smear blood on the side doorknob
7. Take discharge folder from the psychiatric unit with the payment plan and destroy it
8. Erase Internet searches and reformat the hard drive of the computer
9. Wash hands, put clothes, shoes, gloves, and weapons into the garbage bag, then into the backpack. No traces
10. Turn on the bedroom TV
11. (There's something written, but it's crossed out. It looks like John was speculating about the proper volume for the TV)
12. Toss a few dollars onto the floor to make it look like a robbery, and the robber was in a hurry and didn't have time to stuff all the cash
13. Don't touch anything else
14. Smash back-door glass panel from the outside, so it looks like someone broke into the house
15. Walk backward in the snow with shoeprints pointing toward the house
16. Change clothing and shoes in the car and put everything into the backpack
17. Drive to ACME and torch the car with the backpack in it
18. Ride the bike home and call the police.

Jan continued, "The agenda for this family meeting was John's contract covering reimbursing his parents and the details of his outpatient treatment. He was to get a part-time job and repay the money, even if it took the rest of his life. The problem was that he was only a few days shy of his 18th birthday. I wasn't sure of the status of the agreement after that. All this had just become irrelevant.

"We started the family meeting, and I started to read the list aloud. After just a few words, John said, 'Stop! I know what it is.'

"His parents were unable to speak. His mother started to cry, and his father turned pale. I said to John, 'You and I had a conversation this morning, and I was preparing your discharge from the day hospital, but now I need to understand better what this means. You need to explain yourself before we can think about discharge. Do I need to read more, or can you explain all this?'

"Looking at his parents, John said, 'I didn't want to kill *you*. I just wanted to whack Bizi. He's my steroid dealer.'

"I expected more probing questions from his parents, but instead, John's father just seemed relieved that he and his wife weren't John's intended targets. He asked, 'Do you owe money to anyone else? Tell me. I'll pay it, and we'll just add it to the money you owe us.'

"John answered without hesitation, 'I don't owe money to anybody but you. I just wanted to kill my dealer.'

"Fearing further collusion between John and his parents, I spoke with a stern voice, 'It doesn't matter who you wanted to kill. You're talking murder. My concern is that you were lying all along. Give me a good reason to believe you now.'"

I asked, "Did he 'fess up or try to give you a good reason?"

"No, he kept bullshitting. He insisted that he didn't know where Bizi lives, but his list suggested that he was familiar with the intended murder scene. In fact, the particulars matched his own house, and it says 'when they're drunk'; that's not Bizi. Finally, I asked him to explain his motive to kill Bizi if he didn't owe him any money. John answered that he hated him because Bizi had hooked him on drugs and changed his life forever. 'Bizi is responsible for my craziness, mom's crying, and dad's worrying. That's why Bizi deserves to die.'

"I decided that Sripadisms had gotten me only so far, and now I was stuck. Some patients are impervious to Sripadisms. To go any further with John, I had to rely on my own judgment."

These two sentences filled my heart with joy and pride. The essence of a person's freedom is to act on their *own* judgment. However flattering it may be to know that a patient looks up to you, the knowledge of an autonomously acting patient is infinitely more rewarding.

Jan continued, "I told him, 'There's no doubt that you're smart, but I think you got caught being over-smart. You thought you could fool everybody and carry out your plan. That is now obvious to everybody here, including me. I think you wanted to commit murder. You're dangerous. You need to be back in the inpatient unit *now*. It doesn't really matter how you feel about it. I need time to contact the hospital lawyers and authorities to ensure that you and others are safe. I'm sorry I have to do this, but I believe this is the best way to help you. I have to get to know you better and learn to trust you before I can let you go.'"

I reflected on Jan's statement to John and repeated it aloud, "'You're dangerous. It doesn't matter how you feel about it. I have to readmit you to the hospital.' You couldn't have said this to Amir, but you said it to John and acted on your judgment. This describes your change in a nutshell, from the *then* bookend to the *now* bookend."

Regarding Sripadisms, people will always influence each other: Children influence parents, just as parents influence children; patients influence doctors, just as doctors influence patients. This mutual influence is inevitable, and no party can deny it by claiming to be neutral and, above all, the analyst constantly reviewed it. (In the old school of psychoanalysis, the analyst inquired into influences that became pernicious and dangerous.) I helped Jan climb down from his suicidal depression and retrospectively understand its roots. For some time, I had been concerned that Jan looked up to me excessively and that it was counterproductive for him to regard me too highly. Such excesses are inevitable in love, friendship, and patriotism. I suspected that Jan was a guy searching for other good guys and had assigned me more goodness than I deserved and more than was reasonable. Although I had *helped* him overcome his depression, he had done most of the heavy lifting. Therefore, I was glad that he had found the limits of the Sripadisms and started to replace them with his own gut sense.

Jan continued, "I told John, 'I want to do everything I can to make sure that you won't legally purchase a weapon.'

"This may have been a bluff because I wasn't sure about the law and whether I could make it stick. His mom started crying. Both parents thanked me profusely. I didn't know what they were thanking me for. I felt horrible for them. Then I looked at John. For the first time since I met him, I saw emotions boiling inside of him. I could see that he was getting agitated. His face got red, the veins in his neck were sticking out, his eyes were bulging, and he was breathing heavily. I had a feeling that he was about to blow. So I said to him, 'I know you're upset, but I have to do what I have to do. After a few family sessions and our face-to-face conversations, you agreed upon and signed a few documents, which I put in your discharge folder. However, I realized that you planned to destroy everything we talked about and everything in this folder. It made me sad. We all wanted to believe that you were getting better. However, your plan to kill your parents and torch our agreements means that we all have much more work to do.'

"John didn't say anything. He got even more angry and sullen and said, 'I want a copy of any documentation that comes out of this session. I strongly object to this hospitalization. Do I have the legal right to object to my hospitalization?'

"I said, 'It's my clinical judgment that you are dangerous and need hospitalization. Of course, you have the right to object. If you and I can't work it out, I'll take you to the mental-health court, and a judge will decide.'

"Before the session, as a precaution, I had had two security guards stationed outside the room where we were meeting. So I opened the door just enough so he could see them. Then I said, 'I'll walk you to the inpatient unit.'

"Afterwards, I called the police precinct near his house. I told them I was concerned that John might go out and buy another gun after his discharge. So I asked the officer if I could prevent it.

"The officer patiently explained the difference between my sense of right and wrong and how the law works. He said, 'John has not committed any crime; he has a clean record. If we ask his neighbors, they would likely describe him as a nice boy—cheery, polite, and gentle. They might even say that he cuts the grass in front of his house and helps elderly neighbors. Your ideas are kind of naïve.'"

Death

Maria called to inform me that Jan's father had deteriorated precipitously, and Jan had gone to Poland to see his father. After a few weeks, Jan returned. Soon after returning, his sister called to tell him their father had died. In those few days, Jan was in Chicago, and I did not see him. Jan had returned to Poland for the funeral and services. Jan called and said that he would call me when he got back.

CHAPTER 49

THIS SESSION MARKS THE START of the fifteenth month of Jan's treatment. Jan called and made an appointment. After returning from Poland, he looked somber and shaken in this first session. He had stubble on his face and a faraway look in his eyes.

"My dad died so suddenly. He had been coughing and getting weaker for a few weeks, but after a short stay in the hospital and a course of antibiotics, he had started to feel better. Then, he got sick again, and Sofia took him back to the hospital. This time, his condition didn't improve. He had more difficulty breathing, and, at some point, Sofia and I agreed that he didn't have much time left. When I got to Poland, he was still in the hospital. He was confused and didn't recognize us. He had lost a lot of weight, probably 50 pounds; I noticed it when I helped him get up from his bed to take a bath. After I spoke with his doctor, it became clear that not much more could be done. We took him home the next day.

"I came back to Chicago and, a few days later, my sister called to tell me he had passed away. Although I wasn't close to him and often felt that he wasn't a good dad, I was surprised by my reaction. I thought I would be matter-of-fact, but the news hit me as profoundly as when my mother died. I was shocked. I couldn't speak for a while.

"Then I ran into Alma, one of the doctors I work with, and she asked what was happening, and when I told her that my father had just died, she hugged me and cried. I wasn't thinking clearly at that moment, but I felt the strangeness of the situation. I was surprised by my reaction and hers. I was touched and moved. It was like someone close to me, someone I liked, had died.

"After I got the news of my father's death, I caught the next flight to Poland. Sofia picked me up at the airport, and we drove to our hometown. My father had already been prepared and transported there. The funeral home we had used for my mom had already taken care of the obituary and other funeral arrangements. I was isolated from my feelings. I didn't see the point of talking about my dad and processing my feelings with Sofia. I was relieved when it was over. I'm still not in touch with my emotions.

"The next day, at dawn, I went to the morgue. The streets were deserted. I had to knock on the door a few times before the attendant opened it. Then, finally, there was just him and me and my father's casket in the corner. The attendant was a short man with coarse hands and a red face, suggesting he wasn't a stranger to alcohol or cigarettes. He asked me a question using language that he probably thought was sophisticated, but to me, it sounded peculiar. In English, it was like, 'Would you like to view the corpse?'"

I asked, "What was peculiar or surprising about this sentence?"

"Most people would say *see* instead of *view*, and *body* instead of *the corpse*. I didn't want him to open the casket, but the word *yes* came out of my mouth. I remember my grandmother telling me to touch my dead uncle's finger to prevent him from coming back as a ghost in my dreams. The attendant opened the lid, and my father was there, dressed in a black suit with a striped gray tie. He seemed tiny, like he had shrunk to half his normal life-size. The texture of his skin was unnatural—waxy, if I had to describe it. He looked familiar and, at the same time, foreign, like he was my father's doppelgänger.

"I nodded to the attendant indicating that I was done, and he riveted the casket shut. I watched as they loaded the casket into the hearse outside and drove away. Then I got back into my car and drove to the church. My father's casket was resting on the pedestal in the main aisle, close to the altar, covered with wreaths and flowers when I got there. And there was another surprise waiting for me. As I walked over to sit next to my sister, I saw a group of old men dressed in World War II uniforms carrying ornate Polish military flags that we call *sztandar*."

"Could you describe them for me?"

"Each of the six old soldiers held a standard, three on each side of the casket. They come in many designs, but I clearly remember that one was a Polish Home Army standard. It was about 3 feet by 6 feet, made of heavy red silk, and had a gold laurel wreath. In the middle of the wreath was a crowned eagle embroidered in silver. This eagle is the Polish national symbol. Right below the eagle, you could see *Bog, Honor, Ojczyzna*: God, Honor, Fatherland. In the lower-right corner, there's a Kotwica, a symbol of the *Armia Krajowa,* the Home Army. The letter 'P' appears to end in an anchor, indicating *Polska Walczaca,* Fighting Poland."

"I didn't know any of them. I looked inquiringly at my sister. She seemed equally at a loss and shrugged. Then I looked at my Aunt Malgorzata, who also shook her head in puzzlement. Nobody knew who these guys were. When the religious part of the service was over, the mourners were allowed to speak. Before anybody could get up, the six soldiers started talking, singing praises of my father. They said he was a lieutenant and a World War II hero and described his military exploits. They said that he put his body in harm's way and was shot by Germans while defending the Holy Land of Poland. I was stunned! I remembered my grandmother describing how my father, as a little boy, was shot in the butt by a German soldier as he was riding his bicycle, carrying a message for the Home Army partisans. After that, my grandma grounded my father for the rest of the War.

"So, did he fight in World War II? Is there proof that he was shot?"

"I never believed that my dad fought in the war, but he *did* have a scar on his butt."

I raised my eyebrows, waiting for further details.

"I remember one family vacation at the Baltic Sea. My parents befriended two other couples with children roughly my age. The men partied together almost every night, grilling sausages on an open fire and drinking more than usual. One night, my father and two other guys got drunk and started talking, boasting about their war exploits. One of the guys claimed that he was in charge of a squad of 15 men who surprised and killed a platoon of 50 German soldiers. My father said that the Germans had shot him. After going back and forth for a while, they started undermining each other's stories. Finally, my father asked him some tough questions, and it quickly became clear that the guy had made up his stories. But the guy didn't give up! He pulled up his shirt and showed them a scar across his abdomen. That didn't impress my father, who said maybe it was from a surgery or a work-related injury. The guy challenged my dad to do better. My father pulled down his pants and proudly showed him his scar on the left buttock that, according to him, was unmistakably caused by a bullet. That was the first time I saw my father's war scar.

"So, looking at the six old soldiers carrying standards at his funeral brought back a flood of memories. It was like a dream, unreal. Have you ever had an experience like that?"

"Yes."

"Since I don't feel like talking, why don't you talk?"

"OK. My dad was a captain in the Indian Medical Service in World War II, on the side of the Allies in Burma. He came back from the War with a knife that he took out maybe once a year to clean. Just like your dad's butt scar and the six old Polish soldiers who squeezed into their uniforms and sang praises of him, my dad's knife was real. There are many explanations about the knife in my family. No one in my family knows the whole truth about the knife. Each version of the story creates a different veil. Each version combines truth, memory, wishful thinking, distortion, and uncertainty. There, you didn't want to speak, so now you have my thoughts."

"You never told me before that your father was in World War II," Jan responded. "I respect anyone who fought in that War. It was a great War: The forces of good fought against the forces of evil. Yes, I used to go swimming with my father, and I saw the scar on his butt. That was a fact."

CHAPTER 50

THE BURMA FRONT, DURING WORLD WAR II, was active from 1941 until the end of the War in 1945. As a captain in the Indian Medical Service, my dad served in Burma on the Allies' side and saw action in the Imphal-Kohima battle. The westernmost highwater mark of the Japanese invasion of India was the hill town of Kohima. After fierce fighting, the Allies defeated the Japanese in Kohima and Imphal, and the War went downhill for them after that loss. Historians refer to the Burmese conflict between the Allies and Axis as the "Forgotten War" because its history remains to a large extent untold.

It was a miracle that the Allies won in Burma, as they worked at cross purposes. The British, thrown out of Burma by the Japanese earlier, wanted to reconquer Burma and reestablish the crumbling British Empire. The Americans weren't interested in the British Empire; they wanted democracies to flourish in Asia and beyond. Roosevelt sought freedom for India, but Churchill was vehemently against Indian independence. The U.S. primarily wished to defeat the Japanese, urging the Chinese to fight to keep the Japanese pinned down. Under Chiang Kai-shek's leadership, the Chinese were glad to accept lend-lease equipment, resources, and know-how from the Americans to fight the Japanese. Chiang Kai-shek focused on the civil war in China with Mao Tse-tung after the Second World War, so China engaged in a limited war with Japan. During the War, India was a British colony, and most Indians wanted independence from the British under Gandhi's leadership. Yet, against this sentiment, about two million Indian soldiers volunteered to fight for the British in the British Indian Army. Tens of thousands of Indians even fought on the side of the Japanese. They wanted to gain independence from the British by force.

The Japanese soldiers swore allegiance to Emperor Hirohito and lived according to the Samurai's Bushido code. It includes a belief that dying in battle was purifying and that surrendering was unacceptable. As a result, soldiers resisted capture, often committing suicide instead. If captured, they wouldn't give their name, rank, and service number, as other POWs did. They knew it was considered shameful to them and their families if it became known that they surrendered. In addition, the Japanese military denied military benefits to families of captured soldiers. As a result, many of those POWs became prisoners in their sleep. Some, because they were too sick to kill themselves.

In the battle of Kohima-Imphal, near the northeastern Indian state of Assam, the Japanese vastly outnumbered the British Allies. They surrounded them, about 20,000 Japanese against 5,000 British, Indian, Nepali, African, and Naga soldiers. The conditions were primitive, and there was much hand-to-hand combat. Air support provided by the British and the Americans helped save them. Although the Allies won, many Allied soldiers perished in the battle.

The Kohima Epitaph, commemorating their sacrifice, at the War Cemetery in Kohima, maintained by the Commonwealth War Graves Commission, reads:

When You Go Home, Tell Them Of Us And Say,
For Your Tomorrow, We Gave Our Today.

My dad came back from the War with a knife that he took out maybe once a year to clean. That was when he would talk about the War. I recently took my family to visit my relatives in India, including my 90-year-old mom.

My Uncle Venkat, my mom's younger brother, was visiting. Amma wanted me to videotape her thoughts and bring out my dad's World War II knife, which she stored in a steel cabinet. To make sure that her grandchildren would understand her, she spoke slowly, in English. She told them, and I paraphrase: 'My husband, Captain Sripada Krishnayya [Indians give surname or their last name, first] was a medical officer stationed in Burma in the Indian Medical Service in the British Army during World War II. He died about 20 years ago. This is his knife. When an enemy tried to kill you in the War, you shot him with your gun. But if he was on your neck, and there was no time to put bullets into your gun, you stabbed him with a bayonet, cut him with a knife, or tried to kill him with your bare hands. If you succeeded, you lived; if you failed, you died. Killing in Burma in those days wasn't like modern War. It was more like World War I. Now, you fire a missile, and you can kill an enemy thousands of miles away. You just press a button. In those days in Burma, there were no such buttons. And you could also die of malaria from mosquitoes or from drowning.

'After the Americans dropped atom bombs on Hiroshima and Nagasaki, Emperor Hirohito surrendered and said that the war situation had developed not to Japan's advantage, that the Japanese people would have to *bear the unbearable and endure the unendurable*.[67] The War ended with the signing of the Armistice in 1945. Many Japanese soldiers preferred death to surrender. My husband saw a Japanese officer who committed *harakiri*, cutting open his belly with a knife.' She unsheathed the knife and drew it across her abdomen, acting out what the Japanese officer must have done, and then she put it back in the sheath.

My Uncle Venkat was surprised by Amma's speech. "You never showed the knife to me before," he said. Then he asked my mom if she had any photographs of my dad from Burma. She said, 'No.' He looked disappointed.

Venkat turned to me and asked, "Did you know about the knife?"

"Yes," I replied. "Occasionally, Nanna removed the knife from its sheath, wiped the blade clean, and applied a fresh coat of Vaseline to prevent rust. Often, he talked about the War. Nanna joined the Indian Army in 1942 and was in Rawalpindi, Sialkot, and Bannu before the partition of British India. These places are in current-day Pakistan. He then was posted on the Eastern Front. Then, as a captain in the Indian Medical Service, he saw fighting in the Imphal-Kohima area in British India. He was also in Mandalay, Rangoon, and Kalaw, all in Burma, until 1946. Then, the Army demobilized, and he returned to civilian life."

---

67 On August 15, Emperor Hirohito of Japan recorded a speech to the Japanese public concerning the termination of the War. It read: "The war situation has developed not necessarily to Japan's advantage. Moreover, the enemy has begun to employ a new and most cruel bomb . . . We have resolved to pave the way for a grand peace for all the generations to come by enduring the unendurable and suffering what is unsufferable." https://www.theatlantic.com/international/archive/2015/08/emperor-hirohito-surrender-japan-hiroshima/400328/ August 17, 1945, Emperor Hirohito's surrender rescript was transmitted to the Japanese troops. It read:
". . . We trust that you officers and men of the Imperial forces will comply with our intention and will maintain a solid unity and strict discipline in your movements and that you will bear the hardest of all difficulties, bear the unbearable and leave an everlasting foundation of the nation." http://www.taiwandocuments.org/surrender07.htm

I continued my conversation with Venkat and said, "I recall him telling me the history of the knife, but I can't remember the details, so I don't know from where the knife came. However, I believe it's a typical Gurkha knife, a *kukri*, not a Japanese weapon."

A look of recognition came over Venkat, my Uncle. He seemed to be remembering events that had taken place more than 60 years ago. He became electrified by the story. Venkat unsheathed the knife with much care and posed as a victor would. Then, again, he asked my mom if there was a picture of my dad in Burma.

Again, my mom replied, "No."

Venkat said, "It would have been fitting if there was a picture of the captain posing with this knife on the battlefield in Burma." Then, with increasing excitement, my 88-year-old uncle said, "Captain Sripada Krishnayya is a hero. He was on the Western Front, in Bannu, in northwest Pakistan, along with the Pathans, guarding India against the Russians, and he was on the Eastern Front in Burma, fighting against the Japanese!"

Then, Venkat focused on the knife again. He took the unsheathed knife and drew it across his abdomen as my mom had done a few minutes before. He then put the knife back into the sheath and handed it to me, saying, "I give the *harakiri* knife back to you." It was hilarious to see my mom and her brother play-acting *harakiri*. They were a nonagenarian and octogenarian having fun brandishing my dad's World War II souvenir!

Then Venkat declared again, "Krishnayya is a hero." On what did he base that statement? My dad was an Emergency Commissioned Officer between 1942 and 1946. His job was dealing with wartime injuries, improving the hygiene among the soldiers, and preventing malaria and other tropical diseases. He saw much pain, performed his share of amputations, and dispensed his share of syrettes, single-dose hypodermic needles containing a half-grain dose of morphine. I don't know if that makes him a hero.

I remember other family discussions about the knife. Several years ago, while I was visiting my family, my Cousin Bujji, who is twelve or thirteen years older than me, came to visit us. He had been a successful businessman, but he was ill with end-stage kidney problems at that time. Now he's dead. On that day, he and Amma were talking about life and death. Then, suddenly, he asked Amma, "Could I please take another look at Uncle Krishnayya's *harakiri* knife?"

Amma brought out the knife, and they talked about World War II a bit. Then, Amma got up and said that she would make him some coffee; she was always a generous hostess.

After she left, Bujji and I continued talking. Finally, I asked Bujji why he called it the *harakiri* knife. He said, "Your dad told me that a Japanese officer used this knife to commit *harakiri*."

At that moment, Amma came back with the coffee, and it became a typical Indian afternoon—excited talk about family and politics. But unfortunately, I did not have an opportunity to ask Bujji about what else my dad told him.

My dad was fond of talking about his experiences of the War. He hated the Japanese. Even before World War II, he said that they had perfected the art of deceiving, raping, and killing civilians when they pillaged Nanking. So I read up about the Japanese during the War. In 1942, the Japanese arrived in Burma and India with the slogan 'Asia for Asians,' claiming they wanted to grant independence to Burma and help Indians gain independence from Britain. In Burma, within only a year, they established a whole military administration and encouraged Burmese to learn Japanese. The Burmese initially welcomed them as liberators, but soon the Japanese started treating the Burmese citizens—many of whom were Buddhists like themselves—much as they had treated the Chinese in Nanking. Gang rapes of Burmese women began to occur. They executed Burmese citizens for little or no cause. They started to use live Burmese civilians for bayonet practice. Soon, the Japanese were inflicting so much pain that the Burmese regarded them conquerors, not liberators.

Then the Japanese attacked Assam and the northeast provinces of India. The Japanese depended on captured territories to provide food and shelter for them. General Slim, the Allied British general in charge of confronting the Japanese, anticipated their advance and burned all the fields to ensure they couldn't survive long.

Japanese soldiers would be victorious or die. If surrounded by the enemy, they would die fighting or bring about their death by suicidal attacks. They had a philosophy called *Gyokusai*, jade shards: A soldier who died honorably this way was like a shattered jewel, while a soldier who chose to stay alive by surrendering was a complete roof tile. That's why they had no respect for Allied soldiers who allowed themselves to become POWs.

The Allies learned to be wary even when the Japanese retreated. In many instances, Allied soldiers killed most members of a Japanese unit.

However, the few survivors were ready with machine guns to kill as many Allied soldiers as possible before being killed. Some would feign death, holding a grenade in their hands. When Indian or English soldiers approached, they would detonate it, preserving their honor by killing themselves along with their enemies. After losing several soldiers this way, the English and Indian soldiers decided that any seemingly dead Japanese could be faking it, so they stopped trying to take prisoners and killed every Japanese soldier. To be safe, they shot, slit the throats, or bayonetted those who were dead, dying, or possibly feigning death. When the Japanese soldiers hid in caves, they became targets for the Allied flamethrowers. Although the Japanese looked serene before committing *harakiri*, they lost their composure when hit by flamethrowers and rushed out of the caves screaming. Still, they were unsafe at any distance and took as many Allied soldiers with them as possible.

As a child, I got nervous when Nanna spoke about the War. I remember him talking about *harakiri* and showing the knife to the rest of the children and me. What I remember most weren't his words but his agitated mood and killer attitude toward the Japanese. It's like a kid who watches *Psycho* but shields his eyes with his fingers just as the knife plunges into Janet Leigh. Although he can't be called a witness, he can recall the music, and the scene is still vivid.

Growing up, I found my father's accounts of his life as a physician in the army too gory. However, my unease was not the whole story. I also carried a sense of curiosity and interest in his experiences. My dad wanted me to become a physician and encouraged my curiosity about medicine.

When I was about seven, my parents contracted to build our house, very close to our rented place. During that time, our family often went to take a look. I had the opportunity to watch various construction tradespeople at work and ask questions. The workers even encouraged me to try my hand at some construction odds and ends. Once, I tried to cut a piece of wood with a saw while my dad watched. He saw that I was not getting anywhere, as the saw in my hands roamed all over the wood block's surface. I asked for his help to understand why I could not use the saw. He explained to me the importance of first establishing a groove and expertly cutting the wood. I appreciated his unexpected skill, and I asked him where he learned to use saws. He then told me that he knew to use the saw to perform surgical amputations during the War. Later, he showed me a thin, detachable, thirteen-inch bone saw with a metal handle.

My dad and I went to a barber's shop on Kingsway (named after King George VI of the United Kingdom and now renamed Rashtrapati Road—President's Road) in Secunderabad. Then, when I was about ten years old, after our haircut, as usual, we had a dosa (South Indian pancake with curry) in the nearby Taj Mahal hotel. We came across a secondhand street bookstore as we walked home. The owner spread his books on the pavement, and my dad picked up *The Doctors Mayo*[68] for four annas (equivalent to a quarter). Subsequently, it turned out to be our favorite book.

Nanna and I would often listen to the news and chat. Sometimes he read poems or some part of a book. Then he started reading episodes about Mayo's experience as a country doctor to me. William Worrall Mayo moved from England to the United States and established himself as a country doctor in Rochester, Minnesota, around 1880. He had two sons, who, under his tutelage, learned to apply bandages and splints to patients and help their father. Thus, William James Mayo and Charles Horace Mayo became physicians and founded the Mayo Clinic; they became legends in their lifetimes when they grew up.

Because there were no hospitals in Minnesota, Dr. Mayo performed all his operations in the patients' homes. There was no reliable help for a surgeon in those days, and Dr. Mayo asked the local coroner to serve as the anesthetist. Charlie, his teenage son, was watching. Dr. Mayo planned to remove an ovarian tumor, and the coroner helped administer anesthesia to the patient on a sofa. Here was our familiar dog-eared page. Nanna conveying the drama of the scene, that I still remember, read:

> "Dr. Mayo made a small incision and drained the fluid contents of the tumor into a tub. Then by means of clamps worked by thumbscrews he began to pull the tissue of the growth out through the incision. The base of the tumor was pulled back and forth in the process, producing a peculiar sucking noise like that made 'by a cow's foot in the mud.' This was too much for the nerves of the anesthetist, and he fainted.
>
> After a quick survey of the possibilities, Dr. Mayo kicked over a cracker box at the end of the sofa and said, "Here, Charlie, you stand on this and give the anesthetic." (p. 93)

---

68 Clapesattle, Helen B., (1941). *The Doctors Mayo*, Minneapolis: University of Minnesota Press.

During such readings, Nanna and I imagined that he was Dr. Mayo and I was his son, Charles, and he would ask me to help him with his work. Of course, this was our play. It was fun, and neither was confused about our identities. It was his way of encouraging me to become curious about a physician's life. It got me thinking that I could be a doctor. So, when my mom and my dad came to visit us for our wedding, my wife, then my fiancée, and I drove my parents to Rochester to see the Mayo Clinic. As my dad and I stood by the statue of the Brothers Mayo, Nanna exclaimed words to the effect, "Thanks to this visit to the Mayo Clinic, one of my life's dreams has come true." *The Doctors Mayo* was an American story of doctors—a father and sons; it aligned my dad, sister, and me, also all doctors. I did not become a surgeon or join the military but enjoyed my later life as a physician and analyst. Although I was anxious about his surgery-talk when I was a child, I never doubted his love or goodwill. I was pleased with how my dad guided me as a child and an adolescent.

There is a curious fact about my dad in the War and his family's reaction. My dad came from the *Brahmin*, or priest, caste; they don't eat meat. From our family's point of view, putting meat into his mouth was more significant than the entire World War II. For me, the *kukri*, which he cherished till he died, was the symbol of his proud personal transformation. After the War, he became liberated from common Indian beliefs and practices. Therefore, he treated all people equally regardless of caste and became an alien in his world.

My family has a photograph of Nanna taken in Bannu in 1942 as a lieutenant. Bannu is now a hangout for Al Qaeda in Pakistan. During the colonization of India and especially in the nineteenth century, "The Great Game" came to signify the conflict between Britain and Russia. The British were suspicious of Tsarist designs in Central Asia, which might have included an invasion of India through Afghanistan. However, Bannu was a dangerous place and located in the North-West Frontier, Pakistan, near the border of Afghanistan. Kipling described it well:

When you're wounded and left on Afghanistan's plains,
And the women come out to cut up what remains,
Jest roll to your rifle and blow out your brains
An' go to your Gawd like a soldier.[69]

---

69 Kipling, R. (1892). *Barrack Room Ballads and Other Verses.* Project Gutenberg EBook of Barrack-Room Ballads, by Rudyard Kipling (December 8, 2008 [EBook #2819]).

John Masters, an Indian-born British soldier who served with distinction in India, Burma, and the Middle East during World War II, wrote *Bugles and a Tiger*.[70] Speaking of his experiences concerning Pathans of northwest India (Afghanistan) before the War, Masters wrote:

"Tribesmen who captured any soldiers except Moslems, and especially Sikhs or British, would usually castrate and behead them, and both these operations were frequently done by the women. Sometimes they would torture prisoners with the death by a thousand cuts, pushing grass and thorns into each wound as it was made. Sometimes, they would peg the prisoner out and with a stick force his jaws so wide open that he could not swallow, and then the women urinated into his open mouth till he drowned."

---

70 Masters, J. (1954). *Bugles and a Tiger*. London: Michael Joseph, p. 190.

CHAPTER 51

Jan was talking even before he sat down.

"I've been thinking about my childhood, so I can help David avoid the problems I had. There are many things that I don't understand, even now. From where did all my anger come? Part of it was the gymnasium-like environment where I grew up, where fighting was the way to solve problems. Through fighting, the boys established their pecking order. There has to be another explanation for all the dark forces I felt. I didn't want to be like my dad for most of my life. He hurt me deeply, and I demonized him. Even though he's dead now, I haven't been able to think about him differently. I still see him with horns. I need to redo his horns at some point."

Bravo, I thought.

"I still remember bad things that happened between us, but without much emotion, as though they happened a long time ago or to somebody else. When I talked about him in the past, I had lots of raw feelings right on the surface. I felt he was in me and all around me, even when he was thousands of miles away. I don't feel him now. He's disappeared. And whatever positive or negative influences he had on my life, they are all gone with his death. I have no sense of his existence. Although his body was still there during the past several years, he was totally demented. And now he's gone, completely gone, and it's much easier to think about him.

"I don't know if I told you this before. My hometown was halfway between Warsaw and Lublin. My father's business took him out of town quite often, and it was always a big deal for me, as a boy, when he would take me along. The excitement wasn't about spending time with *him*; I was excited to ride on the tram, see the skyscrapers, go up and down the escalators, and go to the Museum of Evolution in the Palace of Culture and Science. Still, *he* was taking me there. I probably wouldn't have given him any credit for doing it in the past. But, now I can admit that he did. As I was driving back from the funeral, I listened to *Maly Ksiaze*, "Little Prince," the Polish hit from the sixties by Kasia Sobczyk. And, suddenly, our trips to the capital popped into my head out of nowhere, and for the first time, I allowed myself to give him at least some credit."

Jan suddenly began to speak hesitantly, his sentences breaking up before completing them.

"I remember . . . another time . . . my mother thought I was going with him . . . He told her he was taking me . . . a business trip to Warsaw . . . That's a different story."

"You seem to be pursuing several lines of thought. But, unfortunately, I'm having trouble following you."

"So, one day, when I was maybe five or six, my father told me that we would be going to Warsaw, and I was all excited. The following day, we boarded a bus, but the trip was surprisingly short. I knew we weren't in Warsaw, but he tried to convince me that we were. He left me at a restaurant with a lady who smelled of tobacco and probably alcohol, too. She talked to me and tried to be nice, but I didn't like her. There were a couple of other people there, too. It made me uncomfortable and grouchy. When we got back home, my mom asked me how the trip was. I told her I didn't like it and didn't want to talk about it. I knew something was wrong, but I couldn't explain what it was. Why did my father disappear? Why did he leave me with that smelly lady? I wonder if I embellished this story later when I was older. Did I really know what tobacco or alcohol smelled like when I was that age? But I knew something was wrong with the whole situation.

"In the past, if anything reminded me of this event, I just avoided it. But, perhaps because my dad's gone now, I can think about it. I know we didn't go to Warsaw; we went to a nearby town. And my father left me for a few hours with some stinky lady and her companions. Strangers! Over the years, I've wondered why, but now I don't think it matters. He lied to me and left me with strangers. That was just wrong. This memory became a splinter in my heart and set the tone for our future mistrustful relationship."

"It must be painful for you that this memory resurfaced now."

Without acknowledging what I'd said, Jan continued, "Oh, I just remembered: My father told my mom that we had a good time 'in Warsaw,' and I didn't rat on him. Should I have said, 'I don't think we went to

Warsaw'? I felt guilty that I didn't tell my mom that he was lying. I was torn between loyalty toward my father and guilt about respecting my mom. That's why I got anxious every time I thought about it. Now that I've overcome this anxiety, I want to know more about what my father was up to. I think what triggered my anxiety was the thought that he was with some other woman."

When Jan was a child, his dad had put him in an impossible situation: Should Jan have been faithful to himself and told his mom his dad had lied? Or should he have protected his father and stayed silent? He sensed that he was protecting her from devastating news, but he also felt profound guilt for not telling her. I also sensed that Jan was livid on her behalf. Jan dimly sensed, even then, that his father was cheating on his mom, something he confirmed later in his life. If so, in Jan's eyes, not only was his dad worthless, but he had defiled his mom's dignity. I remembered Jan talking about the code of honor killings among Polish Highlanders and felt Jan had become like a Highlander: He believed his father had murdered his mother's soul and wanted to avenge the crime.

"It seems you're a Highlander at heart," I said.

My statement hit Jan like a thunderbolt. Rattled, he said, "I'm sorry, but what is *that* supposed to mean?"

I had been waiting for such a moment for a while and waded in slowly to explain my thinking. Here was the confluence of Jan, his father, and his mother with love, betrayal, fear, anger, and guilt. "Like a Highlander," I began, "you want to kill—"

"—my father, for cheating on my mom. Oh, yes—I had such thoughts, but never any actual plan. And I had more of them when my father tried to exercise his authority by threatening my mother or sister. This happened somewhat regularly. I remember one time when I was 15. It was June, right before the end of the school year. My father was going through lots of problems at work. He was the head of a research lab in a big factory, attempting to kick him out. The more he lost his grasp on power at work, the more he became a tyrant at home. He became impossible to deal with.

"One evening, Sofia came home way past curfew. From my room, I heard him screaming at her. I went to see what was going on and saw him raise his hand like he would strike her. I felt a rush of feelings and grabbed his hand. Then, very calmly, I told him, 'I don't want to fight. I just want you to leave her alone.' I think my calm tone made him even angrier, and he barked, 'I can do whatever I want in my house! Do you want to fight?'

"As a teenager, I was athletic. I lifted weights and was very much into martial arts. At that point, I had been taking classes in *kung fu* and *judo* for more than three years. I practiced for hours every day and never missed a class, so I knew some holds. So I said, 'I don't want to fight, but I'm ready if you do.'

"He took the challenge and tried to hit me. I grabbed his wrist and twisted it, forcing him to sit down. Again, he was furious and struggled to hit me, but I was behind him, and he couldn't reach me. He started foaming at the mouth, but I held him down. I told him I would let him go if he behaved. He squirmed, trying to strike me, but I tightened my grip and repeated the offer. He didn't want to give up and tried to hit me again. It took a while, but he finally stopped resisting me. He knew I meant business. He realized that I was stronger and would let him go only after he agreed not to hit Sofia.

"When he finally said, 'Let me go,' I knew he was defeated. He lost the physical part of the fight, but he still wanted to hurt me, so he said, 'You aren't my son.'

"You know, I don't remember most of my dreams, but the few that I remember never leave me. I just thought about one that we discussed some time ago: the one about finding my father hanged in my apartment. When I originally talked about this dream, I described the anger I felt at him for killing himself in my home, that I was concerned that Maria would discover his body and become scarred for life. Now, it occurs to me that this was *my* dream and *my* home, so *I* could have been the one who killed him."

Heeeeere's Oedipus, I thought, and said, "So, what had seemed like a rotten father who hanged himself is now a rotten father that you possibly hanged," I said. "In this explanation, you're actively involved in his death."

"Yes, but I don't feel so guilty."

Jan was silent for a while and then continued, more in a spirit of inquiry than of self-blame: "Perhaps Amir felt the same way, and that was why I couldn't help him. Amir hated his father for setting impossible standards. He was unaware of that hatred because it had turned inward, and he killed himself instead. I want to understand myself so that David won't become overly angry and guilty like me. I'm not going to be an adulterer like my dad, and I'm not going to make David collude with any kind of lies. I'm still angry at my dad for cheating on my mom, but I can deal with that anger better, thanks to you. Because of our conversations, my father's image as an evil monster has faded; now, I have the image of a troubled man. I've finally been able to bury him. May he rest in peace and also leave me in peace."

"What we talk about here has changed you and how you feel about your dad. It will stick to the extent that your experience and understanding have produced the change. It will fade to the extent that my suggestions or theories influence it. Your understanding organizes your past, explains your present, and will determine who you will become in the future. Your understanding and your life certainly can't be based on lies. Your goal of not living a lie or putting your son in a position to cover your lies is meaningful. You have decided to live a truthful future despite the lies mixed into your past; this is the change you have accomplished."

"I used to think of my past and wonder where my anger and guilt came from. Finally, I am beginning to understand. One day, when I was a teenager, I answered the phone, and the woman on the line obviously thought that she had reached my father and started to talk. It was clear she was the 'other woman.' She sputtered and hung up when she realized that I wasn't him. That time, too, I decided not to tell my mom, and I felt guilty about it.

"Instead, my sister and I encouraged her to get a divorce. I told her, 'Don't worry about us. I know you're staying with him because of us, but we're no longer children, and you should do what's right for you. If leaving him will lessen your pain, leave him.' This way, I could get rid of my father without hurting her with bad news."

"Your focus moved from Amir to your dad and is now moving toward David. Now that your father isn't a living presence, it seems that the tone of your voice is more inquiring. You want self-understanding, and you want to figure out how to be the best dad to David that you can."

"This room is where it all started. For all those years, I didn't have the desire—"

"—to look into it?"

Jan nodded. "I made tentative attempts to discuss my feelings with my sister, but the conversations usually ended with my saying, 'I thought I wanted to talk about it, but I really don't,' or 'It doesn't make sense to talk about it now. Whatever happened is in the past.'"

"Before, dealing with your past involved only *you*, but now it has a bearing on David's future *and* yours," I noted. "Today, there is good reason to look into it. You want to create a path for your son, a path that you didn't have, so that history won't repeat itself."

"My father didn't expose me much to his side of the family. I hated his mother with all my heart. Every time I was supposed to go there, I pretended I was sick. I became an expert at getting the thermometer to exactly 38°

[100.4° Fahrenheit], high enough that I had to stay home but not so high that I had to go to the doctor. I would show it to my mom, make a sick face, and feign exhaustion. That was enough. I wasn't going anywhere, especially not to my grandmother's."

"Why didn't you want to visit your grandmother?"

"I'm sure I told you: She mistreated my Uncle Bozydar. He was in the Polish Underground during World War II. Arranging the killing of collaborators destroyed him, and he escaped into alcohol. To me, he was a hero, but my grandmother made him a pariah and wouldn't let him sit at the table with the rest of the family.

"And I never liked my father's sister, Aunt Malgorzata. I've talked about her, too. She's a very troubled woman. Yes, she lost her son to encephalitis when he was 17, but she's also just a paranoid bigot. She practically lives in the church and always has Jesus on her lips, but she's a hateful person. She thinks anybody who isn't a Catholic deserves to burn in hell.

"She's genuinely toxic, impossible to deal with, even when you try. I am sure you remember. Sofia was taking care of my mother when she was dying, and she asked Aunt Malgorzata to take care of my father for a few days since he was often agitated, which made extra work for her. He also didn't sleep well and made a lot of noise walking around the house at night. He needed constant supervision to prevent him from endangering himself and everybody else. For example, he would put the kettle on the stove and turn on the gas but forget to light it. And when he went to the bathroom, he couldn't—or wouldn't—aim right, so he peed all over the place.

"Well, Aunt Malgorzata went ballistic and accused Sofia of wanting to get rid of him. She said Sofia was heartless, taking a husband away when his wife was dying.

"My mother heard the exchange and told Sofia not to ask Aunt Malgorzata for any favors, that we should manage our dad as best we could by ourselves. She said, 'Don't feel guilty. You weren't trying to get rid of your father. There are some things you can't explain to your aunt.' Two weeks later, she passed away.

"And then there was what happened at my mom's wake. Aunt Malgorzata pulled me aside and told me not to trust people I think are my friends and warned that they would try to undermine my father now that my mother was gone.

"It was the wrong time and place, and she wouldn't stop talking! Finally, I managed to shut her down without using one profanity! I told her, 'My mom just died. The wake is about her, not my father. I understand the great tragedy that you suffered when your son died and that you feel deeply about your brother, but it is wrong to persist in focusing on my father now. I know who my friends are. Unlike you, they reached out to help us all through Mom's illness. I don't feel you are my friend. I barely know you. I don't want you to talk about my family like this.'

"At first, she didn't react. I had always wanted to say those things to her, and it turned out it *was* the right time and place! But then she started talking again, like I hadn't said a thing, rambling on about my family and how they would try to influence me against my father and separate me from him. I was calm, collected, and coherent. Finally, I said, 'I don't want to talk to you now, and if I feel that I want to talk to you in the future, I'll call you. Right now, I need to say goodbye to my mom.'

"Aunt Malgorzata is not an orthodox Catholic; she's a psychotic Catholic. She gave me a hard time when Maria and I married because we didn't have my first marriage annulled. Even though Maria grew up Catholic, she didn't care. And getting an annulment probably would have required me to say bad things about my first wife, and why? I don't have any bad feelings about her. So in a way, my aunt helped me find Maria. Because she was so obnoxious and rigid, I decided to go for it and forget about the religious requirements and rigmarole to get remarried.

"In general, Maria has more reservations about the Catholic Church than I do, mostly for its stance against women priests and the child sexual abuse scandals, which I see as a product of troubled individuals and not the system. Nevertheless, the Catholic tradition must be deeply rooted in me because I still feel that the Church is a positive force. Even though I didn't find my answers there, I believe that the Church, as an institution, plays a significant role in increasing good and decreasing evil in this world.

"My father became more religious after he turned 70. Maybe he wanted to be rescued from his depression and forgiven for his past behavior. Maybe people need religion when they're dying or want to secure a good position in the afterlife. Perhaps it's loneliness. I don't know what it is, but I know many people who became religious in their old age. I haven't seriously thought about my own demise yet and haven't found any comfort in the practice of religion. I just like the feeling I get inside the old churches: the beautiful architecture and artwork, the smell, the silence. The perfect stillness slows my thoughts and makes me feel at peace.

"One day, David will ask questions, and Maria and I will have to take another look at religion to answer them. For me, growing up with the idea of God was protective. It prevented me from making even more mistakes than I did. God is a nice old man with a long white beard who knows everything I do and even everything I think in my earliest memories. This is how my mother and father described Him to me. They said that God is important and that I could always talk to Him and He would listen, but He would never talk back to me.

"I had this dream. A person was going down the stairs, disappearing from my life forever. I realized that it was God. I woke up petrified because I knew in the dream that this was forever."

"When did you have this dream?"

"I was probably ten or eleven. My father was making sure that I said my prayers every night. I had to kneel and recite the *Hail Mary* and *Our Father* without any mistakes. If I made even one, I had to start over. At some point, he stopped sitting next to me during prayers and just asked if I had said them. So one day, I decided, instead of praying every day, I would pray eleven times in one evening, so I didn't have to do it again for another eleven days."

"Mass production!" I laughed.

"Yes, but the mass production got out of hand. It was hard to keep track, and I would forget to restart at the correct time and feel guilty. That was why I had the dream that God left me and would never come back."

"I want to look at some key events related to your guilt. At the age of five or six, you went on a trip, supposedly to Warsaw, where you had an encounter with the smelly woman, and you felt guilty for not telling your mom. At ten or eleven, you felt guilty for trying to cheat on your prayers, so you dreamt that God left you. And at 15, you felt guilty because you encouraged your mom to leave your dad."

"I agree about the first two, but not the third. I didn't feel guilty about advising my mom to leave my dad. As for linking or connecting these instances with main periods in my life, that's not how my mind works. I know that, in analysis, we hope that doing this can help sort out people's guilt, but I'm never sure how to track the events in my personal history with any precision.

"I am curious, however, about how other people sort out their past. Some people, like Alvear-Reverte, can recall the exact dates of events that took place 25 years ago. They remember the names of all their kindergarten friends, the specifics of conversations.

"That isn't how my memory works. I use my own milestones to divide my past into periods and trace my life events somewhere amid them. For example, I can trace some things by remembering what apartment I lived in at the time. Though I may remember seasons, I don't remember exact dates. My recollections aren't in a calendar format.

"I remember very well the conversation in which I encouraged my mother to divorce my father. I remember feeling emotional and trying to hold back my tears. We were on a balcony, and it was fall or spring. I felt my father was a cheater and a traitor in the back of my mind. I hated him, but I didn't want to say that to my mom, so I said, 'If you divorce him, it's fine with us.' It was the second apartment on the third floor; we moved to another one when I started high school, so I was about 15 when we had that conversation.

"Different people have different ways of sorting memories. I bookmark milestones from our conversations and refer to them when I speak to you. I hope that it improves our communication. I focus on what I believe we can use, rather than some ideal or theoretical standard. There is no way of knowing beforehand which interpretation will work; only time will tell. You know, some people believe that clear and vivid memories may be false memories, or they are mashups of several other significant events that have been telescoped, disguised, or merged.

"I think I have some ADD and just can't focus properly on my memories."

"That may be true, but the definition of attention is also important. After your dad died, you were more able to pursue particular thoughts, like the smelly lady. In the past, you wouldn't have paid any attention to that thought."

"Because I didn't want to go there. It was unpleasant."

"Yes, today we did some work to discover why it was unpleasant. Besides, now you're curious, and David has made the job meaningful."

"What do you mean?"

"We have to go with your way of organizing your memories and experience, but today you were able to pursue a thought that you weren't able to in the past. Although you feel you may have ADD, you're a coherent narrator, and I feel continuity in your stream of thought. I don't see you as someone whose stories are out of focus. Today, you focused on your mom and dad and, also, on how to be a father to your son. Your thoughts about David enrich your analysis."

CHAPTER 52

THIS SESSION MARKS THE START of the sixteenth month of Jan's treatment.

"Almost immediately after we spoke last time, I regretted things I said. I was frustrated that I had no closure with my father. We had no communication of any sort for many years, just occasional arguments during my visits home. These were typically about how poorly he treated my mom, but sometimes they dealt with politics or just everyday, stupid things. As a hot-blooded youngster, I often fell into arguments with him, but I got hurt every time.

"He would get personal and say that I was too young to understand; I usually responded by saying that he was too senile to comprehend. He would never admit to any mistake. The things he said during those arguments were hurtful and undermined my self-esteem. He always used hints and insinuations to suggest that he was disappointed in me. Instead of recognizing what I had accomplished, he would hold up some ideal version of me that I should aspire to.

"At my medical school graduation, I was chatting with a few of my close friends, and my father asked about our future plans. When he heard that one of them wanted to be a neurosurgeon, he asked me why I hadn't thought of that. At some point, I just gave up and stopped trying to make peace with him. I saw him less and less often and rarely spoke with him on the phone. However, my mom always picked up the phone. She ended many of the calls by saying, 'I love you very much. I'll tell your father that you called. He's sleeping now.'

"My father was always sleeping, no matter what time of day I called. He slept 16-plus hours a day, stoned on sedatives like Tranxene or Xanax, which he took from medical donations given to the Catholic charities where he volunteered. On the rare occasions when he was awake, she would give him the phone. We would speak briefly, and he would also say, 'I love you very much,' which he had heard my mom say a few minutes earlier.

"My answer was always, 'Thank you. Me, too.' Then, after we hung up, he would torture my mom by comparing my affectionate responses to her, which he had overheard, with my dutiful responses to him."

I asked, "And now, he's dead. Do you think you'd do anything differently if you had a chance?"

"It's possible that I would, only because I've had the chance to talk to you. As our sessions have progressed, my image of my dad has changed from an evil cartoon character to just a troubled, sick man. I went back to say farewell to him, hoping to conclude this chapter of my life. Whatever grudge I held against him was about to end. Unfortunately, although I was true to myself, I still felt hypocritical during the funeral. You probably remember my description of the last hours before my father was buried."

"How could I forget? You saw him as a harmless, shrunken man while the six old soldiers trumpeted him as a war hero."

"You remember well. The only thing I didn't tell you was that, as I touched his finger, I thought, *Rest in peace. It's over for you.*"

I remembered that, when Amir killed himself, Jan felt jealous of him because it was *over* for Amir. I felt any reference to Amir was out of place right now, so I suppressed it. I just asked, "Why?"

"A long time ago, I told you about a custom my grandma taught me: When I was a boy, she took me with her to the open casket of my Uncle Hektor at his funeral. I remember being scared. When morticians lay a dead person in a casket, they try to pose them, so they appear like they're praying. Then, they put a rosary in the person's hands, which, in addition to its religious meanings, helps keep their hands together in the middle. My grandma said, 'Touch his thumb; it has a rosary wrapped around it. If you are brave enough to do it, his *dusza* will never come to you in your dreams.' *Dusza* means 'ghost' or 'soul.'"

"So, back to your father's funeral."

"Yes, I was looking around and feeling like I was participating in some kind of strange drama. I had never met people talking about my father and using his first name. Elderly soldiers dressed in Underground uniforms holding military standards, saluting his coffin, and saying farewell to . . . a war hero."

Jan hesitated and then continued. "You see, I've already said enough. What sense does it make to even talk about it? As I said, I should just let him rest in peace."

There was a moment of silence, and then Jan spoke again.

"I had a dream two days after our last session. The dream took place in my old school, Stefan Batory High School. So many of my friends were there, and we all looked much younger. During a break between classes, we were all in the hallway on the second floor, by the principal's office. I saw the scene through a child's eyes because the hall seemed huge. But, in reality, the halls are small. I realized that during my last class reunion. Now, going back to the dream.

"I looked at the Hall of Fame: walls with framed pictures of prominent alumni and small plaques below each one, describing the person's accomplishments. Then, I went closer to read one of the plaques. It described the exploits of one of the alumni in the Polish Underground during World War II, talking about the war to a group of kids in one of our classes."

"I smiled to myself, partly disgusted and partly ashamed, thinking of my father's so-called exploits because I knew my father was the Baron Munchausen of World War II.[71] I continued looking and noticed that they were genuine sepia-toned war photographs. They were amazing, full of action: a group of partisans running toward a tank, some shooting guns, some throwing grenades.

"I was impressed that these were authentic war photos. Then I looked closer. One of the guys seemed familiar. I suddenly felt chills going down my spine as I stared at it. It was my father, younger but unmistakable. It was him! He was a true war hero!

I was pleased. An angry person is not at peace and thought, *Free at last! Free at last! Free to look up to Dad, even if just for once!*

"My last thought in the dream was that I hadn't given him the credit he deserved. Facts are facts. Was he a true war hero? Was I blinded from the truth?"

Jan laughed and then continued, "But this is not the truth or not as much of the truth as he claimed. Although I want to be fair to him, something drags me back to my old ways. I can't decide which side I'm on. I always despised

---

71 Baron Munchausen was the fictional, impossibly heroic, protagonist of *Baron Munchausen's Narrative of his Marvellous Travels and Campaigns in Russia*, written by Rudolf Erich Raspe, and published in 1785.

my father and called him a liar. This dream made me think that I wanted to be open to the possibility that he was also good. That's bothersome!"

Reflecting on what Jan had said last time, I said, "It's hard to close the casket when you have lingering thoughts."

Jan responded immediately. "Yes, it's hard. As hard as when my grandmother instructed me to touch the cold finger of my uncle."

My view, as an analyst, is that an occasional dream or two is welcome; even a nightmare is. They help one know what wakefulness can't hold and, if understood, also help heal the soul. When successful, thoughts about dreams keep ghosts away. But nothing is always successful. I jokingly said, "Maybe your grandmother's ritual of touching a dead body to ward off visitations from the dead doesn't always work."

Jan chuckled. Then he laughed heartily, and I could see that he had a good retort. "Maybe it *did* work. My father didn't show up as a ghost. Only his picture showed up! Maybe she was right!

"Wow. After all these years, I got a laugh out of my dad! But there's something else important that I want to mention. I want to tell you how my father ended up in the family grave. In Poland, people visit the graves of their loved ones on the first two days of November, All Saints' Day and All Souls' Day; on those days, cemeteries are covered with smoke from burning candles. We also go before major holidays, like Christmas and Easter, and on everyone's name-day anniversaries. So, someone visits our gravesite at least once a week, cleaning it and leaving flowers to honor everybody resting there.

"We were always separated as a family during All Saints' Day and All Souls' Day. My father would leave the day before to be with his sister at his family's gravesite in Terespol. He never tried to find a way for us to be together, like one day here and one day there, and he never asked any of us to go with him. Because of that, I thought he wanted to be buried in his family's plot. But three days after my mom was buried, we went to the gravesite. My demented father pointed to it and said, 'Maybe there will be a place for me here. I want to be by my darling wife's side.' We were speechless.

"So now he is at his wife's side. Luckily, he told us he wanted to be buried there; now, he won't be lonely or neglected. I always felt sad for people whose graves were overgrown with grass and weeds or had a rusty cross and no flowers or candles. Out of her heart's goodness, my mom tried to comfort lonely souls: Whenever she went to the family plot, she took a few extra candles to light by abandoned graves.

"Europeans are less commercial and more personal than Americans when they visit their family graves. Those two days in November are about keeping memories of our loved ones alive. On those days, my family would gather around the grave. We talk about and recall stories about the goodness of our departed family members. Sometimes, these were funny stories. I remember lots of graveside laughter.

"From the time when I was growing up, I remember that people who committed suicide couldn't be buried inside graveyards. That was sacred ground, and suicide was a cardinal sin. People who committed suicide had to be buried outside the cemetery wall. Of course, if at all possible, families would try to hide the fact that their loved one had committed suicide. Now the rules have changed, and anything is possible. The cemeteries are state property, not Church property."

"Would a family ever say that a man was a bad father and didn't deserve to be buried in the sacred ground?" I asked.

"I never heard of such a case, but family members know who a person is or was. Traditionally, the church did not allow murderers and people who committed suicide to be buried in sacred grounds. After World War II, when Poland became a Communist country, some old religious traditions were replaced by new *progressive* folklore. Funerals of Communist Party members were different from church funerals but equally lavish. Their gravestones were also different. I know about two Communists who were known to have been atheists all their lives. Both were buried close to my family plot. They died before I was born, and their gravestones stood out from the rest. No crosses, no mention of God or heaven. Just *Czesc Jego Pamieci*, Hail Comrade. Years later, after 1989, when the Communists lost the elections, some families decided that the Communists had been believers after all. They were labeled believers after they died! You see, you can rejoin the Church from six feet under!

"As you know, Maria was also brought up Catholic. When I decided I was going to marry her, I thought she would want us to get married in the Catholic Church, so I considered going through the procedures of Canon Law and getting a formal divorce from my first wife. I found out that it was quite possible, just time-consuming.

"It requires the testimony of people who knew you as a couple. A local Catholic priest makes the recommendation and puts together a dossier, but Catholic courts decide the divorce itself in the Vatican."

"Is it a divorce or an annulment?"

"You're right. 'Annulment' is correct. Marriage is final. There's no mechanism to undo a marriage in the Catholic Church. What others call divorce, annulment asserts that the marriage never took place. There are different grounds to allow annulments. First, the marriage occurred but unconsummated; the Latin expression is *matrimonium non consummatum*. Second, there might be an undisclosed mental illness in one of the spouses or the use of deception or force on the spouse upon entering the marriage. Third, an annulment is possible if one of the spouses entered the marriage intending to be unfaithful or not have children. Fourth, a difficult ground for granting an annulment is infidelity. Finally, according to the priest, I had sufficient reason to seek an annulment because my first wife didn't have children. He was ready. All I needed was $500 for the fee and extra money for the *ofiara*, the offering, for the parish, which he suggested 'was usually no less than $500.'

"In addition, I would have had to attend religious classes for a few weeks to become a better Catholic. I didn't go through with it primarily because Maria only cared that we loved each other. Also, as we investigated the process, she realized that she didn't believe in Catholic Church formalities."

I suspected that Jan's father also played a part in this decision, so I said, "Perhaps you didn't go through the Catholic ceremony because the love between Maria and you didn't require it. And maybe you didn't want to practice a religion in bad faith, like your father."

"Yes, my father was a faithful follower of the rotten priest Tadeusz Rydzyk and his way of understanding and practicing Catholicism. He was a big fan of the poisonous and politicized *Radio Maryja*. Under Catholic slogans, it preached hatred, anti-Semitism, and homophobia. Even the Vatican was concerned about its broadcasting style, and the head of the Church in Poland reprimanded them for using religion as a political tool. If my father had been a woman, he would have been a *moherowe berety*, a mohair beret."

"What's that?"

"That was the name for a group of crazed elderly women in Poland who worshipped that lousy priest. Their trademark was wearing mohair berets."

"When you first came in today, you mentioned having regret about expressing your feelings about your dad. What was the regret about?"

"Talking badly about a dead person, regardless of whether he was my dad. 'May he rest in peace' conveys this meaning. So there's no point in bringing up those feelings. I can't change the past. And besides, he can't respond. He can't defend himself."

"Like being in a duel with a person who has no gun?"

"It's more than that. It's like having a duel with myself. I know what he would say if he could defend himself. The whole effort is just pointless . . ." Jan chuckled. " . . . and worthless and hopeless . . . It doesn't make sense to me anymore . . . But, as I said, let him rest in peace."

"Yes, rest in peace."

"I'm disappointed that I didn't have these words to say to my family while I was in Poland. Sometimes, you and I laugh when we talk. Things I thought were painful sometimes become bizarre and even comical when I see them through your eyes. I also believe our laughter comes from the fact that you understand how I feel. Unfortunately, I wasn't able to discuss all this with my sister. Maybe it was too early, or perhaps I'll never be able to have this healthy perspective when talking to her about our father. We stood next to each other during the funeral but didn't talk. We spoke to our family members but not to each other. We waited next to the casket, and we still didn't talk. My sister participated in the mass, communion, and confession. I didn't. I looked at the unreal scenes around me and tried to avoid having blasphemous thoughts about my father.

"When the old men in Polish Underground uniforms waved their military standards and sang old patriotic songs, we looked at each other with surprise, but we didn't talk. Then we went to the *stypa*, the wake, and people shared thoughts and memories of our father. It lasted about an hour and a half. I still didn't talk to her. Finally, when I was driving her home, I said, 'Who were they? Who were those old guys in Polish war uniforms, waving flags and calling our father a war hero? It was ridiculous. And how did they even know that Dad died?'

"She said, 'You tell me. I'm the one who lives here, and I should have known if our dad was in the war and, if so, who his war buddies were. I had never met them before. I was more surprised than you were. I think our cousin Filip told them to come.'

"'Lieutenant! An activist in the Underground!' I muttered under my breath. 'Partisan!' I said aloud so that Sofia could hear me. 'I shook with laughter when I saw the shocked faces on his side of the family,' she said. 'Some of them had known him since he was a child and knew nothing of it! It was a theater of the absurd.'

"We didn't talk about it again. That was the extent of my processing my feelings with my sister. I didn't share my true feelings with her. I couldn't find any closure with my dad. In a sense, for me, he died a long time ago. His dementia made sure of that. He was nothing but an empty shell for so many years. His memories gradually faded away and, with them, any chance to make him aware of the pain he had caused me. I wanted closure, but he was incapable of helping me with that in his condition. In the last few years, he had a few moments of recognition and found a few islands of recollection in a sea of oblivion, but he held onto his mean personality until the very end. With only a few neurons still firing, he was capable of torturing his caretakers. When my mom died, he was preoccupied with his wish to have a pedicure *immediately*!

"I was never able to tell him that I felt he was belittling me. Instead, he would say he loved me in an affected tone. I had no option to say anything but, 'I love you, too.' Often, I said, 'OK, me, too.' But then he took his anger out on my mom and said, 'You turned my children against me.' We simply could not talk about the feelings we had for each other. It never happened."

"Yes, he was out of it, and it was impossible to relate to him. You'll never have the opportunity to find closure. That slipped away as his dementia got worse. As you said, he was declining for a few decades."

"Yes, it was a gradual process over many years. But, very likely, it started way before I, or anybody else, realized it. I thought I was talking to a man when, in fact, I may have been talking to his ghost. Maybe that's why I failed to settle things with him before he died."

"Perhaps that's why you've come to the reluctant conclusion that there was nothing more you could do. So the only thing left for you is to let him rest in peace."

"Yes, that's exactly how I started to feel."

I appreciated that Jan was reflecting on the changes in him and the shadows they cast on the changing masks of his father. I also thought of the regret that Jan had referred to at the start of the session. I wondered if this indicated that he was becoming more self-conscious of the hostility he harbored within himself. Nobody can ever be comfortable discovering his own blemishes. I asked, "Do you have any thoughts about the regrets that you mentioned as you started today?"

"I regret having talked about him disparagingly. I regret my sarcasm in describing his stories of being a war hero."

"You don't want him to turn over in his grave. At this time, so soon after his death, you'd rather be silent than say anything negative about him. You also said you felt numb. Perhaps you were avoiding acknowledging how you really felt."

"Yes, but I let out my feelings with you."

"Today, as you reflect on what you said to me, especially in the last session, do you feel I pushed you?"

"No, I don't feel that you're insisting on anything. You're not forcing me to feel or say anything. I did have the dream I told you about. It was definitely related to our conversation last time. No doubt about it. But it will probably be the last time that I'll talk about my dad. When David asks about my dad, I'll polish his image. He'll only know my father through my stories, and I want him to feel good about his heritage; it will contribute to his self-confidence. Where did I come from? What was my life like? My dad will be a grandfather who died a long time ago for David. I was thinking about the book *Diary of My Dad*. My friend Aleksander gave it to me after my dad died. It's a blank book with chapter headings, like 'My father lives in me,' 'Laughing together,' 'His most important lesson.' Each one was supposed to evoke positive feelings. I had nothing to say. The things I could say, I don't want to say. It would be nasty if I spilled my guts, but I know the best use for the book: I'll give it to my son. When he writes in it, I pray he won't face the same dilemma."

I appreciated that Jan had found a rightful place to bury a lifelong hatchet and that his life with David started with hope and good faith.

"Generations change," I said. "People not only change, but they also die. So for good or bad, there can be no more conversations between you and your dad, only memories and feelings."

"Once, when my dad was depressed, we talked. He said that he'd been a lifelong Catholic and had lived by the precepts of the Church. However, he said that he was wrong and there was no God. When I tried to speak to him about the change in his religious beliefs, he said, 'I never said there's no God.' He just denied having said it."

Almost overcome by emotion and with tears in his eyes, Jan said, "I feel bad talking about it. There's no point. What he said was seared into my memory. I'm the only person who knows or can remember that my dad was briefly a disbeliever. My sister has a more positive attitude. She tries to look at the good in him.

"When I'm down, I just look at David and feel good right away. I'm fine. It's hard to be upset about anything. When I go home and see Maria or pick up David, I need nothing else. I feel great. All my worries seem to disappear."

"That's fantastic," I said. "It's great to have people in your life who can uplift you so powerfully."

"I agree. I have proof of change. Compared to the first time I saw you, I'm now a psychiatrist and love my work. But, more than that, I'm always trying to be a good husband and father."

"Life goes on," I said. "Today, you talked about life and its limits. Always trying to be a good husband and father is a good motto. You lived with a father but buried a dad. He's lucky, resting by his wife's side. They will smell flowers for the rest of eternity."

"Yes, everything settles down. Time with my dad is gone. That's final. I feel relief. I'm satisfied."

I pondered the changes Jan had made since he started seeing me. Just as he recounted, Jan was a doctor, husband, and father. His life, promises, and future lay ahead of him. He had made good progress in our 16 months of analysis and still had some way to go. Finally, I reflected on what he just said, "Time with my dad is gone. That's final. I feel relief. I'm satisfied." I, too, was satisfied.

Jan looked at his watch and then at me. We both knew it was time to stop. He nodded, got up, and put his jacket on. I walked with him to the doorway. He turned to look at me. I reached out and patted him gently on the shoulder, acknowledging a tough job well done.

POSTSCRIPT

WHEN *SUICIDE BECKONS* DESCRIBED the first sixteen months of Jan's three-year psychoanalysis, which helped him understand and manage the trauma of Amir's suicide and cope with Amir's mother's accusation that Jan's negligence was responsible for Amir's suicide. Jan experienced anger and rage at his father throughout his life, often accompanied by homicidal fantasies and dreams. Periods of debilitating guilt followed such fantasies or dreams. Nevertheless, he came to care for his demented father compassionately and buried his dad by his mother's side despite his hostility toward him. He realized the futility of his anger and even came to see some redeeming aspects of his father.

Jan's life settled into a stable and satisfactory manner. A loving wife, a newborn son, and ordinary parenting responsibilities changed his life for the better. Noticing the day-to-day changes in his son brought joy to Jan. Jan completed his residency and started life as an attending psychiatrist in a hospital. He was well-appreciated by his patients, peers, and students. Finally, Jan felt that his daily concerns and challenges resembled those of any husband, new father, and breadwinner. Jan thought he had enough understanding of his past problems to avoid similar ones in the future and that he no longer needed to be in analysis. I agreed, and we decided to stop the treatment after three years.

Post-termination collaboration

After the termination, Jan again gave his permission for me to use his case material as part of a book I planned to write. While considering this memoir, both Jan and I realized that while analysis was a therapeutic effort, drafting a book about an analysis was a related but different challenge involving three distinct but interrelated tasks: 1) Deidentifying patients through disguises and complex fictionalization, 2) providing clarity and context to enable the reader to read the book meaningfully, and 3) reconstructing and inserting my reminiscences at appropriate points in the narrative. In addition, I realized that, even with the tape recording of our sessions, there were details about Jan's life involving many Polish particulars and other information, which I could not construct independently. So, I invited Jan to help me, and he accepted. However, he was involved only in the first two aspects mentioned above. We spent time on the clinical sessions detailed in the book during this period. Although Jan had the manuscript of the entire book, we did not co-review any part dealing with my childhood memoirs or my other private asides. Instead, I alone organized the book, inserted my memories and responses to Jan, and managed the third task.

We discussed the difference between being a co-collaborator and a patient or an analyst. A coherent story for a reader requires conscious effort, while free associations and evenly suspended attention are the effects of unconscious automaticity. Occasionally, recordings were poor, and so we reconstructed them. As in any analysis, Jan and I resorted to colloquialisms, verbal shortcuts, and gestures to facilitate therapeutic communication. A reader would find it difficult to follow our conversation at this point. So, in the book, we repaired fractured grammar, filled out the verbal shorthand, and explained the context. We tried to explain the flow of our conversations to an imaginary and interested reader. We double-checked dates, places, and other details regarding World War II, Poland, Burma, Italy, etc. During the analysis, Jan and I spoke briefly about psychoanalysis, which I elaborated on and expanded on in the book.

I reconstructed and summarized the earlier sessions because I obtained Jan's permission to tape our session only after the first three months of treatment. I transcribed the taped sessions described in the book. Sometimes a single transcribed session took five or six sessions to review. We together reviewed each sentence of each session in the book. As we did so, Jan often provided secondary associations to those he had previously spoken about during the analysis. These supplementary associations provided a richer context, enabling us to understand the meaning of a set of associations with greater clarity and conviction.

Jan also asked me to clarify the intent behind my interpretations, explanations and comments, and other interventions. I responded to such requests and had the further chance to explain myself. This collaboration allowed me to reflect upon my work and reconstruct my experience. Our review was leisurely. After our reflections concerning a sentence were complete, we moved to the following sentence. I then sent the drafts to an editor. Unfortunately, the initial editor could not complete the project due to health reasons. So, I engaged another editor and sent the manuscript for review. Both editors had questions concerning the book's basic structure, typos, incoherent statements, and intent in ambiguous passages and historical facts. Reviewing my draft and addressing the concerns of my editors took twelve years; during this period, Jan and I met less regularly than during the analysis and developed identities as collaborators.

Jan was well functioning during this collaborative phase, and no psychological emergency emerged. So freed of clinical concerns, I freely spoke to him as a colleague. Nevertheless, in addition to such functions, incidental clarifications, explanations, and interpretations added an occasional clinical dimension to the post-termination collaboration.

In the post-termination phase, Jan sometimes questioned the accuracy of my transcription of the sessions. He thought I must have made a mistake because he believed he could not have said what my transcription reported. I conceded that he could be correct and that I was wrong. I might have slipped up, and my transcription might have been in error. So, we checked, knowing either of us could be wrong. These were situations where I, the analyst, had no privilege. Yet, each time we went back and reviewed the tape, my transcription was correct. Such direct transference tests of my veracity gave Jan fresh clues about change in the analytic process. From his current self's perspective, Jan discovered that he could not believe parts of his previous self. Verifying that he did say something unbelievable in the past helped Jan to appreciate the extent of his change. Jan felt that closely reviewing the tape and transcript helped to "turbocharge" the treatment. He found the reappraisal to be therapeutically meaningful, adding a measure of testing and extra credibility. This lesson was unexpected. *There may be a benefit to the analyst and patient in explicitly reviewing their progress this way.*

Readers will remember that I intended to provide transference interpretations regarding my long vacation and link it to Jan's early childhood separation from his mother when she needed to be away at a TB sanatorium (Chapters 26 and 31). However, at that very time, an accusatory letter from Amir's mother claiming that his negligence had killed her son traumatized Jan. So, I had held back my interpretation for fear of overburdening him.

During this post-treatment collaborative phase, I revisited this issue following an unexpected event. A hacker took control of my e-mail account. As a result, my contacts received a fake e-mail message originating in my name from London. The e-mail stated that I was stranded because I had lost my passport and urgently requested my friends to send several thousand dollars to some shady address. When he received this e-mail, Jan became alarmed. It took me about a week to reestablish my e-mail account and inform my friends that I was the subject of a hoax. Before he received my message about my hacked e-mail, Jan, flustered, called me. First, we addressed Jan's experience of a post-analytic transference shock dealing with his imaginations of my marooned ordeal and his rescue fantasies that also left him feeling abandoned. Second, this current feeling that he was helpless reminded him of his despair as a toddler, when his mother needed to be away from him while receiving treatment at a TB sanatorium. This emotionally charged hacking incident evoked in Jan a near panic and paralleled Jan's anguish as a child when his mother's TB treatment separated them. It was easy for me to explain to Jan the transference connection and for Jan to accept this post-analytic interpretation with conviction.

In addition, we went over the sessions just before I took an extended vacation during the analysis. I had not offered any transference interpretations concerning our separation during the analysis. Now I did, in a broader context. I explained that interpretative lapse by clarifying that I had felt guilty that, on my extended vacation, Jan would have had to deal with three awakened stresses: 1) Amir's mom's overwhelming and harsh criticisms of Jan 2) the reminders of his mom's stay at the sanatorium, and 3) my actual absence due to my vacation. However, Jan accepted and appreciated my delayed interpretation. Jan added that I was right not to interpret separation in a transference light. He said that, at that time, Amir's mother so tortured him that he would not have been able to hear or process my interpretation. Nevertheless, this deferred explanation helped him understand what I intended to say. Of course, it is best to offer timely analytic interventions, but belated interpretations may also have therapeutic value.

Transference-countertransference

Here I will not attempt to summarize Jan's transference and my countertransference elaborated in the book, but recall a specific instance of both. Jan's usage of *Sripadism* best symbolizes his transference (Chapter 48). When Jan decided he could become a better psychiatrist by identifying with me, the word came into being. However, as he gained self-confidence, he began to rely on himself and abandoned usage of this term. This process led Jan to understand that he overidealized me and that depending on himself provided him with better tools for life. However, despite my analytic efforts, a residue of Jan's idealization of me remained because I could not comprehensively analyze it. I feel that collaborating with Jan helped me. A more in-depth dialogue emerged between us to further clarify what I meant at an earlier time. So, the post-treatment alliance not only produced this book about the psychoanalytic process but became a valuable supplementary tool to answer Jan's questions and clarify my perspective, and elaborate the contents of my evenly suspended attention.

I understood (Chapter 2) that Jan felt free when he said, "spill my guts." However, "spill my guts" evoked in me the thought of *harakiri*. These stem from an entirely personal stream of associations having to do with my fascination with suicide from years of listening to my father's war stories. Therefore, this memoir is an extended countertransference exposition from the perspective of countertransference.

Exploration of Jan's father-son relationships

Jan had a tumultuous relationship with his father. Jan felt that his father treated him with hostility. Jan and his father even had physical confrontations on a few occasions. For example, when his father raised his hand to strike Sofia, Jan's sister, Jan grabbed his father's wrist, and they wrestled. Jan, a frequent visitor to the gym, twisted his father's wrist, forcing him to sit down. Jan freed him only after his father agreed not to hit Sophia. Then, his furious father exclaimed to Jan, 'You're not my son.'" (Chapters 12 and other chapters).

Understandably, in response to his father's chronic demeaning attitude, punishments, and occasional physical confrontations, and finally, his father disowning him, Jan experienced anger and rage at his father. Murderous fantasies toward his father accompanied such feelings. Jan dreamt that he killed his father with a poker. (Chapter 12) However, Jan experienced such murderous fantasies as highly unpleasant, as guilt invariably accompanied them.

In contrast to his father and Catholic priests of his childhood, Jan felt that I listened and tried to understand his rage toward his father. In the analysis, Jan recalled occasional positive interactions memories of his father, and also, his tendency was "not to remember such events." (Chapter 26 and other chapters). In the analysis, Jan dreamt of his father's death by hanging and had associations of poisoning him or shooting him or killing him some other way. Finally, after Jan disclosed the details of parental conflicts and his father's infidelity, I interpreted Jan's Oedipus complex in terms of Jan being a "highlander at heart."

I thoroughly explored the depths of his conscious and unconscious anger and other feelings concerning his father, Amir, and others. In addition, we explored Jan's feelings and frustrations toward me. Finally, I adapted play techniques and introduced relevant movies and poems, and we discussed them as an aspect of the analysis. These afforded workable analytic displacements but were sufficient to continue Jan's analysis and effect change. The birth of a son, joy of parenting, desire and hope of being a better father to his son, and the feeling of belonging to life also changed Jan's attitude toward his father.

Psychoanalysis, myth, and individual experience

Throughout human history and in all civilizations, myths dealt with the heavens and heroes. However, such fabled stories simultaneously guided generations of people to manage their lives and relationships. For example, Freud's Oedipus complex addressed core conflicts between offspring and parents, dealing with competitive, homicidal impulses of a son toward his father and of a father toward his son.

Contemporary psychoanalysis offers other views on the relations between generations. For example, as an alternate to Freud's Oedipal competition and conflict, Kohut's Self-psychology described empathy which can be the basis of parent-child relations. Kohut's "semi-circle of mental health" metaphor illustrates a father's benevolence toward a son. Odysseus, the legendary hero of Greek mythology, tries to avoid military service by feigning madness. The military chiefs assess him by placing his beloved infant son, Telemachus, in the path of his plow. Odysseus plows a semi-circle around the baby to avoid killing him, revealing his sanity and obligating him to go to war.[72]

---

72 Kohut, H. (1981). "Introspection, Empathy, and the Semicircle of Mental Health." In P. H. Ornstein (Ed.), *The Search for the Self: Selected Writings of Heinz Kohut* (Vol. 4). New York: International Universities Press, pp. 537–568.

In this semi-circle metaphor, Kohut described empathy from a father (parent) to a son (children) as essential for healthy narcissism and human survival. Similarly, the case of Jan shows that a son's (person's) compassion and caring for his father (parents), especially when old age or illness debilitates a parent, is equally necessary for the optimal functioning of the institution of the family. Indeed, mutual understanding, kindness, compassion, empathy, and benevolence from parents to children and children to parents promotes societies. Conversely, when such essential caring is not present, its development during the analysis can be seen as a significant sign of analytic progress. Such an accomplishment can allow a person to become a loving parent, even if they have had the misfortune to have hostile or neglectful parents.

Freud and many analysts after him have offered theoretical models to guide psychoanalytic practice. These theories apply to all or most patients. However, rather than be exclusively camped in a single view, increasingly, contemporary analysts are employing mixed models into their practice. Based on my notions of essential psychoanalysis, this book is such an example. In addition to the abstract principles of theories, I describe the usage of the ongoing moment-to-moment experiences evoked by the patient to guide the treatment. Such thoughts, fantasies, emotions, or memory contents are experience-near and connected to the patient in specific, more easily discernible ways and offer therapeutic guidance to the analyst. I specifically refer to an analyst's surprises, prediction errors, mistakes, and incorrect interpretations from which the analyst can learn much to shape and improve the treatment.

In contrast to abstract models, the contents of such ongoing patient-reactive individual analyst responses are calibrated to that patient and draw upon that analyst's unique life experiences. Although they may not conform to a single theory, these discrete experiential guides to treatment are particular to that patient-analyst dyad. Therefore, if the analyst feels free to use such experiences, his actions will be based on immediate experiences evoked by interactions with the patient, which may be better fitted to a specific analytic task, regardless of theory. Finally, when a broad theory or approach seems not to be working or is unsuited to a patient, such experiential contents may also offer clues about the best time to switch analytic strategies or techniques.

The active observer and psychoanalysis

Each analyst understands and describes the goals of analysis in their own manner. Through these variations, psychoanalysis has evolved. For example, the notions of analyst's neutrality and objectivity guided an earlier generation of analysts. Many contemporary analysts, including me, view both the patient and analyst as active observers whose observations mutually influence each other. In analysis, where such dynamic participant-observer relations prevail, objectivity is impossible. Despite this, a person can learn and change beliefs, habits, and preferences, avoid danger, and anticipate better. The analyst's and patient's unavoidable active participant-observer influence is understood differently. The patient and analyst may agree or disagree about the correctness of an interpretation and need to explore their different perspectives and negotiate how to manage such situations. Except when dangers to self or others prevail, the analyst should not overrule the patient's perspective. The analyst and patient can both learn from errors and misunderstandings.

We all experience anger and some relief, if not satisfaction, when we can express it reasonably. However, we feel alienated if anger and frustration are suppressed, repressed, projected, or split off. The awareness of anger, its appropriate expression, and communication make us human. Anger can help let others know the limits of one's tolerance and set boundaries. But sometimes, even expressing anger does not bring satisfaction. Such was the case for Jan in his relationship with his father.

When Jan informed his father that Maria (Jan's wife) was pregnant, his father responded lukewarmly. At this time, his father's chronic dementia had destroyed his cognitive abilities to the extent that it was not always clear to Jan if his father recognized him as his son. At this crucial time, when he was going to have a son, I realized Jan's natural and unshakeable desire for recognition, appreciation, and understanding from his father; but to expect these from a demented person was destined for disappointment. Although aware of the quest of an expectant father, I employed a psychodramatic deliberate anti-empathy to shake Jan to recognize the reality of his father's mental and emotional inability to respond to Jan (Chapter 20).

Even after I helped Jan thoroughly explore his homicidal wishes toward his father, Jan still felt angry and guilty. Jan's demented father was now a shadow of his previous self and could barely recognize Jan. At this point in the analysis, I felt it was meaningless and no longer productive to employ an Oedipal understanding emphasizing conflict and competition between a son and a demented father. The release of his anger gave him no relief. I felt that Jan's continuing anger at an enfeebled man and subsequent guilt were understandable but futile. The sad truth was that, even if Jan's analysis had made it possible, they could no longer have a meaningful relationship, let alone improve it. Jan's anger and guilt were gnawing only at him. Therefore, while having no impact on his father, Jan's intense, unpleasant, and intrusive feelings only hurt Jan. Anger and competition are essential sentiments but do not exhaust the entire range of human emotions. Jan needed a self-transformation that addressed the crippling anger and self-loathing he was experiencing.

The hot-coals metaphor derived from a Buddhist perspective on anger reflected my assessment of the situation and influenced my interventions and actions. This aphorism explains the hot-coal metaphor: "By doing this [being angry], you are like a man who wants to hit another and picks up a burning ember or excrement in his hand and so first burns himself or makes himself stink."[73]

Its language was plain. It deals with unintended consequences. Although a person may intend to hurt another person, his anger, unintentional, may also harm his own self. Every interaction has an effect on the other party and the self. A person must ask: Is it worth expressing one's anger fully if it means getting a stomach ulcer or going to jail? The Sermon on the Mount also teaches, "whosoever shall smite thee on thy right cheek, turn to him the other also."[74] Such religious sentiments, Eastern or Western, represent pearls of universal wisdom formulated by great beings that may apply to all believers of that faith. In a religious or humanitarian context, the "hot coal" or "turn the other cheek" aphorisms may be seen as favoring universal pacifism. While prophets guide humanity to where it should be, analysts try to help individuals where they are. I am not an advocate of pacifist psychoanalysis. I intend it to be an individually tailored analysis that addresses conflicts, feelings, and suffering that considers the effects of actions on others and oneself.

In contrast to universally applicable religious aphorisms, I used "hot coal" to formulate my actions in Jan's unique and particular circumstances. I believed that my hot-coal bias suited Jan, for he was weary of

---

73 Buddhaghosha (5th century CE). Visuddhimagga—The Path of Purification. IX, 23.
74 Bible, King James Version. Matthew 5, Verses 38-39

his anger and guilt and longed for a good night's sleep. As I intend it, the hot-coal technique may apply to a person in treatment who suffers from excessive, prolonged, or maladaptive anger. In the psychoanalytic context, the "hot coal" or "turn the other cheek" may be counterproductive in some anxious, inhibited, or fearful patients. Analytic treatment, in such cases, may involve increasing a patient's awareness of their unexpressed repressed anger and appreciating that "good fences make good neighbors."[75]

There are several examples of the unexpected and unwanted consequences of my actions in the book. The lesson is that analysts are constantly influencing patients. Whether stemming from personal experiences evoked by a patient, or theoretical preferences, the analyst's attitude and perspective are unavoidable and may have a beneficial or harmful effect on the analysis. In general, promoting the patient's freedom is the analyst's job. Barring dangerous situations where the treater must act regardless of the patient's preference, a vital consideration is whether the patient has the power to reject the analyst's conscious or unconscious influences by saying "No" to the analyst's interventions. The patient's "No" efficacy depends on how the analyst responds to it. A privileged analyst may feel entitled to overrule the patient and render it meaningless. So, it is vial to establish relationship based on mutual respect, which favors greater tolerance for each other's personality styles and errors.

My family and Indian culture

The march of history in the West retired the Greek, Roman, and pagan gods, who now primarily populate museums, the pages of classical literature, and psychoanalytic theories. However, the ancient Hindu pantheon, including Kali, dwells in the contemporary beating hearts of Hindus. Kali's primary message to man is to uncover and dispel illusory wishes and beliefs; this may require the preparedness for battle and the engagement in conflict. Hindu culture has been in continuous evolution for millennia. So, it retained many of its archaic beliefs and practices, mythic allegories, and disturbing rawness of the prehistoric idiom. However, like the Greek myths that inspired Freud and Kohut concerning family

---

75 Frost, Robert. "Mending Wall." *Gleeditions*, 17 Apr. 2011, www.gleeditions.com/mendingwall/students/pages.asp?lid=305&pg=5. Originally published in *Tendencies in Modern American Poetry*, edited by Amy Lowell, Macmillan, 1917, pp. 92-93.

life, the Kali myth represents the human concerns of a mother managing her spouse while caring for her infant child. Her divine spousal relations and family life reflect the everyday problems of humankind displaced to the divine. This book rests on psychoanalysis, my chosen profession, and the Hindu culture in which I grew up. Although psychoanalysis and Hindu culture are worlds apart, they share a common feature. Both Western and Hindu mythologies assume that our manifest impressions link to more profound, unconscious, latent, but often recoverable layers of human experience.

My integration of Freud's Oedipal and Kohut's Self-psychological notion of the semi-circle of mental health also relied simultaneously on the experiential direction offered by my ongoing thoughts, feelings, and memories elicited by Jan's free associations and actions. The contents of my continuous, evenly suspended attention in response to Jan provided me with a set of unique thoughts/feelings/memories specific to Jan and me. Other analysts, too, rely on their own insights. Thus, analysts must manage the tensions evoked by choosing between known and tested patterns and the bewildering newness of fresh and untested theories and actions that may arise in analysts who follow their own experiences. For the analyst, the former offers the comfort of known, available, familiar ideas. The latter, though, is fraught with novelty and uncertainty. Yet, it provides the possibility of using the analyst's freedom to link their emerging spontaneous thoughts, feelings, and memories with the patient's associations. As cited earlier in the book, Freud appreciated that other analysts differently constituted might adopt different attitudes to their patients and tasks before them. Thus, while learning from existing psychoanalytic wisdom, analysts can exercise their freedom, develop techniques suited to each patient, and consider their unique thoughts, feelings, and memory responses. It remains to be seen whether a psychoanalytic effort based primarily on the mutually influencing patient-analyst dyads and less on theories benefit patients better. It would undoubtedly increase variety in the forms of psychoanalysis.

My personal analysis, analytic training, supervisors, mentors, and theories made a deep impression on me and contributed to my professional identity. For example, I learned from my child's psychoanalytic training about play techniques and interpreting a child's displaced feelings onto toys. In addition, however, my mom, dad, and culture left an imprint on my personality, guiding my analytic attitude, style, and interpretations. For example, my mom taught me the underlying unity of all gods and goddesses, including Kali and Parvati. They have little in common on the surface, but they are imaginative aspects of the displaced human concerns. My mom used to calm my fears about Kali by telling stories of Kali and Parvati, indicating that each represented different aspects of the goddess; this means that a devotee may consider Kali as an aspect of Parvati, or Parvati as an an aspect of Kali. The mechanism behind such paradoxical- contradictory mythological identities was that the Parvati of one avatar reincarnated into Kali in a different avatar. Her explanation, familiar to many Hindus, assumes the belief in reincarnation for living beings and an analogous reincarnation of divine beings through various avatars that are appropriate to deal with evil at any given era.

Since I did not share this belief, I became agnostic and did not dwell on the reality of the divine. However, I understood that my regular touchable, reachable, and affectionate mom and her occasional untouchable isolated self were two sides of the same person! So I grew to accept the interpenetration of opposites and love and live with all her aspects. In a similar manner, I hope I accept all accepts of my patients and carry my mom's caring and kind spirit in my words and deeds.

My dad and I affectionately played, imagining ourselves to be Drs. William and Charles Mayo, during my childhood (Chapter 50). As a child analyst, I also practiced using play techniques. As a result, I used the medium of movies, poems, literature, and other artifacts to help Jan express himself and address his trauma and conflicts. They allowed me to explore displaced dynamics and provided Jan a safe distance to explore and understand the roots of his conflicts. Initially, Jan could remember his father only as a powerful, angry, and unkind person. In return, Jan felt rageful toward his father and guilty about his hostile fantasies toward his father. However, later in the analysis, Jan mainly described his father as a helpless negative person with few positive qualities for whom he developed compassion. Those playful approaches I made from time to time also helped Jan remember those easily forgotten but few good times with his own father.

Likewise, Lakshmamma's prayer's spontaneous, heartfelt directness inclined me toward plain-spoken interpretations offered in a conversational tone. Finally, this book claims that the early family, culture, and life experiences contribute significantly to an analyst's attitude and interventions, including interpretations.

Jan's previous analyst

With Jan's permission, I gave the psychoanalyst he had initially seen an opportunity to read the manuscript before publication. The analyst wrote back and said that the treatment details and my ongoing commentary moved him and that reading the manuscript was a corrective emotional experience for him. He wrote, "Seeing Jan's psychoanalytic story unfold helped me appreciate that being an effective psychoanalyst requires being who you are, not hiding who you are."

Psychoanalysis and science

Many analysts strive to establish themselves as practitioners of a scientific discipline based on the biological and psychological aspects of the patient's free associations, analyst's interpretations, interventions, the analytic relationship, and uncovering of unconscious meanings leading to better adaptation. Popper (1959)[76], early in the twentieth century, devised the criterion of falsifiability to demarcate and distinguish scientific from unscientific propositions. According to him, a single falsification overrides any number of positive verifications. Although they involve introducing measuring or recording devices, empirically based falsifiable studies of analytic events can help generalize analytical knowledge. However, the limits to empirical studies also need to be acknowledged. Psychoanalysis is an intricate set of ideas and beliefs. Psychoanalytic knowledge and scientific claims are extraordinarily complex and may not yield simple, falsifiable experiments.

Willard Van Orman Quine argued for the unity between science and philosophy. Whereas traditional empiricism took statements of individual observations to be units of empirical data, Quine, in contrast, argued that a significant empirical unit is a set of statements or an entire system of belief(s). Evidence, not based on *a priori* knowledge or philosophic presumptions, supports systems of beliefs or sets of ideas. Furthermore, Quine argued for precision in formulating hypotheses and understood that any proof could only provisionally support a proposition.[77]

Although the processes of analysis are not easily quantifiable, analysts have contributed to understanding consciousness, including the role of the

---

76 Popper, Karl 1959. *The Logic of Scientific Discovery*. New York: Basic Books.

77 Quine, W.V. (1951). "Two dogmas of empiricism." *The Philosophical Review*, 60 (1951), pp. 20–43.

active observer. Moreover, they are poised to make further contributions to science.

Freedom and Essential Psychoanalysis

Freedom is an inherent and essential aspect of the psychoanalytic method.[78] The patient's free associations and the analyst's freedom to use the contents of evenly suspended attention represent different aspects of freedom in the analysis. In an ideal session, the patient freely expresses his thoughts when they occur. A mix of existing theories and the emerging content of evenly suspended attention guide the analyst's actions. Generally, established views are formally organized, contain assumptions and strategies, and apply to most patients. The analyst is the expert on the theory and has the privilege to apply it, but the layperson patient may not understand the analyst's methods. Therefore, there is a power differential between analyst and patient to the extent that treatment depends on theory.

Furthermore, the analyst responds to the patient and the rules and recommendations advocated by his theory. Regardless, the thrust of its premises and principles may or may not fit a particular patient. The patient may feel like a passive subject to whom the analyst's theory is being imposed and less like an active participant when treatment methods fail to match the patient's personality or are applied rigidly or inflexibly.

In addition, the analyst can profitably base interventions on equally suspended attention contents which are the ongoing responses to the patient's free associations. If this is the case, the patient's associations and the analyst's reactions reflect their felt mutual relationship, not a distant, formal theory. Consequently, analyst experiences are specific, immediate, unconsciously, or preconsciously related to the patient, therefore, relevant to the situation. Because analytic events are unique and fresh, their processing depends mostly on patient and analyst negotiations rather than on theory, prior knowledge, or group acceptance. This context can provide patients and analysts with nuanced, new insights. The analyst may have to deal with more uncertainty and doubt than the familiar territory covered by a theory. Therefore, analyzing the situation may require more trial and error. Patients may offer feedback when their views do not align with the analyst's

---

78 Sripada B (2018) Freedom and the Way Forward: Liberating Psychoanalysis. Int J Psychol Psychoanal 4:024. doi.org/10.23937/2572-4037.1510024

view. They need to collaborate, struggle, and negotiate to construct the best possible meaning. Although the analyst and patient have different roles and may contribute asymmetrically to the analysis, there is no privileged analyst. Ultimately, the participants share significant understanding; but other disagreements and unexplored areas remain.

A patient knows the difference between being the subject of a distant theory and feeling the presence of an immediately responsive analyst. The patient understands the importance of the analyst's freedom in choosing material familiar to both parties. As a result, the patient's free associations may become more interactive, spontaneous, and meaningful. As a result, the patient and analyst feel freer to associate and interpret. Thus, psychoanalysts must, guided by their personality and responses elicited by the patient, exercise their freedom and judgment so that the principles of psychoanalysis and the mission of alleviating suffering are at the center of every clinical situation, every theoretical idea, and every research project. Psychoanalysis promotes freedom, subject to ethical, legal, and other reasonable constraints.

Conclusion

Psychoanalysis is a therapeutic venture whose goal is to help the patient. It works by conversations in the analysis, which link symptoms to other experiences in the analysis. As a result, the patient's reconstructed childhood and real-life relationships and emotions emerge superimposed on the transference. Transference includes the patient's conscious and unconscious responses directed to the person of the analyst, his attitude and actions, office, bills, vacations, illnesses, and routine or unexpected events during the treatment. However, such faithful revival of the patient's life in the transference is not the only aim of the treatment. Although it is a necessary first step, adaptive patient change is its final goal. However, there are several routes to advance toward such a result. 1) Any analysis aims to uncover the patient's unconscious and thus reveal maladaptive patterns of beliefs, feelings, thoughts, and actions, 2) Through the transference relationship, interpretations, and explanations, an analyst facilitates understanding, awareness of surprise, error correction, and the capacity for change in a patient; 3) the patient, with better insights, understanding, and compromises, realigns boundaries, conscience, and predictions. Such changes reduce pathological conflicts, stress, and suffering and prompt a sense of well-being, relatedness, and productivity. Actions are the culmination of many factors. Therefore, any analytic action's assessment must include an account of what provoked it, its intent, and its intended and unintended effect(s) on other(s) and the self.

Analyses impact both the analysand and the analyst. The analyst is responsible for the intended and unintended effects on patients. The analytic process can change a patient's beliefs, boundaries, conscience, empathy, error detection and correction, insight, habits, memories, model of the mind—appreciation of other-selves, predictions, relationships, surprises, and self-perception. As psychoanalysis progresses, the patient re-calibrates their sense of safety, danger, anxiety, satisfaction, risk-taking, affective fight-flight, defenses, compromises, style of communication, and behavior. Although not part of its primary purpose, analysts change and learn for each analysis.

The individual analyst can contribute to the vitality of psychoanalysis and even toward its scientific claims by providing detailed and comprehensive descriptions of analyses and personal antecedents to analytic interventions. The wisdom of psychoanalysis lies more in recognizing and realizing the richness of underlying human life that can foster freedom in each individual and less in its abstract theories or dogma. Interactions between the events in the analysis and the analyst's personal history, moment-to-moment awareness, and responsiveness generate interpretations, reconstructions, and clarifications, which contribute to the treatment's tapestry and outcome.

Each psychoanalytic case is unique. Psychoanalysis evolves from an understanding of the roots of the analyst's and patient's expectations, surprises, failures, and successes. I described my life experiences that have influenced my theory and practice. I do not claim correct technique or remarkable results. After safeguarding the identity of the concerned parties and providing context for the reader, the effort merely describes an analysis, warts and all, and welcomes criticism. I urge all analysts to provide deidentified reports of their treatments, including the sources of their interpretations and interventions. Such an integrated effort will benefit future patients and psychoanalysis, and better inform humanity.

INDEX

A

Adalbert (Uncle), 85
Alexander, Franz, 397–398
All Souls' Day, 503
alterego countertransference identification, 42
Alvear-Reverte, Dr., 95, 96–97, 165, 221–222
  Amir's death, 385
  comfortable silence, 404
  depressed patient, 385
  detail recall, 498
  idealizing talk, 406
  not pressuring patients, 405
Amir
  alterego countertransference, 383
  "Amir moments" for Jan, 232–233
  anger in transference, 430
  anger toward, 150
  anniversary of suicide, 317
  assumptions about, 272
  as black hole, 239
  as career-defining patient, 363
  deception, 89

  depression assessment, 215
  early sessions with, 30
  effect on Jan's wedding, 242
  family response to death, 54, 58
  father and, 323–324
  fearfulness, 42
  as groom in dream, 376
  hijra, 32
  homicidal trajectory, 444
  hospitalization, resistance, 369, 382
  identities, integration problems, 53
  Jan and Maria, 141–142
  Jan's description of, 26–27
  Jan's identification with, 42, 260, 324–326
  killer spirit, 376, 445
  as life lesson, 172
  noncompliance, 38–39
  parents, contact after death, 319–334, 348–351, 355–356, 367–368, 370–371, 378–381
  relationship anxiety, 35–38, 213–214

relationship phases with Jan, 100–101
sabotage of Jan, 327, 444
suicidal gambling, 51–52, 369
suicide
  Jan's change in understanding, 425–426
  as lure for Jan, 7
  responsibility, 426
  timing, 39–40
  transference, 442
Amiss, Dr., suicidal patients, 39, 226
Amma, 7, 81–83
  aging, 183
  chosen gods, 452
  death, 184
  first day of school, 451
  illness, 182
  Kali and, 454–455
  story of WWII knife, 483–486
  warning about swimming, 125
'An Elegy on the Death of a Mad Dog' (Goldsmith), 422
Analyze This? movie, 233
Andersen, Hans Christian, The Little Match Girl, 180
Anna O
  Breuer and, 18
  Freud and, 18
  talking cure, 17, 392
Apocalypse Now movie, 35
Apocalypto movie, 294, 295
Arbeit Macht Frei, 297
Archangel Michael, 449
attachment theory, John Bowlby and, 175
Augustine, 41
Auschwitz, 130, 131, 255–256, 297

B
Bakri Eid, 30
Balint, Dr., 327
  analysis and, 441–442
  Incident Review Committee and, 329
Becket movie, 364, 365, 415
Benzoni, veiled Rebecca, 28
bird feeder, 433
black hole, Amir as, 239
Bohr, Nils, xxii
bookends, 469
boundaries
  adaptive patient change and, 524
  analytic process and, 525
  patient and therapist, 349–350, 390
  physicians and, 100
  role, 290
  violations, 392, 400
Bowlby, John, 175
brachytherapy, 88–89
Breuer, Josef, 17–18, 392–393
Bujji (Cousin), 485–486
bullshit
  Analyze This, 223–224
  Communist Polish Thanksgiving, 296
  history of psychoanalysis, 406
burka, attitudes toward women, 37, 38
burnt apples, smell, 46
Bushido code, Samurai, 483

C
camel
  breaking, 22
  sacrifice, 30–32, 34, 52, 90
  dreams, 35
  father's rejection of Amir, 425

killing spirit and, 376
relationship with father, 219
Casablanca movie, *The Good German* and, 437
caste system, 73–82
  post-War father, 489
  relinquished by Sadhus, 414
Chaya, 68–69, 73, 83
Chen, Ms., 35–36, 53, 211, 213–214
Colpidium colpoda, 118
complementarity , xxi
Comrade Rossa, 414
Comte, Auguste, xvi
concentration camps
  Dora, 435
  effects of imprisonment, 130–132
  Frankl, Victor, 224
  Freud's sisters, 416
  Levi, Primo, 131
  modern lack of knowledge, 314
  one-person, 224–225
  The Pianist, 62
  Poland, 255–256
    construction, 259
  Polish jokes, 258
  reasons to be taken, 69
  Sonderkommandos, 130–131
  Soviet, 296
confession, 150–151
  homicidal fantasies, 146
  Jan's confessional spirit, 26
consent, 91–92
Coombs, Keith, 20
Coppola, Francis Ford, 35
Corinthians, 308
corrective emotional experience, 397
countertransference, xxi–xxiv, 349, 383–384, 390, 407

alterego countertransference identification, 42
  Freud, Sigmund, xvii
  hate as, 429
  sex, 391
  transference-countertransference, xxiv–xxvii, 271, 428, 514
  unconscious and, 395, xxv
cruelty, 88–89

D
Dali, Salvador, 155
  The Persistence of Memory, 238
David, 309–310, 312–315, 338, 339, 342–343, 363
  family awareness, 410
  pictures, sharing, 389, 401
The Deer Hunter movie, 35, 38, 51
Deneuve, Catherine, 431
Descartes, Rene, xvi
Dewald, Paul, xxxii
difficult letter, 330, 331
dipstick, 145–146
doll, 116
Donne, John, 379
Dora (Ida Bauer), 3, 417
Dora camp, 435
drowning, 125–129
drowning in self-blame, 7

E
Edelman, G.M., xxii–xxiii
Einstein, Albert, xxi
Elena, 388–389, 402–403
Essential Psychoanalysis, xxx, 516
  freedom and, 523–524

F
false connection, 394
Famuki, 104
Ferenczi, Sándor, 396–397
flight to health, 56, 177
Fossa Lady, 124–125, 129–130, 132–134
Frankl, Victor, 224
Freud, Sigmund, 17
  abreaction, 393
  "Analysis Terminable and Interminable," 70
  Anna O, 18, 392–393
  attitudes toward, 416
  bust, Chicago Institute for Psychoanalysis, 2
  censorship of sexual ideas, 3
  classical science era, xxi
  countertransference, xvii
  death, 405
  essential psychoanalysis and, xxx
  false connections, 394
  feeding hungry patient, 399
  Ferenczi, Sándor, 396–397
  free association, 391, 393–394, xv
  fundamental rule, 19, 22
  Gay, John, 416
  hypnosis, 393
  hysteria case with Breuer, 18
  idealistic attitude, 70–71
  interpretation, 395
  Interpretation of Dreams, 187
  Jung, Carl and, 416
  Kohut and, 519–520
  method of doubt, xvi
  neurotics, 393
  Oedipal complex, 515
  omelet quote, 2
  oral cancer, 404–405, 415
  primal memories, 117
  psychoanalysis definition, 396
  realistic attitude, 70–71
  rule of abstinence, 391
  Schur, Max, 405
  sexual conflict and neurosis, 18
  on suffering, 390
  theoretical models, 516
  transference, 394
Freud: A Life for Our Time (Gay), 416

G
Ganesha, 452
Gay, John, *Freud: A Life for Our Time*, 416
Gertruda (Aunt), 117–118
Gill, Merton, xviii, xxxii, xxxv–xxxvi
Goddess of Victory and Peace, 449
godlike, 279–280
Goldberg, Arnold, xxxv–xxxvi
  The Prisonhouse of Psychoanalysis, 401
Goldsmith, Oliver, 'An Elegy on the Death of a Mad Dog,' 422
good fences make good neighbors, 519
Good German, 434–437
The Good German movie, 434, 437
  Casablanca and, 437
good paranoia, 374
good-enough, 184–185
Greta, 368–370

H
hacker, 513
Hamelin, Pied Piper, 6–7
Hanna-Barbera, 447

hara-kiri, 17
  Nanna's witnessing, 15, 484
  'spill my guts,' 15, 514
  Uncle's knife, 484–487
Havens, Leston, xviii
Heisenberg, Werner, xxii
Highlanders, 449–450, 493
hijra, 32
Hirohito (Emperor), 483, 484
Hitler, 269–270
  Good Germans, 435
Hitler Youth, 270
hot-coals metaphor, 518

I
identification, 42
Indochine movie, 431
infidelity
  annulments and, 505
  Jan's father's, 515
  The Painted Veil movie, 419, 424
Interpretation of Dreams (Freud), 187
Irwin, Steve, 433

J
Jagiellonian University, 41–42
  dormitory suicide, 136
  Polish Jewish Society, 59
Jan
  alterego countertransference, 42,
    384
  analyst vacation, 305–306, 336–337
  anger toward Amir, 38
  antidepressants, 48–50
  attachment and loss, 188
  avoidance, 57–58
  background, xiii–xiv
  bookends, 469

Catholic upbringing, 40–41
  confession, 150–152
  dementia, fear of, 208
  depression
    abandonment of, 55–56
    minimizing, 177
    passivity and, 181
  Dr. Schwartz and, 228
  Dr. Williams and, 349
  dream of father hanging, 135
  earliest memory, 189
  Essential Psychoanalysis, xxx
  father in psychiatric care, 59–61
  fatherhood fears, 244–245, 279–280
  father's death, 478–481
  first session with Amir, 30
  friendship, 409
  groom in dream, 375–377
  guilt, 144, 155, 159–164
  homicidal feelings toward father,
    140–142
  ideas about family, 110–111
  initial meeting, 10–17
  insecurities as resident, 345
  killer angel, 445–449
  memories after father's death,
    492–499
  misunderstandings, healing and,
    328–239
  mother, 115–116
  narcissism, 177–178, 181
  new fatherhood, 112–113
  oncology, 84–87, 408–409
  pacifism, 157
  paranoia, 349–350, 374
  passive-aggressiveness, Dr.
    Schwartz, 286–287
  play, analysis and, xxviii

positive moods, 122
post-termination collaboration, 510–513
prayers, 113–114
pre-parental preoccupations, 315
previous analyst, 522
progress, awareness of, 425–428
Psychiatry Boards, 439–440
repression, 66–67
rest in peace, 501
science project, 118
screaming, 152–153
Sripadism, 514
Student Scientific Society, 123
therapeutic good guy/bad guy, 285
time heals all wounds, 101
Uncle Hektor (Jozef), 179–180, 501
USMLE exam success, 94
jealousy
  dead patient, 11–12
  Jan after Amir's death, 41, 46–47, 50, 233, 239, 445, 501
  Oedipus complex and, 141
The Jerry Springer Show, 312
Jesus, 61
  death, 70
  Jan on Freud, 418
  Jan's grandmother, 114
jhatka, 454
Joanna, 90
John (patient), 458–477
Jones, E., 18
Jung, Carl, 416

K
Kali, 3–7, 448, 452–455, 519–521
Kamala. *See* Amma

Kanti, 78–80
Kasia, 168–169, 202
Kazimierz, 60
Kazipet, 19–20
  caste system and, 81
  schools, 186–187
Kernberg, Otto, 349–350, 417
killer angel, 445–448
The Killer Angels (Shaara), 449
Kipling, Rudyard, 330, 489
  "My Boy Jack," 332–333
Kobierzyn Mental Hospital, 41
Kohima, 482–484
Kohut, Heinz, xv, xvii
  alterego transference, 383
  semi-circle of mental health, 515–516, 520
Krakow
  Auschwitz trips, 255
  Fossa Lady, 124
  Kazimierz, 60
Krakow Academy, 41–42
Krishnayya, Sripada, 483, 485
kukri (Gurkha knife), 14, 15, 485, 489

L
Lakshmamma, 451–455, 521
Laticia, 220–222
Levi, Primo, 131
"Lift not the Painted Veil" (Shelley), 421
Lipton, Samuel, 399
Little Hans, xxxii, 417
The Little Match Girl (Andersen), 180
Lord's Prayer, 99
Lublin, Poland, 124
  Catholic University of Poland, 133
Lydia, 10

M

Malgorzata (Aunt), 120, 144, 166–172, 192, 480, 496–497
mali (gardener), 79–80
Marek, 168, 202
Maria
  attachment theory and, 175
  church, opinions on, 309–310, 497–498
  concern for Jan, 1–3
  family ties, 110–111
  extended family, 173–174
  family's support, 243
  father's visit, 291, 303
  good paranoia and, 374
  Jan and family, 108–112
  Jan's healing, 42
  The Painted Veil movie, 419
  pre-parental preoccupations, 315
  suicide in Jan's dream, 139, 142, 148
Marta, 68–69
masochism, 327
  good paranoia and, 374
  unconscious/reconscious, 373
Masters, John, 490
masturbation
  bestiality porn, 52–53
  confession and, 151
Matthew (Gospel), 61, 349
Maugham, W. Somerset, 415
  The Painted Veil, 421–422
Max (Jan's father)
  absence, 145–146
  abusive behavior, 140–141
  beatings, 146–147
  dementia, 198
  dream of suicide, 135, 141–142, 149
  father transference, 237

Jan's homicidal thoughts, 146, 159
Jan's rage toward, 149
Jan's terminology for, 59, 160–161
Jewishness, 59–62
living with Sophia, 168–169
mental health, 138–140
physical fight, 248
similarities, 207–211
slomiany ogień, 206
Mayo, Charles, 521
Mayo William Worrall, 488
Mielec, Nazi occupation, 68–69
morgue, 479
Museum of Evolution, 492
muttu, 456–457
'My Boy Jack' (Kipling), 332–333

N

Nagesh, 125, 128–129
Nanavati, Kawas, 126–127
Nanna, 7–8, 485
  Dr. Mayo and, 489
  hara-kiri knife, 487
  military service, 484
  railroad, 19–20
  tiffin delivery, 29–30
  transfer, 186–187
  WWII memorabilia, 14–15
Narasimha, 75–76
narcissism, 177–178
Natasha, 36–37, 53, 212
National Cadet Corp, 273, 376
Nazis
  Arbeit Macht Frei, 297
  Auschwitz, 297
  Bettman, Franz, 435
  killing of Jews, 131
    efficiency, 255–256

Mielec occupation, 68–69
  Rachel, 102–103
Nello, 422
Nina, 85–86, 180

O

Occam's razor, xxi–xxii
Odysseus, 515
Oedipus Complex, xxxv, 33, 141–142, 298, 399, 515
Olympics
  national biology Olympics, 329
  National Science Olympics, 118
One Flew Over the Cuckoo's Nest movie, 264, 382

P

The Painted Veil (Maugham), 421
The Painted Veil movie, 419–432
Pappenheim, Bertha, 17. *See also* Anna O
paranoia, 349–350
  good paranoia, 374
  healthy, 374
  Jan's awareness of, 358
  micro-paranoia, 349
  predisposition, 315
  steroid abuse, 466
participant-observer, xvii–xviii, xxi, xxiii, xxiv, xxvi, 517
Parvati, 452, 454–455, 521
peacocks, 21–22
The Persistence of Memory (Dali), 238
phenol, 29, 30
Philip, 85–86
physicians, boundaries and. *See* boundaries
Pia *(The Divine Comedy)*, 422

The Pianist movie, 58, 62
Pied Piper of Hamelin, 6–7
poker (killing father in dream), 140, 144, 514
Polish Underground, 69, 124, 506
  book about, 203
  retaliation, 130
  Uncle Bozydar, 155, 157
  uprising in 1944, 296
Pontius Pilate, 61, 70
Pope
  handshake, 109
  Poland visit, 313
Popper, Karl, 395, 399, 522
predictions, xix
  learning from errors and, xxvii–xxviii
pre-parental preoccupations, 315
presenting complaint, 44
psychoanalysis
  Freud's definition, 396
  versus psychiatry, 22
  science and, 522–523
  self-discovery, 70
psychotropic medications, 23, 49, 398
purohit, 455
Purple Heart recipient, 340–341

Q

Quine, Willard Van Orman, 522

R

Rachel, 101–104, 250–266, 270–272
Red Sea, 101, 257
resistance, 44, 52, 71, 87, 176, 256
  Extensive Psychoanalysis and, xxxi
  transference and, xxx, 396, 416–417

rest in peace
  Amir, 494
  Jan's father, 501–502, 506
Rome
  Amir's suicide, 40, 100–101
  Maria's pregnancy, 231–234
Russian roulette, 425
  Amir's considerations, 51–52
  The Deer Hunter movie, 38, 51

S
Sanhedrin, 61
Schur, Max, 404–405
Schwartz, Dr., 94–100, 228, 258–259
self-discovery, 70
semi-circle of mental health, 186,
    515–516, 520
Shaara, Michael, *The Killer Angels*,
    449
Shastri, Dr., 328, 442
Shelley, Percy Bysshe, 421–422
Shiva, 4, 6, 452, 455
Singh, Baldev, 274
Sofia (Jan's sister)
  father moved in, 168–169
  father's death, 479
  father's threat to strike, 514
  meeting Maria, 293
  mother's funeral, 146, 166
  road trip with mother, 145–146
  sending father money, 140
Sonderkommandos, 130–131
sonogram, 107, 231, 232, 243
Springer, Jerry, 312
Sripada, Venkata Krishnayya. *See*
    Nanna
Sripadism, 514
Star Wars movies, 162, 289

Stefan Batory High School, 502
stinky lady, 492
strawberries, 10, 45–46
stunned, Jan, 425
stypa, 167–168, 506
suicidal gambling, 51–52
suicide
  accidental success, 224
  Alterego Countertransference
      Identification and, 42
  Catholic church and, 104–105,
      253–254, 260, 504
  covert, 424
  Japanese soldiers, 483
  killer angels and, 445
  preventing, 225
  risks for therapists, 178
  Sonderkommando's and, 131
  therapist overwhelm, xiii
  vulnerability to, 93
suicide-doctor, 174
Szpilman, Wladyslaw, 59, 62, 63
sztandar, 479

T
Tahseen, 83
talking cure, 17, 392
Tarasoff ruling, 251, 443
Tarnopol, 269
Ten Commandments, 146, 150, 260,
    263
terrorists, 349, 381
Teutonic Knights, 157
thrust toward the east, 296
tiffin, 29–30
tinctures, 8, 21
The Tortoise and the Hare, 447
Tower, Lucia, xx

transference, xiv, xvi–xxi, xxv–xxx, 394
  alterego countertransference identification, 42
  alterego transference, 383
  Amir's negative transference, 210
  analyst's vacation, 336–337
  dream interpretation, 136
  false connection, 394
  free association and, 395
  Freud, 394–395, 416–417
  Gill and, xxxv
  hysteria, Freud, 18
  interpretation, 337
  Jan to Amir's father, 322
  Jan to Dr. Schwartz, 286
  Jan's post-termination phase, 512, 513
  layering, 346–347
  Lipton, S., 399
  misunderstanding by analyst, 390
  past life and, 396
  patient's childhood relationships, 71
  vignettes, xxxii
transference-countertransference, 271, 428, 514
turbocharging treatment, 512

U
Uncle Bozydar (Richard)
  as father substitute, 162
  German and Russian invaders, opinions, 269–270
  as hero, 155
  Polish resistance, 69, 131–132
  treatment by mother, 496
Uncle Hektor (Jozef), 179–180, 501

unconscious, xiv, xvi, xx
  collaboration, analyst and patient, xxiii
  countertransference and, xxv
  dreams, xxxii
  Essential Psychoanalysis, xxx–xxxi
  play and, xxviii
  self-discovery and, 70–72
  theories, xxix
  transference and, xvii
  unconscious enactment, 305
  vignettes, xxxii
Untermenschen, 255
USMLE (United States Medical Licensing Examination), 225, 317, 432

V
Venkat (Uncle), 126–128, 483–486
vermilion dot, 457

W
Warangal, 81
Warsaw, 296, 492–493, 498
water buffalo, 75–76
  Mahakali puja, 453–454
whip, 366
whistle, engine whistle, 20
'Why not first?,' 329
wild analysis, 398
Williams, Dr., 292, 349, 404, 406, 429, 470
Winnicott, D.W., xxi, xxxii, 382, 429
Wooden Plate play, 159

Y
Yankeelandia, 64, 67, 243
"You aren't my son.," 494

Z

Zanana Women's Hospital, 26–27
Zazueta, Mario, 108–109, 441
Zmory movie, 46
ZOMO (Zmechanizowane Oddzialy Milicji Obywatelskiej), 132–133

ABOUT THE AUTHOR

In his memoir, Bhaskar Sripada, M.D., a psychoanalyst, describes his experience treating a patient with depression using Essential Psychoanalysis. Emotions, thoughts, and memories evoked in him by the patient, more than by abstract theories, guide his actions. Despite the uncertainty created by their active observations and interactions, the patient and analyst maintain different perspectives. Although they share a common understanding concerning many aspects of their interactions, they often attribute  different meanings to their communications. They may sometimes disagree even about what is happening in the analytic sessions. With the help of the analyst, the patient reevaluates his interests, frustrations, conflicts, novelties, and errors, redefines what is desirable, ideal, and good enough, and reshapes his "Self." As in the case he presents, where a patient steps away from the brink of suicide, understanding the unconscious and conscious roots of a patient's suffering leads to insight, change, and healing. Dr. Sripada has been practicing psychoanalysis since 1980 and has taught at the Chicago Institute for Psychoanalysis since 1995. He currently resides and practices in Chicago.